THE ORGANIC CHEMISTRY PROBLEM SOLVER®

REGISTERED TRADEMARK

VOL. I

Staff of Research and Education Association,

Dr . M. Fogiel, Director

 Research and Education Association
505 Eighth Avenue
New York, N. Y. 10018

THE ORGANIC CHEMISTRY PROBLEM SOLVER ®

Printed in the United States of America

Library of Congress Catalog Card Number 78-51952

International Standard Book Number 0-87891-512-5

Revised Printing, 1983

PROBLEM SOLVER is a registered trademark of
Research and Education Association, New York, N. Y. 10018

WHAT THIS BOOK IS FOR

For as long as organic chemistry has been taught in schools, students have found this subject difficult to understand and learn because of the unusually large number of principles and mechanisms involved. Despite the publication of hundreds of textbooks in this field, each one intended to provide an improvement over previous textbooks, organic chemistry remains particularly perplexing and the subject is often taken in class only to meet school/departmental requirements for a selected course of study.

In a study of the problem, REA found the following basic reasons underlying students' difficulties with organic chemistry taught in schools:

(a) No systematic rules of analysis have been developed which students may follow in a step-by-step manner to solve the usual problems encountered. This results from the fact that the numerous different conditions and principles which may be involved in a problem, lead to many possible different methods of solution. To prescribe a set of rules to be followed for each of the possible variations, would involve an enormous number of rules and steps to be searched through by students, and this task would perhaps be more burdensome than solving the problem directly with some accompanying trial and error to find the correct solution route.

(b) Textbooks currently available will usually explain a given principle in a few pages written by a professional chemist who has an insight in the subject matter that is not shared by students. The explanations are often written in an abstract manner with involved mechanisms which leave the students confused as to the application of the principle. The explanations given are not sufficiently detailed and extensive to make the student aware of the wide range of applications and different aspects of the principle being studied. The numerous possible variations of principles and their applications are usually not discussed, and it is left for the students to discover these for themselves while doing exercises. Accordingly, the average student is expected to rediscover that which has been long known and practiced, but not published or explained extensively.

(c) The illustrations usually following the explanation of a principle in organic chemistry are too few in number and too simple to enable the student to obtain a thorough grasp of the principle involved. The illustrations do not provide sufficient basis to enable a student to solve problems that may be subsequently assigned for homework or given on examinations.

The illustrations are presented in abbreviated form which leaves out much material between steps. As a result, students find the illustrations difficult to understand—contrary to the purpose of the illustrations.

Illustrations are, furthermore, often worded in a confusing manner. They do not state the problem and then present the solution. Instead, they pass through a general discussion, never revealing what is to be solved for.

Illustrations, also, do not always include diagrams, wherever appropriate, and students do not obtain the training to draw diagrams to simplify and organize their thinking.

(d) Students can learn the subject only by doing the exercises themselves and reviewing them in class, to obtain experience in applying the principles with their different ramifications.

In doing the exercises by themselves, students find that they are required to devote considerably more time to organic chemistry than to other subjects of comparable credits, because they are uncertain with regard to the selection and application of the principles involved. It is also often necessary for students to discover those "tricks" not revealed in their texts (or review books), that make it possible to solve problems easily. Students must usually resort to methods of trial-and-error to discover these "tricks," and as a result they find that they may sometimes spend several hours to solve a single problem.

(e) When reviewing the exercises in classrooms, instructors usually request students to take turns in writing solutions on the boards and explaining them to the class. Students often find it difficult to explain in a manner that holds the interest of the class, and enables the remaining students to follow the material written on the boards. The remaining students seated in the class are, furthermore, too occupied with copying the material from the boards, to listen to the oral explanations and concentrate on the methods of solution.

This book is intended to aid students in organic chemistry to overcome the difficulties described, by supplying detailed illustrations of the solution methods which are usually not apparent to students. The solution methods are illustrated by problems selected from those that are most often assigned for class work and given on examinations. The problems are arranged in order of complexity to enable students to learn and understand a particular topic by reviewing the problems in sequence. The problems are illustrated with detailed step-by-step explanations of the principles involved, to save the students the large amount of time that is often needed to fill in the gaps that are usually omitted between steps of illustrations in textbooks or review/outline books.

The staff of REA considers organic chemistry a subject that is best learned by allowing students to view the methods of analysis and solution techniques themselves. This approach to learning the subject matter is similar to that practiced in the medical fields, for example, and various scientific laboratories.

In using this book, students may review and study the illustrated problems at their own pace; they are not limited to the time allowed for explaining problems on the board in class.

When students want to look up a particular type of problem and solution, they can readily locate it in the book by referring to the index which has been extensively prepared. It is also possible to locate a particular type of problem by glancing at just the material within the boxed portions. To facilitate rapid scanning of the problems, each problem has a heavy border around it. Furthermore, each problem is identified with a number immediately above the problem at the right-hand margin.

To obtain maximum benefit from the book, students should familiarize themselves with the section, "How To Use This Book," located in the front pages.

To meet the objectives of this book, staff members of REA have selected problems usually encountered in assignments and examinations, and have solved each problem meticulously to illustrate the steps which are usually difficult for students to comprehend. For outstanding effort and competence in this area, special gratitude is due to
                        Steven Schwartzberg

The following persons also have contributed a great deal of support and much patient work to achieve the objectives of the book:

David Friedel	Margaret Polaneczky
Howard Korman	Chak Tom
John McNelis	Alice Wong

Thanks are, furthermore, due to several contributors who devoted brief periods of time to this work.

The manuscript that was evolved with its endless inserts, changes, modifications to the changes, and editorial remarks, must have been an arduous typing task for Agnes Czirjak and Sophie Gerber. These ladies typed the manuscript expertly with almost no complaints about the handwritten material and the numerous symbols that require much patience and special skill.

For their efforts in the graphic-arts required in the layout arrangement, and completion of the physical features of the book, gratitude is expressed to Roberta Corn and Judy Goldenberg. They also helped in the training and supervision of other artists who assisted in the preparation of the book for printing. Included among these were Dorie Arnold, Eija Heino, Jonathan Plummer, and Andrew Taylor.

Finally, special thanks are due to Helen Kaufmann for her unique talents to render those difficult border-line decisions and constructive suggestions related to the design and organization of the book.

Max Fogiel, Ph. D.
Program Director

HOW TO USE THIS BOOK

This book can be an invaluable aid to students in organic chemistry as a supplement to their textbooks. The book is subdivided into 35 chapters, each dealing with a separate topic. The subject matter is developed beginning with structure and properties and extending through spectroscopy, stereochemistry, molecular orbital theory, and all of the principal classes of organic compounds. Sections on natural products, photochemistry, and color have also been included. Wherever applicable, topics include nomenclature, preparation, synthesis and reactions, characterization tests, and spectroscopy.

TO LEARN AND UNDERSTAND A TOPIC THOROUGHLY

1. Refer to your class text and read there the section pertaining to the topic. You should become acquainted with the principles discussed there. These principles, however, may not be clear to you at that time.

2. Then locate the topic you are looking for by referring to the "Table of Contents" in front of this book, "The Organic Chemistry Problem Solver."

3. Turn to the page where the topic begins and review the problems under each topic, in the order given. For each topic, the problems are arranged in order of complexity, from the simplest to the more difficult. Some problems may appear similar to others, but each problem has been selected to illustrate a different point or solution method.

To learn and understand a topic thoroughly and retain its contents, it will be generally necessary for students to review the problems several times. Repeated review is essential in order to gain experience in recognizing the principles that should be applied, and to select the best solution technique.

TO FIND A PARTICULAR PROBLEM

To locate one or more problems related to a particular subject matter, refer to the index. In using the index, be certain to note that the numbers given there refer to problem numbers, not to page numbers. This arrangement of the index is intended to facilitate finding a problem more rapidly, since two or more problems may appear on a page.

If a particular type of problem cannot be found readily, it is recommended that the student refer to the "Table of Contents" in the front pages, and then turn to the chapter which is applicable to the problem being sought. By scanning or glancing at the material that is boxed, it will generally be possible to find problems related to the one being sought, without consuming considerable time. After the problems have been located, the solutions can be reviewed and studied in detail. For this purpose of locating problems rapidly, students should acquaint themselves with the organization of the book as found in the "Table of Contents."

In preparing for an exam, it is useful to find the topics to be covered in the exam from the Table of Contents, and then review the problems under those topics several times. This should equip the student with what might be needed for the exam.

CONTENTS

CHAPTER 1

STRUCTURE AND PROPERTIES

LEWIS STRUCTURES

Provide a likely simple electronic structure for each of the following, assuming them to be completely covalent. Assume that every atom has a complete octet (except hydrogen, of course), and that two atoms may share more than one pair of electrons.

(a) H_2SO_4 (b) N_2H_4 (c) $COCl_2$ (d) HONO   (e) HSO_4^-

(f) C_2H_2 (g) CH_2O_2

Solution: The consideration of the structure of molecules requires an understanding of chemical bonds, the forces that hold atoms together in a molecule.

One type of chemical bond is the covalent bond, which results from sharing of electrons. The bonding force is electrostatic attraction: this time between each electron and both nuclei. The formation of ammonia serves as an example of this and an electronic structure below depicts how the electrons are shared.

$$3H_x \quad + \quad \cdot\overset{\cdot}{\underset{\cdot\cdot}{N}}: \quad \longrightarrow \quad H\overset{\overset{\textstyle H}{\overset{x\bullet}{}}}{\underset{\cdot\cdot}{x}N\overset{x}{}}H \qquad \text{(ammonia)}$$

Each dot or "x" denotes an electron. (The different symbols for the electron are meant for clarity, and not to suggest a difference.) In writing the electronic structures for the formation of ammonia, one had to realize the number of electrons in the incomplete shell. Each hydrogen atom has one and the nitrogen atom has five. These numbers are obtained from inspection of their electronic configurations. By hydrogen and nitrogen bonding, nitrogen obtains a complete octet (8 electrons surrounding it) for stability and completion of outer shell and each hydrogen atom is now surrounded by 2 electrons for completion of its shell.

One can now proceed to write the electronic structures the problem calls for.

(a) H_2SO_4. Consider first the number of electrons in the incomplete shell for each atom. Hydrogen has one, oxygen has six, and sulfur has six. Both sulfur and oxygen must have a complete octet. Hydrogen must have two electrons for a complete shell. To distinguish the electrons for clarity and see how they are arranged in the electronic structure, the following symbols will be used: Hydrogen's electrons will be represented by +, sulfur's by ·, and oxygen's by x. The electronic structure can be written as:

Notice how only this configuration satisfies the requirement that sulfur donates six electrons, oxygen six electrons, and hydrogen one electron.

(b) N_2H_4

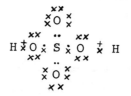

Here, each nitrogen contributes 5 electrons (·) and each hydrogen contributes 1 electron (x).

(c) $COCl_2$ The carbon atom can contribute only 4 electrons (this is the number in its incomplete shell - represented by +) and the chlorine atom can contribute 7 (represented by x). Oxygen's electrons are shown as dots (·).

Notice at arrow that two pairs of electrons must be shared for complete octets to be obtained. This denotes the presence of a double bond. (A triple bond would have three pairs of electrons shared between two atoms.)

(d) HONO   (Oxygen: +, nitrogen: x, and hydrogen: ·)

$$H \; \overset{++}{\underset{++}{+}} \; O \overset{x}{\underset{}{+}} \; \overset{xx}{N} \overset{++}{\underset{+}{x}} \; O\overset{++}{\underset{}{+}}$$

(e) HSO_4^- (Hydrogen: +, sulfur: ·, and oxygen by x)

H × O × S × O ⊖   ⎯ This electron accounts for
negative charge

2

(f) C_2H_2 (Carbon: + and hydrogen: •)

H⁺C⁺⁺⁺⁺C⁺H

(g) CH_2O (Carbon: + , hydrogen: • , and oxygen: x)

H⁺C⁺ Ö×H
++ ××
××
O×
××

Draw Lewis structures for the following substances. Use distinct, correctly placed dots for the electrons. Mark all atoms which are not neutral with charges of the proper sign.

a. propane
b. cyclopropane
c. benzene
d. methyl bromide
e. methanol

f. ethylene oxide
g. sodium acetate $(CH_3CO_2^{\ominus}Na^{\oplus})$
h. methylamine
i. acetamide
j. nitromethane

Solution: In drawing the Lewis structure of the following compounds, it should be noted that each element should have a complete octet (eight electrons in its outer shell). The exception to this rule is hydrogen which has a duet shell.

(a) Propane: C_3H_8

H H H
H×C:C:C×H
H H H

Elements that are in the middle of the periodic table tend to acquire the electrons to complete their octets by sharing electrons.

• C • + 4×H ⟶ H×C×H (with H above and below)

×and • both represent electrons, though from different sources.

(b) Cyclopropane: C_3H_6. In this compound, the 3 carbon atoms mutually share electrons with one another thus forming a ring.

H×C : C×H (with C at top, H below)

(c) benzene: C_6H_6.

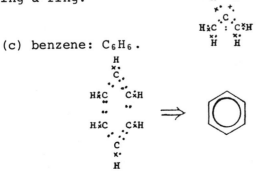

3

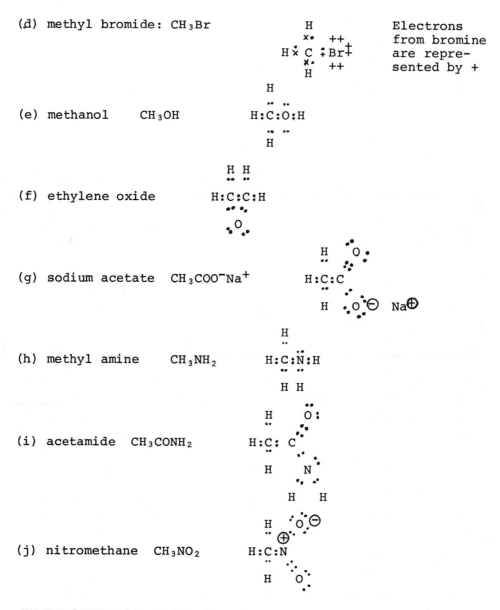

(d) methyl bromide: CH_3Br

Electrons from bromine are represented by +

(e) methanol CH_3OH

(f) ethylene oxide

(g) sodium acetate $CH_3COO^-Na^+$

(h) methyl amine CH_3NH_2

(i) acetamide CH_3CONH_2

(j) nitromethane CH_3NO_2

STRUCTURAL FORMULAS

● **PROBLEM 1-3**

How many isomers of formula CH_3Y would be possible if methane were a pyramid with a rectangular base? What are they?

<u>Solution:</u>   Any compound, no matter how complicated, that contains carbon bonded to four other atoms can be considered as a derivative of methane. For any atom Y, only one substance of the formula CH_3Y has ever been found. Chlorination of methane yields only one compound of formula CH_3Cl; bromination yields only CH_3Br. The same holds true even if

Y were not only an atom, but a group of atoms (i.e., if
the group itself is not too complicated to bring about
isomerism). This means that every hydrogen atom in methane
is equivalent, so that replacement of one hydrogen as
opposed to another always yields the same product.

To answer this problem one makes two identical
pyramidal models of CH_4 (with C at the apex), and then replace, for instance, the upper right-hand H with a different atom Y; in the other model replace the lower right-
hand H. Next determine whether or not, by any manipulations
except bending or breaking bonds, the models can be made
to coincide in all their parts. If the two models are superimposable, then they represent two molecules of the same
structure; if the models are not superimposable, then they
represent molecules of different structures which, since they
have the same molecular formula, are by definition isomers.

All the possible pyramidal structures of CH_3Y are drawn
and shown in figures A through D.

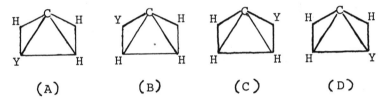

(A)   (B)   (C)   (D)

In each of these structures the Y atom has been
shifted to each of the four corners of the rectangular base.
With close inspection and imagination one can distinguish
only two non-superimposable molecules. Figures A and C are
the same, as are figures B and D. Thus, only 2 isomers of
CH_3Y can be formed if its structure were a pyramid with a
rectangular base.

● PROBLEM 1-4

How many isomers of formula CH_2YZ would be expected from
each of the following structures for methane? (a) Carbon
at the center of a rectangle; (b) Carbon at the center of
a square; (c) carbon at the apex of a square base pyramid;
(d) carbon in the center of a tetrahedron.

Solution: For any atom Y and for any atom Z, only one
substance of the formula CH_2YZ has ever been found. Halogenation of methane yields only one compound of formula CH_2Cl,
only one compound of formula CH_2Br_2, and only one compound
of formula CH_2ClBr.

To answer this problem one must make molecular models
of CH_4 in the particular shape in question. One then proceeds to replace two hydrogen atoms by a Y and Z atom. Next
determine whether or not, by any manipulation except bending or breaking bonds, the models can be made to coincide
in all their parts. If the models are superimposable, then

they represent molecules of the same structure; if the models are not superimposable, then they represent molecules of different structures which are by definition isomers.

(a) Carbon at the center of a rectangle: Draw all the possible structures of CH_2YZ in this arrangement. These are shown in figures A through L.

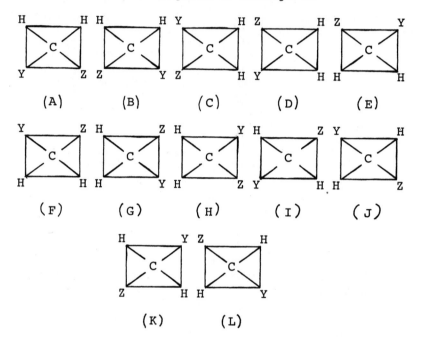

(A)   (B)   (C)   (D)   (E)

(F)   (G)   (H)   (I)   (J)

(K)   (L)

With some intuition one can distinguish only three different structures. Figures A, B, E, and F are the same; figures C, D, G, and H are the same; and figures I, J, K, and L are the same.

(b) Carbon at the center of a square:

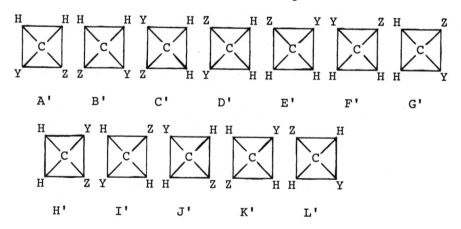

A'   B'   C'   D'   E'   F'   G'

H'   I'   J'   K'   L'

Draw all the possible structures of CH_2YZ in this arrangement. These are shown in figures A' through L'. With some intuition one can distinguish only two different structures or isomers. Figures A', B', C', D', E', F', G', and H' are the same; and figures I', J', K', and L' are the same.

(c) Carbon at the apex of a squarebase pyramid. Draw all the possible structures of CH_2YZ in this arrangement. With a little imagination figures A' through L' can be seen as the top view of a pyramid with a square base. However, care must be taken when rotating these structures; their bases must not be removed from the plane of the paper. With some intuition one can distinguish three different structures or isomers. Figures A', C', E', and G' are the same; figures B', D', F', and H' are the same; and figures I', J', K', and L' are the same. These three figures are redrawn as figures 1, 2, and 3, respectively.

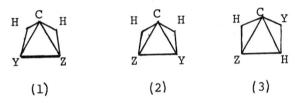

(1)   (2)   (3)

(d) Carbon in the center of a tetrahedron. As stated at the beginning of this problem only one structure of the methane derivative, CH_2YZ, has ever been found. This structure is a tetrahedron and is shown in figure M.

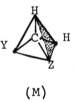

(M)

● **PROBLEM** 1-5

In the complex ion $Co(NH_3)_6^{+3}$, the bonds to the central atom can be pictured as utilizing six equivalent sp^3d^2 (or d^2sp^3) hybrid orbitals. On the basis of maximum separation of orbitals, what geometry would one expect this complex to have?

Solution: An understanding of hybridization will be necessary for the solution. Consider the case of beryllium chloride, $BeCl_2$. Beryllium may be pictured as:

    1s   2s   2p
    ☉   ☉   OOO

S and P represent atomic orbitals. The former is a sphere with its center at the nucleus of the atom, while the latter

7

is dumbbell-shaped. It consists of two lobes with the atomic nucleus lying between them. Since the axis of each P orbital is perpendicular to the axes of the other two, they are differentiated by the names P_x, P_y and P_z. An orbital may be defined as the region in space where an electron is likely to be found. An orbital may hold no more than 2 electrons (the Pauli Exclusion Principle). (Electrons are shown as dots.) The coefficients represent energy levels, with 1s as the lowest energy level and 2s and 2p being positioned at the next highest energy levels.

Inspection of the picture of beryllium shows it has no unpaired electrons. Hence, to account for beryllium combining with two chlorine atoms, one could promote one of 2s electrons to an empty p orbital:

```
1s          2s          2p
⊙           ◐           ◐OO
```

This procedure creates two unpaired electrons which could theoretically bond to chlorine in two different bonds, one using a p orbital, the other a s orbital. However, it is an established fact the two bonds in beryllium are equivalent. Consequently, the orbitals must be combined. The scheme below shows the combination of one s and one p orbitals to produce the mixed (hybrid) orbitals:

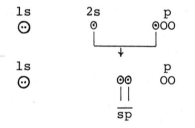

In sp hybridization, two orbitals are produced that represent a mixture of s and p orbitals. These orbitals are equivalent and much more strongly directed than either the s or p orbital. The sp hybrid orbitals point in exactly opposite directions; this arrangement permits them to get as far away from each other as possible. For note that electrons of like spin tend to get as far away from each other as possible, and it is this that mostly determines the geometry or shapes and properties of molecules.

In sp^2 hybridization, one has three orbitals, so that a trigonal (three-corned) arrangement permits the least contact of the orbitals. It can be visualized as shown:

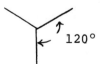

Sp^3 hybridization requires a tetrahedral (angle = 109.5°) arrangement for the least possible overlap of orbitals.

These considerations, then, should provide an important insight into the geometry of $Co(NH_3)_6^{+3}$. In this instance, one has the hybridization sp^3d^2, which indicates that six equivalent orbitals are involved. (The mixture is 3 from p, 2 from d, and 1 from s.) The point is to think of a geometry that will keep these six hybrid orbitals as far apart as possible. The best configuration or geometry would have to be the octahedral as shown:

BONDING

Assign all the electrons in acetaldehyde ($CH_3-CH=O$) to their atomic or molecular orbitals.

Solution: The formation of covalent bonds by the sharing of electrons results from the overlapping and interaction of partially filled atomic orbitals. The molecular orbitals (bonds) so formed are represented adequately by the summation of the geometrical properties of the individual atomic orbitals.

Since bond formation is produced by the interaction of orbitals, which can be highly directional, the most effective bonds will be formed when the relative spatial positions of the atoms are such as to produce the best possible overlap of orbitals.

To be able to assign all the electrons in $CH_3-CH=O$ to their orbitals, first set up the electron dot formula:

$$\overset{\displaystyle H \quad H}{\underset{\displaystyle H}{H:C^1:C^2::\overset{..}{\underset{..}{O}}:}}$$

When an atom forms a compound in which it is attached to four neighbouring atoms by single bonds, sp^3 hybrid orbitals are used to form these bonds. Thus carbon 1 is sp^3 hybridized. All hydrogen atoms have s orbitals, therefore, the three carbon-hydrogen bonds on the first carbon atom are sp^3-s bonds.

The carbon-carbon bond between the first and the second carbon are sp^3-sp^2 bonds. $Sp2$ orbitals are utilized only in the formation of molecules containing double bonds. This gives a trigonal arrangement (planar) in space as opposed to the tetrahedral arrangement of the sp^3 hybrid orbital. Thus the carbon-hydrogen bond on the second carbon atom is an sp^2-s bond, while the double bond on the oxygen

atom is composed of two different bonds. One bond is the
sp^2-p bond and the other (weaker) bond is a p-p bond.

Write an expanded structural formula with a line for each
bond for each of the substances represented below by a
condensed formula:

(a) $CH_3CH(CH_3)_2$ (e) $CH_3CONHCH_3$

(b) CH_3CCCH_3

(c) CH_2ClOCH_2CHO (f) $\overline{CH_2CH_2OCH_2CH_2O}$

(d) $(CH_2)_4$

Solution: (a) In 2-methylpropane, $CH_3CH(CH_3)_2$, 3 hydrogens are joined with the first and third carbons and a
fourth bond with the second carbon (thus acquiring the
four bonds or eight valence electrons in its outer shell).
The second carbon atom is joined together with 3 methyl
groups and a hydrogen atom. The methyl group consists of
a carbon atom bonded with three hydrogen atoms.

```
      H   H   H
      |   |   |
 H -  C - C - C - H
      |   |   |
      H   |   H
        H-C-H
          |
          H
```

(b) CH_3CCCH_3: The first carbon has three hydrogen atoms
and is bonded to the second carbon. The second carbon is
only joined to the first carbon and the third carbon atom.

    In order to complete an octet around the second
carbon it is absolutely necessary for the linkage with the
third carbon atom to be triple bonded. The third carbon
is attached to a methyl group.

```
      H           H
      |           |
 H -  C - C ≡ C - C - H          2-butyne
      |           |
      H           H
```

(c) CH_2ClOCH_2CHO

    The first methyl group has a hydrogen replaced by
a chlorine atom and is attached to an oxygen atom. The
last carbon is attached to a methylene group and an oxygen
atom. Since the oxygen is not linked to any other atom and

in order to be neutral it must be doubly bonded to the last carbon.

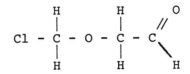

(d) $(CH_2)_4$ Each carbon atom is attached to two other carbon atoms   (in a ring) and two hydrogen atoms:

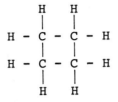

(e) $CH_3CONHCH_3$. A methyl group is attached to the middle carbon. The latter has an oxygen atom but since it needs to bond twice more it should be bonded doubly to either nitrogen or oxygen. But since nitrogen (needing 3 bonds) is linked to hydrogen and a methyl group it can only form a single bond with the middle carbon.

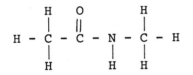

(f) $CH_2-CH_2OCH_2CH_2O$ In this compound the two oxygens are bonded with two $-CH_2-$ groups each and the carbon atoms are linked to an oxygen, another $-CH_2-$ and two hydrogen atoms.

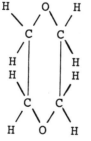

● **PROBLEM** 1-8

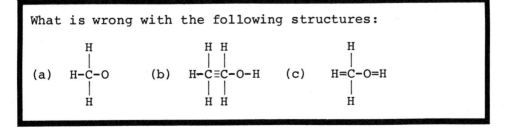

What is wrong with the following structures:

(a)   H-C-O   (b)   H-C≡C-O-H   (c)   H=C-O=H

11

<u>Solution</u>:   Carbon, hydrogen and oxygen each forms a
specific number of bonds when they combine with other
elements. This number is called their valence and is determined by their position in the periodic table. Carbon is in
group IV and thus forms four bonds when it combines with
other elements. Hydrogen is in group I and forms one bond.
Oxygen is in group VI. It does not form six bonds, though.
The actual number of bonds formed by any element is dependent upon the number of electrons in the outer shell of
the atom. In nature, there is a rule that is followed
which states that every element in combining with another
element seeks to attain eight electrons in its outer shell.
This is called the octet rule. Thus, hydrogen in group I
will seek to combine with an element in group VII. This is
because hydrogen has one electron to contribute and an
element in group VII will have seven. Getting back to oxygen;
it is in group VI and will, therefore have six electrons to
share. This means that it needs two more electrons to make
up its octet. Oxygen needs to form two bonds to complete
its octet.

     In each one of the structures above the error is in
the number of bonds drawn to the various elements.

$$\begin{matrix} & H \\ & | \\ \text{(a)} & H-C-O \\ & | \\ & H \end{matrix}$$ Taking the elements one by one, it is

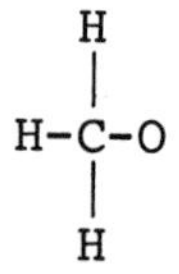

seen that each hydrogen atom forms one bond and is thus
correct; the carbon atom forms four bonds which is also
correct but the oxygen has only formed one bond. This
indicates that there are only seven electrons in its outer
shell and is not correct.

$$\begin{matrix} & H\ H \\ & |\ | \\ \text{(b)} & H-C\equiv C-O-H \\ & | \\ & H \end{matrix}$$ Each of the hydrogen atoms has formed

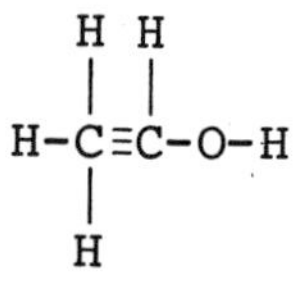

one bond and is thus correct. The carbon atom on the left
has formed three single bonds with the hydrogen atoms and
a triple bond with the other carbon for a total of six
bonds which is incorrect. The carbon on the right also
participates in the triple bond and in single bonds with
the oxygen and hydrogen atoms. This is a total of five
bonds and is also incorrect.

     The oxygen atom has formed two bonds which is correct.

$$\begin{matrix} & H \\ & | \\ \text{(c)} & H=C-O=H \\ & | \\ & H \end{matrix}$$ Here, two hydrogen atoms are drawn with

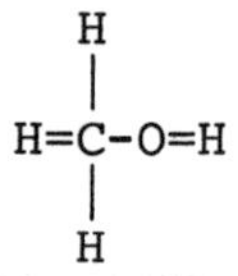

12

one bond and two are drawn with two bonds. The latter two
are incorrect. There is a total of five bonds drawn to the
carbon, which is incorrect. Carbon can form only four bonds.
There are three bonds drawn to the oxygen atom. This is
also incorrect because oxygen can form only two bonds.

● **PROBLEM** 1-9

Would you expect $He_2^{\oplus}$ to be more stable than He_2? than He?

Solution: This problem requires a consideration of bonding and antibonding orbitals. An atomic orbital may be
thought of as a particular volume element at a given distance and direction from the nucleus where there is a probability of finding an electron. According to the Pauli
exclusion principle, no more than two electrons can occupy
an orbital. Two overlapping orbitals can be considered to
combine to give one low-energy bonding orbital and one high-
energy antibonding orbital.

Consider the electron configuration of a helium atom
(He): $1s^2$. We can readily see that the outermost shell of
helium, the s orbital, is filled with 2 electrons, which is
the maximal and stable capacity. Thus the helium atom is
very stable. In fact, it is inert to most chemical reactions
and is for this reason known as one of the inert gases.

To form He_2, each helium atom contributes 2 1s
electrons for a total of 4 electrons. Since the molecular
bonding orbital can accommodate only 2 electrons, the remaining 2 must go into the antibonding orbital. Hence, any
stabilization gained by filling the bonding orbital is
offset by the required filling of the antibonding orbital.
Hence, there exists no net decrease in energy when He_2 is
produced, so that He_2 is less stable than He.

The only difference between He_2 and $He_2^{\oplus}$ is that the
latter has only 1 electron (not 2) in the antibonding
orbital. It possesses two electrons in the bonding orbital
as does He_2, but because of the one less electron in destabilizing antibonding orbital in $He_2^{\oplus}$, it should be more
stable than He_2. (It is, of course, less stable than He
which has no electrons in the antibonding orbital.)

● **PROBLEM** 1-10

When hydrogen chloride dissolves in water, the product is
"hydrochloric acid." Such a solution contains water, $H_3O^{\oplus}$,
and $Cl^{\ominus}$. Which of these species are Lewis acids? Lewis
bases? If you have more than one compound per category,
arrange them in order of decreasing strength.

Solution: According to the Lewis definition,
an acid is any species capable of accepting a pair of
electrons into an unfilled orbital, thereby forming a
mutual bond. A Lewis base may be defined as any species
which possesses a nonbonding or weakly bonding pair of
electrons and which is capable of donating these electrons
to a Lewis acid.

The reaction of hydrogen chloride in water may be
written as:

$$H-\overset{\cdot\cdot}{\underset{\cdot\cdot}{O}}-H \ + \ H-\overset{\cdot\cdot}{\underset{\cdot\cdot}{Cl}}: \longrightarrow H-\overset{\overset{\displaystyle H}{|}}{\underset{\oplus}{O}}-H \ + \ :\overset{\cdot\cdot}{\underset{\cdot\cdot}{Cl}}: \ {}^{\ominus}$$

The initial reaction of HCL with water involves a strong
hydrogen-bonding interaction of the hydrogen of HCL with
an unshared electron pair on the water molecule. Thus one
can consider this to be a Lewis acid-base interaction
between the HCL, which acts as an electron acceptor, and
the water molecule which acts as the electron pair donor.

However, water (H-$\overset{\cdot\cdot}{O}$-H) is the stronger base (that

is, it has the greater tendency to donate a pair of non-
bonded electrons). As such, it donates a pair of electrons
to HCl,which is a Lewis acid.This reaction produces

:$\overset{\cdot\cdot}{\underset{\cdot\cdot}{Cl}}$: ${}^{\ominus}$ which is a Lewis base (it can accept no more pairs

of nonbonded electrons since its outer shell now has the
8 electrons needed to fill it). The hydronium ion

$$\left[H-\overset{\overset{\displaystyle H}{|}}{\underset{\underset{\oplus}{\cdot\cdot}}{O}}-H \right] \ \text{formed may be considered, then, a Lewis acid.}$$

ACIDS AND BASES

● PROBLEM 1-11

What is the Lowry-Brønsted acid in (a) HCl dissolved in
water; (b) HCl (unionized) dissolved in benzene? (c) Which
solution is the more strongly acidic?

Solution: A Lowry-Brønsted acid may be defined as a
substance that gives up a proton (hydrogen nucleus). A
base, according to the Lowry-Brønsted idea, would then be
a substance that accepts the proton.

(a) When HCl is dissolved in water, the water acts
as a base due to the electron pairs available for sharing
around the oxygen. Hence, the HCl can donate a proton
(H$^{\oplus}$) and protonate the oxygen atom in H_2O as shown:

$$HCl + H_2O \rightleftarrows H_3O^{\oplus} + Cl^{\ominus}$$

The hydronium ion ($H_3O^{\oplus}$) generated on the right is
then the Lowry-Brønsted acid in solution, for it can donate
the proton in the reverse reaction and hence acts as an
acid.

(b)   When unionized HCl is added to benzene, a
hydrocarbon (that is, a compound containing only hydrogen
and carbon atoms),the Lowry-Brønsted acid can only be HCl.
No reaction occurs between the benzene and HCl to generate
any other acid.

(c)   The Lowry-Brønsted acid $H_3O^{\oplus}$ is weaker than HCl. The
strength of an acid depends upon its tendency to give up
a proton. HCl gives up its proton very readily, whereas
$H_3O^{\oplus}$ has a greater tendency to hold onto its proton. The
strengths of some common acids are indicated below.

Acid strength $\begin{matrix} H_2SO_4 \\ HCl \end{matrix} > H_3O^{\oplus} > NH_4^{\oplus} > H_2O$

Since HCl is the stronger acid, the HCl in benzene
is the more acidic solution.

● **PROBLEM 1-12**

Account for the fact that nearly every organic compound
containing oxygen dissolves in cold concentrated sulfuric
acid to yield a solution from which the compound can be
recovered by dilution with water.

Solution: The solution to this problem can be obtained
by a consideration of the Lowry-Brønsted definition of
acids and bases.
     In the Lowry-Brønsted sense, an acid is a substance
that gives up a proton, and a base is a substance that
accepts a proton. When the cold concentrated sulfuric acid
is added to the organic compound containing oxygen, it gives
up a proton (hydrogen nucleus) and protonates the oxygen
atom, which possesses electron pairs available for sharing.
The reaction may be illustrated as shown:

$$-\overset{|}{\underset{\cdot\cdot}{O}}: + H_2SO_4 \rightleftarrows -\overset{|}{\underset{\cdot\cdot}{O}}:H^{\oplus} + HSO_4^{\ominus}$$

     The oxygen atom of the organic compound is acting as
the base because it accepts the proton from the sulfuric
acid. It is thus protonation, which is reversible, that
accounts for the organic compound dissolving in the cold
concentrated sulfuric acid.

     The protonation generates (as shown previously) the

following: $-\overset{|}{\underset{\cdot\cdot}{O}}:H^{\oplus}$ and $HSO_4^{\ominus}$

                A   B

"A" is the new acid formed because it can donate the
proton; "A" is a weak acid (it will tend not to give up
the proton readily). "B" is the new base generated, and it
is also weak (it will tend not to accept a proton donated).
If water is added to this solution, the organic compound

15

will be regenerated, because water is a stronger base than $HSO_4^{\ominus}$ so that it will accept the proton from "A". The reaction can be written as:

$$-\overset{|}{\underset{\cdot\cdot}{O}}:H^{\oplus} \;+\; H_2O \;\rightleftarrows\; -\overset{|}{\underset{\cdot\cdot}{O}}: \;+\; H_3O^{\oplus} \; \text{hydronium ion obtained}$$

organic compound recovered

IDENTIFICATION AND STRUCTURE DETERMINATION

A qualitative analysis of Atebrin, an antimalarial drug used extensively by Allied troops during the Second World War, showed carbon, hydrogen, nitrogen, chlorine and oxygen. A quantitative analysis showed 69.1% carbon, 7.5% hydrogen, 10.5% nitrogen, 8.9% chlorine and 4.0% oxygen. What is the empirical formula for Atebrin?

Solution: When the percent composition of a compound is given the percents refer to weight percent unless it is stated otherwise. To calculate the empirical formula for a compound from its composition first assume that 100 g of the compound is present and then determine the mass of each component. From these masses the number of moles of each element can be found and from this the empirical formula.

In 100 g of Atebrin there will be 69.1 g C, 7.5 g H, 10.5 g N, 8.9 g Cl and 4.0 g O.

The molecular weights (MW) of these elements are 12, 1, 14, 35.5 and 16 respectively. Solving for the number of moles of each in 100 g of Atebrin:

$$\text{no. of moles} = \frac{\text{no. of grams}}{\text{MW}}$$

$$\text{no. of moles of C} = \frac{69.1\ g}{12\ g/\text{mole}} = 5.76 \text{ moles}$$

$$\text{no. of moles of H} = \frac{7.5\ g}{1\ g/\text{mole}} = 7.5 \text{ moles}$$

$$\text{no. of moles of N} = \frac{10.5\ g}{14\ g/\text{mole}} = 0.75 \text{ moles}$$

$$\text{no. of moles of Cl} = \frac{8.9\ g}{35.3\ g/\text{mole}} = 0.25 \text{ moles}$$

$$\text{no. of moles of O} = \frac{4.0\ g}{16.0\ g/\text{mole}} = 0.25 \text{ moles}$$

The number of moles of each element in the empirical formula must be integers. The formula that has been derived above is $C_{5.76} H_{7.5} N_{0.75} Cl_{0.25} O_{0.25}$. There are 0.25 moles of each Cl and O, thus multiplying the number of moles of each element by 4 will yield $C_{23}H_{30}ClO$, which is the empirical formula.

● **PROBLEM** 1-14

A gas of molecular weight 58 was found to contain 82.8% C and 17.2% H. What is the molecular formula of this compound?

<u>Solution</u>: The molecular formula for this compound can be written C_xH_y, where x is the number of moles of carbon present in one mole of the compound and y is the number of moles of hydrogen present in each mole of the hydrocarbon.

The number of moles of each compound can be determined by multiplying the molecular weight (MW) of the compound by the fraction of the element present divided by its own MW.

(i)   no. of moles $= \dfrac{\text{fraction of C or H}}{\text{MW of C or H}} \times 58$ g

MW of C = 12; MW of H = 1

Substituting into equation (i):

no. of moles of C $= \dfrac{.828}{12 \text{ g/mole}} \times 58$ g = 4.0 moles

no. of moles of H $= \dfrac{.172}{1 \text{ g/mole}} \times 58$ g = 10.0 moles

The formula for this compound is C_4H_{10}.

● **PROBLEM** 1-15

A sample of aspirin (acetylsalicylic acid) was determined to be 60.0% carbon, 4.4% hydrogen and 35.6% oxygen. The molecular weight is 180. What is the molecular formula for aspirin?

<u>Solution</u>: The molecular formula for a given compound can be calculated from its molecular weight and the percent composition.
One mole of aspirin weighs 180 g; 60.0% of this weight is contributed by carbon. After determining the mass of the carbon present, the number of moles of carbon in one mole of aspirin can be found. (MW of C = 12)

mass of carbon in one mole of aspirin = .60 × 180 g = 108 g

no. of moles $= \dfrac{\text{mass}}{\text{MW}} = \dfrac{108 \text{ g}}{12 \text{ g/mole}}$ = 9 moles

Similar calculations can be made for hydrogen and oxygen to determine the molecular formula. (MW of H = 1)

mass of H in 1 mole of aspirin = 0.044 × 180 g = 8 g

$$\text{no. of moles} = \frac{8 \text{ g}}{1 \text{ g/mole}} = 8 \text{ moles}$$

(MW of O = 16)

mass of O in 1 mole of aspirin = .356 × 180 g = 64 g

$$\text{no. of moles} = \frac{64 \text{ g}}{16 \text{ g/mole}} = 4 \text{ moles}$$

The molecular formula for aspirin is $C_9H_8O_4$. Its structure is shown below.

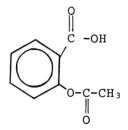

Acetylsalicylic Acid
(Aspirin)

● **PROBLEM 1-16**

What do the differences in properties between lithium acetylacetone (m.p. very high, insoluble in chloroform) and beryllium acetylacetone (m.p. 108°, b.p. 270°, soluble in chloroform) suggest about their structures?

Solution: From their melting and solubility properties, the structures of lithium acetylacetonate and beryllium acetylacetonate are, respectively, ionic or salt-like and non-ionic or covalent.

Melting may be considered to be a change from a highly ordered arrangement of particles to a more random arrangement. When a temperature is reached at which the thermal energy of the particles is great enough to overcome the forces holding the particles together, melting occurs. An ionic compound or salt forms crystals in which the structural units are ions. These ions are held together by the electrostatic forces that derive from an ion of say positive charge being surrounded by ions of opposite charge (negative charge) in the structure. These powerful forces, which are interionic, can be overcome only at a very high temperature. In a non-ionic compound, the atoms are held together by covalent bonds and form crystals in which the structural units are molecules. For melting to occur, the forces holding these molecules together must be overcome. These intermolecular forces are weak compared to the electrostatic forces, so

that a much lower temperature is required for melting.
Since the melting point of lithium acetylacetonate is very
high, and beryllium acetylacetonate relatively low, one
expects the former to be ionic with the latter being non-
ionic.

These same expectations could have been obtained by
examination of the solubilities. For something to dissolve, the structural units-ions or molecules - must become
separated from each other, and the spaces in between become
occupied by solvent molecules. To dissolve an ionic compound, the solvent must be able to form ion-dipole bonds
and have a high dielectric constant, that is, possess high
insulating properties to lower the attraction between
oppositely charged ions once they are solvated (surrounded
by a cluster of solvent molecules). Only water or other
highly polar solvents possess these properties, and hence
can dissolve ionic compounds to a large extent. (A polar
molecule has a positive end and a negative end, so that
there is an electrostatic interaction between a positive
ion and a negative end of a solvent molecule, and between
a negative ion and a positive end of a solvent molecule -
ion-dipole bonds.) Solubility of non-ionic compounds is
determined by their polarity. Non-polar or weakly polar
compounds dissolve readily in non-polar or weakly polar
solvents, whereas highly polar compounds dissolve in highly polar solvents. These facts are often remembered by
the "like dissolves like" rule. Chloroform is a non-
polar solvent, so that it should dissolve only non-polar
compounds. Since beryllium acetylacetonate dissolves in
it, one expects its structure to be non-ionic. Likewise,
since lithium acetylacetonate is not soluble in it, it is
probably ionic or salt-like.

POLARITY

● PROBLEM 1-17

What are the characteristics which ionic, ion-dipole, and
dipole-dipole bonds have in common? How do they differ?

Solution: A bond between two species is defined in terms
of the amount of energy liberated because of adduct formation. The strength of the bond increases as the amount of
heat generated is increased at the expense of the total
energy of the system.

An ionic bond is produced when an electropositive and
an electronegative element react by transferring electrons.
For example, when Na· and :$\overset{\bullet}{\text{C}}$l: react the electropositive
sodium transfers one electron to chlorine; Na^+ and :Cl:$^-$
are produced. This ionic bond is non-directional.

An ion-dipole bond is generated when one of the ions
in an ionic bond is replaced by a highly polar molecule

19

such as water: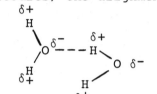

When an ion such as Na^+ reacts with H_2O, the positive ion aligns with respect to the polar molecule as shown:

$$Na^+ + \text{(+ -)} \longrightarrow Na^+ \text{(- +)}$$

Similarly, if another polar molecule replaces the ion in the ion-dipole bond, the formation of a dipole-dipole bond occurs. If we consider two polar molecules (e.g., two H_2O molecules) the alignment of the molecules

is such: The other

hydrogen atoms also attract oxygen atoms in other water molecules.

Ionic bonds form stronger bonds than ion-dipole bonds, and the latter are stronger than dipole-dipole bonds.

● **PROBLEM** 1-18

Why does hydrogen fluoride undergo intermolecular self-association while the other hydrogen halides do not?

<u>Solution:</u>   The fluorine atom is the most electronegative, that is, strongest attractor of electrons, of all the halogen atoms. Since fluorine will tend to attract electrons, the fluorine atom should possess a negative charge and the hydrogen atom a positive charge in HF. That is, HF is a polar molecule with one end (F) electron rich and one end (H) electron deficient. In a solution of HF, the opposite charges can attract each other, that is, one has inter-molecular self-association. When opposite and equal charges are separated by some distance in a molecule (such as HF), a dipole is formed. Hence, the intermolecular self-association can be considered dipole-dipole interaction. This particular kind of interaction is also referred to as hydrogen bonding. It may be pictured as shown:

$$H-F \cdots H-F$$

hydrogen bonding.

The tremendous electronegativity of fluorine is what allows the formation of hydrogen bonds in an HF solution. Since the other halogens possess less of a tendency to attract electrons, they will be less able to form hydrogen bonds required for intermolecular self-association.

(a) Although HCl (1.27 A) is a longer molecule than HF (0.92 A), it has a smaller dipole moment (1.03 D compared to 1.75 D). How do you account for this fact? (b) The dipole moment of CH_3F is 1.847 D, and of CD_3F, 1.858 D. (D is ^2H, deuterium.) Compared with the C-H bond, what is the direction of the C-D dipole?

Solution: (a) Both HCl and HF are polar compounds. This means one end of the bond between the two atoms in the molecule is relatively negative and the other end is relatively positive. In other words, there exists a negative pole and a positive pole. A covalent bond will be polar if it joins atoms that differ in their tendency to attract electrons, that is, atoms that differ in electronegativity. The greater the difference in electronegativity, the more polar the bond. The following relates the electronegativity of some common elements: F>O>Cl,N>Br>C>H.

The molecules HF and HCl constitute dipoles because of this difference in electronegativity. A dipole may be defined as a molecule with two equal and opposite charges separated in space. A dipole possesses a dipole moment, μ, which equals the magnitude of the charge, e, multiplied by the distance, d, between the centers of charge: $\mu = e \times d$.

Since HCl is longer than HF, the "d" will be larger for HCl in the computation of its dipole moment. Thus, to explain why HCL's dipole moment is smaller than HF, one must examine the other parameter, "e". The magnitude of the charge will reflect the extent of the difference in electronegativities of the elements. As previously indicated, the electronegativity of F is greater than Cl by a significant amount. Thus, when both F and Cl are compared with H's electronegativity, the difference is greatest for F. Hence, the magnitude of "e" must be much larger for HF than HCl. Consequently, the dipole moment is larger in HF. In essence, then, the greater electronegativity of F is responsible for the larger dipole moment.

(b) The fact that the dipole of CH_3F is less than CD_3F means that D must be attracting the electrons less than H does. If one assumes there exists no difference in "d",or the distance between the charges,when D is substituted for H, then the difference in dipole moment can only stem from magnitude of charge, "e". If the electronegativity of D is less than H, that is, it tends to attract less electrons, then F is more negative so that the magnitude of "e" is increased, which would account for higher dipole moment of CD_3F. What this means is that the dipole is less directed toward D than toward H.

Predict the direction of polarization of the following
bonds, considering only the relative electronegativity
of the atoms involved.

C-H;   B-H;   N-Br;   I-Cl

Solution: The electronegativity of an element is a
measure of the ability of an atom of the element to
attract electrons to itself in a chemical bond. It is
generally found that electronegativity increases from
left to right across the periodic table and decreases on
on going down any group. The most electronegative elements
are therefore found in the top right-hand corner (O, **F**, Cl)
and the least electronegative (most electropositive) in
the bottom left-hand corner (Ba, Cs, Rb). A qualitative
list of relative electronegativity is given below, but it
should be realized that the molecular environment of an
atom may affect its electronegativity to a limited extent.

The relative electronegativities of some common
elements occur in the following order:

F>O>Cl,N>Br>I,S,C>P,H>B>Mg>Li>Na

The distribution of electrons in a single covalent
bond between two atoms is not equally shared. In a
symmetrical molecule A-A (e.g. H_2, Cl_2) the two nuclei,
in whose neighborhood the bonding electrons are found, are
indistinguishable, and in the absence of any external
effects the electron distribution will be symmetrical. If,
however, a molecule such as A-X is considered where A and
X are different (e.g. HF, ICl), then the nuclei are distinct
and the atoms A and X may differ greatly in electronegativity. In these circumstances the distribution of electrons
may be asymmetric and the electron density will be greater
near the more electronegative element. This electron displacement carried to an extreme leads to the production of
ions, but in many covalent bonds only causes slight polari-
zation of the bond, represented as $\overrightarrow{AX}$ or $A^{\delta+}\!\!-\!\!X^{\delta-}$ where X
is the more electronegative atom, and $\delta+$, $\delta-$ represent small
electrical charges produced by polarization.

Thus, referring to the relative electronegativities
of the individual atoms, and the above definition of polarization:

$$\begin{array}{cccc}
\delta- \quad \delta+ & \delta+ \quad \delta- & \delta- \quad \delta+ & \delta+ \quad \delta- \\
C - H & B - H & N - Br & I - Cl \\
\longleftarrow\!\!\!+ & +\!\!\!\longrightarrow & \longleftarrow\!\!\!+ & +\!\!\!\longrightarrow
\end{array}$$

CHAPTER 2

SPECTROSCOPY

LINE SPECTRA

● PROBLEM 2-1

Calculate the energy in kcal which corresponds to the absorption of 1 einstein of light of 5893 Å (sodium D line) by sodium vapor. Explain how this absorption of light by sodium vapor might have chemical utility.

Solution: One einstein of light refers to the change in energy (ΔE) that occurs from the absorption of electromagnetic radiation by one gram-atom (or mole) of a monatomic gas such as sodium vapor. The absorption of radiation results in the excitation of the molecule. The energy difference between the excited state and the ground state of the molecule is the change in energy. This change in energy is related to the frequency (ν) or wavelength (λ) by the equations:

$$\Delta E = h\nu = \frac{hc}{\lambda}$$

where   h = Planck's constant

c = velocity of light.

Since Planck's constant and the velocity of light are numerical constants, this equation can be written as:

$$\Delta E = \frac{286,000}{\lambda (\text{Å})} \text{ kcal}$$

where $\lambda (\text{Å})$ indicates that the wavelength is measured in angstrom units (Å). Hence we can calculate the energy, in Kcal (kilocalories), which corresponds to the absorption of one einstein of light at 5893 Å by sodium vapor as follows:

$$\Delta E = \frac{286,000}{5893} \text{ kcal}$$

$$\Delta E = 48.5 \text{ kcal.}$$

23

The energy requirements of many chemical reactions are within the range of 48.5 kcal/mole. Hence when the excited electron in sodium drops to its ground state, the energy transferred (48.5 kcal/mole) can cause a chemical reaction to occur.

INFRARED SPECTROSCOPY

● PROBLEM 2-2

Identify the functional groups in each compound from the following infrared spectra.

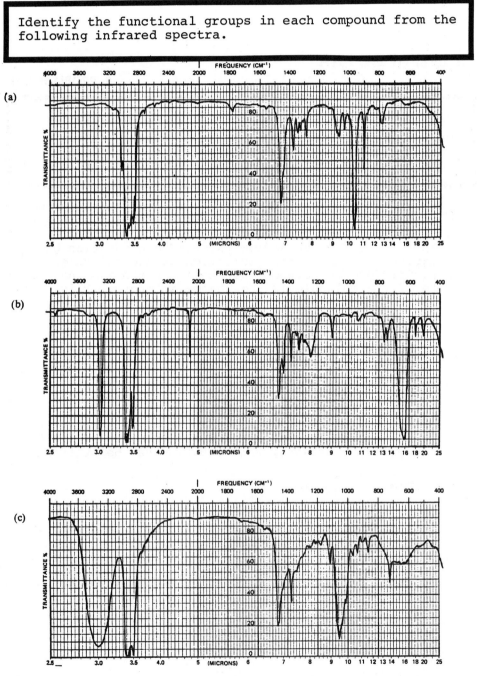

(d)

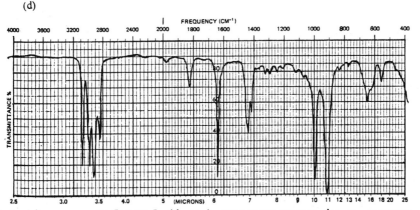

Solution: Infrared (i.r.) spectroscopy is a common technique that is used to identify the major functional groups in a compound. The identification of these groups depends upon the amount of infrared radiation absorbed and the particular frequency (measured in cm^{-1}, wavenumbers) at which these groups absorb. An infrared spectrum measures the degree of the molecular vibration and rotation of the bonds in the molecule. Each type of functionality will absorb at certain characteristic frequencies and with characteristic strengths. With this knowledge at hand, we can identify the major functional groups from the i.r. spectra (a) through (d).

(a)   This spectrum has a moderate band at 3050 cm^{-1} which is characteristic of the =C-H stretch of a dialkylated alkene: RHC = CHR'. There is also a strong sharp band at approximately 965 cm^{-1}, which is the characteristic absorption of the C-H out-of-plane bending of a trans-1,2-dialkylated alkene:

(b)   The strong sharp band at 3300 cm^{-1} is characteristic of a ≡ C ⤒ H stretch and is suggestive of a terminal

alkyne: R-C ≡ C—H. The medium sharp band at 2170 cm^{-1} is the characteristic absorption band of the C ≡ C stretch of terminal alkynes. The strong broad band at 630 cm^{-1} is the absorption of the ≡ C - H bend of R - C ≡ C - H. We can see from this i.r. spectrum that the compound is conclusively a terminal alkyne.

(c)   The broad band centered ay 3350 cm^{-1} is indicative of a bonded O—H stretch. The complex absorption pattern at 1050 cm^{-1} is the C—O vibrations of a primary alcohol, RCH_2OH.

(d)   The strong sharp bands at 995 cm^{-1} and 905 cm^{-1} are characteristic of the C - H out-of-plane bend of monoalkylated alkenes: RHC = CH_2. This is strongly supported by the other spectral evidence. The moderate sharp band at 3080 cm^{-1} is the absorption of the = C - H stretch and the medium sharp band at 1640 cm^{-1} is the C = C stretch absorption.

25

Give a structure or structures consistent with each of the following infrared spectra.

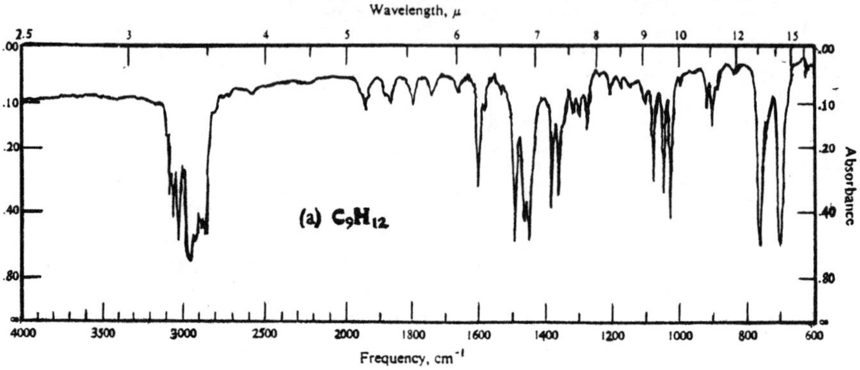

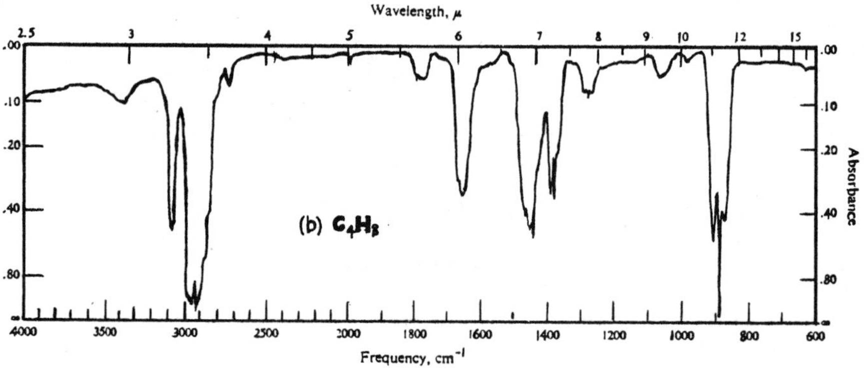

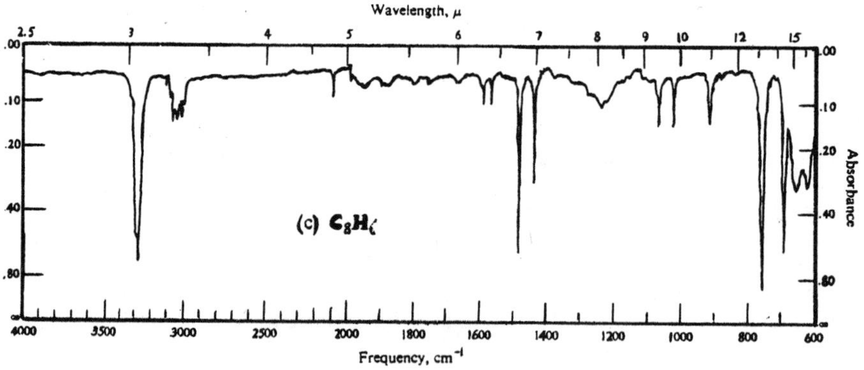

Wavelength, μ

(a) C_9H_{12}

Wavelength, μ

(b) C_4H_8

Wavelength, μ

(c) $C_8H_?$

Solution: Infrared (i.r.) spectra can reveal the molecular structure of an organic compound. It is based on the fact that a molecule is constantly vibrating. Chemical bonds stretch (and contract) and bend with respect to each other. The absorption of infrared light (that is, light lying beyond the red end of the visible spectrum - lower frequency, longer wavelength, less energy) causes changes in vibrations of a molecule.

An infrared spectrum may be referred to by its wavelength or, preferably, by its frequency which is expressed in wavenumbers, cm^{-1}, as can be seen in the

spectra given in the problem. (Wavenumbers may be defined
as the number of waves per centimeter.)

Two substances that possess identical infrared
spectra are identical in thousands of different physical
properties; they must almost certainly be the same compound.
The infrared spectrum reveals the molecular structure by
indicating what groups are present (or absent) in the
molecule. This is based on the fact that a group of atoms gives
rise to characteristic absorption bands. In other words, a
particular group absorbs light of certain frequencies that
are essentially the same from compound to compound. For
example, the carbonyl group (C=O) of ketones absorbs at
1710 cm^{-1}. Now, the absorption band of a particular group
of atoms can be shifted by various structural features such
as angle strain, van der Waals strain, conjugation, electron
withdrawal, and hydrogen bonding. Hence, the interpretation
of an infrared spectrum may not be easy. The table provided
lists some characteristic infrared absorption frequencies.
In solving for the molecular structure, try to correlate
the frequencies in the table with those for bands indicated
in the problem.

(a)   A band is present in the 3000-3100 cm^{-1} region; this
indicates an aromatic ring. This can be confirmed by the
presence of a band in the 1500, 1600 regions which would
indicate the stretch of the C═══C bond in the ring. Such
a band is present. Therefore, one knows that six of the
nine carbons in C_9H_{12} belong to an aromatic portion: a
benzene ring. The weak finger-like bands from 2000 cm^{-1}
to 1700 cm^{-1} are characteristic of the absorption of mono-
substituted aromatic rings.   Hence the remaining three
carbons must be part of a single substituent. The aromatic
bands account also for five hydrogen atoms, so that the
substituent possesses seven hydrogen atoms. There exist
two possibilities for an organic structure with three
carbons and seven hydrogens: isopropyl (-CH(CH$_3$)$_2$) and
propyl (-CH$_2$CH$_2$CH$_3$). That it is isopropyl can be determined from the isopropyl split at about 1400 cm^{-1}. So,

CH(CH$_3$)$_2$

the structure in (a) can be written as [benzene ring]

The diagram below assigns groups of atoms to each bond
for further clarity.

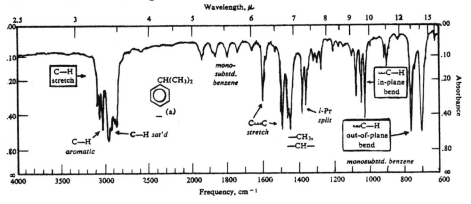

(b)   That this is an alkene can be seen from the strong
band present in the 1640-1680 cm^{-1} region, due to the
C=C stretch. Also, the molecular formula given, C_4H_8,
fits the general formula for an alkene, C_nH_{2n}. There

exists a band in the region of 3020-3080 cm^{-1} which
indicates the C-H absorption for alkenes. The diagram
below assigns structures to the bands which lead to the
conclusion that the structure is $(CH_3)_2C=CH_2$, isobutylene.

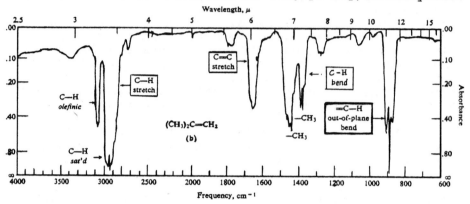

(c)   That the structure is phenylacetylene may be determined by examining two prominent bands. There exist the
C-H stretch of aromatics(confirmed by the C====C stretch
at 1500, 1600 cm^{-1})at 3000-3100 cm^{-1} and the -C≡C-
stretch characteristic of alkynes at 2100-2260 cm^{-1}.

One concludes therefore, that C_8H_6 represents   ⟨O⟩-C≡CH,

phenylacetylene. Other bands are assigned structures in
the diagram.

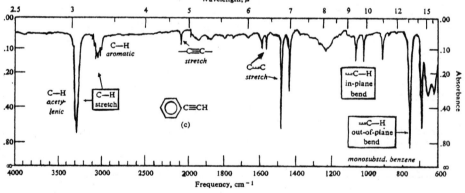

• PROBLEM 2-4

Which (if any) of the following compounds could give rise
to each of the infrared spectra shown?

    isobutyraldehyde   ethyl vinyl ether
    2-butanone   cyclopropylcarbinol
    tetrahydrofuran   3-buten-2-ol

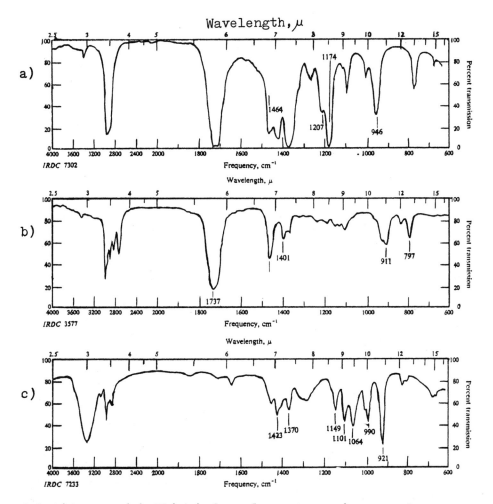

Wavelength, μ

IRDC 7302

Wavelength, μ

IRDC 3577

Wavelength, μ

IRDC 7233

Solution: (a) This infrared spectrum shows a strong
absorption near 1720 cm^{-1}. This is the characteristic
absorption of a C=O stretch for saturated aldehydes and
saturated acyclic ketones. The weak absorption at
3400 cm^{-1} is the C=O overtone and it further supports
our conclusion that we are dealing with a carbonyl compound.
The C=O overtone is noticeable in the spectrum because the
C=O stretch is such an intense absorption. The only given
carbonyl compounds are isobutyraldehyde (an aldehyde,

$$\overset{O}{\overset{\|}{}}$$

RCHO) and 2-butanone   (a ketone, RCR'). The C-H stretch
of the aldehyde proton characteristically shows absorptions
at 2820 cm^{-1} and 2720 cm^{-1}. The i.r. spectrum shows only
a strong band at 2900 cm^{-1} in this vicinity. Hence the
compound is not the aldehyde and must be the ketone, 2-
butanone. The band at 2900 cm^{-1} is the characteristic
absorption band of the C-H stretch of methyl and methylene
groups. 2-Butanone has the structure:

$$CH_3 - \overset{O}{\overset{\|}{C}} - CH_2 - CH_3$$

(b)   This i.r. spectrum shows a strong absorption at

29

1737 cm^{-1}. This is suggestive of the C=O stretch of a saturated aldehyde because the frequency at which aldehydes absorb infrared radiation is greater than that of ketones. The sharp bands at 2820 cm^{-1} and 2740 cm^{-1} are the absorptions of the C-H stretch of an aldehyde. Hence the compound is an aldehyde and must be isobutyraldehyde.

(c)   This spectrum shows a strong broad band at 3400 cm^{-1}, which is indicative of a bonded O-H stretch of an alcohol. Our choice is therefore narrowed down to cyclopropylcarbinol

$\left(\text{▷—CH}_2\text{OH, a primary alcohol}\right)$ and 3-buten-2-ol ($CH_2=$

CH-CHOHCH$_3$, a secondary alcohol). The C-O stretch of primary alcohols characteristically absorbs at 1050 cm^{-1} and that of secondary alcohols absorbs at 1100 cm^{-1}. Since the spectrum shows a complex absorption pattern in this range, we must look for other clues. There is a weak absorption at 1640 cm^{-1}. This is the characteristic absorption of the C=C stretch of terminal alkenes (RHC=CH$_2$ or R$_2$C=CH$_2$). Hence the compound must be 3-buten-2-ol because it possesses a double bond whereas cyclopropylcarbinol has none.

● **PROBLEM** 2-5

The infrared spectra shown in Figures 1 a and b are for compounds of formula C$_3$H$_6$O and C$_4$H$_6$O$_2$, respectively. Deduce a structure for each of these substances from its infrared spectrum. Indicate clearly which lines in the spectra you identify with the groups in your structures.

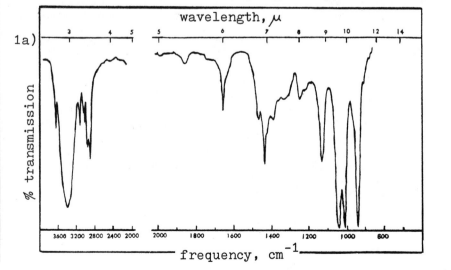

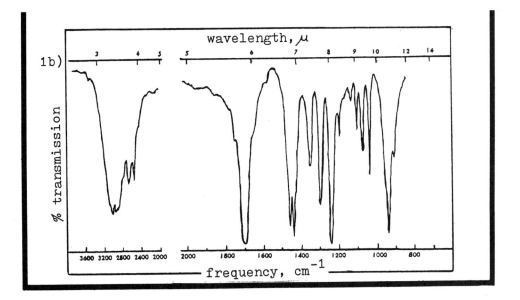

1b)

wavelength, μ

% transmission

3600 3200 2800 2400 2000   2000   1800   1600   1400   1200   1000   800

frequency, cm^{-1}

Solution: (a) The most noticeable feature in this infra-red spectrum is the strong broad band at 3400 cm^{-1}. This absorption is characteristic of the bonded O-H stretch of alcohols. We can furthermore deduce that the compound is a primary alcohol by noticing the strong sharp C-O stretch absorption at 1050 cm^{-1}. The C-O stretch of secondary and tertiary alcohols absorbs at frequencies greater than 1050 cm^{-1}. Another significant band in this spectrum is the weak sharp absorption at 1650 cm^{-1}. This is the charac-teristic absorption band of the C=C stretch of monoalkylated alkenes ($RHC=CH_2$) and dialkylated terminal alkenes ($R_2C =CH_2$). These types of alkenes are distinguished by their methylene C-H out-of-plane bending. The spectrum shows two strong sharp bands at 1010 cm^{-1} and 930 cm^{-1}, the characteristic absorption bands of the C-H out-of-plane bend of monoalkylated alkenes. As if this were not enough proof, the molecular formula of the compound (C_3H_6O) re-stricts it to three carbons; the smallest dialkylated terminal alkene requires four carbons:

$$\begin{array}{c} CH_3 \\ \diagdown \\ \quad\quad C=CH_2 \\ \diagup \\ CH_3 \end{array}$$. A monoalkylated alkene of three carbons is

$CH_3CH=CH_2$. Hence the compound is a monoalkylated alkene and is also a primary alcohol. Since there is only one carbon attached to the $-CH=CH_2$ portion, it must contain the -OH functionality (the sp^2-hybridized carbons cannot bear the -OH, for it would not account for the spectrum shown). Hence, the compound is an allyl alcohol and has the structure $CH_2=CHCH_2OH$. The principle absorptions of the infrared spectrum are labeled below:

31

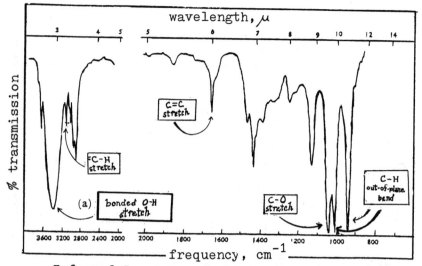

Infrared Spectrum of Allyl Alcohol

(b)   The major feature of this spectrum is the strong sharp
absorption at 1700 cm^{-1}. This is the typical absorption of

the C=O stretch of a carboxylic acid (R-$\overset{\overset{\displaystyle O}{\|}}{C}$OH). The strong
band at 1240 cm^{-1} is the C-O stretch. Further spectral
evidence of a carboxylic acid is the strong O-H bend near
1455 cm^{-1} and 950 cm^{-1}, and the very broad O-H stretch
centered at 2800 cm^{-1}. If we subtract the molecular

formula (M.F.) of the known portion (-$\overset{\overset{\displaystyle O}{\|}}{C}$OH) from the M.F.
of the compound ($C_4H_6O_2$), we will have the M.F. of the
unidentified portion of the compound. We find that a
C_3H_5 portion remains to be identified. By manipulating the
atoms in various arrangements we see that there are only
four possibilities for the structure of a C_3H_5 group. They
are:

(1) $H_2C=CH-CH_2-$

(2) $CH_3-CH=CH-$

(3)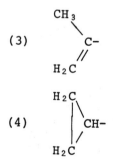

(4) $\begin{matrix} H_2C \\ | \\ H_2C \end{matrix} \!\! \begin{matrix} \diagdown \\ \diagup \end{matrix} \!\! CH-$

    Structures (1), (2) and (3) each has   one π bond;
structure (4) does not due to its cyclic nature. The
spectral data show   that structure (4) is the C_3H_5 portion

of the compound. The methylene C-H stretch of the cyclopropyl group absorbs at 3075 cm^{-1}. The methine C-H stretch
absorbs at 3000 cm^{-1}. These absorptions are difficult to
notice because they overlap with the broad band of the
O-H stretch. Structures (1), (2) and (3) can be ruled out
as the C_3H_5 group because the i.r. spectrum shows none of
the characteristic bands for alkenes. For example, there
are no strong sharp bands at 700 cm^{-1}, 890 cm^{-1}, 910 cm^{-1}
or 990 cm^{-1}, which is characteristic of the C-H out-of-
plane bending of alkenes. There is, however, a strong broad
band at 950 cm^{-1} which is the O-H bend. Hence the compound
is cyclopropylcarboxylic acid and has the structure

$$
\begin{array}{c}
H_2C \\
\quad \diagdown \\
\qquad \quad \overset{O}{\overset{\|}{CH\text{-}C\text{-}OH}} \\
\quad \diagup \\
H_2C
\end{array}
$$

. The principle absorption bands of the

infrared spectrum are labeled below:

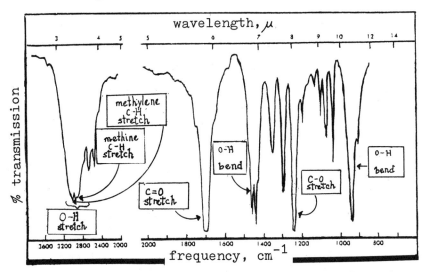

Infrared Spectrum of Cyclopropylcarboxylic Acid

RAMAN SPECTROSCOPY

• PROBLEM 2-6

Classify the following molecules according to the
general characteristics expected for their infrared and
Raman spectra: (a) Cl_2; (b) HCl; (c) CO; (d) $CF_2=CH_2$
(double bond stretch only).

Solution: Raman spectroscopy is often used in conjunction
with infrared spectroscopy in the identification of organic
functionalities. Raman spectra arise from the absorption
of monochromatic light by a sample before it is emitted as

scattered light. As in infrared spectra, Raman spectra are recorded in wavenumbers. Frequently a Raman spectrum will reveal something that was missed in the infrared spectrum. This is because a bond which has no dipole moment (i.e., is electrically symmetrical) will appear in the Raman spectrum but will not appear in the infrared spectrum. With this information we can predict the general characteristics expected for the infrared and Raman spectra of compounds (a) through (d).

(a) The Cl-Cl bond of the chlorine molecule has no dipole moment because, like all other diatomic molecules (H_2, O_2, Br_2), the two identical atoms exert equal and opposite electronegative effects upon each other. Hence the infrared spectrum of Cl_2 will show no absorptions and the Raman spectrum will show a strong Cl-Cl absorption.

(b) The H-Cl bond of hydrogen chloride is fairly polar due to the considerable difference in electronegativity of hydrogen and chlorine, whose electronegativities are 2.1 and 3.0, respectively. As a result, both the infrared and Raman spectrum of HCl will show a strong H-Cl stretch. The dipole moment of HCl is directed toward the chlorine (because of its greater electronegativity) as shown:

H $+\!\longrightarrow$ Cl

(c) Carbon monoxide is a polar molecule and its structure can be shown by two main resonance structures:

$:\!\overset{-}{C}\!\equiv\!\overset{+}{O}:$ $\longleftrightarrow$ $:\!C\!=\!\overset{..}{\overset{..}{O}}.$

Note: Resonance structures do not exist independently; they only approximate what the molecule really looks like. That is, the molecule is actually a hybrid of the resonance structures.

The principal characteristic of the infrared and Raman spectra will be the strong C=O stretch.

(d) The C=C double bond of 1,1-difluoroethylene is polar because of the powerful electron withdrawing effects of the two fluorine atoms:

The net result is:

F_2C $\longleftarrow\!\!+$ CH_2

The C=C bond will appear as a strong band in both the infrared and Raman spectra.

ULTRAVIOLET SPECTROSCOPY

The ultraviolet spectrum of 3,6,6-trimethylcyclohex-2-en-1-one, is shown below. The concentration is 1.486×10^{-5} g ml^{-1} in ethanol and the path length is 1.0 cm. Calculate ε and compare λ_{max} with the value predicted by Woodward's rules.

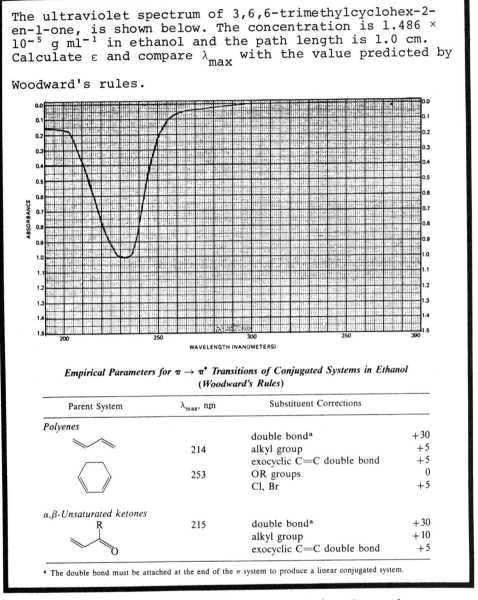

Empirical Parameters for $\pi \rightarrow \pi^*$ Transitions of Conjugated Systems in Ethanol
(Woodward's Rules)

Parent System	λ_{max}, nm	Substituent Corrections	
Polyenes			
		double bond[a]	+30
	214	alkyl group	+5
		exocyclic C=C double bond	+5
	253	OR groups	0
		Cl, Br	+5
α,β-Unsaturated ketones			
R	215	double bond[a]	+30
		alkyl group	+10
		exocyclic C=C double bond	+5

[a] The double bond must be attached at the end of the π system to produce a linear conjugated system.

Solution: Ultraviolet spectroscopy involves the excitation of an electron in its ground state level to a higher energy level. This is accomplished by irradiating a sample with ultraviolet light (electromagnetic radiation with wavelengths in the range of 200 nanometers (nm) to 400 nm). The wavelength of maximum absorption (λ_{max}) can be calculated by using Woodward's Rules.

λ_{max} has a specific degree of absorbance associated with it. The absorbance at a particular wavelength is dependent upon the intensity or molar absorptivity, ε, of the incident light. The molar absorptivity is related to the absorbance by the equation

$$\varepsilon = \frac{\log\ (I_0/I)}{c\ \ell}$$

where I_0 = initial light intensity

          I = final light intensity

          c = concentration of sample in moles per liter

          ℓ = path length of sample tube in centimeters

Beer's Law relates the absorbance A to I_0 and I by the equation:

     $A = \log\ (I_0/I)$

Hence the equation for molar absorptivity can be written as:

$$\varepsilon = \frac{A}{c\ell}$$

where A = absorbance at λ_{max} .

To calculate λ_{max} by Woodward's Rules, we must look at the parent system of 3,6,6-trimethylcyclohex-2-en-1-one:

The parent compound is an α,β-unsaturated ketone, therefore λ_{max} is at least 215 nm. There are two alkyl substituents on the parent system of our compound:

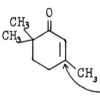 this sp²-hybridized carbon has two alkyl groups attached

For each alkyl group substituted on the α,β-unsaturated ketone, a correction of + 10 nm must be made according to Woodward's Rules. Therefore, the calculated λ_{max}

$\left(\lambda_{max}^{calc}\right)$ for 3,6,6-trimethylcyclohex-2-en-1-one is

215 nm for the parent system $\left(\begin{array}{c} \text{[structure with R, O]} \end{array} \right)$ plus 2

(10 nm) or 20 nm for the two alkyl groups substituted on the β-carbon of the α,β-unsaturated ketone.

$$\lambda_{max}^{calc} = 215 \text{ nm} + 20 \text{ nm}$$

$$\lambda_{max}^{calc} = 235 \text{ nm}$$

By looking at the ultraviolet spectrum of our compound, we see that λ_{max}^{calc} is very close to the experimental λ_{max}

$\left(\lambda_{max}^{expl} \right)$. The λ_{max}^{expl} is 233 nm whereas the λ_{max}^{calc} is 235 nm;

this discrepancy of 2 nm falls within the experimental margin of error and confirms the validity (and accuracy) of Woodward's Rules.

The molar absorptivity (ε) may be calculated by using the aforementioned equation

$$\varepsilon = \frac{A}{c\ell}$$

where   A = absorbance at λ_{max}^{expl}

    c = concentration of sample in moles per liter

    ℓ = path length of sample tube in centimeters.

By looking at the ultraviolet spectrum, we see that the absorbance at λ_{max}^{expl} (233 nm) is 1.0. There are no units for absorbance and the molar absorptivity is expressed in liters per mole per centimeter (liters mole^{-1} cm^{-1}). The path length of the sample tube is given as 1.0 centimeter. The concentration of the sample in ethanol is given in grams (g) per milliliter (ml). This must be converted to moles per liter. Since 1 liter = 1000 ml, multiplying the given concentration by 1000 will give us the concentration in grams per liter:

$$1.486 \times 10^{-5} \text{ (g/ml)} \times 10^3 \text{ (ml/liter)} =$$

$$1.486 \times 10^{-2} \text{ (g/liter)}$$

We must now convert grams to moles to give us the proper unit. Since moles = $\frac{g}{MW}$ (MW is the molecular weight of the sample), and the MW of 3,6,6-trimethylcyclohex-2-en-1-one is 138, we can calculate the concentration in moles per liter as shown:

$$1.486 \times 10^{-2} \; (g/liter) \times \frac{1}{138 \; (g/mole)}$$

$$= 1.08 \times 10^{-4} \; (moles/liter)$$

The molar absorptivity may now be calculated as follows:

$$\varepsilon = \frac{1.0}{1.08 \times 10^{-4} \; (moles/liter) \times 1.0 \; (cm)}$$

$$\varepsilon = 9260 \; liters \; mole^{-1} \; cm^{-1}$$

● PROBLEM 2-8

Calculate the percentage of the incident light which would be absorbed by an 0.010-M solution of acetone in cyclohexane contained in a quartz cell 0.1 cm long at 2800 Å and 1900 Å.

Some Electronic Transitions of Simple Organic Molecules

Compound	Type	λ_{max}, A	ε_{max} [a]	Solvent [b]
$(CH_3)_2C=O$	$n \rightarrow \pi*$	2800	15	cyclohexane
	$\pi \rightarrow \pi*$ [c]	1900	1,100	
	$n \rightarrow \sigma*$ [c]	1560	strong	
$CH_2=CH_2$	$\pi \rightarrow \pi*$	1620	10,000	vapor
$CH_2=CH—CH=CH_2$	$\pi \rightarrow \pi*$	2170	20,900	hexane
$CH_3—CH=CH—CH=CH—CH_3$	$\pi \rightarrow \pi*$	2270	22,500	hexane
$CH_2=CH—CH_2—CH_2—CH=CH_2$	$\pi \rightarrow \pi*$	1850	20,000	alcohol
$CH_3—C\equiv CH$	$\pi \rightarrow \pi*$	1865	450	cyclohexane
$CH_2=CH—C=O$	$n \rightarrow \pi*$	3240	24	alcohol
|	$\pi \rightarrow \pi*$	2190	3,600	
CH_3				
CH_4	$\sigma \rightarrow \sigma*$ [d]	1219	strong	vapor
$CH_3—CH_3$	$\sigma \rightarrow \sigma*$ [d]	1350	strong	vapor
$CH_3—Cl$	$n \rightarrow \sigma*$ [e]	1725	weak	vapor
$CH_3—Br$	$n \rightarrow \sigma*$ [e]	2040	200	vapor
$CH_3—I$	$n \rightarrow \sigma*$ [e]	2575	365	pentane
$CH_3—O—H$	$n \rightarrow \sigma*$ [e]	1835	150	vapor
$CH_3—O—CH_3$	$n \rightarrow \sigma*$ [e]	1838	2,520	vapor
$(CH_3)_3N$	$n \rightarrow \sigma*$ [e]	2273	900	vapor

[a] The molar extinction coefficient ε is a measure of the absorption efficiency at the wavelength λ_{max}. Since the amount of absorption will be proportional to the concentration (c moles/liter) and thickness of the sample (l cm), ε is obtained from the equation

$$\varepsilon = \frac{1}{cl} \log_{10} \frac{I_0}{I}$$

where I_0/I is the ratio of intensity of incident light I_0 to transmitted light I. The per cent transmission of a solution is $(I/I_0) \times 100$. Substances for which ε is independent of concentration are said to obey Beer's law (or the Beer-Lambert law).

[b] It is necessary to specify the solvent since λ_{max} and ε_{max} vary somewhat with solvent.

[c] These assignments are not certain.

[d] Transitions $\sigma \rightarrow \sigma*$ correspond to excitation of an electron of a single bond (designated σ) to a higher antibonding state (designated $\sigma*$).

[e] Transitions $n \rightarrow \sigma*$ correspond to excitation of an electron of an unshared (i.e., nonbonding) pair to an antibonding state ($\sigma*$) of a σ bond in the molecule.

Solution: The percentage of light absorbed is related to the percentage of light transmitted by the equation

$$\% \text{ A} = 100 - \% \text{ T}$$

where % A = % absorbance

% T = % transmittance

The absorbance (A) is related to the initial intensity (I_0) and the final intensity (I) by Beer's Law:

$$A = \log\left(\frac{I_0}{I}\right)$$

We can therefore relate the transmittance (T) to I_0 and I as:

$$T = \frac{I}{I_0}$$

The absorbance of the incident light of a sample solution may be calculated by using the equation for molar absorptivity (ε):

$$\varepsilon = \frac{1}{c\ell} \log\left(\frac{I_0}{I}\right)$$

where ε = molar absorptivity in liters mole^{-1} cm^{-1}

c = concentration of sample in moles per liter

ℓ = path length of sample tube in centimeters

At a wavelength of 2800 $\overset{\circ}{\text{A}}$ (Angstrom; 10 $\overset{\circ}{\text{A}}$ = 1 nm), a solution of acetone in cyclohexane solvent has a molar absorptivity of 15 liters mole^{-1} cm^{-1}. The path length is 0.1 cm and the molar concentration is 0.01. The absorbance can be calculated as follows:

$$\varepsilon = \frac{1}{c\ell} \log\left(\frac{I_0}{I}\right)$$

$$15 = \frac{1}{(0.01)(0.1)} \log\left(\frac{I_0}{I}\right)$$

$$0.015 = \log\left(\frac{I_0}{I}\right)$$

$$\frac{I_0}{I} = 1.04$$

Since T = $\frac{I}{I_0}$, then:

$$T = \frac{1}{\frac{I_0}{I}} = \frac{1}{1.04} = 0.9615$$

$$\% \text{ T} = 100 \times \text{T}$$

$$\% \text{ T} = 100 \times 0.9615$$

$$\% \text{ T} = 96.15$$

$$\% \text{ A} = 100 - \% \text{ T}$$

$$\% \text{ A} = 100 - 96.15$$

$$\% \text{ A} = 3.85$$

Hence at 2800 Å there is 3.85% absorption of the incident light. At a wavelength of 1900 Å the molar absorptivity is 1100 liters mole^{-1} cm^{-1}. The percentage absorbance may be calculated as:

$$\varepsilon = \frac{1}{c\ell} \log \left(\frac{I_0}{I} \right)$$

$$1100 = \frac{1}{(0.01)(0.1)} \log \left(\frac{I_0}{I} \right)$$

$$1.10 = \log \left(\frac{I_0}{I} \right)$$

$$\frac{I_0}{I} = 12.6$$

$$\text{T} = \frac{1}{\frac{I_0}{I}} = \frac{1}{12.6} = 0.0794$$

$$\% \text{ T} = 100 \times \text{T} = 100 \times 0.0794$$

$$\% \text{ T} = 7.94$$

$$\% \text{ A} = 100 - \% \text{ T} = 100 - 7.94$$

$$\% \text{ A} = 92.06$$

Hence at 1900 Å there is 92.06% absorption of the incident light by a 0.01 M solution of acetone in cyclohexane.

● **PROBLEM 2-9**

Compounds A, B and C have the formula C_5H_8, and on hydrogenation all yield n-pentane. Their ultraviolet spectra show the following values of λ_{max}: A, 176 nm; B, 211 nm; C, 215 nm. (1-Pentene has λ_{max} 178 nm.) (a) What is a likely structure for A? For B and C? (b) What kind of information might enable you to assign specific structures to B and C?

Solution: (a) The molecular formula of compounds A, B and C is of the general form C_nH_{2n-2}. This formula indicates

that the compounds are hydrocarbons with either one carbon-carbon triple bond (an alkyne), two carbon-carbon double bonds (a diene), two rings, or one ring and one carbon-carbon double bond; that is, the compounds have two units of unsaturation. Since hydrogenation of the compounds yield n-pentane, and hydrogenation of alkynes and dienes does not change the carbon skeleton, all the compounds must be straight-chained. Hence the compounds are normal five-carbon alkynes or dienes.

Compound A has maximum absorption at a wavelength of 176 nm (λ_{max}). Since this is very close to the λ_{max} of

1-pentene, compound A must have a chromophore similar to that of 1-pentene. A chromophore is a functional group that gives rise to an absorption with characteristic λ_{max} and ε

(molar absorptivity) values. Hence compound A's chromophore, like 1-pentene, is an isolated double bond. The only structure of a normal five-carbon compound with two units of unsaturation and isolated double bonds is 1,4-pentadiene:

$H_2C=CH-CH_2-HC=CH_2$

1,4-pentadiene

(Compound A)

Compounds B and C have λ_{max} of 211 nm and 215 nm,

respectively. These values are greater than that of compound A and are of lower energies (longer wavelength (λ), lower frequency, lower energy). One thing that could account for this is if B and C were conjugated dienes. Conjugated dienes are compounds that have two double bonds separated by one single bond (R-CH=CH-CH=CH-R'). The extra stability of conjugated dienes as compared to the analogous non-conjugated dienes is due to electron delocalization in the former. This extra stability lessens the energy difference between the ground state and excited state. Hence the frequency necessary for the maximum absorption of the compound is less than expected and the wavelength (λ_{max})

will be greater. Therefore compounds B and C must be geometric isomers of the conjugated compound, 1,3-pentadiene. These are the "E" and "Z" isomers:

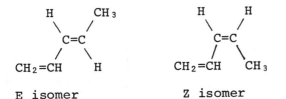

E isomer   Z isomer

(b) The E and Z isomers of the diene can be distinguished by their heats of hydrogenation. The Z isomer is less stable

41

than the E isomer because of steric considerations, due to the proximity of the vinyl and methyl groups. This means that the Z isomer will have a higher heat of hydrogenation than the E isomer.

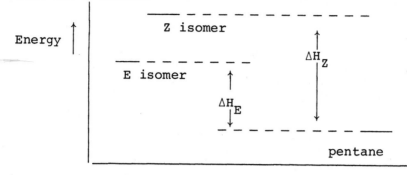

Reaction coordinate $\longrightarrow$

where $|\Delta H_Z| > |\Delta H_E|$

ΔH_Z = heat of hydrogenation

for the Z isomer

ΔH_E = heat of hydrogenation

for the E isomer.

NMR SPECTROSCOPY

● PROBLEM 2-10

Deduce the structure corresponding to each of the following nmr spectra:

(a) $C_2H_3Cl_3$

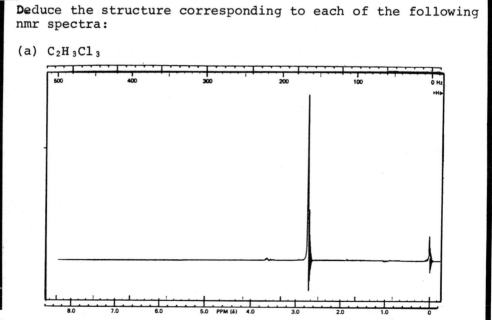

(b) $C_2H_3Br_3$

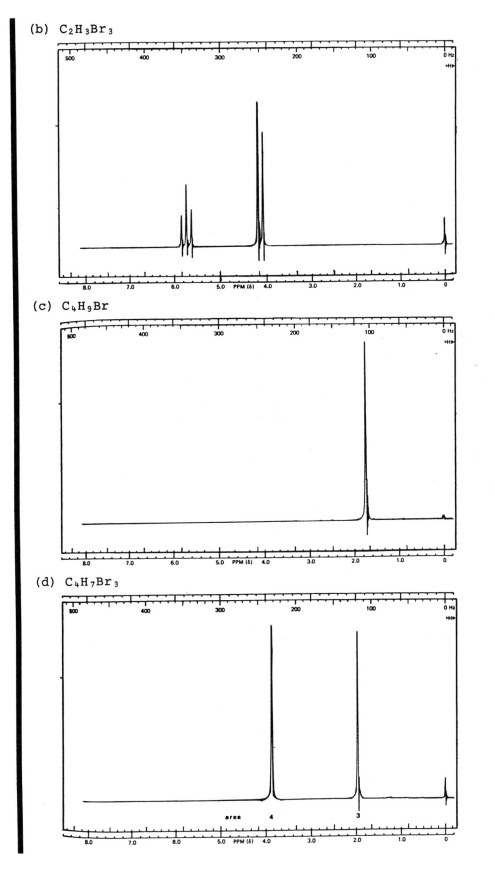

(c) C_4H_9Br

(d) $C_4H_7Br_3$

area   4   3

(e) $C_2H_4Br_2$

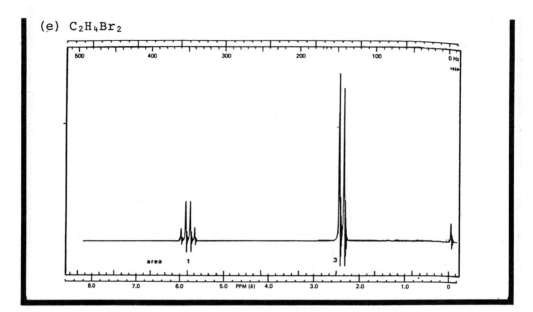

Solution: Certain atoms have a nuclear spin similar to
the spin of an electron. The spinning of charged particles
(the proton(s) in the nucleus bears a positive charge)
generates a magnetic field. When an atom is placed in an
external magnetic field, the magnetic field generated by
the nucleus will be aligned with or against the external
magnetic field. At some frequency of electromagnetic
radiation, the nucleus will absorb energy and "flip" over
so that it reverses its alignment with respect to the
external magnetic field. This is known as the nuclear
magnetic resonance (nmr) phenomenon. It is generally
concerned with the nuclear magnetic resonance of hydrogen
atoms and is therefore sometimes called proton magnetic
resonance (pmr).   It is also standard practice for the
frequency of radiation to be kept constant while the
strength of the external magnetic field is varied. At some
value of the magnetic field strength, the energy required
to flip the proton matches the energy of the radiation.
Absorption will occur and a signal will be observed. The
spectrum that results from all these absorptions is called
an nmr spectrum. Absorptions that occur at relatively low
field strengths are downfield relative to those that occur
at higher field strengths. The field strength at which a
proton will absorb energy is called the chemical shift
(measured in parts per million, ppm or δ, relative to
the absorbance of $Si(CH_3)_4$, tetramethylsilane). The
chemical shift of a proton depends upon the proton's
electronic environment. Electron withdrawing atoms (or
groups) that are nearby a proton will decrease the electron
density about that proton; this is known as a deshielding
effect. The proton's absorption will occur downfield from
what is expected. Specifically, the proton will absorb at
a smaller field strength than a proton experiencing no
deshielding effects. Electron releasing atoms (or groups)
that are nearby a proton will increase the proton's
electron density; the proton is experiencing a shielding
effect. The proton's absorbance will occur upfield (higher
magnetic field strength) from what is expected.

The signal that arises from a proton's absorption may occur as a singlet, a doublet, a triplet, etc. The number of peaks in the signal depends upon the neighboring protons. Protons that are in identical electronic environments are equivalent protons; those that are in non-identical electronic environments are non-equivalent protons. A proton that has n non-equivalent adjacent protons will have a signal with n + 1 peaks, called a n + 1 multiplet. This is the result of spin-spin splitting of the protons. For example, all the protons of ethane (CH_3-CH_3) are in identical electronic environments and are therefore equivalent. Hence there will be no spin-spin splitting of the protons; the nmr spectrum will contain only singlets (signals with one peak). Furthermore, since all the protons in ethane are equivalent they will have identical chemical shifts, and will occur as one signal. Hence the nmr spectrum of ethane will have one singlet. An example where spin-spin splitting occurs is propane. The methylene protons are non-equivalent to the methyl protons. As a result, the six non-equivalent adjacent methyl protons will split the methylene proton's signal into a heptet (seven peak multiplet).

The relative areas under the signals in an nmr spectrum indicate the relative number of protons that give rise to each signal.

With our basic understanding of nuclear magnetic resonance, we can now deduce the structures of (a) through (e).

(a) The compound's molecular formula ($C_2H_3Cl_3$) is of the type C_2*_6, where * represents an atom that forms a single bond with carbon. The formula C_2*_6 is of the form C_n*_{2n+2} and indicates that the carbon compound is saturated; there are only σ bonds in this compound. The nmr spectrum shows a singlet at about 2.7 δ. Since the signal is a singlet there is no spin-spin splitting. This means that the three protons in the compound are equivalent. Since the two carbons are adjacent all three protons must be on one carbon for no spin-spin splitting to occur. Hence the compound is 1,1,1-trichloroethane and has the structure:

```
    H Cl
    | |
H-C-C-Cl
    | |
    H Cl
```

(b) As in part (a), the molecular formula ($C_2H_3Br_3$) is of the form C_n*_{2n+2}, and is hence a saturated carbon compound. The nmr spectrum has a doublet near 4.2 δ and a triplet near 5.7 δ. These multiplets occurred as a result of spin-spin splitting. Since there is a doublet and a triplet in the spectrum, and there are three hydrogen atoms in the compound, we can conclude that there is one hydrogen adjacent to two non-equivalent hydrogens. This means that the carbon with one hydrogen has two bromines

and the carbon bearing two hydrogens has one bromine. The
compound is 1,1,2-tribromoethane:

The lone $-CHBr_2$ hydrogen split the $-CH_2Br$ signal
into a doublet; the two $-CH_2Br$ hydrogens split the $-CHBr_2$
signal into a triplet. The $-CHBr_2$ signal occurred downfield from the $-CH_2Br$ signal because the deshielding
effect of two bromine atoms is greater than that of one
bromine atom.

(c)   The molecular formula (C_4H_9Br) is of the form
C_n*_{2n+2} and is therefore a saturated carbon compound. The
nmr spectrum has a singlet at 1.7 δ; this indicates that
there is no spin-spin splitting. Hence, all the hydrogens
are equivalent; they are in identical electronic environments. The only manner in which all the hydrogens are
equivalent is if there are three methyl ($-CH_3$) groups. This
leaves us with a $-CBr$ portion. The only possible structure
is:

$$
\begin{array}{c}
CH_3 \\
| \\
CH_3-C-Br \\
| \\
CH_3
\end{array}
$$

2-bromo-2-methylpropane

(d)   As in parts (a) through (c) the molecular formula
($C_4H_7Br_3$) of the compound indicates that the compound is
saturated. The nmr spectrum shows a singlet at 3.9 δ
and another singlet at 2.0 δ, having relative intensities
(relative areas) of four and three, respectively. The
absence of multiplets means that no spin-spin splitting
occurred. If all the protons were equivalent, the spectrum
would show only one signal because equivalent protons
have identical chemical shifts. The fact that there
are two signals indicates that there are two sets of
non-equivalent protons. Since there are seven hydrogens
in the compound, and the sum of the relative intensities
is seven, the relative intensities show the actual number
of protons absorbing per molecule. The signal at 2.0 δ
with a relative intensity of three must have arisen from
the absorption of a methyl group's protons. This is because
in a saturated four-carbon compound, a methyl group is
the only group that has three equivalent hydrogens. Since
no spin-spin splitting occurred the methyl group must be
separated from the other hydrogens by a carbon bearing no
hydrogens. In order for the four remaining hydrogens to be
equivalent (they gave rise to the same signal), they must
be part of equivalent groups. The signal that occurs at
3.9 δ is characteristic of an $R-CH_2-Br$ chemical shift.
With this in mind we can conclude that the four remaining

hydrogens are part of two -CH₂Br groups. The structure of
the compound is:

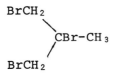

2-bromomethyl-1,2-dibromopropane

(e) Once again we are dealing with a saturated carbon
compound, this one having a molecular formula of $C_2H_4Br_2$.
The nmr spectrum shows a doublet at 2.4 δ and a quartet
at 5.8 δ, with relative intensities of three and one,
respectively. The presence of these multiplets means
that spin-spin splitting occurred. The protons that gave
rise to the doublet were split by one non-equivalent
proton. The proton that gave rise to the quartet was split
by three non-equivalent protons. Since we are restricted
to two carbons, the only possible compound is 1,1-di-
bromoethane:

```
     H  Br
     |  |
 H-C-C-H
     |  |
     H  Br
```

● **PROBLEM** 2-11

(a) On catalytic hydrogenation, compound A, C_5H_8, gave
cis-1,2-dimethylcyclopropane. On this basis, three
isomeric structures were considered possible for A. What
were they? (b) Absence of infrared absorption at
890 cm⁻¹ made one of the structures unlikely. Which one
was it? (c) The nmr spectrum of A showed signals at δ 2.22
and δ 1.04 with intensity ratio 3:1. Which of the three
structures in (a) is consistent with this? (d) The base
peak in the mass spectrum was found at m/e 67. What ion
was this peak probably due to, and how do you account for
its abundance? (e) Compound A was synthesized in one step
from open-chain compounds. How do you think this was done?

Solution: (a) Catalytic hydrogenation of alkenes
(compounds with a carbon-carbon double bond) yields the
corresponding alkanes (saturated hydrocarbons). The reaction
proceeds with the cis addition of two hydrogen atoms to the
double bond; the hydrogens add onto the same side of the
double bond.

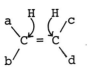 →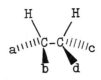

47

Note: ▶ = bond coming towards reader

|ιιιιι· = bond going away from reader

Compound A underwent catalytic hydrogenation to yield
cis-1,2-dimethylcyclopropane:

C_5H_8 catalytic
Compound A   hydrogenation →

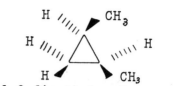

cis-1,2-dimethylcyclopropane

    Since compound A's molecular formula (C_5H_8) contains
two less hydrogens than the hydrogenation product's
molecular formula (C_5H_{10}), there must have only been one
double bond in compound A because only one mole of hydrogen
gas was consumed in the reaction. There are three possible
positions for a double bond to be created in cis-1,2-di-
methylcyclopropane. There can be a double bond coming off
the ring to a methylene group:

There can be a tetrasubstituted alkene:

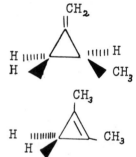

    The third possibility is a trisubstituted alkene:

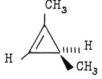

    Catalytic hydrogenation of these three compounds all
yield cis-1,2-dimethylcyclopropane. Note that the tetrasubstituted alkene yields only the cis product upon
catalytic hydrogenation. The other two yield cis and trans
products, depending upon which side of the double bond was
hydrogenated.

(b)   Disubstituted terminal alkenes ($R_2C=CH_2$) characteristically have a strong band at 890 cm^{-1} in the infrared
spectrum. This is the absorption of the C-H out-of-plane
bending vibrations. Since the infrared spectrum of compound
A has no such band, we can eliminate the terminal alkene

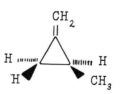

as a possible structure for A.

48

(c)   Since there are eight hydrogens in compound A, and
the sum of the relative intensities is four, the relative
intensities represent one half the number of protons
absorbed per molecule. Hence for every molecule there are
six protons absorbing at δ 2.22 and two protons absorbing
at δ 1.04. The presence of two signals in the nmr spectrum
indicates that there are two sets of non-equivalent protons
(that have different chemical shifts, hence different
signals). Of the three possible structures for compound A
in part (a), only the tetrasubstituted alkene has two sets
of non-equivalent hydrogens. The six methyl hydrogens are
non-equivalent to the two methylene hydrogens:

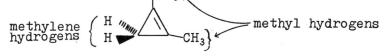

methylene hydrogens

methyl hydrogens

The terminal alkene that was previously suggested as
a possible structure for A has five sets of non-equivalent
hydrogens. The trisubstituted alkene that was suggested has
four sets of non-equivalent hydrogens. Hence the only structure from part (a) that is consistent with the nmr spectrum
is the tetrasubstituted alkene, 1,2-dimethylcyclopropene:

(d)   The base peak in a mass spectrum is the peak which
corresponds to the positively charged species of highest
stability upon a compound's fragmentation. The cation with
molecular weight 67 must be formed by loss of a hydride
anion from compound A which has a molecular weight of 68.
This cation will be consistent with the proposal that
compound A is 1,2-dimethylcyclopropene in that the subsequently formed cation will contain two π electrons and
be aromatic. Its aromaticity is determined by Hückel's
rule which states that a cyclic, conjugated π system of
4n+ 2π electrons (where n is an integer) is aromatic.
Aromaticity and its associated electron delocalization
confer stability upon the cation, agreeing with the
spectral data. The cyclopropenyl ion has the following
structure:

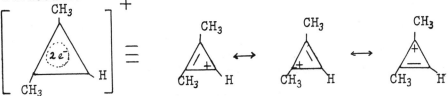

(e)   The only way to synthesize this cyclopropene ring
from open chain reagents would be through the use of the
carbene, methylene (CH_2:) and the acetylene derivative,
2-butyne. The carbene is generated via diazomethane's
loss of nitrogen upon heating, and its free pair of
electrons allow it to be reactive enough to add to sites
of unsaturation such as a triple bond. On occasion, it may

even add to alkenes. Thus the synthesis would be as follows:

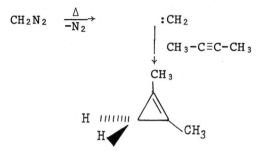

$$CH_2N_2 \xrightarrow[-N_2]{\Delta} \quad :CH_2$$

The Figure below shows the proton n.m.r. spectrum of
$(CH_3)_2C(OH)CH_2COCH_3$ with tetramethylsilane as standard.
The stepped line is an electronic integration of the areas
under the signal peaks. (a) List the chemical shift of
each proton signal in ppm, and deduce, from the trace of
the integrated areas, the identity of the protons that give
rise to each line. (b) List the line positions in cps
relative to tetramethylsilane expected at 100 Mcps.
(c) Sketch out the spectrum and integral expected for
$CH_3COC(CH_3)_2CHO$ at 60 Mcps.

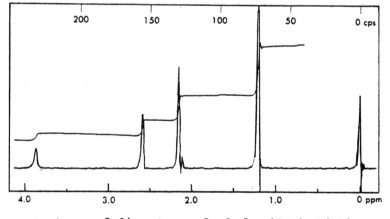

N.m.r. spectrum of diacetone alcohol, $(CH_3)_2C(OH)CH_2COCH_3$
at 60 Mcps relative to TMS 0.00 ppm. The stepped line
is the integrated spectrum.

Solution: (a) To assign the identity of the protons to
the spectral lines, we must look at the different types of
protons within the molecule. Once we have identified all
the non-equivalent protons in the molecule, we must determine their relative chemical shifts. When we have deduced
the relative order of chemical shifts, we can read off the
chemical shift of each signal and assign these values to
particular protons. Diacetone alcohol has the following
structure:

$$\begin{array}{ccc} \text{OH} & & \text{O} \\ | & & || \\ \text{CH}_3\text{-C-CH}_2\text{-C-CH}_3 \\ | \\ \text{CH}_3 \end{array}$$

There are no two adjacent carbons in this molecule that bear non-equivalent hydrogens. This is supported by the fact that all the signals in the nmr spectrum are singlets; no spin-spin splitting took place. The methylene ($-CH_2-$) and hydroxyl ($-OH$) protons are unique in this molecule and hence constitute their own type of proton.

The protons of the ketone methyl group ($-\overset{\overset{\textstyle O}{||}}{C}-CH_3$) are non-equivalent to the protons of the other methyl groups by inspection. The protons of the two methyl groups bonded to the carbinol carbon ($(CH_3)_2COH-$) are in identical electronic environments (made possible by the ability of the carbinol carbon to rotate about its single bonds) and are therefore equivalent. Hence there are four sets of non-equivalent protons in diacetone alcohol; they are labeled below as   a   through   d :

$$\begin{array}{cccc} & a & & \\ & \text{OH} & \text{O} & \\ b & | & || & d \\ \text{CH}_3\text{-C} & \text{---} & \text{CH}_2\text{-C-CH}_3 & \\ & | & c & \\ & \text{CH}_3 & & \\ b & & & \end{array}$$

The nmr signal of proton   a   will be downfield from all the other signals; it will absorb energy at a lower field strength (higher chemical shift) than any other proton   in the molecule. This is due to the powerful de-shielding effect of oxygen; this proton's electron density is the least of all the protons in the molecule. The next most deshielded protons are those of the methylene (c) group. The electron withdrawing effects of the adjacent carbonyl group

$$\begin{array}{c} \text{O} \\ || \\ (\text{-C-}) \end{array}$$ and the nearby hydroxyl group ($-OH$) have a powerful combined deshielding effect. The ketone methyl group ex-periences deshielding from only the carbonyl group, and the   b   protons experience deshielding from only the nearby hydroxyl group. Since the carbonyl group has greater electron-

withdrawing capabilities than the carbinol group ($-\overset{\overset{\textstyle OH}{|}}{\underset{|}{C}}-$), the

ketone methyl group is more deshielded than the   b   protons. Hence the relative order of deshielding and chemical shift values of the proton types   a   through   d   are:

$$a \; > \; c \; > \; d \; > \; b$$

By looking at the nmr spectrum of diacetone alcohol, we can see that the chemical shifts of the four signals are 3.85, 2.6, 2.15 and 1.2. By using the relative amounts of deshielding of each type of proton, we can assign the

51

protons to a particular chemical shift as follows:
        -OH proton, 3.85 ppm; -CH$_2$- proton, 2.6 ppm;

-COCH$_3$ proton, 2.15 ppm; (CH$_3$)$_2$C-OH proton, 1.2 ppm.

(b) The signals in an nmr spectrum are measured relative to
an internal standard such as tetramethylsilane (Si(CH$_3$)$_4$)
for matters of convenience. Traditionally the chemical shift
is measured in ppm (parts per million), but it can also be
measured in cps (cycles per second) or H$_z$ (Hertz). The line
positions in cps relative to TMS (tetramethylsilane) expected
at a frequency of 100 Mcps (1 mega cps = 1 million cps) can
be calculated by using the line positions of the spectrum
at 60 Mcps. This is accomplished by using a direct
proportion:

$$\frac{60 \text{ Mcps}}{100 \text{ Mcps}} = \frac{\text{relative cps at } \nu = 60 \text{ Mcps}}{\text{expected cps at } \nu = 100 \text{ Mcps}}$$

        The line positions in cps of the nmr spectrum shown
at 60 Mcps are:- OH proton, 232 cps; -CH$_2$- proton, 157 cps;

-COCH$_3$ proton, 128 cps; (CH$_3$)$_2$C- proton, 72 cps. We can
calculate the expected line positions in cps relative to
TMS at 100 Mcps as shown.

        For the -OH proton:

$$\frac{60 \text{ Mcps}}{100 \text{ Mcps}} = \frac{232 \text{ cps (at } \nu = 60 \text{ Mcps)}}{\text{expected cps (at } \nu = 100 \text{ Mcps)}}$$

expected cps = 387

        For the -CH$_2$- proton:

$$\frac{60 \text{ Mcps}}{100 \text{ Mcps}} = \frac{157 \text{ cps}}{\text{expected cps}}$$

expected cps = 262

        For the -COCH$_3$ proton:

$$\frac{60 \text{ Mcps}}{100 \text{ Mcps}} = \frac{128 \text{ cps}}{\text{expected cps}}$$

expected cps = 213

        For the (CH$_3$)$_2$C- proton:

$$\frac{60 \text{ Mcps}}{100 \text{ Mcps}} = \frac{72 \text{ cps}}{\text{expected cps}}$$

expected cps = 120
        The expected line positions in cps relative to TMS
at 100 Mcps are: - OH proton, 387 cps; -CH$_2$- proton, 262 cps;

-COCH$_3$ proton, 213 cps; (CH$_3$)$_2$-C- proton, 120 cps.

(c)   The compound CH$_3$COC(CH$_3$)$_2$CHO is 2,2-dimethyl-3-oxo-
butanal and has the structure:

$$\underset{\displaystyle CH_3}{\underset{\displaystyle |}{CH_3-\overset{\displaystyle O}{\overset{\displaystyle ||}{C}} - \overset{\displaystyle CH_3}{\overset{\displaystyle |}{\underset{|}{C_{\text{②}}}}} - \overset{\displaystyle O}{\overset{\displaystyle ||}{C_{\text{①}}}}-H}}$$

        The ketone methyl group is non-equivalent to the other
methyl groups by inspection. These other methyl groups,
bonded to carbon number 2, are in identical electronic

environments (because of carbon 2's ability to rotate about its single bonds) and are hence equivalent to each other. Therefore there are three sets of non-equivalent protons in the compound. They are labeled as:

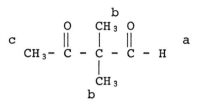

At a frequency of 60 Mcps, an aldehydic proton (a) will characteristically absorb between 9.4 and 10.4 ppm. Hence proton   a   will absorb in this range. The protons of a ketone methyl group (c) characteristically absorb between 2.1 and 2.4 ppm. The protons of the two equivalent methyl groups   (b)   are slightly deshielded by the carbonyl groups and will absorb between 1.0 and 1.4 ppm. Note that the signal of proton   c   will occur downfield from that of proton   b   due to greater deshielding effects; proton   c is adjacent to the carbonyl group whereas proton   b   is separated from the carbonyl groups by one carbon.

The integration curve of an nmr spectrum indicates the relative intensities or relative areas of the peaks. The signal for proton   a   will have a relative intensity of one. Likewise, the signals for protons   b   and   c   will have relative intensities of six and three, respectively. These relative intensities will be represented on the integration curve as the relative changes in height at each peak. The nmr spectrum of 2,2-dimethyl-3-oxo-butanal is sketched below:

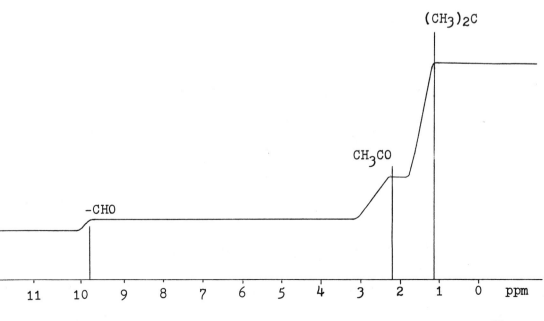

MASS SPECTROSCOPY

An unknown compound contains only carbon and hydrogen. Its mass spectrum is shown. Propose a structure for the compound.

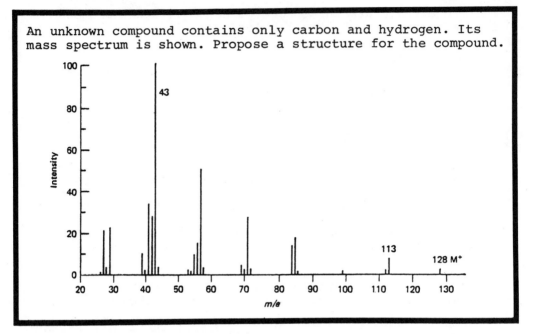

Solution: Mass spectroscopy is a technique used to deter-mine the molecular weight, formula and structure of a com-pound. It differs from infrared, raman, ultraviolet and nuclear magnetic resonance spectroscopy in that it is a destructive spectroscopy; the sample is fragmented by the technique and cannot be recovered in its original form. Mass spectroscopy involves the bombardment of a sample with an electron beam of a particular energy. If the sample is subjected to a low energy electron beam (about 10 eV-electron volts) the molecule will lose an electron to produce the molecular ion, $M^{\cdot \oplus}$.

$$M: \quad \xrightarrow{\text{10 eV}} \quad e^{\ominus} \quad + \quad M^{\cdot \oplus}$$

sample   electron   molecular ion

If the sample is subjected to a high energy electron beam (about 70 eV) the molecule will undergo fragmentation to yield various ionic species.

$$A\text{-}B\text{-}C: \quad \xrightarrow{\text{70 eV}} \quad A\text{-}B\text{-}C^{\cdot \oplus} \quad\quad + e^{\ominus}$$

sample   molecular ion

$$A\text{-}B\text{-}C^{\cdot \oplus} \quad \xrightarrow[\text{70 eV}]{\text{fragmentation}} \quad A^{\oplus} \quad + \quad B\text{-}C^{\cdot}$$

The mass spectrum of a compound plots the relative intensity of the ionic species versus the mass to charge ratio of each species. Note that only cationic species (those species that bear positive charge(s)) are recorded in the mass spectrum. The mass spectrum of a compound is taken by sequentially bombarding the sample with a low energy electron beam and a high energy electron beam. Bombardment by a low energy electron beam principally produces the molecular ion. The molecular ion has a charge of + 1 and has the same molecular weight as the sample compound and therefore its mass to charge ratio (m/e) will be the molecular weight of the compound. As a result the molecular ion peak indicates the molecular weight of the compound and is called the parent peak (generally indicated by M^+ in the mass spectrum). One may reason that the peak with the greatest m/e is the parent peak, but this is not necessarily true. The existence of isotopes will produce small peaks with m/e values of M + 1, M + 2, etc. The relative abundance or intensity of these peaks reflect the relative abundance of the isotopes. For example C^{13} and C^{12} are isotopes of carbon with relative abundances of 1% and 99%, respectively. In the mass spectrum of methane, CH_4, the parent peak will be at m/e = 16. There will however be a peak at m/e = 17, which was derived from the methane molecules containing C^{13}. The peak at 17 will be 1/99 the intensity of the peak at 16.

The parent peak is usually of moderate intensity and may sometimes be the peak of greatest intensity. There is another type of peak in the mass spectrum that is essential in determining the structure of the compound. This peak is the one that arises from the most abundant species that resulted from the fragmentation of the compound, which occurred upon bombardment by the high energy electron beam. This species is often the most stable one that resulted from the fragmentation of the compound. Its peak is the one of greatest intensity and is called the base peak. Sometimes the base peak and the parent peak may be the same, as in the case of methane, although this usually does not happen. For example, the mass spectrum of isobutane

$$\left(\begin{array}{c} CH_3 \\ | \\ CH_3-C-CH_3 \\ | \\ H \end{array} \right)$$

has its parent peak at m/e = 58 and its base

peak at m/e = 57. The species that gives rise to the base

peak is $CH_3-\overset{CH_3}{\underset{\oplus}{C}}-CH_3$, which was formed by the loss of a

hydrogen atom from the molecular ion, $\left[\begin{array}{c} CH_3 \\ | \\ CH_3-C-CH_3 \\ | \\ H \end{array} \right]^{\cdot\oplus}$

Note that $CH_3-\overset{CH_3}{\underset{\oplus}{C}}-CH_3$ is the most abundant fragment because of the relatively high stability of a tertiary carbocation, a trialkylated carbon bearing a positive charge. (the relative order of carbocation stability is:

tertiary > secondary > primary > $CH_3^{\oplus}$.)

With these basic principles of mass spectroscopy, we may now attempt to identify the compound whose mass spectrum is shown. The spectrum indicates that the parent peak (M^+) is the one with m/e = 128; hence the molecular weight of the compound is 128. Since the compound is a hydrocarbon (contains only carbon and hydrogen) the molecular weight restricts the number of carbons to nine or ten. The possible molecular formulas are C_9H_{20} and $C_{10}H_8$. Note that the compound cannot contain eight carbons because the molecular formula would then be C_8H_{32}; the greatest number of hydrogens an eight-carbon compound can accommodate is 18. Hence the compound must contain more than eight carbons. A compound with a molecular formula of C_9H_{20} is a saturated hydrocarbon and is in the class of alkanes. A compound with a molecular formula of $C_{10}H_8$ has seven units of unsaturation. This is determined by the fact that a fully saturated ten-carbon compound has twenty-two hydrogens and for each unit of unsaturation gained, there is a loss of two hydrogens. Since the parent peak has a small relative intensity, the compound is more likely to be the saturated hydrocarbon (C_9H_{20}) than the unsaturated one ($C_{10}H_8$). This is because fragments with multiple bonds have higher stability and less tendency to rearrange than saturated fragments. The unsaturated compound will therefore have a great relative intensity for its parent peak whereas the saturated compound will not. We can conclude that the compound is a saturated hydrocarbon with the molecular formula C_9H_{20}.

Examining the mass spectrum further, we note that the peak with the greatest relative intensity (possessing a value of 100) has a m/e value of 43. This peak, the base peak, most probably represents the isopropyl cation

$$\left(\begin{array}{c} H \\ | \\ CH_3CCH_3 \\ \oplus \end{array} \right)$$
and therefore the compound contains one or

more isopropyl fragments. A n-propyl fragment would have the same molecular weight but would not have such a high relative intensity value. The absence of any significant peak for m/e = 29 tells us that the compound does not produce the ethyl cation ($C_2H_5^{\oplus}$) and therefore is not of the type $R-C_2H_5$ because compounds of this type would produce the pertinent cation. Thus, the compound seems to have branched terminal groups, probably isopropyl portions. Assuming this, we have accounted for 85 grams of the molecular weight of 128 grams. Hence, we hypothesize the unknown compound to have one of the following three structures:

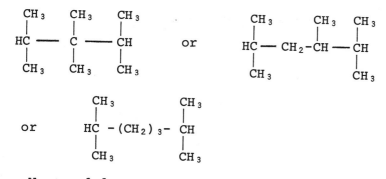

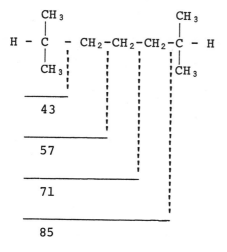

We can deduce that the compound has the third structure in that there is only a moderate peak at m/e = 113 which corresponds to the compound's loss of a methyl fragment. (The other structures have five or six methyl groups.) More importantly, we can relate the different moieties to their m/e values in the mass spectrum upon fragmentation of the molecule along the chain.

We note that peak at m/e value of 57 is particularly intense and this can be related to the formation of the stable t-butyl cation, exemplifying the problem of carbocation rearrangements that plague alkyl cations and make analysis of mass spectra more difficult.

● PROBLEM 2-14

Show how the molecular weights of acetone, propionaldehyde, and methyl ethyl ketone can be estimated from the mass spectra in the figure below. Suggest a possible origin for the strong peaks of mass 57 in the spectra of methyl ethyl ketone and propionaldehyde, which is in accord with the fact that this peak is essentially absent in acetone, although acetone shows a strong peak at 43.

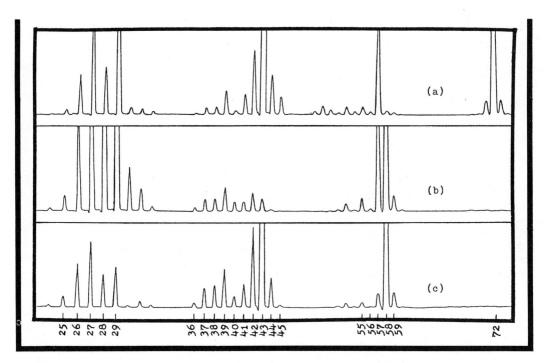

Solution: The parent peak in a mass spectrum is derived from the molecular ion, M^+. The m/e value of the parent peak indicates the molecular weight of the compound. In the mass spectra shown above, the m/e of the parent peak and hence the molecular weight of the compounds is: (a) 72 (b) 58, (c) 58. Hence spectrum (a) is that of methyl ethyl

ketone $\left(\begin{matrix} O \\ \parallel \\ CH_3CCH_2CH_3 \end{matrix} \right)$ and spectra (b) and (c) are those of

acetone $\left(\begin{matrix} O \\ \parallel \\ CH_3CCH_3 \end{matrix} \right)$ and propionaldehyde $\left(\begin{matrix} O \\ \parallel \\ CH_3CH_2CH \end{matrix} \right)$ which have identical molecular weights. Since we know from the problem that propionaldehyde has a strong peak at m/e = 57 and acetone does not, we can conclude that spectrum (b) is that of propionaldehyde and spectrum (c) is that of acetone. The species responsible for the strong peaks of m/e = 57 for methyl ethyl ketone and propionaldehyde and that of m/e = 43 for acetone is an acylium ion ($R-\overset{\oplus}{C}=O$). The acylium ion is very abundant due to its relative stability. The acylium ion is stabilized by resonance. The two principal resonance structures are:

$$R-\overset{\oplus}{C}=O \quad \leftrightarrow \quad R-C\overset{\oplus}{\equiv}O$$

Note that resonance structures do not exist as independent molecules; they only serve to approximate what the real molecule looks like. That is, the molecule is actually a hybrid of its resonance structures.

The acylium ion is formed from ketones $\left(\begin{array}{c} O \\ \| \\ R-C-R \end{array} \right)$ by
fragmentation occurring at the C-R bond and from aldehydes
$\left(\begin{array}{c} O \\ \| \\ R-C-H \end{array} \right)$ at the C-H bond.

The peak at m/e = 57 in spectrum (a) is derived from
the species $CH_3CH_2C=O^{\oplus}$. This species was formed by the loss
of a methide ion ($CH_3^{\ominus}$) from methyl ethyl ketone. A methide
ion is lost in preference to an ethide ion ($^{\ominus}CH_2CH_3$) because
the order of carbanion stabilities is: $CH_3^{\ominus} > 1° > 2° > 3°$.

The peak at m/e = 57 in spectrum (b) is derived from
the species $CH_3CH_2C=O^{\oplus}$. This species was formed by the loss
of a hydride ion ($H^{\ominus}$) from propionaldehyde.

The peak at m/e = 43 in spectrum (c) is derived from
the species $CH_3C=O^{\oplus}$ which is formed by the loss of a methide
ion from acetone.

● **PROBLEM** 2-15

Explain how a mass spectrometer, capable of distinguishing
between ions with m/e values differing by 1 part in 50,000,
could be used to tell whether an ion of mass 29 is $C_2H_5^{\oplus}$
or $CHO^{\oplus}$.

Solution: The exact mass of the ethyl and formyl cations
is not 29. By using the international atomic weights based
on the C^{12} isotope, we can calculate the exact mass of both
ions as shown:

C^{12} = 12.0000

H = 1.0080

O = 15.9994

MW of $CHO^{\oplus}$ = 12.0000 + 1.0080 + 15.9994 = 29.0074

MW of $C_2H_5^{\oplus}$ = 2(12.0000) + 5(1.0080) = 29.0400

The difference in weights is 0.0326. A mass spectrometer
that can distinguish between ions with m/e values differing
by one part in 50,000 means one that is able to resolve ions
that differ in weight by 1/50,000 or 0.00002. Since $CHO^{\oplus}$ and
$C_2H_5^{\oplus}$ differ in weight by more than 0.00002, they can readily
be resolved in the mass spectrum.

ELECTRON SPIN RESONANCE

Although all electrons spin, only molecules containing
unpaired electrons - only free radicals - give esr spectra.
Why is this? (Hint: Consider the possibility (a) that one
electron of a pair has its spin reversed, or (b) that both
electrons of a pair have their spins reversed.)

<u>Solution</u>:   Electron spin resonance (esr) is a phenomenon
involving electrons that occurs in a similar fashion as
nuclear magnetic resonance. The odd electron of a free
radical generates a magnetic moment by spinning; the free
radical therefore has a net magnetic moment. Each electron
of an electron pair also generates a magnetic moment but of
equal and opposite magnitude (because the two electrons have
equal and opposite spins); the electron pair therefore has
no net magnetic moment. When a free radical is placed in
a magnetic field, the magnetic moment generated by the odd
electron may be aligned with or against the external magnetic
field. When this system is exposed to electromagnetic radiation of the proper frequency, the odd electron absorbs the
radiation and reverses its spin; like the proton in nmr, the
electron "flips" over in esr. An absorption spectrum is
obtained which is called an electron spin resonance (esr)
spectrum or an electron paramagnetic resonance (epr)
spectrum.

The signals of an esr spectrum may show splitting for
the same reason that nmr signals maybe split. The esr signal
will be split by n neighboring protons into n + 1 peaks.
The protons that are responsible for splitting the signal
indicates the distribution of the odd electron in the free
radical.

(a)   Every electron that resides in an atomic or molecular
orbital can be described by a set of four quantum numbers.
Quantum numbers are used to depict the relative energies
and distribution of electrons. The first quantum number
is called the principal quantum number (n); it gives the
order of increasing distance of the average electron
density from the nucleus. The second quantum number is the
orbital quantum number (ℓ); it gives the subshell in which
the electron resides and the spatial geometry of the electron
distribution. The third quantum number is the magnetic quantum
number (m); it describes the circulation of the electric
charge which generates a magnetic moment. The fourth quantum
number is the spin quantum number (s); it describes the
orientation of electron spin and can be either +1/2 or
- 1/2.

The Pauli exclusion principle states that no two
electrons in the same atom are identical, that is, no two
electrons in the same atom have an identical set of quantum
numbers. Each electron of an electron pair differs only by
their spin orientation; they have identical principal,
orbital and magnetic quantum numbers. One electron has a

spin quantum number of + 1/2 and the other one of the pair
has a spin quantum number of - 1/2. If one electron of a
pair had its spin reversed, it would have a set of quantum
numbers identical to the other electron. This is a violation
of the Pauli exclusion principle and will hence not occur.
As a result, no esr spectrum is expected to arise in this
manner.

(b)   If both electrons of a pair have their spins reversed,
there is no net change in the energy because the resulting
electron pair is identical to the initial electron pair in
all respects. Hence there will be no absorption signals
and no esr spectrum.

In each of the following cases, tell what free radical
is responsible for the esr spectrum, and show how the
observed splitting arises. (a) X-irradiation of methyl
iodide at low temperatures: a four-line signal, (b) γ-
irradiation at 77°K of propane and of n-butane: symmetrical signals of, respectively, 8 lines and 7 lines.
(c) Triphenylmethyl chloride + zinc: a very complex
signal.

Solution: (a) A four line signal in the esr spectrum
indicates that there are three nearby (adjacent) hydrogens
that split the signal. This is deduced from the fact that
the esr signal will be split by n adjacent protons into
n + 1 peaks. Hence the free radical that gave rise to the
esr spectrum has three hydrogens near the odd electron
and must be CH_3.

$$CH_3I \quad \xrightarrow[\text{low temp.}]{\text{X-rays}} \quad CH_3\cdot \quad + \quad I\cdot$$

   methyl iodide

(b)   The eight line esr signal of propane indicates that
there are seven neighboring hydrogens about the odd
electron. The only way in which a free radical of propane
can have this arrangement is if the odd electron is on
the middle carbon, an isopropyl radical, $CH_3\dot{C}HCH_3$.   The
seven neighboring hydrogens split the esr signal into eight
peaks.

$$CH_3CH_2CH_3 \quad \xrightarrow[\text{77°K}]{\gamma\text{- rays}} \quad CH_3\dot{C}HCH_3 \quad + \quad H\cdot$$

   propane

      The seven line esr signal of n-butane indicates that
there are six neighboring hydrogens about the odd electron.
There are two possible free radicals that n-butane can

form: $CH_3CH_2CH_2CH_2\cdot$ and $CH_3CH_2\dot{C}HCH_3$. The former has four
neighboring hydrogens about the odd electron and will give

an esr signal having five lines. The latter has six neighboring hydrogens and will give a seven line esr signal. Hence the free radical is $CH_3CH_2\dot{C}HCH_3$ and is formed as shown:

$$CH_3CH_2CH_2CH_3 \xrightarrow[77°K]{\gamma\text{-rays}} CH_3CH_2CHCH_3 + H\cdot$$

n-butane

(c) The fact that the esr signal of a mixture of triphenylmethyl chloride and zinc is very complex indicates that there are many neighboring hydrogens about the odd electron. This means that the odd electron is delocalized.

Triphenylmethyl chloride reacts with zinc to produce zinc chloride and a free radical that is stabilized by resonance. This triphenylmethyl radical

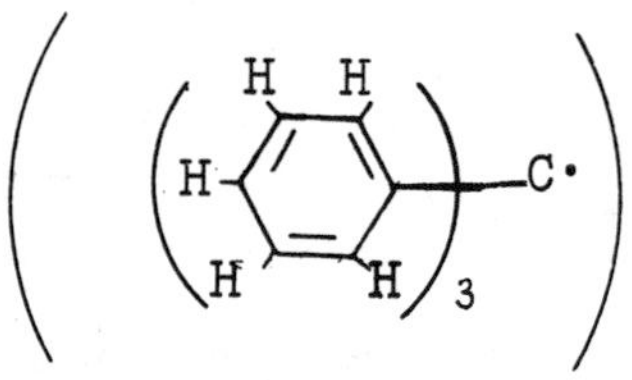

distributes the odd electron about the three phenyl rings. As a result the odd electron is surrounded by many neighboring hydrogens which split the esr signal into a very complex one. The formation of the triphenylmethyl radical and the distribution of the odd electron in the radical is shown below:

C-Cl + Zn $\xrightarrow[\text{radiation}]{\text{electromagnetic}}$

$ZnCl_2$ +

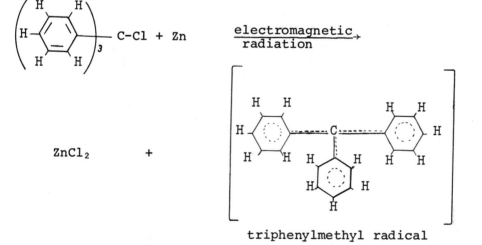

triphenylmethyl radical

Thiphenylmethyl radical's odd electron distribution is also indicated by:

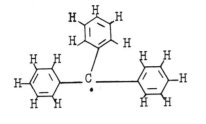 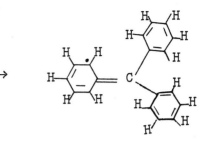

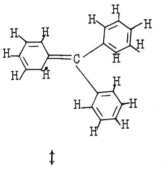 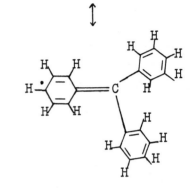

etc.

Note: the structures above are resonance structures and are indicated by resonance arrows (⟷). Resonance structures do not exist independently; they only approximate what the actual species looks like.

CHAPTER 3

ALKANES

NOMENCLATURE AND STRUCTURE

What is an alkane?

Solution: An alkane is a saturated hydrocarbon with the formula C_nH_{2n+2}, where n is the number of carbon atoms. As can be seen from the formula, an alkane consists of only carbon and hydrogen atoms. In a saturated hydrocarbon each carbon atom is bound to four other atoms by sigma bonds. An example of an alkane is propane, a three carbon alkane.

propane

The general formula for an alkane is often written RH. Here R is called an alkyl group; in propane the alkyl group is called a propyl group and is written $CH_3CH_2CH_2 \cdot$. Notice that if a hydrogen atom is added to the last carbon, the propyl group becomes propane.

(i) $CH_3CH_2CH_2 \cdot$ +   H   = $CH_3CH_2CH_3$

           propyl group   propane

(ii)   R·   +   H   =   RH

           alkyl group   alkane

Name the following alkanes.   (a) CH_4

(b) CH_3CH_3 (c) $CH_3-CH_2 \overset{\displaystyle CH_3}{\overset{\displaystyle |}{}}$ (d) $CH_3CH_2CH_2CH_3$

Solution: Four steps can be followed in naming alkanes.

Step I: In naming open-chain alkanes, first find the
            longest chain of carbon atoms.

Step II: Write down the parent name.

Step III: Identify any side chains.

Step IV: Number these side chains and add their names
            and locations as a prefix to the name of the
            parent compound.

These steps are illustrated in the naming of the four
compounds above.

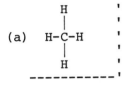

(a)   This compound contains only one
       carbon atom and is the simplest

of all the alkanes. It is called methane.

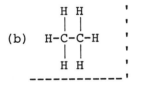

(b)   This is a two carbon alkane. A
       chain of two carbon atoms is given
the root 'eth'. The parent names of alkanes are formed
by adding the suffix 'ane' to the root name of the
longest carbon chain. This compound is called ethane.

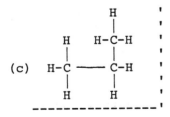

(c)   The longest chain in this com-
       pound is three carbons long. It

is not significant that the chain is bent. The root used
in naming three carbon chains is 'prop'. The name of this
compound is propane.

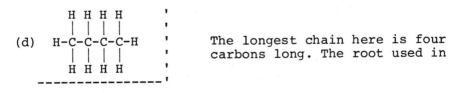

(d)   The longest chain here is four
       carbons long. The root used in

naming four carbon chains is 'but'. The name of this
compound is butane.

65

Distinguish between primary, secondary and tertiary carbons.

Solution: Carbon atoms are often characterized as being either primary, secondary or tertiary. A primary (1°) carbon is attached to only one other carbon atom, a secondary (2°) carbon is attached to two other carbon atoms and a tertiary (3°) carbon is attached to three other carbons. In the diagram below the carbons are labelled as 1°, 2°, or 3°.

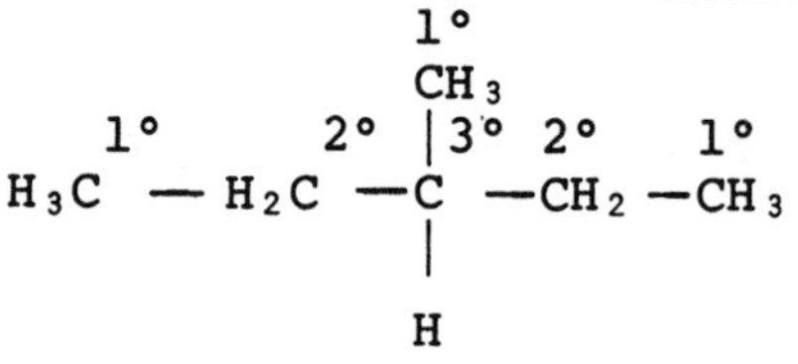

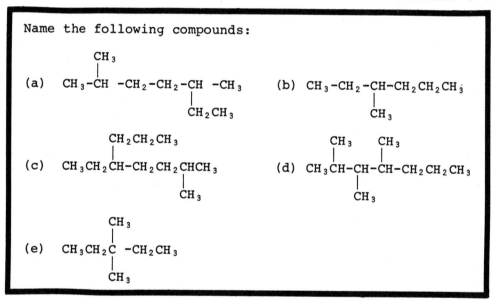

$$1°$$
$$CH_3$$
$$\underset{H_3C}{1°} - \underset{H_2C}{} \underset{}{2°} \underset{C}{|3°} \underset{-CH_2}{2°} \underset{-CH_3}{1°}$$
$$|$$
$$H$$

3-methylpentane

Name the following compounds:

(a) CH_3
      |
      $CH_3-CH -CH_2-CH_2-CH -CH_3$
                          |
                          CH_2CH_3

(b) $CH_3-CH_2-CH-CH_2CH_2CH_3$
                    |
                    CH_3

(c) $CH_2CH_2CH_3$
      |
      $CH_3CH_2CH-CH_2CH_2CHCH_3$
                          |
                          CH_3

(d) CH_3 CH_3
      | |
      $CH_3CH-CH-CH-CH_2CH_2CH_3$
                |
                CH_3

(e) CH_3
      |
      $CH_3CH_2C -CH_2CH_3$
      |
      CH_3

Solution: In brief, the rules for naming organic compounds are as follows:

(a) determine and identify the longest continuous carbon chain

(b) locate and name any side chains

(c) add the names and positions of the side chains as a prefix to the name of the parent compound.

After looking at the structures above, it is seen that all of the compounds are saturated hydrocarbons or alkanes. They all have the formula C_nH_{2n+2} where n is the number of carbon atoms. Another characteristic of alkanes is that the compounds contain only single or sigma bonds.

(a) 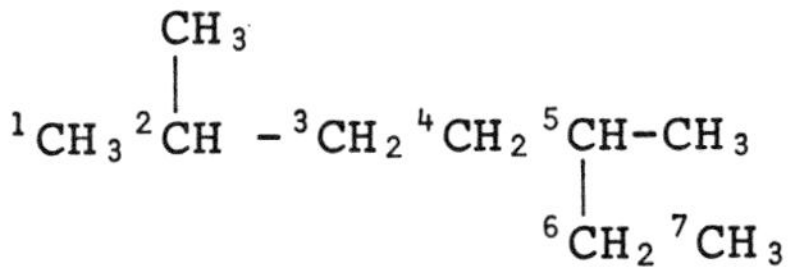
$$^1CH_3\ ^2CH\ -\ ^3CH_2\ ^4CH_2\ ^5CH-CH_3$$
with a CH_3 group attached to ^2CH, and $^6CH_2\ ^7CH_3$ attached to ^5CH.

The longest continuous chain contains seven carbons. These carbons

have been numbered in the accompanying diagram.

The root of the name of a seven carbon chain is 'hept-'.

The carbons are numbered from lowest to highest beginning with the end of the chain which contains the side chain of greatest molecular weight closest to the end of the chain. The substituents on this chain are two CH_3-groups placed one at C2 and one at C5. The CH_3- side chain has one carbon and is called methyl. The name of this compound is 2,5-dimethylheptane.

(b) 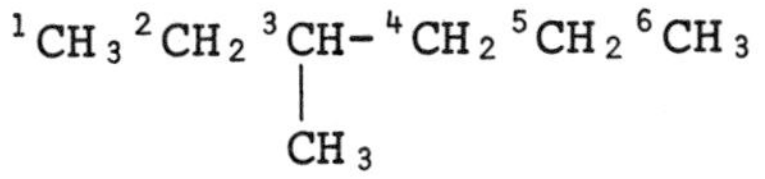
$$^1CH_3\ ^2CH_2\ ^3CH-\ ^4CH_2\ ^5CH_2\ ^6CH_3$$
with a CH_3 group attached to ^3CH.

As shown in the accompanying figure, the longest carbon

chain contains six carbons. The root of the names of compounds containing a six carbon chain is 'hex-'. In this compound there is also a methyl group at C3. The compound is called 3-methylhexane.

(c) 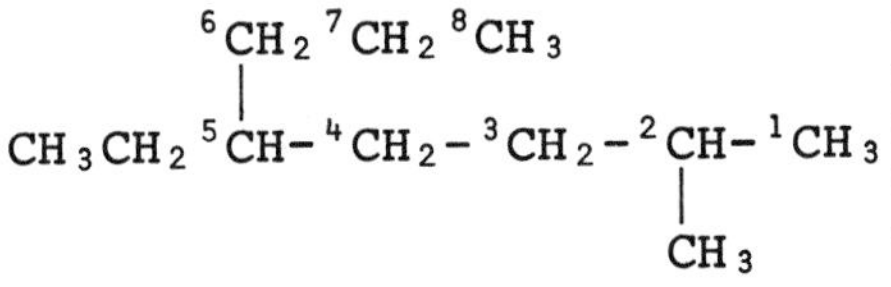
$$CH_3CH_2\ ^5CH-\ ^4CH_2-\ ^3CH_2-\ ^2CH-\ ^1CH_3$$
with $^6CH_2\ ^7CH_2\ ^8CH_3$ attached to ^5CH, and a CH_3 attached to ^2CH.

As shown, the longest carbon chain contains

eight carbons. The root used in naming eight carbon chains is 'oct-'. As the accompanying figure shows, the numbering of the carbons proceeds from the right end of the molecule towards the left. The methyl group here is given precedence over the ethyl group because it is closer to an end of the chain. The two methyl groups attached to C2 are equivalent. The name of this compound is 2-methyl-5-ethyloctane.

(d) 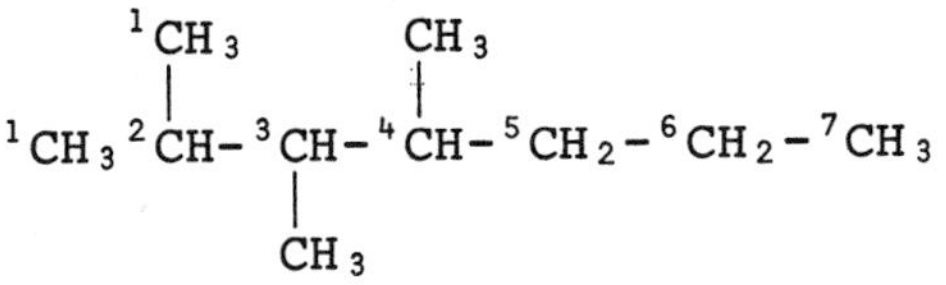
$$^1CH_3\ ^2CH-\ ^3CH-\ ^4CH-\ ^5CH_2-\ ^6CH_2-\ ^7CH_3$$
with $^1CH_3$ and CH_3 attached to ^2CH, CH_3 attached to ^3CH, and CH_3 attached to ^4CH.

The longest chain in this compound contains seven

carbons. There are methyl groups present at C2, C3, and C4. The compound is named 2,3,4-trimethylheptane.

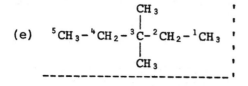

(e) $^5CH_3-^4CH_2-^3C-^2CH_2-^1CH_3$ The longest chain is five carbons long. There are two methyl groups attached

to C3. The root used in naming five carbon chains is 'pent-'; thus the name of this compound is 3,3-dimethylpentane.

Give the structural formula of:

(a)   2,3-dimethylbutane
(b)   2,2-dimethylpropane (neopentane)
(c)   3,4-dimethylheptane
(d)   2,4-dimethyl-4-ethylheptane.

Solution: To derive the structural formula from the name of a compound follow the following steps:

(1) determine the parent compound

(2) identify and position the side chains.

These steps will be illustrated in the examples below.

(a)   2,3-dimethylbutane. The parent compound here is butane which can be drawn:

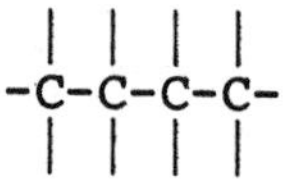

The lines around the carbon atoms indicate bonds to other atoms. This compound contains two methyl groups as indicated by the prefix dimethyl. They are placed at the second and third carbon of the chain. Both ends of the chain are equivalent, therefore the carbons can be numbered from either end. Here they will be numbered from right to left.

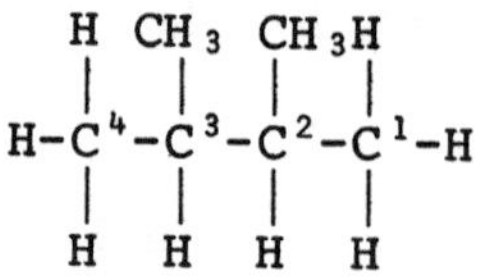

$$H \quad CH_3 \quad CH_3 H$$
$$H-C^4-C^3-C^2-C^1-H$$
$$H \quad H \quad H \quad H$$

2,3-dimethylbutane

(b)   2,2-dimethylpropane. Here, the same procedure can be followed as was used for part a. The parent compound is propane, which is drawn:

The two methyl groups are placed at the two position.

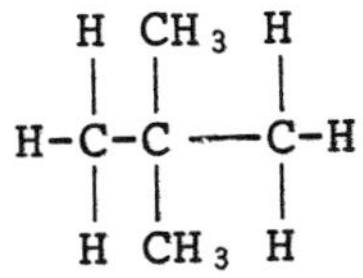

2,2-dimethylpropane

(c)   2-ethyl-3-methylhexane: The parent compound, hexane, is drawn:

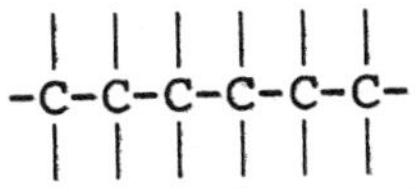

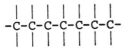

By numbering the carbons from right to left, the required structure can be written.

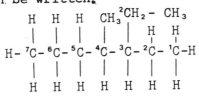

3,4-dimethylheptane

(d)   2,4-dimethyl-4-ethylheptane: The parent structure is heptane.

-C-C-C-C-C-C-C-

heptane

After drawing in the side chains, the following structure is obtained.

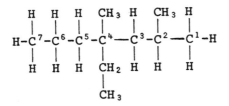

2,4-dimethyl-4-ethylheptane

● PROBLEM 3-6

Draw all the isomers of C_5H_{12}.

Solution: A systematic approach for drawing all the

structures of a compound is necessary. First, start with the straight chain isomer. Next, draw the possible structures using a straight chain of carbon length one less than the first isomer. Repeating this second step will lead to the formation of all of the isomers. This method will be illustrated using pentane (C_5H_{12}). The straight chain isomer is

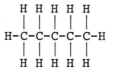

Straight chained isomers are designated by adding the prefix n to the name of the compound. This isomer is called n-pentane.

The next shortest chain contains four carbons. The fifth carbon appears as a methyl group at C2. There is only this one isomer with a chain length of four.

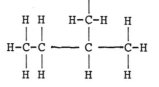

This structure is called 2-methylbutane.

When the chain is reduced to three carbons, one further isomer can be drawn.

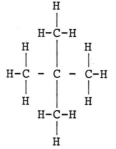

The name of this structure is 2,2-dimethyl propane or neopentane.

When the carbon chain is reduced to two carbons, the isomer 2-methylbutane is produced again. It is exactly the same isomer as the one with 4 carbon atoms in the straight chain.

● **PROBLEM 3-7**

Draw perspective formulas and Newman projections for the eclipsed and staggered forms of propane.

Solution: Propane (C_3H_8) is a member of the paraffins

(saturated hydrocarbons). The eclipsed and staggered forms
of a molecule are different conformations of that molecule.
Conformations of a molecule are structures of that molecule
that differ only in the torsional angle of carbon-carbon
single bonds. Since perspective formulas are three
dimensional we can represent them on paper by having a
dashed bond represent a projection away from the reader,
the heavy wedge bond projecting towards the reader, while
a normal bond would represent the plane of the paper.

In the eclipsed form of propane there is more steric
hindrance than in the staggered form. There is also a
greater torsional strain in the eclipsed form. As a result,
the eclipsed form is expected to be higher in energy than
the staggered form. Therefore the staggered conformation is
more stable. The perspective formulas and Newman projections
are sketched below:

Perspective Formula   Newman Projection

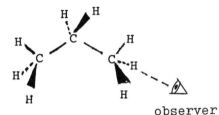

observer

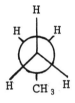

Staggered

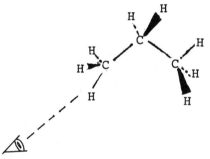

observer

Eclipsed

PHYSICAL PROPERTIES

● PROBLEM 3-8

Without referring to a table, place the following hydrocarbons in order of increasing boiling points.

(a) methane   (d) neopentane
(b) n-hexane   (e) 2,3-dimethylbutane
(c) n-undecane

Solution: For a compound to change states, i.e. go from

71

solid to liquid (melt) or liquid to gas (boil), energy must
be added to the system. This energy is used to weaken the
intermolecular forces holding the molecules together. These
intermolecular forces are greater the larger the molecule
is. As a general rule, except for very small alkanes, the
boiling point rises 20 to 30 degrees for each carbon that
is added to the chain. A branched chain isomer has a lower
boiling point than a straight chain.

In the group of alkanes given above, the straight chain
isomers are methane, n-hexane and n-undecane. There is one
carbon in methane, six in n-hexane and eleven in undecane.
Since shorter chains have lower boiling points the order of
increasing boiling points for these compounds is methane,
n-hexane and n-undecane.

The other two compounds that must be considered are
neopentane and 2,3-dimethylbutane. The latter compound
has six carbons and neopentane or 2,2-dimethylpropane has
five, but since 2,3-dimethylbutane is much more branched
than neopentane it will have a lower boiling point. These
two compounds will fit in between methane and n-hexane in
the above order because straight chain compounds generally
boil higher than branched compounds and hydrocarbons with
greater number of carbons also boil at higher temperatures.
The order of increasing boiling points is:

 methane < 2,3-dimethylbutane < neopentane < n-hexane <
n-undecane.

The actual boiling points of these compounds are
shown in the following table.

Compound	Boiling Point (°C)
methane	− 162
2,3-dimethylbutane	− 129
neopentane	− 17
n-hexane	69
n-undecane	196

● **PROBLEM** 3-9

Isobutane is thermodynamically more stable than butane.
Which has the lower boiling point? Is there any relationship between thermodynamic stability and boiling point?
Would you expect such a relationship between thermodynamic
stability and melting point?

Solution: Thermodynamic stability refers to the intramolecular forces (Van der Waals forces) acting within the

molecular structure of a compound. Thus benzene

which has a low ground state energy, is considered to be

thermodynamically stable. An enormous amount of energy is required for the degradation of this compound. However, the boiling point is related to the intermolecular forces in a given compound. When the temperature is raised, thus increasing the kinetic energy, the molecular collisions are greatly enhanced and the distance between molecules is widened. The transition from the liquid to the vapor phase occurs and the relatively cohesive liquid is transformed to wandering molecules in the gaseous phase.

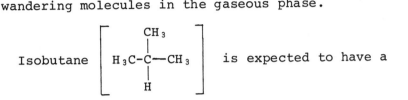

Isobutane   is expected to have a

lower boiling point (b.p. = - 12°C) than the straight chain isomer (b.p. = 0°C). The boiling points of alkanes rise as the molecules get larger. Branching decreases the boiling point because the shape of the molecule approaches that of a sphere, thus decreasing the surface area. This results in the weakening of the intermolecular forces which are overcome at a lower temperature.

Considering the above descriptions of stability and boiling points, there is absolutely no correlation between the two.

● **PROBLEM** 3-10

Examine a molecular model of adamantane. Give a rough estimate of its b.p. Would you expect the m.p. to be far below the b.p.? Give another example to illustrate its properties.

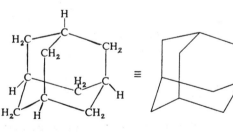

Solution: The numbering of adamantane, a tricyclic hydro-

carbon is: 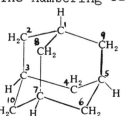   . Its name is

73

tricyclo$[3.3.1.1^{1,7}]$ decane. The melting point is the temperature at which the substance undergoes a transition from
a solid state to a liquid one. The movement of molecules is
greatly increased and instead of vibrating about a fixed
axis, they can wander without any restriction except for leaving the container in which they are held. The boiling point
is defined as the temperature at which the vapor pressure
of the compound is equal to external pressure (at S.T.P.,
760 mmHg).

Adamantane has a very symmetrical appearance. Crystal
lattices are easily formed and therefore a high melting
point and low boiling point would be expected. Sublimation
is possible when adamantane is heated;it will directly change from the solid state to the gaseous state upon
heating. The melting point could be about 250°C while its
boiling point could be about 258°C.

Another example of a compound that readily sublimates
would be camphor,which also has a high degree of symmetry
and spherical character within the structure.

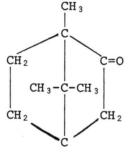

Camphor

PREPARATION AND REACTIONS

● **PROBLEM** 3-11

Write equations for the preparation of n-butane from:

(a) n-butyl bromide   (d) 1-butene, $CH_3CH_2CH=CH_2$
(b) sec-butyl bromide   (e) 2-butene, $CH_3CH=CHCH_3$
(c) ethyl chloride

<u>Solution:</u>   The structure of n-butane (C_4H_{10}) may be
written as:

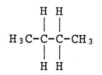

(a)   To prepare n-butane from n-butyl bromide
$(CH_3CH_2CH_2CH_2Br)$, first take note that both compounds have

74

the same carbon content. This means the reactions to remove the bromide must not alter the carbon skeleton. To replace the bromine atom with a hydrogen atom without altering the carbon skeleton, employ a reaction that results in the reduction of the alkyl halide. Two such reactions are the hydrolysis of a Grignard reagent and the reduction by metal and acid.

When a solution of alkyl halide is placed in dry ethyl ether with metallic magnesium, a vigorous reaction takes place - a Grignard reagent is formed. The Grignard reagent has the general formula RMgX, where R is an alkyl or aryl group and X is a halogen atom. The Grignard reagent is extremely reactive. It reacts with numerous inorganic and organic compounds. If water is added, hydrolysis occurs to produce R-H, a hydrocarbon of the same carbon skeleton. The hydrolysis may be viewed as the reaction of a salt (the Grignard reagent) with an acid (H_2O) to produce a weaker acid (R-H). This reaction which can produce the n-butane desired, is illustrated in the following reaction sequence:

$$CH_3CH_2CH_2CH_2Br \xrightarrow[\text{Ether (Dry)}]{Mg} CH_3CH_2CH_2CH_2MgBr \xrightarrow{H_2O}$$

(n-butyl bromide)   (n-butylmagnesium bromide)

$$CH_3CH_2CH_2CH_3 \quad + \quad Mg(OH)Br$$

(n-butane)

Reduction of n-butyl bromide with metal and acid will accomplish the same thing as shown:

$$CH_3CH_2CH_2CH_2Br + Zn + H^+ \rightarrow CH_3CH_2CH_2CH_3 + Zn^{+2} + Br^-$$

(b) Sec-butyl bromide may be written as:

$CH_3CH_2CHCH_3$. Here, again, hydrolysis of Grignard reagent
$\quad\quad\quad |$
$\quad\quad\quad Br$

or reduction by metal and acid gives the desired product, n-butane.

$$CH_3CH_2CHCH_3 \xrightarrow[\text{Ether (dry)}]{Mg} CH_3CH_2CHCH_3 \xrightarrow{H_2O} CH_3CH_2CH_2CH_3$$
$\quad\quad |$ $|$
$\quad\quad Br$ $MgBr$

$$CH_3CH_2CHCH_3 + Zn + H^+ \rightarrow CH_3CH_2CH_2CH_3 + Zn^{+2} + Br^-$$
$\quad\quad |$
$\quad\quad Br$

(c) Ethyl chloride possesses only a 2 carbon backbone: CH_3CH_2Cl. To produce n-butane, which has four carbons, one must use a reaction that will add two carbons. To manufacture an alkane of higher carbon number than the starting material will require the formation of carbon-carbon bonds. This is most directly accomplished by the coupling together of two alkyl groups. An excellent method of doing this was developed by Corey and House. It is the coupling of alkyl halides with organometallic compounds. Coupling takes place between a lithium dialkylcopper, R_2CuLi, and an alkyl halide, $R'X$ (R' may be different or the same as R). The general reaction may be illustrated as shown:

$$R_2CuLi \; + \; R'X \rightarrow \; R-R' \; + \; RCu \; + \; LiX$$

(Alkane)

The lithium dialkylcopper is prepared by adding lithium to the alkyl halide which may be primary, secondary or tertiary. After this, one adds cuprous halide, CuX. Overall,

$$RX \; \xrightarrow{\text{Li}} \; RLi \; \xrightarrow{\text{CuX}} \; R_2CuLi$$

(Alkyl   (Lithium dialkylcopper)
lithium)

The alkyl halide ($R'X$) which will be added to R_2CuLi (to produce R-R') should be primary to obtain good yields. The reaction sequence that generates n-butane from ethyl chloride can now be written:

$$CH_3CH_2Cl \; \xrightarrow{\text{Li}} \; CH_3CH_2Li \; \xrightarrow{\text{CuX}} \; (CH_3CH_2)_2CuLi$$

$$(CH_3CH_2)_2CuLi \; + \; CH_3CH_2Cl \rightarrow \; CH_3CH_2CH_2CH_3 \; + \; CH_3CH_2Cu \; + \; LiCl$$

(d) and (e) Alkenes (compounds with double bonds) such as 1-butene and 2-butene can be readily converted to the corresponding alkane with a hydrogenation reaction. In this reaction, hydrogen gas is passed over the alkene in the presence of Pt, Pd, or Ni, which act as catalysts. The hydrogen adds across the double bond to produce an alkane of the same carbon number. Hydrogenation of 1-butene and 2-butene directly produces the desired product as shown:

$$CH_3CH_2CH=CH_2 \; + \; H_2 \; \xrightarrow{\text{Pt, Pd or Ni}} \; CH_3CH_2CH_2CH_3$$

(1-butene)

$$CH_3CH=CHCH_3 \; + \; H_2 \; \xrightarrow{\text{Pt, Pd or Ni}} \; CH_3CH_2CH_2CH_3$$

● **PROBLEM** 3-12

On the basis of certain evidence, including its infrared spectrum, an unknown compound of formula $C_{10}H_{22}$ is suspected of being 2,7-dimethyloctane. How could you confirm or disprove this tentatively assigned structure?

Solution: It is possible to obtain a pure sample of 2,7-dimethyloctane by synthesizing it using the Corey-House method. If the compound's infrared spectrum coincides with the IR of the suspected 2,7-dimethyloctane, and if the other properties are similar to the compound in doubt we could ascertain the nature of $C_{10}H_{22}$.

An interesting feature about the structure of 2,7-dimethyloctane

$$\left[CH_3\overset{\overset{\displaystyle CH_3}{|}}{C}HCH_2CH_2-CH_2CH_2\overset{\overset{\displaystyle CH_3}{|}}{C}HCH_3 \right]$$

is that it is symmetrical; it is composed of two identical alkyl groups

$$\left(-CH_2CH_2\overset{\overset{\displaystyle CH_3}{|}}{C}HCH_3 \right).$$

This characteristic, along with the knowledge that alkyl halides could be coupled with organometallic compounds to form hydrocarbons, makes it possible to synthesize 2-7, dimethyloctane by starting with isopentylbromide

$$\left(Br-CH_2CH_2\overset{\overset{\displaystyle}{}}{C}H\ CH_3 \atop {|\atop CH_3} \right).$$

The mechanism for coupling with these organometallic compounds could be illustrated as follows. First an organolithium (RLi) compound is prepared from the alkyl halide. In this case the alkyl halide is isopentylbromide.

$$CH_3\overset{\overset{\displaystyle CH_3}{|}}{C}HCH_2CH_2CH_2Br + Li \rightarrow CH_3\overset{\overset{\displaystyle CH_3}{|}}{C}HCH_2CH_2CHLi.$$

isopentyl Lithium

If cuprous halide (e.g. CuX) is added to isopentyl lithium, cuprous lithium diisopentane is formed. On addition of isopentyl bromide (since isopentyl bromide is a primary halide the yield of the reaction would be high. The alkyl group in the organometallic group could be either primary, secondary or tertiary without affecting the yield), the alkyl group (isopentyl) is transferred from copper. The alkyl group leaves with two electrons and attaches itself to the other alkyl halide by displacing the halide ion (bromide) by nucleophilic aliphatic substitution.

$$\left(CH_3\overset{\overset{\displaystyle CH_3}{|}}{C}HCH_2CH_2CH_2 \right)_2 - CuLi + CH_3\overset{\overset{\displaystyle}{}}{C}H\ CH_2CH_2CH_2Br \atop {|\atop CH_3} \rightarrow$$

$$CH_3\overset{\overset{\displaystyle}{}}{C}H\ CH_2CH_2 - CH_2CH_2\overset{\overset{\displaystyle}{}}{C}H\ CH_3 \atop \quad {|\atop CH_3}\qquad\qquad {|\atop CH_3}\qquad\qquad .$$

● **PROBLEM** 3-13

A chemist was asked to determine the identity of a clear liquid. He sniffed it and found that it smelled like lighter fluid. He performed a quantitative analysis and calculated that the liquid was 83.3% carbon and 16.7% hydrogen. He decided that the compound was n-pentane. Was it? Assume that this chemist was working during the summer and that his lab was 29°C.

Solution: The molecular formula for n-pentane is $CH_3CH_2CH_2CH_2CH_3$, or C_5H_{12}. Since there is no common denominator except the number one for 5 and 12, the empirical formula for n-pentane is also C_5H_{12}. The empirical formula can be derived from the weight percentages of carbon and hydrogen.

Assume that 100 g of the liquid is available. By using the weight percentages it is seen that there is 83.3 g. carbon and 16.7 g. hydrogen. In each mole of n-pentane there exists 5 moles of carbon and 12 moles of hydrogen. If this liquid is n-pentane the ratio of the number of moles of carbon to the number of moles of hydrogen must be 5:12 or .417:1. To determine this ratio from the data given, calculate the number of moles of carbon in 83.3 g. and the number of moles of hydrogen in 16.7 g. (MW of C = 12, MW of H = 1).

$$\text{no. of moles} = \frac{\text{mass}}{\text{MW}}$$

$$\text{no. of moles of C} = \frac{83.3 \text{ g}}{12 \text{ g/mole}} = 6.94 \text{ moles}$$

$$\text{no. of moles of H} = \frac{16.7 \text{ g}}{1 \text{ g/mole}} = 16.7 \text{ moles}$$

The ratio of C:H is

$$\frac{\text{moles of C}}{\text{moles of H}} = \frac{6.94}{16.7} = .416 : 1,$$

which proves that the formula for the compound is C_5H_{12}. There are compounds which have the formula C_5H_{12} other than n-pentane but these branched isomers have boiling points lower than 29°C and will be gases at this temperature.

COMBUSTION AND BOND DISSOCIATION ENERGY

● **PROBLEM** 3-14

Kilogram for kilogram, would the combustion of gaseous methane or of liquid n-decane (to liquid water) give more heat? Refer to the table below.

Bond Energies (kcal/mole at 25°C)

Diatomic Molecules

H-H	104.2	F-F	36.6	H-F	134.6
O=O	119.1	Cl-Cl	58.0	H-Cl	103.2
N≡N	225.8	Br-Br	46.1	H-Br	87.5
C=O[b]	255.8	I-I	36.1	H-I	71.4

C-H	98.7	C-C	82.6	C-F	116
N-H	93.4	C=C	145.8	C-Cl	81
O-H	110.6	C≡C	199.6	C-Br	68
S-H	83	C-N	72.8	C-I	51
P-H	76	C=N	147	C-S	65
N-N	39	C≡N	212.6	C≡S[c]	128
N=N	100	C-O	85.5	N-F	65
O-O	35	C=O[d]	192.0	N-Cl	46
S-S	54	C=O[e]	166	O-F	45
N-O	53	C=O[f]	176	O-Cl	52
N=O	145	C=O[g]	179	O-Br	48

[b]Carbon monoxide.
[c]For carbon disulfide.
[d]For carbon dioxide.
[e]For formaldehyde.
[f]Other aldehydes.
[g]Ketones.

Solution: This problem calls for the determination of the heat of combustion of gaseous methane and liquid n-decane, given the various bond energies. First we must sketch the balanced equation of the combustion of the two hydrocarbons in the presence of oxygen.

$$CH_4(g) + 2 O_2(g) \rightarrow CO_2(g) + 2 H_2O (\ell)$$

Note that carbon dioxide and water are the only products of combustion.

ΔH for methane could be calculated by 4(98.7), the energy for the C-H bonds.

bonds broken-
endothermic
and
ΔH>0

$$H:C:H \rightarrow \cdot \dot{C} \cdot + 4H \cdot \quad \Delta H = +4 \times 98.7$$
$$= 394.8 \text{ kcal.}$$

Energy of double bond in O_2 = 119.1 kcal

$$2:O::O: \rightarrow 4:O: \quad \Delta H = 2 \times 119.1 \text{ kcal}$$
$$= 238.2 \text{ kcal}$$

bonds formed-
exothermic
and
ΔH<0

2[C=O] bonds in carbon
dioxide = (- 192 × 2) kcal
= - 384.0 kcal

Each of the O-H bonds in
water = - 110.6 kcal

Since 4 O-H bonds are present in
2 molecules of water ΔH=4 × 110.6 kcal
=- 442.4

$$\Sigma\Delta H = 394.8 + 238.2 - 384.0 - 442.4 = - 193.4 \text{ kcal}$$

The heat of vaporization for water is represented by

$$H_2O \ (g) \ \rightarrow \ H_2O \ (\ell)$$

$$\Delta H = -10.4.$$

Since 2 molecules of water are present $\Delta H_v = 2 \times -10.4 = -20.8$ kcal.

1000 g constitute 1 kilogram, M.W. of methane = 16;

$$\text{no. of moles} = \frac{1000 \ g}{16 \ g/mole} = 62.5 \text{ moles}$$

Total $\Delta H = -193.4 - 20.8 = -214.2$ kcal/mole.

Heat evolved by 1000 g methane

$$= 62.5 \text{ moles} \times -214.2 = -13,400 \text{kcal}$$

In order to determine the heat evolved from n-decane we will follow a similar procedure as above. The balanced equation for the combustion of n-decane is:

$$C_{10}H_{22} \ + \ \frac{31}{2} \ O_2 \ \rightarrow \ 10 \ CO_2 \ + \ 11 \ H_2O$$

$C_{10}H_{22}$ has 9 C-C bonds and 22 C-H bonds broken.

$$\Delta H = 9 \times 82.6 + 22 \times 98.7 = 2,914.8.$$

$$\Delta H_{O_2} \ = \ \frac{31}{2} \ (119.1) \qquad = 1846.05$$

$$\Delta H_{CO_2} \ = 10 \ (2 \times -192.0) \quad = -3840.0$$

$$\Delta H_{H_2O} \ = 11 \times 2 \ (-110.6) \quad = -2433.2$$

$$\Delta H_{vap.} \ = 11 \ (-10.4) \qquad = -114.4$$

$$\Sigma\Delta H \ = 2914.8 + 1846.05 - 3840.0 - 2433.2 - 114.4$$

$$= -1630.0 \text{ kcal/mole.}$$

$$\text{no. of moles of n-decane} = \frac{1 \ kg \times 1000 \ g/kg}{\text{M.W.: } 142}$$

$$\text{Amount of heat evolved} = \frac{1000}{42} \text{ moles} \times -1630 \text{ kcal/mole}$$

$$= -11500 \text{ kcal.}$$

Thus methane yields about 14% more heat than n-decane per mole.

5.82 g of a compound was burned in the presence of oxygen. The products were 17.1 g of carbon dioxide and 10.5 g of water. Calculate the empirical formulas for this compound. What is its name? Find the percent yield of this reaction.

Solution: A compound whose sole products of combustion are carbon dioxide and water must be a hydrocarbon. Hydrocarbons consist of only carbon and hydrogen atoms; alkanes, alkenes and alkynes fall into this category.

The general equation for the combustion of a hydrocarbon could be represented by

$$C_nH_x + (n + \frac{x}{4}) O_2 \xrightarrow{\Delta} nCO_2 + \frac{x}{2} H_2O.$$

Notice that this reaction is balanced. Indentical amounts of atoms of the various constituents are present in both the products and reactants.

The empirical formula of the hydrocarbon C_nH_x can be calculated as follows:

$$C_n H_x + \left[n + \frac{x}{4}\right] O_2 \xrightarrow{\Delta} nCO_2 + \frac{x}{2} H_2O.$$

17.1 g of CO_2 is produced;

$$\text{no of moles of } CO_2 = \frac{17.1}{44} = .388 \text{ moles}$$

10.5 g of H_2O is produced;
$$\text{no. of moles of water produced} = \frac{10.5}{18} = .5833.$$

Next, we determine the ratio of water to carbon dioxide:

$$\frac{\text{moles } H_2O}{\text{moles } CO_2} = \frac{\frac{x}{2}}{n} = \frac{.5833}{.388} = \frac{3}{2}$$

Hence, $\frac{x}{2} = 3$, or x = 6 and n = 2.

So the empirical formula of the hydrocarbon = C_2H_6.

The general form of C_2H_6 could be written as C_nH_{2n+2}. Therefore, it comes under the class of alkanes (saturated hydrocarbons). Since there are two carbon atoms, its name is

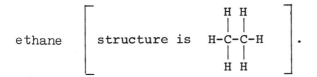

ethane   structure is

To determine the % yield we must first calculate how much ethane is required to produce the amounts of CO_2 and H_2O.

$$C_2H_6 + \frac{7}{2} O_2 \xrightarrow{\Delta} 2\ CO_2 + 3\ H_2O.$$

This is the balanced equation for the combustion of ethane.

$$\text{No. of moles of } CO_2 \text{ produced} = \frac{17.1}{44} = .388 \text{ moles.}$$

Since 2 moles of CO_2 are evolved from 1 mole of ethane, the amount of ethane needed for .388 moles of CO_2 = .388/2 = 194 moles.

$$\text{Wt. of ethane reacting} = .194 \times (MW_{ethane})$$

$$= .194 \times 30 = 5.82$$

$$\text{Hence, the \% yield} = \frac{\text{Reacted ethane} \times 100 \text{ \%}}{\text{Initial amount of ethane}}$$

$$= \frac{5.82}{5.82} \times 100 \text{ \%} = 100\%$$

● **PROBLEM** 3-16

(a) If a rocket were fueled with kerosine and liquid oxygen, what weight of oxygen would be required for every liter of kerosine? (Assume kerosine to have the average composition of n-$C_{14}H_{30}$ and a density of 0.764 g/ml).(b) How much energy would be required to fragment the molecules in one liter of kerosine? (Assume 157 kcal mole for each $-CH_2-$ group and 186 kcal mole for each $-CH_3-$ group.)

Solution: To answer this problem we must first determine the balanced equation for the combustion of kerosine in the presence of oxygen. Since any hydrocarbon on combustion produces carbon dioxide and water, the skeleton equation could be written as n-$C_{14}H_{30} + O_2 \rightarrow CO_2 + H_2O$. To balance this equation we could balance each type of atom separately. 14 atoms of carbon are present in kerosine, therefore there must be 14 molecules of CO_2 evolved for each molecule of kerosine; 30 molecules of hydrogen present in kerosine contribute to 15 molecules of water. Therefore the balanced equation could be represented by:

$$n\text{-}C_{14}H_{30} + \frac{43}{2} O_2 \rightarrow 14\ CO_2 + 15\ H_2O.$$

Since the density of kerosine (0.764 g/ml) is given, the weight of 1 liter of kerosine is:

$$\text{vol.} \times \text{density} = 1 \; \ell \times \frac{1000 \; m\ell}{1 \; \ell} \times \frac{0.764 \; g}{m\ell} = 764 \; g.$$

$$\text{no. of moles of kerosine:} \; \frac{\text{weight}}{\text{M.W.}} = \frac{764 \; g}{198 \; g/\text{mole}}$$

From the balanced equation we can accurately predict that one mole of kerosine requires 43/2 moles of oxygen for total combustion.

Hence $\frac{764}{198}$ moles need $\frac{764}{198} \times \frac{43}{2}$ moles = 83.0 moles of oxygen required.

Weight of oxygen: 83.0 moles $\times$ 32 g/mole = 2,660 g.

(b) When each $-CH_2-$ and CH_3- group disintegrates to form the products of combustion, the former requires 157 kcal/mole, whereas CH_3- requires 186 kcal/mole. The structural formula for kerosine ($n-C_{14}H_{30}$) is $CH_3-(CH_2)_{12}-CH_3$.

The total amount of heat required per mole is

$$(157 \text{ kcal/mole} \times 12) + (186 \text{ kcal/mole} \times 2) = 2{,}256 \text{ kcal/mole}$$

$$\text{One liter of kerosine} = \frac{764}{198} \text{ moles}$$

$$\text{Total energy per liter kerosine} = \frac{764}{198} \times 2{,}256 = 8{,}710 \text{ kcal.}$$

● PROBLEM 3-17

Suppose we assume the following bond energies (kcal):

$\equiv$C-H   110.7   C$\equiv$C   175.6

$=\overset{|}{C}$-H   102.7   C$=$C   129.8

$-\overset{|}{\underset{|}{C}}$-H   98.7   C-C   82.6

What corresponding values would we have to assign to C-Br bonds if the ΔH values calculated for the reactions HC$\equiv$CH + Br$_2$ → BrHC$=$CHBr and BrHC$=$CHBr + Br$_2$ → CHBr$_2$CHBr$_2$ are to be exactly the same as those calculated using just the bond energies from the table given?

Bond Energies (kcal/mole at 25°C)

Diatomic Molecules

H-H	104.2	F-F	36.6	H-F	134.6
O=O	119.1	Cl-Cl	58.0	H-Cl	103.2
N≡N	225.8	Br-Br	46.1	H-Br	87.5
C=O[b]	255.8	I-I	36.1	H-I	71.4

C-H	98.7	C-C	82.6	C-F	116
N-H	93.4	C=C	145.8	C-Cl	81
O-H	110.6	C≡C	199.6	C-Br	68
S-H	83	C-N	72.8	C-I	51
P-H	76	C=N	147	C-S	65
N-N	39	C≡N	212.6	C=S[c]	128
N=N	100	C-O	85.5	N-F	65
O-O	35	C=O[d]	192.0	N-Cl	46
S-S	54	C=O[e]	166	O-F	45
N-O	53	C=O[f]	176	O-Cl	52
N=O	145	C=O[g]	179	O-Br	48

[b]Carbon monoxide.
[c]For carbon disulfide.
[d]For carbon dioxide.
[e]For formaldehyde.
[f]Other aldehydes.
[g]Ketones.

Solution: In order to evaluate the values for the bond energies of =C-Br and -C-Br we must first determine the ΔH values using the table of the Bond Energies:

First equation: HC≡CH + Br_2 → BrHC=CHBr.

$$\Delta H = + 199.6 + 2(98.7) + 46.1 - [145.8 + 2(98.7) + 2(68)]$$

$$= - 281.8 + 245.7 = - 36.1 \text{ kcal/mole.}$$

Due to further bromination :

BrHC=CHBr + Br_2 → Br_2HC - $CHBr_2$.

$$\Sigma H = 145.8 + 2(98.7) + 2(68) + 46.1 - [82.6 +$$

$$2(98.7) + 4(68)]$$

$$= - 26.7 \text{ kcal/mole.}$$

If we now use the assumed bond energies and allow =C-Br to be x and -C-Br to be y :

H-C≡C-H + Br_2 → BrHC=HBr .

$$\Sigma\Delta H = 175.6 + 2(110.7) + 46.1 - [129.8 + 2(102.7) + 2x]$$

$$= 443.1 - 335.2 - 2x = - 36.1$$

$$- 2x = - 143 → x = 71.5 \approx 72 \text{ kcal/mole.}$$

BrHC=HBr + Br_2 → Br_2HC-$CHBr_2$.

$$\Sigma\Delta H = 129.8 + 2(102.7) + (71.5)2 + 46.1 - [82.6 +$$

$$2(98.7) + 4y] = - 72.8$$

$$524.3 - 280 - 4y = -26.7$$

$$y = \frac{-26.7 - 244.3}{-4} \approx 68 \text{ kcal.}$$

Calculate ΔH (bond dissociation energy) for the following reactions:

(a) $t\text{-}C_4H_{10} + Br_2 \rightarrow t\text{-}C_4H_9Br + HBr$

(b) $CH_4 + I_2 \rightarrow CH_3I + HI$

(c) $C_6H_6 + Cl_2 \rightarrow C_6H_5Cl + HCl$

(d) $n \cdot C_3H_8 + CH_4 \rightarrow 2 \; C_2H_6.$

Table 1   BOND DISSOCIATION ENERGIES, KCAL/MOLE

$A\text{:}B \longrightarrow A\cdot + \cdot B \quad \Delta H = \text{Bond Dissociation Energy or } D(A\text{-}B)$

H—H	104				CH$_3$—H	104
H—F	136	F—F	38		CH$_3$—F	108
H—Cl	103	Cl—Cl	58		CH$_3$—Cl	84
H—Br	88	Br—Br	46		CH$_3$—Br	70
H—I	71	I—I	36		CH$_3$—I	56

CH$_3$—H 104	CH$_3$—CH$_3$ 88	CH$_3$—Cl 84	CH$_3$—Br 70
C$_2$H$_5$—H 98	C$_2$H$_5$—CH$_3$ 85	C$_2$H$_5$—Cl 81	C$_2$H$_5$—Br 69
n-C$_3$H$_7$—H 98	n-C$_3$H$_7$—CH$_3$ 85	n-C$_3$H$_7$—Cl 82	n-C$_3$H$_7$—Br 69
i-C$_3$H$_7$—H 95	i-C$_3$H$_7$—CH$_3$ 84	i-C$_3$H$_7$—Cl 81	i-C$_3$H$_7$—Br 68
t-C$_4$H$_9$—H 91	t-C$_4$H$_9$—CH$_3$ 80	t-C$_4$H$_9$—Cl 79	t-C$_4$H$_9$—Br 63
H$_2$C=CH—H 104	H$_2$C=CH—CH$_3$ 92	H$_2$C=CH—Cl 84	
H$_2$C=CHCH$_2$—H 88	H$_2$C=CHCH$_2$—CH$_3$ 72	H$_2$C=CHCH$_2$—Cl 60	H$_2$C=CHCH$_2$—Br 47
C$_6$H$_5$—H 112	C$_6$H$_5$—CH$_3$ 93	C$_6$H$_5$—Cl 86	C$_6$H$_5$—Br 72
C$_6$H$_5$CH$_2$—H 85	C$_6$H$_5$CH$_2$—CH$_3$ 70	C$_6$H$_5$CH$_2$—Cl 68	C$_6$H$_5$CH$_2$—Br 51

<u>Solution:</u>   The amount of energy consumed or liberated when a bond is broken or formed is called the bond dissociation energy, D. The ΔH for a reaction can be determined by subtracting the bond dissociation energies of the products from those of the reactants. The ΔH values for various compounds are given in the accompanying table.

(a) $t\text{-}C_4H_{10} + Br_2 \rightarrow t\text{-}C_4H_9Br + HBr$

This reaction can be rewritten to show the bonds that are being broken and those being formed.

$t\text{-}C_4H_9\text{-}H + Br\text{-}Br \rightarrow \quad t\text{-}C_4H_9\text{-}Br + H\text{-}Br$

The hyphens indicate the bonds involved in the reactions. ΔH for this reaction is found by using the following equation:

$$\Delta H = \left(\Delta H_{t\text{-}C_4H_9\text{-}H} + \Delta H_{Br\text{-}Br}\right) - \left(\Delta H_{t\text{-}C_4H_9\text{-}Br} + \Delta H_{H\text{-}Br}\right)$$

Using the values from the table:

$$\Delta H = (91 \text{ kcal/mole} + 46 \text{ kcal/mole}) - (63 \text{ kcal/mole} + 88 \text{ kcal/mole})$$
$$= 137 \text{ kcal/mole} - 151 \text{ kcal/mole} = -14 \text{ kcal/mole}$$

(b) $CH_4 + I_2 \rightarrow CH_3I + HI$

Rewriting the reaction to show the bonds involved:

$CH_3-H + I-I \rightarrow CH_3-I + H-I$

Solving for ΔH:

$$\Delta H = \left(\Delta H_{CH_3-H} + \Delta H_{I-I}\right) - \left(\Delta H_{CH_3-I} + \Delta H_{H-I}\right)$$

$$= (104 \text{ kcal/mole} + 36 \text{ kcal/mole}) - (56 \text{ kcal/mole} + 71 \text{ kcal/mole})$$
$$= 140 \text{ kcal/mole} - 127 \text{ kcal/mole} = 13 \text{ kcal/mole}$$

(c) $C_6H_6 + Cl_2 \rightarrow C_6H_5Cl + HCl$

Rewriting the equation to show the bonds:

$C_6H_5-H + Cl-Cl \rightarrow C_6H_5-Cl + H-Cl$.

Solving for ΔH:

$$\Delta H = \left(\Delta H_{C_6H_5-H} + \Delta H_{Cl-Cl}\right) - \left(\Delta H_{C_6H_5-Cl} + \Delta H_{H-Cl}\right)$$

$$= (112 \text{ kcal/mole} + 58 \text{ kcal/mole}) - (86 \text{ kcal/mole} + 103 \text{ kcal/mole})$$
$$= 170 \text{ kcal/mole} - 189 \text{ kcal/mole} = -19 \text{ kcal/mole}.$$

(d) $n-C_3H_8 + CH_4 \rightarrow 2 C_2H_6$

Rewriting this equation to show the bonds:

$n-C_2H_5-CH_3 + CH_3-H \rightarrow C_2H_5-H + CH_3-CH_3$

Solving for ΔH:

$$\Delta H = \left(\Delta H_{n-C_2H_5-CH_3} + \Delta H_{CH_3-H}\right) - \left(\Delta H_{C_2H_5-H} + \Delta H_{CH_3-CH_3}\right)$$

$$= (85 \text{ kcal/mole} + 104 \text{ kcal/mole}) - (98 \text{ kcal/mole} + 88 \text{ kcal/mole})$$

$$= 189 \text{ kcal/mole} - 186 \text{ kcal/mole} = 3 \text{ kcal/mole}$$

HALOGENATION

● PROBLEM 3-19

Why would the bromination of ethane to ethyl bromide be a more efficient synthesis than the bromination of hexane to 1-bromohexane?

Solution: There is only one possible monobrominated product formed from ethane, that is, ethyl bromide. This is true because the two carbons making up the ethane molecule are equivalent and the bromine radical will attack either one with equal frequency. This makes the synthesis of ethyl bromide from ethane an extremely efficient process.

This is not true of the production of 1-bromohexane from hexane. The six carbon atoms comprising hexane are not equivalent and will not be attacked by the bromine radical with equal frequency. In hexane there are two sets of equivalent carbons. One set is composed of the two carbons at the ends of the chain. These carbons are referred to as primary carbons because they are bound to only one other carbon atom. The four carbons in the center of the chain comprise the other set. These carbons are referred to as secondary carbons because they are each bound to two other carbon atoms. Secondary carbons are more reactive than primary carbons and will bind the bromine radical more readily. This will cause the production of more 2 and 3-bromohexane than 1-bromohexane. As a synthesis for 1-bromohexane, monobromination of hexane is a rather inefficient procedure.

● **PROBLEM** 3-20

A possible mechanism for the reaction of chlorine with methane would be to have collisions where a chlorine molecule removes a hydrogen according to the following scheme:

$$CH_3:H + :\overset{..}{\underset{..}{Cl}}:\overset{..}{\underset{..}{Cl}}: \xrightarrow{\text{slow}} CH_3\cdot + H:\overset{..}{\underset{..}{Cl}}: + :\overset{..}{Cl}\cdot$$

$$CH_3\cdot + :\overset{..}{\underset{..}{Cl}}\cdot \xrightarrow{\text{fast}} CH_3:\overset{..}{\underset{..}{Cl}}:$$

Use appropriate bond energies to assess the likelihood of this reaction mechanism. What about the possibility of a similar mechanism with elemental fluorine and methane?

Solution: Refer to the table on bond energies of various molecules in a previous problem. Given the bond energies we can determine whether the reaction requires energy or whether it liberates energy to the surroundings. This quantity of energy is known as the change in enthalpy (ΔH) of the reaction. When $\Delta H > 0$, external energy is required for the reaction to proceed, whereas if $\Delta H < 0$, then the reaction occurs spontaneously. Since in this problem external energy is not provided, the reaction will not proceed unless $\Delta H < 0$.

$$CH_3: H + :\overset{..}{\underset{..}{Cl}}:\overset{..}{\underset{..}{Cl}}: \xrightarrow{\text{slow}} CH_3\cdot + H:\overset{..}{\underset{..}{Cl}}: + :\overset{..}{\underset{..}{Cl}}:$$

From the table of bond energies, C-H = 98.7 kcal /mole, Cl-Cl = 58.0 , and H-Cl = 103.2.

$\Sigma\Delta H = + 98.7 + 58.0 - 103.2 = 53.5$ kcal.

Since $\Delta H = + 53.5$ is very high, it is improbable that this reaction will proceed in the direction indicated in the equation.

The equation for fluorine and methane would be given by :

$$CH_3:H + :\overset{..}{\underset{..}{F}}:\overset{..}{\underset{..}{F}}: \rightarrow CH_3\cdot + H:\overset{..}{\underset{..}{F}}: + :\overset{..}{F}\cdot$$

F-F = 36.6, C-F = 116, H-F=134.6.

Hence, $\Sigma\Delta H = 98.7 + 36.6 - 134.6 = + 0.7$ kcal.

It is possible for this reaction to take place because $\Delta H \approx 0$; but in order to determine whether fluoro-methane is the end product or not we have to calculate ΔH for the second step.

$$CH_3\cdot + \cdot\overset{..}{\underset{..}{F}}: \rightarrow CH_3:\overset{..}{\underset{..}{F}}:$$

$\Sigma\Delta H = (98.7)\ 3 + 0 - [3(98.7) + 116] = - 116$ kcal.

$\Delta H = - 116 < 0$ implies that the second step occurs with ease. Therefore the reaction that produces fluoro-methane is more probable than that which produces chloro-methane.

● **PROBLEM** 3-21

Suggest a reason for the fact that ultraviolet light causes Cl_2 (gas) to cleave homolytically, to produce two chlorine radicals, rather than heterolytically, to produce Cl^+ and Cl^-.

Solution: The fragmentation of molecules is associated with the consumption of energy ; however, when the converse occurs, i.e. when atoms combine, energy is liberated. The quantity of energy involved during the breakage or formation of bonds is known as the bond dissociation energy.

Let us consider a molecule A:B. The fragmentation of the A-B bond could be presented by:

$$A : B \rightarrow A\cdot + B\cdot$$

or

$$A : B \rightarrow A + :B$$

In the first case the two atoms break and leave with an equal share of electrons (one each). This is known as homolytic cleavage whereas in the latter reaction, both the electrons are deposited with one atom making that atom more electronegative than the other. The second type of fragmentation could also be viewed in terms of the production of ions, i.e. A^+ and B^-.

Recall that like charges repel and unlike charges attract. Since the two ions are opposite in charge they will tend to attract each other and the energy required to overcome this powerful electrostatic attractive force is in the order of about 100 kcal/mole. The fragments of homolysis on the other hand, are neutral in charge and therefore a molecule will need less dissociation energy in this type of reaction.

Since chlorine is in the gaseous state, cleavage occurs more easily by homolysis.

● **PROBLEM** 3-22

Predict the proportions of isomeric products from chlorination at room temperature of: (a) propane; (b) isobutane; (c) 2,3-dimethylbutane; (d) n-pentane (Note: There are three isomeric products); (e) isopentane.

Solution: The answer to this problem involves a consideration of orientation, the factors that determine where in a molecule reaction is most likely to occur. Orientation is determined by the relative rates of competing reactions.

Suppose one compared the rate of abstraction of primary hydrogens with the rate of abstraction of secondary hydrogens. What are the factors that determine the rates of these two reactions?

(1) Collision frequency. Since both reactions involve collision of the same particles, a specific alkene and a halogen, this must be the same for the two reactions. (2) Probability factor. If a primary hydrogen is to be abstracted, the alkane must be so oriented at the time of collision that the halogen atom strikes a primary hydrogen. Likewise, if a secondary hydrogen is to be abstracted, the alkane must be so oriented that the halogen atom strikes a secondary hydrogen. Now, if the alkane has, say, six primary hydrogens and only two secondary hydrogens, it could be estimated that the probability factor favors abstraction of primary hydrogens by the ratio of 6:2, or 3:1. (3) Energy of activation (E_{act}) is more for abstraction of a primary hydrogen than for abstraction of a secondary hydrogen. In fact, the E_{act} is greater for abstraction of a secondary hydrogen than for abstraction of a tertiary hydrogen. Hence, abstraction of hydrogens is found to follow the sequence 3°>2°>1° in reactivity. In chlorination at room temperature, the relative rates per hydrogen atom are 5.0:3.8:1.0.

With this information, the proportions of isomeric products from chlorination can be predicted.

(a) Propane's isomeric products (from chlorination):

$$CH_3CHCH_3$$
$$|$$
$$Cl$$

$$CH_3CH_2CH_2Cl$$

(iso-propyl chloride)   (n-propyl chloride)

To figure out the relative amounts of these products, remember that the probability and reactivity (E_{act}) of the hydrogens must be examined. In n-propyl chloride, the chlorine halogen abstracted a primary hydrogen (1°H) of relative rate 1, whereas in iso-propyl chloride the halogen abstracted a secondary hydrogen (2°H) of relative rate 3.8. The calculation of isomeric proportion is as follows:

$$\frac{\text{n-PrCl}}{\text{i-PrCl}} = \frac{\text{no. of 1° H}}{\text{no. of 2° H}} \times \frac{\text{reactivity of 1° H}}{\text{reactivity of 2° H}}$$

$$= \frac{6}{2} \times \frac{1.0}{3.8} = \frac{6.0}{7.6} .$$ Hence, the percentage of

1° isomeric product (that is, n-propyl chloride) is equal

to $\frac{6.0}{6.0 + 7.6} \times 100 = 44\ \%$. Consequently, percentage of

2° isomeric product (that is, iso-propyl chloride) is 56 %,

which is $\frac{7.6}{6.0 + 7.6} \times 100$.

(b) Isobutane's isomeric products:

$$\begin{array}{c} CH_3 \\ | \\ CH_3-C-CH_3 \\ | \\ Cl \end{array}$$

$$\begin{array}{c} CH_3 \\ | \\ CH_3-C-CH_2Cl \\ | \\ H \end{array}$$

(tert-butyl chloride)   (iso-butyl chloride)

The method of calculation of their proportion is the same as in (a).

$$\frac{\text{tert-butyl-chloride}}{\text{iso-butyl chloride}} = \frac{\text{no. of 3° H}}{\text{no. of 1° H}} \times \frac{\text{reactivity of 3° H}}{\text{reactivity of 1° H}}$$

$$= \frac{1}{9} \times \frac{5}{1} = \frac{5}{9} .$$ Therefore, the

percentage of t-butyl-chloride = $\frac{5}{5 + 9} \times 100 = 36\ \%$.

The percentage of iso-butyl chloride must be $\frac{9}{9 + 5} \times 100 = 64\ \%$.

(c)   2,3-dimethylbutane's isomeric products:

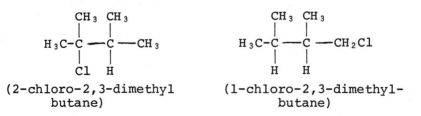

$$\begin{array}{cc} CH_3 & CH_3 \\ | & | \\ H_3C-C & -C-CH_3 \\ | & | \\ Cl & H \end{array}$$

$$\begin{array}{cc} CH_3 & CH_3 \\ | & | \\ H_3C-C & -C-CH_2Cl \\ | & | \\ H & H \end{array}$$

(2-chloro-2,3-dimethyl   (1-chloro-2,3-dimethyl-
     butane)   butane)

$$\frac{\text{2-chloro}}{\text{1-chloro}} = \frac{\text{no. of 3° H}}{\text{no. of 1° H}} \times \frac{\text{reactivity of 3° H}}{\text{reactivity of 1° H}}$$

$$= \frac{2}{12} \times \frac{5}{1} = \frac{10}{12} = \frac{5}{6}. \text{ Consequently, } \frac{5}{5 + 6} \times 100 =$$

45% is the percentage of 2-chloro-2,3-dimethylbutane, while

$\frac{6}{6 + 5} \times 100 = 55\%$ is the amount of 1-chloro-2,3-dimethyl-butane.

(d) n-pentane's isomeric products:

CH$_3$CH$_2$CH$_2$CH$_2$CH$_2$Cl   CH$_3$CH$_2$CH$_2$CHCH$_3$ CH$_3$CH$_2$CHCH$_2$CH$_3$

(n-pentyl chloride)   Cl   Cl

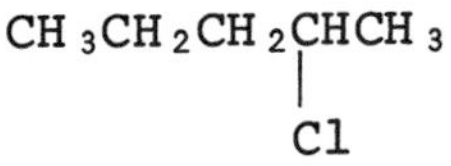

         (2-chloropentane) 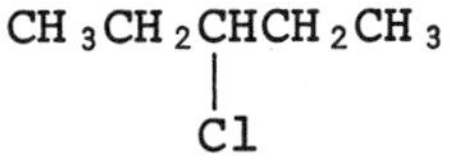 (3-chloro-
                pentane)

n-pentyl chloride: 6 primary hydrogens with reactivity of 1.0, so that 6 × 1.0 = 6.

2-chloropentane: 4 secondary hydrogens with reactivity of 3.8, so that 4 × 3.8 = 15.2.

3-chloropentane: 2 secondary hydrogens with reactivity of 3.8, so that 2 × 3.8 = 7.6.

The total number x reactivity = 6.0 + 15.2 + 7.6 = 28.8. Hence, the percentage of n-pentyl chloride is

$\frac{6}{28.8} \times 100 = 21$ %.

2-chloropentane: $\frac{15.2}{28.8} \times 100 = 53$ %

3-chloropentane: $\frac{7.6}{28.8} \times 100 = 26$ %.

(e) Isopentane's isomeric products:

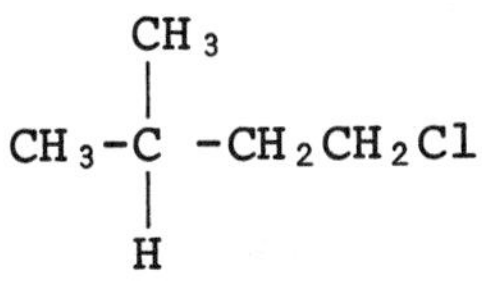

    CH$_3$ CH$_3$
    | |
CH$_3$-C -CH$_2$CH$_2$Cl   CH$_3$-C -CH$_2$CH$_3$
    | |
    H   Cl

(1-chloro-3-methyl-   (2-chloro-2-methyl-
  butane)   butane)

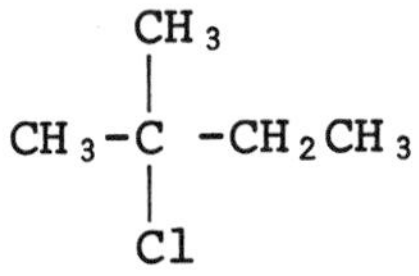

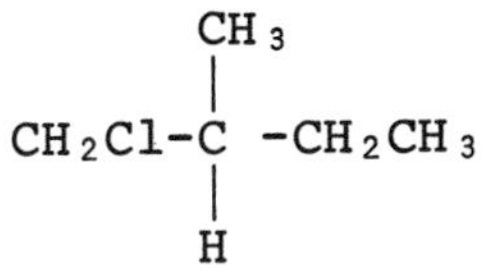

     CH$_3$ CH$_3$
     | |
CH$_2$Cl-C -CH$_2$CH$_3$ CH$_3$-C -CHCH$_3$
     | | |
     H   H   Cl

(1-chloro-2-methyl   (3-chloro-2-methyl-
  butane)   butane)

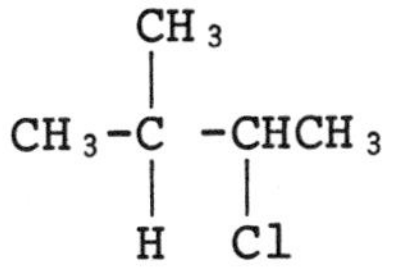

1-chloro-3-methylbutane: 3 primary hydrogens with reactivity of 1.0. 3 × 1 = 3.

2-chloro-2-methylbutane: 1 tertiary hydrogen with reactivity of 5.0. 5 × 1 = 5.

1-chloro-2-methylbutane: 6 primary hydrogens with reactivity of 1.0. 6 × 1 = 6.

3-chloro-2-methylbutane: 2 secondary hydrogens with reactivity of 3.8. 2 × 3.8 = 7.6.

The total number × reactivity = 3 + 5 + 6 + 7.6 = 21.6.

The percentages for the four isomeric compounds are as follows:

1-chloro-3-methylbutane: $\frac{3}{21.6}$ × 100 = 14 %

2-chloro-2-methylbutane: $\frac{5}{21.6}$ × 100 = 23 %

1-chloro-2-methylbutane: $\frac{6}{21.6}$ × 100 = 28 %

3-chloro-2-methylbutane: $\frac{7.6}{21.6}$ × 100 = 35 %

● **PROBLEM 3-23**

The reaction of the unusual hydrocarbon spiropentane with chlorine and light is one of the best ways of preparing chlorospiropentane.

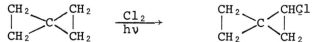

spiropentane   chlorospiropentane

(a) Explain why chlorination is such a useful preparative method in this case. (b) Write the reaction mechanism.

Solution: (a) Since all the hydrogen atoms in spiro-

pentane [structure] are equivalent, there is only

one possible monochlorinated product. If any dichlorospiropentane is formed it can be separated from the monochloro spiropentane by fractional distillation. This is possible because the boiling point of the dichlorinated compound is higher than the monochlorinated compound.

(b)   In any reaction mechanism there are three general
steps: initiation, propagation and termination. In the
initiation step, light catalyzes the homolytic cleavage of
a chlorine molecule to produce two chlorine radicals.
Further reactions which are believed to occur are sketched
below:

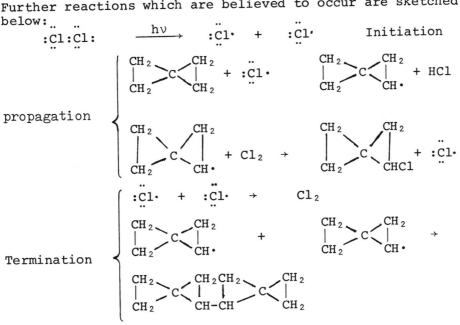

• **PROBLEM 3-24**

A commonly used free-radical initiator is AIBN (azobisiso-
butyronitrile). What are the products of its decomposition
in an inert solvent?

$$CH_3-\underset{\underset{CH_3}{|}}{\overset{\overset{CN}{|}}{C}} - N=N - \underset{\underset{CH_3}{|}}{\overset{\overset{CN}{|}}{C}} - CH_3$$

AIBN

Solution: Aliphatic azo compounds in general decompose
on heating, with the formation of nitrogen and two radicals.

$$CH_3-\underset{\underset{CH_3}{|}}{\overset{\overset{CN}{|}}{C}} - N=N - \underset{\underset{CH_3}{|}}{\overset{\overset{CN}{|}}{C}} - CH_3 \quad \xrightarrow{\Delta} \quad N = N$$

$$+ \quad CH_3-\underset{\underset{CH_3}{|}}{\overset{\overset{CN}{|}}{C}}\cdot \quad + \quad CH_3\underset{\underset{CH_3}{|}}{\overset{\overset{CN}{|}}{C}}\cdot$$

93

Because of the high propensity of the formation of radicals, AIBN is used extensively for the synthesis of polymers where a radical is the initiator of a reaction.

These two radicals can undergo disproportionation, where, through the process of hydrogen transfer, two equivalent amounts of saturated and unsaturated compounds are produced:

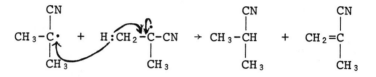

Since each of the six hydrogens are equivalent it does not matter which of the two places the double bond is placed.

A different reaction (dimerization) could also occur whereby two radicals join together:

SPECTROSCOPY

● PROBLEM 3-25

Give a structure or structures consistent with each of the following sets of nmr data.

(a) $C_3H_3Cl_5$
a triplet, δ 4.52, 1H
b doublet, δ 6.07, 2H

(b) $C_3H_5Cl_3$
a singlet, δ 2.20, 3H
b singlet, δ 4.02, 2H

(c) $C_{10}H_{14}$
a singlet, δ 1.30, 9H
b singlet, δ 7.28, 5H

(d) $C_{10}H_{14}$
a doublet, δ 0.88, 6H
b multiplet, δ 1.86, 1H
c doublet, δ 2.45, 2H
d singlet, δ 7.12, 5H

(e) $C_{10}H_{13}Cl$
a singlet, δ 1.57, 6H
b singlet, δ 3.07, 2H
c singlet, δ 7.27, 5H

Solution: (a) The molecular formula ($C_3H_3Cl_5$) suggests that the compound is a penta-chloro substituted propane. This is because there are 8 substituents (3 hyrdogens, 5 chlorines) for 3 carbons. A propane (3 carbon alkane) has the general formula C_3*_8, where * represents all the substituents in the molecule. The nuclear magnetic resonance (nmr) spectrum of the compound shows a doublet downfield from a triplet. The splittings indicate that the protons that gave rise to the doublet are deshielded relative to the protons that gave rise to the triplet; that is, the electron density about the "doublet protons" is less than that about the "triplet protons". This means that there are more chlorine atoms on the carbons with the "doublet protons" than there are on the carbons with the "triplet protons". Since there are only two signals in the nmr spectrum, two of the three protons must be in identical environments. The only situation that can satisfy this re-quirement as well as the molecular formula is:

```
      Cl H  Cl
      |  |  |
  H-C -C -C -H    1,1,2,3,3-pentachloropropane
      |  |  |
      Cl Cl Cl
```

The two terminal protons gave rise to the doublet and the middle proton gave rise to the triplet.

(b) The molecular formula ($C_3H_5Cl_3$) suggests that the compound is a tri-chloro substituted propane. The nmr spectrum shows that there is no spin-spin splitting. This means that all the protons are on the terminal carbons; there are none on the middle carbon (if there were, splitting would occur). The only possible structure could be:

```
       H Cl H
       | |  |
  Cl-C-C -C-H,    1,2,2-trichloropropane.
       | |  |
       H Cl H
```

The singlet at 2.20 δ is the methyl protons' signal and the singlet at 4.02 δ is the methylene protons' signal.

The methylene protons occur quite downfield because of the deshielding effects of the chloro groups.

(c) The nmr spectrum of the compound $C_{10}H_{14}$ shows a singlet at 7.28 δ. This is indicative of a benzene ring. If we subtract the phenyl group (C_6H_5-) from the molecular formula ($C_{10}H_{14}$) we are left with a $-C_4H_9$ portion. The fact that these nine remaining protons occur as a singlet indicates that they are in identical environments (they are equivalent). The only $-C_4H_9$ group that has all its protons in identical environments is a t-butyl group:

```
  CH 3
  |
-C -CH 3 .  This is attached to the benzene ring; the compound
  |
  CH 3
```

is t-butylbenzene:

C(CH$_3$)$_3$

(d) The singlet at 7.12 δ indicates the presence of a benzene ring. Subtracting the phenyl group (C_6H_5-) from the molecular formula ($C_{10}H_{14}$) gives us a $-C_4H_9$ portion. This group's protons must account for the remaining signals. The protons responsible for the doublets were split by a single proton and hence must be adjacent to a carbon bearing one hydrogen. The fact that one of the doublets has a relative intensity of 6H indicates that there must be at least two methyl groups attached to the carbon bearing one hydrogen. Since we are limited to four carbons to account for these signals, there must be only two methyl groups bonded to the carbon with one hydrogen. The other doublet has a relative intensity of 2H and a methylene group must have given rise to this signal. The $-C_4H_9$ portion must be an isobutyl group: $-CH_2-CH(CH_3)_2$. The isobutyl group is bonded to the benzene ring. The compound is isobutylbenzene:

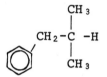

This compound is a structural isomer of the one in part (c).

(e) There is a singlet at 7.27 δ; hence a benzene ring is in the compound. Subtraction of the phenyl group (C_6H_5-) from the molecular formula ($C_{10}H_{13}Cl$) leaves us with a $-C_4H_8Cl$ portion. The protons in this portion must account for the remaining signals. The fact that there is a singlet with relative intensity 6H indicates that there are two methyl groups in identical environments. Since there is no splitting in the nmr spectrum, the two methyl groups must be bonded to a carbon with no hydrogens; this implies that

the chlorine group is bonded to this carbon: $-\underset{\underset{Cl}{|}}{\overset{\overset{CH_3}{|}}{C}}-CH_3$. The

singlet with relative intensity of 2H must be a methylene protons signal. This is because it is the only group that will bond to the $-\underset{\underset{Cl}{|}}{C}(CH_3)_2$ portion to satisfy the required

molecular formula (C_4H_8Cl). This group is bonded to the benzene ring. The compound is 2-chloro-2-methyl-1-phenyl-propane:

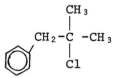

CHAPTER 4

CYCLOALKANES

NOMENCLATURE

● PROBLEM 4-1

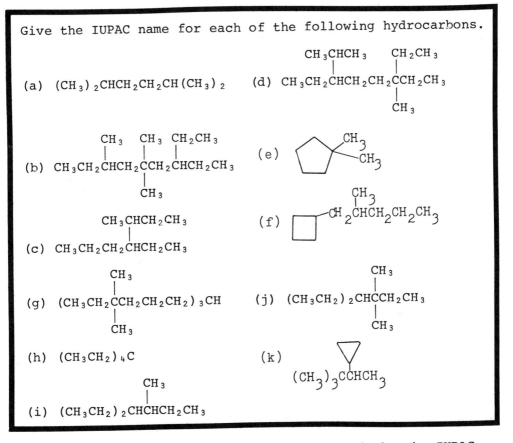

Give the IUPAC name for each of the following hydrocarbons.

(a) $(CH_3)_2CHCH_2CH_2CH(CH_3)_2$

(b)
$$CH_3CH_2CHCH_2CCH_2CHCH_2CH_3$$
with substituents CH_3, CH_3, CH_2CH_3 and CH_3

(c) $CH_3CH_2CH_2CHCH_2CH_3$ with substituent $CH_3CHCH_2CH_3$

(d) $CH_3CH_2CHCH_2CH_2CCH_2CH_3$ with substituents CH_3CHCH_3, CH_2CH_3 and CH_3

(e) cyclopentane with two CH_3 groups

(f) cyclobutane with $CH_2CHCH_2CH_2CH_3$ (substituent CH_3)

(g) $(CH_3CH_2CCH_2CH_2CH_2)_3CH$ with substituents CH_3 and CH_3

(h) $(CH_3CH_2)_4C$

(i) $(CH_3CH_2)_2CHCHCH_2CH_3$ with substituent CH_3

(j) $(CH_3CH_2)_2CHCCH_2CH_3$ with substituents CH_3 and CH_3

(k) cyclopropane with $(CH_3)_3CCHCH_3$

Solution: The naming of organic compounds by the IUPAC system follows certain procedures:

(1) Determine and identify by inspection the longest continuous carbon chain in the molecule or compound.

(2) Locate and name all the side chains attached to the longest continuous carbon chain.

(3) Indicate the names and positions and numbers of each type of side chain by means of prefixes to the name of the parent chain. The side chains are named in alphabetical order.

(4) Since cycloalkanes are basically saturated hydrocarbons, they are given the same name as their corresponding chain alkane, with the addition of the prefix cyclo- to signify the presence of a ring structure.

(a)   We can rewrite the compound in its expanded form in order to make the structure more evident.

$$
\begin{array}{ccc}
CH_3 & & CH_3 \\
| & & | \\
CH_3-CH-CH_2CH_2CH-CH_3 & &
\end{array}
$$

The longest continuous carbon chain consists of 6 carbon atoms, and one methyl group is attached to each of the two terminal carbons. The IUPAC name is thus 2,5-dimethylhexane.

$$
\overset{2}{CH_3} \quad \overset{1}{CH_2CH_3}
$$
(b) $\overset{9}{CH_3}-\overset{8}{CH_2}-\overset{7}{CH}-\overset{6}{CH_2}-\overset{5\ 4}{\underset{CH_3}{C}}-CH_2-\overset{3}{\underset{CH_3}{CH}}-CH_2-CH_3$

The longest chain contains 9 carbon atoms. A methyl group is attached to the 7th carbon; 2 methyl groups are attached to the 5th carbon; and an ethyl group is bonded to the third carbon. The name of this compound is thus 3-ethyl-5,5,7-trimethylnonane.

$$
\overset{5}{CH_3}-\overset{6}{CH}-\overset{7}{CH_2}-CH_3
$$
(c) $\overset{1}{CH_3}-\overset{2}{CH_2}-\overset{3}{CH_2}-\overset{4}{CH}-CH_2-CH_3$

The longest chain has 7 carbon atoms. The 3rd carbon has a methyl group attached to it and the 4th carbon an ethyl group. The name given to this compound is 4-ethyl-3-methylheptane (alphabetical order has precedence over numerical order in side chains).

$$
CH_3-CH-CH_3 \qquad CH_2CH_3
$$
(d) $\overset{8}{CH_3}-\overset{7}{CH_2}-\overset{6}{CH}-\overset{5}{CH_2}-\overset{4}{CH_2}-\overset{3}{C}-\overset{2}{CH_2}-\overset{1}{CH_3}$
$$
| \\
CH_3
$$

Using the same principles illustrated above, this compound is named 3-ethyl-6-isopropyl-3-methyloctane.

(e)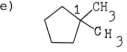

This structure is a 5-carbon ring (cyclopentane)
having 2 methyl groups attached to the same carbon (con-
ventionally designated as C_1). The name of the structure
is 1,1-dimethylcyclopentane.

(f)

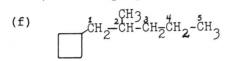

The longest chain has 5 carbon atoms. The ring is
composed of four carbon atoms and is therefore cyclobutane.
Thus, the name of the compound is 1-cyclobutyl-2-methyl-
pentane.

(g) Written in expanded form:

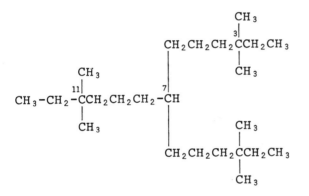

The longest chain has 13 carbon atoms (tridecane).
The seventh carbon has one 4,4-dimethylhexyl group
attached to it; in addition 2 methyl groups are bonded
to both the 3rd and the eleventh carbon. The IUPAC name
of the compound is written as 7-(4,4-dimethylhexyl)-
3,3,11,11-tetramethyltridecane.

(j) 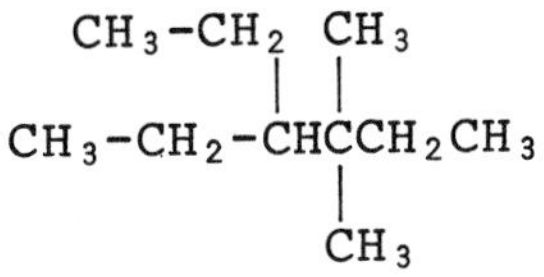 $CH_3-CH_2-CHCCH_2CH_3$ with CH_3-CH_2 and CH_3 above and CH_3 below

$$CH_3-CH_2\ \ CH_3$$
$$|\qquad|$$
$$(j)\quad CH_3-CH_2-CHCCH_2CH_3$$
$$|$$
$$CH_3$$

The longest chain has 6 carbons. The name of the
compound is 3-ethyl-4,4-dimethylhexane.

(k)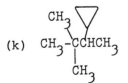

The longest chain has 4 carbon atoms. The name of
this compound is 2-cyclopropyl-3,3-dimethylbutane.

Write expanded structures showing the C-C bonds for each of the following condensed formulas. Name each substance by an accepted system.

a. $(CH_2)_{10}$ (saturated compound only)
b. $(CH_2)_5CHCH_3$

c. $(CH_3)_2C(CH_2)_6CHC_2H_5$
d. The isomers of trimethylcyclobutane
e. $(CH_2)_6CHCH_2C(CH_3)_2CH_2Cl$
f. $[(CH_2)_2CH]_2C(CH_3)C_2H_5$

Solution:

(a) $(CH_2)_{10}$

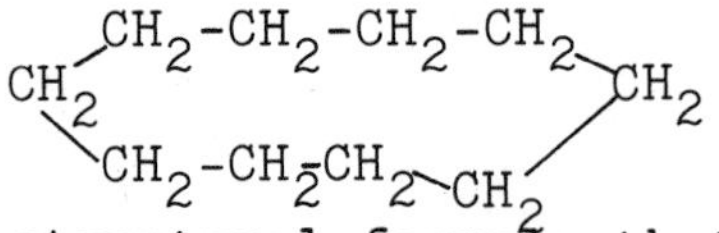

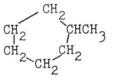

This is the only structural formula that satisfies a saturated compound with 10 CH_2 groups. Note that the structure must be a ring since there are no suitable end groups.

The name of this ring is cyclodecane.

(b) $(CH_2)_5CHCH_3$

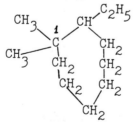

The formula given indicates that there is only one group that could possibly serve as an end group, namely CH_3. Since a chain type structure would require two end groups, this compound must be in ring form, with the CH_3 as a substituent. The structure indicated is a 6-membered ring, with a methyl substituent. It can be named methyl-cyclohexane.

(c) $(CH_3)_2C(CH_2)_6CHC_2H_5$

The bar between the two carbon atoms indicates that they are linked into a ringtype structure. In expanded form, then, the structure is:

This compound can be named 1,1-dimethyl-2-ethylcyclooctane.

(d)   The isomers of trimethylcyclobutane.   Isomers are
defined as compounds that have exactly the same kind and
number of atoms, but have different structural forms with
different bonding relationships between the atoms.   Tri-
metylcyclobutane can be represented structurally as

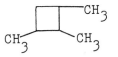

and named 1,2,3-trimethylcyclobutane.   The methyl groups
could just as well be attached to any other carbon atom(s)
in the ring, and thus the compound can be modified structurally into two other isomeric forms:

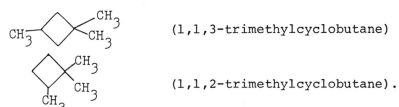

(1,1,3-trimethylcyclobutane)

and   (1,1,2-trimethylcyclobutane).

Therefore a total of three isomeric forms are possible
for trimethylcyclobutane.

(e) $(CH_2)_6CHCH_2C(CH_3)_2CH_2Cl$ can be written as

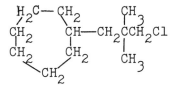

Since there are 7 carbon atoms in the ring attached to a
dimethyl propyl chloride group, this structure is named
2,2-dimethyl-3-cycloheptylpropyl chloride.

(f) $[(CH_2)_2CH]_2C(CH_3)C_2H_5$

Two rings, each consisting of 3 carbon atoms, are attached
to the second carbon of butane.   This can be written as

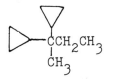

where the triangle (Δ) represents the cyclopropyl group,
i.e.,

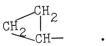   .

The name given to this structure is 2,2-dicyclopropyl-
butane.

101

Write structural formulas for all of the possible cis-
trans isomers of the following compounds:

a. 1,2,3-trimethylcyclopropane
b. 1,3-dichlorocyclopentane
c. 1,1,3-trimethylcyclohexane
d. (3-methylcyclobutyl)-3-methylcyclobutane

Solution: The first step undertaken in writing
the structural formula for a compound is to draw the
structure for the longest continuous carbon chain, which
is indicated in the name.   The next step is to attach the
subgroups, denoted in the prefixes, to the parent chain
at the positions indicated.

(a)   1,2,3-trimethylcyclopropane.   Cyclopropane is planar
and is a 3-carbon ring (△) structure.   Here, one methyl
group is bonded to each carbon in the ring.   Each methyl
group can either be attached above the plane of the cyclopropane ring or below the plane.   Only 2 different combinations of methyl group attachment are possible for this
compound, resulting in two isomers.

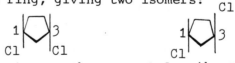

The structural formulas can also be represented by

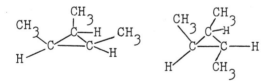

respectively, but we will use the first type of representation in our solutions due to its clarity.

(b)   1,3-dichlorocyclopentane.   The last part of the name
tells us that the compound is a 5-carbon ring structure.
Again, the substituents of the ring can be attached either
above or below the ring, giving two isomers:

When both substituents are above or   below the ring,
they are cis with respect to the ring.   If one is above
and one is below the ring, they are trans.

(c) 1,1,3-trimethylcyclohexane.   With some careful inspection one will notice that there is only one isomer
present if the compound has a planar structure.   However,

102

because cyclohexane in reality is not planar, there are
two conformational isomers of 1,1,3-trimethylcyclohexane:

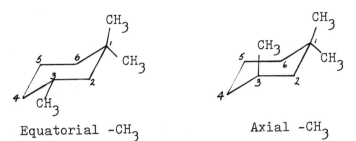

Equatorial -CH₃   Axial -CH₃

Since in room temperature these two forms undergo
rapid interconversion, it is very difficult to distinguish
them from each other.

(d) (3-methylcyclobutyl)-3-methylcyclobutane. A 3-
methylcyclobutyl group is attached to the first carbon
atom of 3-methylcyclobutane. Three possible arrangements
of the two methyl groups exist:

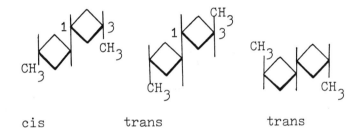

cis   trans   trans

Note that the two trans forms cannot be made to superimpose upon each other and are therefore not identical
compounds.

● **PROBLEM** 4-4

Name each of the following compounds by an accepted system.

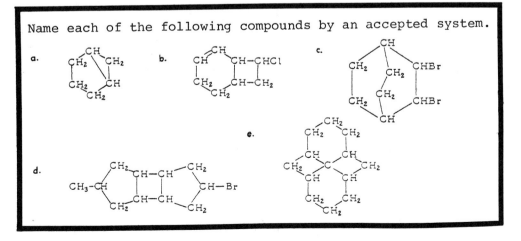

Solution: (a)

This is an example of a polycycloalkane, an alkane with
more than one ring. Compounds of this type are named
systematically by attaching the prefix "bicyclo',
'tricyclo', etc., as the case may be, to the name of an
open chain hydrocarbon with the same number of carbon
atoms as the polycycloalkane. The number of carbon atoms
in each linkage is noted in a square bracket immediately
following the prefix.

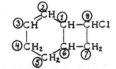

     Here, the presence of two rings calls for the prefix
'bicyclo'. There are a total of 6 carbon atoms in the
two rings, and so the compound is a bicyclohexane. The
different carbon atoms have been numbered for convenience.
Going in the order of increasing carbon number, there are
3 carbon atoms following C_1 up to its bonded partner,
$\overline{C}_5$ ($C_2 \rightarrow C_4$), and 1 carbon atom following C_5 (C_6). The
linkage responsible for forming a second ring is between
C_1 and C_5 and there are no internal carbon atoms (0)
within this linkage.

     These numbers are placed in decreasing order within
brackets and are separated by periods. We can thus write
the name for the above compound as bicyclo[3.1.0]hexane.

(b)

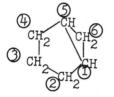

     This is a bicyclic compound (because the carbon atoms
form two rings) consisting of 8 carbon atoms in all, which
are numbered as shown. Look at the linkages between C_1
and C_6. Four carbon atoms follow C_1 ($C_2 \rightarrow C_6$), while 2
atoms follow C_6 ($C_7 \rightarrow C_8$). There are no atoms internal
to the C_1 - C_6 bond itself. Since a chlorine atom is
bonded to C_8, we can name this compound as 8-chloro
bicyclo[4.2.0]-2-octene. 2-octene signifies the presence
of a double bond between C_2 and C_3 in a 8-carbon compound.

(c)

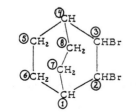

104

There are two rings and 8 carbon atoms in this compound. The central linkage between C_1 and C_4 contains 2 internal carbon atoms (C_7 and C_8). There are 2 carbon atoms following both C_1 ($C_2 \rightarrow C_3$) and C_4 ($C_5 \rightarrow C_6$). Bromine atoms are bonded to both C_2 and C_3. Therefore, the correct name for the compound is 2,3-dibromobicyclo[2.2.2]octane.

(d)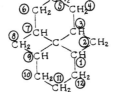

This compound consists of 10 carbon atoms grouped into 3 rings (hence tricyclodecane) to which is attached a methyl group at C_9 and a bromine atom at C_4. Looking at the bonding between C_1 and C_7, we see there are 5 carbon atoms following C_1 ($C_2 \rightarrow C_6$) and 3 atoms following C_7 ($C_8 \rightarrow C_{10}$). There are no carbon atoms within the linkage between C_1 and C_7. We designate any further bonds, after the first has been established, by the number of carbon atoms internal to the bonds (here C_2 and C_6 with 0 atoms in between). A superscript names the carbons between which that bond occurs. Therefore, the name of the compound is 4-bromo-9-methyltricyclo[5.3.0.0^{2,6}]decane.

(e)

There are a total of four rings and 13 carbon atoms in this structure, hence it is a tetracyclotridecane.

Looking first at the linkages between C_1 and C_9, we find there are 7 carbon atoms following C_1 ($C_2 \rightarrow C_8$) and 3 carbon atoms following C_9 ($C_{10} \rightarrow C_{12}$). There is one carbon atom within the bond (C_{13}).

There is a bond between C_3 and C_{13} with no atoms in between, and a bond between C_7 and C_{13}, again with no atoms in between.

The name of the compound is thus tetracyclo [7.3.1.0^{3,13}.0^{7,13}]tridecane.

CONFORMATIONS

• PROBLEM 4-5

(a) How many pairs of eclipsed hydrogens are present in planar cyclobutane?   (b)   In puckered cyclobutane?

Solution: First let us look at the structure of planar cyclobutane.

(a) planar cyclobutane

As we can see, eight pairs of hydrogens in planar cyclobutane are eclipsed:

1 and 2	5 and 6
2 and 3	6 and 7
3 and 4	7 and 8
4 and 1	8 and 5

In puckered cyclobutane, we can tell from examining its structure that no eclipsed hydrogens are present.

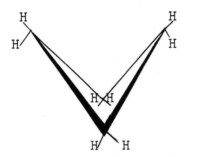

(b) puckered cyclobutane

The student should use a model if the above is not clear.

● **PROBLEM** 4-6

The energy barrier for rotation about the C-C bond in ethane is about 3 kcal, which suggests that the energy required to bring one pair of hydrogens into an eclipsed arrangement is 1 kcal. Calculate how many kilocalories the planar form and extreme boat form of cyclohexane are likely to be unstable relative to the chair form on account of H-H eclipsing and flagpole interactions.

Solution: First let us study the structure of planar cyclohexane:

planar cyclohexane

In this structure, we expect a considerable degree of instability due to the 12 pairs of eclipsed hydrogens. Since 1 pair of eclipsed hydrogens requires 1 kcal of energy, 12 pairs of eclipsed hydrogens in planar cyclohexane will present an eclipsing strain of 12 kcal.

In the extreme boat form of cyclohexane, 4 pairs of eclipsed hydrogens are present:

flagpole interaction

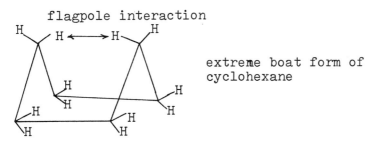

extreme boat form of cyclohexane

Here, 4 kcal of eclipsing strain is involved. In addition, a pair of hydrogens are forced to come together in a flagpole type of interaction. It is experimentally measured that each flagpole interaction (where the hydrogens are about 1.83 Å apart) carries 3 kcal of energy. Therefore the extreme boat form of cyclohexane has a total of 7 kcal of energy more than the most stable chair form; in which there are no eclipsed hydrogen pairs.

● PROBLEM 4-7

(a) trans-1,2-Dimethylcyclohexane exists about 99% in the diequatorial conformation; trans-1,2-Dibromocyclohexane on the other hand, exists about equally in diequatorial and diaxial conformations. Furthermore, the fraction of the diaxial conformation decreases with increasing polarity of the solvent. How do you account for the contrast between the dimethyl and dibromo compounds?

(b) If trans-3-cis-4-dibromo-tert-butylcyclohexane is subjected to prolonged heating, it is converted into an equilibrium mixture (about 50:50) of itself and a di-astereomer. What is the diastereomer likely to be? How do you account for the approximately equal stability of these two diastereomers? (Here, and in (c), consider the more stable conformation of each diastereomer to be the one with an equatorial tert-butyl group).

(c) There are two more diastereomeric 3,4-dibromo-tert-butylcyclohexanes. What are they? How do you account for the fact that neither is present to an appreciable extent in the equilibrium mixture?

Solution: (a) Two types of strain are about equally important in trans 1,2-dibromocyclohexane. First, steric strain dictates that the compound exist in the diequatorial conformation. By having the two bromo groups pointing away from the ring in equatorial positions (see Figure) non-bonded interactions between hydrogen and bromine atoms, which will occur in diaxial conformation, will be prevented.

However, since the bromine atom is electron-rich,
two bromine atoms in the diequatorial conformation will
repel each other. This dipole-dipole repulsion will be
relieved as the bromine atoms become axially oriented in
the diaxial conformation. Thus at equilibrium, trans
1,2-dibromocyclohexane will exist in both the diequatorial
and the diaxial conformations in approximately equal parts,
since the two forms are of about equal energy.

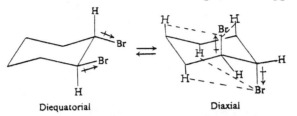

Diequatorial   Diaxial

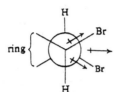   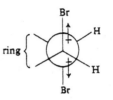

steric strain low   dipole-dipole repulsion low
dipole-dipole repulsion high   steric strain high

(Dotted line indicates steric interaction; arrow indicates
direction of dipole moment.)

      As polarity of the solvent is increased, any dipole-
dipole repulsion is relieved through interaction with the
solvent. Therefore, the favored form is the polar one,
that is, the diequatorial conformation, since both its
steric strain and its dipole-dipole repulsion will be low.

      Trans 1,2-dimethylcyclohexane exists mainly in the
diequatorial conformation. This is because the repulsion
between $-CH_3$ groups is much weaker, and steric strain is
the controlling factor.

(b) As trans-3-cis-4-dibromo-tert-butylcyclohexane is
heated, a diastereomer, cis-3-trans-4-dibromo-tert-
butylcyclohexane is formed. An equilibrium mixture shows
the following:

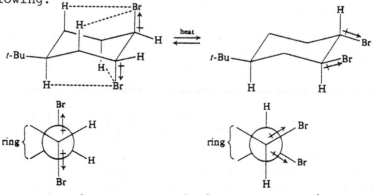

(i) trans-3-cis-4-dibromo   (ii) cis-3-trans-4-dibromo
     (both -Br's axial)   (both -Br's equatorial)

In (i) there are four 1,3-diaxial interactions between Br's and H's; but there is relief of dipole-dipole repulsion. In (ii) there are no 1,3-diaxial interactions between Br's and H's, but there is increased dipole-dipole repulsion. Dipole-dipole repulsion and 1,3-diaxial interactions just about balance each other; thus (i) and (ii) are of about equal stability.

(c) Two other possible diastereomers are:

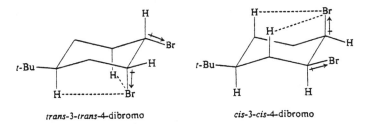

trans-3-trans-4-dibromo   cis-3-cis-4-dibromo

In each, there are both considerable 1,3-diaxial interactions and unrelieved dipole-dipole repulsion. Hence they are relatively unstable and do not occur in appreciable amounts in the equilibrium mixture.

● **PROBLEM** 4-8

Would you expect cis- or trans-1,2-dimethylcyclopropane to be the more stable? Explain.

Solution: The trans form is expected to be more stable than the cis form. As we can see, the former has its methyl groups farther apart from each other than the latter. The non-bonded interaction between the hydrogen and the methyl group in the trans conformation is smaller than that between the two methyl groups in the cis conformation. Thus the cis form has a greater strain, and is less stable.

non-bonded interaction

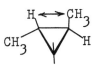 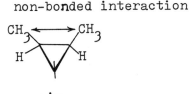

trans   cis

ANGLE STRAIN

● **PROBLEM** 4-9

(a) Estimate the amount of eclipsing strain in planar

cyclopentane.   (b)   Is the amount of eclipsing strain
decreased in going from the planar to the pickered form?

Solution: Eclipsing strain has a value of approximately
1 Kcal/mole for two adjacent, eclipsed bonds.   In planar
cyclopentane 10 pairs of eclipsed hydrogens are found, thus
10 Kcal of eclipsing strain is present.

As planar cyclopentane folds, the number of eclipsed
hydrogens decreases, and thus eclipsing strain decreases.

In puckered cyclopentane, only two pairs of eclipsed
hydrogens are found: 1   and   3 , 2   and   4 .   Hence only
2 Kcal of eclipsing strain is present.

Therefore, as planar cyclopentane becomes puckered,
a loss of 8 Kcal of eclipsing strain enables the puckered
form to become more stable.

● **PROBLEM** 4-10

Calculate and compare the total angle strain in kcal for
planar cyclobutane and for a folded cyclobutane with all
C-C bond lengths of 1.54 Å and the carbons on opposite
corners 2.04 Å apart (which corresponds to a dihedral
angle of about 120°, see Figure).   Assume that the energy
of changing a C-C-C bond angle is 17.5 kcal per degree^2
per mole.   Estimate relief in hydrogen-hydrogen eclipsing
interactions which would be associated with bending a
cyclobutane ring in this way.

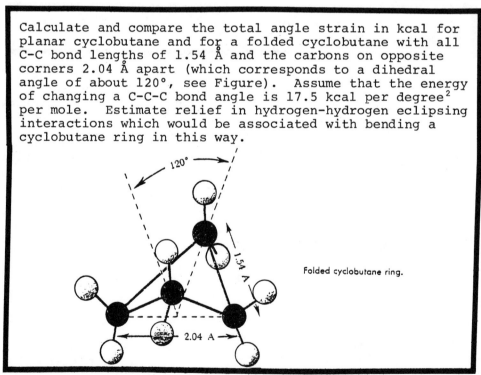

Folded cyclobutane ring.

Solution: From the given information we can calculate
the value of the C-C-C bond angles in the 60°-folded

110

cyclobutane:

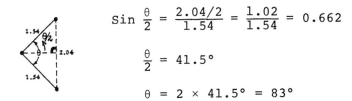

$$\text{Sin } \frac{\theta}{2} = \frac{2.04/2}{1.54} = \frac{1.02}{1.54} = 0.662$$

$$\frac{\theta}{2} = 41.5°$$

$$\theta = 2 \times 41.5° = 83°$$

Since the stable angle of a C-C-C bond in hydrocarbons is 109.5° (tetrahedral angle), keeping the angles in puckered cyclobutane at 83° requires additional energy. This energy is called the angle strain. The total angle strain for a mole of puckered cyclobutane is calculated from the following:

$$\text{angle strain} = 17.5 \times 4 \times (109.5 - 83)^2 \text{ kcal}$$

$$= 49.2 \text{ kcal}$$

where 4 is the number of C-C-C bond angles in cyclobutane. The 49.2 kcal is the total energy required to keep the four C-C-C bond angles each at 83° rather than the more stable value of 109.5°.

In planar cyclobutane, each C-C-C bond angle measures 90°. Thus the angle strain is

$$17.5 \times 4 \times (109.5 - 90)^2 \text{ kcal or 26.6 kcal.}$$

The greater angle strain present in the folded form of cyclobutane (49.2 kcal) as compared to that in the planar form (26.6 kcal) indicates that the former is more unstable than the latter. But this is true judging on the basis of angle strain alone. We have to take into account the energy involved in hydrogen-hydrogen eclipsing interactions which we find are stronger in planar cyclobutane than puckered cyclobutane. Considering the structures of the two forms,

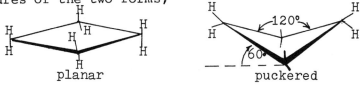

planar   puckered

we can see that the planar form requires that all 8 hydrogens be kept in eclipsing positions. Their repulsion of each other presents an eclipsing strain which decreases as the planar form becomes puckered, and the hydrogens are moved somewhat apart. Thus hydrogen-hydrogen eclipsing strain alone dictates that the puckered form be more stable than the planar.

It is experimentally observed that as a pair of hydrogens loses their eclipsing relationship, about 1 kcal of energy is released. So as planar cyclobutane is folded, so that all hydrogen-hydrogen eclipsing interations are lost, 8 kcal (8 × 1 kcal) of energy is liberated.

111

Most cyclobutanes in nature show a 30°-folding corresponding to C-C-C bond angles of 88° and a calculated angle strain of 32.4 kcal, which is a compromise between the planar and the 60°-folded form.

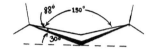

30°-folded cyclobutane

Investigate the thermodynamic feasibility of the following propagation steps for opening the rings of cycloalkanes with n = 2-6 by a free-radical mechanism.

(1) $(CH_2)_n$ + Br$^{\cdot}$ → $BrCH_2 \{CH_2\}_{n-2} CH_2 \cdot$

(2) $BrCH_2 \{CH_2\}_{n-2} CH_2^{\cdot} + Br_2$ → $(CH_2)_{n-2} (CH_2Br)_2$ + Br$^{\cdot}$

Use 83 kcal for the bond-dissociation energy of a normal C-C bond and 68 kcal for the bond-dissociation energy of a C-Br bond. (An easy way to solve a problem of this type is to first calculate ΔH of each step for cyclohexane where there is no strain, and then make suitable corrections for the strain which is present for small values of n.) Refer to the following table for your answer.

Table 1. Total Strain of Cycloalkanes

Cycloalkane $(CH_2)_n$	n	Total strain (kcal/mole)
ethylene	2	22.4
cyclopropane	3	27.6
cyclobutane	4	26.4
cyclopentane	5	6.5
cyclohexane	6	0.0

Solution: ΔH of a reaction is the energy change as a reactant gives rise to a product. Since chemical substances contain energy in chemical bonds, a change in energy (ΔH) can be considered as a change in total bond energy as a reactant (or reactants) yields a product (or products). In other words,

$$\Delta H = E_{product} - E_{reactant} ,$$

where E = bond energy. If ΔH carries a positive sign, the energy of the products is greater than that of the reactants, and the reaction is defined as endothermic, meaning that energy must be absorbed in order for the reaction to occur. If ΔH is negative, the energy of the products is less than that of the reactants; the reaction is said to be exothermic, meaning energy is released as a result of the reaction. Exothermic reactions are feasible whereas endothermic reactions are not, since the latter requires a net input of energy.

In solving the problem, we must find the sign of the ΔH of the reaction in order to tell whether the reaction is feasible.

When n = 6, the cycloalkane is a cyclohexane. In the first step of the given reaction,

$$(CH_2)_6 + Br^{\cdot} \rightarrow BrCH_2-(CH_2)_4-CH_2\cdot$$

one bond - the C-C bond in cyclohexane - is broken, and one bond - the C-Br bond in the product - is formed. We know that a C-C bond carries with it 83 kcal of energy, and a C-Br bond 68 kcal. Thus in this reaction, 83 kcal is absorbed in order to break a C-C bond while only 68 kcal is released as a C-Br bond forms. There is a net absorption of 15 kcal (83 - 68) of energy. ΔH therefore is + 15 kcal and the reaction is endothermic. Endothermic reactions are not readily feasible.

In calculating the ΔH's for the same reaction involving smaller ring sizes (n = 2, 3, 4, 5) we need to know the additional energy stored in the cycloalkanes due to angle strain. As n decreases, angle strain becomes stronger. In addition, there is also the hydrogen-hydrogen eclipsing strain that has to be taken into consideration. The total strain, then, equals to the sum of angle strain and eclipsing strain. When the ring is opened in reaction (1), the additional energy required to maintain the strain in the cyclic form is released. We can find the ΔH's for smaller cycloalkanes by subtracting the total strain (given in Table 1) from the + 15 kcal found previously for the ΔH of cyclohexane's ring-opening reaction. Therefore, when

Total
strain
↓
n = 5	ΔH = + 15 kcal -	6.5 kcal =	+ 8.5 kcal
n = 4	ΔH = + 15 kcal -	26.4 kcal =	- 11.4 kcal
n = 3	ΔH = + 15 kcal -	27.6 kcal =	- 12.6 kcal
n = 2	ΔH = + 15 kcal -	22.4 kcal =	- 7.4 kcal

As we can see, only ring-opening reactions of n = 2, 3, and 4 will be exothermic (with negative ΔH's). Thus only these reactions will be feasible.

In the second step of the reaction,

$$BrCH_2-(CH_2)_{n-2}CH_2^{\cdot} + Br_2 \rightarrow (CH_2)_{n-2}(CH_2Br)_2 + Br^{\cdot},$$

there is simply a Br-addition onto the CH radical.
Strains related to ring structures do not apply, since no
breakage of the ring structure occurs. The ΔH of this
reaction will then be the same for all n's. In this step
one Br-Br bond is broken while another C-Br bond is
formed. The energy absorbed in breaking a Br-Br bond is
experimentally found to be 46 kcal. The ΔH can then be
calculated from 46 kcal - 68 kcal, which gives - 22 kcal.

STEREOISOMERISM

● **PROBLEM** 4-12

You have two bottles labeled "1,2-Cyclopentanediol," one
containing a compound of m.p. 30°, the other a compound
of m.p. 55°; both compounds are optically inactive. How
could you decide, beyond any doubt, which bottle should
be labeled "cis" and which "trans"?

Solution:

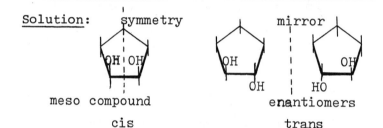

meso compound   enantiomers

cis   trans

The mirror image of cis-1,2-cyclopentanediol is
identical to and superimposable upon the cis compound
itself. By examining the structure a bit more closely,
we find that the compound is actually a meso compound.
By definition, its mirror images are identical and so
unresolvable, and the compound is optically inactive.

Trans-1,2-cyclopentanediol has non-superimposable
mirror images, and so can exist as two enantiomers. When
equal parts of enantiomers are mixed, trans-1,2-cyclo-
pentanediol is a racemic modification and appears to be
optically inactive. This is because the equal parts of
enantiomers rotate light to the same degree but in
opposite directions, and the net effect is no observable
optical activity. However, the trans compound can be
resolved into its enantiomers by special methods, such as
reacting them with reagents that are themselves optically
active.

Thus, if the solution is resolvable into two optically active compounds, it must contain the trans
isomers.

● **PROBLEM** 4-13

Which of the following compounds are resolvable, and which

are non-resolvable? Which are truly meso compounds? Use
models as well as drawings.

(a) cis-1,2-cyclohexanediol   (d) trans-1,3-cyclohexanediol
(b) trans-1,2-cyclohexanediol (e) cis-1,4-cyclohexanediol
(c) cis-1,3-cyclohexanediol   (f) trans-1,4-cyclohexanediol

Solution: Every compound has a mirror image. But not
all mirror images are superimposable on each other.
Mirror images that are nonsuperimposable are called
enantiomers. Enantiomers can be resolved and are characterized by optical activity. A compound with a chiral
center (atom bonded to 4 different groups) has enantiomers,
whereas one with no chiral center has no enantiomers.
However, there are compounds with chiral carbons whose mirror-
images are superimposable.   These compounds are called
meso compounds. Meso compounds cannot be resolved.

(a)   cis-1,2-cyclohexanediol

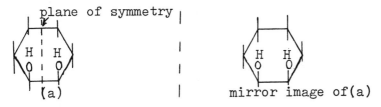

These mirror images are actually identical and
superimposable on each other. On closer inspection one
half of the compound is superimposable on its other half.
This is equivalent to saying that there is a plane of
symmetry in the compound. Cis-1,2-cyclohexanediol is a
meso compound and is not resolvable, although it contains
two chiral carbons.

(b)   trans-1,2-cyclohexanediol

These mirror images are not superimposable. Note
also that there is no internal plane of symmetry in (b).
Trans-1,2-cyclohexanediol therefore exists as enantiomers
which are resolvable.

(c)   cis-1,3-cyclohexanediol

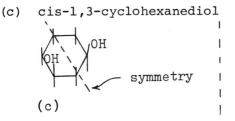

115

These two forms are superimposable. They are actually identical. In addition, an internal symmetry exists making cis-1,3-cyclohexanediol a meso compound. Meso compounds are not resolvable.

(d)   trans-1,3-cyclohexanediol

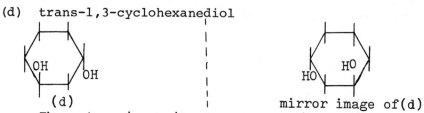

These two mirror images are enantiomers and are therefore resolvable.

(e)   cis-1,4-cyclohexanediol

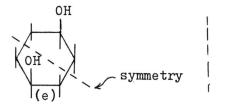

These two compounds are perfectly superimposable and thus non-resolvable. They are actually identical compounds.

(f)   trans-1,4-cyclohexanediol

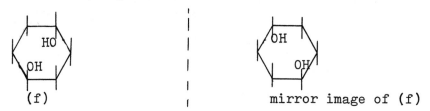

Like compound (e), these are identical compounds and not enantiomers. They cannot be resolved.

Note that (e) and (f) are not meso compounds since they contain no chiral carbons.

POLYCYCLOALKANES

● **PROBLEM** 4-14

Use ball-and-stick models to assess the degree of stability to be expected for a decalin with chair-form rings and an axial-axial ring fusion.

<u>Solution:</u>   Trans-decalin is formed by fusion of two chair-form cyclohexane molecules via two equatorial-type bonds:

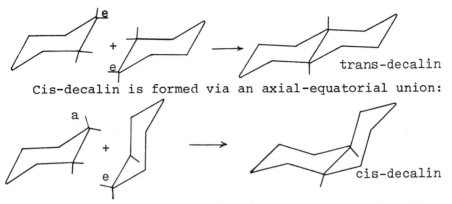

Cis-decalin is formed via an axial-equatorial union:

An axial-axial type of fusion is not possible for steric reasons.

There are two isomers of decalin. One is of higher energy and the other is more stable. Which is the stabler form? Why?

Solution: To answer this question we have to look into the structures of the two forms. Trans-decalin is formed by two equatorial-type bonds while cis-decalin is formed via an axial-equatorial fusion of two cyclohexane molecules:

non-bonded
interactions

trans-decalin   cis-decalin

As we can see, within the concave area of cis-decalin, there is a considerable amount of non-bonded interactions between hydrogen atoms. The repulsion of the closely spaced hydrogen atoms causes instability of the cis compound. In the trans form, non-bonded hydrogen interactions are less and the compound is more stable than the cis isomer.

CHAPTER 5

STEREOCHEMISTRY

OPTICAL ACTIVITY

● **PROBLEM** 5-1

Draw stereochemical formulas for all the possible stereoisomers of the following compounds. Label pairs of
enantiomers, and meso comounds. Tell which isomers, if
separated from all other stereoisomers, will be optically
active.

  (a) 1,2-dibromopropane   (b) 1,2,3,4-tetrabromobutane

<u>Solution</u>:   A knowledge of enantiomers, diastereomers,
meso compounds, chirality, and optical activity will be
necessary to solve this problem.

    Stereoisomers may be defined as isomers that are
different from each other only in the way the atoms are
oriented in space. Non-superimposable mirror-image stereoisomers are referred to as enantiomers.

    These two models are not superimposable. Although
two substituent groups may coincide as they are twisted
and turned, the other two do not. When molecules are not
superimposable on their own mirror images, they are chiral.
A compound whose molecules are chiral can exist as enantiomers; a compound whose molecules are without chirality
(achiral) cannot exist as enantiomers. Enantiomers have
identical physical and chemical properties, except for
the direction of rotation of the plane of polarized light
and the reaction with optically active reagents. Because
enantiomers can rotate the plane of polarized light, they
are called optically active substances. Stereoisomers that
are not mirror images of each other are called diastereomers.
A meso compound is defined as one whose molecules are superimposable on their mirror images, even though they contain

chiral centers. Therefore, meso compounds contain chiral centers but nevertheless are not chiral. For example, 2,3-dichlorobutane would be a meso compound with an internal plane of symmetry (indicated by a dotted line):

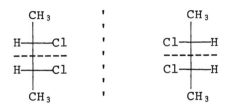

superimposable

In solving this problem, we need to draw the compounds and look for possible configurations that would give rise to enantiomers, diastereomers, or meso compounds. One method of drawing the compound is to use a cross in which the intersection marks the location of the chiral carbon and the four groups attached to the carbon are at the ends of the cross.

(a)   1,2-dibromopropane ($CH_3CHBrCH_2Br$). This structure may be drawn as follows:

Note what happens if we rewrite this as

BrCH₂——CH₃ . This is indeed the mirror image of the

first structure. Try to superimpose these two forms. The fact is that they cannot be made to superimpose.

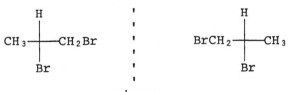

mirror

Hence, for 1,2-dibromopropane there exist two enantiomers, which when separated will rotate the plane of polarized light to the same degree but in opposite directions.

(b)   1,2,3,4-tetrabromobutane ($BrCH_2CHBrCHBrCH_2Br$). Three stereochemical formulas may be drawn in this case. Two of the three represent enantiomers that would be optically active if separated, whereas the third is an optically inactive meso compound.

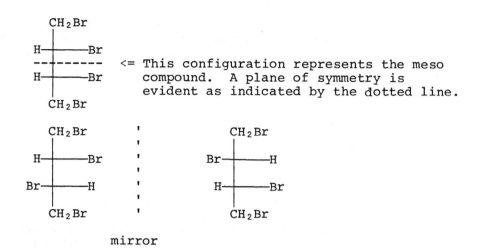

This configuration represents the meso compound. A plane of symmetry is evident as indicated by the dotted line.

mirror

These two mirror images cannot be superimposed. They are enantiomers.

● PROBLEM 5-2

The concentration of cholesterol dissolved in chloroform is 6.15 g per 100 ml of solution. (a) A portion of this solution in a 5-cm polarimeter tube causes an observed rotation of - 1.2°. Calculate the specific rotation of cholesterol. (b) Predict the observed rotation if the same solution were placed in a 10-cm tube. (c) Predict the observed rotation if 10 ml of the solution were diluted to 20 ml and placed in a 5-cm tube.

Solution: An optically active substance may be defined as one that rotates the plane of polarized light. This rotation is measured and detected by an instrument called the polarimeter. The amount of rotation observed will reflect the number of molecules the light encounters in passing through the polarimeter tube. The specific rotation may be defined as the number of degrees of rotation observed if a 1-decimeter tube is used, and the compound being examined is present to the extent of 1g/cc. The following equation is employed:

$$[\alpha] = \frac{\alpha}{1 \times d} , \quad \text{that is,}$$

$$\text{specific rotation} = \frac{\text{observed rotation (degrees)}}{\text{length (dm)} \times \text{g/cc}} ,$$

where g/cc represents density for a pure liquid or concentration for a solution. To calculate (a), (b), and (c), we can use this equation and the given information.

(a) The observed rotation, α, is - 1.2° in a 5-cm. or 0.5-dm polarimeter. Since the concentration of cholesterol dissolved in chloroform is 6.15 g per 100 ml of solution,

$$d = \frac{6.15}{100} \frac{g}{ml} . \quad \text{Substituting:}$$

$$[\alpha] = \frac{\alpha}{1 \times d} = \frac{-1.2°}{0.5 \times \frac{6.15}{100}} = -39.0°$$

(b) Here, the same situation exists except that the tube is 10 cm or 1 dm, that is, it is twice as long. A doubled observed rotation should be anticipated, that is, α should now be - 2.4°. This is confirmed by the following calculation:

$$-39.0 = \frac{\alpha}{1.0 \times \frac{6.15}{100}} ; \quad \alpha = -2.4°.$$

(c) Here, the concentration has been halved by diluting from 10 ml. to 20 ml. Hence, it can be expected that the observed rotation should be halved from part (a) since the number of molecules is halved. In other words, α should be - 0.6°. This is indeed found to be the case by calculation:

$$-39.0 = \frac{\alpha}{0.5 \times \frac{6.15}{200}} ; \quad \alpha = -0.6°.$$

CHIRALITY

● PROBLEM 5-3

(a) Neglecting stereoisomers for the moment, draw all isomers of the formula C_3H_6DCl. (b) Decide which of these are chiral.

Solution: Chiral organic molecules are those that contain at least one chiral carbon, that is, a carbon with four different groups attached to it.

(a) The isomers of C_3H_6DCl are:

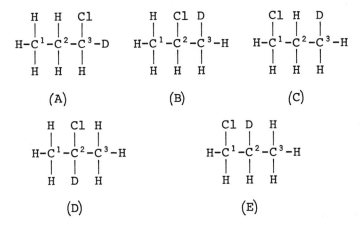

(b) To tell whether a molecule is chiral one must locate
the chiral carbon, if it exists. Thus in structure A, C^3
is a chiral carbon and this isomer is chiral. In structure
B, C^2 is a chiral carbon and this isomer is chiral.
Isomers C and D contain no chiral carbons and are thus not
chiral. Isomer E is a chiral molecule because C^2 is a
chiral carbon.

● **PROBLEM** 5-4

Which of the following formulas are chiral?

(a) 1-chloropentane   (e) 2-chloro-2-methylpentane
(b) 2-chloropentane   (f) 3-chloro-2-methylpentane
(c) 3-chloropentane   (g) 4-chloro-2-methylpentane
(d) 1-chloro-2-methylpentane   (h) 1-chloro-2-bromobutane

Solution: To answer this question, one must first
determine if a particular molecule or compound contains
at least one carbon atom with four different groups attached
to it. If it does then the molecule is chiral.

(a)   1-chloropentane

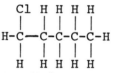

There is no chiral carbon in this molecule since no
carbon contains four different substituent groups. The
molecule is therefore not chiral.

(b)   2-chloropentane

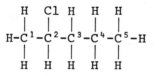

C^2 is a chiral carbon since it has four different
groups attached to it: H_3C-, $Cl-$, $H-$ and $CH_3CH_2CH_2-$. It
can better be represented as:

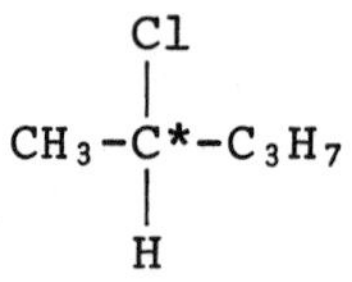

(c)   3-chloropentane

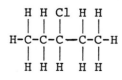

122

This molecule contains no chiral center since no carbon atom contains four different groups.

(d) 1-chloro-2-methylpentane

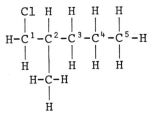

C² is a chiral carbon, thus this molecule is chiral. It can be better represented as:

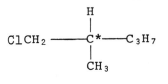

(e) 2-chloro-2-methylpentane

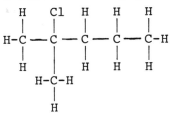

This molecule contains no chiral center and is not chiral.

(f) 3-chloro-2-methylpentane

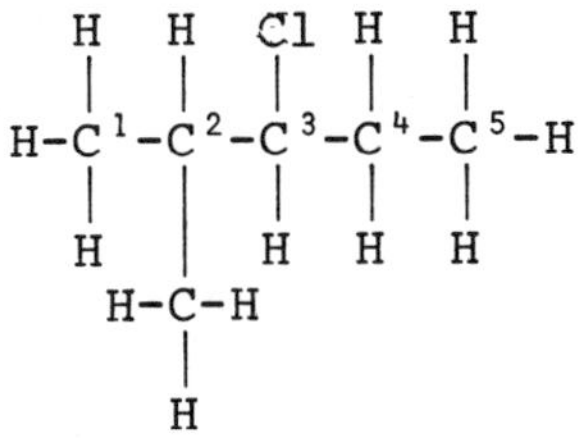

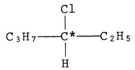

C³ is a chiral carbon and thus the molecule is chiral. It can be better represented as:

$$C_3H_7 \underline{\quad} C* \underline{\quad} C_2H_5$$

(g) 4-chloro-2-methylpentane

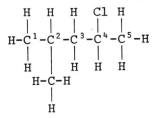

C^4 is a chiral carbon and thus the molecule is chiral. It can be better represented as:

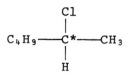

(h) 1-chloro-2-bromobutane

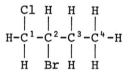

C^2 is the chiral carbon and thus this molecule is chiral. It can be better represented as:

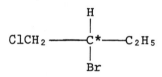

Thus, only molecules b, d, f, g, and h contain chiral carbons and are thus chiral.

● **PROBLEM** 5-5

Each of the following compounds is involved in biological chemistry or medicine. Identify all of the chiral centers and indicate how many stereoisomers of each compound are possible. (Note that the biological activity is usually associated with a particular stereoisomer.)

(a) general formula for a hexose sugar

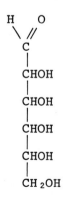

(b)   glucose (blood sugar)

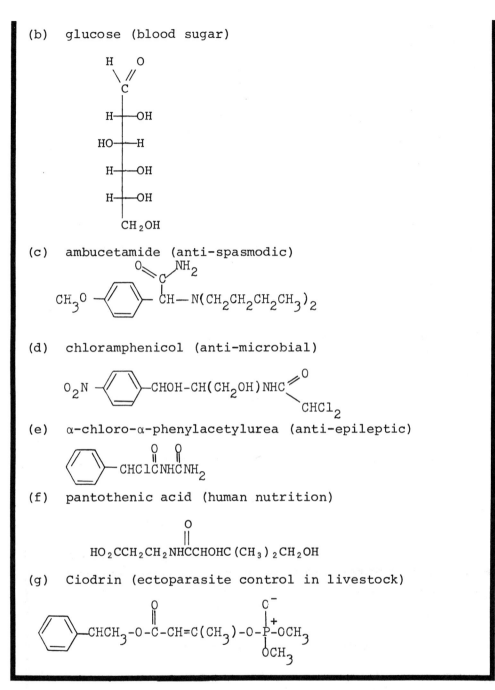

(c)   ambucetamide (anti-spasmodic)

CH_3O —⟨ ⟩— $\overset{\overset{\displaystyle O\diagdown \quad NH_2}{\diagup C\diagup}}{CH}$—$N(CH_2CH_2CH_2CH_3)_2$

(d)   chloramphenicol (anti-microbial)

O_2N —⟨ ⟩—$CHOH$-$CH(CH_2OH)NHC\overset{\diagup O}{\diagdown CHCl_2}$

(e)   α-chloro-α-phenylacetylurea (anti-epileptic)

⟨ ⟩— $CHCl\overset{O}{\overset{||}{C}}NH\overset{O}{\overset{||}{C}}NH_2$

(f)   pantothenic acid (human nutrition)

$HO_2CCH_2CH_2NH\overset{O}{\overset{||}{C}}CHOHC(CH_3)_2CH_2OH$

(g)   Ciodrin (ectoparasite control in livestock)

⟨ ⟩—$CHCH_3$-O-$\overset{O}{\overset{||}{C}}$-$CH=C(CH_3)$-$O$-$\overset{\overset{\displaystyle C^-}{|}}{\underset{\underset{\displaystyle OCH_3}{|}}{\overset{+}{P}}}$-$OCH_3$

Solution: In general, the maximum number of stereo-isomers that are possible for a compound with n chiral centers is given by 2^n. For example, a compound with 3 chiral centers can have a maximum of 2^3 or 8 stereoisomers.

(a) $\overset{O}{\overset{||}{C}}-\overset{*}{C}H-\overset{*}{C}H-\overset{*}{C}H-\overset{*}{C}H-CH_2OH$
$\diagup \quad | \quad | \quad | \quad |$
$H \quad OH \ OH \ OH \ OH$

The chiral centers are marked by *. There are 2^4 or 16 stereoisomers possible.

(b) This molecule is one of the 16 possible stereoisomers of (a). So this molecule can have 15 possible stereoisomers.

(c) There is only one chiral center in this structure:

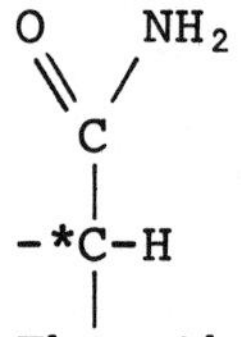

Thus there are 2^1 or two possible stereoisomers.

(d) There are two chiral centers in this structure:

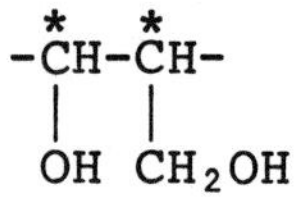

$$\overset{*}{-CH}-\overset{*}{CH}-$$
$$\begin{array}{cc} | & | \\ OH & CH_2OH \end{array}$$

Four possible stereoisomers are thus present.

(e) 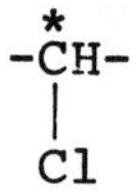 $-\overset{*}{CH}-$ one chiral center
    $|$
    Cl .·. two possible stereoisomers

(f) 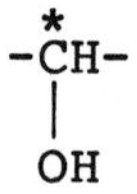 $-\overset{*}{CH}-$ one chiral center,
    $|$
    OH .·. two possible stereoisomers

(g) $-\overset{*}{CH}CH_3-$ one chiral center
    .·. two possible stereoisomers

● **PROBLEM** 5-6

Many biologically important compounds contain prochiral centers. Identify all of the prochiral centers in the following:

(a) nitroglycerin (coronary vasodilator)

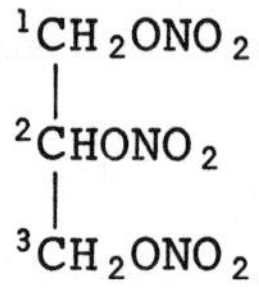

$$^1CH_2ONO_2$$
$$|$$
$$^2CHONO_2$$
$$|$$
$$^3CH_2ONO_2$$

(b) Phorate (systemic insecticide)

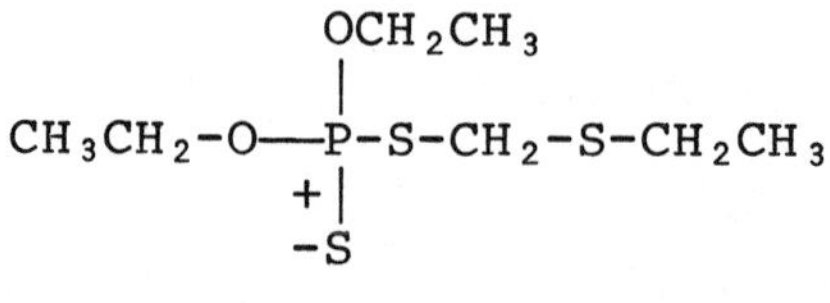

$$OCH_2CH_3$$
$$|$$
$$CH_3CH_2-O\!\!-\!\!\!-\overset{+}{\underset{-S}{P}}-S-CH_2-S-CH_2CH_3$$

(c)   sorbitol   (humectant; candy manufacture)

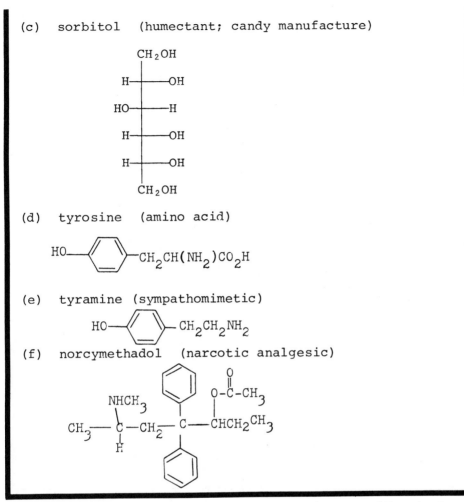

(d)   tyrosine   (amino acid)

HO—⟨benzene ring⟩—$CH_2CH(NH_2)CO_2H$

(e)   tyramine   (sympathomimetic)

HO—⟨benzene ring⟩—$CH_2CH_2NH_2$

(f)   norcymethadol   (narcotic analgesic)

Solution: A prochiral center contains two identical and two unidentical substituents, and is thus not chiral. However, replacement of one of the identical substituents with a completely different one (which is not identical to any of the other substituents) will convert the prochiral center into a chiral center.

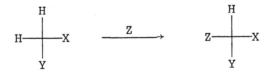

      prochiral center   chiral center

(a)   All three carbons are prochiral centers.   The first and third carbon atoms can become chiral by replacement of either hydrogen.   The middle carbon can become chiral if replacement of either of the $-ONO_2$ groups on carbons 1 and 3 or of an entire $-CH_2ONO_2$ group occurs.

(b)   All $-CH_2$ groups have prochiral carbons, and replacement of their hydrogens would give chirality.   The P atom is prochiral, and replacement of either $-OCH_2CH_3$ group would result in a chiral P.

(c) Replacement of the hydrogens of C_1 and C_6 would convert these carbons to chiral centers. All other carbons are already chiral.

(d) Both the CH_2 and the NH_2 group have prochiral centers, and substitution of hydrogen atoms would give chirality. (The unshared pair of electrons in $-NH_2$ can be thought of as a substituent.)

(e) Replacing the H's of the CH_2 groups or the H's of the NH_2 group would give rise to chiral centers.

(f) The carbons of the CH_2 groups are prochiral. The central carbon atom is prochiral, with replacement of either phenyl group leading to chirality.

ENANTIOMERISM

● **PROBLEM** 5-7

Which of the following idealized objects is capable of existing as pairs of enantiomers?

(a)   a spool of thread
(b)   a spool of thread with all the thread and labels removed
(c)   a conch shell
(d)   a coiled cable connecting a telephone receiver to the instrument

<u>Solution</u>:   Enantiomers are   compounds that are non-superimposable mirror images of each other. They contain identical subunits which are oriented differently.
Enantiomers are a class of stereoisomers.

Stereoisomers are compounds with the same molecular formula, but different molecular structures due to different spatial arrangement or orientation of substituent atoms or groups.

(a) A spool of thread can exist as a pair of enantiomers. This is because the thread has a direction which it is wound in. Two spools of thread

can exist which are wound in opposite direction to each other.

(b) A spool of thread with all the thread and labels

128

removed could not exist as an enantomeric pair. This is because there is nothing on the symmetric spool to show direction. The mirror image of the spool will be super-imposable upon it.

(c) A conch shell could exist as an enantiomeric pair. The spirality of the shell can be in two possible direc-tions which are opposite to each other, like two spirals wound in different directions. These two spirals

mirror

cannot be superimposed. They are therefore not identical.

(d) A coiled cable connecting a telephone receiver to the instrument is capable of existing as a pair of enantiomers. The coil of the telephone is similar to the spiral in (c). There are two possible directions to the coil (clockwise and counterclockwise) so that the coil and its mirror image cannot be made to superimpose.

mirror

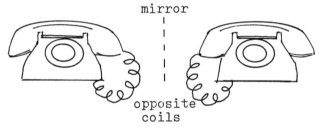

opposite
coils

• **PROBLEM** 5-8

Identify one pair of enantiotopic groups in each of the following:

(a) CH_2ClBr (d) $ClCH_2CH_2Br$
(b) $CHCl(CH_3)_2$ (e) $ClCH_2CH_2Cl$
(c) $CHCl(CH_2CH_3)_2$

Solution: (a) Replacement of either of the two methylene protons (by R) would give a pair of enantiomers.

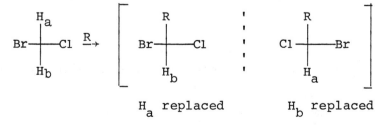

H_a replaced   H_b replaced

Such pairs of protons (H_a and H_b) are called enantiotopic protons.

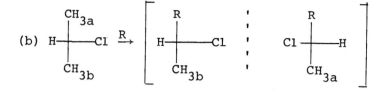

(b)

The two methyl groups are enantiotopic groups. So we see that not only protons (H) may be enantiotopic, but entire groups of atoms can be enantiotopic.

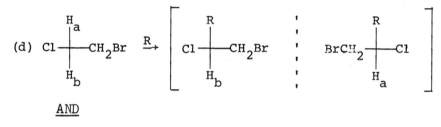

(c)

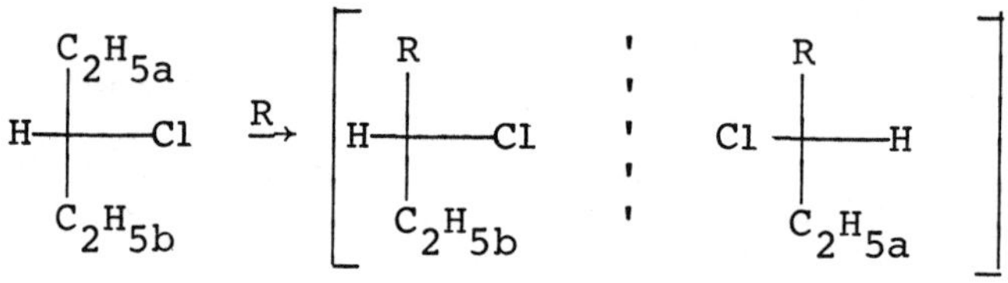

Replacement of either ethyl group gives a pair of enantiomers. Thus the two ethyl groups are enantiotopic.

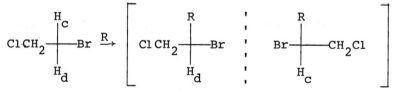

(d)

AND

Thus, there are two pairs of enantiotopic protons: H_a and H_b, and H_c and H_d.

(e) $ClCH_2CH_2Cl$. In the same way as in problem (d) we can see that the hydrogens of either methylene group are enantiotopic hydrogens.

● **PROBLEM** 5-9

Draw the structures of all the different staggered conformations possible for (+)-tartaric acid (shown below). Are any of these identical with their mirror images? How many optically active forms of tartaric acid could there be altogether if rotation were **not** possible about the C_2-C_3 bond and only the staggered conformations were allowed.

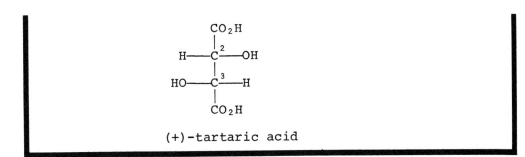

(+)-tartaric acid

Solution: Different conformations of a molecule result from rotation about single bonds. The bonding between atoms does not change, so different conformational isomers have the same configuration about their chiral centers.

Three different staggered conformations of (+)-tartaric acid result from rotation about the C_2-C_3 bond. These (along with their mirror images) are:

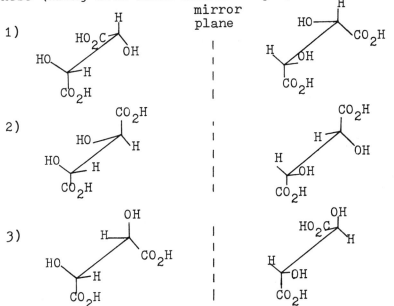

mirror plane

1)

2)

3)

(+)-tartaric acid   (-)-tartaric acid

None of the staggered conformations of (+)-tartaric acid have superimposable mirror images.

If rotation were not possible about the C_2-C_3 bond, then any molecule of tartaric acid would be "locked" in one conformation. Assuming that only staggered conformers are allowed, there would be three enantiomeric pairs of tartaric acid possible (or a total of six isomers that are staggered).

If rotation about the C_2-C_3 bond were allowed to occur, interconversion between the conformers would render the three forms indistinguishable from each other.

CONFIGURATION

Arrange the following sets in order of decreasing priority.

(a) $-H$, $-CH_3$, $-C_2H_5$, $-C(CH_3)_3$, $-CH(CH_3)_2$

(b) $-CH_2CH_2CH_3$, $-CH_2CH(CH_3)_2$, $-CH(CH_2CH_3)_2$

(c) $-CHCH_3CH_2CH_3$, $-C(CH_3)_2CH_2CH_2CH_3$, $-C(CH_3)_2CH_2CH_3$

Solution: To answer this question we must know the rules used to assign priority. Priority is given to the substituent atom highest in atomic number. Thus I has priority over Br and Br has priority over Cl. Here are some more examples:

$$Cl > O > N > H$$

But when two atoms in comparison are identical and hence have equal priority, precedence is given to the one that has substituent groups of higher atomic number, or one that has a greater number of heavy substituent atoms. For example,

$$-CHCl_2 > -CH_2Cl,$$

because in the first group, the carbon is attached to two chlorine atoms, while in the other structure the carbon is bonded to only one chlorine.

(a) structure (1) $-\overset{\displaystyle CH_3}{\underset{\displaystyle CH_3}{C}}-CH_3$, (2) $-\overset{\displaystyle CH_3}{\underset{\displaystyle CH_3}{C}}-H$, (3) $-\overset{\displaystyle H}{\underset{\displaystyle H}{C}}-CH_3$, (4) $-CH_3$, (5) $-H$

   (1)   (2)   (3)   (4)   (5)

In structure 1 we have three carbons bonded to the central carbon. In structure 2 we have only two carbons bonded to the central carbon. In structure 3 there is only one carbon bonded to the central carbon. Structure 4 has only one carbon, while structure 5 has only a hydrogen atom. So we have in order of decreasing priority:

$$-C(CH_3)_3 > -CH(CH_3)_2 > -C_2H_5 > -CH_3 > -H$$

(b) $-\overset{\displaystyle C_2H_5}{\underset{\displaystyle C_2H_5}{C}}-H$ > $-\overset{\displaystyle H}{\underset{\displaystyle H}{C}}-\overset{\displaystyle CH_3}{\underset{\displaystyle CH_3}{C}}-H$ > $-\overset{\displaystyle H}{\underset{\displaystyle H}{C}}-\overset{\displaystyle H}{\underset{\displaystyle H}{C}}-CH_3$

(c) $-\overset{\displaystyle CH_3}{\underset{\displaystyle CH_3}{C}}-CH_2-CH_2-CH_3$ > $-\overset{\displaystyle CH_3}{\underset{\displaystyle CH_3}{C}}-CH_2-CH_3$ > $-\overset{\displaystyle CH_3}{CH}-CH_2-CH_3$

Draw and specify as R or S the enantiomers of:

(a)   3-chloro-1-pentene
(b)   3-chloro-4-methyl-1-pentene
(c) $HOOCCH_2CHOHCOOH$, malic acid
(d) $C_6H_5CH(CH_3)NH_2$

Solution: This problem deals with configuration, the arrangement of atoms that characterizes a particular stereoisomer.   One method of assigning configuration, called the Cahn-Ingold-Prelog Method, is by use of the prefixes R and S.   Two steps are involved in this process: In step 1, a set of sequence rules is followed.   A sequence of priority is assigned to the four atoms or groups of atoms attached to the chiral center.   (Recall, an atom to which four different groups are attached is a chiral center.)   In step 2, the molecule is oriented so that the group of lowest priority is directed <u>away</u> from us.   We observe, then, the arrangement of the remaining groups. If our eye travels in a clockwise direction in going from the group of highest priority to the groups of lower priority, the configuration is specified R.   If eye movement is counterclockwise, the configuration is specified S.

    At this point, the problem is how do we assign priority, that is, what are the sequence rules?   For simplicity, we can note three sequence rules:

    Sequence Rule 1:   If the four atoms attached to the chiral center are all different, then priority depends on atomic number, with the atom of higher atomic number getting higher priority.   In the case of two atoms being isotopes of the same element, the atom of higher mass number has the higher priority.

    Sequence Rule 2:   If sequence rule 1 fails to establish priority, then a similar comparison of the next atoms attached to the groups is made.   In other words, if two atoms attached to the chiral center are the same, the atoms attached to each of these first atoms are compared.

    Sequence Rule 3:   Both atoms are considered to be duplicated or triplicated when there exists between them a double or triple bond.   For example:

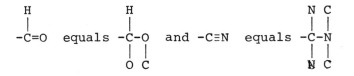

    Now that we know how to specify configuration, we need to know a method that allows us to draw these enantiomers.   One method is to draw a cross (+) and attach to the four ends the four groups that are bonded to the

chiral center; the point where the lines cross denotes the
location of the chiral center. For example, 2-chloro-
butane ($CH_3CHClCH_2CH_3$) may be represented by

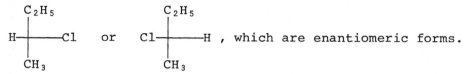

C_2H_5

H————Cl   or   Cl————H , which are enantiomeric forms.

CH_3 CH_3

It is important to recognize the fact that in such
representation the horizontal lines denote bonds coming
toward us out of the plane of the paper, whereas the
vertical lines represent bonds going away from us behind
the plane of the paper.

With this information, it is now possible to draw
and specify as R or S the following enantiomers (mirror-
image isomers):

(a)   3-chloro-1-pentene   ($CH_2=CHCHClCH_2CH_3$)

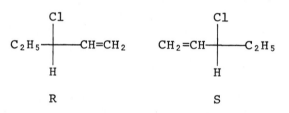

Explanation: These enantiomers are drawn so that the
chiral carbon of each structure is located at the intersection of the lines. The four groups attached to the
chiral center are positioned at the four ends. To establish configuration, the priority of the groups must be
determined. To do this recall that sequence rules must be
followed. As mentioned in sequence rule 1, priority depends
on atomic number. Chlorine has the highest atomic number,
so that it has the highest priority. Hydrogen, with the
lowest atomic number, has the lowest priority. The two
other atoms bonded to the chiral center are carbon atoms.
But note that one carbon atom is involved in a double
bond, so (in accordance with rule 3) it is duplicated and
has the higher priority. Overall, then, we can rank in
increasing priority the following groups of atoms:

H, C_2H_5, $CH=CH_2$,   Cl
increasing priority ————→

At this point, recall that the group of lowest
priority must be directed away from us. Note that the
drawings given accomplish this. The hydrogen atom, the
group of the lowest priority, is at the end of a vertical
line. Consequently, it is directed away from us behind the
plane of the paper. Finally, note that in the first configuration (the one to the left), our eyes move in clockwise (↻) direction in going from the group of highest
priority (-Cl) to the groups of second ($CH=CH_2$) and third
priority ($-C_2H_5$). Hence, this configuration is considered

to be R.   In the other configuration (the one to the right)
our eyes move counterclockwise ( ), so that S should be
assigned to this configuration.

     In (b) - (d), the same kind of reasoning is used
to obtain the following:

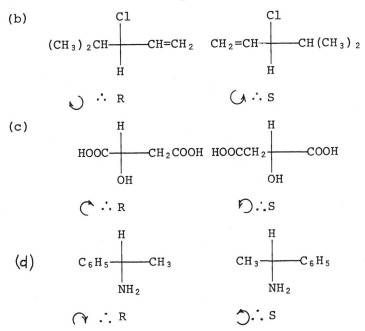

(b)

$(CH_3)_2CH$———CH=CH$_2$ CH$_2$=CH———CH(CH$_3$)$_2$

with Cl on top, H on bottom

 ∴ R   ∴ S

(c)

HOOC———CH$_2$COOH HOOCCH$_2$———COOH

with H on top, OH on bottom

 ∴ R   ∴ S

(d)

C$_6$H$_5$———CH$_3$ CH$_3$———C$_6$H$_5$

with H on top, NH$_2$ on bottom

 ∴ R   ∴ S

● **PROBLEM 5-12**

Draw and label the enantiomers of each of the following
compounds as either R or S:

(a) 4-chloro-2-pentene   (c) isopentylbenzene
(b) isobutyl alcohol   (d) phenylalanine

Solution: (a) 4-chloro-2-pentene

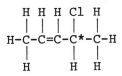

```
        H H H Cl H
        | | | |  |
      H-C-C=C-C*-C-H
        |     | |
        H     H H
```

     Since there is one chiral center (C*),two (2^1)
enantiomeric forms exist for this compound:

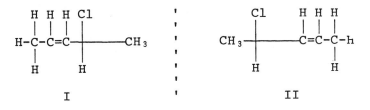

```
      H H H Cl                    Cl       H H H
      | | | |                     |        | | |
    H-C-C=C———CH$_3$       CH$_3$———C=C-C-h
      |     |                     |        |   |
      H     H                     H        H   H
```

        I   II

135

According to the rules of sequence, the order of priority for the four groups is:

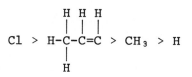

$$Cl > H\text{-}C\text{-}C\text{=}C > CH_3 > H$$

H, the atom of the lowest priority, is visualized as extending away from us behind the plane of the paper. Now follow the three remaining groups in decreasing priority. In doing this, figure I leads our eye into a counterclockwise movement, thus the chiral carbon of this structure is assigned an absolute configuration of S. Figure II leads our eye into a clockwise movement, thus II has an absolute configuration of R. Notice that since these two structures are enantiomers, they are assigned opposite absolute configurations as expected.

(b) Isobutyl alcohol

$$H\text{-}C\text{-}C\text{-}C^*\text{-}C\text{-}H$$

C* is a chiral center. We can immediately see that two enantiomers are possible for this compound:

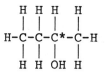

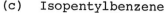

I   II

The order of priority is $OH > C_2H_5 > CH_3 > H$. With H visualized as projecting away from us, we can see that the remaining groups are arranged, according to decreasing priority, in a clockwise manner in I and in a counter-clockwise manner in II. Thus I has an absolute configuration of R while that of II is S.

Using the same reasoning, we can determine the configuration of the enantiomers of (c) and (d).

(c) Isopentylbenzene

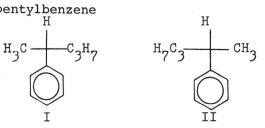

I   II

	I	II
Priority	$C_6H_5 > C_3H_7 > CH_3 > H$	
Arrangement of substituents in decreasing priority	counterclockwise	clockwise
Configuration	S	R

(d) Phenylalanine

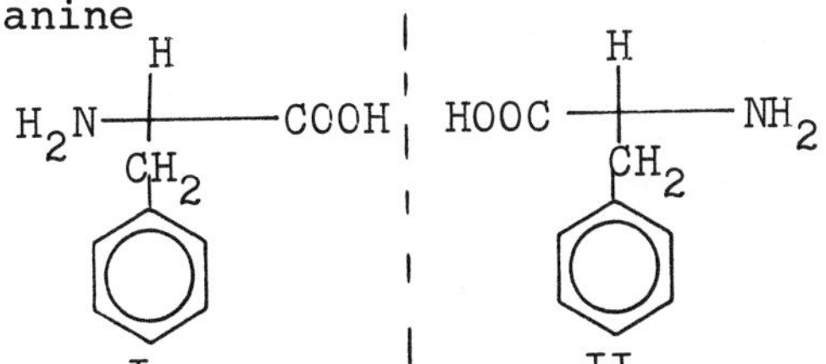

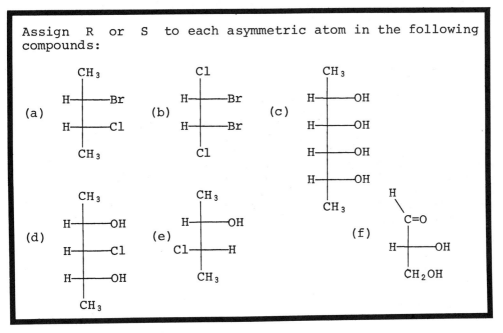

	I	II
Priority	$NH_2 > COOH > CH_2C_6H_5 > H$	
Arrangement	clockwise	counterclockwise
Configuration	R	S

● **PROBLEM** 5-13

Assign R or S to each asymmetric atom in the following compounds:

(a)
```
      CH3
       |
  H----+----Br
       |
  H----+----Cl
       |
      CH3
```

(b)
```
      Cl
       |
  H----+----Br
       |
  H----+----Br
       |
      Cl
```

(c)
```
      CH3
       |
  H----+----OH
       |
  H----+----OH
       |
  H----+----OH
       |
  H----+----OH
       |
      CH3
```

(d)
```
      CH3
       |
  H----+----OH
       |
  H----+----Cl
       |
  H----+----OH
       |
      CH3
```

(e)
```
      CH3
       |
  H----+----OH
       |
  Cl---+----H
       |
      CH3
```

(f)
```
    H
     \
      C=O
     
  H----+----OH
       |
      CH2OH
```

137

<u>Solution:</u>   This problem differs from the previous two
only in that it calls for the determination of absolute
configuration for more than 1 chiral carbon in the same
compound.   The solution to this problem makes use of the
knowledge we have gained previously concerning priority
determination and R-S assignment.

(a)

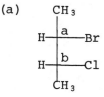

As we can see immediately, there are two chiral
carbons in this structure (C_a and C_b).   The order of
priority of the substituent groups with the chiral
center at C_a is

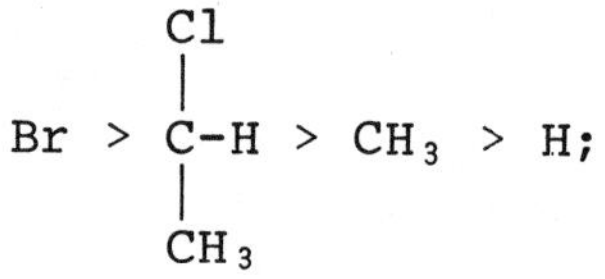

$$Br > \overset{\displaystyle Cl}{\underset{\displaystyle CH_3}{\overset{|}{\underset{|}{C}}-H}} > CH_3 > H;$$

the order of priority with the chiral center at C_b is

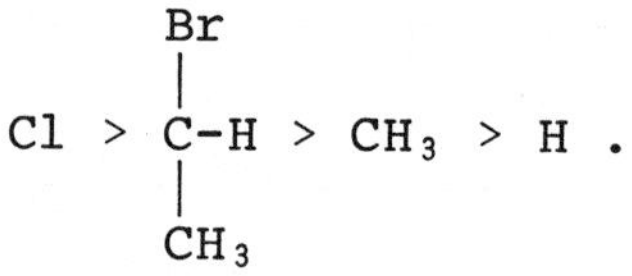

$$Cl > \overset{\displaystyle Br}{\underset{\displaystyle CH_3}{\overset{|}{\underset{|}{C}}-H}} > CH_3 > H .$$

Focusing our attention first on chiral carbon a, we
can draw the following:

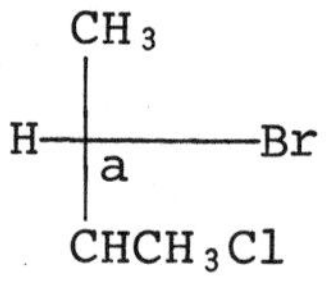

Recall that in this type of representation horizontal
lines indicate bonds coming toward us out of the plane of
the paper, and vertical lines bonds that point away from
us behind the plane of the paper.   We can draw an equivalent
structure in which H, the lowest priority group, is at the
end of a vertical line and pointing away from us (in accordance with step 2 in the method for R-S assignment. See
last two solutions.):

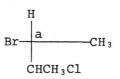

138

Now, with H visualized as extending away from us, follow the remaining groups in decreasing priority. This will lead our eye into a counterclockwise movement. Thus C_a has a S configuration.

Let us now focus on chiral carbon b. Using the same approach we can find that C_b has a R configuration.

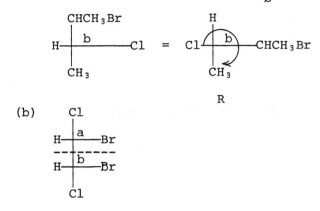

(b)

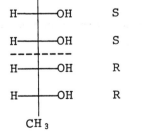

Again, there are two chiral carbons in this structure (C_a and C_b). This is a meso compound.

Focusing on one chiral center at a time, we can find that C_a has a configuration of R while C_b a configuration of S.

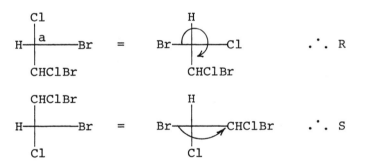

Using the same approach, we can assign R-S configuration to the chiral centers in compounds (c) to (f).

(c)

	CH$_3$	
H—	—OH	S
H—	—OH	S
H—	—OH	R
H—	—OH	R
	CH$_3$	

meso compound

(with 4 chiral centers)

(d)

	CH$_3$	
H—	—OH	S
----H—	—Cl-----	
H—	—OH	R
	CH$_3$	

meso compound

(with 2 chiral centers)

(e) 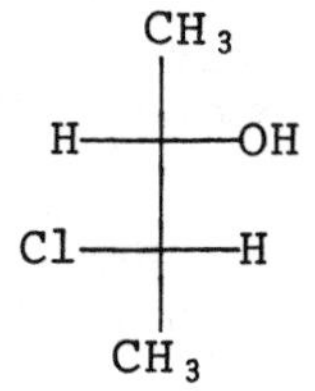 S S

(2 chiral centers)

(f) 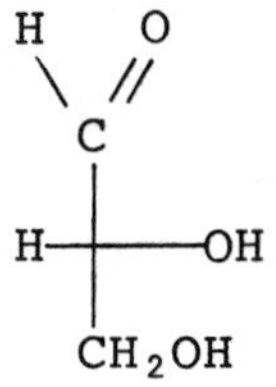

R

(1 chiral center)

• PROBLEM 5-14

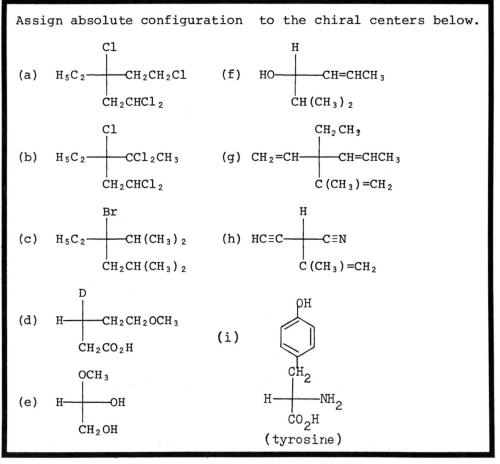

Assign absolute configuration to the chiral centers below.

(a) 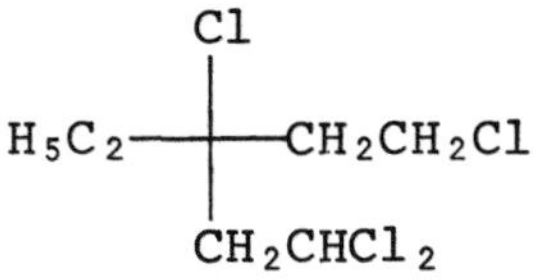

(b) 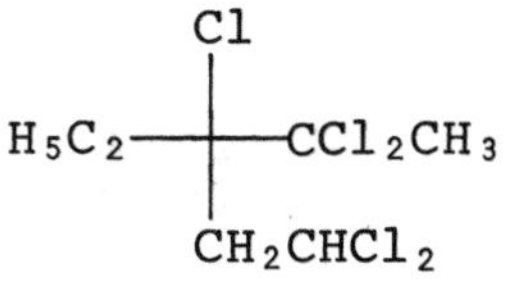

(c) 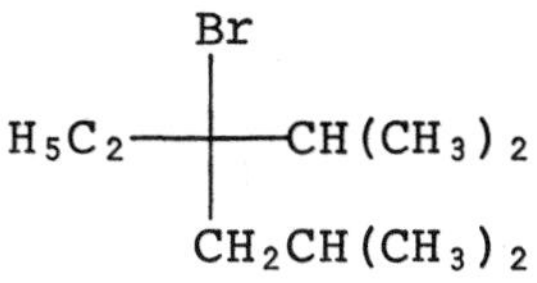

(d) 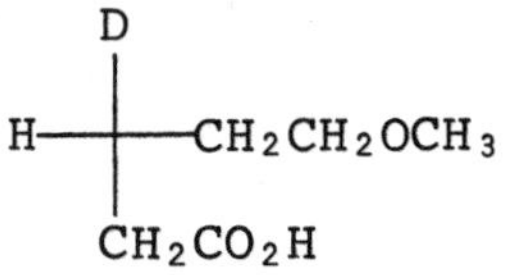

(e) 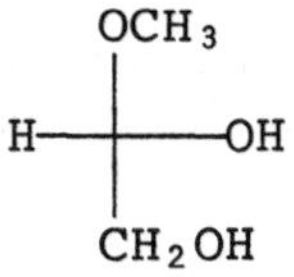

(f) 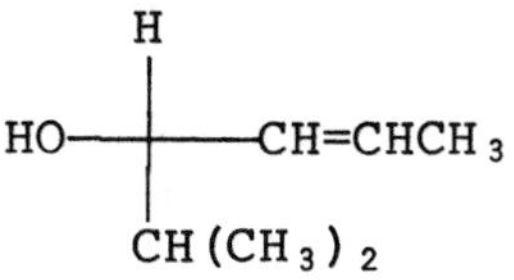

(g) 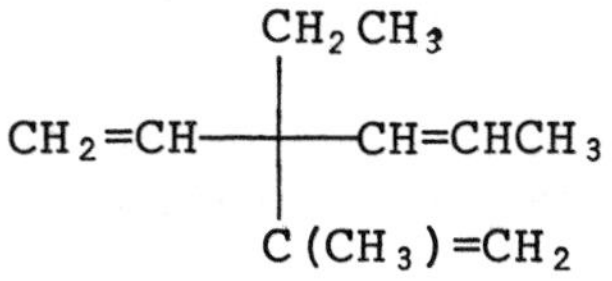

(h) 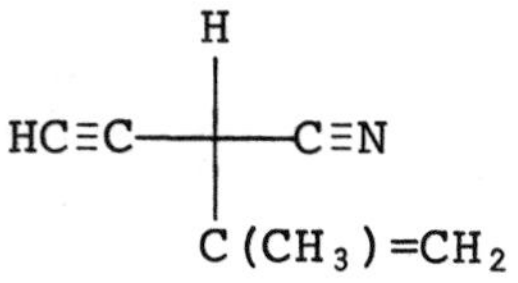

(i) 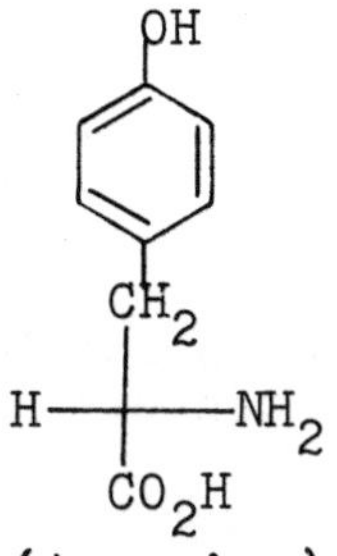

(tyrosine)

Solution:

(a) 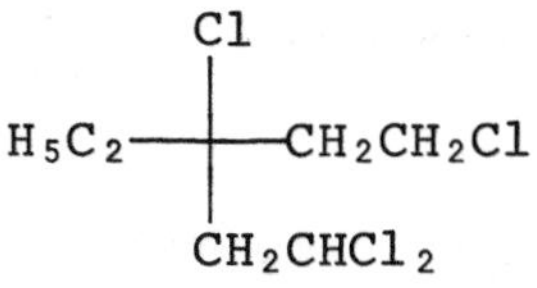

The order of priority of the substituent groups in this compound is

$$Cl > CH_2CHCl_2 > CH_2CH_2Cl > C_2H_5.$$

Rewriting the structure so that C_2H_5, the group of the lowest priority, is at the end of a vertical line (symbolizing a bond pointing away from us) gives the following:

4th priority

C_2H_5

3rd priority ClH_2CH_2C———Cl 1st priority

CH_2CHCl_2

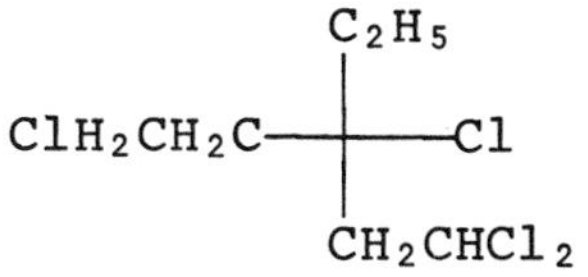

2nd priority

We can now see that the substituent groups are arranged in a clockwise ($\circlearrowright$) manner according to priority, and the chiral center therefore has a R-configuration.

Cl

(b) 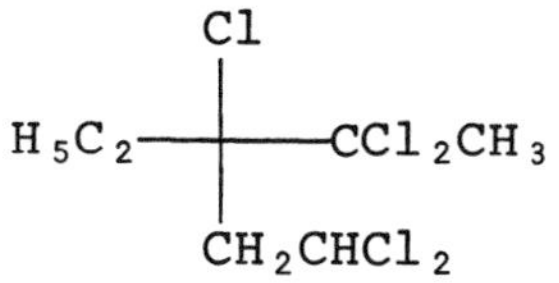 H_5C_2———CCl_2CH_3

CH_2CHCl_2

The order of priority is $Cl > CCl_2CH_3 > CH_2CHCl_2 > C_2H_5$. Redrawing the structure gives

4th

C_2H_5

2nd H_3CCl_2C———Cl 1st

CH_2CHCl_2

3rd

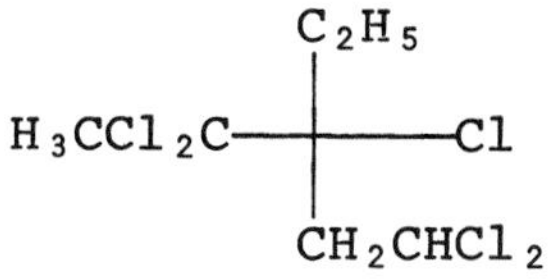

in which C_2H_5, the lowest priority group, is directed away from us. The substituents show a counterclockwise arrangement according to priority, and the absolute configuration about the chiral center is therefore S.

Br

(c) 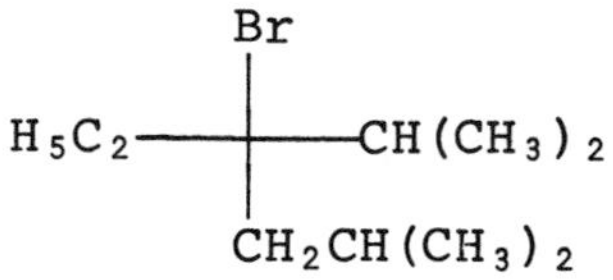 H_5C_2———$CH(CH_3)_2$

$CH_2CH(CH_3)_2$

Redrawing gives

4th

C_2H_5

2nd $(CH_3)_2CH$———Br 1st

$CH_2CH(CH_3)_2$

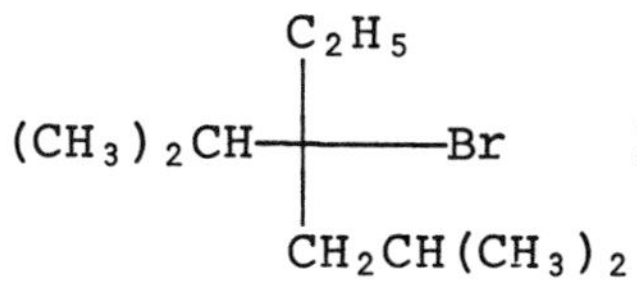

3rd

The chiral center has a configuration of S.

(d)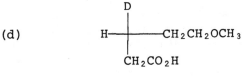

Redrawing gives

4th

Note:
H and D are isotopes of the same element, D being the heavier of the two.

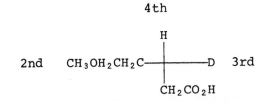

2nd   CH₃OH₂CH₂C————D   3rd

1st

The chiral center of this structure should be assigned a R configuration.

(e)

Redrawing gives

4th

H

2nd   HO————OCH₃   1st

CH₂OH

3rd

The correct configuration therefore is S.

(f)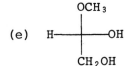

Recall that Sequence Rule # 3 states that atoms involved in a double bond are duplicated, and those in a triple bond are triplicated.

Redrawing the structure gives us the following:

4th

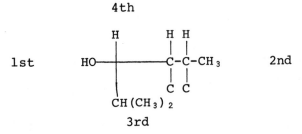

1st   HO————C-C-CH₃   2nd

3rd

The correct configuration assigned to the chiral center of this structure is therefore R.

(g)

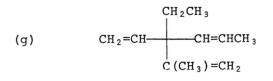

The expanded form of this structure is

4th

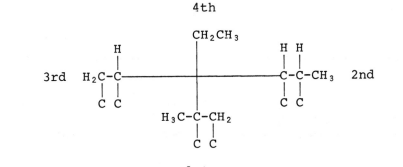

1st

The configuration therefore is S.

(h)

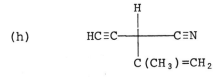

The expanded form is

4th

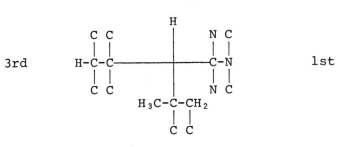

2nd

The chiral center of this structure has a R configuration.

(i)

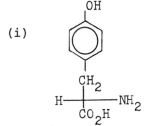

Redrawing gives:

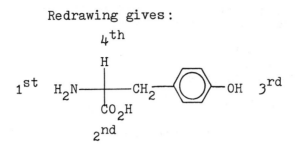

S is the correct configuration.

The enantiomer of (+)-(R)-malic acid occurs in many fruits and is called "apple acid." Draw a three-dimensional structure of apple acid. What is its sign of rotation? What is its absolute configuration?

<u>Solution</u>: The sign of rotation tells us the direction that the molecule will rotate the plane of polarization: to the right if it is (+) or to the left if it is (-). The signs of rotation of a pair of enantiomers are always opposite.

The arrangement of atoms that characterizes a particular stereoisomer is called its configuration. To assign absolute configuration we use the R and S system. A pair of enantiomers will always have opposite absolute configurations.

Hence, the enantiomer of (+)-(R)-malic acid must be (-)-(S)-malic acid, also called "apple acid".

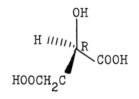

(+)-(R)-malic acid

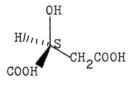

(-)-(S)-malic acid

Designate which of the following configurations of glyceraldehyde are D and which L:

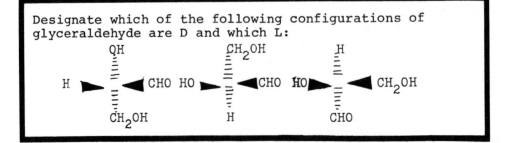

<u>Solution</u>:   The use of D and L to specify the configuration about a chiral carbon is the Fischer Convention.   It is an older method now used primarily for sugars.

In the Fischer Convention, the type of structural formula used is the Fischer projection.   Thus we should convert the structural representation of the glyceraldehydes given in the problem into the Fischer projection.   First, a cross is drawn.   The location of the chiral (assymmetric) carbon is represented by the intersecting point of the two lines of the cross.   The horizontal lines extending to the left and right of this point represent bonds extending forward, above the plane of the paper.   The vertical lines represent bonds extending back, below the plane of the paper.

Now we can proceed with the conversion.

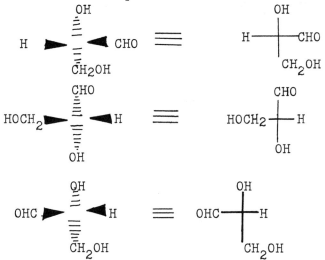

As we can see, all these molecules are enantiomers. In the Fischer system, each member of a pair of enantiomers is specified as either D or L. An isomer is said to be D

D-glyceraldehyde   L-glyceraldehyde

if, when it is written with the aldehyde group at the top and the other carbon-containing group   at the bottom in the Fischer projection, the OH group is on the right hand side.   Its enantiomer is said to be L.   (Note that D or L does not refer to the sign of rotation of the plane of polarized light which is indicated by (+) or (-).   D or L isomers may be either positive or negative depending on the particular compound involved.)

In order to put the molecule into the correct configuration (CHO at the top, CH_2OH at the bottom) one may interchange any two pairs of substituents and still retain the same configuration. (If only one pair of substituents is interchanged, the enantiomer is generated.)

Applying these principles to the configurations of glyceraldehyde given:

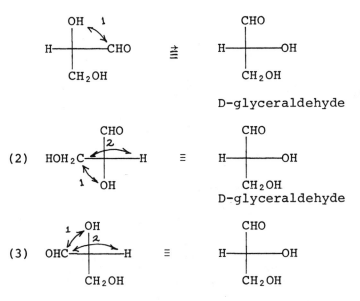

(1)

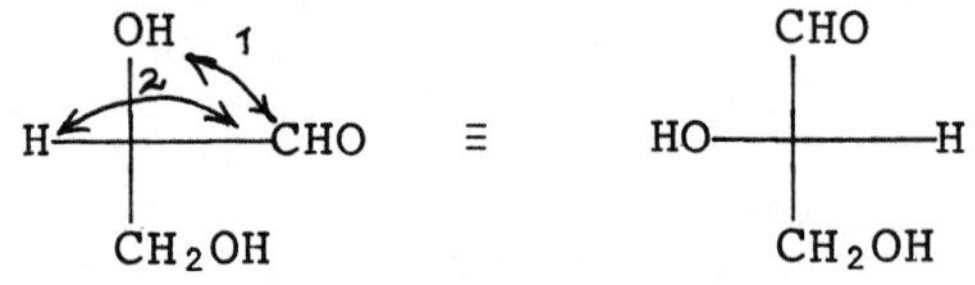

≡

L-glyceraldehyde

The OH is on the left, so the molecule is L-glyceraldehyde. Note that exchanging only one pair of substituents would give rise to the D isomer, its enantiomer:

D-glyceraldehyde

(2)

≡

D-glyceraldehyde

(3)

≡

D-glyceraldehyde

In (2) and (3), the OH is on the right. The molecules are D-glyceraldehyde.

DIASTEREOMERISM

● **PROBLEM 5-17**

Write structures showing the configuration of each of the possible products to be expected from the following reactions. Which diastereomer would you expect to be formed preferentially, assuming that the substituents decrease in size in the order $C_6H_5 > C_2H_5 > CH_3 > OH > H$?

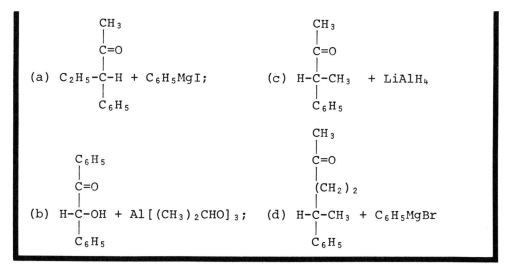

(a) $C_2H_5-\overset{\overset{\displaystyle CH_3}{\overset{\displaystyle |}{\underset{\displaystyle |}{C}=O}}}{\underset{\displaystyle C_6H_5}{|}}-H + C_6H_5MgI;$

(c) $H-\overset{\overset{\displaystyle CH_3}{\overset{\displaystyle |}{\overset{\displaystyle C=O}{|}}}}{\underset{\displaystyle C_6H_5}{|}}-CH_3 + LiAlH_4$

(b) $H-\overset{\overset{\displaystyle C_6H_5}{\overset{\displaystyle |}{\overset{\displaystyle C=O}{|}}}}{\underset{\displaystyle C_6H_5}{|}}-OH + Al[(CH_3)_2CHO]_3;$

(d) $H-\overset{\overset{\displaystyle CH_3}{\overset{\displaystyle |}{\overset{\displaystyle C=O}{|}{(CH_2)_2}}}}{\underset{\displaystyle C_6H_5}{|}}-CH_3 + C_6H_5MgBr$

Solution: An understanding of the mechanism of the four reactions is necessary in order to be able to predict the predominating product of each reaction.

All four reductions involve attack of the carbonyl group. Since the atoms of the carbonyl group lie in a plane, attack can occur from either of the two sides of the plane, that is, either from above or below the plane and perpendicular to it. Because of the two possible directions of attack, the resultant tetrahedral carbon (originally of the carbonyl group), if chiral, will have one of two possible configurations (R or S). The predominating product of the reduction will result from the more sterically favored and thus more frequent attack.

(a)

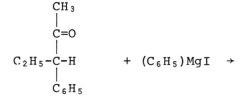

$C_2H_5-\overset{\overset{\displaystyle CH_3}{\overset{\displaystyle |}{\overset{\displaystyle C=O}{|}}}}{\underset{\displaystyle C_6H_5}{|}}-H \quad + (C_6H_5)MgI \rightarrow$

First, it is helpful to picture the compound in a three dimensional manner. (Use models if necessary.)

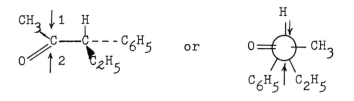 or

The two possible directions of attack of the carbonyl group are indicated by arrows so we have the following possible reaction mechanisms:

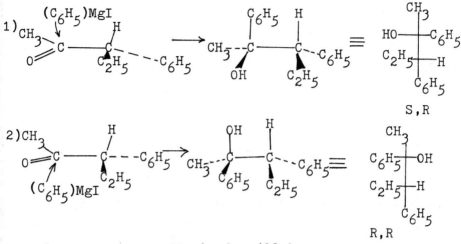

As we can see, attack 2 will have to overcome more steric hindrance (due to $-C_2H_5$ and $-C_6H_5$ groups) than attack 1. Therefore, the S, R product will predominate over the R,R product.

(b)

$$C_6H_5$$
$$|$$
$$C=O$$
$$|$$
$$H-C-OH \quad + \quad Al[(CH_3)_2CHO]_3 \rightarrow$$
$$|$$
$$C_6H_5$$

Again, the two possible directions of attack will lead to two products.

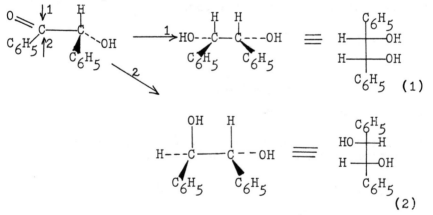

Attack 1 is more sterically favored, therefore, the first product will be formed preferentially.

(c)

$$CH_3$$
$$|$$
$$C=O$$
$$|$$
$$H-C-CH_3 \quad + \quad LiAlH_4 \rightarrow$$
$$|$$
$$C_6H_5$$

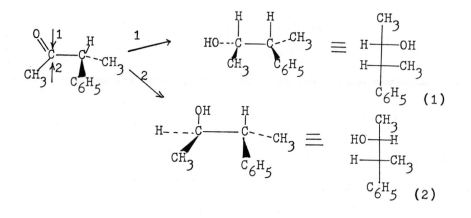

Product 1 will be formed in preference to product 2.

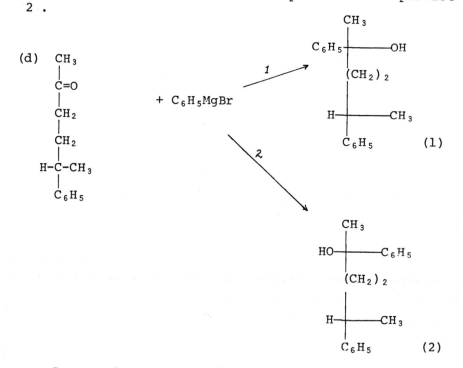

Due to the presence of the two $-CH_2$ groups, which increases the distance between the carbonyl group and the bulky $-CH_3$ and $-C_6H_5$ substituents, there is no significant difference in the steric environment of the carboxyl group in formation of either product. Thus, 1 and 2 will be formed in approximately equal amounts.

● PROBLEM 5-18

Camphor has two asymmetric carbons, but only two optical isomers are known. Explain. (Models will be helpful.)

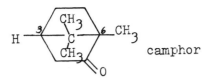

camphor

Solution: C_2 and C_6 are asymmetric carbons and there-fore chiral centers. Theoretically, the number of possible stereoisomers of a molecule with n chiral centers is 2^n. In this case, $2^n = 2^2$ or 4. Drawing the possible isomers:

1)

2)

3)

4)

It is obvious that isomers 3 and 4 are impossibly strained. These isomers would not normally be formed. Note that isomers 3 and 4 would have been diastereomers of isomers 1 and 2. Therefore, camphor exists only in two enantiomeric forms (1 and 2).

● **PROBLEM** 5-19

In the following structures, indicate if H_a and H_b are identical, enantiotopic, or diastereotopic.

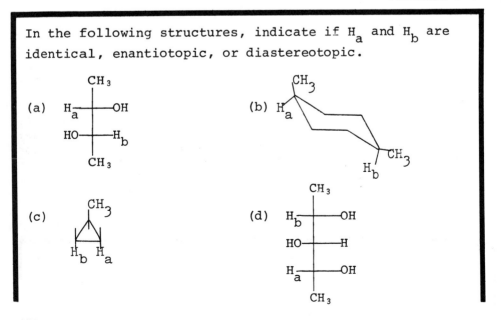

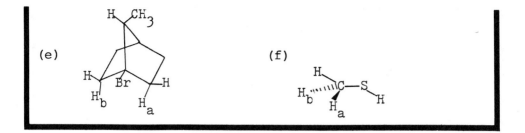

(e)

(f)

Solution: (a)   If we replace either H_a or H_b we get identical structures, therefore we can call these two hydrogens identical.

(b)   Here H_a and H_b are diastereotopic protons.   Note that one hydrogen (H_b) is axial while the other (H_a) is equatorial. Since the environments of these two protons are not mirror images and lack a chiral center, replacing either of the two H's will yield a pair of diastereomers:

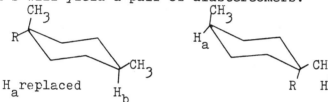

H_a replaced H_b
R   R H_b replaced

These two protons can be identical if we allow the ring to undergo inversion.

(c) H_a and H_b are enantiotopic protons in this structure. Replacement of either of the two protons results in a pair of enantiomers;

H_a replaced H_b replaced

Note that if the H's were positioned on the same side of the ring as $-CH_3$, the protons would be identical.

(d)   Notice that both the carbons to which H_a and H_b are attached are chiral.   Replacement of either H_a or H_b gives us a pair of enantiomers, hence the hydrogens are enantiotopic.

(e) H_a and H_b are enantiotopic.   The reason is the same as that given in (d).

(f)   The carbon to which H_a and H_b are attached is achiral. Replacement of either H_a or H_b gives us two identical structures and so the protons are identical.

Give the stereoisomers of:

(a) 2-butene
(b) 2-pentene
(c) 2,4-hexadiene

(d) 1-bromo-1-chloropropene
(e) 2-bromo-1-chloropropene
(f) 1-bromo-1,2-dichloroethene

Indicate for each the isomer that is expected to predominate in an equilibrium mixture. Justify your answer.

Solution: Isomers differing from one another only in the way the atoms are oriented in space (but are like one another with respect to which atoms are attached to which other atoms) belong to the general class of stereoisomers. The particular kind of stereoisomers that owe their exist- ence to hindered rotation about double bonds are called geometric isomers. Geometric isomerism can exist only when both atoms of the double bond carries two different substituent groups.

Geometric isomers have different physical properties: different melting points, boiling points, refractive indices, solubilities, densities, and so on. Therefore in principle geometric isomers can be separated from each other.

(a) Stereoisomers of 2-butene

2-Butene exists in two forms due to the presence of a double bond. The two geometric isomers of 2-butene are:

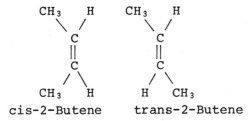

cis-2-Butene   trans-2-Butene

In cis-2-butene, the methyl groups are on the same side of the double bond. In trans-2-butene they are on opposite sides. Thus cis isomers have the substituted groups on the same side of the double bond, while trans isomers have the substituted groups on opposite sides.

(b) Stereoisomers of 2-pentene

Two geometric isomers of 2-pentene exist:

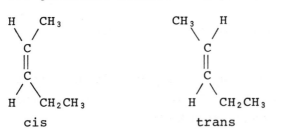

cis   trans

(c)　Stereoisomers of 2,4-hexadiene

Owing to the presence of 2 double bonds, 3 geometric isomers are present:

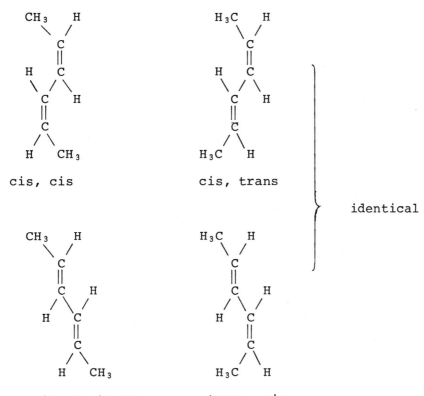

cis, cis

cis, trans

identical

trans, trans

trans, cis

In general, because of greater steric strain present in the cis isomer due to closer spacial relationship of the substituted groups, the cis isomer is less stable than the trans.　In an equilibrium mixture the trans isomer is expected to predominate on the basis of thermodynamic stability.　Thus, trans-2-butene will predominate over cis-2-butene and trans-2-pentene will predominate over cis-2-pentene.　In 2,4-hexadiene, the order of stability of the isomers is: trans, trans > trans, cis (same as cis, trans) > cis, cis.　Therefore, the trans, trans isomer will predominate in an equilibrium mixture.

For the geometric isomers of (d), (e), and (f) the cis and trans prefixes are not useful.　For them we use a different system of specification.　We take the group of higher priority (determined by the Cahn-Ingold-Prelog Method) on the one carbon of the double bond and the group of higher priority on the other carbon, and see whether they are on the same side of the double bond or on opposite sides.　If they are on the same side, the molecule is specified as Z (German: zusammen, together), if they are on opposite sides, the molecule is specified as E (German: entgegen, opposite).

(d) Stereoisomers of 1-bromo-1-chloropropene

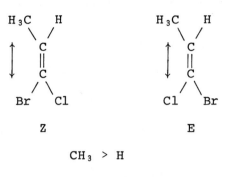

Z   E

CH$_3$ > H

Br > Cl

The non-bonded interaction between -CH$_3$ and -Br in the Z isomer is greater than that between -CH$_3$ and -Cl in the E isomer. Therefore, the latter is more stable and is expected to predominate in equilibrium.

(e) Stereoisomers of 2-bromo-1-chloropropene

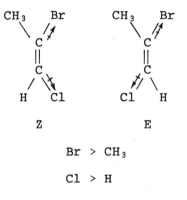

Z   E

Br > CH$_3$

Cl > H

The strong electrostatic repulsion between the electron-rich bromine and chlorine atoms in the Z isomer renders it less stable than the E isomer.

(f) Stereoisomers of 1-bromo-1,2-dichloroethene

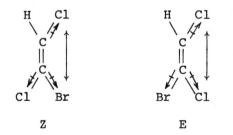

Z   E

Cl > H

Br > Cl

Electrostatic repulsion is strong in both geometric
isomers. The steric strain however is stronger in the Z
structure (due primarily to non-bonded Br ↔ Cl interaction) than in the E structure (due primarily to
Cl ↔ Cl interaction) for Br has a larger atomic size
than Cl. Therefore the latter is a more stable form. It
will, at least in principle, predominate in the equilibrium
mixture.

RACEMIZATION

● **PROBLEM** 5-21

Compound A racemizes readily on heating to 100° but the rate
is not affected by chloride ion and is the same in chloroform and acetic acid. Racemization in deuteroacetic acid
(CH_3CO_2D) gives only undeuterated racemic A. Devise a
mechanism for the reaction in accord with all the experimental facts.

(A)

<u>Solution:</u>   Racemization is the process which leads to
formation of a racemic modification, a mixture of equal
parts of enantiomers.

In compound A, there is only one asymmetric carbon (*).
Chloride ion could promote racemization by a S_N2-type of
reaction:

Cl⁻ ⟶ Ring ... ⇌ ... Cl—C---H + Cl⁻

Attack by Cl⁻ inverts the configuration at the chiral
carbon. Since the reaction is reversible, a racemic mixture will form as equilibrium is established. We are told,
however, that chloride ion does not affect the rate of
racemization. This is due likely to hindrance of chloride
ion attack by the ring structure. Therefore, racemization
probably does not proceed via the S_N2 mechanism.

Chloroform and acetic acid are both acidic solvents and
may cause racemization by way of enol-keto tautomerism:

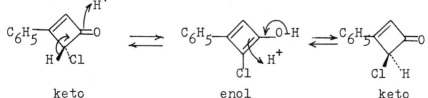

keto   enol   keto

If the racemization indeed proceeded via enol-keto interconversion, deuteroacetic acid could give deuterated racemic A in the following manner:

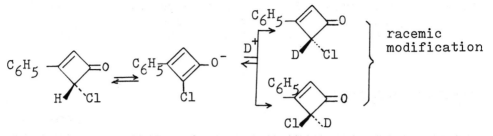

} racemic modification

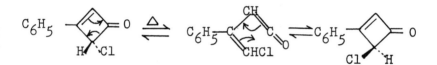

However, reaction with CH_3CO_2D does not result in any deuterated A, so we can conclude that racemization does not occur via enolization.

The racemization is therefore most reasonably explained by a simple thermal reaction at 100°. Heat could cause reversible ring opening in the following manner:

Since the reaction is reversible, equilibrium will give the racemic mixture. Note that the reaction proceeds via electron exchange, and no substitution or addition of atoms occurs. Therefore, the reaction rate would not be affected by acids or chloride ions.

SPECTROSCOPY

● PROBLEM 5-22

The fluorine nmr spectrum of 1,2-difluoro-tetrachloro-ethane, $CFCl_2CFCl_2$, shows a single peak at room temperature, but at -120° shows two peaks of unequal area. Explain.

Solution: This observation is caused by the presence of conformational isomers of $CFCl_2CFCl_2$. Conformational isomers result from the rotation of groups of atoms about a single bond. (Recall that a single bond, in contrast to a double bond, allows free rotation.) Since they differ only in the way the atoms are oriented in space, conformational isomers are also stereoisomers. However, they should not be confused with other kinds of stereoisomers, which differ in their configurations about a chiral atom. For example, different configurational isomers can be either the R or the S forms of a compound. Yet each of

the two forms has its own set of conformational isomers.
All the conformational isomers of either form have the
same configuration, but their subunits' orientation in
space is different due to difference in the degree of
bond rotation.

Since interconversion between conformational isomers
involves only the rotation of a bond, the energy barrier
between these isomers is relatively small, and thus interconversion will be rapid once the energy barrier is
trespassed. (Interconversion between configurational
isomers — R ↔ S — would involve the breaking of covalent
bonds, which requires a greater amount of energy.)

$CFCl_2CFCl_2$ has three possible staggered conformational
isomers (the eclipsed conformers are too unstable to exist
in significant amounts):

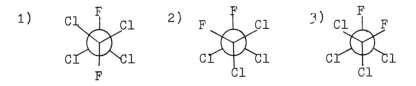

At room temperature, the speed of rotation about the
C-C bond is fast, and the interconversion between the
three isomers is rapid. A fluorine nmr spectrum of the
molecule will then reflect only the average of the three
environments (resulting from the three isomers) of the
fluorine atoms. Thus only a single average signal is
observed.

At - 120°, the speed of bond rotation is considerably slowed down. At this temperature there is not enough
thermal energy to overcome the barriers, interconversion
is therefore very slow; so slow that separate signals are
observed in the fluorine nmr, one for each environment.
In isomers 2 and 3, the positions of the fluorine atoms
with respect to each other and to the chlorine atoms are
equivalent, so they are reflected by a single peak in the
nmr.   The environment of the fluorine atoms in isomer 1
is clearly different from that in 2 or 3, and it will give
a separate peak (of only half the area of the other signal
which results from the contributions of two isomers).

PREPARATION

● **PROBLEM** 5-23

(a) In a study of chlorination of propane, four products
(A, B, C and D) of formula $C_3H_6Cl_2$ were isolated. What
are their structures?

(b)   Each was chlorinated further, and the number of tri-
chloro products ($C_3H_5Cl_3$) obtained from each was determined

by gas chromatography. A gave one trichloro product; B gave two; and C and D each gave three. What is the structure of A? Of B? Of C and D?

(c) By another synthetic method, compound C was obtained in optically active form. Now what is the structure of C? Of D?

(d) When optically active C was chlorinated, one of the trichloropropanes (E) obtained was optically active, and the other two were optically inactive. What is the structure of E? Of the other two?

Solution: (a) There are a number of possible ways in which two chlorine atoms can bind to propane. Indeed there are four isomers of the formula $C_3H_6Cl_2$.

$$CH_3CH_2CH_3 \xrightarrow{\quad Cl_2 \quad}$$

1) $Cl_2CHCH_2CH_3$ +

2) $ClCH_2\overset{\displaystyle Cl}{\underset{\displaystyle |}{C}}HCH_3$ +

3) $ClCH_2CH_2CH_2Cl$ +

4) $CH_3\overset{\displaystyle Cl}{\underset{\displaystyle |}{\underset{\displaystyle Cl}{C}}}CH_3$

(b) If each isomer were chlorinated further, each would produce its own trichloro-substituted isomers.

1) $Cl_2CHCH_2CH_3 \quad \rightarrow \quad Cl_3CCH_2CH_3$ +

$Cl_2CHCH_2CH_2Cl$ +

$Cl_2CH\overset{\displaystyle H}{\underset{\displaystyle |}{\underset{\displaystyle Cl}{C}}}CH_3$

2) $ClCH_2\overset{\displaystyle Cl}{\underset{\displaystyle |}{C}}HCH_3 \quad \rightarrow \quad Cl_2CH\overset{\displaystyle Cl}{\underset{\displaystyle |}{C}}HCH_3$ +

$ClCH_2\overset{\displaystyle Cl}{\underset{\displaystyle |}{\underset{\displaystyle Cl}{C}}}CH_3$ +

$ClCH_2\overset{\displaystyle Cl}{\underset{\displaystyle |}{C}}HCH_2Cl$

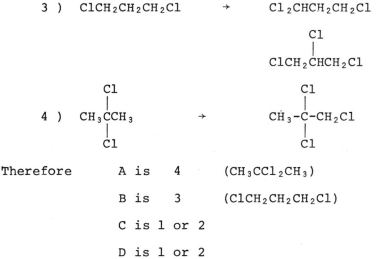

3) ClCH$_2$CH$_2$CH$_2$Cl   →   Cl$_2$CHCH$_2$CH$_2$Cl   +

$$ClCH_2\overset{\overset{\displaystyle Cl}{|}}{C}HCH_2Cl$$

4) CH$_3\overset{\overset{\displaystyle Cl}{|}}{\underset{\underset{\displaystyle Cl}{|}}{C}}CH_3$ →   CḢ$_3$-$\overset{\overset{\displaystyle Cl}{|}}{\underset{\underset{\displaystyle Cl}{|}}{C}}$-CH$_2$Cl

Therefore   A is   4   (CH$_3$CCl$_2$CH$_3$)

B is   3   (ClCH$_2$CH$_2$CH$_2$Cl)

C is 1 or 2

D is 1 or 2

(c) If C is optically active, it must possess a chiral center. Let us look at the structures of 1 and 2.

1) $\underset{\underset{\displaystyle Cl}{|}}{\overset{\overset{\displaystyle H}{|}}{C}}$l-C—$\overset{\overset{\displaystyle H}{|}}{\underset{\underset{\displaystyle H}{|}}{C}}$-$\overset{\overset{\displaystyle H}{|}}{\underset{\underset{\displaystyle H}{|}}{C}}$-H

2) Cl-$\overset{\overset{\displaystyle H}{|}}{\underset{\underset{\displaystyle H}{|}}{C}}$-$\overset{\overset{\displaystyle H}{|}}{\underset{\underset{\displaystyle Cl}{|}}{C}}$*-$\overset{\overset{\displaystyle H}{|}}{\underset{\underset{\displaystyle H}{|}}{C}}$-H

It is evident that isomer 1 has no chiral center. In isomer 2 however, C* is chiral and this isomer is optically active. Therefore

C is 2 (ClCH$_2$CHClCH$_3$) - optically active

D is 1 (Cl$_2$CHCH$_2$CH$_3$) - optically inactive

(d) Let us look more closely at the trichloropropane isomers formed when C was chlorinated further.

(i)   Cl-$\overset{\overset{\displaystyle H}{|}}{\underset{\underset{\displaystyle Cl}{|}}{C}}$—$\overset{\overset{\displaystyle Cl}{|}}{\underset{\underset{\displaystyle H}{|}}{C}}$*-$\overset{\overset{\displaystyle H}{|}}{\underset{\underset{\displaystyle H}{|}}{C}}$-H

(ii) Cl-$\overset{\overset{\displaystyle H}{|}}{\underset{\underset{\displaystyle H}{|}}{C}}$-$\overset{\overset{\displaystyle Cl}{|}}{\underset{\underset{\displaystyle Cl}{|}}{C}}$—$\overset{\overset{\displaystyle H}{|}}{\underset{\underset{\displaystyle H}{|}}{C}}$-H

(iii) Cl-$\overset{\overset{\displaystyle H}{|}}{\underset{\underset{\displaystyle H}{|}}{C}}$-$\overset{\overset{\displaystyle Cl}{|}}{\underset{\underset{\displaystyle H}{|}}{C}}$—$\overset{\overset{\displaystyle H}{|}}{\underset{\underset{\displaystyle H}{|}}{C}}$-Cl

Isomers ii and iii have no chiral centers. In isomer i, C* is a chiral carbon and the isomer is thus optically active. Therefore E is Cl$_2$CHCHClCH$_3$ (i).

Isopentane is allowed to undergo free-radical chlorination, and the reaction mixture is separated by careful fractional distillation. (a) How many fractions of formula $C_5H_{11}Cl$ would you expect to collect? Draw structural formulas, stereochemical where pertinent, for the compounds making up each fraction. Specify each enantiomer as R or S.
(b) Which if any, of the fractions, as collected, would show optical activity? Account in detail for the optical activity or inactivity of each fraction.

Solution: (a) Since the products of the chlorination of isopentane can be separated by fractional distillation, they must be isomeric forms of $C_5H_{11}Cl$. They will differ in respect to which carbon atom the chlorine attacks and then bonds to.

$$\overset{1}{C}H_3\overset{2}{C}H_2\overset{3}{C}H\overset{4}{C}H_3 \quad \underset{}{\overset{\cdot Cl}{\longrightarrow}}$$
$$\underset{\overset{|}{\overset{5}{C}H_3}}{}$$

isopentane

1) $CH_2ClCH_2CHCH_3$ C_1 attacked
$$\underset{\overset{|}{CH_3}}{}$$

2) $CH_3\overset{*}{C}HCHCH_3$ C_2 attacked
$$\underset{\overset{|}{Cl}\ \overset{|}{CH_3}}{}$$

3) $CH_3CH_2\overset{\overset{Cl}{|}}{C}-CH_3$ C_3 attacked
$$\underset{\overset{|}{CH_3}}{}$$

4) $\begin{cases} CH_3CH_2\overset{*}{C}HCH_2Cl \\ \quad\quad\quad\; \underset{CH_3}{|} \\ CH_3CH_2\overset{*}{C}HCH_3 \\ \quad\quad\quad\; \underset{CH_2Cl}{|} \end{cases}$ C_4 attacked

             C_5 attacked

Note that these two are identical.

(* indicates a chiral center)

As we can see, four fractions of $C_5H_{11}Cl$ will result from distillation.

Fraction 1: There is no chiral center in this isomer, so it exists as only one isomer.

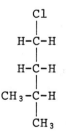

(Look at the mirror images; they are superimposable.)

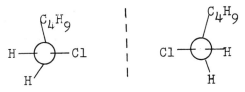

Fraction 2: C_2 is chiral, so molecules of this fraction exist as enantiomers.

Recall that enantiomers have the same physical properties, therefore they cannot be separated by fractional distillation.

Fraction 3: Again, there is no chiral center in this isomer, so it exists in only one, optically inactive, form.

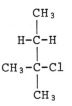

Fraction 4: C_3 is chiral, so this fraction consists of enantiomers.

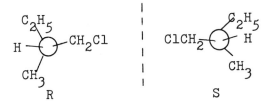

(b) Fraction 2: Because the hydrogen atoms on a tetrahedral carbon are equivalent, the chlorine will not replace one hydrogen preferentially over the other. Therefore the two enantiomers exist in equal proportions, and the fraction is a racemic modification. Since the result of a racemic mixture is cancellation of optical activity (as one enantiomer rotates light in one direction to a certain degree, and the other rotates light in the opposite direction and to the same degree), fraction 2 will show no optical activity.

Fraction 1, 3: Since the isomers have no chiral center, and their mirror images are superimposable, these fractions will show no optical activity.

Fraction 4: Again, replacement by chlorine of any hydrogen on either of the two methyl groups attached to C_3 is equally probable, so that the enantiomers exist in equal proportions. The fraction is racemic, and shows no optical activity.

On treatment with permanganate, cis-2-butene yields a glycol of m.p. 34°, and trans-2-butene yields a glycol of m.p. 19°. Both glycols are optically inactive. The glycol of m.p. 19° is resolvable (through reaction with optically active salts) into two fractions of equal but opposite rotation. The glycol of m.p. 34° is not.

(a) What are the configurations of the two glycols?

(b) Assuming these results are typical (they are), what is the stereochemistry of hydroxylation with permanganate? (syn or anti?)

(c) Treatment of the same alkenes with peroxy acids gives the opposite results: the glycol of m.p. 19° from cis-2-butene, and the glycol of m.p. 24° from trans-2-butene. What is the stereochemistry of hydroxylation with peroxy acids?

<u>Solution:</u>   (a) The general reaction of either cis- or trans-2-butene with permanganate forms a glycol, 2,3-butanediol.

$$CH_3CH=CHCH_3 + KMnO_4 \rightarrow$$

$$
\begin{array}{cc}
OH & OH \\
| & | \\
CH_3-C{\longrightarrow}C-CH_3 \\
| & | \\
H & H
\end{array}
$$

2,3-butanediol

Now we know that the hydroxylation of cis- and trans-2-butane yields two fractions of glycols with the same formula ($CH_3CHOHCCH_3CHOH$) but having different melting points. The two fractions formed must therefore be stereoisomers. Since their chemical properties (here m.p.'s) are similar but not identical, they are not enantiomers of each other (which by definition differ <u>only</u> in optical rotation), but diastereomers. Note that the glycol contains two chiral centers, C_2 and C_3, which is compatible with diastereomer formation.

Since the total possible number of stereoisomers is 2^n, where n equals the number of chiral centers, the glycol has 2^2 or 4 possible stereoisomers.

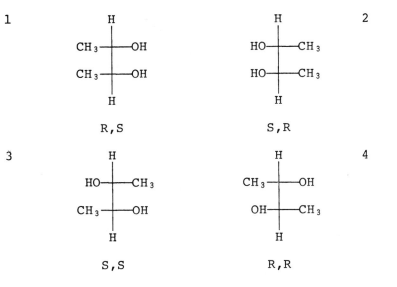

1

CH₃——OH
CH₃——OH

R,S

2

HO——CH₃
HO——CH₃

S,R

3

HO——CH₃
CH₃——OH

S,S

4

CH₃——OH
OH——CH₃

R,R

Isomers 1 and 2 are identical. Isomers 3 and 4 are enantiomers.

Since the fraction of m.p. 19° is optically inactive, but resolvable, it must be a racemic mixture of enantiomers. The other fraction is not resolvable. Therefore, the two isomers composing it must be superimposable mirror images, even though they contain chiral centers, and so must be meso compounds. Looking at the two fractions, it becomes evident that compounds 1 and 2 are superimposable and are meso compounds. Therefore the fraction of m.p. 34° is actually the meso compound of 2,3-butanediol. The fraction of m.p. 19° is a racemic mixture of isomers 3 and 4, which we see are enantiomers.

(b)   We know then that cis-2-butene yields meso-2,3-butanediol, and trans-2-butene yields racemic-2,3-butanediol.

Looking at the possible addition mechanisms in the hydroxylation of cis-2-butene,

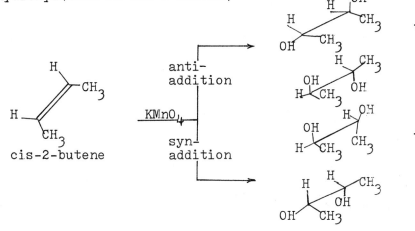

we see that only syn-addition yields the meso compound. Anti-addition gives two enantiomers. Thus permanganate gives syn-hydroxylation.

We can verify this by looking at the reaction with trans-2-butene.

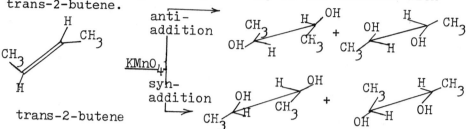

trans-2-butene

Here, anti-hydroxylation would have resulted in the meso compound. Only syn-hydroxylation gives the two enantiomers.

(c)   Here, the opposite results are obtained, with cis-2-butene yielding the racemic mixture and trans-2-butene yielding the meso compound. These results are compatible with anti-hydroxylation.

RESOLUTION OF STEREOISOMERS

● **PROBLEM** 5-26

Describe the technique of resolution of DL alanine.

Solution: Amino acids that are synthesized by the usual methods are obtained as racemates. One method that may be used for the resolution of amino acids involves converting them into diastereomeric salts. The amino group is usually converted into an amide so that the material is not amphoteric. For example, alanine reacts with benzoyl chloride in aqueous base to give N-benzoyl-alanine, which is a typical acid.

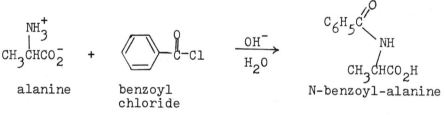

alanine   benzoyl   N-benzoyl-alanine
                   chloride

The racemic N-benzoyl-alanine is resolved with brucine or strychnine. If brucine is used, it is the brucine salt of D-alanine that is less soluble. If strychnine is used, the strychnine salt of L-alanine crystallizes. Acidification of the salts yields the D- and L-enantiomers of N-benzoylalanine. Basic hydrolysis then gives the pure enantiomeric amino acids. The process is outlined schematically as follows:

DL-alanine
↓
N-benzoyl-DL-alanine

| brucine

brucine salt of   brucine salt of
N-benzoyl-D-alanine   N-benzoyl-L-alanine
"insoluble"   "soluble"

↓ H_3O^+ ↓ H_3O^+

N-benzoyl-D-alanine   N-benzoyl-L-alanine

1. OH^-, H_2O, Δ   1. OH^-, H_2O, Δ

2. H_3O^+ 2. H_3O^+

D-alanine (optically pure)   L-alanine (optically impure)

In cases such as that outlined, the enantiomer that forms the less soluble salt is usually obtained in an optically pure state. The other enantiomer is usually obtained in an impure state, because some of the less soluble salt invariably remains in solution. In the case diagrammed, the impure N-benzoyl-L-alanine may be treated with strychnine to give the insoluble strychnine salt. In this way, both enantiomers may be obtained in an optically pure state.

● **PROBLEM** 5-27

Compounds of the type shown below have been found to be resolvable into two optically active forms. Explain.

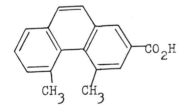

Solution: Compounds composed of fused benzene rings are usually planar, due to the presence of conjugated double bonds. The groups attached to the fused rings lie in the same plane as the rings.

However, in the compound given, such a planar arrangement would result in the two ortho methyl groups lying very close together. The steric hindrance resulting from this may be sufficient to force the methyl groups out of the plane of the ring. The groups would necessarily position themselves as far apart from each other as

possible, in the more sterically favorable trans conformation. Thus, with one methyl group above and the other
below the plane of the rings, the compound now exists in
enantiomeric forms which can be resolved by virtue of
their optical activity.

Notice that this compound actually has no chiral
center. This is an example of compounds with chirality
in the absence of chiral centers.

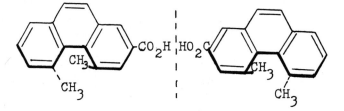

CHAPTER 6

ALKENES

NOMENCLATURE AND STRUCTURE

● PROBLEM 6-1

What is an alkene?

Solution: Hydrocarbons with one or more double bonds are known as alkenes, or sometimes called olefins . This class of hydrocarbons is unsaturated, and since alkenes differ from alkanes in this respect, their nomenclature must be modified. Refer to the following examples to attain an idea of unsaturation:

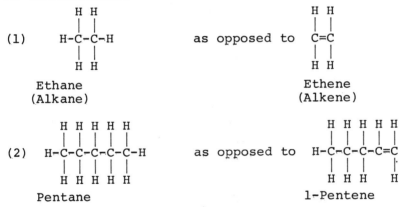

From the examples, note that the parent part of the name (eth- and pent-) remains the same for alkenes, and only the suffix changes to -ene. This is true for all alkenes that possess only one double bond.

If alkenes have more than one double bond, it is referred to as a polyunsaturated alkene. These compounds require another modification in nomenclature. Specifically, an alkene with two double bonds has the suffix -diene, and one with three double bonds has the suffix -triene. For example:

H H H H H H	H H H H H
| | | | | |	| | | | |
H-C-C=C-C=C-C-H	H-C-C=C=C-C=C-H
| |	|
H H	H
2,4-Hexadiene	1,3,4-Hexatriene

In the compound 1,3,4-hexatriene, the double bonds are counted from the right side, because a compound must always be named beginning with the double bond (or functional group) closest to one end. The following examples will make this concept clear:

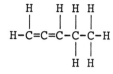

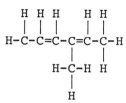

1,2-Pentadiene

(NOT: 3,4-Pentadiene)

3-Methyl-2,4-hexadiene

(NOT: 4-Methyl-2,4-hexadiene)

● PROBLEM 6-2

Name the following compounds using the IUPAC system of nomenclature:

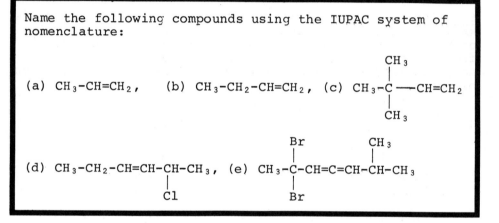

(a) $CH_3-CH=CH_2$,   (b) $CH_3-CH_2-CH=CH_2$, (c) $CH_3-\overset{\overset{\displaystyle CH_3}{|}}{\underset{\underset{\displaystyle CH_3}{|}}{C}}-CH=CH_2$

(d) $CH_3-CH_2-CH=CH-\overset{}{\underset{\underset{\displaystyle Cl}{|}}{CH}}-CH_3$, (e) $CH_3-\overset{\overset{\displaystyle Br}{|}}{\underset{\underset{\displaystyle Br}{|}}{C}}-CH=C=CH-\overset{\overset{\displaystyle CH_3}{|}}{CH}-CH_3$

Solution: (1) Select as the parent structure the longest continuous chain that contains the carbon-carbon double bond; then consider the compound to have been derived from this structure.

(2) Indicate by a number the position of the double bond. The position is designated by the number of the first doubly bonded carbon encountered when numbering from the end of the chain nearest the double bond.

(3) Indicate by numbers the positions of the alkyl groups or other functional groups attached to the parent chain.

With this in mind, the names become:

(a) $CH_3-CH=CH_2$ Propene

(b) $CH_3-CH_2-CH=CH_2$ 1-Butene

(c) $CH_3-\overset{\overset{\displaystyle CH_3}{|}}{\underset{\underset{\displaystyle CH_3}{|}}{C}}-CH=CH_2$ 3,3-Dimethyl-1-butene

(d) $CH_3-CH_2-CH=CH-CH-CH_3$ 2-Chloro-3-hexene
                         |
                         Cl

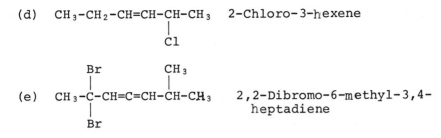

(e) $CH_3-\overset{\overset{\displaystyle Br}{|}}{\underset{\underset{\displaystyle Br}{|}}{C}}-CH=C=CH-\overset{\overset{\displaystyle CH_3}{|}}{CH}-CH_3$ 2,2-Dibromo-6-methyl-3,4-heptadiene

   To illustrate how these names were obtained, consider
structure (c). The longest continuous chain that contains
the double bond is made up of 4 carbons. Therefore, the
parent chain is butene, the "ene" indicative of the presence of a double bond. The double bond is situated on
carbon #1 so that it is 1-butene. The two substituents,
both methyl groups (CH_3), are positioned on carbon #3
because the numbering system is from the end of the parent
chain nearest the double bond. Hence, for (c) the nomenclature is 3,3-Dimethyl-1-butene.

                                        ● **PROBLEM 6-3**

Write the IUPAC names for each of the following chemical
structures:

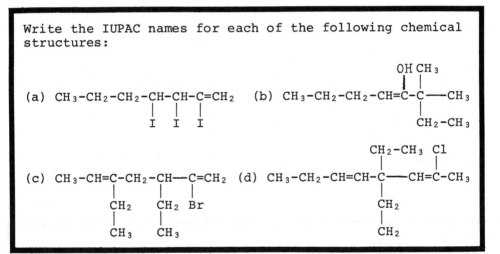

Solution: To write the IUPAC names for these alkenes,
use the following rules:

   (1) Select the parent structure of each compound by
       choosing the longest chain that contains the
       carbon-carbon double bond.

   (2) Denote by number the position of the double
       bond in the parent chain. Designate its position
       by the number of the first doubly bonded carbon
       encountered when numbering from the end of the
       chain nearest the double bond.

   (3) Indicate the positions of all functional groups
       attached to the parent chain by number.

With this in mind, the names of the compounds become:

169

(a) 2,3,4-Triiodo-1-heptene

(b) 3,3-Dimethyl-4-hydroxy-4-octene

(c) 3,5-Diethyl-2-bromo-1,5-heptadiene

(d) 4,4-Diethyl-2-chloro-2,5-octadiene.

To understand the reasoning behind this naming, consider (b):

$$CH_3-CH_2-CH_2-CH=\overset{\overset{\displaystyle OH}{|}}{C}-\overset{\overset{\displaystyle CH_3}{|}}{\underset{\underset{\displaystyle CH_2CH_3}{|}}{C}}-CH_3$$

The longest continuous chain that contains the carbon-carbon double is eight carbons in length. Hence, the name must include the word "octene". The number of the first doubly bonded carbon encountered is four. (In this instance, numbering can be from either end because the double bond is located exactly equidistant from the ends.) Consequently, one has 4-octene. At this point, consider the substituents on the parent chain. Two methyl groups (CH_3) and a hydroxyl group (OH) are present. The methyls are said to be on the third carbon, while the hydroxyl is on the fourth carbon. In this fashion, the lowest possible numbers are used. (For example, if numbering started from the other end of the molecule, the hydroxyl would be on the fifth carbon and the methyls on the sixth carbon.) Overall, then, the name becomes 3,3-Dimethyl-4-hydroxy-4-octene.

The other names of the compounds follow readily from this process.

● PROBLEM 6-4

Write the chemical structures for each compound listed.

(a) 1-Hexene   (b) 3-Methyl-1-butene   (c) 2,4-Hexadiene

(d) 1-Iodo-2-methyl-2-pentene (e) 2-Chloro-3-methyl-2-hexene

(f) 6,6-Dibromo-5-methyl-5-ethyl-2,3-heptadiene

Solution: (1) Look at the complete name of the compound and pick out the parent name. It is usually the last word of the complete name and it denotes the longest continuous chain that contains the carbon-carbon double bond. (All of the structures are alkenes.)

(2) Write out the carbon skeleton that makes up the parent chain. Determine the number of double bonds present by examining the suffix of the parent name. For example, "ene" means one double bond, where as "diene" means two.

(3) Position the double bond (or bonds) in the carbon skeleton as specified by the number directly (usually) in front of the parent name. For example, if the compound is 2-pentene, one would write C-C-C=C-C. (Recall, the position

```
                                        5 4 3 2 1
```

of the double bond is given by the number of the first doubly bonded carbon encountered when numbering from the end of the chain nearest the double bond.)

(4) Position the functional group substituents on the chain as specified by the number directly in front. For example, 3-methyl-2-pentene would be:

```
    C
    |
C-C-C=C-C
5 4 3 2 1
```

The structures of the compounds in (a)-(f) become:

(a) $CH_3CH_2CH_2CH_2CH=CH_2$

(b)
```
CH2=CH-CH-CH3
       |
       CH3
```

(c) $CH_3-CH=CH-CH=CH-CH_3$

(d)
```
CH3CH2CH=C —CH2I
         |
         CH3
```

(e)
```
CH3CH2CH2C ==C-CH3
          |   |
          CH3 Cl
```

(f)
```
                  CH3 Br
                  |   |
CH3-CH=C=CH-C ——C-CH3
                  |   |
                  CH2 Br
                  |
                  CH3
```

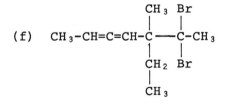

To see how this process works, examine how structure (f) was written. The parent name is heptadiene. The prefix "hepta" indicates that seven carbons are present in the skeleton: C-C-C-C-C-C-C. The 2,3 indicates the positions of the two double bonds - it is a diene. So, one can write C-C=C=C-C-C-C. With this numbering system, the

```
          1 2 3 4 5 6 7
```

substituents are now added as specified by the 6 for the bromines and 5 for the methyl (CH_3) and ethyl groups.

```
          CH3 Br
          |   |
C-C=C=C-C ——C-C
1 2 3 4 |   | 7
        CH2 Br
        |
        CH3
```

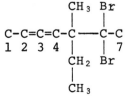

And now only the hydrogens need be added to obtain:

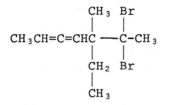

PHYSICAL PROPERTIES

The dipole moment of 1,2-dichloroethane is 1.12 D at room temperature. Show how one could use this dipole moment to calculate the proportions of the possible conformations that are expected to be present.

Solution: When the center of negative charge does not coincide with the center of positive charge in a molecule, it is said to be polar. The molecule constitutes a dipole: two equal and opposite charges separated in space. The molecule possesses a dipole moment which is equal to the magnitude of the charge multiplied by the distance between the centers of charge. In carbon tetrachloride,

Cl ⟷ ⊢ C ⟶ Cl , the dipole moment is zero; the

individual bonds are polar but because of the symmetrical arrangement, they exactly cancel each other out. So, the dipole moment of a molecule depends not only upon the polarity of its individual bonds but also upon the way the bonds are directed, that is, upon the shape of the molecule. Consequently, in calculating the proportions of the possible conformations (shapes) of 1,2-dichloroethane, one wants to consider the dipole moment of each conformation and assign a percentage to each so that the sum of all the individual dipole moments yields the value 1.12 D at room temperature.

A useful representation of the conformations of 1,2-dichloroethane is the Newman projection; . 1,2-dichloroethane possesses two possible conformations (a and b) as illustrated:

(a)   (b)

In figure "a", the polar C-Cl bonds are directed opposite to each other. A symmetrical relationship is established (as was the case with CCl_4) so that there exists a dipole moment of zero. The polarity of the individual bonds is cancelled out by the arrangement.

In figure "b", the polar bonds do not cancel each other so that a dipole exists. The dipole moment of each C-Cl bond is approximately 2.2 D. But, the dipole moment of "b" is not $2 \times 2.2 = 4.4$ D but 3.1 D. Remember, the vector sum must be taken - the direction must always be noted. (The direction is indicated by the dotted line in the figure.)

With this in mind, one can now predict the proportions of "a" and "b". If "b" has a dipole moment of 3.1 D and 1,2-dichloroethane has 1.12 D at room temperature, then the "b" conformation cannot be the shape of most of the molecules. In fact, it represents only 36%. For note: .36 of 3.1 D is 1.12 D, the observed value. What about the other 64%? It can only be conformation "a" with dipole moment zero, and .64 of 0.00 D is, of course, 0.00 D.

In summary, then, one has 64% of "a" with dipole moment zero and 36% of "b" with dipole moment 3.1 D.

● **PROBLEM** 6-6

The trans alkenes are generally more stable than the cis alkenes. Give two examples of unsaturated systems where you would expect the cis form to be more stable and explain the reason for your choice.

Solution: To solve this problem, look for factors affecting stability of conformations. Two such factors include angle strain and van der Waals strain (steric strain).

Any atom tends to have bond angles that match those of its bonding orbitals: tetrahedral (109.5°) for sp^3-hybridized carbon, for example. If there is a deviation from the "normal" bond angles, then angle strain results.

Non-bonded groups or atoms that just touch each other - that is, that are about as far apart as the sum of their van der Waals radii - attract each other. If the groups or atoms are brought any closer together, they repel each other. This crowding produces steric strain.

Consequently, when selecting two examples where a cis form will be more stable than a trans form, consider a situation where the trans conformation produces angle and/or steric strain and the cis does not, or does so to a lesser extent.

One example is cycloalkenes with small to medium sized rings. Cyclobutene fits in this category. The cis and trans forms are illustrated below:

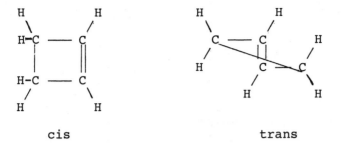

cis   trans

As can be seen in the diagram, the trans form would possess tremendous angle strain. Hence, the cis conformation would be more stable.

The second example of a situation where cis is favored over trans occurs in compounds such as:

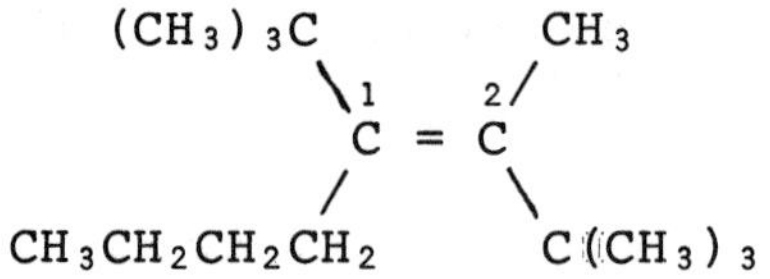

$$(CH_3)_3C \qquad CH_3$$
$$\underset{1}{\diagdown} \qquad \underset{2}{\diagup}$$
$$C = C$$
$$\diagup \qquad \diagdown$$
$$CH_3CH_2CH_2CH_2 \qquad C(CH_3)_3$$

Note that the highest priority group of the carbon labeled 1, $CH_3CH_2CH_2CH_2$, and the highest priority group of the carbon labeled 2, $C(CH_3)_3$, are on the same side of the molecule. Hence, this is the cis (NOT trans) conformation. This conformation is favored in stability over the trans form shown:

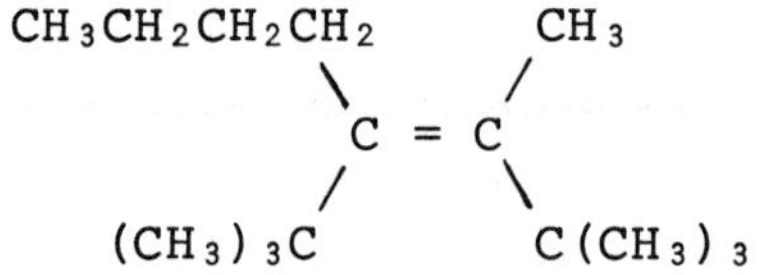

$$CH_3CH_2CH_2CH_2 \qquad CH_3$$
$$\diagdown \qquad \diagup$$
$$C = C$$
$$\diagup \qquad \diagdown$$
$$(CH_3)_3C \qquad C(CH_3)_3$$

The reason stems from the fact that $C(CH_3)_3 \left(H_3C-\overset{\overset{\textstyle CH_3}{\textstyle |}}{\underset{\underset{\textstyle CH_3}{\textstyle |}}{C}}-CH_3 \right)$ is more bulky than $CH_3CH_2CH_2CH_2$ and, as such, creates more steric strain when positioned next to another $C(CH_3)_3$ as is the situation in the trans conformation.

GEOMETRIC ISOMERISM

● **PROBLEM** 6-7

Indicate which of the following compounds show geometric (cis-trans) isomerism, draw the isomeric structures, and specify each as Z or E.

(a) 1-butene   (g) 2-pentene
(b) 2-butene   (h) 1-chloropropene
(c) 1,1-dichloroethene   (i) 1-chloro-2-methyl-2-butene
(d) 1,2-dichloroethene   (j) 3-methyl-4-ethyl-3-hexene
(e) 2-methyl-2-butene   (k) 2,4-hexadiene
(f) 1-pentene $(CH_3CH=CHCH=CHCH_3)$

Solution: If two isomeric substances differ from one another only in the way the atoms are oriented in space (but are like one another with respect to which atoms are attached to which other atoms), they are considered stereoisomers. Stereoisomers that are not mirror images of each other are called diastereomers. The particular kind of diastereomers that result from hindered rotation about double bonds are called geometric isomers.

The arrangement that characterizes a stereoisomer is referred to as its configuration. Configurations are differentiated in their names by the prefixes cis   (on this side) and trans   (across). For example:

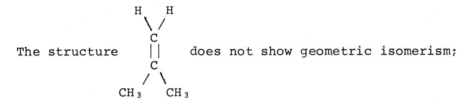

Cis and trans indicate here whether the methyl groups are on the same side or on opposite sides of the molecule.

The structure  does not show geometric isomerism;

geometric isomerism cannot exist if either carbon carries two identical groups. While the prefixes cis and trans work well for disubstituted ethylenes and some trisubstituted ethylenes, it would be difficult to assign a configuration to

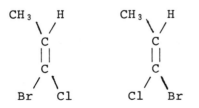

1-Bromo-1-chloropropene

The problem is which group represents the reference. This problem can be solved by looking at each doubly bonded carbon in turn. Of the two atoms or groups of atoms on the one carbon, take the atom or group of atoms of highest priority (highest atomic number) and compare it with the atom or group of atoms of highest priority on the other atom. Now check whether they are on the same side of the double bond or opposite sides. If they are on the same side, use the letter Z to indicate that configuration; if on opposite sides, use the letter E.

Therefore, to solve this problem, one writes out the structures of the compounds given, and looks for that relationship among the groups attached to the doubly-bonded carbons. Then, configuration is assigned using the letters Z and E.

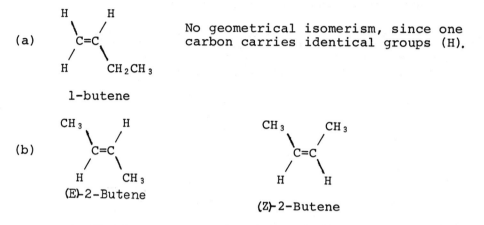

(a)   No geometrical isomerism, since one carbon carries identical groups (H).

1-butene

(b)

(E)-2-Butene

(Z)-2-Butene

In (E)-2-butene, the highest priority groups, CH_3, are on opposite sides of the double bond, therefore it is so named. In (Z)-2-butene, the methyl groups are on the same side of the double bond. Note that the molecule's geometric isomers can also be named by the cis-trans system in this case. (E)-2-butene can also be named trans-2-butene, and (Z)-2-butene cis-2-butene.

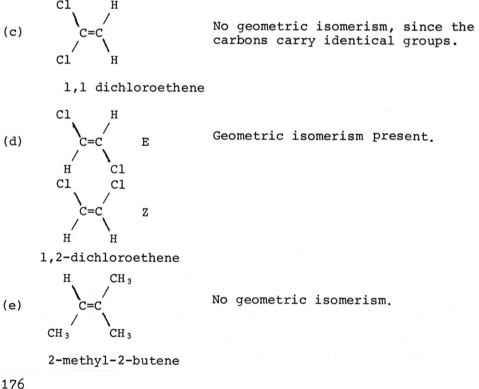

(c)   No geometric isomerism, since the carbons carry identical groups.

1,1 dichloroethene

(d)   E   Geometric isomerism present.

Z

1,2-dichloroethene

(e)   No geometric isomerism.

2-methyl-2-butene

176

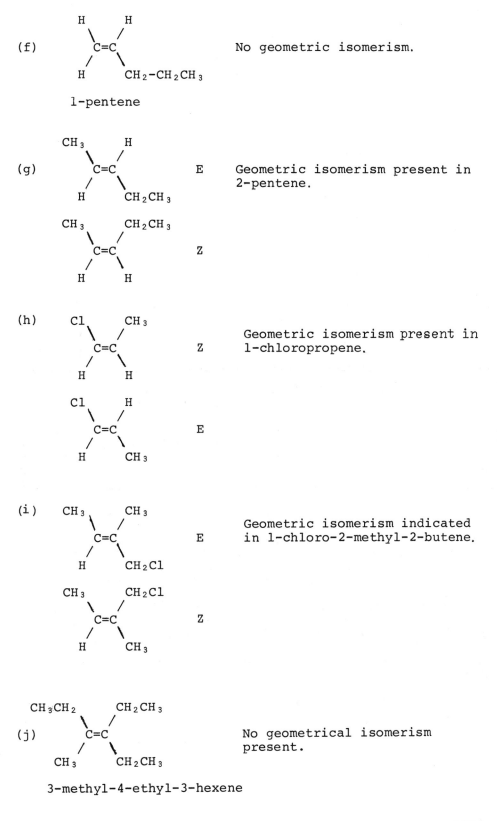

(f) 1-pentene — No geometric isomerism.

(g) E — Geometric isomerism present in 2-pentene.

Z

(h) Z — Geometric isomerism present in 1-chloropropene.

E

(i) E — Geometric isomerism indicated in 1-chloro-2-methyl-2-butene.

Z

(j) 3-methyl-4-ethyl-3-hexene — No geometrical isomerism present.

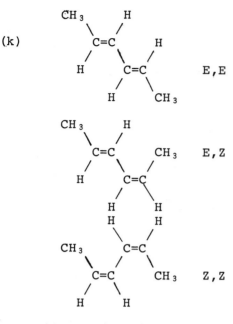

(k)   E,E   Geometrical isomerism
                                                   indicated for 2,4-
                                                   hexadiene.

                                             E,Z

                                             Z,Z

Note: These structures were written by taking the configuration about each carbon-carbon double bond separately.

● **PROBLEM** 6-8

(a) Indicate the direction of the net dipole moment for
each of the dihaloethenes. (b) Would cis-2,3-dichloro-2-
butene have a larger or smaller dipole moment than cis-
1,2-dichloroethene? (c) Indicate the direction of the net
dipole moment of cis-1,2 -dibromo-1,2-dichloroethene. Will
it be larger or smaller than the dipole moment of cis-1,2-
dichloroethene? Why?

Solution: When two atoms are held by a covalent bond,
the bond can be expected to be polar (that is, possess a
negative pole and a positive pole) if the two atoms differ
in their tendency to attract electrons; that is, if the two
atoms differ in electronegativity. The greater the difference in electronegativity, the more polar the bond. When
the center of negative charge does not coincide with the
center of positive charge of such a molecule, a dipole is
said to exist. A dipole moment (μ) equals charge multiplied
by distance between the centers of charge.

(a) All of the dihaloethenes can exist in cis or trans
forms as indicated:

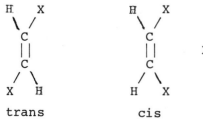

X= a halogen atom
(Cl, F, Br, I)

trans   cis

178

The halogens are strongly electron attracting, so
that the halogen will acquire a negative charge. This
means the dipole between a halogen and a carbon atom
will point to the halogen atom as illustrated:

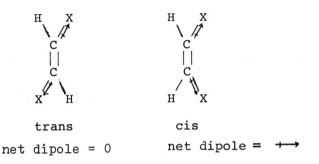

trans   cis

net dipole = 0   net dipole = ⟼

The trans configuration has the dipoles pointing in
two opposite directions so that the net dipole moment is 0,
whereas for the cis configuration the net dipole lies in
the plane of molecule along the bisector of angle between the
Cl atoms.

(b)

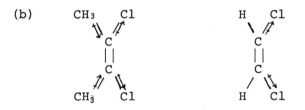

cis-2,3-dichloro-2-   cis-1,2-dichloroethene
       butene

Inspection of the structures of the two compounds
reveals that the four-carbon compound has the larger
dipole moment. This is due to the extra electron release by the two CH_3 groups in the same direction as the
C-Cl dipole.

(c)

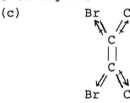

cis-1,2-dibromo-1,2-dichloroethene

Even though the bromine and chlorine are attracting
the electrons in opposite directions, chlorine is the
more electronegative element. This fact accounts for the
direction of the dipole moment. It also explains why the
dipole moment should be less than the moment of cis-1,2-
dichloroethene; the C-Br dipoles oppose the C-Cl dipoles
in cis-1,2-dibromo-1,2-dichloroethene.

179

How many stereoisomers are there for each of the following?

(a) CH_3CH_2 \ $C=CHCH_3$ / CH_3CH_2 (b) $CH_3ClC=$◇   (c) $CH_3HC=C$ with CH_2CH_3 and CH_3

Solution: Stereoisomers may be defined as compounds with identical molecular formulas whose atoms, while linked together in the same order, are arranged differently in space. Stereoisomers must be either enantiomers or diastereomers. Enantiomers refer to stereoisomers that are mirror images of each other, whereas diasteriomers are stereoisomers that are not mirror images of each other. Diastereomers that result from different arrangements of atoms about a double bond are called geometrical isomers.

For (a), there is only one stereoisomer. To see this, let

CH_3CH_2 \ /H $C=C$ / \ CH_3CH_2 CH_3 be the arrangement of atoms given

in (a). The mirror images can now be written as shown:

CH_3CH_2 \ /H $C=C$ / \ CH_3CH_2 CH_3 | mirror | H \ / CH_2CH_3 $C=C$ / \ CH_3 CH_2CH_3

But as we can see, the two mirror images are identical compounds. Also, because (a) has no chiral carbons, it can not exist as a pair of enantiomers .

also does not exist as a pair

of geometric isomers. Its other arrangement of atoms about the double bond: is actually identical

to itself. Thus (a) exists in only one form.

For (b), there is again only one stereoisomer. It may be reasoned in the same manner as was done in (a).

For (c) there exist two stereoisomers which are geometric isomers of each other:

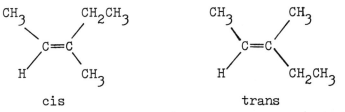

cis   trans

The cis conformation has the highest priority groups of each doubly bonded carbon on the same side of the double bond, whereas the trans conformation has the highest priority groups on opposite sides.

PREPARATION

● **PROBLEM** 6-10

How are alkenes prepared?

Solution: There are four basic methods of preparing alkenes which are as follows:

   (1) Dehydrohalogenation of alkyl halides

   (2) Dehydration of alcohols

   (3) Dehalogenation of vicinal dihalides

   (4) Reduction of alkynes

The most important of these methods of preparation - since they are the most generally applicable - are the dehydro-halogenation of alkyl halides and the dehydration of alcohols.

   Alkenes containing up to five carbon atoms can be obtained in pure form from the petroleum industry. Pure samples of more complicated alkenes must be prepared by methods like those outlined above.

   The introduction of a carbon-carbon double bond (C=C) into a molecule containing only single bonds must necessarily involve the elimination of atoms or groups from two adjacent carbons:

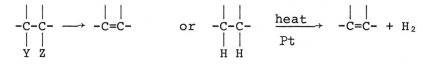

The elimination reactions not only can be used to make simple alkenes, but also provide the best general ways to introduce carbon-carbon double bonds into molecules of all kinds.

The four basic methods of preparing alkenes are outlined below:

(1) Dehydrohalogenation of alkyl halides

$$-\overset{\displaystyle |}{\underset{\displaystyle H}{C}}-\overset{\displaystyle |}{\underset{\displaystyle X}{C}}- \quad + \quad KOH \quad \xrightarrow{\text{alc.}} \quad -\overset{\displaystyle |}{C}=\overset{\displaystyle |}{C}- \quad + \; KX \; + \; H_2O$$

The ease of dehydrohalogenation: $3° > 2° > 1°$

(2) Dehydration of alcohols

$$-\overset{\displaystyle |}{\underset{\displaystyle H}{C}}-\overset{\displaystyle |}{\underset{\displaystyle OH}{C}}- \quad \xrightarrow{\text{acid}} \quad -\overset{\displaystyle |}{C}=\overset{\displaystyle |}{C}- \quad + \; H_2O$$

The ease of dehydration: $3° > 2° > 1°$

(3) Dehalogenation of vicinal dihalides

$$-\overset{\displaystyle |}{\underset{\displaystyle X}{C}}-\overset{\displaystyle |}{\underset{\displaystyle X}{C}}- \quad + \quad Zn \quad \longrightarrow \quad -\overset{\displaystyle |}{C}=\overset{\displaystyle |}{C}- \quad + ZnX_2$$

(4) Reduction of alkynes

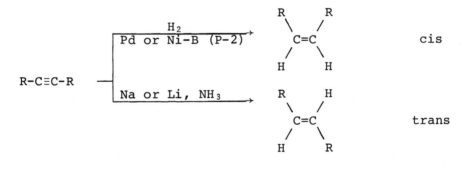

$$R-C\equiv C-R$$

$$\xrightarrow[\text{Pd or Ni-B (P-2)}]{H_2}$$ cis

$$\xrightarrow{\text{Na or Li, NH}_3}$$ trans

● **PROBLEM** 6-11

Describe dehydrohalogenation of alkyl halides to obtain an alkene.

Solution: Alkyl halides are converted into alkenes by the process known as dehydrohalogenation, which is the elimination of the halogen atom together with a hydrogen atom from a carbon adjacent to the one bearing the halogen. The general equation for this process is:

$$-\overset{\displaystyle |}{\underset{\displaystyle |}{C}}-\overset{\displaystyle |}{\underset{\displaystyle |}{C}}- \quad + \quad KOH \text{ (alcoholic)} \longrightarrow \quad -\overset{\displaystyle |}{C}=\overset{\displaystyle |}{C}- \quad + \quad KX \quad + \quad H_2O$$
$$\overset{\displaystyle |}{H} \quad \overset{\displaystyle |}{X}$$

It is known from general chemistry that

$$\frac{acid}{(HCl)} + \frac{base}{(KOH)} \longrightarrow \frac{salt}{(KCl)} + \underset{(H_2O)}{water,} \qquad \text{so it is not}$$

surprising that the reagent required for the elimination of what amounts to a molecule of acid is a strong base.

The alkene is prepared by heating together the alkyl halide and a solution of potassium hydroxide in alcohol. For example:

(1) $CH_3CH_2CH_2Cl$ $\xrightarrow{\text{KOH (alc)}}$ $CH_3CH=CH_2 + KCl + H_2O$

    n-Propyl chloride   Propylene

(2) $CH_3CH_2CH_2CH_2Cl$ $\xrightarrow{\text{KOH (alc)}}$ $CH_3CH_2CH=CH_2 + KCl + H_2O$

    n-Butyl chloride   1-Butene

In dehydrohalogenation, the more stable the alkene, the more easily it is formed as can be seen by the fact that the sequence for ease of formation of alkenes, $R_2C=CR_2>R_2C=CHR>R_2C=CH_2$, $RCH=CHR>RCH=CH_2$, is the same for stability of alkenes. As one moves through the series of alkyl halides, that is, from 1° to 2° to 3°, the structure becomes more branched at the carbon carrying the halogen. Branching provides a greater number of hydrogens for attack by base, and hence a more favorable probability factor toward elimination, and it leads to a more highly branched, more stable alkene, and hence a more stable transition state and lower E_{act}. The result is that in dehydrohalogenation the order of reactivity of RX is 3°>2°>1°.

The orientation of elimination reflects the stability of the alkene that would result. For example:

$CH_3CH_2CHBrCH_3$ $\xrightarrow{\text{KOH (alc)}}$ $CH_3CH=CHCH_3$ and
                                         81%

$CH_3CH_2CH=CH_2$
  19%

2-butene (81%) predominates over 1-butene (19%) because the preferred alkene is the one with the greater number of alkyl groups attached to the doubly bonded carbon atoms as shown above in the sequence for ease of formation of alkenes.

● **PROBLEM 6-12**

Describe dehydration of alcohols to obtain an alkene.

Solution: An alcohol is converted into an alkene by a
process known as dehydration, which is the elimination of
a molecule of water. Dehydration requires the presence of
an acid and the application of heat. The general reaction
for this method of preparation is as follows:

$$-\underset{\underset{\text{H}}{|}}{\overset{|}{C}}-\underset{\underset{\text{OH}}{|}}{\overset{|}{C}}- \quad \xrightarrow[\text{heat}]{\text{acid}} \quad -\overset{|}{C}=\overset{|}{C}- \; + \; H_2O$$

     This method for obtaining an alkene is generally
carried out in either of two ways:

     (a) Heating the alcohol with sulfuric acid or
         phosphoric acid (H_2SO_4, H_3PO_4, respectively)
         to temperatures as high as 200°C, or

     (b) Passing the alcohol vapor over alumina, Al_2O_3,
         at 350-400°C.

     Alcohols are organic compounds of the general formula
ROH, where R is any alkyl group and OH, the hydroxyl group,
is characteristic of alcohols. An alcohol is named by
naming the alkyl group that holds the hydroxyl group and
following this by the word alcohol, for example:

$$CH_3-CH_2OH \qquad \overset{\textstyle CH_3}{\underset{\textstyle CH_3}{\diagdown \diagup}}CHOH \qquad CH_3-\underset{\underset{\text{CH}_3}{|}}{\overset{\overset{\text{CH}_3}{|}}{C}}\!-\!OH$$

   Ethyl Alcohol   Isopropyl Alcohol   t-Butyl Alcohol

     In dehydration of alcohols, these various classes
differ widely in reactivity and conditions. In other
words, some alcohols dehydrate easier than others, depending upon whether the alcohol is primary, secondary or
tertiary. The ease of dehydration of alcohols is 3°>2°>1°.

     The following examples show how these differences in
reactivity affect the experimental conditions of the dehydration.

     Primary Alcohol Dehydration:

   CH_3CH_2OH $\xrightarrow[170°]{95\% \text{ } H_2SO_4}$ $CH_2=CH_2 + H_2O$

     Ethyl Alcohol   Ethylene

     Secondary Alcohol Dehydration:

   $CH_3CH_2\underset{\underset{\text{OH}}{|}}{CH}-CH_3$ $\xrightarrow[100°]{60\% \text{ } H_2SO_4}$ $CH_3CH=CHCH_3 + H_2O$

     sec-Butyl Alcohol   2-Butene
                                        chief product

184

Tertiary Alcohol Dehydration:

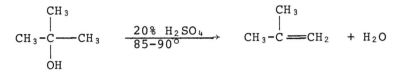

t-Butyl Alcohol   Isobutylene

● **PROBLEM** 6-13

Describe dehalogenation of vicinal dihalides to obtain an alkene.

Solution: Dehalogenation of vicinal dihalides is the process of eliminating two halogens to yield an alkene. The two halogens must be vicinal (Latin: vicinalis, neighboring) in order for a double bond to be formed. The general reaction for this process is:

$$-\underset{\underset{X}{|}}{\overset{|}{C}}-\underset{\underset{X}{|}}{\overset{|}{C}}- \; + \; Zn \; \longrightarrow \; -\overset{|}{C}=\overset{|}{C}- \; + \; ZnX_2$$

Note that this reaction must employ the use of a metal such as zinc or magnesium. A good example of the reaction is:

$$CH_3CH-CH-CH_3 \xrightarrow{\;Zn\;} CH_3CH=CHCH_3 \; + \; ZnBr_2$$
$$\underset{Br \;\; Br}{}$$

2,3-Dibromobutane   2-Butene

Dehalogenation of vicinal dihalides is severely limited by the fact that these dihalides are themselves generally prepared from the alkenes. However, it is sometimes useful to convert an alkene to a dihalide while some operation on another part of the molecule is being performed, and then regenerate the alkene by treatment with zinc.

● **PROBLEM** 6-14

When isopropyl bromide is treated with sodium ethoxide in ethanol, propylene and ethyl isopropyl ether are formed in a 3:1 ratio. If the hexadeuteroisopropyl bromide, $CD_3CHBrCD_3$ is used, $CD_3CH=CD_2$ and $(CD_3)_2CHOC_2H_5$ are formed in a ratio of 1:2. Explain.

Solution: Isopropyl bromide is an alkyl halide. To solve this problem, it will be necessary to consider the typical reactions of alkyl halides.

185

The halide ion may be characterized as a weak base. It can readily be displaced by stronger bases that possess an unshared pair of electrons and seek a relatively positive site. Such basic, electron-rich reagents are nucleophilic reagents. Consequently, one typical reaction of alkyl halides is nucleophilic substitution:

$$R : X \quad + \quad : Z \quad \longrightarrow \quad R : Z + : X^-$$
(Alkyl halide) (Nucleophilic Reagent)   (leaving group)

One type of nucleophilic substitution is called S_N2, which means bimolecular nucleophilic substitution. Bimolecular deals with the kinetics of the reaction; it indicates that the rate determining step involves collision of two particles. For example:

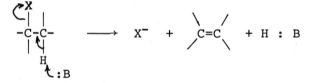

$$(CH_3Br)$$

In S_N2 reactions, the order of reactivity of RX is $CH_3X > 1^\circ > 2^\circ > 3^\circ$. As the number and size of substituents attached to the carbon bearing the halogen is increased, the reactivity toward S_N2 decreases.

Another typical reaction of alkyl halides is bimolecular elimination (called E_2) to produce alkenes. A base abstracts a hydrogen ion away from carbon, and simultaneously a halide ion separates. It is depicted below:

$$-\overset{X}{\underset{H}{C}}-C- \quad \longrightarrow \quad X^- \quad + \quad \overset{\diagdown}{\diagup}C=C\overset{\diagup}{\diagdown} \quad + H : B$$

$$:B$$

This reaction has an isotope effect in that deuterium-carbon bonds are broken more slowly than C-H bonds. The order of reactivity of alkyl halides toward E_2 elimination is $3^\circ > 2^\circ > 1^\circ$. It reflects the relative stabilities of the alkenes being formed.

The structure of isopropyl bromide may be written as

$$\overset{H}{\underset{Br}{CH_3-C-CH_3}}.$$ Hence this alkyl halide is secondary

(2°). This means that in the presence of the strong base sodium ethoxide in ethanol, both the S_N2 and E_2 reactions occur; that is, they compete with each other. This explains why two products, propylene and ethyl isopropyl ether, are obtained.

186

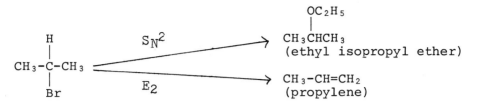

$$CH_3-\underset{\underset{Br}{\overset{\overset{H}{|}}{|}}}{C}-CH_3 \quad \underset{E_2}{\overset{S_N2}{\rightleftharpoons}}$$

$$\underset{CH_3CHCH_3}{\overset{OC_2H_5}{|}}$$
(ethyl isopropyl ether)

$$CH_3-CH=CH_2$$
(propylene)

The ratio of the alkene to the ether is 3:1.

With hexadeuteroisopropyl bromide, $CD_3CHBrCD_3$, the ratio changes to 1:2. This is to be expected for the loss of deuterium in E_2 is slower than hydrogen (the isotope effect). The S_N2 reaction that produces the ether begins to predominate. It may be pictured in the following manner:

$$\underset{CD_3CHCD_3}{\overset{OC_2H_5}{|}} \quad \underset{\text{same rate}}{\overset{S_N2}{\longleftarrow}} \quad CD_3CHBrCD_3 \quad \underset{\text{slower}}{\overset{E_2}{\longrightarrow}} \quad CD_3CH=CD_2$$

The deuterium isotope effect may be calculated as shown:

$$\frac{K_D}{K_H} (E_2) = \frac{1/2}{3/1} = \frac{1}{6} .$$

HYDROGENATION

Describe the catalytic hydrogenation reaction of alkenes.

Solution: Catalytic hydrogenation is the addition of hydrogen atoms across the carbon-carbon double bond of alkenes. The general reaction is:

$$-\underset{|}{\overset{|}{C}}=\underset{|}{\overset{|}{C}}- \quad + \quad H_2 \quad \xrightarrow{\text{Pt, Pd, or Ni}} \quad -\underset{\underset{H}{|}}{\overset{|}{C}}-\underset{\underset{H}{|}}{\overset{|}{C}}- \quad ,$$

where the function of the catalyst (Pt, Pd, or Ni) is to lower the energy of activation so that the reaction can proceed rapidly at room temperature. An example of catalytic hydrogenation is:

$$CH_3CH=CH_2 \quad + \quad H_2 \quad \xrightarrow{\text{Ni}} \quad CH_3CH_2CH_3$$

Propene   Propane

Predict the product after catalytic hydrogenation of each of the following reactants:

187

(a) $CH_3-CH-CH=CH_2$
      |
      CH_3

(b)
$$CH_3-\overset{\overset{\displaystyle CH_3}{|}}{\underset{\underset{\displaystyle CH_3}{|}}{C}}-CH_2CH=CH_2$$

3-Methyl-1-butene

4,4-Dimethyl-1-pentene

(c) $CH_2=CH-CH_2CH_2CH_2CH_2CH_3$

(d) $H_2C=CH_2$

1-Heptene

Ethylene

Solution: When alkenes are shaken under the presence of hydrogen gas at low pressure, including a small amount of catalyst (Pt, Pd, or Ni), they are converted smoothly and quantitatively into alkanes of the same carbon skeleton by hydrogen adding across the carbon-carbon double bond. This reaction, called catalytic hydrogenation, may be illustrated as:

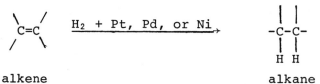

alkene   alkane

   All of the reagents in this problem are alkenes, so that catalytic hydrogenation produces the alkane as shown:

(a) $CH_3-CH-CH=CH_2$ $\xrightarrow[\text{Pt, Pd or Ni}]{H_2}$ $CH_3CH-CH_2-CH_3$
      | |
      CH_3 CH_3

3-Methyl-1-butene   Isopentane

(b) $CH_3-\overset{\overset{\displaystyle CH_3}{|}}{\underset{\underset{\displaystyle CH_3}{|}}{C}}-CH_2CH=CH_2$ $\xrightarrow[\text{Pt, Pd or Ni}]{H_2}$ $CH_3-\overset{\overset{\displaystyle CH_3}{|}}{\underset{\underset{\displaystyle CH_3}{|}}{C}}-CH_2CH_2CH_3$

4,4-Dimethyl-1-pentene   2,2-Dimethylpentane

(c) $CH_2=CH-CH_2CH_2CH_2CH_2CH_3$ $\xrightarrow[\text{Pt, Pd or Ni}]{H_2}$ $CH_3CH_2CH_2CH_2CH_2CH_2CH_3$

1-Heptene   Heptane

(d) $H_2C=CH_2$ $\xrightarrow[\text{Pt, Pd or Ni}]{H_2}$ H_3C-CH_3

Ethylene   Ethane

● PROBLEM 6-17

For each pair of compounds, which one do you expect to show the greater (more negative) heat of hydrogenation? Explain.

188

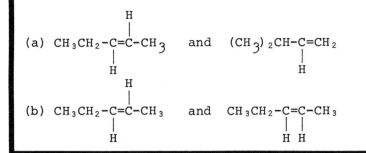

(a) $CH_3CH_2-\overset{\overset{\displaystyle H}{|}}{C}=\overset{\overset{\displaystyle }{|}}{\underset{\underset{\displaystyle H}{|}}{C}}-CH_3$ and $(CH_3)_2CH-\overset{\overset{\displaystyle }{|}}{C}=CH_2$

(b) $CH_3CH_2-\overset{\overset{\displaystyle H}{|}}{C}=\overset{\overset{\displaystyle }{|}}{\underset{\underset{\displaystyle H}{|}}{C}}-CH_3$ and $CH_3CH_2-\overset{\displaystyle }{\underset{\underset{\displaystyle H\ H}{|\ |}}{C=C}}-CH_3$

Solution: Information on the meaning of heat of hydrogenation and how it is related to stability of alkenes will be necessary to solve this problem.

Heat of hydrogenation (ΔH_H) is the enthalpy of the reaction when 1 mole of an unsaturated compound is hydrogenated as shown:

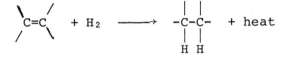

$$\overset{\diagdown}{\diagup}C=C\overset{\diagup}{\diagdown} + H_2 \longrightarrow -\underset{\underset{\displaystyle H\ H}{|\ |}}{\overset{\overset{\displaystyle |\ |}{}}{C-C}}- + \text{heat}$$

Since the reaction is exothermic (that is, evolves heat), ΔH_H is a negative number; the difference in strength of a C=C bond and a C-C bond is 62 Kcal/mole.

If one alkene is less stable than an isomeric unsaturated compound, the internal energy of the former will be higher. This means more heat should be released on hydrogenation of the less stable alkene, and the heat of hydrogenation will have a larger negative value. Hence, for (a) and (b), the compound that shows the greater (more negative) heat of hydrogenation will be the less stable.

What will determine the stability of the isomeric alkenes? One factor is cis-trans conformations. In 2-butene, for example, the cis conformation

$$\begin{pmatrix} CH_3 \quad\quad CH_3 \\ \diagdown \quad\quad \diagup \\ C=C \\ \diagup \quad\quad \diagdown \\ H \quad\quad\quad H \end{pmatrix}$$ is less stable than the trans conformation

$$\begin{pmatrix} H \quad\quad CH_3 \\ \diagdown \quad\quad \diagup \\ C=C \\ \diagup \quad\quad \diagdown \\ H_3C \quad\quad H \end{pmatrix}$$ due to the fact that in the cis conformation,

two bulky substituents on the double bond crowd each other, creating steric compression in the molecule, and raising the van der Waals strain energy. The strain is enhanced as the substituents grow larger.

189

Another factor that influences the stability of isomeric alkenes is the alkyl groups attached to the carbon-carbon double bond. Results indicate that the alkenes which are highly substituted by alkyl groups are more stable. It is believed the inductive effects of alkyl groups and an effect called hyperconjugation are of importance in determining the following order of stability of unstrained alkenes:

$R_2C=CR_2 > R_2C=CHR > R_2C=CH_2 \sim trans-RCH=CHR > cis-RCH=CHR > RCH=CH_2$

$> CH_2=CH_2$

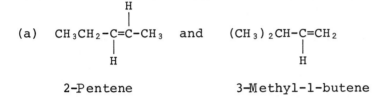

(a) $CH_3CH_2-C=C-CH_3$ and $(CH_3)_2CH-C=CH_2$

    2-Pentene   3-Methyl-1-butene

Examination of these isomeric alkenes shows that 3-methyl-1-butene should give the greater (more negative) heat of hydrogenation; it is the less stable of the pair because it is less substituted with alkyl groups as compared to 2-pentene.

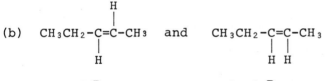

(b) $CH_3CH_2-C=C-CH_3$ and $CH_3CH_2-C=C-CH_3$

    trans-2-Pentene   cis-2-Pentene

This cis conformation of 2-pentene should give the greater heat of hydrogenation for the reasons mentioned earlier - there exists steric repulsion between the alkyl groups.

● **PROBLEM 6-18**

Consider the feasibility of a free-radical chain mechanism for hydrogenation of ethylene in the vapor state at 25° by the following propagation steps:

$$CH_3-CH_2 \cdot + H_2 \rightarrow CH_3-CH_3 + H \cdot$$

$$CH_2=CH_2 + H \cdot \rightarrow CH_3CH_2 \cdot$$

Solution: To determine whether the mechanism is feasible at room temperature (25°C), it will be necessary to calculate ΔH, the heat of the reaction. By convention, the ΔH is given a negative sign when heat is evolved (exothermic reaction) and a positive sign when heat is absorbed (endothermic reaction). If one of the propagation steps of the proposed free-radical mechanism for hydrogenation of ethylene has a positive ΔH, that reaction is unfavorable and will not

190

proceed at room temperature, so that the overall mechanism will not be feasible.

To calculate the heat of reaction, the bond dissociation energies of the reactants must be noted. In $CH_3CH_2\cdot + H_2 \rightarrow CH_3CH_3 + H\cdot$, the hydrogen molecule is broken into a hydrogen radical which, in turn, reacts with the ethyl radical to produce ethane. Now, it takes 104.2 Kcal/mole at 25°C ($\Delta H=+104.2$) to break the H-H bond to form two H· radicals. The addition of one of the H· radicals to the ethyl radical (to give ethane) releases 96 Kcal/mole ($\Delta H= -96.0$). Overall, the heat of reaction is +104.2-96.0= +8.2 Kcal/mole. Since the sign is positive, heat is being absorbed (overall); hence, the reaction is unfavorable. The second reaction, $CH_2=CH_2 + H\cdot \rightarrow CH_3CH_2\cdot$, turns out to have an overall $\Delta H= -36$ Kcal. Even though this reaction releases a large amount of energy (enough to make the overall ΔH favorable: $-36 + 8.2 = -27.8$), the reaction with $\Delta H = +8.2$ makes the mechanism not feasible.

● **PROBLEM 6-19**

Synthesize pentane from 2,3-dibromopentane using any inorganic reagents.

Solution: The structure of 2,3-dibromopentane,

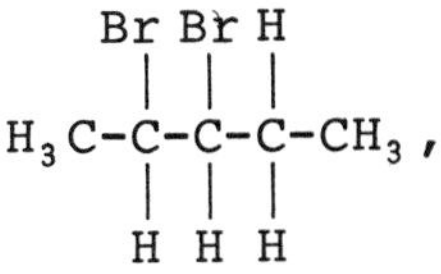

$$\begin{array}{ccc} Br & Br & H \\ | & | & | \\ H_3C-C-C-C-CH_3 \\ | & | & | \\ H & H & H \end{array}, \text{ indicates it is a dihalide. To obtain}$$

pentane ($H_3C-CH_2-CH_2-CH_2-CH_3$) from this compound, the

intermediate 2-pentene ($H_3C-\overset{H}{\overset{|}{C}}=\overset{H}{\overset{|}{C}}-CH_2-CH_3$) would be useful. For from 2-pentene, a hydrogenation reaction can be performed to obtain pentane. To perform this reaction, 2-pentene is required. This can be obtained directly from 2,3-dibromopentane by the addition of zinc (Zn):

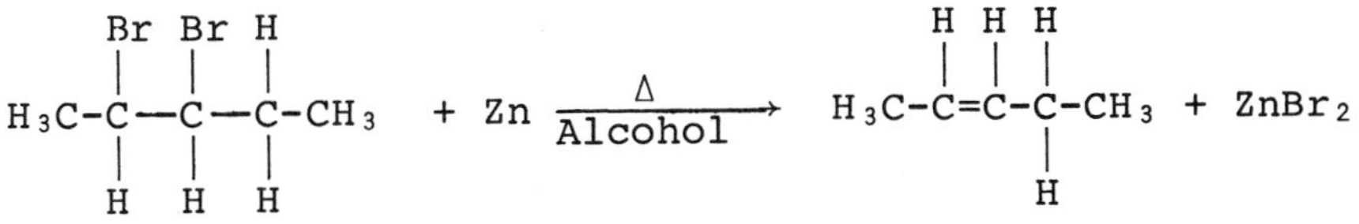

$$\begin{array}{ccc} Br & Br & H \\ | & | & | \\ H_3C-C-C-C-CH_3 \\ | & | & | \\ H & H & H \end{array} + Zn \xrightarrow[\text{Alcohol}]{\Delta} \begin{array}{ccc} H & H & H \\ | & | & | \\ H_3C-C=C-C-CH_3 \\ & & | \\ & & H \end{array} + ZnBr_2$$

This reaction is called the dehalogenation of vicinal dihalides, i.e. it is the abstraction of two halogens from adjacent carbon atoms to yield the alkene. The metal Zn acts as a donor of electrons.

With 2-pentene formed, hydrogenation is the next reaction. This characteristic reaction of alkenes is the addition of hydrogen across the double bond in the presence of a catalyst such as Pt, Pd, or Ni. The catalyst serves to speed up the reaction by lowering the energy of activation. The reaction can then be written as:

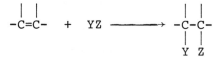

2-Pentene   Pentane

ADDITION REACTIONS

● **PROBLEM** 6-20

What are addition reactions of alkenes?

Solution: To understand addition reactions of alkenes, there must first be a good understanding of the nature of the double bond. The double bond consists of a strong sigma (σ) bond and a weak pi (π) bond. Therefore, it is expected that the reaction would involve breakage of the weaker bond. The typical reactions of the double bond are of the sort where the weaker π bond is broken and stronger σ bonds are formed:

$$-C=C- \quad + \quad YZ \quad \longrightarrow \quad -\underset{Y}{\overset{|}{C}}-\underset{Z}{\overset{|}{C}}- \qquad \text{Addition}$$

A reaction in which two molecules combine to yield a single molecule of product is called an addition reaction. The various types of addition reactions are:

(1) Catalytic Hydrogenation - Addition of Hydrogen

(2) Addition of Halogens

(3) Addition of Hydrogen Halides

(4) Addition of Sulfuric Acid

(5) Addition of Water - Hydration

(6) Halohydrin Formation

(7) Dimerization

(8) Alkylation

(9) Oxymercuration - Demercuration

(10) Hydroboration - Oxidation

(11) Addition of Free Radicals

(12) Polymerization

(13) Addition of Carbenes

(14) Hydroxylation. Glycol Formation.

● **PROBLEM 6-21**

What product is formed when X_2 ($X = Br, Cl$) is added to alkenes in the dark? Explain the mechanism of the reaction.

Solution: The addition of halogens such as Br_2 and Cl_2 to alkenes results in the formation of 1,2-dihalides. The reaction can be written as:

$$\overset{\diagdown}{\underset{\diagup}{C}}=\overset{\diagup}{\underset{\diagdown}{C}} \quad \text{(alkene)} + X_2 \text{ (halogen)} \longrightarrow -\overset{|}{\underset{X}{C}}-\overset{|}{\underset{X}{C}}- \quad \text{(1,2-dihalide)}.$$

The mechanism of this reaction begins by recognizing the fact that X_2 is polarized on contact with the double bond due to the negatively charged π electron cloud of the bond. One end of the halogen molecule becomes positively charged, with the other negatively charged, i.e., $^{\delta-}X\text{-}X^{\delta+}$. The positively charged end is attracted to the negative electron cloud. This results in the cleavage of the X-X bond; the negatively charged $X^{\delta-}$ leaves as shown:

Through a nucleophilic attack, the X^- adds to this species to give the dihalide:

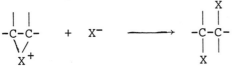

● **PROBLEM 6-22**

Write the products of addition of halogens to each of the following reactants:

(a) $CH_3CH=CH_2$
     Propene

(b) $\overset{\overset{\textstyle CH_3}{|}}{CH_3-C}=CH_2$
     Isobutylene

193

(c) $CH_3CH=CH-CH_2CH_3$

2-Pentene

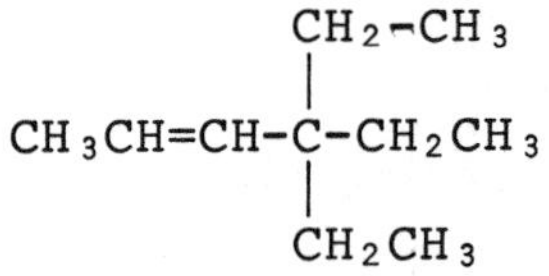

(d)
$$CH_3CH=CH-\overset{\overset{\displaystyle CH_2-CH_3}{|}}{\underset{\underset{\displaystyle CH_2CH_3}{|}}{C}}-CH_2CH_3$$

4,4- Diethyl -2-hexene

Use Cl_2 or Br_2.

Solution: Alkenes can be readily converted by chlorine or bromine into saturated compounds that contain two atoms of halogen attached to adjacent carbons; iodine generally fails to react.

The reaction takes place readily by mixing together the alkene with chlorine or bromine in an inert solvent such as carbon tetrachloride. The general reaction is:

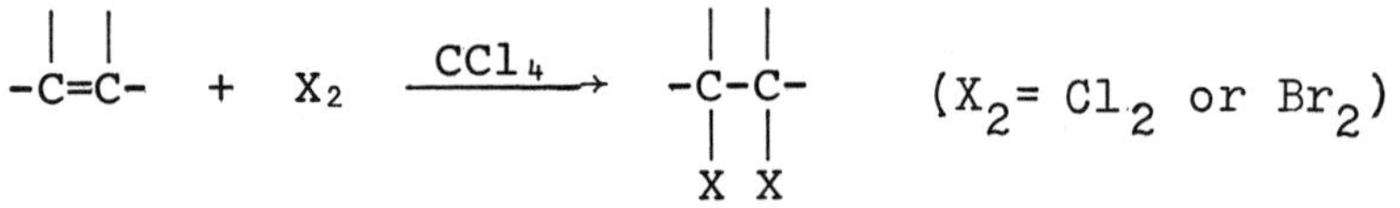

$$-\overset{|}{C}=\overset{|}{C}- \; + \; X_2 \xrightarrow{\;CCl_4\;} -\overset{|}{\underset{\underset{\displaystyle X}{|}}{C}}-\overset{|}{\underset{\underset{\displaystyle X}{|}}{C}}- \qquad (X_2 = Cl_2 \text{ or } Br_2)$$

Keeping this in mind, the product of each reaction can be written:

(a) 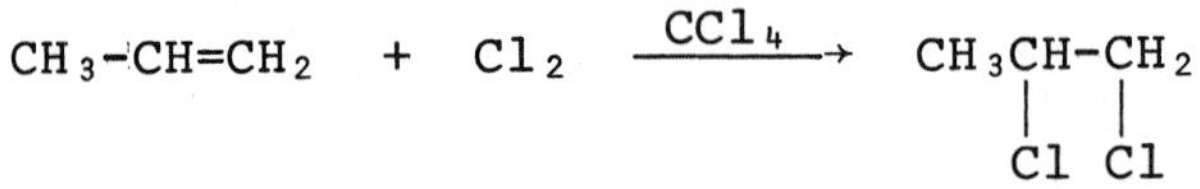 $CH_3-CH=CH_2 \; + \; Cl_2 \xrightarrow{\;CCl_4\;} CH_3\underset{\underset{\displaystyle Cl}{|}}{CH}-\underset{\underset{\displaystyle Cl}{|}}{CH_2}$

Propene $\qquad\qquad$ 1,2-Dichloropropane

(b) 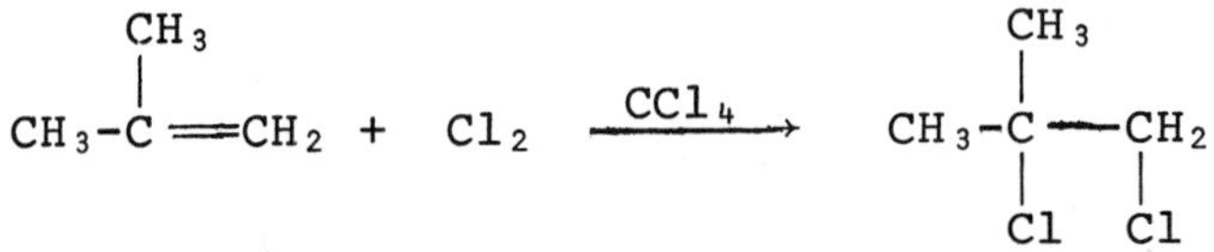 $CH_3-\overset{\overset{\displaystyle CH_3}{|}}{C}=\!=\!=CH_2 \; + \; Cl_2 \xrightarrow{\;CCl_4\;} CH_3-\overset{\overset{\displaystyle CH_3}{|}}{\underset{\underset{\displaystyle Cl}{|}}{C}}\!-\!\!-\!\!-\underset{\underset{\displaystyle Cl}{|}}{CH_2}$

Isobutylene $\qquad\qquad$ 1,2-Dichloro-2-methyl-
propane

(c) 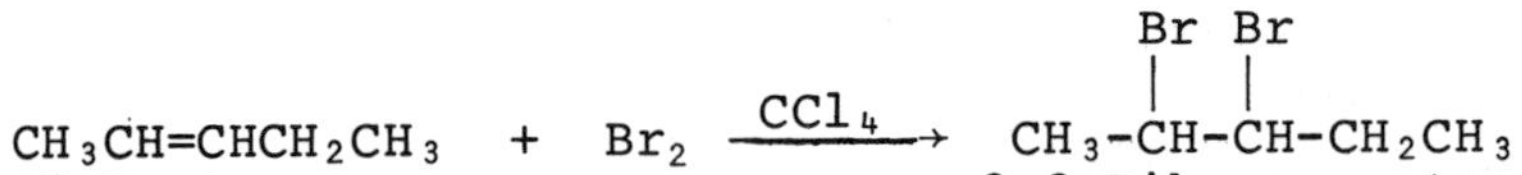 $CH_3CH=CHCH_2CH_3 \; + \; Br_2 \xrightarrow{\;CCl_4\;} CH_3-\overset{\overset{\displaystyle Br}{|}}{CH}-\overset{\overset{\displaystyle Br}{|}}{CH}-CH_2CH_3$
    2-Pentene $\qquad\qquad\qquad\qquad$ 2,3-Dibromopentane

(d) 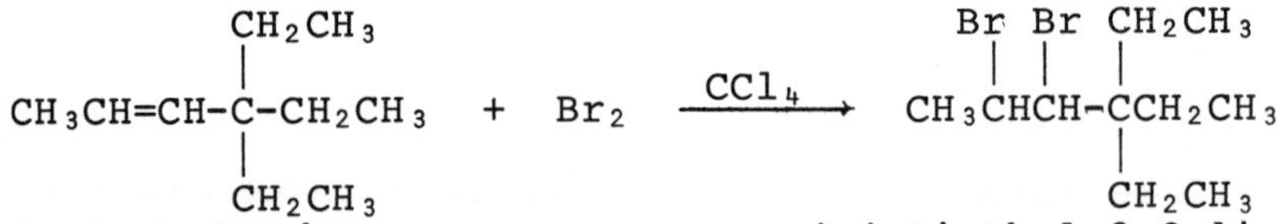 $CH_3CH=CH-\overset{\overset{\displaystyle CH_2CH_3}{|}}{\underset{\underset{\displaystyle CH_2CH_3}{|}}{C}}-CH_2CH_3 \; + \; Br_2 \xrightarrow{\;CCl_4\;} CH_3\overset{\overset{\displaystyle Br}{|}}{CH}\overset{\overset{\displaystyle Br}{|}}{CH}-\overset{\overset{\displaystyle CH_2CH_3}{|}}{\underset{\underset{\displaystyle CH_2CH_3}{|}}{C}}CH_2CH_3$

4,4-Diethyl-2-hexene $\qquad\qquad\qquad$ 4,4-Diethyl-2,3-di-
bromohexane

● PROBLEM 6-23

From the following alkene precursors, show products of halohydrin formation.

194

(a) $CH_3CH=CHCH_2CH_3$ (b) $CH_3-CH=CH_2$

      2-Pentene   Propylene

$$
\begin{array}{ccc}
& CH_3 & \quad CH_3 \\
& | & \quad | \\
(c)\ CH_2=C & -CH_2-C & -CH_3 \\
& & | \\
& & CH_3
\end{array}
$$

            2,4,4-Trimethyl-1-pentene

Solution: Halohydrin formation is the process of adding chlorine or bromine in the presence of water to an alkene to yield compounds containing halogen and hydroxyl groups on adjacent carbon atoms. This reaction changes an alkene to an alcohol that is halogenated, and the product is referred to as a halohydrin. The general reaction is:

$$
-\overset{|}{C}=\overset{|}{C}- \ +\ X_2\ +\ H_2O \longrightarrow -\overset{|}{\underset{X}{C}}-\overset{|}{\underset{OH}{C}}- \ +\ HX\ (X = Cl\ or\ Br)
$$

The products in these reactions also have a modification in nomenclature which is used more than the IUPAC names in some cases. For example:

$$
CH_2=CH_2 + Br_2 + H_2O \longrightarrow \overset{|}{\underset{OH}{C}H_2}-\overset{|}{\underset{Br}{C}H_2} + HBr
$$

       Ethylene   Ethylene bromohydrin
       (Ethene)   (2-Bromoethanol)

This example shows that the double bond is broken when reacted with Br_2 in the presence of water, and the product becomes an alcohol with a halogen. Remembering the general formula of the reaction, it can be written that:

$$
(a)\ CH_3CH=CH-CH_2CH_3 \xrightarrow{Br_2+H_2O} CH_3\overset{\overset{Br}{|}}{C}H-\overset{\overset{OH}{|}}{C}HCH_2CH_3 + HBr
$$

       2-Pentene   2-Bromo-3-pentanol

$$
(b)\ CH_3CH=CH_2 \xrightarrow{Cl_2,\ H_2O} CH_3\overset{\overset{OH}{|}}{C}H-\overset{\overset{Cl}{|}}{C}H_2 + HCl
$$

       Propylene   Propylene chlorohydrin
                                  (1-Chloro-2-propanol)

$$
\begin{array}{l}
\quad\quad CH_3 \quad\quad CH_3 \\
\quad\quad | \quad\quad\quad\ | \\
(c)\ CH_2=C-CH_2-C-CH_3 \xrightarrow{Br_2+H_2O} \\
\quad\quad\quad\quad\quad\quad\ | \\
\quad\quad\quad\quad\quad\quad CH_3
\end{array}
$$

$$
\begin{array}{l}
H \quad CH_3 \quad\quad CH_3 \\
| \quad\ | \quad\quad\quad\ | \\
CH-C-CH_2-C-CH_3 + HBr \\
| \quad\ | \quad\quad\quad\ | \\
Br\ OH \quad\quad\quad CH_3
\end{array}
$$

    2,4,4-Trimethyl-1-pentene   2,4,4-Trimethyl-1-bromo-
                                       2-Pentanol

How can the orientation of the halogen and hydroxyl be explained in these reactions? For example, in propylene chlorohydrin, the chlorine is attached to the terminal carbon, not the middle one. This orientation, and the others, can be accounted for by the mechanism of halohydrin formation. It involves intermediate carbonium ions.

The stability of carbonium ions is $3° > 2° > 1° > CH_3{}^+$. The greater the number of alkyl groups, the more stable the carbonium ion. Now, in halohydrin formation, the halogen adds to the carbon-carbon double bond of the alkene to generate the most stable carbonium ion. Only after this will the hydroxyl be added.

Let us now consider the case of propylene (b) as an illustration. The initial addition of Cl (from Cl_2) to propylene can generate two types of carbonium ions, shown below:

(1) $CH_3CH=CH_2 + Cl_2 \rightarrow CH_3\overset{+}{CH}-CH_2Cl$ (2° carbonium ion)

(2) $CH_3CH=CH_2 + Cl_2 \rightarrow CH_3\underset{|}{\overset{+}{CH}}-CH_2{}^+$ (1° carbonium ion).
Cl

As mentioned above, the 2° carbonium ion is more stable, and will predominate over the 1° carbonium ion. Hence, the hydroxyl adds to $CH_3\overset{+}{CH}-CH_2Cl$, not $CH_3\underset{|}{CH}-CH_2{}^+$, to obtain
Cl

$CH_3\underset{|}{CH}CH_2Cl$, the observed product.
OH

● PROBLEM 6-24

Predict the products of the following reactants after addition of hydrogen halides:

(a) $CH_3\underset{|}{C}=CH-CH_3$
CH_3

2-Methyl-2-butene

(b) $CH_3CH=CHCH_3$

2-Butene

(c) $CH_3CH=C\underset{|}{}-CH\underset{|}{}-CH_3$
$CH_3 CH_3$

3,4-Dimethyl-2-pentene

(d) $CH_3CH=CH_2$

Propylene

Solution: Alkenes can be converted to saturated compounds by addition of hydrogen halides   such as hydrogen chloride, hydrogen bromide, or hydrogen iodide. The general reaction for this process is:

$$-\overset{|}{C}=\overset{|}{C}- \ + \ HX \longrightarrow \ -\overset{|}{\underset{\overset{|}{H}}{C}}-\overset{|}{\underset{\overset{|}{X}}{C}}- \qquad (HX= HCl, \ HBr \ or \ HI)$$

The product is generally referred to as an alkyl halide, and it is produced by passing dry gaseous hydrogen halide through the alkene.

In ionic addition of an acid (such as hydrogen halide) to the carbon-carbon double bond of an alkene, the hydrogen of the acid attaches itself to the carbon atom that already holds the greater number of hydrogens. This principle is known as Markovnikov's Rule. Remembering this principle, the products are written as:

(a) $\quad CH_3-\overset{|}{\underset{\overset{|}{CH_3}}{C}}=CH-CH_3 \quad + \quad HI \quad \longrightarrow \quad CH_3-\overset{\overset{\displaystyle I}{|}}{\underset{\overset{|}{CH_3}}{C}}-CH_2-CH_3$

2-Methyl-2-butene

tert-Pentyl iodide
(2-Iodo-2-methylbutane)

(b) $\quad CH_3CH=CHCH_3 \quad + \quad HBr \quad \longrightarrow \quad CH_3\overset{|}{\underset{\overset{|}{Br}}{CH}}CH_2CH_3$

2-Butene

2-Bromobutane

(c) $\quad CH_3CH=\overset{|}{\underset{\overset{|}{CH_3}}{C}}-\overset{|}{\underset{\overset{|}{CH_3}}{CH}}CH_3 \quad + \quad HCl \quad \longrightarrow \quad CH_3-CH_2-\overset{\overset{\displaystyle Cl}{|}}{\underset{\overset{|}{CH_3}}{C}}-\overset{|}{\underset{\overset{|}{CH_3}}{CH}}-CH_3$

3,4-Dimethyl-2-pentene

3-Chloro-2,3-dimethyl-
pentane

(d) $\quad CH_3-CH=CH_2 \quad + \quad HI \quad \longrightarrow \quad CH_3-\overset{\overset{\displaystyle I}{|}}{CH}-CH_3$
Propylene

Isopropyl iodide

● PROBLEM 6-25

In the dark at room temperature, a solution of chlorine in tetrachloroethylene can be kept for long periods with no sign of reaction. When irradiated with ultraviolet light, however, the clorine is rapidly consumed, with the forma-tion of hexachloroethane; many molecules of product are formed for each photon of light absorbed, and the reaction is slowed down markedly when oxygen is bubbled through the solution.
    (a) How do you account for the absence of reaction in the dark? (b) Outline all steps in the most likely mechanism for the photochemical reaction. Show how it accounts for the facts, including the effect of oxygen.

Solution: The information strongly points to a free-radical addition of chlorine to tetrachloroethylene. The fact that the reaction does not take place in the dark, forms many molecules of hexachloroethane with massive consumption of chlorine upon exposure to U.V., and is inhibited by the addition of oxygen can all be explained readily by a free-radical process.

In such a mechanism, a free-radical must be formed. Chlorine exists as Cl_2, but a radical must be an atom or group of atoms possessing an unpaired electron. For a chlorine radical ($Cl \cdot$) to be formed, the Cl_2 molecule must undergo homolysis, which is the cleavage of the chlorine-chlorine bond in a symmetrical way so that each atom retains one electron of the pair that formed the covalent bond. For this to occur, energy must be supplied. The energy is supplied by either heat or light. Hence, the reaction cannot take place in the dark.

Free-radicals often are involved in a chain reaction. Here, a reaction involves a series of steps, each of which generates a reactive substance that brings about the next step. When the chlorine radical produced by addition of U.V. light collides with tetrachloroethylene, it produces another radical, $Cl_3C-\overset{\bullet}{C}Cl_2$,   which acts in a chain propagating step. This radical reacts with a chlorine molecule to produce the product, hexachloroethane, and another radical, $Cl \cdot$, which can go back and react with tetrachloroethylene. In other words, once a reactive particle is consumed, another reactive particle is produced, so that everything is propagated. This accounts for the many molecules of hexachloroethane formed per photon of light.

The inhibition of the process with oxygen can be explained by its combining with a free radical such as $Cl \cdot$. This makes it much less reactive, so that it can do little to continue the chain; this prevents the formation of many molecules, and, as such, slows down the reaction tremendously by breaking down the chain.

The overall mechanism of the reaction can be written as follows:

(1) $Cl_2 \xrightarrow{\text{light}} 2Cl \cdot$ Chain initiation

(2) $Cl \cdot + Cl_2C=CCl_2 \longrightarrow Cl_3C-\overset{\bullet}{C}Cl_2$

        (tetrachloroethylene)   Chain

                                                    Propagation

(3) $Cl_3C-\overset{\bullet}{C}Cl_2 + Cl_2 \longrightarrow Cl_3C-CCl_3 + Cl \cdot$

                (hexachloroethane)

then (2), (3), (2), (3), etc.

198

What are the products of the following alkenes after hydration?

$$CH_3$$
|
(a) $CH_3-C=CH_2$

(b) $CH_2=CH_2$

Solution: Hydration of alkenes involves the addition of a water molecule in the presence of acid to yield an alcohol. This addition reaction follows Markovnikov's rule.

$$-\overset{|}{C}=\overset{|}{C}- \quad + \quad H_2O \quad \xrightarrow{H^+} \quad -\overset{|}{\underset{H}{C}}-\overset{|}{\underset{OH}{C}}-$$

Knowing the definition and the general principles, it can now be written:

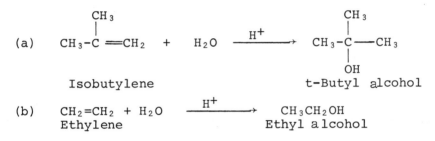

(a)
$$CH_3$$
|
$CH_3-C=CH_2 \quad + \quad H_2O \quad \xrightarrow{H^+} \quad CH_3-\overset{CH_3}{\underset{OH}{\overset{|}{C}}}-CH_3$

Isobutylene \qquad\qquad t-Butyl alcohol

(b) $CH_2=CH_2 + H_2O \xrightarrow{H^+} CH_3CH_2OH$
Ethylene \qquad\qquad Ethyl alcohol

Predict the products of the following reactants after addition of sulfuric acid:

$$CH_3$$
|
(a) $CH_3CH=CH_2$, (b) $CH_2=CH_2$, (c) $CH_3CH_2C=CH_2$.
(propylene) \quad (ethylene) \quad (2-methyl-1-butene)

Solution: Alkenes react with cold, concentrated sulfuric acid (H_2SO_4) to form compounds known as alkyl hydrogen sulfates ($ROSO_3H$). These products are formed by addition of hydrogen ion to one side of the double bond and bisulfate ion to the other. It is important to notice that carbon is bonded to oxygen and not to sulfur. The general reaction is:

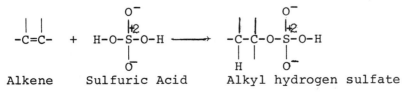

Alkene \qquad Sulfuric Acid \qquad Alkyl hydrogen sulfate

The concentration of sulfuric acid required for reaction depends upon the particular alkene involved. It must also be understood that Markovnikov's rule is involved in this type of addition reaction.

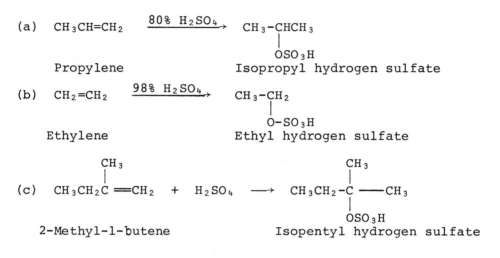

(a) $CH_3CH=CH_2$ $\xrightarrow{80\% \ H_2SO_4}$ CH_3-CHCH_3
                                                      |
                                                    OSO_3H

      Propylene   Isopropyl hydrogen sulfate

(b) $CH_2=CH_2$ $\xrightarrow{98\% \ H_2SO_4}$ CH_3-CH_2
                                                    |
                                                  $O-SO_3H$

      Ethylene   Ethyl hydrogen sulfate

             CH_3 CH_3
              |
(c) $CH_3CH_2C=CH_2$ + H_2SO_4 $\longrightarrow$ $CH_3CH_2-C-CH_3$
                                                                |
                                                              OSO_3H

   2-Methyl-1-butene   Isopentyl hydrogen sulfate

● **PROBLEM 6-28**

Compound X has the molecular formula C_4H_8. Compound Y is obtained when hydrogen bromide is added to X. Compound Y reacts with AgOH to form a tertiary alcohol. Identify all structures.

Solution: Compound X's molecular formula fits the general formula of an alkene, C_nH_{2n}. The presence of the double bond in compound X means asymmetrical reagents such as HA (where A = Br, Cl) can be added across the bond to obtain the alkyl halide. This is exactly what occurs when hydrogen bromide (HBr) is added to compound X. The general reaction can be written as follows:

        Alkene   H A

                          Alkyl halide

     The alkyl halide produced in this reaction (compound Y) reacts with silver hydroxide to produce an alcohol. This reaction illustrates a method of generating alcohols as shown:

       $R - X$ + AgOH $\xrightarrow[\text{ether}]{\text{moist}}$ $R-OH$ + AgX

   Alkyl halide

The fact that a tertiary alcohol $\left(\begin{array}{c} R \\ | \\ R-C-R \\ | \\ OH \end{array} \right)$ is produced can tell what the actual structures of X and Y are. If no carbon atoms are added in a reaction sequence, then the initial number of carbon atoms should equal the final number (assuming no degradation). The tertiary alcohol should, therefore, contain only four carbon atoms. The only way to arrange a 3° alcohol with 4 carbons is to surround a central carbon with three others. In other words, the

tertiary alcohol must be 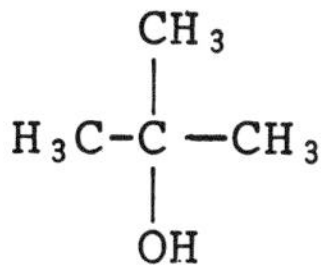
$$H_3C-\overset{\overset{\displaystyle CH_3}{|}}{\underset{\underset{\displaystyle OH}{|}}{C}}-CH_3 \quad \text{(t-butyl alcohol)}.$$

Working backwards, one can determine the structure of the other compounds. Only the alkyl halide t-butyl bromide could have reacted with AgOH to produce this tertiary alcohol:

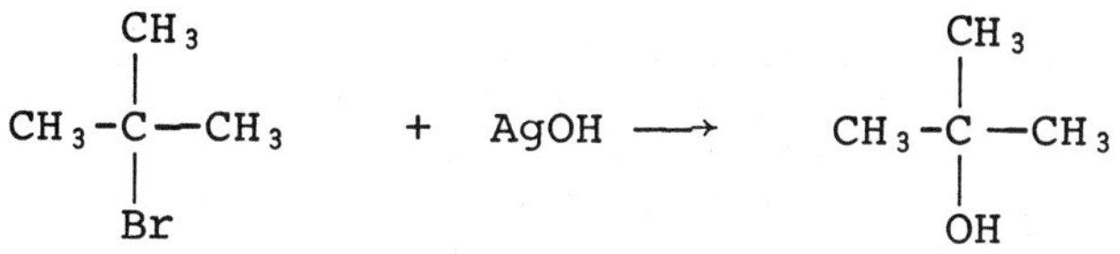

$$CH_3-\overset{\overset{\displaystyle CH_3}{|}}{\underset{\underset{\displaystyle Br}{|}}{C}}-CH_3 \quad + \quad AgOH \longrightarrow \quad CH_3-\overset{\overset{\displaystyle CH_3}{|}}{\underset{\underset{\displaystyle OH}{|}}{C}}-CH_3$$

(t-butyl bromide, compound Y)

With similar reasoning, it can be concluded that compound X has the following structure:

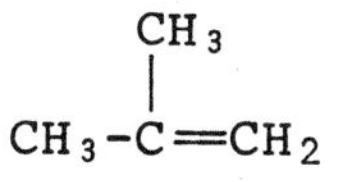

$$CH_3-\overset{\overset{\displaystyle CH_3}{|}}{C}=CH_2 \quad \text{(isobutylene, compound X)}$$

One will notice that when HBr is added (keeping in mind Markovnikov's rule) compound Y is obtained.

● **PROBLEM 6-29**

Treatment of $C_7H_{15}Br$ with strong base gave an alkene mixture that was shown by careful gas chromatographic analysis and separation to consist of three alkenes, C_7H_{14}, A, B, and C. Catalytic hydrogenation of each alkene gave 2-methylhexane. Reaction of A with B_2H_6 followed by H_2O_2 and OH^- gave mostly an alcohol, D. Similar reaction of B or C gave approximately equal amounts of D and an isomeric alcohol E. What structural assignments can be made for A to E on the basis of these observations? What structural element is left undetermined by these data alone?

Solution: The problem indicates that $C_7H_{15}Br$ produces a mixture of three alkenes in the presence of strong base. The formula $C_7H_{15}Br$ suggests the compound is an alkyl halide. In the presence of strong base, dehydrohalogenation of alkyl halides occurs to produce alkenes as illustrated:

$$\underset{\substack{\text{Alkyl halide}}}{\underset{\substack{| \ | \\ H \ X}}{-\overset{|}{C}-\overset{|}{C}-}} \quad + \ \underset{\text{Base}}{KOH} \quad \xrightarrow{\text{alcohol}} \quad \underset{\substack{| \ |}}{-\overset{|}{C}=\overset{|}{C}-} \quad + \ KX + H_2O$$

Alkyl halide   Base   Alkene

Hence, a dehydrohalogenation reaction produced the mixture of alkenes.

In catalytic hydrogenation, H_2 adds across the double bond of the alkene and converts it into the alkane as shown:

$$\underset{\text{Alkene}}{-\overset{|}{C}=\overset{|}{C}-} \quad + \ H_2 \quad \xrightarrow{\text{Pt, Pd, or Ni}} \quad \underset{\substack{| \ | \\ H \ H \\ \text{Alkane}}}{-\overset{|}{C}-\overset{|}{C}-}$$

In this problem, all the alkenes gave rise to 2-methyl-hexane $\left(\underset{\substack{| \\ CH_3}}{CH_3-CHCH_2CH_2CH_3} \right)$ after catalytic hydrogenation. This provides information on the structure of the $C_7H_{15}Br$. The compound must have the same carbon skeleton as 2-methyl-hexane; no carbon atoms were added or degraded. In fact, if one writes the formula for 2-methylhexane, C_7H_{16}, one sees the two compounds differ by a bromine atom which replaces one of the hydrogens. Hence, to write the structure of $C_7H_{15}Br$, one needs only to replace one of the hydrogens in 2-methylhexane with Br. The question is which hydrogen is to be replaced? This can be answered by using the fact that three alkenes are obtained after dehydrohalogenation. One asks: where is it possible to place the Br to give three different alkenes on dehydrohalogenation? Now, through trial and error, one finds the Br must be positioned as shown:

$$\underset{\substack{| \\ CH_3}}{CH_3-CH}\overset{\overset{\textstyle Br}{\textstyle |}}{-}CHCH_2CH_2CH_3$$

2-Methyl-3-bromohexane

One notices that on dehydrohalogenation three alkenes are produced:

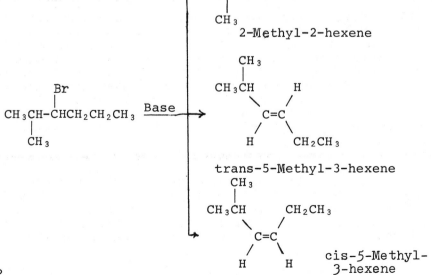

4

202

The structures drawn show that two of the three alkenes are cis-trans geometric isomers.

These alkenes fit the formula, C_7H_{14} and represent A, B, and C. (Note: The Br at the 5th position will also give 3 alkenes, but the remaining reactions with B_2H_6, H_2O_2 and OH^- rule this out. The 5th position Br would give 5-methyl-1-hexene and cis and trans 5-methyl-2-hexenes. However, the cis-trans alkenes cannot give the same alcohol, 5-methyl-1-hexanol, which 5-methyl-1-hexene produces on reaction with B_2H_6, H_2O_2 and OH^-. Consequently, since the problem states that A, B, and C, that is, all the alkenes, can generate the same alcohol (D), this possibility is eliminated.)

At this point, one cannot assign particular structures to A, B, and C. The reagents B_2H_6, H_2O_2 and OH^- will aid in pinpointing the structures. These reagents that generate the alcohols D and E add the hydroxyl group in anti-Markovnikov fashion. Hence, 2-methyl-2-hexene gives mostly one alcohol as shown:

$$CH_3-\underset{\underset{CH_3}{|}}{C}=CHCH_2CH_2CH_3 \xrightarrow{B_2H_6} \xrightarrow[OH^-]{H_2O_2} CH_3-\underset{\underset{CH_3}{|}}{CH}-\overset{\overset{OH}{|}}{C}HCH_2CH_2CH_3$$

$$(D)$$

(Very little $CH_3\underset{\underset{CH_3}{|}}{\overset{\overset{OH}{|}}{C}}-CH_2CH_2CH_2CH_3$ would be produced because

the reaction would have been in Markovnikov fashion.) This fits the information for compound A giving mostly the alcohol D. Therefore, it can be concluded that compound A is 2-methyl-2-hexene. Consequently, B and C must be the cis-trans geometric isomers. From the data provided, it cannot be determined whether B is cis or trans. The structure of the alcohols, D and E, can be discerned as indicated below:

$$CH_3CH_2CH=CHCH(CH_3)_2 \xrightarrow{B_2H_6} \xrightarrow[OH^-]{H_2O_2}$$

B + C, cis and trans

$$CH_3CH_2CH_2\underset{\underset{OH}{|}}{C}HCH(CH_3)_2 \quad + \quad CH_3CH_2\overset{\overset{OH}{|}}{C}HCH_2CH(CH_3)_2$$

$$D \qquad\qquad\qquad\qquad E$$

OXIDATION

Describe the mechanism of the peroxide effect.

Solution: In the absence of peroxides, hydrogen bromide adds to alkenes in agreement with Markovnikov's rule; that is, the hydrogen of HBr goes to that carbon of the double bond that carries the greater number of hydrogens. In the presence of peroxides, the addition proceeds in a reverse direction, or anti-Markovnikov. This phenomenon is known as the peroxide effect.

The main point of the mechanism is that hydrogen and bromine add to the double bond as atoms rather than as ions; the intermediate is a free radical rather than a carbonium ion. As in halogenation of alkanes, this is a chain reaction, this time involving addition rather than substitution.

Step 1 of the mechanism is the decomposition of the peroxide to yield free radicals. The free radical thus formed abstracts hydrogen from hydrogen bromide (step 2) to form a bromine atom.

(1)   peroxides ⟶ Rad ·

(2)   rad · + H : Br ⟶ Rad : H   + Br ·

The bromine atom then adds to the double bond converting the alkene into the most stable radical (step 3). This free radical abstracts hydrogen from hydrogen bromide (step 4).

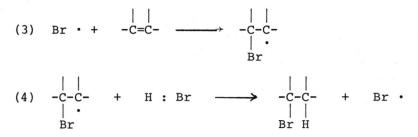

Addition is now complete, and a new bromine atom has been generated to continue the chain.

Determine the oxidation number of each atom in the following:
(a) propene   (e) (E)-2-chloro-2-butene
(b) 1-butene   (f) 1,1-dichloropropane
(c) cis-2-butene   (g) acetic acid, CH_3CO_2H
(d) 1-chloro-2-butene   (h) methanethiol, CH_3SH

Solution: In general chemistry, the term oxidation means loss of electrons and reduction means gain of electrons. The change in degree of oxidation or reduction can be recognized by a change in oxidation number.

   In organic chemistry, this approach cannot be used because the changes accompanying reaction involve covalent bonds and there is no clear ownership of bonding electrons. Consequently, ownership is assigned based upon the electro- negativity of the elements. The rules are as follows:
(1) Electronegative elements (such as O, N, S, Br) are con- sidered to make a +1 contribution to the oxidation number of the carbon to which it is attached. (2) A hydrogen atom, being less electronegative, makes a -1 contribution to the carbon to which it is attached. (3) A zero contribution occurs when a carbon is bonded to another carbon.
(4) Multiple bonds are counted according to the multipli- city of the bond. For example, in C=O, the oxygen con- tributes +2 because it is a double bond.

(a) Propene: $CH_3-CH=CH_2$
                $\quad$ -3 -1 -2

Explanation: In the CH_3 portion, there are three H's each of which makes a -1 contribution for a total of -3.   In CH_2, there exist two hydrogens for a contribution of -2. CH has only a -1 contribution for only one hydrogen is present. The carbons bonded together make no contribution.

   (b) - (h) follow readily with such reasoning.

(b) 1-Butene: $CH_3-CH_2-CH=CH_2$
                $\quad$ -3 $\quad$ -2 -1 -2

(c) cis-2-Butene: $\overset{\displaystyle H\ \ H}{\underset{\displaystyle -3\ -1\ -1\ -3}{CH_3-C=C-CH_3}}$

(d) 1-Chloro-2-butene: $CH_3-CH=CH-CH_2-Cl$
                         $\quad$ -3 -1 -1 -1 -1

Note: The CH_2 portion contributes -1 because the two hydrogens yield -2 and Cl, more electronegative than carbon, imparts +1 to the carbon to which it is attached.

(e) (E)-2-Chloro-2-butene:

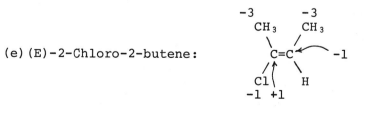

(f) 1,1-Dichloropropane: $\overset{\displaystyle -3\ \ -2\ \ +1\ -1}{CH_3-CH_2-CH-Cl}$
                         $\qquad\qquad\qquad\quad \underset{\displaystyle -1}{\overset{\displaystyle |}{Cl}}$

205

Note: Each chlorine imparts +1 (for a total of +2) to the
carbon to which it is attached, but H imparts -1 for a net
of +1.

(g) Acetic acid:
$$CH_3\overset{\overset{\displaystyle O}{\|}}{\underset{\underset{+3}{-3\ \uparrow\ -2}}{C}}\text{-O-H}$$

with the O labeled -2.

The +3 charge of the carbon comes about as follows: The
doubly bonded oxygen contributes +2 (twice +1 because of
the double bond) and the singly bonded oxygen +1. The
charge on the oxygen atom itself is -2.

(h) Methanethiol: $\quad CH_3S\text{-}H$
$\qquad\qquad\qquad\qquad\ \ -2\ \ -2$

The three hydrogens contribute a -3 but the electronegative
sulfur imparts +1 to the carbon to which it is attached for
a net of -2. (The S, itself, is -2.)

● **PROBLEM 6-32**

In the presence of a trace of peroxide or under the influence
of ultraviolet light, 1-octene reacts:
(a) with $CHCl_3$ to form 1,1,1-trichlorononane;
(b) with $CHBr_3$ to form 1,1,3-tribromononane;
(c) with $CBrCl_3$ to form 1,1,1-trichloro-3-bromononane;
(d) with $H\text{-}S\text{-}CH_2COOH$ (thioglycolic acid) to yield
$n\text{-}C_8H_{17}\text{-}S\text{-}CH_2COOH$;
(e) with aldehydes, $R\text{-}\underset{\underset{\displaystyle H}{|}}{C}\text{=}O$, to yield ketones, $n\text{-}C_8H_{17}\text{-}\underset{\underset{\displaystyle O}{\|}}{C}\text{-}R$.

Show all steps of a likely mechanism for these reactions.

Solution: In the presence of peroxides numerous reagents can add to alkenes through free-radical addition.
Likewise, free-radical addition occurs in the presence of
light. Peroxides decompose to yield free radicals, while
light generates free radicals by causing homolytic cleavage
across covalent bonds. Only trace amounts of peroxide or
light are needed, for once the reaction has been initiated,
the consumption of one radical generates another so that
there exist chain propagating steps. The following mechanism
has been proposed (illustrated with $CHCl_3$):

(1) $\qquad\qquad\qquad$ Peroxide $\longrightarrow$ Rad·

(2) $\quad$ Rad· + $CHCl_3$ $\longrightarrow$ Rad:H + ·CCl_3

(3) $\quad$ ·CCl_3 + $CH_2\text{=}CH\text{-}(CH_2)_5\text{-}CH_3$ → $Cl_3C\text{-}CH_2\text{-}CH\text{-}(CH_2)_5\text{-}CH_3$
$\qquad\qquad\qquad$ (1-octene)

(4) $Cl_3C\text{-}CH_2\text{-}CH\text{-}(CH_2)_5\text{-}CH_3 + CHCl_3 → Cl_3C\text{-}CH_2CH_2(CH_2)_5CH_3$
$\qquad\qquad\qquad\qquad\qquad$ (1,1,1-trichlorononane)

$\quad$ + ·CCl_3

then (3), (4), (3), (4), etc.

The peroxide radical abstracts a hydrogen atom from the $CHCl_3$ to produce another radical, $\cdot CCl_3$. This, in turn, adds across the double bond of l-octene to produce the next radical, $Cl_3C-CH_2-\overset{\cdot}{C}H-(CH_2)_5-CH_3$, which reacts with $CHCl_3$ to yield 1,1,1-trichlorononane and $\cdot CCl_3$ which can repeat the process.

The same mechanism occurs in (b)-(e), except with radicals in steps (2) and (4) abstracting: (b) Br, (c) Br, (d) H from S, (e) H.

● **PROBLEM 6-33**

The following physical properties and analytical data pertain to two isomeric hydrocarbons A and B, isolated from a gasoline:

	b.p.	m.p.	%C	%H
A	68.6°	-141°	85.63	14.34
B	67.9°	-133°	85.63	14.34

Both A and B readily decolorize bromine and permanganate solutions and give the same products on ozonization. Suggest possible structures for A and B. What experiments would you consider necessary to further establish the structure and configuration of A and B?

Solution: One of the best ways an alkene can be characterized is by its ability to decolorize both a solution of bromine in CCl_4 and a cold, dilute, neutral permanganate solution as shown:

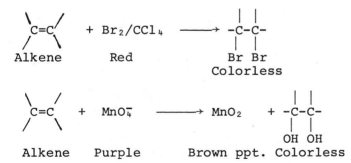

The fact that both A and B decolorize these solutions indicates they possess double bonds, that is, they are alkenes.

The problem states that the same products are obtained from A and B after ozonization, a process that cleaves the carbon-carbon double bond to produce aldehydes and ketones as illustrated:

$$\underset{\text{Alkene}}{-\overset{|}{\underset{}{C}}=\overset{|}{\underset{}{C}}-} \quad \xrightarrow{O_3} \quad \xrightarrow[\text{Zn}]{H_2O} \quad \underset{\text{Cleavage Products}}{-\overset{|}{\underset{}{C}}=O \;+\; O=\overset{|}{\underset{}{C}}-}$$

The fact that the same cleavage products are obtained from A and B must mean that the groups originally attached to the doubly bonded carbons were the same in both molecules. If this is the case, it would appear that A and B are the same compound. And yet, how can one account for the different physical properties of the two compounds indicated in the table? One way is to consider the possibility of geometric isomerism, that is, cis-trans conformations.

The information provided indicates the percentages of carbon and hydrogen in both A and B to be 85.63 and 14.34, respectively. A likely formula for such percentages is C_6H_{12}. That this is the formula may be shown in the following manner: the molecular weight of C_6H_{12} is $12(6)+1(12)=84$. The carbons total $12(6)=72$. Hence, the percentage of carbon is $72/84 \times 100 \sim 85.63$. The percentage of hydrogen, $12/84 \times 100 \sim 14.34$, checks also.

With this in mind, the possible structures are the cis-trans isomer of 2-hexene or the cis-trans isomer of 3-hexene as shown:

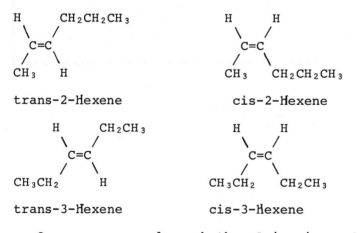

One can narrow down whether A is cis or trans and likewise B. Examination of the melting and boiling points shows that compound A has the lower melting point and higher boiling point which probably suggests the conformation of A is cis. (Except for 3-hexenes, cis isomers have lower melting points and higher boiling points than trans isomers.)

To pinpoint whether the molecule is 2-hexene or 3-hexene, one could use nuclear magnetic resonance. One could also analyze the products of ozonization; they should be identified as acetaldehyde and butyraldehyde in the case of 2-hexene or only as propionaldehyde in the case of 3-hexene.

208

Write the equation for the oxidation of propene by $KMnO_4$
solution at pH = 7.0. Show any intermediates. Assume
cold and dilute conditions.

Solution: Alkenes such as propene $\left(CH_3-\overset{\overset{\displaystyle H}{|}}{C}=CH_2\right)$ can be
hydroxylated with potassium permanganate solution
($KMnO_4$) under cold, dilute and neutral conditions. The 1,2-
diol products that form are almost exclusively syn-adducts.
This stereospecificity of the reaction can be explained by
the formation of a cyclic ester intermediate. The overall
mechanism is given below.

$\underset{\text{Propene}}{\overset{\displaystyle CH_2}{\underset{\displaystyle H-C-CH_3}{||}}}$ + $KMnO_4$ $\longrightarrow$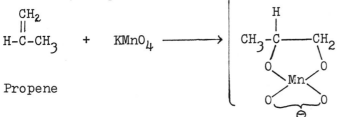

Cyclic ester intermediate

$\longrightarrow$ $\underset{\underset{\displaystyle HO \quad OH}{|\quad\;\;|}}{CH_3-\overset{\overset{\displaystyle H}{|}}{C}-\overset{\overset{\displaystyle H}{|}}{C}-H}$ Syn-adduct:
1,2-dihydroxylpropane

On ozonolysis of a hydrocarbon two equivalents of formaldehyde and one equivalent of

$$O=CH-C(CH_3)_2-\overset{\overset{\displaystyle O}{||}}{C}-C_2H_5$$ were obtained. Give the

structure of the hydrocarbon.

Solution: Ozonolysis is a characteristic reaction
of alkenes. It degrades alkenes to aldehydes

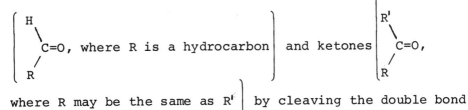

with ozone (O_3) in the presence of zinc dust (Zn) and acid (H^+).

The mechanism of the reaction is as follows: ozone is passed through the alkene which causes the formation of ozonides; the ozonides, which are explosive, are converted into aldehydes and ketones in the presence of zinc dust and acid.

$R_2C=CR_2$ (alkene) + O_3 (ozone) ⟶

$$\xrightarrow{\qquad} R_2C \underset{O}{\overset{O-O}{\diagdown \diagup}} CR_2 \text{ (ozonide)} \xrightarrow[Zn, H^+]{H_2O} R_2C=O +$$

$O=CR_2$ (ketones) + H_2O

The products of ozonolysis can be used to identify the structure from which they came.

The position of the double bond in the original alkene will be indicated by the carbonyl (i.e., C=O) formed in the products after ozonolysis.

In this problem, $O=CH-C(CH_3)_2-\underset{\underset{O}{\|}}{C}-C_2H_5$ and 2 equivalents of

formaldehyde $\left[\begin{array}{c} H \\ \diagdown \\ \diagup C=O \\ H \end{array} \right]$ are given as the products of ozon-

olysis. There are two carbonyls in $O=CH-C(CH_3)_2-\underset{\underset{O}{\|}}{C}-C_2H_5$,

which indicate the locations of the two double bonds. There-fore,

$\underset{H}{\overset{H}{\diagdown}} C=CH-C(CH_3)_2-\underset{\underset{\underset{H \quad H}{\diagup \diagdown}}{C}}{\overset{\|}{C}}-C_2H_5$ can be deduced to be

the structure of the hydrocarbon; ozonolysis of it across its double bonds yields two equivalents of formaldehyde

and one of $O=CH-C(CH_3)_2-\underset{\underset{O}{\|}}{C}-C_2H_5$, as experimentally

observed.

An unknown compound A rapidly decolorized a solution of bromine in carbon tetrachloride. When A was subjected to ozonolysis, the products were butanone and propanal. What might be the structure of A?

Solution: Bromine in carbon tetrachloride is a standard test for olefins. It uses the fact that bromine can add across a carbon-carbon double bond by an electrophilic addition reaction. As the reaction proceeds, the depletion of Br_2 decolorizes the reddish-brown bromine solution. The reaction is so rapid that this decolorization is almost instantaneous.

    Since A decolorizes a bromine solution, it is an olefin. This is further confirmed by the fact that A undergoes ozonolysis, which is an oxidation reaction of olefins. In this oxidation process, the carbon-carbon double bond is cleaved, producing two separate carbonyl compounds. The general reaction may be written as:

$$-\overset{|}{C}=\overset{|}{C}- \quad \xrightarrow{O_3} \quad \xrightarrow[Zn]{H_2O} \quad -\overset{|}{C}=O \quad + \quad O=\overset{|}{C}-$$

        Alkene

Cleavage products: aldehydes and ketones

    As can be seen, in the cleavage products a doubly bonded oxygen is found attached to each of the originally doubly bonded carbons. Knowing the structure of the cleavage products allows one to work back to the structure of the alkene or olefin. Since compound A gives rise to the cleavage products below,

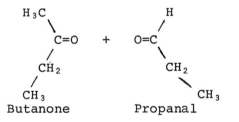

        Butanone   Propanal

unknown A has the following carbon skeletal structure:

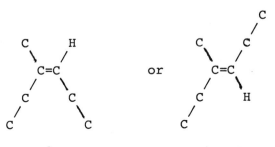

        cis   trans

211

Therefore, compound A can be either cis or trans-3-methyl-3-hexene.

POLYMERIZATION

Give the structure of the monomer from which each of the following polymers would most likely be made:
(a) Orlon (fibers, fabrics), ∿CH₂CH(CN)CH₂CH(CN)∿;
(b) Saran (packaging film, seat covers) ∿CH₂CCl₂CH₂CCl₂ ∿;
(c) Teflon (chemically resistant articles), ∿CF₂CF₂CF₂CF₂∿.

Solution: Each of the polymers indicated results from a process called polymerization. It may be defined as the joining together of many small molecules to make large molecules. The compound made up of many smaller units is termed the polymer, whereas the simple compounds from which polymers are made are referred to as monomers.

Polymerization requires the presence of a minute amount of initiator. Peroxides serve as initiators by breaking down to form a free radical. The free radical adds across the double bond of an alkene, which creates another radical. This radical then can add to another alkene to create a still larger radical, and so on. This type of sequence is known as chain-reaction polymerization and can be illustrated as follows:

Peroxide $\longrightarrow$ rad·

Rad· + CH₂═CH $\longrightarrow$ RadCH₂─CH·
                | |
                R   R

RadCH₂-CH· + CH₂=CH $\longrightarrow$ RadCH₂-CH-CH₂-CH·
        | | | |
        R   R   R   R

This continues until termination, such as the union of two radicals, that consume but do not generate radicals.

Hence, to find the monomer that generates a polymer, look for the sequence that constantly repeats; this sequence represents the smallest building block, the alkene monomer, which adds to others with the help of the radical initiators.

(a) Orlon, ∿CH₂CH(CN)CH₂CH(CN)∿. The repeating sequence is (by inspection) CH₂CH(CN). The monomer must be CH₂=CH-CN, acrylonitrile.

(b) Saran, ∿CH₂CCl₂CH₂CCl₂∿. Since the repeating sequence is CH₂CCl₂, the monomer must be CH₂=CCl₂, 1,1-dichloro-ethene.

(c) Teflon, $\sim\!\!CF_2CF_2CF_2CF_2\!\!\sim$. Since the repeating sequence is CF_2CF_2, the monomer can only be $CF_2{=}CF_2$, tetrafluoro-ethylene.

ALKYLATION

● **PROBLEM** 6-38

When ethylene is alkylated by isobutane in the presence of acid, there is obtained not neohexane, $(CH_3)_3CCH_2CH_3$, but chiefly 2,3-dimethylbutane. Account in detail for the formation of this product.

<u>Solution:</u>   This problem can be solved by a consideration of the mechanism of alkylation and the rearrangement of carbonium ions through an alkyl and/or hydride shift.

Alkylation involves three basic steps. The first two steps are identical to the dimerization reaction, while the 3rd step involves a carbonium ion (that is, a group of atoms that contains a carbon atom bearing only six electrons so that it possesses a positive charge) abstraction of a hydrogen atom with its pair of electrons (a hydride ion) from a molecule of alkane.

Addition of acid in the presence of the alkene ethylene results in the formation of ethyl cation, a carbonium ion, as shown:

$$CH_2{=}CH_2 \xrightarrow{\ H^+\ } CH_3{-}CH_2{}^+$$

    Ethylene   Ethyl cation

Carbonium ions undergo reactions that provide electrons to complete the octet of the positively charged carbon atom. Hence, one reaction that $CH_3{-}CH_2{}^+$ can undergo is to abstract a hydride ion from isobutane,

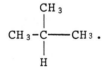

It does this in a manner so that the most stable carbonium is obtained. (Remember, the stability of carbonium ions is $3°{>}2°{>}1°{>}CH_3{}^+$.) The abstraction of the hydride ion can be illustrated as follows:

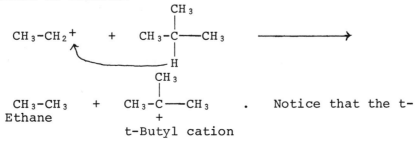

213

butyl cation is a 3° carbonium ion and, therefore, the most stable.

What will the t-butyl cation do? As mentioned, the carbonium wants to complete its octet. The carbon-carbon double bond of ethylene is an excellent electron source to complete its octet, so that the carbonium ion may go there in quest of electrons as shown:

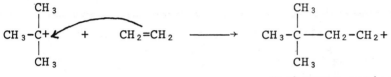

Neohexane cation

A new carbonium ion is formed. Now, if neohexane had been produced, it would have resulted from the cation abstracting a hydride ion from isobutane, which would, in turn, produce the t-butyl cation to start the entire cycle over again:

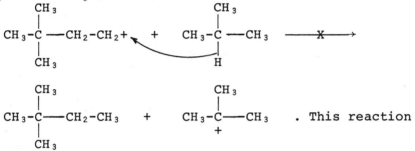

Neohexane

does NOT occur. The reason can be found from inspection of the neohexane cation; it is a primary carbonium ion. This is not a very stable carbonium. By a 1,2 shift of a hydrogen and alkyl group it can yield a more stable carbonium, a tertiary one as shown:

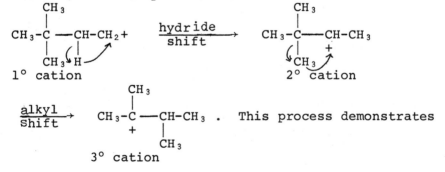

carbonium ion rearrangement. The rule to note is that if a 1,2 shift of hydrogen or alkyl can form a more stable carbonium ion, then such a rearrangement will occur.

The 3° cation, $CH_3-\overset{\overset{\displaystyle CH_3}{|}}{\underset{+}{C}}-\overset{\overset{\displaystyle }{}}{\underset{\underset{\displaystyle CH_3}{|}}{CH}}-CH_3$, can now abstract

the hydride ion from isobutane to produce the 2,3-di-
methylbutane. This reaction also produces the t-butyl
cation, which continues the chain.

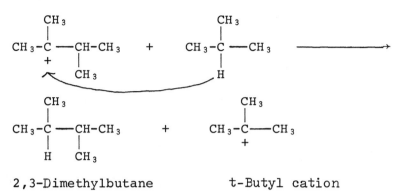

2,3-Dimethylbutane   t-Butyl cation

• **PROBLEM** 6-39

Using only isobutene and any inorganic reagents synthesize
2,2,4-trimethylpentane.

Solution: 2,2,4-trimethylpentane $\begin{pmatrix} & CH_3 & H & CH_3 \\ & | & | & | \\ H_3C-C & -C & -C-CH_3 \\ & | & | & | \\ & CH_3 & H & H \end{pmatrix}$ can

be made from isobutene $\begin{pmatrix} CH_3-C=CH_2 \\ | \\ CH_3 \end{pmatrix}$ by performing a di-

merization reaction followed by hydrogenation.

   Dimerization is a reaction that allows one to obtain
higher molecular weights of alkene than the starting
material. Carbonium ion mechanism explains the formation
of a dimer.

Step 1: Acid is added to isobutene to form the most stable
carbonium ion.

$$
\begin{array}{ccc}
CH_3 & & CH_3 \\
| & & | \\
CH_3-C=CH_2 + H^+ \text{ (acid)} & \rightarrow & CH_3-C-CH_3 \\
& & + \\
\end{array}
$$

      The acid adds across the double bond of isobutene
to give a 3° carbonium ion (i.e., one with 3 alkyl groups
attached to the positive-charged carbon) rather than
      CH_3
      |
CH_3-C-CH_2+, which is a 1° carbonium ion (i.e., one with
      H

1 alkyl group attached to the positive-charged carbon). A

3° carbonium ion is more stable than a 2° or 1° carbonium for the alkyl groups stabilize the charge by feeding in electrons.

Step 2: The 3° carbonium ion can now add to another isobutene in a dimerization by electrophilic addition:

$$CH_3\overset{\displaystyle CH_3}{\underset{\displaystyle CH_3}{-\overset{|}{\underset{|}{C}}+}} \ + \ CH_2=\overset{\displaystyle CH_3}{\overset{|}{C}}-CH_3 \ \rightarrow \ CH_3-\overset{\displaystyle CH_3}{\underset{\displaystyle CH_3}{\overset{|}{\underset{|}{C}}}}-CH_2-\overset{CH_3}{\underset{+}{\overset{|}{C}}}-CH_3$$

A pair of electrons is donated by the pi cloud of isobutene to the t-butyl cation, resulting in a dimer. Again,

$$CH_3-\overset{\displaystyle CH_3}{\underset{\displaystyle CH_3}{\overset{|}{\underset{|}{C}}}}-CH_2-\overset{CH_3}{\underset{+}{\overset{|}{C}}}-CH_3 \quad \text{is formed, not} \quad CH_3-\overset{\displaystyle CH_3}{\underset{\displaystyle CH_3}{\overset{|}{\underset{|}{C}}}}\!\!-\!\!\overset{\displaystyle CH_3}{\underset{\displaystyle CH_3}{\overset{|}{\underset{|}{C}}}}-CH_2+$$

due to the fact that a 3° carbonium ion is more stable than a 2° carbonium ion.

Step 3: $CH_3-\overset{\displaystyle CH_3}{\underset{\displaystyle CH_3}{\overset{|}{\underset{|}{C}}}}-CH_2-\overset{CH_3}{\underset{+}{\overset{|}{C}}}-CH_3$ can eliminate a proton (H$^+$) to

form $CH_3-\overset{\displaystyle CH_3}{\underset{\displaystyle CH_3}{\overset{|}{\underset{|}{C}}}}-CH=\overset{CH_3}{\overset{|}{C}}-CH_3$, 2,4,4-trimethyl-2-pentene. (2,4,4-trimethyl-1-pentene is also formed, but only in minor amounts since the other alkene is more stable.)

From 2,4,4 -trimethyl-2-pentene, 2,2,4-trimethylpentane is obtained by a hydrogenation reaction:

$$CH_3-\overset{\displaystyle CH_3}{\underset{\displaystyle CH_3}{\overset{|}{\underset{|}{C}}}}-CH=\overset{CH_3}{\overset{|}{C}}-CH_3 \ + \ H_2 \ \xrightarrow{\text{catalyst}} \ CH_3-\overset{\displaystyle CH_3}{\underset{\displaystyle CH_3}{\overset{|}{\underset{|}{C}}}}-CH_2-\overset{CH_3}{\underset{H}{\overset{|}{C}}}-CH_3$$

SYNTHESIS

• PROBLEM 6-40

Indicate how you would synthesize each of the following compounds from any one of the given organic starting materials and inorganic reagents. Specify reagents and the

reaction conditions. Starting materials: propylene, isobutylene.

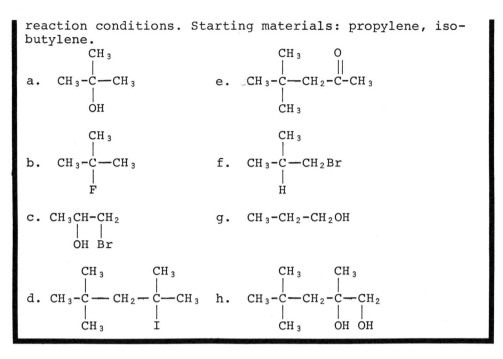

a. $CH_3-\overset{\overset{\displaystyle CH_3}{|}}{\underset{\underset{\displaystyle OH}{|}}{C}}-CH_3$

e. $CH_3-\overset{\overset{\displaystyle CH_3}{|}}{\underset{\underset{\displaystyle CH_3}{|}}{C}}-CH_2-\overset{\overset{\displaystyle O}{||}}{C}-CH_3$

b. $CH_3-\overset{\overset{\displaystyle CH_3}{|}}{\underset{\underset{\displaystyle F}{|}}{C}}-CH_3$

f. $CH_3-\overset{\overset{\displaystyle CH_3}{|}}{\underset{\underset{\displaystyle H}{|}}{C}}-CH_2Br$

c. $CH_3\underset{\underset{\displaystyle OH}{|}}{CH}-\underset{\underset{\displaystyle Br}{|}}{CH_2}$

g. $CH_3-CH_2-CH_2OH$

d. $CH_3-\overset{\overset{\displaystyle CH_3}{|}}{\underset{\underset{\displaystyle CH_3}{|}}{C}}-CH_2-\overset{\overset{\displaystyle CH_3}{|}}{\underset{\underset{\displaystyle I}{|}}{C}}-CH_3$

h. $CH_3-\overset{\overset{\displaystyle CH_3}{|}}{\underset{\underset{\displaystyle CH_3}{|}}{C}}-CH_2-\overset{\overset{\displaystyle CH_3}{|}}{\underset{\underset{\displaystyle OH}{|}}{C}}-\underset{\underset{\displaystyle OH}{|}}{CH_2}$

Solution: The chemistry in this problem involves the
reactions of the carbon-carbon double bond in alkenes.
Alkenes usually undergo electrophilic and free-radical
addition across the double bond; one-half of the double
bond is broken and two new groups are attached to give a
saturated compound.

The double bond of alkenes consists of a strong sigma
bond and a weak pi bond. The loosely held π (pi) electrons
are readily available to a reagent that seeks electrons.
Hence, the double bond acts as a source of electrons, that
is, it acts as a base. Compounds deficient in electrons
(acids), such as electrophilic reagents (which seek a pair
of electrons) and free radicals (which seek an electron),
react with the bond.

(a) To produce $CH_3-\overset{\overset{\displaystyle CH_3}{|}}{\underset{\underset{\displaystyle OH}{|}}{C}}-CH_3$, an alcohol, one could hydrate

isobutylene, $CH_3-\overset{\overset{\displaystyle CH_3}{|}}{C}=CH_2$, with H_2O and a 10% solution
of H_2SO_4 at 25°. The reaction can be written as follows:

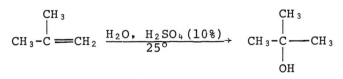

$$CH_3-\overset{\overset{\displaystyle CH_3}{|}}{C}=CH_2 \xrightarrow[25°]{H_2O, \ H_2SO_4 \ (10\%)} CH_3-\overset{\overset{\displaystyle CH_3}{|}}{\underset{\underset{\displaystyle OH}{|}}{C}}-CH_3$$

Water adds to the more reactive alkenes in the presence of
acids to yield alcohols.

217

Note: The addition of H_2O follows Markovnikov's rule, which may be stated as follows: in the addition of HX to an un-symmetrical carbon-carbon double bond, the hydrogen of HX goes to that carbon of the double bond that carries the greater number of hydrogens. This rule is by no means universal, but in this problem it applies. In

$$CH_3-\overset{\overset{\displaystyle CH_3}{|}}{C}=\overset{*}{C}H_2,$$ the starred carbon has two hydrogens, whereas the other carbon involved in the double bond has no attached hydrogens. Hence, the hydrogen of HOH adds to the CH_2, whereas OH adds to the other carbon.

(b) $$CH_3-\overset{\overset{\displaystyle CH_3}{|}}{\underset{\underset{\displaystyle F}{|}}{C}}-CH_3,$$ an alkyl halide, may be prepared from iso-

butylene by the addition of the hydrogen halide HF as shown:

$$CH_3-\overset{\overset{\displaystyle CH_3}{|}}{C}=CH_2 \quad \xrightarrow[-60°]{HF} \quad CH_3-\overset{\overset{\displaystyle CH_3}{|}}{\underset{\underset{\displaystyle F}{|}}{C}}-CH_3$$

The reaction follows Markovnikov's rule. A low temperature is used to reduce polymerization.

(c) To synthesize $CH_3\underset{\underset{\displaystyle OH}{|}}{C}H-\underset{\underset{\displaystyle Br}{|}}{C}H_2$, one may start with propylene,

$CH_3CH=CH_2$, and allow halohydrin formation to occur with Br and NaOH at 25°. Addition of bromine (or chlorine) with water or sodium hydroxide results in compounds containing halogen and hydroxyl groups on adjacent carbon atoms. The reaction is:

$$CH_3CH=CH_2 \quad \xrightarrow[25°]{Br_2,\ NaOH} \quad CH_3\underset{\underset{\displaystyle OH}{|}}{C}H-\underset{\underset{\displaystyle Br}{|}}{C}H_2$$

The bromine is attached to the terminal carbon, not the middle one, for if the mechanism of this reaction is studied, the initial addition of bromine in this fashion yields the more stable carbonium ion, a secondary cation. If the bromine had added to the middle carbon, a primary carbonium would have been produced. The order of stability of carbonium ions is $3°>2°>1°$, so that the terminal addition of bromine is favored.

(d) $$CH_3-\overset{\overset{\displaystyle CH_3}{|}}{\underset{\underset{\displaystyle CH_3}{|}}{C}}-CH_2-\overset{\overset{\displaystyle CH_3}{|}}{\underset{\underset{\displaystyle I}{|}}{C}}-CH_3 \qquad$$ can be synthesized from the

218

starting material isobutylene in two steps. In the first step, a 60% H₂SO₄ solution is added to isobutylene at 70°. This results in polymeration as indicated:

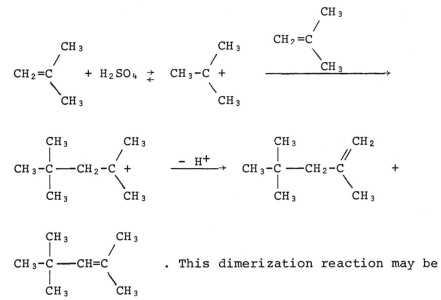

. This dimerization reaction may be described in the following way: a proton from the acid, H₂SO₄, adds to the alkene to yield the most stable carbonium ion. Then another isobutylene molecule donates an electron pair to the cation, forming a larger cation. This carbonium can then lose a hydrogen ion from either side of the positively charged carbon to obtain two products. (See above.)

In the second step, the hydrogen halide, HI, is added to either one of the above products to obtain

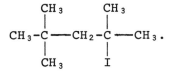

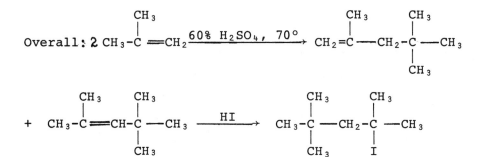

219

(e) $CH_3-\underset{\underset{CH_3}{|}}{\overset{\overset{CH_3}{|}}{C}}-CH_2-\overset{\overset{O}{\|}}{C}-CH_3$, a ketone, may be produced by starting

with isobutylene and allowing it to undergo dimerization
in 60% H_2SO_4 at 70° in the same reaction as illustrated in
step 1 of part (d). One obtains, as indicated in the previ-
ous section, $CH_2=\overset{\overset{CH_3}{|}}{C}-CH_2-\underset{\underset{CH_3}{|}}{\overset{\overset{CH_3}{|}}{C}}-CH_3$. To obtain the ketone, a

reaction must be performed on this substance that yields a
carbonyl group, C=O. Such a reaction is ozonization. Carbon-
carbon double bonds may be cleaved with ozone (O_3) and then
Zn and H_2O into aldehydes and ketones as illustrated:

$$-\overset{|}{C}=\overset{|}{C}- \xrightarrow{O_3} \xrightarrow[Zn]{H_2O} -\overset{|}{C}=O \quad + \quad O=\overset{|}{C}- \text{ . Consequently,}$$

aldehydes & ketones

to produce the desired product, perform ozonolysis as
illustrated:

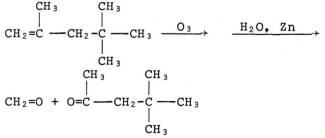

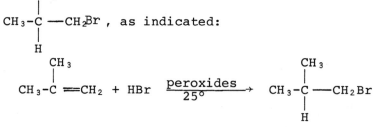

(f) Using the starting material isobutylene and adding HBr
in the presence of peroxides at 25° gives the desired product,
$CH_3-\underset{\underset{H}{|}}{\overset{\overset{CH_3}{|}}{C}}-CH_2Br$, as indicated:

$$CH_3-\overset{\overset{CH_3}{|}}{C}=\!\!=CH_2 + HBr \xrightarrow[25°]{\text{peroxides}} CH_3-\underset{\underset{H}{|}}{\overset{\overset{CH_3}{|}}{C}}-CH_2Br$$

It appears that this reaction violates Markovnikov's rule,
for the hydrogen of HBr does not add to the carbon with the
greatest number of hydrogens. The explanation lies in the
mechanism of the reaction. It is typical of free-radical
addition. The peroxides decompose to free-radicals. The
free radical abstracts hydrogen from HBr to form a bromine
atom, which, in turn, adds to the double bond of the alkene,
and so converts the alkene into a free radical. The stability of free radicals is 3°>2°>1° $CH_3\cdot$. Now examine the

free radicals formed when the bromine atom adds to isobutylene:

$$CH_3-\underset{\underset{CH_3}{|}}{C}=CH_2 \quad \xrightarrow{Br\cdot} \quad CH_3-\underset{\underset{\cdot}{|}}{\underset{\underset{}{|}}{C}}\overset{\overset{CH_3}{|}}{}-CH_2Br, \text{ a } 2° \text{ free radical is}$$

obtained. Now, if the Br· had added in the other fashion:

$$CH_3-\underset{\underset{CH_3}{|}}{C}=CH_2 \quad \xrightarrow{Br\cdot} \quad CH_3-\underset{\underset{Br}{|}}{\overset{\overset{CH_3}{|}}{C}}-CH_2\cdot, \text{ a } 1° \text{ free radical}$$

would have been produced. From the order of free radical
stability given previously, we know that the 2° free
radical will be favored over the 1°. This explains the
anti-Markovnikov type of addition.

(g) $CH_3CH_2CH_2OH$ may be obtained directly from propylene
using B_2H_6 and H_2O_2 as shown:

$$CH_3CH=CH_2 \quad \xrightarrow[2\cdot\ H_2O_2,\ OH^-]{1\cdot\ B_2H_6} \quad CH_3CH_2CH_2OH$$

This reaction (termed hydroboration-oxidation) is an
excellent method of making alcohols of anti-Markovnikov
orientation. The addition of water to the carbon-carbon
double bond in anti-Markovnikov fashion probably occurs
because the boron group attaches first to the terminal
doubly bonded carbon to give the most stable transition
state. However, no carbonium ion is formed in this reaction.

(h) If one of the products from the dimerization reaction
of part (d) is used

$$\left(CH_3-\underset{\underset{CH_3}{|}}{\overset{\overset{CH_3}{|}}{C}}-CH_2-\overset{\overset{CH_3}{|}}{C}=CH_2 \right), \text{ then } CH_3-\underset{\underset{CH_3}{|}}{\overset{\overset{CH_3}{|}}{C}}-CH_2-\underset{\underset{OH}{|}}{\overset{\overset{CH_3}{|}}{C}}-\underset{\underset{OH}{|}}{CH_2}$$

may be obtained readily from it via a hydroxylation with
$KMnO_4$ and H_2O. $KMnO_4$ is an oxidizing reagent that reacts
with alkenes, under mild conditions, to give, as the overall result, addition of hydrogen peroxide as HO-OH. In
other words, a glycol results as shown:

$$\underset{\text{(alkene)}}{-\overset{|}{C}=\overset{|}{C}-} \quad \xrightarrow{\text{Cold } KMnO_4} \quad \underset{\underset{\text{(glycol)}}{OH\ OH}}{-\underset{|}{\overset{|}{C}}-\underset{|}{\overset{|}{C}}-}$$

(Note:This reaction may also be performed with peroxyformic
acid, HCO_2OH.) Hence, the synthesis to be performed is:

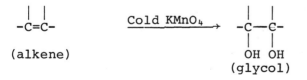

SPECTROSCOPY

Deduce the structures of the substances whose infrared
spectra are shown. Assign as many of the bands as you can
to specific stretching and bending vibrations.

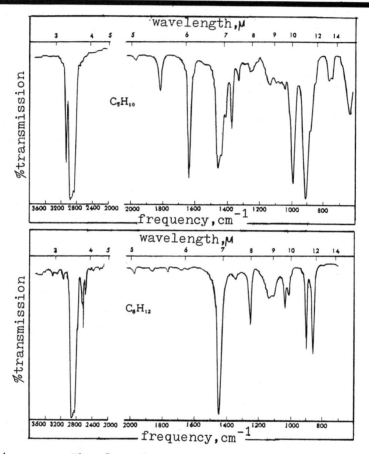

Solution: The formula C_5H_{10} may represent an alkene or
a cycloalkane. That it is an alkene may be determined from
the two strong bands between 800 and 1000 cm^{-1}. These bands
are characteristic of the out-of-plane bending of the
alkenes. The band near 1650 cm^{-1} may represent the carbon-
carbon stretching for double bonds. (This band may be
unreliable for it may disappear entirely for fairly sym-
metrically substituted alkenes.) Between 3000-3100 cm^{-1}
bands are present. The bands present in this location may
reflect the carbon-hydrogen stretching which occurs for
trigonal carbons, which denote alkenes (and aromatic rings).
This information strongly points to the presence of an
alkene, not a cycloalkane.

For more detail about the structure of the alkene,
concentrate on the 800-1000 cm^{-1} region. As mentioned, this
area is indicative of out-of-plane bending for alkenes.
The exact location of the bands reflects the nature and
number of substituents. The two bands are extremely close

to 910-920 cm^{-1} and 990-1000 cm^{-1}. This is typical of the structure RCH=CH$_2$. Therefore, R need only be determined. The CH=CH$_2$ accounts for all atoms except C$_3$H$_7$ in C$_5$H$_{10}$. C$_3$H$_7$, which represents R, can be arranged in two ways:

$$CH_3CH_2CH_2 \quad or \quad \overset{\overset{\textstyle H}{|}}{\underset{\underset{\textstyle CH_3}{|}}{CH_3-C}} \quad . \text{ So, RCH=CH}_2 \text{ can be either}$$

$$CH_3CH_2CH_2CH=CH_2 \quad or \quad \overset{\overset{\textstyle H}{|}}{\underset{\underset{\textstyle CH_3}{|}}{CH_3-C-CH=CH_2}}. \quad \text{If the latter}$$

structure were the true one, then a characteristic band at 1170 cm^{-1} would be present to denote the existence of the isopropyl, $\overset{}{\underset{\underset{\textstyle CH_3}{|}}{CH_3C-H}}$.

What is present is a band 1430-1470 cm^{-1} that indicates carbon-hydrogen bending for methyl and methylene groups. Also, the small band at 1375 cm^{-1} confirms the methyl. R can only be CH$_3$CH$_2$CH$_2$, so that C$_5$H$_{10}$ is CH$_3$CH$_2$CH$_2$CH=CH$_2$, or 1-pentene.

The formula C$_6$H$_{12}$ may also represent an alkene or cycloalkane. However, this time the cycloalkane is the correct choice. The possibility of an alkene may be eliminated because there exists no band at 1650 cm^{-1} to denote carbon-carbon stretching of double bonds. Also, the band for out-of-plane bending is not present.

Between 2850 and 3000 cm^{-1} one finds the C-H stretching of alkanes. There must be methylene groups (-CH$_2$-) present because the band for their characteristic C-H bending is found at 1400 to 1470 cm^{-1}. When there are no alkyl substituents on the ring, the characteristic bending frequencies of methyl groups at 1380 cm^{-1} are absent. Such is the case here. If there are no alkyl substituents on the cycloalkane C$_6$H$_{12}$, the only possible structure is

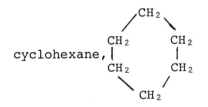

cyclohexane,

● **PROBLEM 6-42**

Deduce the structures of the substances whose n.m.r. spectra are shown. Analyze the spectra in as much detail as you can in terms of chemical shifts and spin-spin splitting.

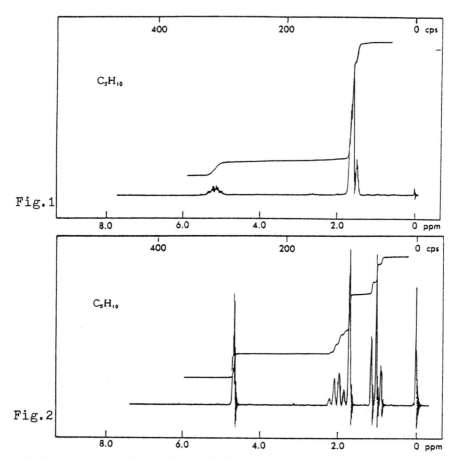

Fig.1

C_5H_{10}

Fig.2

C_5H_{10}

Solution: A review of the various aspects of the n.m.r. spectrum will aid in solving this problem. The number of signals provides information on the number of different kinds of protons in a molecule; the positions of the signals indicate something about the electronic environment of each kind of proton; the intensities of the signals tell how many protons of each kind are present; the splitting of a signal into several peaks gives information about the environment of a proton with respect to other, nearby protons.

In the first n.m.r. spectrum, the formula given, C_5H_{10}, fits the general formula for an alkene or cyclo-alkane (C_nH_{2n}). To distinguish between the two, try to locate the chemical shift of the vinylic proton (C=C-H) that would be indicative of the double bond of the alkene. From a table of characteristic proton shifts, absorption for a vinylic proton should occur between 4.6 and 5.9 ppm. Indeed, in this area absorption is seen. Hence, C_5H_{10} is probably an alkene. At approximately 1.8 ppm, an intense peak can be seen. This chemical shift often derives from allylic protons (C=C-CH_3). The intensity suggests a larger number of such protons is present. (Recall, the area under an n.m.r. signal is directly proportional to the number of protons giving rise to the signal.) At this point, the skeletal structure must be C=C-CH_3 or C=C-CH_3.

H	H

Note that in these structures 3 carbons and 4 hydrogens
have been accounted for. This leaves only 2 carbons and
6 hydrogens to determine. The possibilities are as follows:
C_2H_6 could represent two methyl groups, each of them
attached to a carbon that participates in the double bond.
This would give rise to (from either C=C-CH$_3$ or C=C-CH$_3$)

$$\begin{matrix} & | & & | \\ & H & & H \end{matrix}$$

$$\begin{matrix} CH_3 \\ | \\ CH_3-C=C-CH_3 \\ | \\ H \end{matrix} \; ; \quad \text{the other possibility is that one of the}$$

hydrogens of C_2H_6 is a vinyl one, with C_2H_5 representing
the ethyl group as shown:

$$\begin{matrix} H \\ | \\ H-C=C-CH_3 \\ | \\ CH_2CH_3 \end{matrix}$$

Examination of the first spectrum eliminates

$$\begin{matrix} H_2C=C-CH_3 \\ | \\ CH_2CH_3 \end{matrix} \quad \text{to leave} \quad \begin{matrix} CH_3-CH=C-CH_3 \\ | \\ CH_3 \end{matrix}$$

as the structure. To understand why, look at the spin-spin
splitting. The protons of the ethyl group are adjacent and
non-equivalent, so that if H$_2$C=C-CH$_3$ were correct,

$$\begin{matrix} | \\ CH_2CH_3 \end{matrix}$$

the typical three-four spin-spin splitting for ethyl should
be seen. It is not. In fact, the spin-spin splitting indi-

$$\begin{matrix} CH_3 \\ | \end{matrix}$$

cated could only support CH$_3$-C=CH-CH$_3$ as the structure.
The vinylic proton is split into a 1:3:3:1 quartet by the
adjacent methyl. It is somewhat obscured by long range
effects. Half of the doublet expected for the terminal
methyl falls under the (CH$_3$)$_2$ resonances; the other half
is the low part on the high field side of the 1.8 ppm peak.

It turns out that the second n.m.r. spectrum with

$$\begin{matrix} CH_2CH_3 \\ | \end{matrix}$$

formula C_5H_{10} is H$_2$C=C-CH$_3$, the structure rejected in the
first spectrum. As before, the chemical shifts indicate
the existence of allylic and vinylic protons. This time,
however, the typical three-four ethyl pattern shows at
1.1 and 2.0 ppm to establish the structure

$$\begin{matrix} H_2C=C-CH_3 \\ | \\ CH_2CH_3 \end{matrix} \quad \text{as the correct one.}$$

225

CHAPTER 7

ALKYNES

• PROBLEM 7-1

What is an alkyne?

Solution: An alkyne is an organic compound distinguished by the carbon-carbon triple bond. The simplest member of the alkyne family is acetylene, with the formula C_2H_2 or $H-C\equiv C-H$. The general formula for alkynes is C_NH_{2N-2}.

The alkynes are named according to two systems:

(1) They are considered to be derived from acetylene by replacement of one or both hydrogen atoms by alkyl groups. For example,

(a) $HC\equiv CCH_2CH_3$ — ethylacetylene

(b) $CH_3C\equiv CCH_3$ — dimethylacetylene

(2) For more complicated alkynes the IUPAC names are used. The rules are exactly the same as for the naming of alkenes, except that the ending -yne replaces -ene. The parent structure is the longest continuous chain that contains the triple bond, and the positions both of substituents and of the triple bond are indicated by numbers. The triple bond is given the number of the first triply-bonded carbon encountered, starting from the end of the chain nearest the triple bond. For example,

$$\begin{array}{c} CH_3-C\equiv C-\underset{\displaystyle CH_3}{\underset{|}{CH}}-CH_3 \end{array}$$

4-methyl-2-pentyne

• PROBLEM 7-2

How many sites of unsaturation does a compound with the formula $C_8H_{12}O_2$ contain?

Solution: Carbon compounds which have no multiple bonds
are defined as saturated compounds. They can be distinguished from unsaturated compounds which contain double
bonds, triple bonds, or rings.

If it is first assumed that the compound is saturated,
then we can predict the number of hydrogen atoms that must
be present to meet this assumption. This is calculated by
using the general formula of a saturated compound, C_nH_{2n+2}.
Since the compound in question possesses 8 carbon atoms,
we expect $2(8) + 2$ or 18 hydrogen atoms to be present if
the compound is saturated. But in $C_8H_{12}O_2$ only 12 such
atoms are present. The deficiency in hydrogen atoms =
$18 - 12 = 6$.

The degree of unsaturation is the number of double
bonds, triple bonds, or rings present in a particular

compound. For example, C_2H_6 (Ethane), written as $H-\overset{\overset{H}{|}}{C}-\overset{\overset{H}{|}}{C}-H$,

is saturated, where C_2H_4 (Ethene), structural formula

$H-\overset{}{\underset{\underset{H}{|}}{C}} = \overset{}{\underset{\underset{H}{|}}{C}} - H$, has one double bond (one site of unsatura-

tion) and two hydrogen atoms less than its fully saturated
counterpart. So, two hydrogen atoms are associated with
every site of unsaturation. Since each site of unsaturation
is associated with the loss of two hydrogen atoms, the
number of sites of unsaturation for $C_8H_{12}O_2$ must be
$6 \div 2$ or 3.

PREPARATION

• PROBLEM 7-3

Write equations for all steps in the manufacture of
acetylene starting from limestone and coal.

Solution: Acetylene can be prepared by the action of
water on calcium carbide (CaC_2), which itself is prepared
by the reaction between calcium oxide and coke at very high
temperatures. The calcium oxide and coke are in turn
obtained from limestone and coal, respectively. Acetylene
is thus obtained by a few steps from water, coal, and
limestone as shown below:

Coal $\longrightarrow$ Coke $\Big\rbrace$ $\xrightarrow{2,000°C}$ CaC_2 $\xrightarrow{H_2O}$ $H-C{\equiv}C-H$

Limestone $\longrightarrow$ CaO

Prepare an alkyne from each alkene precursor by the de-hydrohalogenation of alkyl dihalides method.

(a) $CH_3CH=CH_2$

propene

(b) $\overset{\displaystyle CH_3}{\overset{\displaystyle |}{CH_3CH_2CHCH=CH_2}}$

3-methyl-1-pentene

Solution: A carbon-carbon triple bond is formed in the same way as a double bond: elimination of atoms or groups from two adjacent carbons. The groups eliminated and the reagents used are essentially the same as in the preparation of alkenes.

In the first reaction of the synthesis, either Br_2 or Cl_2 is bubbled through the precursor alkene yielding an

alkyl dihalide, $\overset{\displaystyle H\ H}{\underset{\displaystyle X\ X}{-\overset{|}{\underset{|}{C}}-\overset{|}{\underset{|}{C}}-}}$. This product is then treated with

an alcohol-potassium hydroxide solution to form a vinyl

halide, $\overset{\displaystyle H}{\underset{\displaystyle X}{-\overset{|}{C}=\overset{|}{C}-}}$. Sodamide ($NaNH_2$) is added to the vinyl

halide to produce a carbon-carbon triple bond, an alkyne. Overall, the synthetic preparation is:

$$\overset{H\ H}{\underset{}{-\overset{|}{C}=\overset{|}{C}-}} \xrightarrow{X_2} \overset{H\ H}{\underset{X\ X}{-\overset{|}{\underset{|}{C}}-\overset{|}{\underset{|}{C}}-}} \xrightarrow{KOH\ (alc)} \overset{H}{\underset{X}{-\overset{|}{C}=\overset{|}{C}-}} \xrightarrow{NaNH_2} -C\equiv C-$$

Vinyl halides are very unreactive so that under mild conditions the dehydrohalogenation stops here. Only under more vigorous conditions - use of a strong base ($NaNH_2$) is the alkyne generated.

Employing the general reaction of synthesis, problems (a) and (b) can be solved.

(a) $CH_3CH=CH_2 \xrightarrow{Br_2} \overset{}{\underset{Br\ Br}{CH_3CH-CH_2}} \xrightarrow{KOH\ (alc)} CH_3CH=CHBr \xrightarrow{NaNH_2}$

propene   1,2-dibromo-propane   1-bromo-1-propene

Propyne $CH_3C\equiv CH$

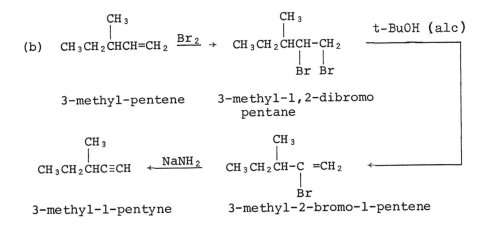

(b) CH$_3$CH$_2$CHCH=CH$_2$ $\xrightarrow{Br_2}$ CH$_3$CH$_2$CHCH-CH$_2$ with CH$_3$ on top carbon

3-methyl-pentene   3-methyl-1,2-dibromo pentane

CH$_3$CH$_2$CHC≡CH $\xleftarrow{NaNH_2}$ CH$_3$CH$_2$CH-C=CH$_2$

3-methyl-1-pentyne   3-methyl-2-bromo-1-pentene

ADDITION REACTIONS

● **PROBLEM** 7-5

Describe the reduction of alkynes to obtain an alkene.

Solution: Reduction of an alkyne to form an alkene is the conversion of the carbon-carbon triple bond of the alkyne to the carbon-carbon double bond of the alkene. Unless the triple bond is at the end of the alkyne, the reaction will yield either a cis-alkene or a trans-alkene. The predominant isomer depends entirely upon the reducing agent used. Examples will make this concept clearer.

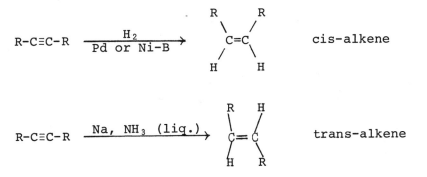

By reduction of alkynes with sodium in liquid ammonia, the trans-alkene will predominate. On the other hand, almost entirely cis-alkene (as high as 98%) is obtained by hydrogenation of alkynes with specially prepared palladium called Lindlar's catalyst or a nickel boride called P-2 catalyst.

● **PROBLEM** 7-6

(a) Write the equation for the two-stage addition of bromine to 2-butyne. (b) How will the first two bromine atoms affect the reactivity of the double bond? (c) How will this in-

Solution: (a) The addition reactions of alkynes are
similar to addition to alkenes, except that two molecules
of reagent can be consumed for each triple bond. In the
addition reactions, it is possible, by proper selection
of conditions, to limit reaction to the first stage of
addition, formation of alkenes. The addition of halogens to
alkynes may be generalized as:

$$-C\equiv C- \xrightarrow[\text{(first stage)}]{X_2} \underset{X\ X}{-C=C-} \xrightarrow[\text{(second stage)}]{X_2} \underset{X\ X}{\overset{X\ X}{-C-C-}} ,$$

where X_2 = Cl_2, Br_2.

     This means that the two stage addition of bromine to
2-butyne becomes:

$$H_3C-C\equiv C-CH_3 \xrightarrow{Br_2} \underset{Br\ Br}{H_3C-C=C-CH_3} \xrightarrow{Br_2} \underset{Br\ Br}{\overset{Br\ Br}{H_3C-C-C-CH_3}} .$$

     (b) The first two bromines decrease the reactivity of
the double bond to further addition. To understand this,
recall that addition of halogen proceeds via an intermediate
carbonium ion. Halogens tend to withdraw electrons so that
the bromine atoms would intensify the positive charge and
destabilize the carbonium ion.

     (c) Since the 2-butyne lacks the electron-withdrawing
halogens, it should favorably compete with the 2,3-dibromo-
2-butene $\left(\underset{Br\ Br}{H_3C-C=C-CH_3} \right)$ for halogen. The 2-butyne

carbonium ion will be more stable relative to the carbonium
ion of 2,3-dibromo-2-butene. In other words, the dibromo
compound is made a poor competitor.

     (d) If the 2-butyne reagent is added in excess, then
at any one moment it should predominate over the dibromo
compound. In this way, there is little dibromo compound
relative to 2-butyne to continue to react past the first
stage.

     (e) In order to keep 2-butyne in excess throughout the
reaction, it would be advisable to drip Br_2 into a solution
of 2-butyne.

Reaction of 4-octyne with n-propylamine, $CH_3CH_2CH_2NH_2$, produces two enamines in unequal amounts. Explain.

Solution: Alkynes can participate in nucleophilic addition reactions. When amines are added to alkynes, enamines, nitrogen analogs of enols, are produced. The general reaction is shown below:

$$R-C \equiv C-R \quad + \quad R'NH_2 \longrightarrow RCH = C-R$$
$$\underset{\text{(an enamine)}}{\overset{|}{NHR'}}$$

When 4-octyne ($CH_3CH_2CH_2-C\equiv C-CH_2CH_2CH_3$) is added to n-propylamine ($CH_3CH_2CH_2NH_2$), two enamines result. This can be accounted for on the basis of   Z-E   geometric isomerism. The two isomers may be written as follows:

$$\begin{array}{cc} C_3H_7 \quad NHC_3H_7 \\ \diagdown \quad | \\ C=C \\ \diagup \quad | \\ H \quad C_3H_7 \\ \text{Z-isomer} \end{array} \qquad \begin{array}{cc} C_3H_7 \quad C_3H_7 \\ \diagdown \quad | \\ C=C \\ \diagup \quad | \\ H \quad NHC_3H_7 \\ \text{E-isomer} \end{array}$$

The E-isomer should predominate over the Z-isomer on the basis of steric hinderance. The NHC_3H_7 is bulkier than the C_3H_7, so that there exists less stability when the C_3H_7 and NHC_3H_7 are located on the same side of the double bond(Z)as compared to when the C_3H_7 and C_3H_7 are located on the same side of the double bond (E).

Give structures and names of the organic products expected from the reaction of l-butyne with the following:

(a) 1 mole H_2, Ni   (b) 2 moles Br_2 (c) 2 moles HCl

Solution: Addition of hydrogen to alkynes leads to the formation of alkenes, if reaction can be limited to the first stage of addition. Two molecules of reagent can be consumed for each triple bond. If the reaction proceeds in two stages, alkanes are formed. In (a), only one mole of H_2 is added, so that the alkene results.

(a) $CH_3CH_2C\equiv CH \quad + \quad H_2 \xrightarrow{\text{Ni}} CH_3CH_2CH=CH_2$

            l-butyne   1-butene

Alkynes react with halogens by addition reactions also. In (b), two moles of the halogen Br_2 react with the triple bond to form a tetrahalide. The reaction scheme appears as:

(b) $CH_3CH_2C{\equiv}CH$ + 2 Br_2 → $CH_3CH_2\underset{\underset{\displaystyle Br}{|}}{\overset{\overset{\displaystyle Br}{|}}{C}}-\underset{\underset{\displaystyle Br}{|}}{\overset{\overset{\displaystyle Br}{|}}{C}}-H$

        1-butyne   1,1,2,2-tetrabromobutane

Reaction (c) involves the addition of hydrogen halide. The general equation for the reaction is:

$$RC{\equiv}CH \xrightarrow{HX} \underset{\underset{\displaystyle X}{|}}{R-C{=}CH_2} \xrightarrow{HX} \underset{\underset{\displaystyle X}{|}}{R\overset{\overset{\displaystyle X}{|}}{C}-CH_3}$$

Hydrogen chloride, bromide, or iodide adds to alkynes in two steps. The reaction may be stopped after the first step to give the vinyl halide, or a second molecule of HX may be allowed to react to give a gem-dihalide. (The prefix "Gem." from the latin geminus, twin, signifies that both halogens are on the same carbon.)

The reaction of 1-butyne with hydrogen chloride follows:

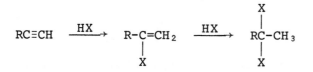

$$CH_3CH_2C{\equiv}CH \xrightarrow{HCl} \underset{\underset{\displaystyle Cl}{|}}{CH_3CH_2C{=}CH_2} \xrightarrow{HCl} \underset{\underset{\displaystyle Cl}{|}}{CH_3CH_2\overset{\overset{\displaystyle Cl}{|}}{C}-CH_3}$$

1-butyne   2-chloro-1-   2,2-dichloro-
                      butene   butane

• **PROBLEM** 7-9

Acetylene has an acid ionization constant (K_A) of ∿ 10^{-22}.

(a) Calculate the concentration of acetylide ion expected to be present in a 14 M solution of potassium hydroxide that is 0.01 M in acetylene (assuming ideal solutions).

(b) Outline a practical method (or methods) that you think might be suitable to determine an approximate experimental value of K_A for acetylene, remembering that water has K_A of about 10^{-14}.

(c) Would you expect H-C≡N to be a stronger acid than H-C≡C-H? Why?

Solution: (a) The acid ionization constant (K_A) for acetylene (HC≡CH) is determined by the ratio of the concentrations of the products to the concentrations of the reactants in the following equation:

$$HC \equiv CH \; \rightleftharpoons \; HC \equiv C^- \; + \; H^+ .$$

$$K_A = \frac{[HC \equiv C^-][H^+]}{[HC \equiv CH]} \sim 10^{-22} \qquad \text{(given)}$$

In the presence of potassium hydroxide,

$$HC \equiv CH \; + \; {}^-OH \; \rightleftharpoons \; H_2O \; + \; HC \equiv C^-$$

For this reaction, the K_A becomes

$$\frac{[H_2O][HC \equiv C^-]}{[HC \equiv CH][{}^-OH]} \;, \text{ which can be rewritten as}$$

$$\frac{[H_2O][HC \equiv C^-][H^+]}{[H^+][OH^-][HC \equiv CH]} \;, \text{ where } \frac{[HC \equiv C^-][H^+]}{[HC \equiv CH]} \sim 10^{-22} .$$

The ionization constant for water is 10^{-14}. This means $[H^+][OH^-]$ is equal to 10^{-14}. Substituting this value in

$$\frac{[H_2O]\,10^{-22}}{[H^+][OH^-]} \;, \text{ we obtain } \frac{[H_2O]\,10^{-22}}{10^{-14}} \text{ or } [H_2O]\,10^{-8}$$

for the K_A of acetylene in potassium hydroxide.

Let X be the concentration of acetylide ion in KOH. If the initial concentration of acetylene is .01 M, then we have left .01 - X of acetylene at equilibrium. Likewise, 14 - X should be the concentration of hydroxide at equilibrium. Hence, the expression for K_A (ionization constant) can be written as $\dfrac{X\,(H_2O)}{(.01 - X)(14 - X)}$. From above, we calculated K_A to be equal to $[H_2O]\,10^{-8}$. Consequently,

$$\frac{X\,(H_2O)}{(.01 - X)(14 - X)} = (H_2O)\,10^{-8} \text{ or } \frac{X}{(.01 - X)(14 - X)} = 10^{-8}$$

Solving for X, X = 1.4×10^{-9} moles/liter, which is the concentration of acetylide ion.

(b) The ionization equilibria of very weak acids, such as acetylene, can only be measured in solvents which are less acidic than water. For example, ammonia, ether, or (possibly) hydrocarbons. The problem is that no solvent can usually be found in which a very weak acid ($K_A < 10^{-22}$) will dissociate significantly. This means the strengths of such acids are determined relative to one another by determining the position of the equilibrium. This measurement of relative acidities permits the assignment of approximate ionization constants to weak acids.

(c) We would expect $H-C \equiv N$ to be the stronger acid than $H-C \equiv C-H$ due to the greater electronegativity (tendency to attract electrons) of the nitrogen as compared to the carbon. As such, the cyanide ion ($^-C \equiv N$) possesses more stability than the acetylide ion ($^-C \equiv CH$).

Outline all steps in the synthesis of

(a)   1 -butyne   and   (b) 2-butyne

from acetylene using any needed organic or inorganic reagents.

Solution: Alkynes of chain length longer than two carbons can be formed from acetylene by using sodamide ($NaNH_2$) in ether and alkyl halides.

A triply-bonded carbon acts as a more electronegative element. As a result, hydrogen attached to triply-bonded carbon, as in acetylene, shows appreciable acidity. Hence, addition of $NaNH_2$ to acetylene produces sodium acetylide in an acid-base reaction as shown:

$$HC \equiv CH + NaNH_2 \xrightarrow{\text{ether}} HC \equiv C^- Na^+ + NH_3$$

(Sodium
Acetylide)

Sodium acetylide can react with alkyl halides in a substitution reaction to produce higher alkynes. The re-action involves substitution of acetylide ion for halide ion as shown:

Now, the acetylide ion could also have caused elimina-tion to give the alkene. The proportion of the elimination product increases as the structure of the alkyl halide is changed from primary to secondary to tertiary.

To synthesize 1-butyne, we add an ethyl halide, say ethyl bromide, to sodium acetylide as illustrated:

$$HC \equiv C^- Na^+ + CH_3CH_2Br \rightarrow HC \equiv C-CH_2CH_3 + NaBr$$

(1-butyne)

Since the alkyl halide is primary, the elimination re-action will be minimal.

The synthesis of 2-butyne is a little more complicated. The initial steps are, however, the same. We commence by re-acting acetylene with $NaNH_2$ in ether (or alternatively sodium in liquid ammonia) to give the sodium acetylide:

$$H-C \equiv C-H + NaNH_2 \xrightarrow{\text{ether}} H-C \equiv C^- Na^+ + NH_3$$

At this point, a methyl halide should be added. For example, methyl bromide. This results in the synthesis of propyne as shown:

$$H-C\equiv C^- \ Na^+ \ + \ CH_3Br \ \rightarrow \ H-C\equiv C-CH_3 \ + \ NaBr$$

(Propyne)

Propyne can be converted to the alkali metal acetylide by addition of $NaNH_2$ in ether:

$$H-C\equiv C-CH_3 \ + \ NaNH_2 \xrightarrow{\text{ether}} Na^+ \ ^-C\equiv C-CH_3 \ + \ NH_3$$

From this species, the 2-butyne is produced by the addition of methyl bromide.

$$CH_3-C\equiv C^- \ Na^+ \ + \ CH_3 \ Br \ \longrightarrow \ CH_3-C\equiv C-CH_3 \ + \ NaBr$$

(2-butyne)

● **PROBLEM 7-11**

Give the equations and mechanisms for the reactions of sodium methyl acetylide with:

(a) 1-bromobutane   (b) 2-bromobutane.

Solution: Sodium methyl acetylide ($CH_3C\equiv C:Na$) is the precursor in both reactions and involves the addition of a halogenated alkane. The expected product from each reaction is a longer chain alkyne, with the general mechanism appearing as:

$$CH_3C\equiv C:Na \ + R-X \ \rightarrow \ CH_3C\equiv C-R + Na^+ \ X^-$$

Since sodium methyl acetylide is the salt of the extremely weak acid, methyl acetylene, the acetylide ion is a stronger base, thus this reaction involves substitution of acetylide ion for halide ion. From this it can readily be seen that the metal ion, sodium, bonds to the released halide ion and the acetylide ion bonds to the alkyl group yielding a higher alkyne, plus a metal halide as the by-product.

The reactions and their mechanisms are:

(a) $CH_3C\equiv C:Na + CH_3CH_2CH_2CH_2-Br \rightarrow CH_3C\equiv CCH_2CH_2CH_2CH_3 \ +NaBr$

    sodium methyl   1-bromo-   2-heptyne
    acetylide   butane

(b) $CH_3C\equiv C:Na + CH_3CH_2CHCH_3 \rightarrow CH_3CH_2CHC\equiv C-CH_3 \ + \ NaBr$
                             Br   CH_3

    sodium   2-bromobutane   4-methyl-2-
    methyl   hexyne
    acetylide

SYNTHESIS

> Outline all steps in the synthesis of propyne from acetylene using any needed organic or inorganic reagents.

Solution: The synthesis should be the one that gives a reasonably pure product in reasonably good yield. The synthetic equation is as follows:

$$HC\equiv CH \xrightarrow{\text{NaNH}_2} Na\overset{+}{C}\equiv CH \xrightarrow{CH_3I} CH_3C\equiv CH$$

   (Acetylene)   (Propyne)

Alkynes of chain length longer than two carbons can be formed from acetylene by using sodamide ($NaNH_2$). Sodamide reacts with acetylene in an acid-base type of reaction. The hydrogen attached to the triply-bonded carbon shows appreciable acidity. Hence,

$$HC\equiv CH + Na^+ NH_2^- \rightleftharpoons HC\equiv C^- Na^+ + NH_3$$

Stronger   Stronger   Weaker   Weaker
 acid   base   base   acid
                        (Sodium acetylide)

Sodium acetylides react with primary alkyl halides in a substitution reaction to give alkynes of carbon skeleton greater than two. Hence, if methyl iodide is added to sodium acetylide, propyne results:

$$HC\equiv C^- Na^+ + CH_3I \rightarrow HC\equiv CCH_3 + NaI$$

                        Propyne

> Using propyne as the starting material, carry out the necessary reaction sequences to give the following products:
>
> (a) 2-butyne   (b) 2-butene
> (c) 2-bromobutane   (d) pentane.

Solution: In this set of reactions, propyne ($CH_3C\equiv CH$) is used as the precursor to obtain all of the various products desired.

Beginning with problem (a), the general reaction sequence is:

$$R-C\equiv CH \xrightarrow{\text{NaNH}_2} RC\equiv\overset{-+}{C}Na \xrightarrow{CH_3I} RC\equiv C-CH_3$$

where sodamide ($NaNH_2$) reacts with an alkyne ($R-C\equiv CH$) to produce a sodium alkyl acetylide $(RC\equiv\overset{-}{C}\overset{+}{Na})$. This intermediate reacts very well with primary alkyl halides, such as methyl iodide, to produce a longer chain alkyne. With the above concepts, the first synthesis proceeds as follows:

(a) $CH_3C\equiv CH$ $\xrightarrow{NaNH_2}$ $CH_3C\equiv\overset{-}{C}\overset{+}{Na}$ $\xrightarrow{CH_3I}$ $CH_3C\equiv C-CH_3$ + NaI

     Propyne   Sodium methyl   2-butyne
                          acetylide

In problem (b), 2-butene is desired, and is obtained by the same method as problem (a). The only modification is the addition of one mole of H_2 to 2-butyne across the triple bond in a catalytic hydrogenation reaction. The solution to (b) is as follows:

(b) $CH_3C\equiv CH$ $\xrightarrow{NaNH_2}$ $CH_3C\equiv\overset{-}{C}\overset{+}{Na}$ $\xrightarrow{CH_3I}$ $CH_3C\equiv CCH_3$ + NaI

     Propyne   Sodium methyl   2-butyne
                          acetylide

$$Ni \downarrow H_2$$

$$CH_3CH=CHCH_3$$

2-butene

Problem (c) can also be done the same way as syntheses (a) and (b) with the addition of one more reaction. This reaction is the addition of hydrogen bromide, HBr, across the carbon-carbon double bond of 2-butene.

(c) $CH_3C\equiv CH$ $\xrightarrow{NaNH_2}$ $CH_3C\equiv\overset{-}{C}\overset{+}{Na}$ $\xrightarrow{CH_3I}$ $CH_3C\equiv CCH_3$ + NaI

     Propyne   Sodium methyl   2-butyne
                          acetylide

$$\overset{Br}{\underset{|}{CH_3CHCH_2CH_3}} \xleftarrow{HBr} \quad Ni\downarrow H_2 \quad CH_3CH=CHCH_3$$

    2-bromobutane   2-butene

Problem (d) involves some of the same reagents as the first three syntheses. Ethyl iodide will be used in the place of methyl iodide. This reagent will add two carbons to the sodium methyl acetylide.

After the addition of the ethyl group, the product, 2-pentyne, can be hydrogenated to the corresponding alkane, pentane. Thus:

(d) $CH_3C\equiv CH$ $\xrightarrow{NaNH_2}$ $CH_3C\equiv \overset{-}{C}\overset{+}{N}a$ $\xrightarrow{CH_3CH_2I}$ $CH_3C\equiv CCH_2CH_3$ +NaI

　　　Propyne　　　　　　　Na methyl　　　　　　　　2-pentyne
　　　　　　　　　　　　acetylide

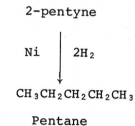

　　　　　　　　　　　　　　　　　　Ni $\Big|$ $2H_2$

　　　　　　　　　　　　　　　$CH_3CH_2CH_2CH_2CH_3$

　　　　　　　　　　　　　　　　　　Pentane

● **PROBLEM** 7-14

Outline all steps in the synthesis of propyne from each of
the following compounds, using any needed organic or inorganic reagents.

(a) 1,2-dibromopropane　　　(e) n-propyl alcohol
(b) propylene　　　　　　　　(f) 1,1-dichloropropane
(c) isopropyl bromide　　　(g) acetylene
(d) propane　　　　　　　　　(h) 1,1,2,2-tetrabromopropane.

<u>Solution:</u>　　(a) 1,2-dibromopropane:

```
  Br Br H
   |  |  |
H-C -C -C-H    C3H6Br2.
   |  |  |
   H  H  H
```

　　　Propyne can be prepared by introducing a triple bond
by eliminating two molecules of hydrogen bromide. The dehydrohalogenation proceeds in two steps. Sodium amide
$(\overset{+}{Na} \overset{-}{NH_2})$ in liquid ammonia is used to create the triple bond:

$$Br-CH_2-\underset{Br}{\overset{H}{\underset{|}{\overset{|}{C}}}}-CH_3 \rightarrow CH \overset{H}{=} \underset{Br}{\overset{|}{C}}-CH_3 + HBr \rightarrow CH\equiv CCH_3 + HBr.$$

(b)　propylene: $CH_3CH=CH_2$.

　　　As there is no direct way to change the double bond to
a triple bond it is however possible to produce the 1,2-
dibromopropane by brominating in the presence of carbon
tetrachloride and then proceeding in the same process outlined in (a).

　　　　$CH_3CH=CH_2 + Br_2$ $\xrightarrow{CCl_4}$ $CH_3CHBrCH_2Br$

　　　　　　　　　　　　　　　　　1,2-dibromopropane

(c) isopropyl bromide: $(CH_3)_2CHBr$.

Isopropyl bromide cannot be directly transformed to
propyne. Reacting with $Na\overset{+}{N}\overset{-}{H_2}$ would not give the desired

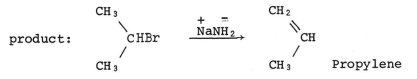

product: Propylene

However, propylene can be converted to propyne in the
synthesis given in part (b).

$$CH_3CH=CH_2 + Br_2 \rightarrow CH_3CHBrCH_2Br$$

$$CH_3CHBrCH_2Br \xrightarrow[NH_3]{Na\overset{+}{N}\overset{-}{H_2}} CH_3-C\equiv CH.$$

(d) propane: C_3H_8 . Since this compound is completely
saturated it can't be halogenated by Br_2 and CCl_4. But by
free radical chain reaction, however, we could chlorinate
propane.

1-chloropropane

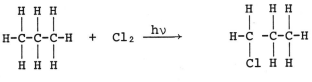

Two isomers are formed:

2-chloropropane.

If both these isomers are dehydrohalogenated by
potassium   hydroxide in alcohol propylene will result.

$$CH_2Cl - CH_2-CH_3 \xrightarrow[alcohol]{KOH} CH_2= CH -CH_3$$

Propylene could be converted to propyne by the method
outlined in part (b).

(e) n-propyl alcohol: $CH_3CH_2CH_2OH$.

First propylene can be produced by the dehydration of
n-propyl alcohol (to eliminate the hydroxy group).

$$CH_3CH_2CH_2OH + H_2SO_4 \xrightarrow[- H_2O]{heat} CH_3CH= CH_2.$$

The hot conc. acid protonates the -OH of the alcohol; subsequent loss of H_2O and H^+ forms the alkene. Propylene can then be converted to propyne as illustrated in part (b).

(f)   1,1-dichloropropane:

$$\overset{\displaystyle Cl}{\underset{\displaystyle Cl}{H-\overset{|}{\underset{|}{C}}-CH_2CH_3}}$$

By dehydrohalogenation of the dichloropropane we can produce propyne.

$$\overset{\displaystyle Cl}{\underset{\displaystyle Cl}{H-\overset{|}{\underset{|}{C}}-CH_2CH_3}} \xrightarrow{\overset{+}{Na}\ \overset{-}{NH_2}/NH_3} HC{\equiv}C-CH_3 .$$

(g)   Starting from acetylene $HC{\equiv}CH$ the carbanion $HC{\equiv}C^-$ must be obtained. By using $\overset{+}{Na}\ \overset{-}{NH_2}$, which is basic relative to acetylene, the end products are $HC{\equiv}C^-\ \overset{+}{Na}$ + NH_3. It is necessary to increase the carbanion by a methyl group to get the desired product, propyne. Since $HC{\equiv}C^-\ \overset{+}{Na}$ is fairly nucleophilic it will participate in an S_N2 displacement reaction with methyl iodide.

$$HC{\equiv}C^-\ \overset{+}{Na} + CH_3I \rightarrow HC{\equiv}CCH_3 + \overset{+}{Na}\ \overset{-}{I} .$$

(h)   1,1,2,2-tetrabromopropane:

$$\overset{\displaystyle Br\ Br}{\underset{\displaystyle Br\ Br}{H-\overset{|}{\underset{|}{C}}-\overset{|}{\underset{|}{C}}-CH_3}}$$

Instead of dehydrohalogenation, it would be sufficient to remove all the bromine atoms from the molecule and thus form 2 sites of unsaturation (a triple bond) between the first two carbon atoms. Zinc is a highly reactive element and readily forms zinc bromide.

$$2\ Zn + CHBr_2CBr_2CH_3 \xrightarrow{heat} 2\ ZnBr_2 + HC{\equiv}CCH_3 .$$

● PROBLEM 7-15

From isopentyl alcohol (3-methyl-1-butanol), acetylene, and any required straight chain primary alcohols, derive a practical synthesis for 2-methylheptadecane, the sex-attractant for the Tiger moth.

<u>Solution</u>:   First the isopentyl alcohol has to be converted to isopentyl bromide. This reaction is brought about by nucleophilic substitution; the protonated alcohol being the substrate and bromide ion as the nucleophile. The mechanism is as follows:

(1) $(CH_3)_2CHCH_2CH_2OH \xrightarrow{H_2SO_4} (CH_3)_2CHCH_2CH_2\overset{+}{O}H_2$

(2) S_N2 displacement of the protonated hydroxyl group:

$(CH_3)_2CHCH_2 \overset{+}{CH_2OH_2}$ + H-Br → $(CH_3)_2CHCH_2CH_2Br$ + H_2O.

If phosphorous tribromide is used instead, then the bromine anion will be formed by ionization of Br^- from PBr_3. The Br^- will then react with isopentyl alcohol to produce isopentyl bromide.

Next undecanol is reacted with HBr/H_2SO_4 or PBr_3, thus obtaining $CH_3(CH_2)_9CH_2Br$. The mechanism is similar to the one outlined above.

Acetylene is next reacted with $NaNH_2$ and liquid ammonia to produce the carbanion $HC\equiv C^-$, acetylene being much more acidic than ammonia:

$HC\equiv CH + Na\overset{+}{N}H_2^-$ → $HC\equiv C^- \overset{+}{Na} + NH_3$.   Then:

$HC\equiv C^-$ + $(CH_3)_2CHCH_2CH_2-Br$ → $(CH_3)_2CHCH_2CH_2C\equiv CH$ + Br^-

The carbanion $HC\equiv C^-$ (being fairly nucleophilic) participates readily in S_N2 displacement reactions.

In order to lengthen the chain to the desired number of carbon atoms the carbanion is reproduced by the addition of $NaNH_2$ and liquid ammonia:

$(CH_3)_2CHCH_2CH_2C\equiv CH + Na\overset{+}{N}H_2^-$ → $(CH_3)_2CHCH_2CH_2C\equiv C^- \overset{+}{Na} + NH_3$

If $CH_3(CH_2)_9CH_2Br$ (which was previously obtained) were reacted with the carbanion, we would get the appropriate alkyne.

$(CH_3)_2CHCH_2CH_2C\equiv C^-$ + $CH_3(CH_2)_9CH_2-Br$ $\longrightarrow$

$(CH_3)_2CHCH_2CH_2C\equiv C(CH_2)_{10}-CH_3$ + Br^-.

Catalytic hydrogenation yields the desired product.

$(CH_3)_2CHCH_2CH_2C\equiv C(CH_2)_{10}CH_3$ + 2 H_2 $\xrightarrow{Pt}$

$$(CH_3)_2CHCH_2CH_2 - \overset{\overset{\displaystyle H}{|}}{\underset{\underset{\displaystyle H}{|}}{C}} - \overset{\overset{\displaystyle H}{|}}{\underset{\underset{\displaystyle H}{|}}{C}} - (CH_2)_{10}\ CH_3$$

which may be written compactly as $(CH_3)_2CH(CH_2)_{14}CH_3$.

Muscalure, cis-9-tricosene, is the sex-attractant insect pheromone of the common housefly. Give a practical synthesis of this compound from acetylene and straight chain alcohols.

Solution: The formula for cis-9-tricosene is $CH_3(CH_2)_7CH=CH(CH_2)_{12}CH_3$, where the octanyl and tridecanyl groups are cis to each other.

In order to synthesize cis-9-tricosene, we start with a straight chain alcohol $CH_3(CH_2)_6CH_2OH$. Hydrogen bromide is added in the presence of a catalyst (H_2SO_4) and the following reaction takes place:

$$CH_3(CH_2)_6CH_2OH \xrightarrow{H_2SO_4} CH_3(CH_2)_6CH_2OH_2^+ \xrightarrow{HBr}$$

$$CH_3(CH_2)_6CH_2Br + H_2O.$$

The hydroxyl group is replaced by the bromine ion thus forming the alkyl bromide. This is an S_N2 (bimolecular nucleophilic substitution) reaction with H_2O as a leaving group and bromide ion as the nucleophile.

OR: Bromination can also be brought about by phosphorus tribromide. The alcohol and PBr_3 react to produce the bromide, $CH_3(CH_2)_6CH_2Br$.

Acetylene is then reacted with $Na^+NH_2^-$ and liquid ammonia to produce the carbanion $HC\equiv C^-$. Acetylene is much more acidic (pKa = 25) than ammonia (pKa = 35). Thus the amide ion reacts in the following manner:

$$HC\equiv CH + NH_2^- \rightleftharpoons HC\equiv C^- + NH_3.$$

The carbanion $HC\equiv C^-$ undergoes an S_N2 reaction with the bromide, producing $CH_3(CH_2)_6CH_2C\equiv CH$.

$$HC\equiv C^- + CH_3(CH_2)_6CH_2-Br \rightarrow HC\equiv CCH_2(CH_2)_6CH_3 + Br^-.$$

In order to lengthen the chain, $NaNH_2$ is added to the alkyne to form the carbanion $CH_3(CH_2)_6CH_2C\equiv C^-$. This is obtained by the mechanism previously outlined. This carbanion is reacted with $CH_3(CH_2)_{11}CH_2Br$, which is formed in the reaction:

$$CH_3(CH_2)_{11}CH_2OH \xrightarrow[HBr]{H_2SO_4} CH_3(CH_2)_{11}CH_2Br$$

The product obtained from the reaction of $CH_3(CH_2)_{11}CH_2Br$ with $CH_3(CH_2)_6CH_2C\equiv C^-$ is $CH_3(CH_2)_7C\equiv C(CH_2)_{12}CH_3$. This fulfills the total requirements of carbon atoms in 9-tricosene.

The alkyne is then hydrogenated to the cis-alkene. This is accomplished by using palladium, barium sulfate and quinoline; the hydrogen adds on the same side of the triple bond. The reaction is:

$$CH_3(CH_2)_7C{\equiv}C(CH_2)_{12}CH_3 + H_2 \xrightarrow[\text{quinoline}]{\text{Pd/BaSO}_4}$$

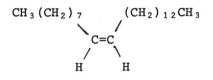

cis-9-tricosene

SPECTROSCOPY

● PROBLEM 7-17

The chemical shifts (2.4 ppm) of acetylenic hydrogens (RC≡C-H) are considerably more toward higher magnetic fields than those of alkene hydrogens (4.6 to 6.9 ppm). Show how this shielding effect might be explained in terms of the atomic orbital representation of acetylenes.

Solution: If a molecule is placed in a magnetic field the electrons are caused to move around and in circulating they induce secondary magnetic fields. This is the under-lying concept behind the determination of an n.m.r. spectrum. Circulation of such electrons about a proton generates a field which aligns itself so as to decrease the applied magnetic field, thus diminishing the field felt by the proton. This is known as shielding. Shielding shifts the absorption upfield and the ppm decreases. The unit of measurement of these chemical shifts is in parts per million, abbreviated by ppm.

     In the case of RC≡C-H (2.4 ppm), the atomic orbitals' π electrons will circulate in a cylindrical region around the axis of the triple bond. This will generate a magnetic field which will tend to decrease an applied magnetic field when directed parallel to the axis of the triple bond. The magnetic field generated by the π electrons of alkenes is not as great as in alkynes. This is because alkenes have only one π bond whereas alkynes have two π bonds. As a result, the chemical shift of alkenes will be downfield (higher ppm) relative to those of alkynes. The magnetic field generated by the π electrons of the alkyne RC≡CH is illustrated in the following:

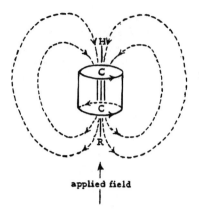

applied field

Indicate the features you would expect for the infrared
and n.m.r. spectra of the following substances.

(a) $CH_3C \equiv CCH_3$
(b) $CH_3C \equiv CH$ (expect a long-range n.m.r. coupling of 3 cps)
(c) $CH_3CH_2C \equiv CCH_2CH_3$

Solution: (a) A bond that is electrically symmetrical
has no dipole moment and will not absorb infrared radiation.
As a result, such bonds will not be seen in infrared spectra.
The infrared spectrum of 2-butyne would show, then, only two
identifying bands: the stretching of the C-H bond near
2900 cm^{-1} (reciprocal centimeters) and the bending vibrations
of the C-H bond at 1400 cm^{-1}. The carbon-carbon triple bond
of 2-butyne will not appear in the infrared spectrum because
of symmetry. In the nuclear magnetic resonance (n.m.r.)
spectrum, the two methyl groups occur as a singlet and
absorb near 1.0 δ. The methyl groups resonate at the same
frequency because their protons are in identical environments; they are equivalent.

     (b) The infrared spectrum of propyne would show the
C≡C bond stretching near 2100 cm^{-1}. The C≡C stretch appears
because the molecule is not electronically symmetrical; it
has a dipole moment. The ≡C-H bond will stretch near
3300 cm^{-1}. Like 2-butyne (part a), propyne will show the
methyl group C-H stretching and bending near 2900 cm^{-1} and
1400 cm^{-1}, respectively. The n.m.r. spectrum of propyne
will have a quartet near 2.5 δ and a doublet near 1.0 δ.
These multiplets occur as a result of spin-spin splitting
between the -CH_3 protons and the ≡C-H proton. Although spin-
spin splitting is expected to occur only between non-
equivalent adjacent protons, splitting may occur between
protons that are further removed from each other, particularly if π bonds intervene. The presence of two π bonds
in propyne facilitates spin-spin splitting to occur between
the methyl protons and the ≡C-H proton. The three methyl
protons split the ≡C-H signal into a quartet and the lone
≡C-H proton splits the methyl signal into a doublet. The
≡C-H signal occurs downfield from the methyl signal because
the lower electron density of the ≡C-H proton causes it to

be deshielded relative to the methyl protons. This de-shielding causes the chemical shift to move downfield. The $\equiv$C-H proton has a lower electron density than the methyl proton because the sp-hybridized carbon of the $\equiv$C-H is more electronegative than the sp^3-hybridized carbon of the -CH_3; this makes the $\equiv$C-H hydrogen more positive than the -CH_3 hydrogen.

(c) The molecule 3-hexyne is electronically symmetrical; it has no dipole moment. Hence the C$\equiv$C bond will not appear in the infrared spectrum. The only bands will be the C-H stretch near 2900 cm^{-1} and the C-H bending near 1400 cm^{-1}. The n.m.r. spectrum of 3-hexyne will show a triplet near 1.0 δ and a quartet near 1.5 δ. These signals occur as a result of spin-spin splitting between the methylene (-CH_2-) protons and the methyl protons. The two methylene protons split the methyl signal into a triplet and the three methyl protons split the methylene signal into a quartet. The methylene signal occurs downfield from the methyl signal because its protons are deshielded more than the methyl protons.

CHARACTERIZATION TESTS

● PROBLEM 7-19

You are given a mixture of 1-butyne (bp 8°) and 2-butyne (bp 27°). How could you separate, and then recover, each of these compounds using chemical means?

Solution: The acidity of $CH_3CH_2C\equiv CH$ is prevalent due to the high degree of s character in the sp orbital used to bond the carbon (the one which is triply bonded to the other carbon atom) to hydrogen. The greater s character increases the electronegativity and therefore makes it more suitable to react with bases. 2-butyne $CH_3C\equiv CCH_3$ is not as acidic since it does not have a hydrogen bonded to the sp hybridized carbon atom; for this reason it does not give any reaction with heavy metals. 1-butyne on the other hand undergoes nucleophilic substitution with heavy metals as represented by the following reaction:

$$CH_3CH_2C\equiv CH \ + \ Ag(NH_3)_2 \ NO_3 \ \rightarrow \ CH_3CH_2C\equiv C\text{-}Ag$$

(precipitate)

2-butyne however does not react with $Ag(NH_3)_2NO_3$, since it lacks acidic hydrogens (H-C$\equiv$) and will not form the carbanion necessary for the reaction to occur.

The 2-butyne can be separated from the mixture by filtration.

We can obtain 1-butyne from $CH_3CH_2CH_2\equiv C$—Ag by dis-placing the silver atom with a hydrogen atom.

Since silver (I) forms a very stable complex with cyanide ions, silver acetylides regenerate the acetylene by reacting with cyanide ion in H_2O:

$$CH_3CH_2CH_2C\equiv C\text{-}Ag \xrightarrow[H_2O]{CN^-} CH_3CH_2CH_2C\equiv CH + Ag(CN)_2^- + OH^-$$

The 1-butyne can be separated from the mixture by filtration.

● **PROBLEM** 7-20

Suppose you were given four unlabeled bottles, each of which is known to contain one of the following compounds: n-pentane, 1-pentene, 2-pentyne, and 1-pentyne. Explain how you could use simple chemical tests (preferably test-tube reactions) to identify the contents of each bottle. (Note that all four compounds are low-boiling liquids.)

Solution: n-Pentane is different than the other three compounds, as it is saturated and therefore will not react with cold dilute potassium permanganate. $KMnO_4$ reacts with double or triple bonds to give vicinal diols (commonly known as glycols) and carboxylic acids, respectively. This causes the intense purple colored potassium permanganate to decolorize. n-Pentane does not cause any color change.

Bromine in carbon tetra-chloride can also be used to identify the presence of the saturated n-pentane. The unsaturated compounds will add bromine to their double and triple bonds forming multibrominated compounds. This causes the reddish-brown color of bromine to disappear. n-Pentane does not cause decolorization and it can be labeled.

The three unsaturated compounds remain to be identified. On adding a silver-ammonia solution to a sample from each of the three 1-pentyne will be observed to form a precipitate. 1-Pentyne ($HC\equiv C\text{-}CH_2CH_2CH_3$) has an acidic hydrogen ($H\text{-}C\equiv$) and in NH_3 solution forms the carbanion $CH_3(CH_2)_2C\equiv C^-$. This is fairly nucleophilic and reacts with the silver ion to form a precipitate:

$$CH_3(CH_2)_2C\equiv C^- + Ag^+ \xrightarrow{NH_3 \text{ sol.}} CH_3(CH_2)_2C\equiv C\text{-}Ag$$

2-Pentyne ($CH_3C\equiv CCH_2CH_3$) has no available acidic hydrogens and cannot form a carbanion and react with the silver ion. 1-pentene ($H_2C=CH\text{-}(CH_2)_2CH_3$) does not give any reaction because there are no hydrogen atoms that would readily leave the molecule so as to make a carbanion.

The two compounds 1-pentene and 2-pentyne cannot be classified by any qualitative analysis. However by measuring the amount of bromine required for total bromination and recognizing that 2-pentyne consumes more bromine we could differentiate between them.

first: $CH_3C{\equiv}CCH_2CH_3 + Br_2 \xrightarrow{CCl_4}$ $CH_3\overset{\displaystyle Br}{\overset{|}{C}} = \overset{\displaystyle Br}{\overset{|}{C}}-CCH_2CH_3$

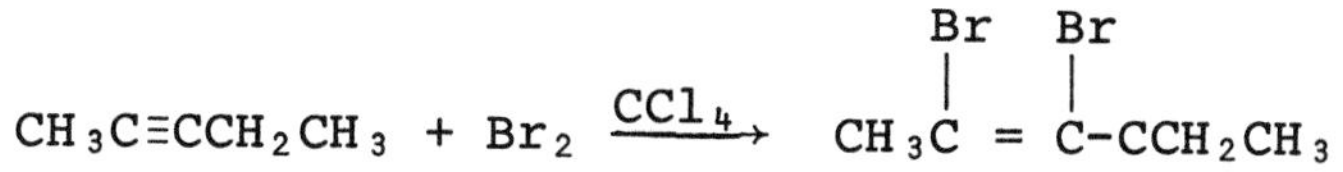

2,3-dibromo, 2-pentene

second: $CH_3\overset{\displaystyle Br}{\overset{|}{C}} = \overset{\displaystyle Br}{\overset{|}{C}}-CH_2CH_3 + Br_2 \xrightarrow{CCl_4}$ $CH_3-\overset{\displaystyle Br}{\underset{\displaystyle Br}{\overset{|}{\underset{|}{C}}}} - \overset{\displaystyle Br}{\underset{\displaystyle Br}{\overset{|}{\underset{|}{C}}}CH_2CH_3}$

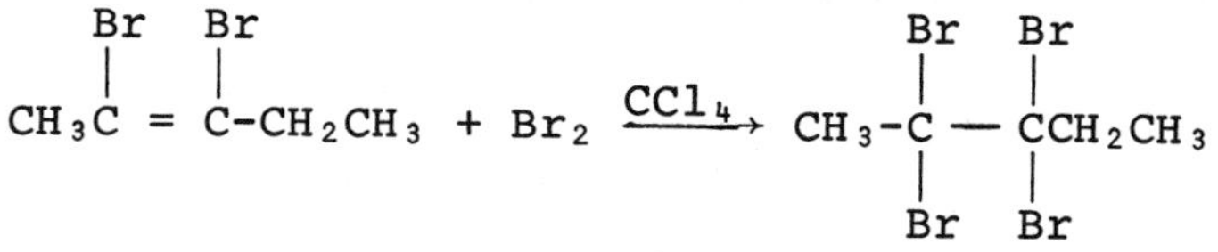

2,2,3,3 tetra bromo
pentane

2 moles of bromine are required for each mole of 2-pentyne for complete saturation.

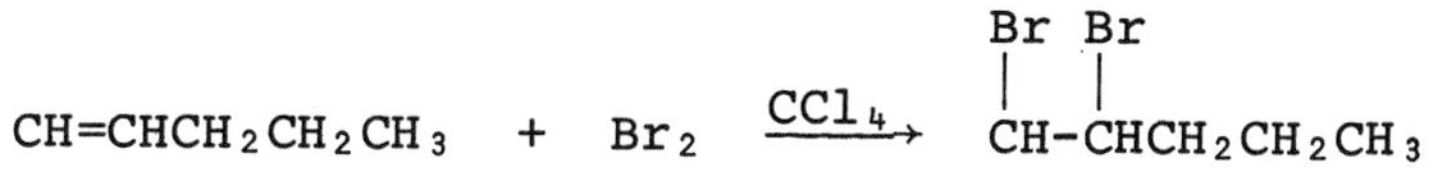

$CH{=}CHCH_2CH_2CH_3 + Br_2 \xrightarrow{CCl_4}$ $\overset{\displaystyle Br}{\overset{|}{CH}}-\overset{\displaystyle Br}{\overset{|}{CH}}CH_2CH_2CH_3$

1,2, dibromopentane

Only 1 mole of bromine is required for each mole of 1-pentene.

CHAPTER 8

MOLECULAR ORBITAL THEORY

FUNDAMENTALS

(a) Define the following terms, and draw a diagram showing their relationship to each other.

    Amplitude
    Nodes
    Nodal plane
    Phase
    "Out of phase"
    Wave equation

(b) How do they pertain to molecular orbitals?

Solution: (a) The terms given above all pertain to wave theory, and in particular to standing waves. The amplitude of a wave is defined as its vertical displacement; the nodes as the points at which the amplitude is equal to zero; the nodal plane as the plane passing through the nodal points; the phase as the upward or downward displacement (distinguished by positive and negative signs, respectively). If two waves were exactly out of phase, then the crests of one would line up with the troughs of the other and the sum of their amplitudes would therefore be zero. The wave equation is little more than the differential equation which describes the wave.

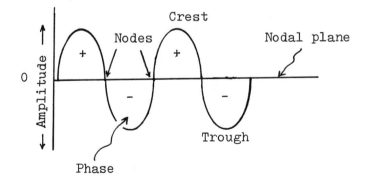

(b)   Electron waves are described by a wave equation
similar to that of standing waves.   The solution to the
wave equation given by $\phi(x)$, where x = distance, is the
amplitude.   Electron waves can have nodes, and amplitudes
of different signs.   It should be noted that the two lobes
of a p orbital lie between a nodal plane.

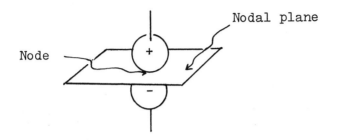

It should further be noted that, while $\phi(x,y,z)$
is the orbital, ϕ^2 has an actual physical meaning; ϕ^2
is the probability of finding an electron within a given
volume. The shapes of orbitals are actually crude representations of the region within which ϕ^2 has a particular
value, or the space within which electrons are significantly likely to be found (> 95% probability).

● **PROBLEM 8-2**

Draw the LCAO model of ethylene in the bonding and antibonding orbitals.   Distinguish the ground state of ethylene
from its excited state.   Distinguish π^2 from $\pi^*\pi$.

Solution: In drawing the LCAO form of ethylene, only
the π-orbital form will be drawn, as these orbitals are the
subject of chief interest here.   Hence, the bonding orbital
of ethylene should appear as below:

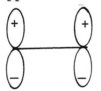

Ethylene: bonding orbital

Conversely, using the definition of antibonding
orbitals, the anti-bonding orbital for ethylene may be
written as:

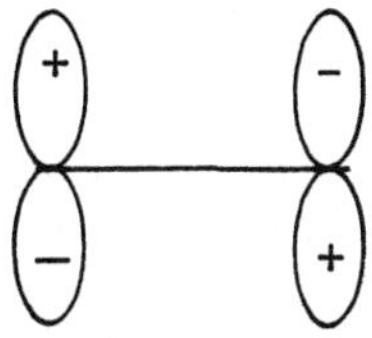

Ethylene: antibonding orbital

The ground state of a molecule occurs when the electrons have the lowest energy levels. The excited state is when the electrons of a molecule rise to higher energy levels. This is usually upon application of an external energetic stimulus (e.g., light).

π^* _____

π ↑↓

Ground state
of ethylene

π^* ↓

π ↑

First excited state
of ethylene

The ground state of ethylene is referred to as being in the π^2 configuration, in that both electrons are in the π bonding orbital. The notation used to describe this excited state of ethylene is $\pi^*\pi$. This shows that one electron is in the π antibonding orbital and one electron is in the π bonding orbital.

● **PROBLEM** 8-3

Show the molecular orbital structure of H_2. Explain the molecular orbital structure both in terms of electron configuration and LCAO. Show the bonding orbital and antibonding orbital, and calculate the bond order.

Solution: When **two** atomic orbitals come together, **two** molecular orbitals are formed - one of higher energy and one of lower energy. The lower-energy one is termed the bonding orbital, which is more stable than the component orbitals. The higher-energy one is the antibonding orbital and is less stable than the component orbitals.

The bonding between the atoms of H_2 involves molecular orbitals of the lowest possible energy states:

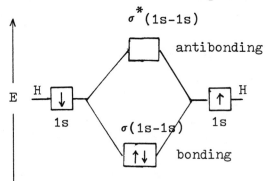

$\sigma^*(1s-1s)$ antibonding

E   H 1s ↓   H 1s ↑

$\sigma(1s-1s)$

↑↓ bonding

It should be noted that in molecular bonding, bonding orbitals (being orbitals of lower energy levels) will fill first and each will accommodate a pair of electrons, which must have opposite signs. It should further be seen that electrons in a bonding orbital will stabilize the mole - cule, whereas electrons in an antibonding orbital will destabi-

lize the molecule.. Furthermore, the effect of an electron
in a bonding orbital will negate the effect of an electron
in an antibonding orbital. The bond order is defined as
half the number of bonding electrons less half the number
of antibonding ones.

Bond order = $\frac{1}{2}$(no. bonding electrons - no. anti-

bonding electrons)

Using this expression, the bond order of H_2 is
found to be 1.

Bond order = $\frac{1}{2}$ (2 - 0) = 1

These concepts may be solidified in the confused
reader by examining the case of H_2^-. Since it is formed
by the anion of two 1s orbitals, it may be represented
as below.

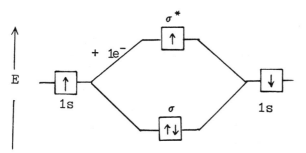

H_2^- differs from H_2 in that it possesses three
electrons, instead of two. Since only two electrons are
permitted per orbital, a third electron (in H_2^-) must be
forced into the energetically unfavorable antibonding sigma
orbital ($\sigma*$). Hence, this will have a net effect of cancelling one of the electrons in the σ bonding orbital.

Bond order = $\frac{1}{2}$ (2 - 1) = $\frac{1}{2}$

Similarly, in the case of H_2^+,

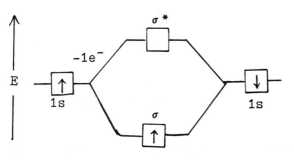

bond order = $\frac{1}{2}$ (1 - 0) = $\frac{1}{2}$

251

And in the case of H_2^{-2},

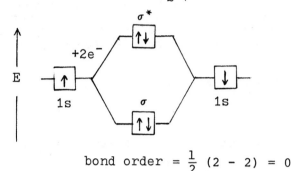

$$\text{bond order} = \frac{1}{2} (2 - 2) = 0$$

This concept may further be expressed using LCAO (linear combination of atomic orbitals). This is, as the name implies, an expression of the molecular orbital in terms of its component atomic orbitals in a linear equation.

$$\psi = \phi_1 + \phi_2$$

where ψ = molecular orbital

ϕ_1 = the first atomic orbital

ϕ_2 = the second atomic orbital

Addition of atomic orbitals will result in the stabilizing bonding orbital, and subtraction will result in the destabilizing antibonding orbital.

$$\psi = \phi_1 + \phi_2$$

$$\psi^* = \phi_1 - \phi_2$$

Schematically, this may be represented as:

ϕ_1 ϕ_2 $\phi_1 + \phi_2$ σ bonding

ϕ_1 ϕ_2 $\phi_1 - \phi_2$ σ^* antibonding

● **PROBLEM 8-4**

Explain the molecular orbital structure of O_2.   Calculate the bond order.

Solution: When reading the   last problem, one may have come to the realization that not all molecular orbitals are as simple as the case presented for H_2. Oxygen, for instance, presents the problem of forming molecular orbitals from atomic p orbitals. To examine this, one must first examine the electron configuration of oxygen.

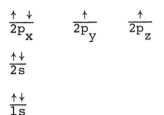

The two s orbitals will form σ bonds in a manner similar to those in H_2.

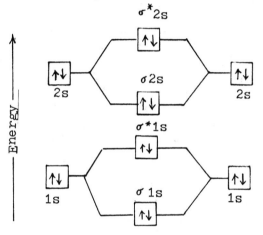

Since both the sigma bonding orbitals and the sigma anti-bonding orbitals are filled, the net effect of these will be zero. They may be neglected in discussing the molecular bonding of oxygen.

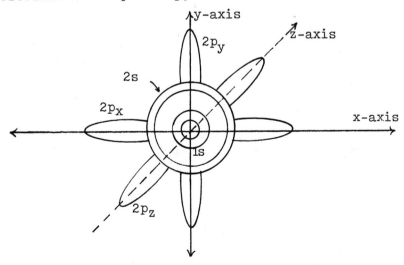

Above is shown the orbital picture of the oxygen

atom. If one remembers the three dimensional configuration of the p orbitals, the difficulties can be seen. Which p sub-orbital (P_x, P_y or P_z) will bond with which? As a rule each P_y or P_z orbital will bond with a corresponding p sub-orbital to give one π-bonding orbital and one π^* antibonding orbital. In the case of P_x, one σ bonding and one σ^* antibonding orbital are formed.

In its bonded state, therefore, O_2 can be represented as:

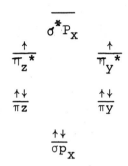

(plus 8 electrons in 2 σ s and 2 σ^* s orbitals)

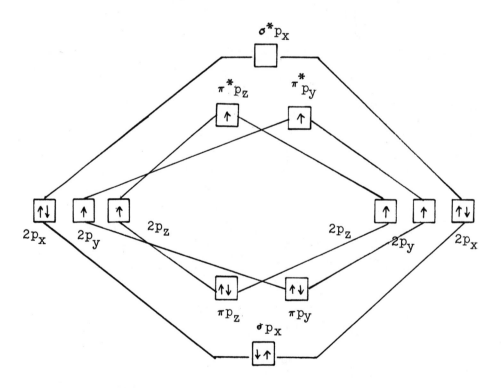

Electronic Configuration of Oxygen (O_2)

Therefore, the bond order can be calculated as $\frac{1}{2}(6 - 2)$, or two. The reader may convince himself of this by drawing a Lewis dot diagram (:O::O:).

The LCAO models may readily be understood by viewing each orbital as a wave function, whereby like phases will add, and opposite phases will tend to cancel each other. As two methods of approach between two bonds are possible, then two types of orbitals will form.

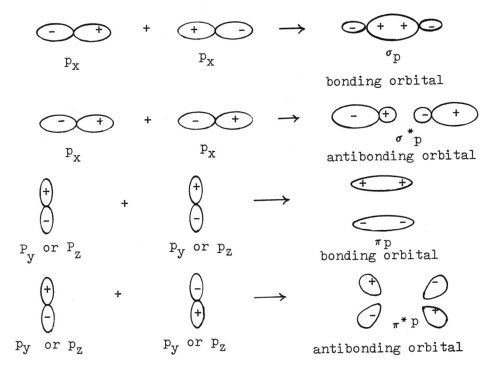

As can be seen from the above diagrams, the addition of like orbitals will result in the formation of favorable bonding orbitals; the addition of opposite orbitals will result in the formation of unfavorable antibonding orbitals.

● PROBLEM 8-5

The LCAO molecular orbitals of the cyclopentadienate system (C_5H_5) have schematic energies as follows:

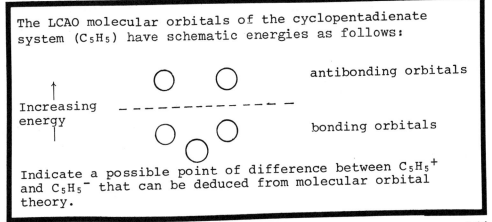

Indicate a possible point of difference between $C_5H_5^+$ and $C_5H_5^-$ that can be deduced from molecular orbital theory.

255

Solution:

The anion is a closed, cyclic, planar system with 6 π electrons, all of which satisfy Hückel's rule for aromaticity. The cation is clearly nonaromatic and its formation is thus not favored thermodynamically.

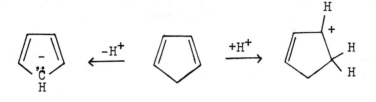

anion   cyclopentadiene   cation

Another way to evaluate the stability, or bond energy of the cyclopentadienate system is by examining its molecular orbitals. A conventional way of drawing the closed-shell π-electronic configuration of a cyclic molecule includes the following steps:

1) Draw the structure of the molecule as resting on one corner.

2) Extend a broken line through the center of the molecule ----- this line represents the non-bonding energy level; below it lies the bonding orbital(s), π, and above it lies the antibonding orbital(s), π*.

3) For each of the corners in the structure mark a line; this represents a molecular orbital available to accommodate one pair of electrons.

4) Following Pauli's principle and Hund's rule, place electrons into the orbitals. There can be only two electrons - and of opposite spin - in each orbital, with orbitals of lower energy being filled up first. For orbitals of equal energy, each gets an electron before any one of them gets a pair of electrons.

Using this convention, we arrive at the following π-electronic configuration of the cyclopentadienate system:

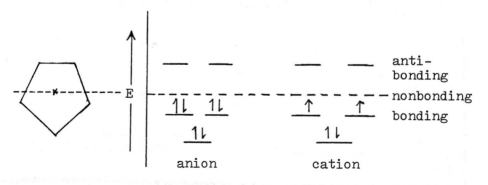

We can see from the above diagram that all the bonding orbitals are filled in $C_5H_5^-$; this is responsible for the aromaticity and stability of the anion. In $C_5H_5^+$, there will be two unpaired electrons, and this diradical character imparts instability to the cation.

● **PROBLEM** 8-6

Discuss the various bonding and antibonding orbitals of 1,3-butadiene. Place them in order of increasing energy. What is the electronic configuration of butadiene in both the ground and the excited state.

Solution:

$$CH_2=CH-CH=CH_2$$

1,3-Butadiene

Since there are four p orbitals, four LCAO structures exist for 1,3-butadiene:

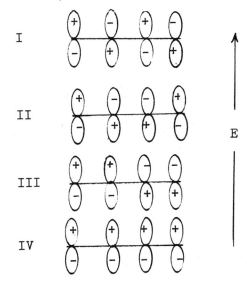

Two of these structures with high energy levels represent antibonding orbitals, while the other two of lower energy represent bonding orbitals.

Placing LCAO structures in increasing order of energy is tricky. The best way to go about this is to calculate the number of bonding interactions and the number of antibonding interactions. The structure with the greatest number of bonding interactions will be the most stable and hence the structure of least energy. The structure with the least number of bonding interactions, and hence the greatest number of antibonding interactions, will be the least stable and hence the structure of highest energy.

257

Examining each LCAO structure, we find

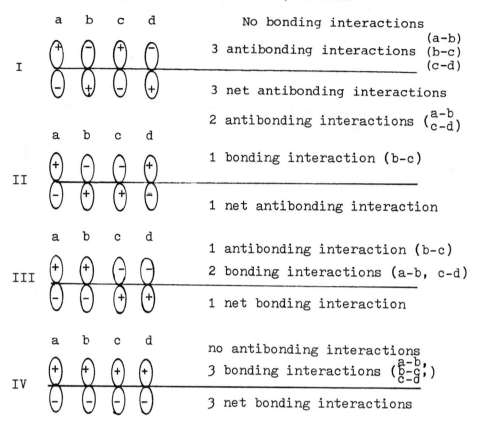

a   b   c   d   No bonding interactions

3 antibonding interactions (a-b) (b-c) (c-d)

I

3 net antibonding interactions

2 antibonding interactions ($^{a-b}_{c-d}$)

a   b   c   d

1 bonding interaction (b-c)

II

1 net antibonding interaction

a   b   c   d

1 antibonding interaction (b-c)

2 bonding interactions (a-b, c-d)

III

1 net bonding interaction

a   b   c   d

no antibonding interactions

3 bonding interactions ($^{a-b}_{c-d}$;)

IV

3 net bonding interactions

As can readily be seen, the order of the four structures in increasing energy is IV, III, II, I.

The four molecular orbital (ψ) levels are thus:

I   —— ψ_4

II   —— ψ_3 antibonding

- -

III   —— ψ_2 bonding

IV   —— ψ_1

Since there are four π electrons, the ground state of 1,3-butadiene would have the following electronic configuration:

—— ψ_4

—— ψ_3 antibonding

- -

↑ ↓ ψ_2 bonding

↓ ↑ ψ_1

This can be expressed as $\psi_1{}^2\psi_2{}^2$ bonding.

Upon ultraviolet stimulation, an electron from ψ_2 will jump to the ψ_3 antibonding orbital. This excited state configuration is shown below and can be expressed as $\psi_1{}^2\psi_2\psi_3$ bonding.

ψ_4 ___

ψ_3 ↓ antibonding

ψ_2 ↑ bonding

ψ_1 ↑ ↓

ELECTROCYCLIC REACTIONS

● **PROBLEM** 8-7

What catalysts may be utilized in order to achieve the following one step transformations?

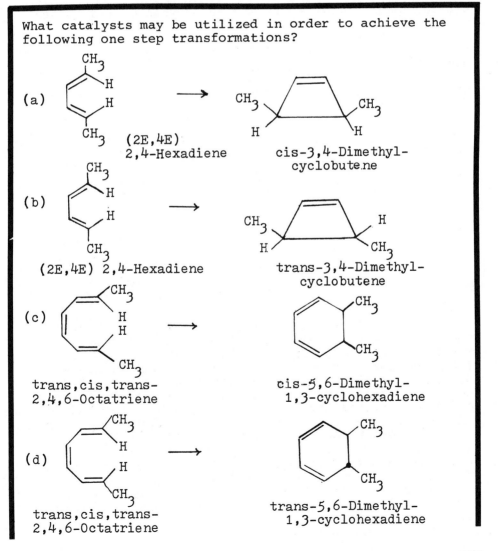

(a) (2E,4E) 2,4-Hexadiene → cis-3,4-Dimethyl-cyclobutene

(b) (2E,4E) 2,4-Hexadiene → trans-3,4-Dimethyl-cyclobutene

(c) trans,cis,trans-2,4,6-Octatriene → cis-5,6-Dimethyl-1,3-cyclohexadiene

(d) trans,cis,trans-2,4,6-Octatriene → trans-5,6-Dimethyl-1,3-cyclohexadiene

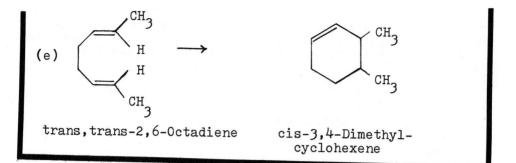

(e)

trans,trans-2,6-Octadiene

cis-3,4-Dimethyl-
cyclohexene

Solution: Electrocyclic reactions are concerted, therefore they are completely stereospecific. The exact
stereochemistry of the product depends upon the number of
double bonds in the polyene; molecular orbital theory
allows us to predict this stereochemistry. Let us look
at the electron configuration of butadiene, a four-π-
electron system, in the ground state and in the first
excited state (achieved by the absorption of radiation):

HOMO of the
1st excited ψ_3
state

HOMO of the
ground state ψ_2

ψ_1

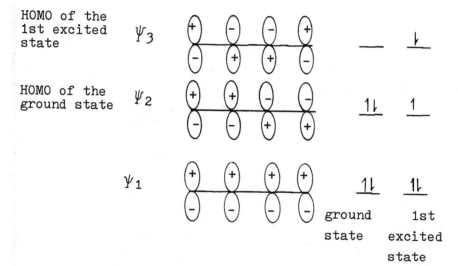

ground   1st
state   excited
state

     The electron that is least tightly held, and
therefore the one that is involved in the reaction, is
the electron in the highest occupied molecular orbital
(HOMO) of the polyene. As we can see from the above
diagram, the highest occupied molecular orbital of the
conjugated diene in the ground state is ψ_2; it is the
electrons in this orbital that will form the bond
that closes the ring. Bond formation requires overlap
of the lobes on the terminal carbons (C_1 and C_4 in
this case). Only a conrotatory motion, in which the p
orbitals of the terminal carbons rotate in the same
direction, can bring together lobes of the same phase.
A disrotatory motion, in which the orbitals rotate in
opposite directions, would on the other hand bring together lobes of opposite phases, resulting in the
formation of an antibonding orbital:

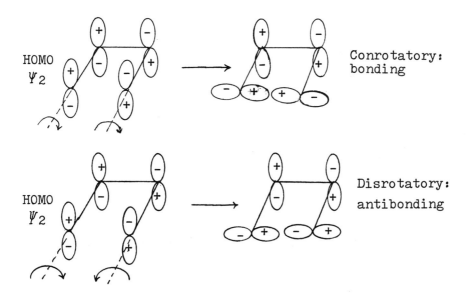

HOMO ψ_2 → Conrotatory: bonding

HOMO ψ_2 → Disrotatory: antibonding

For photocyclic reactions, the HOMO is ψ_3, hence only disrotatory motion would result in effective cyclization of a diene:

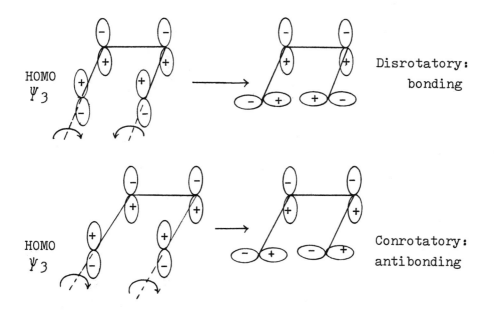

HOMO ψ_3 → Disrotatory: bonding

HOMO ψ_3 → Conrotatory: antibonding

Therefore, thermal electrocyclic reactions of four π electrons can only occur in a conrotatory manner, while photochemical electrocyclic reactions of four π electrons can only occur in a disrotatory manner. This is summarized by the Woodward-Hoffman rules for electrocyclic reactions (given in Table 1 below).

261

Table 1   Woodward-Hoffman Rules for Electrocyclic
          Reactions

Number of π electrons	Reaction	Motion
4n (n=any integers)	Thermal	Conrotatory
4n	Photochemical	Disrotatory
4n + 2	Thermal	Disrotatory
4n + 2	Photochemical	Conrotatory

(a)   Since the cis product is desired, a disrotatory
motion is required. From the Woodward-Hoffman rules,
a 4n(n=1)-π-electron system undergoing disrotatory
motion must be a photochemical reaction:

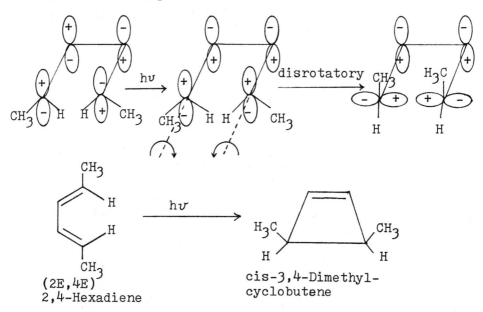

(2E,4E)
2,4-Hexadiene

cis-3,4-Dimethyl-
cyclobutene

(b)   Since the trans isomer is desired, a conrotatory
motion is required.   Therefore, a thermal reaction
is required:

262

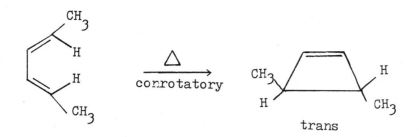

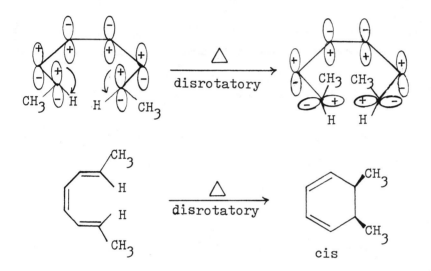

(c) Since the cis product is desired, a disrotatory motion is required. From the Woodward-Hoffman rules, a 4n + 2(n=1)-π-electron system undergoing disrotatory motion must be a thermal reaction:

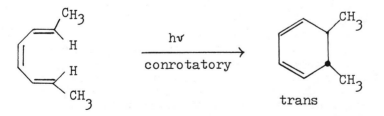

(d) Since the trans isomer is desired, conrotatory motion is required. According to the Woodward-Hoffman rules, a 4n + 2(n=1)-π-electron system undergoing conrotatory motion must be a photochemical reaction. Therefore:

(e) Since this polyene is not in conjugated form, no electrocyclic reaction will occur.

● **PROBLEM** 8-8

The commonly observed conversion of cyclopropyl cations into allyl cations is considered to be an example of an electrocyclic reaction. (a) What is the HOMO of the

Cyclopropyl cation   Allyl cation

allyl cation? How many π electrons has it? (b) Would
you expect conrotatory or disrotatory motion? (c) What
prediction would you make about interconversion of allyl
and cyclopropyl anions? (d) About the interconversion of
pentadienyl cations and cyclopentenyl cations?

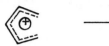

Pentadienyl cation   Cyclopentenyl cation

Solution: (a) The molecular orbitals for the allyl
system in the form of their linear combinations of atom
orbitals (LCAO's) are

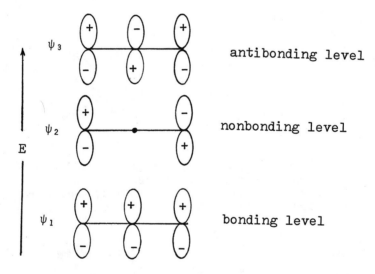

ψ_3 antibonding level

ψ_2 nonbonding level

E

ψ_1 bonding level

    Note that the energy of the molecular orbital in-
creases as the number of non-bonding interactions increases. The allyl cation will have the first molecular
orbital (ψ_1) filled. This orbital, at the bonding level,
is considered to be the highest occupied molecular orbital
(HOMO) and it has two π electrons

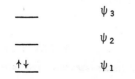

(b) The Woodward-Hoffmann Rules dictate that the
thermally induced electrolytic ring closure of a polyene
of 4n π electrons will involve a conrotatory motion of

264

the terminal p orbitals; conversely, a polyene of 4n + 2 π electrons will have its terminal p orbitals undergoing disrotatory motion. The allyl cation with 2 π electrons falls into the latter category and we would expect the ring closure to involve disrotatory motion.

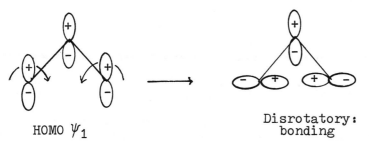

HOMO ψ_1

Disrotatory: bonding

(c) Using the same approach as in (b), we predict that the allyl anion, with 4 π electrons, would involve con-rotatory motion of the terminal p orbitals in its thermal cyclization.

Another way to arrive at this prediction is by examining the HOMO of the allyl anion. With 4 π electrons, 2 electrons are forced into the nonbonding orbital (ψ_2).

ψ_3 ___

ψ_2 ↑↓

ψ_1 ↑↓

ψ_2 is now   the HOMO state, and only conrotatory motion of the terminal p orbitals will allow effective cyclization.

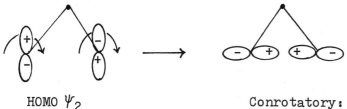

HOMO ψ_2

Conrotatory: bonding

(d) In the pentadienyl cation, there are 4 π electrons. Thus, by the Woodward-Hoffman rules, the thermal ring closure forming the cyclopentenyl cation would involve conrotatory motion.

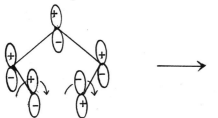
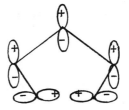

HOMO ψ_2

Conrotatory: bonding

265

CYCLOADDITION REACTIONS

Discuss the direct, concerted addition of H_2 to an alkene from the standpoint of orbital symmetry. (a) In the absence of catalyst, and (b) in the presence of photo-chemical stimulation.

Solution: It is best to begin with a review of the molecular orbital basis of a concerted addition reaction.

(1) In concerted addition, two new σ bonds are formed. The electrons involved in new bond formation come from the highest occupied molecular orbital (HOMO) because they are the least tightly held and thus most reactive.

(2) Since the HOMO of each reactant already contains two electrons, it must overlap an empty orbital of the other reactant. In doing this, it picks the most stable of these, the lowest unoccupied molecular orbital (LUMO). In the transition state of the addition, then, stabiliza-tion comes chiefly from overlap between the HOMO of one reactant and the LUMO of the other.

(3) In the absence of a catalytic agent (such as light or chemicals), only the ground state HOMO and LUMO are the reacting orbitals. For the converse, excited state HOMO and LUMO may take part in orbital overlap.

(a)   In the concerted reaction between H_2 and ethylene, the molecular orbitals of chief focus are:

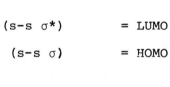

Note that since the hydrogenation is noncatalyzed, the reacting molecules have ground state configurations in accordance with (3) above. Also, according to (2), such reaction involves the overlap of the HOMO of one

reactant with the LUMO of the other.   Hence we have two
possible orbital combinations - (i) $HOMO_{H_2}$ + $LUMO_{C_2H_4}$
and (ii) $LUMO_{H_2}$ + $HOMO_{C_2H_4}$:

(i)

H_2　　　　　HOMO　　　　　(σ)

C_2H_4　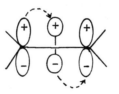　LUMO　　　　　$(\pi*)$

symmetry forbidden

(ii)

H_2　　　LUMO　　　　　$(\sigma*)$

C_2H_4　　HOMO　　　　　(π)

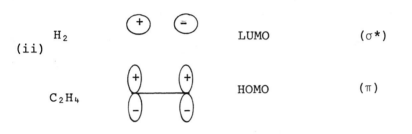

symmetry forbidden

    As the above shows, lobes of opposite phase
(indicated by opposite signs) would approach each other.
Since H_2 is only two atoms long, a suprafacial-antara-
facial reaction is sterically very difficult:

Hence, concerted hydrogenation of ethylene in the absence
of a catalyst is not possible.

(b)   In the presence of photochemical stimulation, some
molecules will exist in excited state.   The HOMO of an
excited molecules can actually overlap in a suprafacial-
suprafacial manner with the LUMO of a ground-state molecule, allowing orbital symmetry and effective bond formation.   Thus catalyzed concerted addition of H_2 to ethylene
will result in hydrogenation.

H_2　　　　　　　LUMO of ground state $(\sigma*)$

C_2H_4　　　　　　HOMO of excited state $(\pi*)$

symmetry allowed

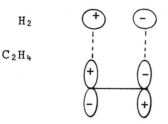

H₂

C₂H₄

HOMO of excited state ($\sigma*$)

LUMO of ground state ($\pi*$)

symmetry allowed

● **PROBLEM** 8-10

Starting with any organic compounds of less than four carbon atoms and any inorganic or physical reagents that may be required, synthesize

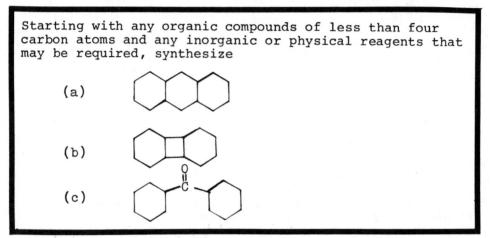

(a)

(b)

(c)

Solution: Diels-Alder reactions, as well as other electrocyclic reactions are very valuable synthetic tools.   They enable the chemist to perform ring closings, build up molecules and are used extensively in the syntheses of drugs.

(a)

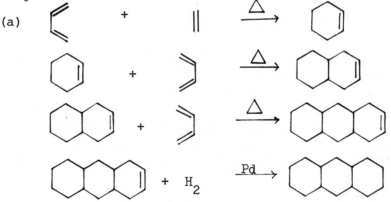

(b)   This reaction is a slight variation on the Diels-Alder.   The first step consists of the formation of cyclohexene.

Now, if two cyclohexenes are exposed to ultraviolet light the desired moity will be obtained.

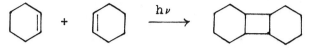

(c) This reaction involves little more than cyclo-hexane formation followed by two Grignard reactions.

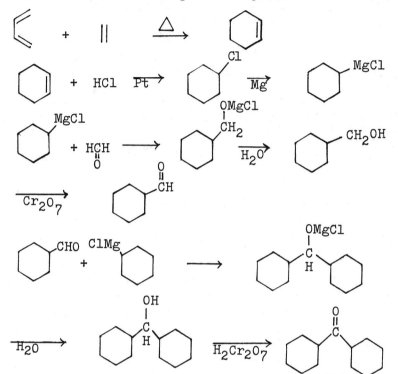

RESONANCE THEORY

● **PROBLEM** 8-11

In 1,3-butadiene, the observed length of the C_2-C_3 bond is 1.48 Å, while the "standard" single bond distance is gener-ally accepted to be 1.54 Å. Explain this discrepancy and calculate the π bond order of the C_2-C_3 butadiene bond. (Hint, consider the resonance effects and the molecular orbital structure).

Solution:

$$\underset{\text{1,3-Butadiene}}{H_2C=\overset{\overset{\displaystyle H}{|}}{C}-\overset{\overset{\displaystyle H}{|}}{C}=CH_2}$$

269

The above structure is the accepted structure for 1,3-butadiene. This structure, however, is not altogether correct in that 1,3-butadiene has several resonance forms which originate from the interactions of the π-cloud electrons.

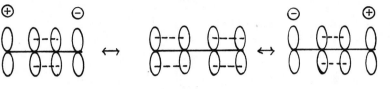

$$\overset{\oplus}{CH_2}-CH=CH-\overset{\ominus}{CH_2} \leftrightarrow CH_2=CH-CH=CH_2 \leftrightarrow \overset{\ominus}{CH_2}-CH=CH-\overset{\oplus}{CH_2}$$

It should be stressed that the correct structure of 1,3-butadiene is a hybrid of these structures, not an equilibrium condition of the three forms.

Hence, the best representation of 1,3-butadiene would be,

$$CH_2 \text{========} CH \text{=======} CH \text{======} CH_2$$

So, as one can see, the C_2-C_3 bond, which was previously represented as a single bond, is really a single bond with some double bond character. The C_1-C_2 and C_3-C_4 bonds, conversely, are double bonds with some single bond character. Empirically the C_2-C_3 bond length has been observed at 1.48 Å, while the "standard" single bond distance (as found in ethane) is 1.54 Å.

In recent years, a second theory has developed which not only account for shorter bond distances, but predicts them as well. If the bonding about the various carbons is examined, it will be seen that the C_2-C_3 single bond is a bond between two sp^2-hybridized carbons, which would have a shorter length than a bond between two sp^3-hybridized carbons.

$$\overset{H\quad H}{CH_2=C - C=CH_2}$$

$$sp^2 \quad sp^2 \quad sp^2 \quad sp^2$$

The shortness of the C_2-C_3 butadiene bond is attributable to both the sp^2 hybridization and to resonance stabilization.

The π bond order is simply a measure of the double bond character of a given bond. The C_2-C_3 single bond should possess some double bond character. The general formula for the calculation of the π bond order order (πBO) is:

$$\pi BO = \frac{r_s - r}{2r - 3r_d + r_s}$$

where   r = observed bond length

r_s = normal single bond length (1.54 Å)

r_d = normal double bond length (1.33 Å)

$$\pi BO_{C_2-C_3} = \frac{(1.54 - 1.48)}{(2 \times 1.48) - (3 \times 1.33) + 1.54} = .12$$

● **PROBLEM** 8-12

Evaluate the importance of resonance of the following
types:

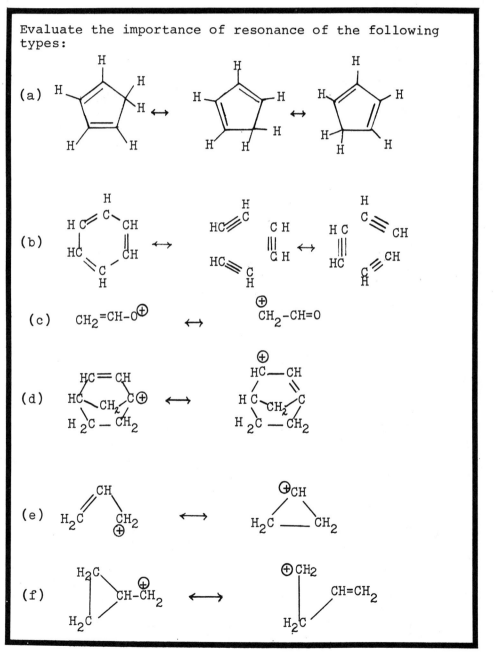

(a)

(b)

(c)

(d)

(e)

(f)

271

Solution: In solving these problems, one should keep in mind the three criteria for resonance:

(1)   There is no change in the positions of nuclei in resonance structures, the only change involved is in electron distribution.

(2)   Structures with filled octets are more important than structures with unfilled octets.

(3)   More important structures involve a minimum of charge separation.

(a)

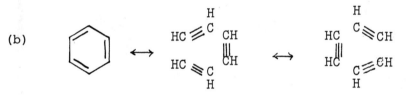

The above resonance is expected to be relatively unimportant.   The carbon atoms in these resonance structures would have to vary between sp^3 and sp^2 hybridizations.   This involves a change in molecular bonding, and as such represents a change in bond angles and nuclear positions.

(b)

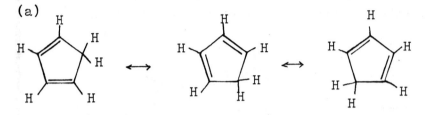

This   resonance   is considered to be unimportant, as they involve the existence of acetylene molecules in highly strained conformation.

Acetylene prefers a linear molecular arrangement with bond angles of 180° rather than 120° as assumed in the resonance contributing structures.

(c) $CH_2=CH-\overset{\oplus}{O}$ ⟷ $CH_2\doteq CH\doteq\overset{\oplus}{O}$

In going from one resonance form to the other, there is no change in the nucleic configuration of the molecule.

272

Each has an unfilled octet as well as an identical positive charge. Therefore this type of resonance is expected to be important.

Of the two, $\overset{\oplus}{C}H_2-CH=O$ will be slightly more favorable, as a positive charge on oxygen is less stable than a positive charge on carbon.

(d)   A superficial examination would indicate that these resonance structures satisfy the three criteria for resonance.   There is no change in the nucleic configuration. The structures are alike in having one unfilled octet, and also in having the same charge separation.

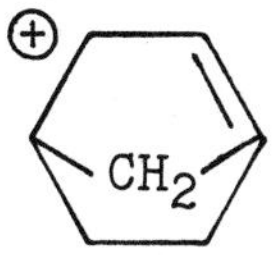

II

Resonance form II, however, violates Bredt's rule which states that for steric reasons a double bond at a bridgehead carbon is forbidden.   Therefore, the resonance is not important.

(e)

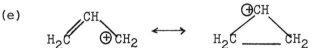

This type of resonance is considered unimportant, since the cyclic cation involves an unfavorable conformation with highly strained bond angles.   The conformation in which the allyl carbon will most likely be found is:

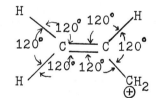

(f)

The above resonance will be of importance since it follows the three criteria of resonance.   In addition, a primary cation is highly unstable, therefore the tendency for the cation to be in a conformation which would allow for the cyclic resonance form is high.

Which chloride of each of the following pairs would be expected to lose chloride ion most readily and form a carbonium ion? Explain.

(a) $CH_2=CH-CH_2-CH_2Cl$ and $CH_2=CH-CH_2Cl$

(b) $CH_2=CH-CH-CH=CH_2$ and $CH_2=CH-CH=CH-CH_2Cl$
　　　　　　　|
　　　　　　　Cl

Solution: (a) To determine which chloride will be likely to become a carbocation most readily, it is best to look at the various resonance forms of the carbocations. The carbocation with the most resonance forms will be the most stable due to resonance energy.

Examining allyl chloride first, we find the following resonance:

$$CH_2=CH-CH_2Cl \xrightarrow{-Cl^{\ominus}} CH_2=CH-\overset{\oplus}{CH}$$
$$\updownarrow$$
$$H_2\overset{\oplus}{C}-\overset{H}{C}=CH_2$$

4-Chloro-1-butene will not undergo any appreciable resonance stabilization upon ionization (loss of Cl^-); therefore the positive charge will not be stabilized by electrons from the double bond.

(b) In this case, these two isomers will form identical resonance structures.

$$CH_2=CH-\underset{\underset{Cl}{|}}{CH}-CH=CH_2 \xrightarrow{-Cl^{\ominus}} CH_2=CH-\overset{\oplus}{CH}-CH=CH_2$$

$$CH_2=CH-CH=CH-\overset{\oplus}{CH_2} \longleftrightarrow \overset{\oplus}{CH_2}-CH=CH-CH=CH_2$$

$$CH_2=CH-CH=CH_2-CH_2Cl \xrightarrow{-Cl^{\ominus}} CH_2=CH-CH=CH_2-CH_2\overset{\oplus}{}$$
$$\updownarrow$$
$$CH_2=CH-CH-CH=CH_2$$
$$\overset{\oplus}{\updownarrow}$$
$$\overset{\oplus}{CH_2}=CH=CH-CH=CH_2$$

Since the conjugated compound ($CH_2=CH-CH=CH-CH_2Cl$) is more stable thermodynamically than the nonconjugated compound ($CH_2=CH-CHCl-CH=CH_2$), the energy of activation (E_{act}) in the ionization process is greater for the former than the latter. Hence the nonconjugated compound will lose Cl^- more easily than the conjugated one.

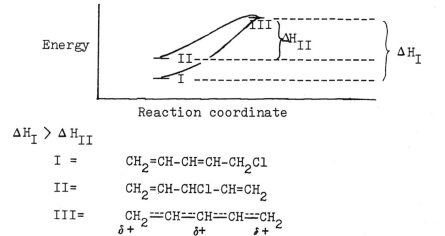

Reaction coordinate

$\Delta H_I > \Delta H_{II}$

I   = $CH_2=CH-CH=CH-CH_2Cl$

II= $CH_2=CH-CHCl-CH=CH_2$

III= $CH_2\!=\!=\!=\!CH\!=\!=\!CH\!=\!=\!CH\!=\!=\!=\!CH_2$
              $\delta+$ $\delta+$ $\delta+$

CHAPTER 9

ALKADIENES

● **PROBLEM** 9-1

What are dienes? Briefly discuss their properties and system of nomenclature.

Solution: Dienes are alkenes which contain two carbon-carbon double bonds. These double bonds can be either adjacent (called cumulated double bonds), or separated by one carbon-carbon single bond (conjugated), or separated by two or more carbon single bonds (isolated).

The nomenclature of dienes is analogous to that of alkenes, with certain modifications to indicate the extra double bond. The numbering of carbons is the same as that of alkenes. The numbers of the olefinic carbons are placed at the beginning of the name, which is suffixed by -diene instead of -ene. For example, a compound of the structure

$$\overset{5}{C}H_3\overset{4}{C}H=\overset{3}{C}H-\overset{2}{C}H=\overset{1}{C}H_3 \text{ is called 1,4-pentadiene, where "1,4"}$$

indicates the positions of the double bonds.

The properties of dienes depend upon the arrangement of the double bonds and the other substituents. If the double bonds are widely separated(as in isolated dienes),the compound behaves like a simple alkene. If the compound is conjugated, there is potential delocalization of the π electrons. Conjugated double bonds are, in general, more stable than isolated double bonds because of the resonance effect. Cumulated double bonds (allenes) are more unstable than isolated double bonds because of their geometry and electron density.

Of all the dienes studied so far, the most important one is 1,3-butadiene, $CH_2=CH-CH=CH_2$. It is used in making synthetic rubber by free-radical polymerization.

● **PROBLEM** 9-2

Name or draw structures for the following compounds.

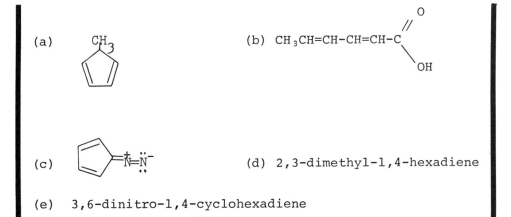

(a)

(b) $CH_3CH=CH-CH=CH-C\diagleftdownarrow^{O}_{OH}$

(c)

(d) 2,3-dimethyl-1,4-hexadiene

(e)   3,6-dinitro-1,4-cyclohexadiene

Solution: The IUPAC system of naming for dienes is
similar to that for simple alkenes, except that it is pre-
fixed by two numbers to indicate the positions of the double
bonds, and suffixed by -diene instead of -ene. The numbers
are assigned so as to have the lowest combination.

(a) [structure: 5-methyl-cyclopentadiene, carbons numbered 1-5 with CH₃ at 5]   is a cyclic compound containing five

carbons in the ring, a methyl substituent, and two carbon-
carbon double bonds. The name of the compound is 5-methyl-
1,3-cyclopentadiene.

(b) $CH_3-CH=CH-CH=CH-C\diagleftdownarrow^{O}_{OH}$ contains six carbons in a
      6   5   4   3   2   1

chain, two carbon-carbon double bonds, and a carboxyl
functional group. Since the COOH group takes precedence
over diene in naming, the compound is named as a derivative
of hexanoic acid. The numbering of carbons in carboxylic
acid starts with the carbonyl carbon as number one. Thus,
the name of the compound is 2,4-dienehexanoic acid.

(c) [structure: cyclopentadiene ring numbered 1-5 with N=N: group]   is a cyclic diene with the double bonds

at carbons 1 and 3. At carbon number 5 there is a diazo
substituent. The IUPAC name for the compound is 5-diazo-
1,3-cyclopentadiene.

(d)   2,3-Dimethyl-1,4-hexadiene has a straight chain of six
carbons with double bonds at carbons 1 and 4. At carbons 2
and 3, there are methyl substitutions. Therefore, the structure of the compound is:

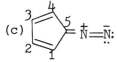

$$\underset{1\quad 2\qquad\; 3\qquad\; 4\quad 5\quad 6}{H_2C=\overset{\overset{\displaystyle CH_3}{|}}{C} - \overset{\overset{\displaystyle CH_3}{|}}{CH} - CH=CH-CH_3}$$

(e)   3,6-Dinitro-1,4-cyclohexadiene is a six-carbon cyclic
compound with double bonds at carbon numbers 1 and 4. At

carbons 3 and 6, there are two nitro $\left(\begin{array}{c} O \\ \parallel \\ -N\overset{\oplus}{} \\ \diagdown \\ \underset{\ominus}{O} \end{array}\right)$ sub-

stitutions. The structure of the compound is:

CONJUGATED DIENES

• **PROBLEM** 9-3

Account for the fact that 2-methyl-1,3-butadiene reacts
(a) with HCl to yield only 3-chloro-3-methyl-1-butene and
1-chloro-3-methyl-2-butene; (b) with bromine to yield only
3,4-dibromo-3-methyl-1-butene and 1,4-dibromo-2-methyl-2-
butene.

Solution: (a) In acid solution, one of the double bonds
in a diene becomes protonated. As in the case of alkenes,
protonation will occur to form the most stable cation. 2-
methyl-1,3-butadiene is protonated at carbon #1 because it
forms the most stable cation; there is electron delocalization involving the remaining double bond which stabilizes
the cation:

$$CH_2 = \overset{\overset{\textstyle CH_3}{|}}{C}-CH = CH_2 \quad \xrightarrow{H^+} \quad CH_3-\overset{\overset{\textstyle CH_3}{|}}{\underset{+}{C}}-CH = CH_2$$

$$CH_3-\overset{\overset{\textstyle CH_3}{|}}{\underset{+}{C}}-CH= CH_2 \quad \longleftrightarrow \quad CH_3-\overset{\overset{\textstyle CH_3}{|}}{C}= \underset{+}{CH}-CH_2$$

     Had protonation occurred at carbons # 2 or 3, no
electron delocalization would have been possible; the cation
would be relatively unstable. Had protonation occurred at
carbon # 4, electron delocalization is possible. However,
protonation of carbon # 4 distributes the positive charge
between a secondary and primary carbon, whereas protonation
of carbon # 1 distributes the charge between a tertiary and
primary carbon.

$$\underset{\text{CH}_3}{\overset{\text{CH}_3}{\underset{|}{\text{CH}_2\!=\!\text{C}-\text{CH}\!=\!\text{CH}_2}}} \xrightarrow{\text{H}^+} \underset{+}{\overset{\text{CH}_3}{\underset{|}{\text{CH}_2\!=\!\text{C}-\text{CH}-\text{CH}_3}}}$$

$$\overset{\text{CH}_3}{\underset{|}{\text{CH}_2\!=\!\text{C}-\overset{+}{\text{C}}\text{H}-\text{CH}_3}} \quad \longleftrightarrow \quad \overset{\text{CH}_3}{\underset{|}{+\ \ \text{CH}_2-\text{C}\!=\!\text{CH}-\text{CH}_3}}$$

Above: Protonation and stabilization at carbon # 4.

Since tertiary carbon stabilizes a positive charge more than a secondary carbon, the cation formed by protonation of carbon # 1 is more stable than the one formed by protonation of carbon #4. Hence, 2-methyl-1,3-butadiene will be protonated by HCl as follows:

$$\text{Cl}-\text{H} + \underset{\text{CH}_3}{\overset{\text{CH}_3}{\underset{|}{\text{CH}_2\!=\!\text{C}-\text{CH}\!=\!\text{CH}_2}}} \rightarrow \overset{\text{CH}_3}{\underset{|}{\text{CH}_3-\underset{\delta+}{\text{C}}\!=\!=\!=\!\text{CH}\!=\!=\!=\!\underset{\delta+}{\text{CH}_2}}} + \text{Cl}^-$$

The chloride will react with the diene cation to form two products. This is because the positive charge is distributed between two carbons (# 2 and # 4); hence there are two sites to which the chloride could attach.

$$\overset{\text{CH}_3}{\underset{|}{\text{CH}_3-\underset{\delta+}{\text{C}}\!=\!=\!=\!\text{CH}\!=\!=\!=\!\underset{\delta+}{\text{CH}_2}}} + \text{Cl}^- \rightarrow \underset{\text{Cl}}{\overset{\text{CH}_3}{\underset{|}{\text{CH}_3-\text{C}-\text{CH}\!=\!\text{CH}_2}}} + \underset{\text{Cl}}{\overset{\text{CH}_3}{\underset{|}{\text{CH}_3-\text{C}\!=\!\text{CH}-\text{CH}_2}}}$$

The overall reaction can be written as:

$$\underset{\text{CH}_3}{\overset{\text{CH}_3}{\underset{|}{\text{CH}_2\!=\!\text{C}-\text{CH}\!=\!\text{CH}_2}}} + \text{HCl} \rightarrow \underset{\text{Cl}}{\overset{\text{CH}_3}{\underset{|}{\text{CH}_3-\text{C}-\text{CH}\!=\!\text{CH}_2}}} + \overset{\text{CH}_3}{\underset{|}{\text{CH}_3-\text{C}\!=\!\text{CH}-\text{CH}_2\text{Cl}}}$$

| 2-methyl-1,3-butadiene | 3-chloro-3-methyl-1-butene | 1-chloro-3-methyl-2-butene |

3-chloro-3-methyl-1-butene is referred to as the "1,2" adduct. This is because addition of hydrogen halide took place at carbons #1 and 2. 1-chloro-3-methyl-2-butene is referred to as the "1,4" adduct because addition occurred at carbons # 1 and 4. The product distribution kinetically will favor the "1,2" adduct over the "1,4" adduct because the former actually resulted from a more stable carbonium ion than the latter, as shown in the following.

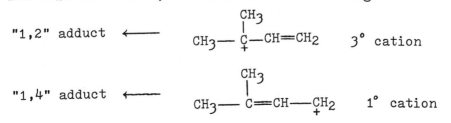

"1,2" adduct ⟵ $\underset{+}{\overset{\text{CH}_3}{\underset{|}{\text{CH}_3-\text{C}-\text{CH}\!=\!\text{CH}_2}}}$ 3° cation

"1,4" adduct ⟵ $\overset{\text{CH}_3}{\underset{|}{\text{CH}_3-\text{C}\!=\!\text{CH}-\underset{+}{\text{CH}_2}}}$ 1° cation

279

Products: $\overset{\displaystyle CH_3}{\underset{\displaystyle Cl}{\overset{\displaystyle |}{\underset{\displaystyle |}{CH_3C}}}}-CH=CH_2$ > $\overset{\displaystyle CH_3}{\overset{\displaystyle |}{CH_3C}}=CH-CH_2Cl$

The product distribution will thermodynamically favor the "1,4" adduct over the "1,2" adduct. This is because an internal double bond ("1,4" adduct) is more stable than a terminal double bond ("1,2" adduct); that is, the more substituted an alkene, the more stable the molecule. Hence, the product distribution depends totally upon the reaction conditions.

(b) Reaction of 2-methyl-1,3-butadiene with bromine is similar to part (a) in that addition occurs at carbons # 1 and 2 and at carbons # 1 and 4. The difference is that in part (a) the diene undergoes a hydrohalogenation whereas in part (b) the diene is halogenated. The electron-rich carbon # 1 - carbon # 2 double bond polarizes the bromine molecule so that a Br^+ is added to carbon # 1. The Br^- can then add to carbon # 2 or carbon # 4. The reaction occurs as:

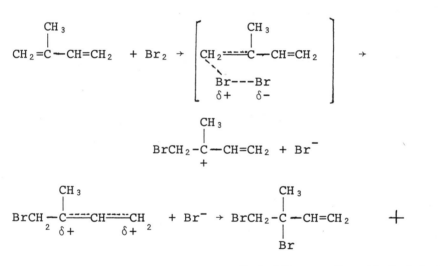

3,4-dibromo-3-methyl-1-butene

$$\overset{\displaystyle CH_3}{\overset{\displaystyle |}{BrCH_2-C}}=CH-CH_2Br$$

1,4-dibromo-2-methyl-2-butene

The overall reaction can be written as:

$$\overset{\displaystyle CH_3}{\overset{\displaystyle |}{CH_2}}=C-CH=CH_2 \ + \ Br_2 \ \rightarrow \ \overset{\displaystyle CH_3}{\underset{\displaystyle Br}{\overset{\displaystyle |}{\underset{\displaystyle |}{BrCH_2-C}}}}-CH=CH_2 \ + \ \overset{\displaystyle CH_3}{\overset{\displaystyle |}{BrCH_2-C}}=CH-CH_2Br$$

Draw energy diagrams analogous to Figure 1   for simple addition of H^+ to 1,3-pentadiene and 1,4-pentadiene so as to give the most stable carbonium ions possible. It turns out that the 1,3-isomer is both the more reactive and the more energetically stable diene. Explain how this information can be used to deduce the relative stabilities of the carbonium ions formed from these dienes.

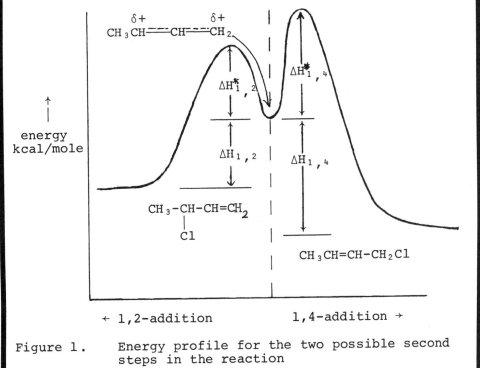

Figure 1.   Energy profile for the two possible second steps in the reaction

Solution: Protonation of 1,3-pentadiene occurs so that the resulting positive charge can be delocalized, involving the second double bond's π electrons. This will increase the stability of the carbocation. 1,3-pentadiene will be protonated at carbon # 1 to facilitate electron delocalization which stabilizes the positive charge. This is shown as:

$$CH_2=CH-CH=CH-CH_3 \xrightarrow{H^+} CH_3-\overset{+}{C}H-CH=CH-CH_3 \longleftrightarrow CH_3-CH=CH-\overset{+}{C}H-CH_3$$

This electron delocalization can alternately be represented as:

$$\overset{\delta+}{CH_3-CH} --- CH --- \overset{\delta+}{CH-CH_3}$$

Protonation at carbons # 2 and 3 does not occur because the resulting species would be relatively unstable; no electron delocalization could occur. Protonation at carbon # 4 also does not occur despite the fact that the resulting species would undergo electron delocalization. The reason for this is that the positive charge would be distributed

281

between a secondary and a primary carbon, whereas protonation
of carbon # 1 results in the positive charge distributed
between two secondary carbons. Since secondary carbons can
stabilize a positive charge more than primary carbons, protonation will preferentially occur at carbon # 1.

The double bonds of 1,4-pentadiene are equivalent and
it will not matter which one becomes protonated. What is
important is which carbon of the double bond becomes protonated. Protonation at carbon # 1 gives a secondary
carbocation whereas protonation of carbon # 2 gives a
primary carbocation. Neither species can undergo electron
delocalization. Since secondary carbocations are more
stable than primary carbocations, protonation will occur
at carbon # 1.

Since 1,3-pentadiene is more reactive to protonation
than 1,4-pentadiene, the activation energy for an addition
reaction is lower for 1,3-pentadiene than for 1,4-pentadiene.
From the problem we know that 1,3-pentadiene is energetically more stable than 1,4-pentadiene. This, coupled with the
fact that the activation energy is less for 1,3-pentadiene
can lead us to conclude that the cation of the 1,3-diene
is more energetically stable than the cation of the 1,4-
diene. An energy diagram of the protonation of both dienes
is shown below:

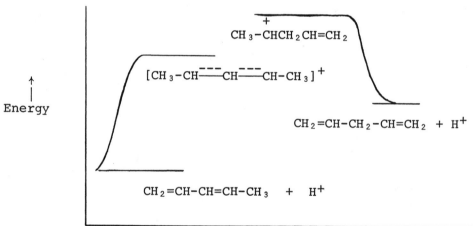

↑
|
Energy

Reaction coordinate   →

● **PROBLEM** 9-5

vic-Dibromides usually react with bases to produce more
alkyne than conjugated diene. What factor(s) may be
controlling this?

$$\begin{array}{c} \text{H H H H} \\ | \; | \; | \; | \\ -C-C-C-C- \\ | \; | \; | \; | \\ \text{Br Br} \end{array} \xrightarrow{\;-2HBr\;} \begin{array}{c} \text{H}\quad\;\;\text{H} \\ |\qquad\; | \\ C-C\equiv C-C- \\ |\qquad\; | \end{array} > \;\; \diagdown C=CH-CH=C\diagup$$

Two exceptions to this behavior are 1,2-dibromo-cyclohexane and 2,3-dichloro-2,3-dimethylbutane. How do you account for these exceptions?

Solution: The hydrogens that are bonded to the carbons bearing the bromine atoms are more acidic than the hydrogens on the adjacent carbon atoms. This is due to the inductive effect of the bromide group [i.e., its powerful electron withdrawing effect makes the hydrogen (H_a in diagram below) partially positively charged].

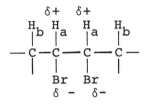

Hence, the proton H_a is more easily removed from the molecule than the proton H_b. This results in elimination occurring principally between the carbons bearing the bromine atoms. Therefore, triple bond formation is favored over the formation of two separate double bonds. In 1,2-dibromocyclohexane, triple bond formation is impossible due to ring strain. In other words, sp-hybridized carbons cannot exist in a cyclic structure. Thus only the cyclo-alkadiene is produced from this compound in the presence of base.   Therefore:

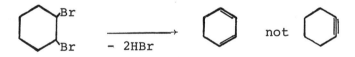

2,3-Dichloro-2,3-dimethylbutane will form only the conjugated diene (2,3-dimethyl-1,3-butadiene) and not the alkyne because there are no hydrogens on the carbons bearing the chloro groups; elimination will not occur between these two carbons.

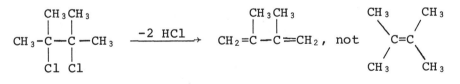

DIELS-ALDER REACTIONS

● **PROBLEM** 9-6

What products would you expect from the Diels-Alder addition of tetracyanoethylene to cis,trans-2,4-hexadiene and cis,cis-2,4-hexadiene? Explain.

Solution: The Diels-Alder reaction is a cycloaddition
reaction that occurs between a conjugated diene and an
alkene. This reaction is thermally induced and can be called
a [4+2] process because it involves the reaction of a system
of four π electrons (the diene) with a system of two π
electrons (the alkene). The alkene in the Diels-Alder reaction is called the dienophile; the diene reacts with the
dienophile to form a cyclohexene derivative. The Diels-
Alder reaction has some strict stereochemical requirements.
First, the diene must be in the s-cis configuration to react with the dienophile. The s-cis configuration is in
equilibrium with the s-trans configuration; they are
conformational diastereomers. The equilibrium between the
s-cis and s-trans isomers of 1,3-butadiene is shown as:

s-trans   s-cis

        This equilibration takes place by rotation about the
carbon-carbon single bond. Another requirement of the Diels-
Alder reaction is that the diene must add onto the dienophile
in a suprafacial process; that is, both bonds are formed on
the same face of the dienophile. The last requirement of the
Diels-Alder reaction is that the addition of a diene to a
dienophile bearing an unsaturated group will occur in an
endo fashion; that is, the unsaturated group will lie near
the developing double bond in the diene portion. Cis,trans-
2,4-hexadiene exists in s-trans - s-cis equilibrium as shown:

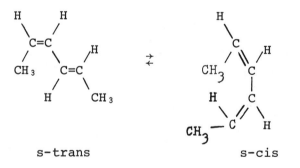

        s-trans   s-cis

        The molecule in the s-cis geometry will react with the
dienophile (tetracyanoethylene) in a suprafacial process.
Since the dienophile has unsaturated groups (the cyano
groups), the reaction should occur in an endo fashion. But
note that the dienophile has four equivalent unsaturated
groups; hence, it does not matter how the dienophile is
oriented for the reaction to occur. Cis,trans-2,4-hexadiene
undergoes a Diels-Alder reaction with tetracyanoethylene
as shown:

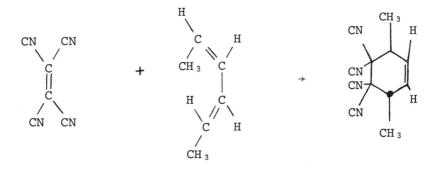

Note: The two methyl groups are trans to each other.

Cis,cis-2,4-hexadiene exists in s-trans - s-cis equilibrium as follows:

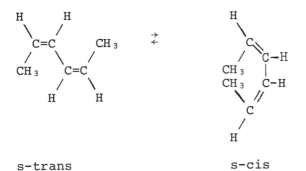

s-trans   s-cis

The molecule in the s-cis geometry will react with the
dienophile (tetracyanoethylene) in a suprafacial process.
Cis,cis-2,4-hexadiene undergoes a Diels-Alder reaction with
the dienophile as follows:

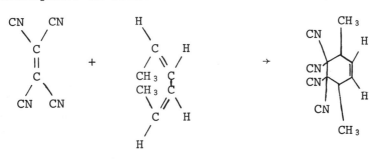

Note: The two methyl groups are cis to each other.

● PROBLEM 9-7

Consider whether formation of ionic rather than diradical
intermediates would affect the argument in favor of a two-
step mechanism for the Diels-Alder reaction. What information does the fact that typical Diels-Alder additions
occur in the vapor state give about free-radical vs. ionic
reaction mechanisms?

Let's look at a specific Diels-Alder reaction and proposed mechanisms for ionic and diradical intermediates. The Diels-Alder reaction between trans-piperylene

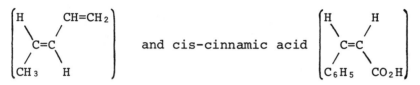

and cis-cinnamic acid

produces only one product due to the stereospecificity of the reaction. A proposed free radical mechanism is:

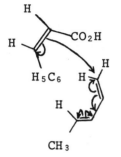

$\xrightarrow{\text{first step}}$

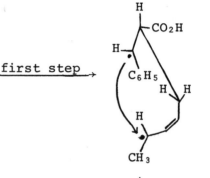

 second step

Arrows indicate movement of one electron.

(Note: All ring substituents are cis to each other.)

The fact that there is only one product formed indicates that the second step occurs faster than does rotation about the carbon-carbon single bonds in the diradical intermediate. The diradical intermediate has a free electron on carbon # 3 (and not carbon # 2) of cis-cinnamic acid because it can undergo resonance stabilization involving the phenyl group. A proposed ionic mechanism for the same Diels-Alder reaction is:

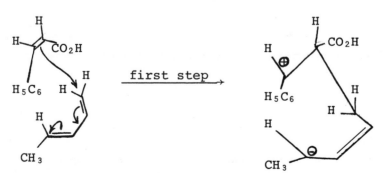

$\xrightarrow{\text{first step}}$

286

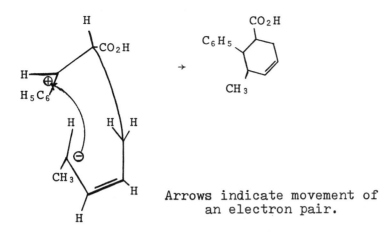

Arrows indicate movement of
an electron pair.

As in the free radical mechanism, the ring is formed
in the second step faster than rotation about the
carbon-carbon single bond. Hence, this explains how only
one product is formed. The fact that Diels-Alder reactions
can occur in the vapor state suggests that the reaction
does not occur through an ionic mechanism. Ions cannot
easily exist in the vapor state. The ions must be solvated;
that is, the charges must be separated by a solvent. In
the vapor phase, there is no solvent. Since free radicals
can easily exist in the vapor state, the Diels-Alder reaction seems to occur more through a free radical mechanism
than an ionic mechanism.

1,2-CYCLOADDITION REACTIONS

● **PROBLEM** 9-8

Assuming the mechanism of 1,2-cycloaddition is similar to
1,4-cycloaddition (i.e., the Diels-Alder reaction), is the
product obtained from the addition of cyclopentadiene and
ketene the expected one? Explain.

Solution: It is thought that 1,4-cycloaddition reactions
proceed through a mechanism involving a diradical intermediate. If we assume that the mechanism of 1,2-cycloaddition
is similar to 1,4-cycloaddition, there are four possible
products from the reaction of cyclopentadiene and ketene.
The reactions and their mechanisms are presented below
(arrows show movement of one electron):

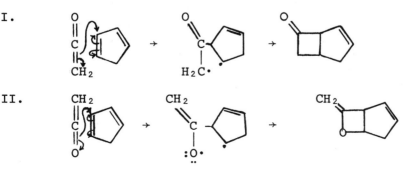

III.

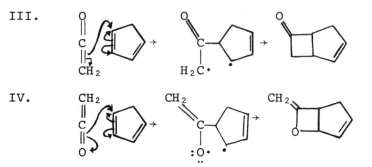

IV.

CH₂
‖
C
‖
O

→

CH₂
‖
C
|
:O·

→

The expected product would be the one that proceeds through the most stable intermediate. The intermediates in reactions III and IV have allylic radicals; they will be stabilized by electron delocalization of the type:

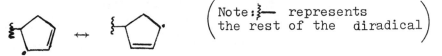

$$\left(\begin{array}{l}\text{Note:}\text{\textemdash represents}\\ \text{the rest of the diradical}\end{array}\right)$$

The intermediates in reactions I and II are less stable than those in reactions III and IV; this is because I and II intermediates do not undergo resonance stabilization. The product from reaction III will be expected over the product from reaction IV because

$$\left|\Delta H_{III}\right| > \left|\Delta H_{IV}\right|.$$

This means that reaction III is more exothermic than reaction IV, and the product of reaction III is thermodynamically more stable than the product of reaction IV. Hence, the expected product is the one formed in reaction III. This is in fact the actual product obtained from the 1,2-cycloaddition reaction of ketene with cyclopentadiene.

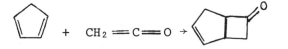

ALLENES

• PROBLEM 9-9

(a) Make a model of allene, $CH_2=C=CH_2$, a cumulated diene. What is the spatial relationship between the pair of hydrogens at one end of the molecule and the pair of hydrogens at the other end? (b) Substituted allenes of the type RCH=C=CHR have been obtained in optically active form. Is this consistent with the shape of the molecule in (a)? Where are the chiral centers in the substituted allene? (c) Work out the electronic configuration of allene. (Hint: How many atoms are attached to the middle carbon? To each of the end carbons?) Does this lead to the same shape of molecule that you worked out in (a) and (b)?

Solution: (a) Allene is the simplest cumulated diene;
its molecular formula is C_3H_4. The two pairs of methylene
hydrogens lie in planes that are perpendicular to each
other. This spatial relationship is the only one that will
allow for efficient overlap of 2p-2p orbitals in the π
bonds.

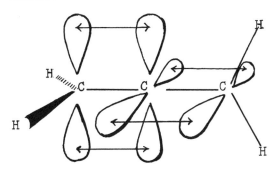

Above: Diagram showing 2p-2p orbital overlap in allene.

     (b)   Compounds of the type RCH=C=CHR have the same
molecular shape as allene. This is because the carbons involved in π bonding for allene have the same hybridization
as those in RCH=C=CHR. There are no chiral carbons in RCH=
C=CHR, but the molecule itself is chiral; that is, there is
no plane of symmetry in the molecule. As the molecule is
chiral, it will be optically active. Note that a compound
of the type $R_2C=C=CH_2$ is achiral because there are two
planes of symmetry (R_2C- plane and the $-CH_2$ plane).

     (c) Each of the end carbons in allene is bonded to
three atoms and possesses one double bond. All chemical
double bonds contain a sigma (σ) bond and a pi (π) bond.
The π bond involves the overlap of two 2p electron orbitals.
The remaining three bonds of the end carbons (the σ bond
of the double, and the two single bonds to the hydrogens)
must be hybridized. The orbitals involved in bonding for
carbon are one 2s orbital and three 2p orbitals. Since for
each end carbon in allene one of the 2p orbitals are
involved in π bonding, this leaves one 2s orbital and two
2p orbitals to be involved in the hybridization. The end
carbons in allene are sp^2-hybridized carbons; there are
three $2sp^2$ orbitals involved in σ bonds and one 2p orbital
involved in a π bond.   The trigonal   planar configuration
of the end carbons' orbitals (as seen in the diagram in
part a) supports our conclusion; the end carbons are sp^2
hybridized. The middle carbon is bonded to two atoms and
has two double bonds; that is, it has two σ bonds and two
π bonds. Each π bond involves a 2p orbital. The remaining
two bonds of the middle carbon must be involved in orbital
hybridization. Since two 2p orbitals have been accounted
for, it must be the remaining 2s orbital and 2p orbital that
are hybridized. The middle carbon is sp hybridized; there
are two 2sp orbitals involved in σ bonding and two 2p
orbitals involved in π bonding. The linear configuration
of the orbitals (as seen in the diagram in part a) supports
our conclusion; the middle carbon is sp hybridized. Below
is a diagram of allene indicating the orbitals involved
in the different types of bonds:

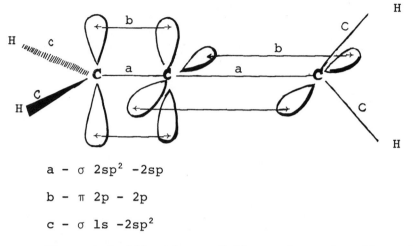

a - σ 2sp² -2sp

b - π 2p - 2p

c - σ 1s -2sp²

These hybridizations of the carbons in allene lead to the same shape that we worked out in part (a) and part (b).

● **PROBLEM** 9-10

(a) Predict the heat of hydrogenation of allene, $CH_2=C=CH_2$.
(b) The actual value is -71 kcal. What can you say about the stability of a cumulated diene?

Solution: (a) The general range of heats of hydrogenation of alkenes is from -27 to -31 kcal/mole. Here we are dealing with the hydrogenation of double bonds between two sp^2-hybridized carbons and an sp-hybridized carbon. We will assume a ΔH (heat of hydrogenation) value of -28 to -30 kcal/mole for each double bond in allene.

$CH_2=C=CH_2$ + $2H_2$ → $CH_3CH_2CH_3$

   allene   propane

ΔH = (2 × -28) to (2 × -30)

ΔH = - 56 to -60 kcal/mole.

(b) The lower ΔH value means that the reaction is more exothermic than predicted; there is more energy actually released than we expected . This indicates that allene is more reactive, and hence more unstable relative to compounds having conjugated or isolated double bonds.

POLYMERIZATION

● **PROBLEM** 9-11

Formulate chain initiation, propagation, and termination steps for the polymerization of butadiene by a peroxide

catalyst. Consider carefully possible structures for the
growing-chain radical. Show the expected structure of the
polymer.

Solution: Peroxides are very unstable compounds which
are often used as a catalyst for free radical polymerization
reactions. The peroxide breaks down into two alkoxy radicals
as shown:

$$ROOR´ \longrightarrow RO· + R´O·$$

peroxide   alkoxy radicals

This is the initiation step of a free radical polymerization process. Free radical polymerizations, like all addition
polymerization reactions, produce head to tail polymerization;   that is, the growing end of the polymer is the most
stable possible radical. In the case of 1,3-butadiene the
alkoxy radical attacks an end carbon and not an internal
carbon. This is because attack of an end carbon forms a
resonance stabilized free radical whereas attack of an internal carbon forms a radical with no such stabilization.
Hence, the end carbon will be attacked by the alkoxy
radical to form the more stable species. This is shown as:

$$RO·+CH_2=CHCH=CH_2 \rightarrow ROCH_2-\overset{·}{C}H-CH=CH_2 \leftrightarrow ROCH_2-CH=CH-\overset{·}{C}H_2$$

The resulting radical will attack an end carbon of
another 1,3-butadiene molecule. There are three possible
products which all depend on where the end carbon of the
diene is bonded to the radical. Note that the free electron
of the radical $ROCH_2\overset{·}{C}HCH=CH_2$ distributes its time between
carbons # 2 and 4 (where carbon # 1 is the $RO-CH_2-$ carbon).

Polymerization can occur as a 1,2-addition or a 1,4-
addition; that is, the radical can attack a diene molecule
with the free electron on either carbon # 2 or carbon # 4.
This accounts for two possible polymerization products,
but there is a third one. Note that the growing polymer in
1,4-addition can have two different configurations: cis and
trans. The radical can add to a diene by 1,4-addition to
produce a trans or a cis product:

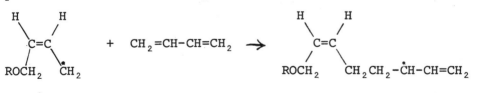

cis

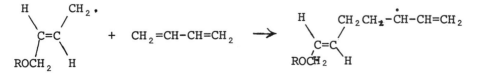

trans   1,4-addition

291

The radical adds to the diene by 1,2-addition as shown:

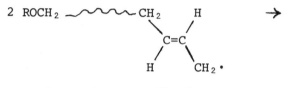

The chain lengthening of the polymeric radical is the propagation step. The polymer can be formed as any combination of 1,2-, 1,4-cis or 1,4-trans additions; the polymer can be a result of one or all of the three addition processes. The termination step of a polymerization reaction puts a stop to the growing polymer. In free radical polymerization, the termination step rids the growing polymer of its free electron. This generally proceeds by any one of three different methods: dimerization, disproportionation and abstraction. Dimerization involves the joining of two growing polymer radicals. It can be shown as:

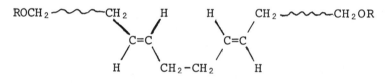

growing polymer radical

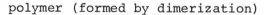

polymer (formed by dimerization)

Disproportionation reactions involve the transfer of a hydrogen radical from one growing polymer radical to another. This results in the joining of a hydrogen radical with a growing polymer radical and the formation of a carbon-carbon bond in the other growing polymer radical. This is shown as:

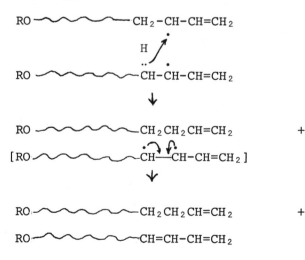

292

Abstraction involves the loss of a hydrogen atom to form a carbon-carbon bond. This is shown as:

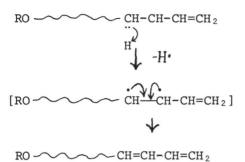

• **PROBLEM 9-12**

Gutta percha is a non-elastic naturally-occurring polymer used in covering golf balls and underwater cables. It has the same formula $(C_5H_8)_n$, and yields the same hydrogenation product and the same ozonolysis product as natural rubber. Using structural formulas, show the most likely structural difference between Gutta percha and rubber.

Solution: Natural rubber or poly-cis-isoprene has the structure:

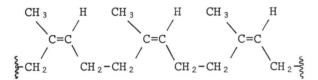

The hydrogenation product of natural rubber is poly-2-methylbutane or poly-isopentane:

$$\xi\text{-} CH_2\text{-}\overset{\overset{\displaystyle CH_3}{|}}{C}HCH_2CH_2\text{-}CH_2\text{-}\overset{\overset{\displaystyle CH_3}{|}}{C}HCH_2CH_2 \text{-}\xi$$

Hydrogenation of Gutta percha yields the same product. Hence, there are six possible structural formulas that correspond to the molecular formula of Gutta percha, $(C_5H_8)_n$. They are:

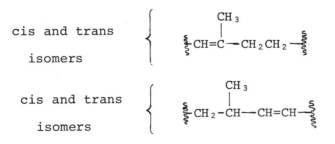

293

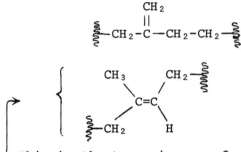

This is the trans isomer of natural rubber (that is, poly-trans-isoprene).

Ozonolysis of natural rubber yields 4-oxo-pentanal:

$$\underset{CH_3}{\overset{\overset{O}{\|}}{C}}\underset{}{\overset{}{CH_2}}\underset{}{\overset{}{CH_2}}\underset{}{\overset{\overset{O}{\|}}{CH}}$$

Since ozonolysis of Gutta percha gives the same product as natural rubber, the only structural formula for Gutta percha (from our list of possibles) would be the trans isomer of natural rubber. Hence, Gutta percha is also known as poly-trans-isoprene:

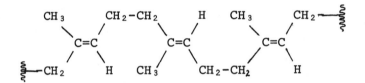

SYNTHESIS

• PROBLEM 9-13

Show the last step in a synthesis of each of the following substances (give approximate reaction conditions):

(a) CH_2=CHCHBrCH$_3$

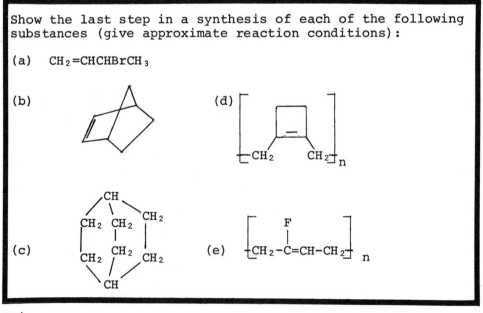

294

Solution: (a) We can synthesize the desired product, 3-bromo-1-butene, by reacting 1,3-butadiene with hydrobromic acid. There will be competition between the 1,2- and 1,4-addition processes. Since our desired product is a result of 1,2-addition, we want to set the reaction conditions so that the 1,2-addition product is the major one. Since the 1,2-addition product is kinetically more stable than the 1,4-addition product, we would want to slow down the reaction so that it is easy for "1,2"-adduct and difficult for "1,4"-adduct to form. We can slow the reaction by maintaining a low temperature.

$$CH_2{=}CH{-}CH{=}CH_2 \quad \xrightarrow[0°C \text{ or less}]{HBr}$$

$$CH_2{=}\;CH{-}CHBr{-}CH_3 \qquad \text{(main product)}$$

(b) Many bridged bicyclic alkenes can be prepared by a Diels-Alder reaction. The desired product can be prepared by a Diels-Alder reaction involving cyclopentadiene and ethylene. Since Diels-Alder reactions are thermally induced, a high temperature must be maintained throughout the reaction.

$$+ \quad \begin{array}{c} CH_2 \\ || \\ CH_2 \end{array} \quad \xrightarrow{150°C}$$

(c) Catalytic hydrogenation of bridged bicyclic alkenes will yield bridged bicyclic alkanes (which is our desired product). A Diels-Alder reaction between 1,3-cyclohexadiene

and ethylene will yield :

$$+ \quad \begin{array}{c} CH_2 \\ || \\ CH_2 \end{array} \quad \xrightarrow{150°C} \quad$$ If this compound under-

went catalytic hydrogenation, it would form our desired product.

$$\xrightarrow{H_2/Pt} \qquad \begin{array}{c} CH_2 \\ | \\ CH_2 \end{array}$$

(d) The desired product is formed by polymerization of

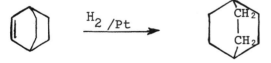

. This compound is made by a [2+2] cycloaddi-

tion reaction (a system with two π electrons acting upon another system with two π electrons). Allene will react

295

with itself to produce Polymerization can be

accomplished by using peroxides. A peroxide will break down to an alkoxy free radical; free radical polymerization will then occur.

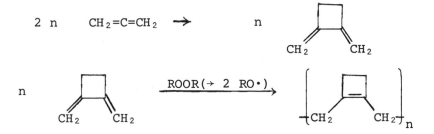

(e) The desired product can be made by the free radical polymerization of $CH_2=CF-CH=CH_2$. The desired product is one that results from a 1,4-addition process.

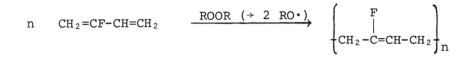

SPECTROSCOPY

● **PROBLEM** 9-14

Sketch out the n.m.r. spectra, including spin-spin splitting (if any), expected for the following compounds:

(a) $BrCH=C=CH_2$
(b) $CH_3CH_2C≡CH$
(c) $(CH_3)_3CCH=C=CHCH_2OCH_3$

Solution: Generally, we can expect spin-spin splitting to occur only between non-equivalent adjacent protons. When there is a significant amount of π bond interaction in a molecule, non-equivalent protons that are separated by one carbon (where there is significant π bonding) will undergo spin-spin splitting.

(a)   Cumulated dienes have significant π bond interaction about the =C= carbon. As a result, there will be spin-spin splitting between the protons adjacent to the central carbon. The methylene (=CH₂) protons will be split into a doublet by the bromomethylene (BrCH=) proton. The methylene signal will be near 5.5 δ due to   deshielding by the nearby π electrons. The bromomethylene proton will be split into a triplet by the two methylene protons. The bromomethylene proton will absorb near 4.5 δ. It is upfield from the methylene signal because of the shielding effect of the bromo group.

(b) Alkynes also have significant π bond interaction about the -C≡C- bond. The n.m.r. spectrum of terminal alkynes will show spin-spin splitting between the terminal proton (-C≡C-H) and the -CH₂-C≡C- protons. The n.m.r. spectrum of 1-butyne has the -C≡C-H proton split into a triplet by the two methylene protons. The -C≡C-H signal will be near 2.4 δ. This is due to the deshielding effect of the π electrons. The methyl protons will be split into a triplet by the two methylene protons. The methyl group will absorb at the characteristic value of 0.9 δ. The methylene protons will be split by the non-equivalent methyl and terminal protons. The methylene protons are split into a doublet by the terminal proton; these in turn are split into a quartet by the three methyl protons. The signal that results is an octet. It occurs near 1.3 δ, which is slightly down-field from the characteristic methylene absorption. This is because of the deshielding effect of the π electrons.

(c) This compound is a cumulated diene and will have the same type of splitting described in part (a). The methyl protons of the t-butyl group will not be split and will occur as a singlet near 0.9 δ. The t-Bu-CH=C= proton will be split into a doublet by the =C=CH- proton and will absorb near 5 δ. The =C=CH- proton will be split into a doublet by the t-Bu-CH=C= proton. This in turn will be split into a triplet by the two methylene protons (=C=CH-CH₂-). As a result, the =C=CH- signal will appear as a sextet. This signal occurs near 5 δ and is slightly up-field (lower δ value) relative to the t-Bu-CH=C= signal. This is because the =C=CH- proton is closer to the oxygen and will be shielded more than the t-Bu-CH=C= proton. The methylene signal will be split into a doublet by the =C=CH- proton; it will occur near 2.1 δ. This is because the methylene is adjacent to the electron withdrawing oxygen. The -OCH₃ protons will not be split and will occur at 3.3 δ.

● **PROBLEM** 9-15

Why is the electronic spectrum of the compound shown below more like that of tetramethylethylene than that of hexamethyl-1,3-butadiene? (Hint: Build a model.)

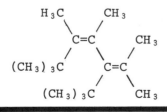

Solution: As the electron delocalization in a molecule increases, the maximum wavelength absorption in the electronic spectrum will also increase. The electron delocalization of a conjugated diene such as 1,3-butadiene is great enough so that the electronic spectrum will not appear as "two ethylenes." That is, 1,3-butadiene will have its own characteristic electronic spectrum and constitutes a different chromophore from a compound with two isolated double bonds. In the compound shown above (Z-2,4,5,6,6-pentamethyl-3-t-butyl-2,4-heptadiene), the steric repulsion between the t-butyl groups prevents coplanarity of the double bonds. As a result, there is some loss of electron delocalization. The loss in electron delocalization causes a decrease in the maximum wavelength absorption in the electronic spectrum. This decrease in absorption is great enough that the electronic spectrum of the compound is more like an ethylene chromophore spectrum than a conjugated diene chromophore spectrum. Hence, the electronic spectrum of the compound is more like that of tetramethylethylene than that of hexamethyl-1,3-butadiene.

CHARACTERIZATION TESTS

● **PROBLEM** 9-16

On the basis of physical properties, an unknown compound is believed to be one of the following:

n-pentane (b.p. 36°)   1-pentyne (b.p. 40°)
2-pentene (b.p. 36°)   methylene chloride (b.p. 40°)
1-chloropropene (b.p. 37°)   3,3-dimethyl-1-butene (b.p.41°)
trimethylethylene (b.p. 39°) 1,3-pentadiene (b.p. 42°)

Describe how you would go about finding out which of the possibilities the unknown actually is. Where possible, use simple chemical tests; where necessary, use more elaborate chemical methods like quantitative hydrogenation and cleavage. Tell exactly what you would do and see.

Solution: We can separate the saturated compounds from the unsaturated compounds by testing with $KMnO_4$ (potassium permanganate). Potassium permanganate is a strong oxidizing agent and will oxidize alkenes to vicinal diols and alkynes to carboxylic acids. Manganese dioxide (MnO_2) is the reduced $KMnO_4$ product; $KMnO_4$ is purple and MnO_2 is brown. Hence, all the compounds except n-pentane and methylene chloride will show a color change in $KMnO_4$ solution (purple → brown). To distinguish between methylene chloride and n-pentane, we will test each for the presence of halogen; only methylene chloride should give a positive test. In this case, we can't just add silver ion and expect to see a silver chloride precipitate from methylene chloride. We must first liberate chloride ion from methylene chloride. This can be accomplished by using an S_N2 reaction; the

chloride is a good leaving group and will go into solution. n-Pentane has no good leaving groups and will not undergo an S_N2 reaction. If both compounds are treated with silver

hydroxide, methylene chloride will show a white silver chloride precipitate and n-pentane will not.

$$CH_2Cl_2 \; + \; Ag^{\oplus}OH^{\ominus} \rightarrow \; Cl-CH_2OH \; + \; Ag^{\oplus}Cl^{\ominus}$$

colorless   white

$$CH_3CH_2CH_2CH_2CH_3 \; + \; Ag^{\oplus}OH^{\ominus} \; \rightarrow \; \text{no reaction}$$

colorless   colorless

Now we can turn to the unsaturated compounds. Of these, 1-pentyne is the only alkyne. Terminal alkynes ($R-C\equiv C-H$), when treated with ammoniacal silver nitrate ($Ag^{\oplus}(NH_3)_2NO_3^{\ominus}$), will give a precipitate of silver acetylide ($R-C\equiv C-Ag$). 1-Pentyne can be distinguished from the other unsaturated compounds by this method.

$$CH_3CH_2CH_2-C\equiv CH \xrightarrow{\;Ag^{\oplus}(NH_3)_2NO_3^{\ominus}\;} CH_3CH_2CH_2-C\equiv C-Ag$$

solution   precipitate

Of the remaining compounds, 1-chloropropene is the only one that has a halogen. In the presence of silver amide in ammonia, an elimination reaction will occur to yield propyne; this will liberate chloride ion into the solution. As a result, the white silver chloride precipitate will form:

$$Cl-CH=CHCH_3 \xrightarrow[NH_3]{\;Ag^{\oplus}NH_2^{\ominus}\;} HC\equiv C-CH_3 \; + \; Ag^{\oplus}Cl^{\ominus}$$

colorless   white

We are now left with four compounds; three are alkenes and one is a diene. By quantitative catalytic hydrogenation, we can identify the diene (1,3-pentadiene). Quantitative catalytic hydrogenation is accomplished by treating the compound with a known amount of hydrogen gas in the presence of a catalyst (Pd, Ni or Pt). After the reaction is completed, the amount of hydrogen gas remaining is measured. From this it can be determined how many moles of H_2 gas was consumed by the compound. All the compounds will be reduced to an alkane. 1,3-pentadiene will consume two moles of H_2 gas whereas the other compounds will consume one mole of H_2 gas.

$$CH_2=CH-CH=CHCH_3 \; + \; 2\;H_2 \xrightarrow{Pt} CH_3CH_2CH_2CH_2CH_3$$

1,3-pentadiene

$$CH_3CH=CHCH_2CH_3 \; + \; 1\;H_2 \xrightarrow{Pt} CH_3CH_2CH_2CH_2CH_3$$

2-pentene

$$(CH_3)_2C=CHCH_3 \; + \; 1\;H_2 \xrightarrow{Pt} (CH_3)_2CHCH_2CH_3$$

trimethylethylene

$$CH_2=CHC(CH_3)_3 \quad + \quad 1 \ H_2 \quad \xrightarrow{Pt} \quad CH_3CH_2C(CH_3)_3$$

3,3-dimethyl-1
  butene

    Of the three remaining compounds, two will form methyl

carbonyl compounds $\left(\begin{smallmatrix} O \\ \| \\ -C-CH_3 \end{smallmatrix}\right)$ upon ozonolysis with reductive

workup. In general, methyl carbonyl compounds can be identified by using an iodoform reaction. The iodoform reaction
is one between methyl carbonyl compounds and iodine in
alkaline solution. The methyl group is converted to $-CI_3$,
which then leaves the molecule when a hydroxide ion attacks
the carbonyl carbon. This produces a yellow precipitate,
iodoform (CHI_3).

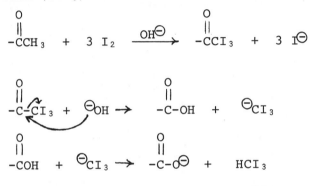

$$\begin{array}{c} O \\ \| \\ -CCH_3 \end{array} \quad + \quad 3 \ I_2 \quad \xrightarrow{OH^{\ominus}} \quad \begin{array}{c} O \\ \| \\ -CCI_3 \end{array} \quad + \quad 3 \ I^{\ominus}$$

$$\begin{array}{c} O \\ \| \\ -C-CI_3 \end{array} + \ {}^{\ominus}OH \rightarrow \begin{array}{c} O \\ \| \\ -C-OH \end{array} + \ {}^{\ominus}CI_3$$

$$\begin{array}{c} O \\ \| \\ -COH \end{array} + \ {}^{\ominus}CI_3 \rightarrow \begin{array}{c} O \\ \| \\ -C-O^{\ominus} \end{array} + \ HCI_3$$

                                    yellow

    3,3-Dimethyl-1-butene will not yield a methyl carbonyl
compound upon ozonolysis with reductive workup. Hence, it
will subsequently not give a positive iodoform reaction.
The other two compounds, after ozonolysis, will give positive iodoform reactions.

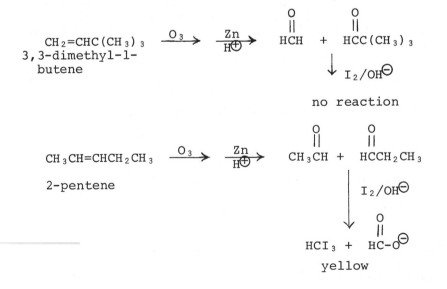

2-pentene

$$(CH_3)_2C=CHCH_3 \xrightarrow{O_3} \xrightarrow[H\oplus]{Zn} \underset{\text{O}}{CH_3\overset{\|}{C}CH_3} + \underset{\text{O}}{H\overset{\|}{C}CH_3}$$

trimethylethylene

$$\underset{\text{O}}{CH_3\overset{\|}{C}CH_3} + \underset{\text{O}}{H\overset{\|}{C}CH_3} \xrightarrow{I_2/OH\ominus} \underset{\text{O}}{\ominus O-\overset{\|}{C}-O\ominus} + \underset{\text{O}}{H\overset{\|}{C}-O\ominus}$$

$$+ \ 3 \ HCI_3$$

yellow

Of the two remaining compounds, 2-pentene and tri-methylethylene, only 2-pentene will show an upfield triplet and downfield quartet (typical of ethyl groups) in its n.m.r. spectrum.

CHAPTER 10

BENZENE

AROMATIC CHARACTER AND PROPERTIES

● PROBLEM 10-1

Which of the following structures are aromatic according to Hückel's rule?

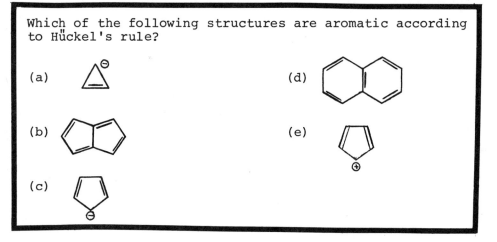

(a)

(b)

(c)

(d)

(e)

Solution: Aromatic systems are found to be unusually stable. These systems are composed of cyclic structures with conjugated double bonds. Conjugated double bonds are sets of bonds which alternate between single and double bonds. Conjugated double bonds are seen in benzene.

Benzene

Not all conjugated systems are aromatic, though. Aromaticity can be determined by using Hückel's rule. Using theoretical data, Hückel formulated the 4n + 2 rule which states that exceptional resonance stability is to be expected with π electron systems containing 4n + 2 electrons in planar, cyclic structures, where n is an integer. This applies to a continuous series of p orbitals which are capable of effective overlapping. For example, benzene has 6, or 4(1) + 2 (with n=1), π electrons. Therefore, according to Hückel's rule, benzene is aromatic and is stabilized by resonance.

(a) This structure is called the cyclopropenyl anion. In this system two π electrons are donated by the double bond and two by the lone pair. This gives a total of four π electrons. Solving for n:

$$4n + 2 = 4$$

$$n = 0.5.$$

n is not an integer and therefore the system is not aromatic.

(b)  There are four double bonds each contributing two π electrons. The total number of π electrons is eight. Solving for n:

$$4n + 2 = 8$$

$$n = 1.5$$

Therefore, the system is not aromatic.

(c) In this system four π electrons are donated by the double bonds and two by the lone pair. The total number of π electrons is six. Solving for n:

$$4n + 2 = 6$$

$$n = 1.0$$

Because n is an integer, this system is aromatic.

(d) This ten carbon structure is known as napthalene. There are two π electrons contributed by each double bond. The total number of π electrons is ten. Solving for n:

$$4n + 2 = 10 \quad \text{and} \quad n = 2$$

Napthalene is aromatic because n is an integer.

(e) There are four π electrons in this system, two donated by each double bond. As has already been shown, systems containing four π electrons are not aromatic.

● **PROBLEM** 10-2

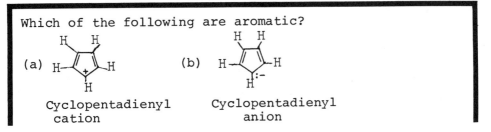

Which of the following are aromatic?

(a) Cyclopentadienyl cation

(b) Cyclopentadienyl anion

303

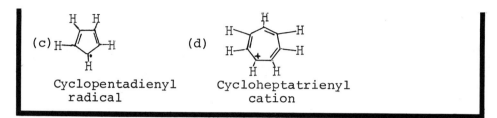

(c) Cyclopentadienyl radical   (d) Cycloheptatrienyl cation

Solution: In order to answer this question, a knowledge of the properties of aromatic compounds is necessary.

An aromatic compound is a cyclic structure that contains continuous π electron clouds above and below the plane of the molecule. The π clouds must also contain a total of 4n+2 π electrons, where n can be any integer. This requirement is called the 4n+2 rule or Hückel's rule and is derived from quantum mechanics. Thus, to determine whether any given compound is aromatic, first inspect the structure to see if it is cyclic and planar.   Then determine the number of π electrons and see if all these satisfy Huckel's rule.

(a)   The cyclopentadienyl cation possesses a total of four π electrons.   Hence, it does not agree with Huckel's 4n + 2 rule and therefore is not an aromatic compound.

(b)   All five carbons of the cyclopentadienyl anion are sp^2-hybridized and the compound therefore lies in a plane. Six π electrons are delocalized about the ring, one being responsible for the net negative charge.   According to Huckel's rule, then, the compound is aromatic.

(c)   The cyclopentadienyl radical possesses five π electrons, one of which is a nonpaired electron.   Since five electrons do not agree with Huckel's rule, the compound is not aromatic.

(d)   The cycloheptatrienyl cation has a total of six π electrons which account for the compound's aromaticity.

● **PROBLEM** 10-3

The anion of benzene $C_6H_5^-$, is aromatic although it contains a total of eight "free" electrons. How do you account for this?

phenyl anion

Solution: Let us first look at the orbital representation of the phenyl anion:

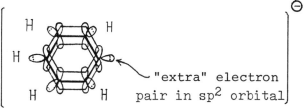

From this, we can see that the "extra" electron pair is in an orbital perpendicular to the π cloud. Since only electrons in the plane of the π cloud can participate in it, these two "extra" electrons cannot participate in the π cloud. In effect, there are only six electrons in the π cloud, which is an aromatic number, according to Hückel's 4n + 2 rule for aromaticity (for n = 1).

● **PROBLEM 10-4**

For which of the following might you expect aromaticity (geometry permitting)?

(a) The annulenes containing up to 20 carbons. (Annulenes are monocyclic compounds of the general formula $[-CH=CH-]_n$.)
(b) The monocyclic polyenes C_9H_{10}, $C_9H_9{}^+$, $C_9H_9{}^-$.

Solution: (a)To be aromatic, a cyclic compound must follow Hückel's 4n + 2 Rule for π electrons.

$$n = 1 : 4n + 2 = 6 \; \pi \text{ electrons}$$

$$n = 2 : 4n + 2 = 10 \; \pi \text{ electrons}$$

$$n = 3 : 4n + 2 = 14 \; \pi \text{ electrons}$$

$$n = 4 : 4n + 2 = 18 \; \pi \text{ electrons}$$

Therefore, the annulenes that are aromatic are: [6] annulene (benzene); [10] annulene; [14] annulene; [18] annulene. (The number in the bracket indicates the number of π electrons.) For [10] and [14] annulenes, the geometry is unfavorable due to the crowding of hydrogens inside the ring. This crowding prevents planarity and would therefore interfere with the formation of the π cloud. The use of models is highly recommended, in order to see the crowding of hydrogens inside the ring.

(b)

C_9H_{10}

There are only 8 π electrons, therefore this system is not aromatic (see part a - Hückel's Rule).

305

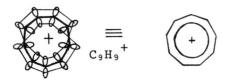

There are only 8 π electrons, which is not an aromatic number.

The pictorial representation for $C_9H_9^-$ is the same as that for $C_9H_9^+$ (see above), except there is now 10 π electrons in a circle, instead of 8. Ten π electrons fit Hückel's

rule for n = 2, therefore this anion is aromatic.

● **PROBLEM** 10-5

Biphenyl, $C_6H_5-C_6H_5$, has a conjugation energy of 71 kcal/mole. (a) Draw an atomic orbital picture of biphenyl. (b) What are its most important resonance con- tributing structures? (c) Estimate the heat of hydrogena- tion of biphenyl.

Solution: (a) The atomic orbital picture should show the p orbitals in a π cloud.

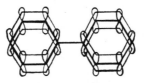

Biphenyl

(b)   The most important resonance structures are the ones without separation of charge. We will use the arrow con- vention of moving electrons to get the different resonance structures.

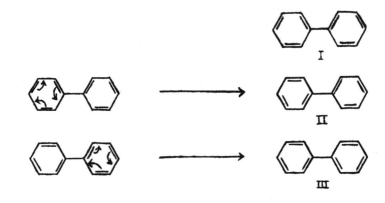

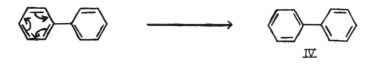

IV

All other structures will result in a separation of charge.

(c)   The heat of hydrogenation is the quantity of heat evolved when one mole of an unsaturated compound is hydrogenated. The heat of hydrogenation is the ΔH (change in heat) of the reaction:

$$-\overset{|}{C}=\overset{|}{C}- \quad + \quad H-H \quad \rightarrow \quad -\overset{|}{\underset{\overset{|}{H}}{C}}-\overset{|}{\underset{\overset{|}{H}}{C}}-$$

The heat of hydrogenation for cyclohexene is 28.8 kcal/mole:

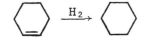   ΔH = - 28.8 kcal/mole.

Since there are six C=C bonds in biphenyl: 28.8 × 6 = 172.8 kcal/mole; but biphenyl is aromatic, therefore, we must subtract the 71 kcal of resonance stabilization energy (conjugation energy) from our calculated heat of hydrogenation:

172.8 kcal/mole - 71 kcal/mole ≒ 101.8 kcal/mole =

estimated heat of hydrogenation

● PROBLEM 10-6

For a large number of organic compounds, the heat of combustion actually measured agrees rather closely with that calculated by assuming a certain characteristic contribution from each kind of bond, e.g. 54.0 kcal for each C-H bond, 49.3 kcal for each C-C bond, and 117.4 kcal for each C=C bond (cis-1,2-disubstituted). (a) On this basis, what is the calculated heat of combustion for benzene?   (b) How does this compare with the measured value of 789.1 kcal for benzene?

Solution: Benzene has the following structure:

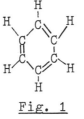

Fig. 1

Since benzene rings are so often used in organic chemistry, the carbons and hydrogens are often left out, and the structure is simply drawn as:

Fig. 2

The hydrogens are implicit, since carbon must have 4 bonds connected to it.

The calculated heat of combustion is determined by adding up all the bond energies of the various bonds. There are 3 different types of bonds in benzene. By adding these up, we get:

6 C-H bonds : 6 × 54.0 = 324.0 kcal

3 C=C bonds : 3 × 117.4= 352.2 kcal

3 C-C bonds : 3 × 49.3 = 147.9 kcal

The calculated heat of
combustion   = 824.1 kcal

(b)   To compare the   different values, we take the difference:

824.1 - 789.1 = 35.0 kcal

(calc.)   (meas.)

The calculated value is 35.0 kcal greater than the measured value. The reason for this huge discrepancy is   the resonance effect of benzene. The 35.0 kcal of energy is called resonance energy , and is responsible for the aromatic properties of benzene. The resonance effect is due to the delocalization of electrons in the benzene ring. Besides the structure shown in Fig. 1, the structure of benzene can also be drawn as:

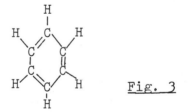

Fig. 3

These two structures of benzene are the Kekulé's structures, named after August Kekulé, who first proposed them in 1865. As resonance structures, they do not exist in equilibrium, nor do they exist independently; rather, they are used to represent the actual structure of benzene. Another representation of benzene is shown below.

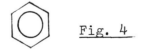

Fig. 4

Fig. 4 represents the resonance hybrid of the two Kekulé's structures shown earlier. The circle stands for the cloud of six delocalized π electrons, while the straight lines represent bonds joining the carbon atoms.

Since equivalent structures can be drawn for benzene (see figures) the π electrons therefore participate in several bonds. The π electrons are delocalized, and the molecule is therefore more stable.

Benzene is aromatic because its π electrons are de-localized in a cyclic cloud above and below the plane of the molecule, and its π cloud contains 4n+2 π electrons (where n = 1 for benzene). This stipulation, known as Hückel's 4n+2 Rule, is the defining condition for aroma-ticity. This special stability, due to the property of aromaticity, is based on quantum mechanics and has to do with the filling up of the bonding orbitals of the π electrons.

STRUCTURE OF BENZENE

● **PROBLEM** 10-7

For a time the prism formula VI, proposed in 1869 by Albert Ladenburg of Germany, was considered as a possible structure for benzene, on the grounds that it would yield one mono-substitution product and three isomeric disubstitution products.

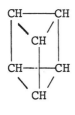

VI

(a) Draw Ladenburg structures of three possible isomeric dibromobenzenes.
(b) On the basis of the Körner method of absolute orienta-tion, label each Ladenburg structure in (a) as ortho, meta, or para.
(c) Can the Ladenburg formula actually pass the test of isomer number?
(Derivatives of Ladenburg "benzene," called prismanes, have actually been made.)

Solution: The three isomeric "dibromobenzenes" are:

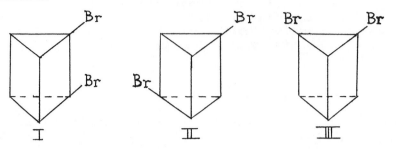

I	II	III

These three structures are different isomers because
isomer I has the two bromines between the edges of two
squares; isomer II has one bromine on the corner of one triangle, and the other bromine on the corner of the other
triangle; isomer III has the two bromines on the two corners
of the same triangle. These are the only three possible
isomeric Ladenburg dibromobenzenes.

(b)   According to the Körner method of absolute orientation,
the dibromobenzene isomer that reacts to form one isomer of
dibromonitrobenzene is the para-dibromobenzene; the one that
forms two isomers is the ortho-dibromobenzene; the one that
forms three isomers is the meta-dibromobenzene. By drawing
the possible isomeric dibromonitrobenzenes for each isomer
of dibromobenzene, we can label each Ladenburg structure in
(a) as ortho, meta, or para:

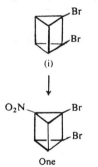

Since there is only one possible isomeric product, this
dibromobenzene is the para isomer.

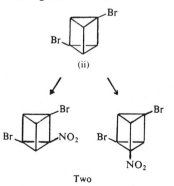

There are two isomeric products, therefore this is
ortho-dibromobenzene.

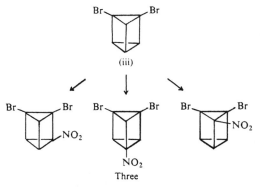

(iii)

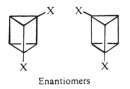

NO₂

Three

There are **three** isomeric products, therefore this is meta-dibromobenzene.

(c)   No. All three disubstituted benzenes are not chiral. For the Ladenburg formula, the ortho isomer is chiral; thus enantiomeric structures are possible. (Recall that molecules that are not superimposable on their mirror images are chiral and that enantiomers are mirror-image isomers):

Enantiomers

● **PROBLEM 10-8**

In Kekulé's day, one puzzling aspect of his dynamic theory for benzene was provided by 1,2-dimethylbenzene. According to his theory, there should be two distinct such compounds, one with a double bond between the two methyl-substituted carbons and one with a single bond in this position.

Only a single 1,2-dimethylbenzene is known, however.

(a) Does Ladenburg's formula solve this problem?
(b) Explain with modern resonance theory.

Solution: Ladenburg's structure for benzene is a tetracyclic one (notice the absence of double bonds):

Fig. 1

This structure accounts for the fact that benzene has only
one monosubstitution product and three isomeric disubstitution products. However, Ladenburg's formula is not able to
solve the problem of there being only one 1,2-dimethyl-
benzene. According to this formula, there would be two
possible isomers for this compound:

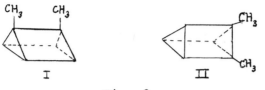

Fig. 2

The two methyl groups in isomer I are shared by the edges
of two squares, while those of isomer II are shared by the
edges of a square and a triangle. Since the methyl groups
in these two structures have different spatial orientations,
they are isomers of each other, thereby contradicting the
experimental observation of one isomer.

(b)   Modern resonance theory says that the π electrons are
delocalized in a π cloud. A pictorial representation of the
π cloud in the benzene ring is:

Fig. 3

The thin lines depict delocalization of the 6 π electrons.
One structural representation of this system is the Kekulé's
structure (shown in Fig. 4.).

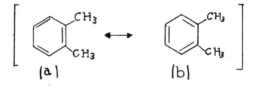

Fig. 4

The double-headed arrow   and the brackets are used to
indicate that the two structures are resonance structures.
Remembering the concept of resonance (that is, the delocalization of electrons), we can see why these two structures
are equivalent. Using the arrow convention of moving electrons, we have:

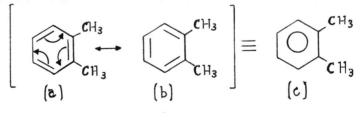

Fig. 5

312

These two resonance structures (Fig. 5a and 5b) can also be represented by Fig. 5c, with the circle representing the cloud of six delocalized π electrons.

NOMENCLATURE AND STRUCTURE OF BENZENE DERIVATIVES

● **PROBLEM** 10-9

Draw structures of:

(a) p-dinitrobenzene
(b) m-bromonitrobenzene
(c) o-chlorobenzoic acid
(d) m-nitrotoluene
(e) p-bromoaniline
(f) m-iodophenol
(g) mesitylene (1,3,5-tri-methylbenzene)

(h) 3,5-dinitrobenzenesulfonic acid
(i) 4-chloro-2,3-dinitrotoluene
(j) 2-amino-5-bromo-3-nitro-benzoic acid
(k) p-hydroxybenzoic acid
(l) 2,4,6-trinitrophenol (picric acid)

Solution: All of these structures are derivatives of benzene. Hence, a consideration of the nomenclature of benzene derivations will aid in the drawing of these compounds.

For many derivatives, the name of the substituent is prfixed to the word -benzene, as in iodobenzene

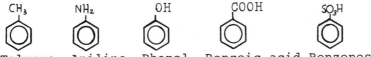

Others possess special names which show no resemblance to the name of the attached substituent group. For example, methylbenzene is termed toluene. The most important compounds in this class include:

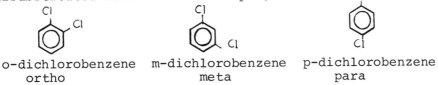

Toluene   Aniline   Phenol   Benzoic acid Benzenesulfonic acid

When several groups are attached to the benzene ring, the positions as well as the names of the substituents must be indicated. The words ortho (o), meta (m), and para (p) are used to designate the three possible isomers of a disubstituted benzene. For example,

o-dichlorobenzene   m-dichlorobenzene   p-dichlorobenzene
    ortho   meta   para

If the two groups are different, and neither group imparts a special name to the compound, then the two groups are named successively and end the word with -benzene. For example:

313

m-chloronitrobenzene   p-bromoiodobenzene

If one of the two groups does impart a special name, then
the compound is named as a derivative of that special compound. For example:

m-nitrobenzoic acid   o-nitrotoluene

   When more than two groups are attached to the benzene,
numbers are used to indicate their relative positions. For
example:

1,2,4-tribromo   2-chloro-4-nitrophenol   3-bromo-5-chloro
   benzene   nitrobenzene

   When the groups are all the same, each is given a
number; the sequence being the one that gives the lowest
combination of numbers. When the groups are different, the
last named group is understood to be in position 1 and
the other numbers conform to that, as in 3-bromo-5-chloro-
nitrobenzene. When one of the groups that gives a special
name exists, then the compound is named as having the
special group in position 1; thus, in 2,6-dinitrotoluene

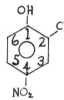   the methyl group is considered to be at

the 1-position.

   From their names, the chemical structure of the
given compounds can now be determined.

(a) p-dinitrobenzene   (b) m-bromonitrobenzene

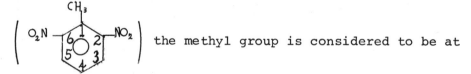

(c) o-chlorobenzoic acid   (d) m-nitrotoluene

314

(e) p-bromoaniline

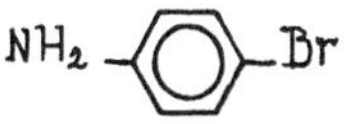

 NH₂ —⟨ ⟩— Br

(f) m-iodophenol

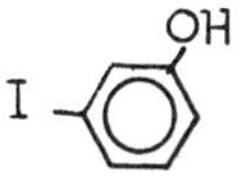

I —⟨ ⟩ with OH

(g) mesitylene

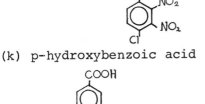

H₃C —⟨ring with CH₃ top and CH₃⟩

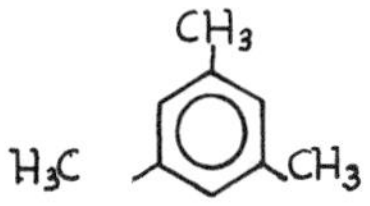

(h) 3,5-dinitrobenzene
sulfonic acid

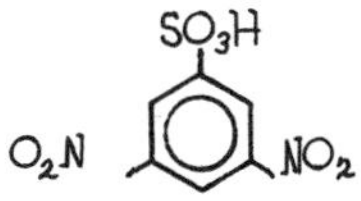

O₂N —⟨ring SO₃H top⟩— NO₂

(i) 4-chloro-2,3,-dinitro-
toluene

CH₃ / NO₂ / NO₂ / Cl

(j) 2-amino-5-bromo-3-
nitrobenzoic acid

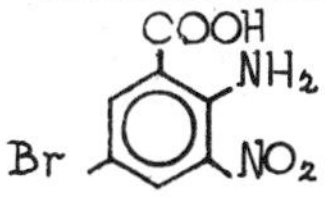

COOH / NH₂ / Br / NO₂

(k) p-hydroxybenzoic acid

COOH / ring / OH

(l) 2,4,6-trinitrophenol

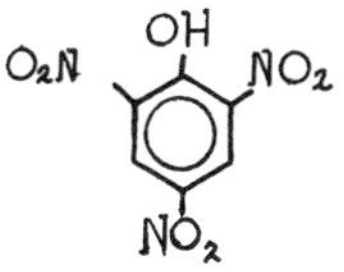

O₂N — OH — NO₂ / NO₂

• PROBLEM 10-10

Draw structures for each of the following:

(a) m-Bromonitrobenzene
(b) o-Ethyltoluene
(c) p-Xylene
(d) 3-Nitrobenzene

(e) 2,4-Dibromomesitylene
(f) Phenylcyclohexane
(g) Biphenyl
(h) Benzyl cyanide

Solution: Benzene belongs to the class of cyclic unsaturated compounds called aromatics. In benzene (C₆H₆)
all the C-C bonds have equal lengths and all the C-C-C
bond angles are equal (120°).

     The terms ortho, meta, and para (abbreviated o, m,
and p) are used to indicate the relative positions of substituents in disubstituted benzenes:

Cl / Cl   Cl / Cl   Cl —⟨ ⟩— Cl

o-Dichlorobenzene   m-Dichlorobenzene 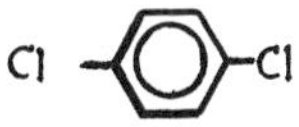   p-Dichlorobenzene

     For more complicated derivatives, the positions on the
ring are numbered 1 to 6.

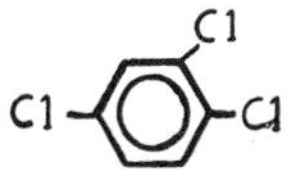

Cl / Cl —⟨ ⟩— Cl

1,2,4-Trichlorobenzene

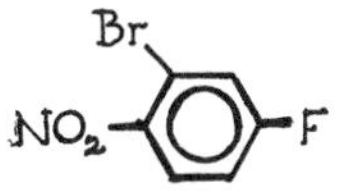

Br / NO₂ —⟨ ⟩— F

1-Bromo-2-nitro-4-fluorobenzene

315

The group 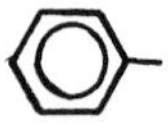 , in which one hydrogen is replaced, is known as the phenyl group (abbreviated as C_6H_5- or sometimes Ph).

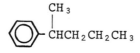

2-Phenylpentane 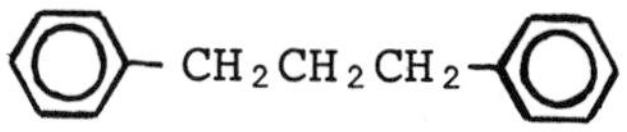   1,3-Diphenylpropane

The symbol Ar(aryl) is used to stand for any aromatic substituent group in a way analogous to the use of R to mean any alkyl group. For example, aryl halides (ArX) vs. alkyl halides (RX).

Some of the common mixed aliphatic-aromatic hydrocarbons are:

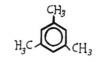

Toluene   o-Xylene   Mesitylene   Cumene
(methylbenzene) (1,2-dimethyl (1,3,5-tri-   (isopropyl-
                 benzene)   methylbenzene)   benzene)

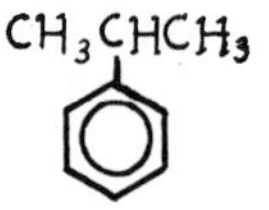

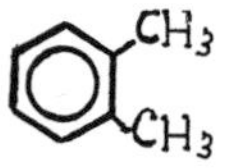

(a) m-Bromonitrobenzene

This compound has a bromo and a nitro group in the meta orientation on the benzene ring. Its structure looks like

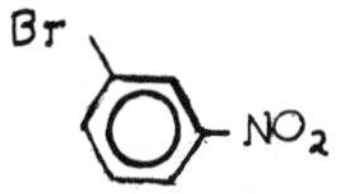

(b) o-Ethyltoluene

This structure contains an ethyl group attached at the ortho position to the toluene molecule. This structure looks like:

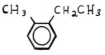

(c) p-Xylene

Xylene is a benzene ring with two methyl groups in place of 2 hydrogen atoms. The p means these 2 groups are para to one another.   The structure is:

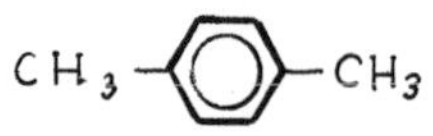

CH₃—⟨O⟩—CH₃

(d) 3-Nitrobromobenzene

This structure contains a bromo and a nitro group attached to a benzene ring. The nitro group, however, is

316

positioned on the third carbon from the carbon containing the bromo group. The structure is

This compound has the same structure as m-bromonitrobenzene.

(e) 2,4-Dibromomesitylene

This structure contains 2 bromo groups located on the second and fourth carbons of the mesitylene structure (1,3,5-trimethylbenzene). This structure can be rewritten as 2,4-dibromo-1,3,5-trimethylbenzene.

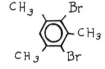

(f) Phenylcyclohexane

Phenylcyclohexane is a benzene ring attached to cyclohexane. The structure is

(g) Biphenyl

This compound is two benzene rings attached together. The structure is

(h) Benzyl cyanide

This compound contains the benzyl group and the cyanide group. The cyanide group consists of a nitrogen atom triply bonded to a carbon atom. The point of attachment to the benzyl group is at the carbon. This group looks like: -C≡N. The benzyl group is a toluene molecule with a hydrogen replaced, as depicted below.

Thus the structure of this compound looks like:

REACTIONS OF BENZENE

1,3,5,7-Cyclooctatetraene, C_8H_8, has a heat of combustion
of 1095 kcal; it rapidly decolorizes cold aqueous $KMnO_4$
and reacts with Br_2/CCl_4 to yield $C_8H_8Br_8$. (a) How should
its structure be represented? (b) Upon what theoretical
grounds might one have predicted its structure and properties? (c) Treatment of cyclooctatetraene with potassium
metal has been found to yield a stable compound $2K^+C_8H_8^{--}$.
Of what significance is the formation of this salt?
(d) Using models, suggest a possible shape (or shapes)
for cyclooctatetraene. What shape would you predict for
the $C_8H_8^{--}$ anion?

Solution: From the name of the compound we know that
it is an eight-carbon ring (cycloocta-), with 4 double
bonds at positions 1, 3, 5, 7 (tetraene). The structure
should therefore be represented as:

Fig. 1

(b)   The number of π electrons is 8, which is not a Hückel
number, therefore, it is not aromatic. Non-aromatic alkenes decolorize cold aqueous $KMnO_4$ and react with
Br_2/CCl_4 to form addition products. The calculated heat of
combustion (total bond energies of the molecule) is:

Fig. 2

8 C-H bonds : 8 ×   54.0 = 432 kcal

4 C-C bonds: 4 ×   49.3 = 197.2 kcal

4 C=C bonds: 4 × 117.4 = 469.6 kcal

calculated heat of combustion=1098.8 kcal

The difference between the calculated value and the
observed value is:

1098.8 - 1095 = 3.3 kcal

This difference of 3.3 kcal is due to resonance
stabilization energy. This energy is much lower than the
resonance energy for the aromatic compounds, for example,
benzene with a resonance stabilization energy of 36 kcal.

(c)   The willingness of cyclooctatetraene to accept two
electrons is significant. The number of π electrons in the
anion is 10, which is a Hückel number (for n = 2).
Stabilization due to aromaticity is enough to outweigh the

318

double negative charge and angle strain. Remember that in order for the anion to be aromatic, the ring must be flat for π overlap. This will cause the carbon-carbon angle to be 135°, which is a large deviation from the tetrahedral angle of 109.5°.

(d)   For cyclooctatetraene, the shape would minimize angle and torsional strain, therefore the most stable conformation would be:

Fig. 3

This conformation is analogous to the boat conformation of cyclohexane. (See the chapter on stereochemistry.)

The shape for $C_8H_8^{--}$ would be a planar (see part c), regular octagon:

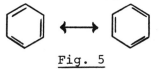

Fig. 4   Cyclooctatetraenyl
dianion

The octagon must be regular because all the bonds in an aromatic ring are the same. This is due to the equivalence of the resonance structures. This last point is best illustrated by the benzene ring:

Fig. 5

Both of these resonance structures are equivalent, therefore all the bonds are equivalent.

● **PROBLEM** 10-12

You have three bottles containing the three isomeric dibromobenzenes; they have the melting points +87°, +6°, and - 7°. By a great deal of work, you prepare six dibromonitrobenzenes ($C_6H_3Br_2NO_2$) and find that, of the six, one is related to (derived from or convertible into) the dibromobenzene of m.p. +87°, two to the isomer of m.p. +6°, and three to the isomer of m.p. -7°.

Label each bottle with the correct name of ortho, meta, or para.

(This work was actually carried out by Wilhelm Körner, of the University of Milan, and was the first example of the Körner method of absolute orientation.)

<u>Solution:</u>   All the hydrogen positions on para-dibromo-
benzene are equivalent; one neighboring carbon carries Br,
while the other neighboring carbon contains H:

Fig. 1

Therefore, the only possible product in a mono-substitution
reaction is:

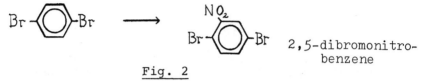

2,5-dibromonitro-
benzene

Fig. 2

There are three sets of hydrogen positions in meta-
dibromobenzene:

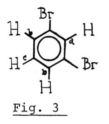

Fig. 3

Therefore, NO₂ can replace hydrogen in 3 different
positions; a, b, and c:

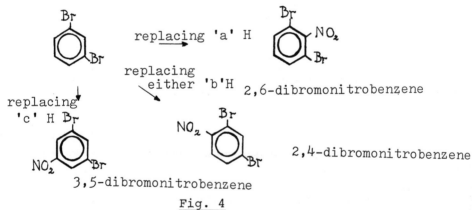

replacing 'a' H

2,6-dibromonitrobenzene

replacing
either 'b'H

replacing
'c' H

3,5-dibromonitrobenzene

2,4-dibromonitrobenzene

Fig. 4

There are two sets of hydrogen positions in ortho-
dibromobenzene:

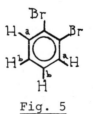

Fig. 5

Therefore, NO_2 can replace hydrogen in 2 different positions, a and b:

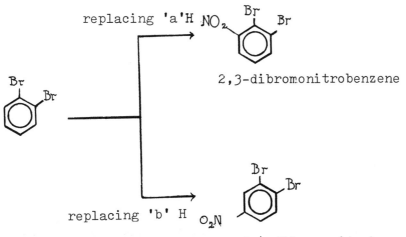

replacing 'a'H

2,3-dibromonitrobenzene

replacing 'b' H

3,4-dibromonitrobenzene

Fig. 6

The bottle of dibromobenzene with the melting point of 87° is the para-isomer; the bottle with the melting point of 6° is the ortho-isomer; the bottle with the melting point of -7° is the meta-isomer.

● PROBLEM 10-13

Complete the following equations. Name each organic product.

(a) ⬡ + Cl_2 $\xrightarrow{FeCl_3}$

(b) ⬡ + SO_3 $\xrightarrow{H_2SO_4}$

Solution: When a substitution reaction is carried out with benzene, only one monosubstituted product can result. When benzene is treated with chlorine in the presence of ferric chloride catalyst, chlorobenzene and hydrogen chloride result. This reaction is called a chlorination reaction.

⬡ + Cl_2 $\xrightarrow{FeCl_3}$ ⬡Cl + HCl

Similarly, other reagents can attack the benzene ring and replace a hydrogen atom.

In substitution reactions, the product is aromatic and a group or atom has been substituted for a hydrogen on

321

the ring. Each of these reactions is carried out under acidic conditions: chlorination with the Lewis acid $FeCl_3$; nitration with sulfuric acid; and alkylation with $AlCl_3$, another Lewis acid.

In the case of sulfonation of benzene, one or more hydrogen atoms are replaced by the sulfonic acid group. $(-SO_3H)$. Sulfonation of benzene with fuming sulfuric acid $(H_2SO_4 + SO_3)$ yields benzenesulfonic acid.

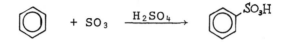

Consider the possible free radical chain chlorination of benzene:

$$C_6H_6 + Cl \cdot \rightarrow C_6H_5 \cdot + HCl$$

$$C_6H_5 \cdot + Cl_2 \rightarrow C_6H_5Cl + Cl \cdot$$

Calculate ΔH for each reaction. Use these results to explain why this method is not a satisfactory way of preparing chlorobenzene.

Solution: ΔH, or enthalpy, is the heat of reaction and is generally associated with bonding. It is calculated by subtracting the sum of the $\Delta H°$s of the reactants from the sum of the $\Delta H°$s of the products, that is, $\Sigma \Delta H°_{(prod.)} -$ $\Sigma \Delta H°_{(react.)}$. ("$\Sigma$" is the mathematical symbol for "the sum of".) $\Delta H°$ is the standard heat of formation of a molecule, and is usually tabulated. Therefore, the ΔH of the first reaction is:

$$C_6H_6 + Cl \cdot \rightarrow C_6H_5 \cdot + HCl$$

$\Delta H°$ 19.8   28.9   80 $-$ 22.1

$$\Delta H_1 = \Sigma \Delta H°_{(prod.)} - \Sigma \Delta H°_{(react.)}$$

$$= (80 - 22.1) - (19.8 + 28.9)$$

$$= 57.9 - 48.7 = + 9.2 \text{ kcal-mole}^{-1}$$

Similarly, the ΔH of the second reaction is:

$$C_6H_5 \cdot + Cl_2 \rightarrow C_6H_5Cl + Cl \cdot$$

$\Delta H°$ 80   0   12.2   28.9

$\Delta H_2 = (12.2 + 28.9) - (80) = - 38.9$ kcal-mole^{-1}

ΔH of the overall reaction $= - 38.9 + 9.2$

$$= - 29.7 \text{ kcal-mole}^{-1}.$$

Although the overall reaction is highly exothermic ($\Delta H = (-) \rightarrow$ exothermic, $\Delta H = (+) \rightarrow$ endothermic), the first step is endothermic, with $\Delta H_1 = + 9.2$. The activation energy for this step is at least 9.2 kcal-mole^{-1}, since the activation energy is always greater than or equal to the ΔH of an endothermic reaction. The rate of reaction is dependent on the activation energy of an elementary reaction. Since the activation energy for this step is high, the rate will be very low, and the chlorine radicals, instead of reacting with benzene, will eventually react with each other. These conditions will not support a chain reaction. Therefore, this method is not a satisfactory way of preparing chlorobenzene.

● **PROBLEM** 10-15

Calculate from appropriate bond and stabilization energies the heats of reaction of chlorine with benzene to give (a) chlorobenzene and (b) 1,2-dichloro-3,5-cyclohexadiene. Your answer should indicate that substitution is energetically more favorable than addition.   Assume the bond dissociation energy for a C=C π bond to be 65 kcal; the resonance stabilization energy of benzene to be 36 kcal, and that of 1,2-dichloro-3,5-cyclohexadiene to be 3 kcal.

Solution: The heat of reaction is the enthalpy, ΔH.   In a reaction, if more stable bonds are formed, ΔH is negative and the reaction is exothermic. A reaction with positive ΔH is endothermic. To solve for ΔH, we substract the sum of the bond dissociation energies of the products from the sum of the bond dissociation energies of the reactants.   In mathematical symbols, if "D" is the bond dissociation energy of the bond formed or broken, then:

$$\Delta H = \Sigma D_{(react.)} - \Sigma D_{(prod.)}$$

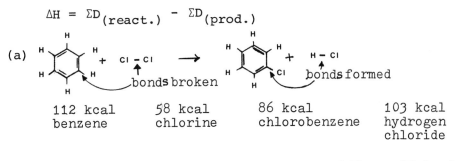

(a)

| 112 kcal | 58 kcal | 86 kcal | 103 kcal |
| benzene | chlorine | chlorobenzene | hydrogen chloride |

$\Delta H = (112 + 58) - (86 + 103) = 170 - 189 = - 19$ kcal

(b)

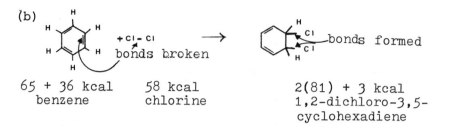

65 + 36 kcal	58 kcal	2(81) + 3 kcal
benzene	chlorine	1,2-dichloro-3,5-cyclohexadiene

$$\Delta H = 65 + 36 + 58 - 2(81) - 3 = -6 \text{ kcal}$$

The 36 kcal of resonance stabilization energy is added to the equation because that amount of energy is expended when we break the aromatic structure of benzene.

The larger negative ΔH (-19 kcal) for the substitution reaction as compared to the one (-6 kcal) for the addition reaction of benzene indicates that the former type of reaction is more exothermic than the latter. In other words, substitution is energetically more favorable than addition for benzene.

● PROBLEM 10-16

When benzene is treated with chlorine under the influence of ultraviolet light, a solid material of m.wt. 291 is formed. Quantitative analysis gives an empirical formula of CHCl. (a) What is the molecular formula of the product? (b) What is a possible structural formula? (c) What kind of reaction has taken place? (d) Is the product aromatic? (e) Actually, the product can be isolated into six isomeric compounds, one of which is used as an insecticide (Gammexane or Lindane). How do these isomers differ from each other? (f) Are more than six isomers possible?

Solution: The empirical formula is the simplest integral formula for a compound. Since the molecular weight of the compound is given, we must first calculate the unit weight of CHCl:

unit wt. of CHCl = atomic weight of C + atomic weight
of H + atomic weight of Cl
= 12 + 1 + 35.5 = 48.5.

To determine the molecular formula, we have to determine the number of units of CHCl per molecule. From unit analysis:

$$\frac{\text{wt. /molecule}}{\text{wt./unit}} = \frac{\text{number of units}}{\text{molecule}}$$

Therefore, we must divide the molecular weight by the unit weight:

$$\frac{\text{M.W.}}{\text{U.W.}} = \frac{291}{48.5} = 6 \text{ CHCl units per molecule.}$$

Therefore, the molecular formula is $C_6 H_6 Cl_6$.

(b)   Since benzene is treated with chlorine, we must have a cyclic structure; a possible compound is 1,2,3,4,5,6-hexachlorocyclohexane:

(c)   The molecular formula for benzene is: C_6H_6, while the molecular formula of this compound is $C_6H_6Cl_6$. Since nothing is substituted or eliminated, the reaction that has taken place is an addition reaction.

$$\text{benzene} + 3Cl_2 \xrightarrow{\text{light}}$$

1,2,3,4,5,6-hexachlorocyclohexane

(d)   Since this compound has no double bonds, and therefore no π electrons, this compound is not aromatic.

(e-f) There are nine possible stereoisomers, consisting of different combinations of cis and trans Cl's in the cyclohexane ring. Structures 8 and 9 are a pair of enantiomers, that is, mirror-image isomers. The other seven structures are achiral. The method for determining chirality is to draw the mirror image of the given structure, and see if the two structures match exactly. If the two structures do not match, they are chiral. Remember that a chiral molecule is a molecule that is not superimposable on its mirror image. The use of models is the best method for determining chirality, as well as determining the possible stereoisomers. The nine possible stereoisomers are:

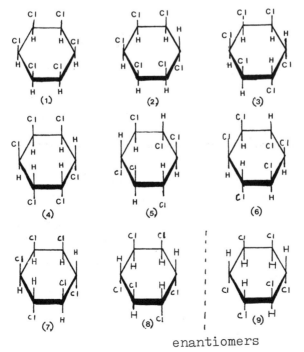

enantiomers

SPECTROSCOPY

Establish the structures of the following benzene derivatives
on the basis of their empirical formulas and n.m.r. spectra.
Remember that equivalent protons do not normally split each
other's resonances.

(a) C_8H_{10}

(b) C_8H_7OCl

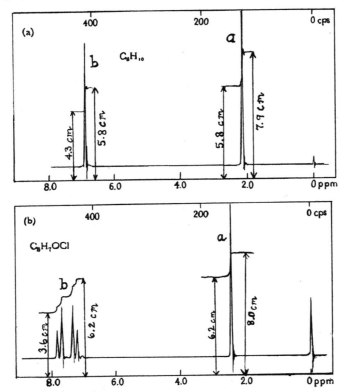

Proton n.m.r. spectra of some benzene derivatives at
60 Mcps with reference to TMS at 0 ppm

Solution: Before we evaluate these nuclear magnetic
resonance (n.m.r.) spectra, let us briefly review the basic
principles of n.m.r. spectroscopy.

At a given radiofrequency, all protons absorb at the
same effective field strength. Note that the effective
field strength is not the same as the applied field strength.
The effective field strength is the magnetic field that the
proton feels, and is therefore dependent on the environment
of the proton. Since every set of equivalent protons has a
different environment from other sets of protons, they will
absorb at different applied field strengths. It is this
applied field strength that is measured, and the absorption

plotted. Aromatic protons, Ar-H̲, absorb far downfield (δ = 6 - 8.5) due to the powerful deshielding effect of the circulating π electrons. Benzylic protons are close enough to the ring to feel a little of the deshielding effect of the π electrons, therefore they absorb at a δ value further downfield, that is, greater δ value from ordinary alkyl protons.

The main aspects of the n.m.r. spectra are:

(1) the number of signals. This tells us how many different sets of protons there are in the molecule.

(2) the position of the signals. This tells us the electronic environment of each kind of proton.

(3) the intensity of the signals. This tells us the number of protons of each kind. To measure the area, we need only measure the height of the step curve above or at the signal.

(4) the splitting of a signal into several peaks. This tells us about the environment of a proton with respect to other nearby protons, specifically protons on a neighboring carbon. The number of splits is equal to the number of neighboring protons plus one.

(a) To evaluate this spectrum, let us go down the above list. (1) Since there are two signals, we can conclude that there are two kinds of protons.

(2) The position of the first signal is approximately 2.2 δ. Looking at the Proton Chemical Shifts Table, the possible groups are:

(1) Acetylenic   -C≡C-H̲ ; δ = 2 - 3

(2) Benzylic   Ar-C-H̲ ; δ = 2.2 - 3

(3) Iodides   I-C-H̲ ; δ = 2 - 4

(4) Esters   ROOC-C-H̲ ; δ = 2 - 2.2

(5) Acids   HOOC-C-H̲ ; δ = 2 - 2.6

(6) Carbonyl Compounds   O=C-C-H̲; δ = 2 - 2.7

(7) Hydroxylic   R-O-H̲ ; δ = 1 - 5.5

(8) Amino   RNH̲$_2$; δ = 1 - 5

The given empirical formula is C_8H_{10}; there are only carbons and hydrogens in this molecule, therefore we can eliminate choices 3 - 8, since they contain atoms other than carbon and hydrogen. This elimination leaves us with two possible groups for signal a:

(1)   Acetylenic $-C\equiv C-\underline{H}$; $\delta = 2 - 3$

(2)   Benzylic $Ar-C-\underline{H}$; $\delta = 2.2 - 3$

The δ value for signal b is approximately 6.8. The only possible group, after eliminating the groups that contain atoms other than carbon and hydrogen is: Aromatic-$Ar-\underline{H}$; $\delta = 6 - 8.5$.

(3) The height of the step curve for:

signal a   = 7.9 cm - 5.8 cm = 2.1 cm.

signal b   = 5.8 cm - 4.3 cm = 1.5 cm.

The molecular formula for this compound is C_8H_{10}, therefore there are 10 protons in the molecule. The fraction of protons responsible for signal a =

$$\frac{\text{(height of a)}}{\text{(height of a + height of b)}} = \frac{2.1}{(2.1 + 1.5)}$$

$$= \frac{2.1}{3.6} = .583$$

$\left(.583 \quad \dfrac{\text{a protons}}{\text{total no. of protons}} \right)$ (10 total no. of protons)

= 5.8 signal a protons

$\sim$ 6 signal a protons

The no. of signal b protons = total no. of protons -
                              no. of signal a protons
                            = 10 - 6 = 4 signal b protons.

With this information, and the fact that signal b is aromatic, we can conclude that set a is not acetylenic. There is only one possible proton per acetylenic group. Since set a has six protons, that would require six acetylenic groups. But there are only two carbons left (subtracting the six carbons for the benzene ring), therefore set a must be benzylic.

(4) Since there are no splitting of signals, the two groups of protons are not neighbors.

Let us now summarize what we know:

(1) There are six benzylic protons.

(2) There are two groups attached to the benzene ring. (Remember that there are 4 protons to set b: 6 possible aromatic protons - 4 existing aromatic protons = 2 aromatic protons that are replaced by substituent groups.)

With the molecular formula of C_8H_{10}, we can now draw

three possible structures for this compound:

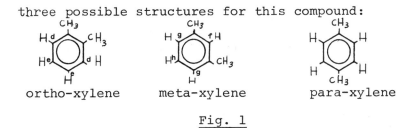

Fig. 1

The ortho-xylene has two sets of aromatic protons. The d protons (see Fig. 1) are different from the e protons since the d protons are next to a carbon carrying a methyl group, while the e protons are only next to carbons carrying aromatic protons. We know that there is no splitting in signal b (see 4 above), therefore ortho-xylene is not the correct structure. Meta-xylene has 3 different sets of aromatic protons (see Fig. 1); we can eliminate this structure based on the above argument with ortho-xylene. The aromatic protons of para-xylene are all equivalent. Each aromatic proton has one neighboring carbon carrying a methyl group, with the other neighboring carbon carrying an aromatic proton. Therefore, the correct structure based on this n.m.r. spectrum is p-xylene.

(b) Using the same method as in part a, we have:

(1) There are two signals, therefore there are two kinds of protons. Note that signal b is one signal split into four peaks, a quartet. We can recognize this signal as a quartet from the even spacings within it and from its symmetrical intensity pattern.

The δ value for signal a is approximately 2.2. The possible groups are:

(a) acetylenic $-C\equiv C\text{-}\underline{H}$; $\delta = 2 - 3$

(b) benzylic $Ar\text{-}C\text{-}\underline{H}$; $\delta = 2.2 - 3$

(c) carbonyl compounds $O=C\text{-}C\text{-}\underline{H};$ $\delta = 2 - 2.7$

(d) hydroxylic $R\text{-}O\underline{H}$; $\delta = 1 - 5.5$

We can eliminate the hydroxylic group because there is an absence of a signal at $\delta = 3.4 - 4$ (the alcohol $HO\text{-}C\text{-}\underline{H}$ group range).

The δ value for signal b is approximately 7.5. The only possible group is: Aromatic - $Ar\text{-}\underline{H}$; $\delta = 6 - 8.5$.

(3) The height of the step curve for:

signal a = 8.0 cm - 6.2 cm = 1.8 cm.

signal b = 6.2 cm - 4.0 cm = 2.2 cm.

The ratio of a : b = 1.8 : 2.2 = 3 : 4

329

Since there are seven protons: set a has 3 protons and set b has 4 protons, we can now eliminate the acetylenic group as a possibility based on the argument in part a of this problem.

Let us now summarize:

(1) There is a group of 3 equivalent protons that are either carbonyl or benzylic.

(2) There is a group of 4 non-equivalent protons that are aromatic.

With the molecular formula of C_8H_7OCl, we can now draw out six possible structures:

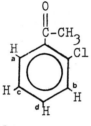

a) o-chloro-
acetophenone

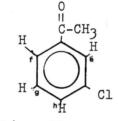

b) m-chloro-
acetophenone

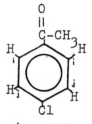

c) p-chloro-
acetophenone

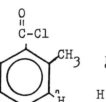

d) o-methyl-
benzoyl chloride

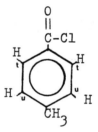

e) m-methyl-
benzoyl chloride

f) p-methyl-
benzoyl chloride

Fig. 2

The ortho and meta structures can be eliminated because signal b is split into a symmetrical quartet, signifying the para structure. The ortho and meta structures have four non-equivalent aromatic protons, therefore, the splitting for these two compounds would be far more complex. Hence, there are two possible structures:

(1) para-chloroacetophenone

(2) para-methyl-benzoyl chloride.

Further information would be necessary to distinguish between these two structures.

330

Identify the two compounds with molecular formula C_7H_7Cl from their infrared spectra shown in the figure below.

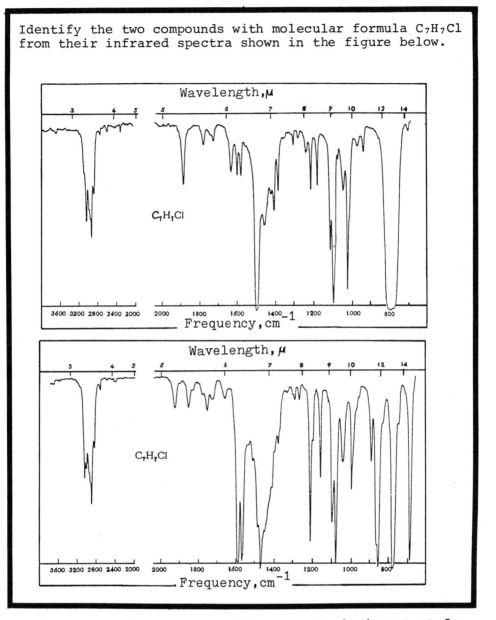

Solution: The infrared (IR) spectrum is important for aromatic compounds because the presence of an aromatic group can be easily distinguished in an IR spectrum.

Aliphatic absorption is strongest at higher frequencies and is almost missing below 900 cm^{-1}; aromatic absorption is strong at lower frequencies; between 650 cm^{-1} and 900 cm^{-1}. We can also determine the number and position of substituent groups on the benzene ring from the IR spectrum.

Before we evaluate the above two IR spectra, let us look at four IR spectra (toluene, o-, m-, and p-xylenes) that show bands typical of benzene compounds. Looking at Fig. 1 notice the 2 bands near 1600 cm^{-1} and 1500 cm^{-1} .

331

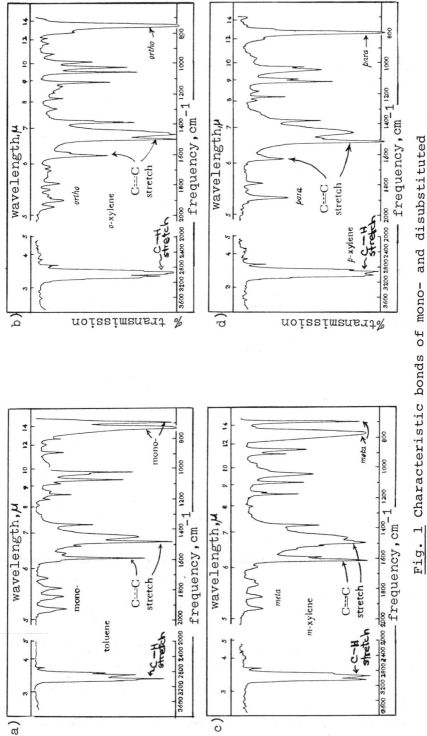

Fig. 1 Characteristic bonds of mono- and disubstituted benzene derivatives

These 2 bonds are characteristic of the C═══C bonds in
aromatic rings. These 2 bands have variable intensities
and a weak band should not be overlooked (see the weak
band in Fig. 1d). The sharp bands near 3000 cm^{-1} are
characteristic of aromatic C-H bonds. The bands between
1650 cm^{-1} and 2000 cm^{-1}, between 1225 cm^{-1} and 950 cm^{-1},
and below 900 cm^{-1} are correlated with the number and
position of the substituent groups on the benzene ring.
Notice the difference between the peaks of Fig. 1a - d
(at 1650 - 2000 cm^{-1}), corresponding to the mono-substituted benzene ring, and the ortho-, meta-, and para-isomers
respectively. Perhaps the most helpful bands in this respect are the ones between 690 cm^{-1} and 840 cm^{-1}. For many
aromatic compounds, absorption occurs at:

(a) mono-substituted: (1) 690 - 710 cm^{-1}

    2 strong peaks   (2) 730 - 770 cm^{-1}

(b) ortho-disubstituted: (1) 735 - 770 cm^{-1}

    1 strong peak

(c) meta-disubstituted: (1) 690 - 710 cm^{-1}

    2 strong peaks   (2) 750 - 810 cm^{-1}

(d) para-disubstituted: (1) 810 - 840 cm^{-1}

    1 strong peak

      Locate these peaks in Fig. 1a - d to familiarize
yourself with these important bands.

(a)   This compound is a derivative of benzene (see Fig. 2a),
as indicated by the bands at 3000 cm^{-1} (=C-H stretch), and
1600 cm^{-1} and 1500 cm^{-1} (C═══C) stretch. The absorption
pattern in the region of 2000 - 1650 cm^{-1} is consistent with

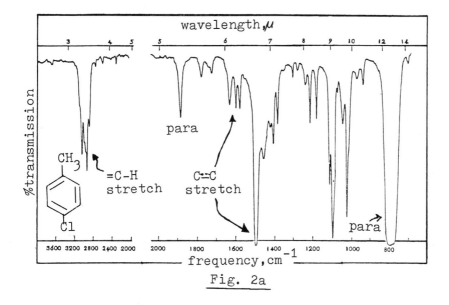

Fig. 2a

333

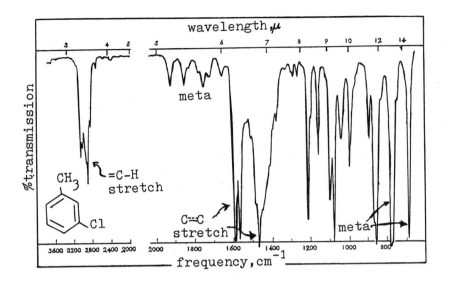

Fig. 2b

this compound being a para-isomer (compare with Fig. 1d).
The single strong band at 800 cm^{-1} clearly shows that this
compound is a <u>para</u>-disubstituted benzene derivative. The
only structure with the molecular formula C$_7$H$_7$Cl that is
consistent with this data is para-chlorotoluene:

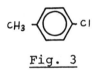

Fig. 3

(b)   This compound is also a benzene derivative, as evidenced
by the 2 bands (see Fig. 2b) at 1460 cm^{-1} and 1580 cm^{-1}
(C$\equiv$C stretch), and at 3000 cm^{-1} (=C-H stretch). The 2 bands
at 690 cm^{-1} and 780 cm^{-1} is characteristic of meta-substituted
benzene derivatives; the absorption pattern at 2000 - 1650 cm^{-1}
is also consistent with this compound being a meta-isomer
(compare with Fig. 1c). The only structure with the molecular
formula C$_7$H$_7$Cl that is consistent with this data is <u>meta-</u>
chlorotoluene:

Fig. 4

CHAPTER 11

ELECTROPHILIC AROMATIC SUBSTITUTION

NITRATION

● PROBLEM 11-1

Draw the principal resonance forms of the nitronium ion.

Solution: Resonance structures differ from each other
only by the arrangement of electrons about the atoms in
the molecule. The actual structure of a molecule is a
hybrid of all the possible resonance structures. When the
contributing structures to the hybrid are of about the same
stability, the resonance is important. The resonance hybrid
is more stable than any of the contributing structures. For
the nitronium ion ($+NO_2$), there exist two resonance forms
as shown:

$$\left[\overset{\ominus}{O} - \overset{+2}{N} = O \right] \longleftrightarrow \left[O = \overset{+2}{N} - \overset{\ominus}{O} \right]^{\oplus}$$

The formal charge on each atom is calculated by using
the equation:

formal charge = A + B - C,   where

A = number of valence electrons in the isolated atom

B = number of covalent bonds to atom

C= number of electrons present

For nitrogen, the number of valence electrons is five
(A = 5). There exist three covalent bonds to the nitrogen
in the nitronium ion, so that B = 3. Each covalent bond is
composed of two electrons for a total of six. Hence,
A + B - C = 5 + 3 - 6 = 2.

● PROBLEM 11-2

Nitration by nitric acid alone is believed to proceed by
essentially the same mechanism as nitration in the
presence of sulfuric acid. Write an equation for the
generation of $NO_2^{\oplus}$ from nitric acid alone.

<u>Solution:</u> Nitration is an example of electrophilic aromatic substitution. These reactions are typical of the benzene ring in which the ring serves as a source of electrons. In nitration, sulfuric acid (H_2SO_4) and nitric acid (HNO_3) are mixed together in the presence of an arene to generate a nitro compound as shown:

$$ArH \quad + \quad HONO_2 \quad \xrightarrow{\ H_2SO_4\ } \quad ArNO_2 \quad + \quad H_2O$$

The electrophile (that is, the acidic, electron-seeking reagent) for nitration reactions is the nitronium ion, $NO_2^{\oplus}$.

Needing electrons the nitronium ion finds them in the π cloud of the benzene ring. Hence, it attaches itself to one of the carbon atoms by a covalent bond to form a

benzenonium ion,

$$C_6H_5 \overset{\oplus}{\underset{\displaystyle NO_2}{\diagdown}} \mkern-30mu \diagup H$$

This ion can then lose a proton by abstraction with HSO_4^- (which came about by $HONO_2 + 2H_2SO_4 \rightleftarrows H_3O^+ + 2HSO_4^- + {}^{\oplus}NO_2$) to create the nitrobenzene. The production of nitronium ion from nitric acid alone may be accounted by a consideration of the Lowry-Brønsted acid-base equilibrium.

Any acid or base is constantly in a Lowry-Brønsted acid-base equilibrium. Nitric acid, therefore, is constantly in acid-base equilibrium where one molecule of nitric acid serves as acid, and another serves as base (step (1), see below). Once a protonated nitric acid molecule is formed, it loses water to give the nitronium ion. (Step (2)).

(1) $\quad HONO_2 \quad + \quad HONO_2 \quad \rightleftarrows \quad \overset{\displaystyle H}{\underset{\displaystyle \oplus}{HONO_2}} \quad + \quad {}^{\ominus}ONO_2$

(2) $\quad \overset{\displaystyle H}{\underset{\displaystyle \oplus}{HONO_2}} \quad \rightleftarrows \quad H_2O \ + \ \overset{\displaystyle \oplus}{NO_2}$

(3) $\quad H_2O \quad + \quad HONO_2 \quad \rightleftarrows \quad H_3O \ \overset{\displaystyle \oplus}{} \quad + \quad {}^{\ominus}ONO_2$

Overall: $\quad 3\ HONO_2 \quad \rightleftarrows \quad \overset{\displaystyle \oplus}{NO_2} \ + \ 2\ {}^{\ominus}ONO_2 \ + \ H_3O^{\oplus}$

● **PROBLEM 11-3**

Account for the fact that fairly reactive arenes (e.g., benzene, toluene, and ethylbenzene) are nitrated with excess nitric acid in nitromethane solution at a rate that is independent of the concentration of the arene (i.e.,

zeroth order). Does this mean that nitration of an equimolal mixture of benzene and toluene would necessarily
give an equimolal mixture of nitrobenzene and nitro-
toluenes? Why or why not?

Solution: The fact that the rate of reaction is
independent of the concentration of arene indicates that
the rate determining step is not the attack of nitronium
ion (+NO$_2$) upon the arene to form the benzenonium ion

$$C_6H_5 \overset{+}{\underset{\diagdown}{\diagup}} \overset{H}{\underset{NO_2}{}}$$
. The rate determining step must be formation of

the nitronium ion.

$$HNO_3 \text{ (excess)} \xrightarrow[CH_3NO_2]{slow} \overset{+}{NO_2} \xrightarrow[C_6H_6]{fast} C_6H_5NO_2 \text{ .}$$

Nitration of an equimolal mixture of benzene and
toluene will not yield an equimolal mixture of nitrobenzene and nitrotoluene. This is because benzene and
toluene react with nitronium ion at different rates.
Toluene reacts faster than benzene because toluene has an
activating group (CH$_3$) on the aromatic ring, whereas
benzene has none. The methyl group is an activating group
because it can stabilize the positive charge of the carbonium ion by releasing electrons in electrophilic aromatic
substitution reactions. This lowers the activation energy
and increases the rate of reaction. The reaction rates of
benzene and toluene with nitronium ion are greater than
the rate determining step. If this were not true, then
the overall rate of nitration would be dependent upon the
concentration of arene.

HALOGENATION

● **PROBLEM** 11-4

Give structures and names of the principal products
expected from the ring monobromination of each of the
following compounds. In each case, tell whether bromination will occur faster than with benzene itself.

(a) iodobenzene   (d) phenetole (C$_6$H$_5$OC$_2$H$_5$)
(b) sec-butylbenzene   (e) diphenylmethane (C$_6$H$_5$CH$_2$C$_6$H$_5$)
(c) acetophenone (C$_6$H$_5$COCH$_3$) (f) benzotrifluoride (C$_6$H$_5$CF$_3$)

Solution: Aromatic compounds with activating groups are
ortho, para directors; they are electron releasing groups
and will direct the electrophile to add ortho and para to
the substituent. Deactivating groups are meta directors;
they are electron withdrawing groups and they will direct

the electrophile to add meta to the substituent. The halogens
are an exception; they are deactivating groups, but they are
ortho, para directors. Halogens, through their inductive
effect, tend to withdraw electrons and thus to deactivate
the intermediate carbonium ions. This effect is felt particularly at the ortho and para positions. Through their
resonance effect, halogens release electrons. This stabilizes the carbonium ion, and it is felt most strongly at
the ortho and para. The reactivity of the species is
controlled by the inductive effect, whereas the resonance
effect seems to govern orientation.

Those aromatic compounds with activating groups have
a faster rate of ring monobromination than benzene. This is
because the activating group helps stabilize the activated
complex. This lowers the energy of activation and increases
the rate of reaction. The opposite holds true for aromatic
compounds with deactivating groups; they react slower than
benzene in a ring monobromination reaction.

(a)   Reacts slower than benzene. The substituent, a halide
      (I), deactivates the ring.

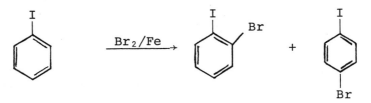

      iodobenzene ⟶ O and p-bromoiodobenzene

(b)   Reacts faster than benzene. The alkyl group (iso-
      propyl) activates the ring.

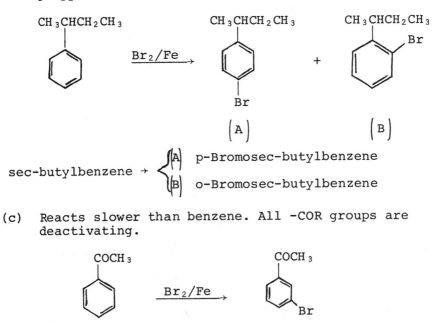

      $\left(A \right)$ $\left(B \right)$

sec-butylbenzene → $\left\{ \begin{matrix} A \\ B \end{matrix} \right.$ p-Bromosec-butylbenzene

                                      o-Bromosec-butylbenzene

(c)   Reacts slower than benzene. All -COR groups are
      deactivating.

      acetophenone ⟶ m-bromoacetophenone

(d) Reacts faster than benzene. -OR groups tend to be moderately activating.

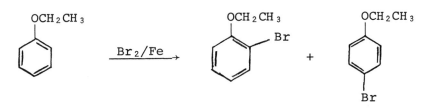

phenetole ———→ o and p-bromophenetole

(e) Reacts faster than benzene.

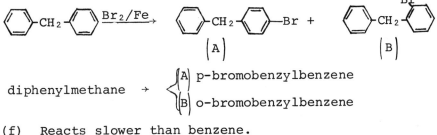

diphenylmethane → [A] p-bromobenzylbenzene
                   [B] o-bromobenzylbenzene

(f) Reacts slower than benzene.

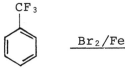

benzotrifluoride ———→ m-bromobenzotrifluoride

● **PROBLEM** 11-5

(a) The bromination of benzene is catalyzed by small amounts of iodine. Consider a possible explanation for this catalytic effect.
(b) The kinetic expression for the bromination of naphthalene in glacial acetic acid involves a term that is first order in naphthalene and second order in bromine. Consider how two molecules of bromine and one of naphthalene could be involved in the rate-determining step of bromination. Suggest a reason why the kinetic expression simplifies to first order in naphthalenes and first order in bromine in 50 per cent aqueous acetic acid.

Solution:

(a) Iodine first reacts with bromine to form iodobromide (IBr).

$$Br_2 + I_2 \longrightarrow 2\ IBr$$

Benzene will polarize the Br-Br bond and will form

339

a π complex. The iodobromide serves to further polarize the Br-Br bond until it breaks the bond.

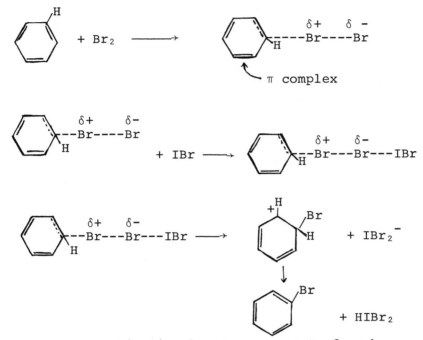

π complex

+ IBr ⟶

⟶

+ IBr$_2^-$

+ HIBr$_2$

The aromatic ring loses a proton to form bromo-benzene.

(b) Naphthalene will form a π complex with the first bromine molecule. A second bromine molecule helps to break the Br-Br bond in the π complex. This would make the reaction first order in naphthalene and second order in bromine. The kinetic expression is:

$$R = K[A][B]^2,$$

where   R = rate of reaction

K = rate constant for the reaction,

[A] = concentration of naphthalene and

[B] = concentration of bromine.

Kinetically, the reaction is third order overall. The reactions for the bromination of naphthalene in glacial acetic acid are given as:

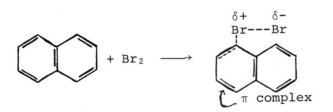

+ Br$_2$ ⟶

π complex

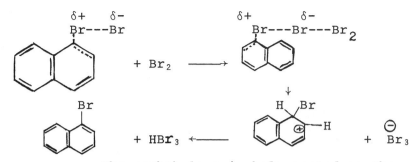

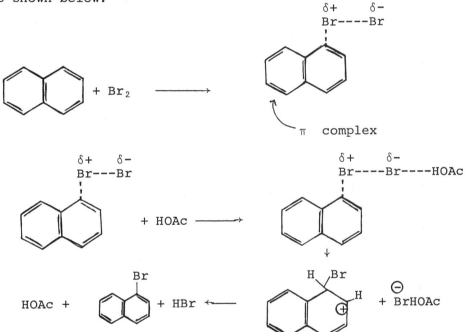

The naphthalene is halogenated at the α position because that is the place where there is greatest stabilization.

In 50% aqueous acetic acid, the kinetic order in bromine is first order because the acid replaces bromine in breaking the Br-Br bond in the π complex. The sequence is shown below:

• PROBLEM 11-6

Certain activated benzene rings can be chlorinated by hypochlorous acid, HOCl, and this reaction is catalyzed by H$^+$. Can you suggest a possible function of H$^+$?

Solution: The mechanism of chlorination of activated benzene rings using hypochlorous acid involves the formation of Cl$^+$. The chlorine cation is extremely reactive because it has only six electrons in its valence shell. Once the chlorine cation has been formed, it undergoes an electrophilic aromatic substitution reaction with benzene.

Hypochlorous acid by itself will not readily form Cl^+ because ^-OH is a poor leaving group, and also because Cl^+ is very reactive and is more stable in the unionized form. In acidic solution, however, the oxygen in hypochlorous acid is protonated. This makes it easier for the Cl^+ to be formed because the leaving group would now be H_2O. Another reason why ionization is easier in acidic solution is that the protonated oxygen tends to give up its positive charge. Once ionization occurs, the Cl^+ is generated and can react with benzene.

In neutral solution:

Difficult { $H - O - Cl \rightleftarrows H - O^- + Cl^+$

In acidic solution:

$$H - O - Cl + H^+ \rightleftarrows H - \overset{H}{\underset{+}{O}} - Cl$$

Easy { $H - \overset{H}{\underset{+}{O}} - Cl \rightleftarrows H_2O + Cl^+$

● PROBLEM 11-7

On what basis (other than a thermodynamic one) could we decide whether or not the following addition-elimination mechanism for bromination of benzene actually takes place?

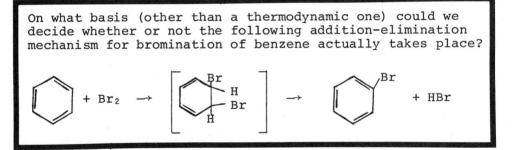

Solution: There are three ways in which we can decide whether bromination of benzene occurs in this fashion.

(1) If the addition product has any appreciable lifetime, it should be possible to trap it by addition to its double bonds. We could do this by using an excess of bromine or an oxidizing agent.

(2) If we brominated something like 1,3,5-trideuteriobenzene, we would expect to get 2,4,6-trideuteriobromobenzene as our major product. This is accounted for by the primary isotope effect, which explains why the carbon-hydrogen bond preferentially breaks to the carbon-deuterium bond. Deuterium is more electronegative than hydrogen. Since carbon is more electronegative than both deuterium and hydrogen, the electronegativity difference between carbon and deuterium is less than that between carbon and hydrogen.

This means that the carbon-hydrogen bond is more polar than the carbon-deuterium bond, and is therefore easier to break. The reaction that would support the addition-elimination mechanism is:

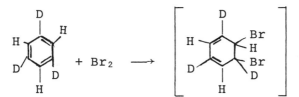

(1,3,5-trideuteriobenzene)

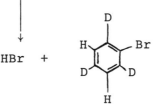

(2,4,6,-trideuteriobromobenzene)

(3) If we brominated benzene in the presence of methanol, we should expect the formation of anisole ($C_6H_5OCH_3$) instead of bromobenzene.

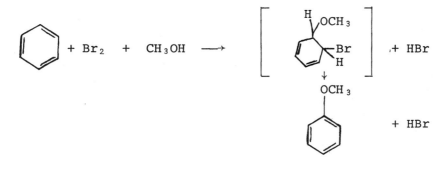

The reason why it is the bromo group and not the methoxy group that leaves in the elimination step is that the bromo group is a better leaving group than the methoxy group. A good leaving group is one with weak basicity, that is, one with little tendency to donate a pair of electrons. This leads to the formation of anisole and not bromobenzene.

FRIEDEL-CRAFTS REACTIONS

● PROBLEM 11-8

Is BH_3 a nucleophile or an electrophile? Explain.

Solution: Electrophilic reagents are species with a deficiency of electrons, e.g. a vacant atomic orbital,

343

sometimes bearing a positive charge. These reagents
attack positions of high electron density or negative
charge. H^+, $AlCl_3$, and SO_3 are examples of electrophiles.

Nucleophilic reagents are species with a lone pair
of electrons, sometimes bearing a negative charge, which
attack positions of low electron density or positive
charge. OH^-, I^-, NH_3 are examples of nucleophiles.

Thus, to answer this question draw the electron dot
formula of BH_3; if BH_3 has a lone pair of electrons or is
deficient in electrons, it will be a nucleophile or an
electrophile, respectively.

The electron dot formula of BH_3 is

$$\overset{\displaystyle H}{H \!:\! \overset{\displaystyle ..}{B} \!:\! H}$$

The B-H bonds are sp^2-hybridized orbitals, therefore there
is an empty p orbital. Since BH_3 is electron-deficient,
it is an electrophile. In fact, it is a lewis acid.

● **PROBLEM** 11-9

Suggest a reason why liquid hydrogen fluoride is preferable
to concentrated, aqueous hydrobromic acid in inducing propene
to react with benzene to produce isopropylbenzene.

Solution:

Hydrogen fluoride and hydrobromic acid are acidic
compounds; both will protonate propene to form the isopropyl
cation ($CH_3\overset{+}{C}HCH_3$) and not the n-propyl cation ($CH_3CH_2\overset{+}{C}H_2$).
This is because secondary carbocations are more stable than
primary carbocations. The isopropyl cation can undergo an
electrophilic aromatic substitution reaction with benzene
or it can react with halide ion (X^-) to form the isopropyl
halide. The reason why hydrogen fluoride (HF) is preferred
over hydrobromic acid (HBr) in inducing formation of isopropylbenzene is that HF will give less addition of halide
ion to the isopropyl cation than will HBr. This is because
of relative nucleophilicities. Nucleophilicity is a measure
of the polarizability of basic, electron rich reagents
called nucleophiles; if the electrons are easily polarizable
(if the outer electron cloud is easily deformed) they will
respond better to a positive charge. In general, polarizability increases as one moves down a group of elements in
the periodic table; this is because the larger the atom,
the more polarizable it is. Bromide is larger and therefore
more polarizable than fluoride. Hence, bromide is more
nucleophilic. The better the nucleophile, the faster it
will react with a source of positive charge. Since bromide
is a better nucleophile than fluoride, there will be more
unreacted isopropyl cation in a solution of HF than in HBr.

This greater amount of isopropyl cation in HF can react with benzene to form isopropyl benzene. Hence, hydrogen fluoride is preferred to hydrobromic acid in inducing formation of isopropylbenzene because hydrogen fluoride will give a greater yield of product.

● **PROBLEM** 11-10

How do you account for the fact that benzene in the presence of AlCl$_3$ reacts: (a) with n-propyl bromide to give isopropylbenzene; (b) with isobutyl bromide to yield tert-butylbenzene; (c) with neopentyl bromide to yield tert-pentylbenzene? (d) By which of the alternative mechanisms for the Friedel-Crafts reaction are these products probably formed?

Solution: Aromatic compounds can be alkylated by using an alkylating agent in the presence of aluminum chloride, the "Friedel-Crafts catalyst." The alkylating agent is an alkyl halide which will form a complex with aluminum chloride. The complex breaks down to form a carbocation. The carbocation will undergo rearrangements if it will lead to a more stable species. Carbocation stability follows the order: tertiary > secondary > primary > $\overset{\oplus}{CH_3}$. The electron rich aromatic ring attacks the carbocation. Subsequent proton loss gives an alkylated aromatic compound.

(a) $CH_3CH_2CH_2-Br + AlCl_3 \rightarrow CH_3CH_2-\overset{\overset{\displaystyle H}{\overset{\displaystyle |}{}}}{\underset{\underset{\displaystyle H}{\displaystyle |}}{C}}\overset{\delta+}{-}--Br-----\overset{\delta-}{AlCl_3}$

   (N-propyl bromide)

$\downarrow$

$CH_3CH_2\overset{\oplus}{CH_2} + \overset{\ominus}{BrAlCl_3}$

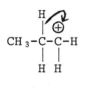

$\xrightarrow{\hspace{1cm}}$

hydride shift to a more stable carbocation

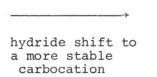

$CH_3-\overset{\oplus}{\underset{\underset{\displaystyle H}{\displaystyle |}}{C}}-CH_3$

The primary carbocation underwent a 1,2-hydride shift to form the more stable secondary carbocation. The benzene ring now reacts with the isopropyl cation to form isopropylbenzene.

(b) $CH_3-\overset{\overset{\displaystyle}{\underset{\underset{\displaystyle CH_3}{\displaystyle |}}{CH}}}{}-CH_2-Br + AlCl_3 \rightarrow CH_3-\overset{}{\underset{\underset{\displaystyle CH_3}{\displaystyle |}}{CH}}\overset{\overset{\displaystyle H}{\overset{\displaystyle |}{}}}{\underset{\underset{\displaystyle H}{\displaystyle |}}{C}}\overset{\delta+}{-}----Br------\overset{\delta-}{AlCl_3} \rightarrow$

   (isobutyl bromide)

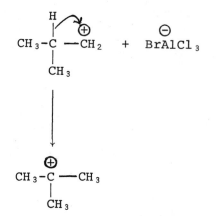

$$CH_3-\overset{\overset{\displaystyle H}{|}}{\underset{\underset{\displaystyle CH_3}{|}}{C}}-\overset{\oplus}{CH_2} + \ominus BrAlCl_3$$

$$\downarrow$$

$$CH_3-\overset{\oplus}{\underset{\underset{\displaystyle CH_3}{|}}{C}}-CH_3$$

The primary carbocation underwent a 1,2-hydride shift to form the more stable tertiary carbocation. The benzene ring now reacts with the t-butyl carbocation to form t-butylbenzene.

(c) $CH_3-\overset{\overset{\displaystyle CH_3}{|}}{\underset{\underset{\displaystyle CH_3}{|}}{C}}-CH_2-Br + AlCl_3 \rightarrow CH_3-\overset{\overset{\displaystyle CH_3}{|}}{\underset{\underset{\displaystyle CH_3}{|}}{C}}-\overset{\overset{\displaystyle H}{|}\overset{\delta+}{}}{\underset{\underset{\displaystyle H}{|}}{C}}----Br\overset{\delta-}{-----}AlCl_3$

(neopentyl bromide)

$$\downarrow$$

$$CH_3-\overset{\overset{\displaystyle CH_3}{|}}{\underset{\underset{\displaystyle CH_3}{|}}{C}}-\overset{\oplus}{CH_2} + \ominus BrAlCl_3$$

$$CH_3-\overset{\overset{\displaystyle CH_3}{|}}{\underset{\underset{\displaystyle CH_3}{|}}{C}}-\overset{\oplus}{CH_2} \longrightarrow CH_3-\overset{\oplus}{\underset{\underset{\displaystyle CH_3}{|}}{C}}-CH_2-CH_3$$

The primary carbocation underwent a 1,2 methyl group shift to form the more stable tertiary carbocation. The benzene ring now reacts with the tertiary carbocation to form t-pentylbenzene.

(d) There are two possible mechanisms for a Friedel-Crafts alkylation: a concerted process and a two step process. In the concerted process, the benzene ring reacts with the alkyl halide-aluminum chloride complex to form the alkylated benzene. In this mechanism, there is no carbocation rearrangement because there is no free carbocation stage. In the two step process, however, there is a free carbocation stage. The alkyl halide complexes with the aluminum chloride. This complex breaks down to form the free carbocation, which can then undergo rearrangement to form a more stable species. The benzene ring can then react with the carbocation to form the alkylated benzene. Therefore, reactions (a), (b) and (c) must have followed the two step mechanism; that is, the carbocation mechanism.

346

Complete the following reactions. Name each organic product.

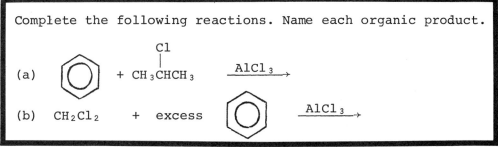

(a)

(b) CH_2Cl_2 + excess

Solution: In alkylation reactions, the alkyl group from any alkyl halide may be substituted on the benzene ring in the presence of a Lewis acid such as aluminum chloride ($AlCl_3$).

In the first reaction the chlorine atom is pulled off the isopropylchloride molecule and replaced by the benzene ring. This reaction is presented in figure A. The product is isopropylbenzene.

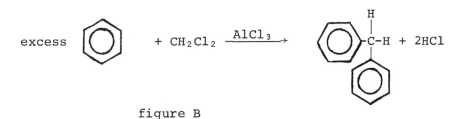

figure A

In the second reaction, the dihalide (methylene chloride) may react with 2 benzene rings to yield a di-phenyl compound. Since benzene is in excess this reaction will take place. The second reaction is presented in figure B and the product is diphenylmethane.

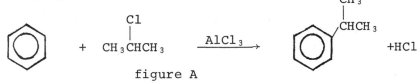

figure B

Complete the following reactions. Name each organic product.

(a) 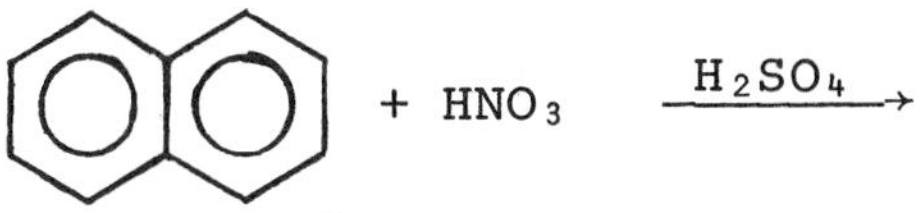 + HNO_3 $\xrightarrow{H_2SO_4}$

(b) 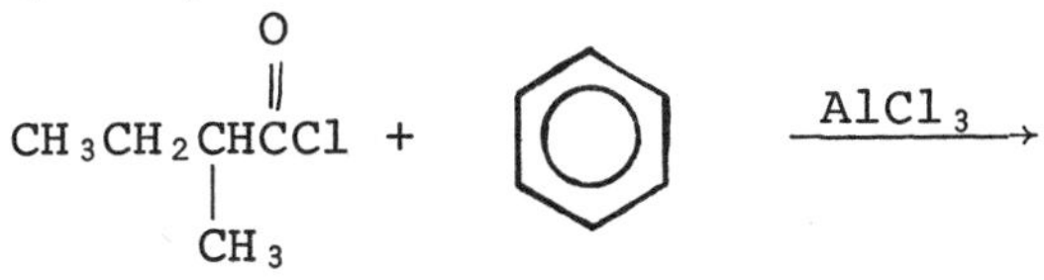 CH_3CH_2CHCCl + $\xrightarrow{AlCl_3}$

347

Solution: Naphthalene and other aromatic hydrocarbons
also undergo aromatic substitution reactions. Naphthalene
(shown in figure A) substitutes at the 1- or α-position
- that is, on a carbon atom adjacent to the other ring.
The numbering of the positions of naphthalene is shown.
It can be seen that naphthalene has four α positions -
at 1,4,5, and 8 - and four β positions - at 2, 3, 6, and 7.

naphthalene

figure A

        The nitration of naphthalene is shown in figure B
and the product is α-nitronaphthalene (1-nitronaphthalene).

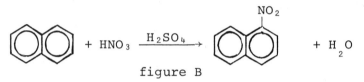

figure B

        The second reaction is an acylation. In the presence
of a Lewis acid, an acid halide also reacts with benzene.
The product of this reaction is a phenyl ketone. The general
acylation reaction is shown in Figure C. The chlorine atom
is replaced by the benzene ring to produce a phenyl ketone.

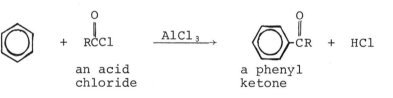

an acid   a phenyl
chloride   ketone

figure C

        The complete reaction for the second equation is
shown in figure D. The product is sec-butyl phenyl ketone.

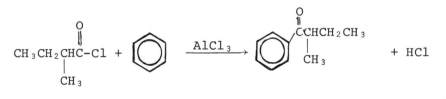

figure D

348

Provide the missing reactant or reaction condition for the following:

(a) Benzene + ___?___ $\xrightarrow{\text{AlCl}_3}$ t-butylbenzene

(b) Dimethyl sulfate + ___?___ → ethylbenzene.

Solution: The reactions of benzene are very important in the study of aromatic compounds. This necessitates the learning of some of the more important reactions that the benzene ring can undergo. One such important reaction is that of alkylation (Friedel-Crafts reaction).

Alkylation (reaction (a)) occurs when alkyl halides react with benzene in the presence of a Lewis acid (ex: AlCl_3) or when alcohols or olefins react with benzene in the presence of a mineral acid. For example,

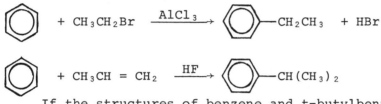

If the structures of benzene and t-butylbenzene are drawn for reaction (a), it will make the reaction clearer.

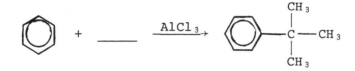

From previous examples of an alkylation reaction, the missing reactant must have the structure of

can be a halogen (Cl, Br, I) or a hydroxyl group (OH). This missing reactant can also be any isobutyl halide or hydroxyl that will rearrange.

Another important reaction which applies not only to aromatic but to all organic compounds is illustrated by reaction (b). This alkylation reaction occurs by way of the Grignard reagent. Grignard reagents are alkylated by very active halides (such as allyl and benzyl) and esters of sulfuric acid. For example,

To find the missing reactant in reaction (b), first
draw the structures of dimethyl sulfate and ethylbenzene.

$$CH_3-OSO_2O-CH_3 \quad + \quad \underline{\quad ? \quad} \quad \longrightarrow \quad \langle\bigcirc\rangle-CH_2-CH_3$$

From the previous examples, the missing reactant
must have the structure of $\langle\bigcirc\rangle-CH_2MgBr$. The bromine
can be replaced by any halogen, so that the general structure for the missing reactant is $\langle\bigcirc\rangle-CH_2MgX$ where X is
any halogen.

● **PROBLEM** 11-14

Prepare a ketone from each of the following precursors by
the Friedel-Crafts acylation method.

(a) $\langle\bigcirc\rangle-COCl$ (b) $CH_3\overset{\overset{O}{\|}}{C}O\overset{\overset{O}{\|}}{C}CH_3$

     Benzoyl Chloride   Acetic Anhydride

Solution: One of the most important syntheses of
ketone preparation is the Friedel-Crafts acylation. This
reaction is modified to involve the use of acid chlorides
and anhydrides rather than alkyl halides. In this reaction
an acyl group, RCO-, is always reacted with the ring of an
aromatic compound, thus forming a ketone. The catalyst
used in these reactions is aluminum chloride, $AlCl_3$, and
having the general equation:

$$R-\underset{\underset{O}{\|}}{C}Cl \; + \; ArH \; \xrightarrow{AlCl_3} \; R-\underset{\underset{O}{\|}}{C}-Ar \quad + \quad HCl$$

     Acid   Aromatic   Ketone
     chloride Hydrocarbon

Acid chlorides are the most common source of compounds
for Friedel-Crafts acylations but they are not the sole
source. Carboxylic acid anhydrides are also used in this
capacity, the other product being a carboxylic acid. The
general equation for this type of reaction   is:

$$R\underset{\underset{O}{\|}}{C}-O-\underset{\underset{O}{\|}}{C}-R \; + \quad ArH \; \xrightarrow{AlCl_3} \; R\underset{\underset{O}{\|}}{C}-Ar \; + \; R\underset{\underset{O}{\|}}{C}OH$$

     Anhydride   Aromatic   Ketone   Carboxylic
                   Hydrocarbon   Acid

350

These reactions, either using acid chlorides or anhydrides yield a ketone as the main product and either an inorganic or an organic acid as the byproduct.

With the above discussion about the Friedel-Crafts acylation, and the general equations for the ketone synthesis, problems (a) and (b) can be derived.

(a)  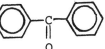 +HCl

      Benzoyl Chloride   Benzene   Benzophenone
                                   (Phenyl Ketone)

(b)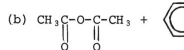

   Acetic Anhydride   Benzene   Acetophenone

+ CH_3COOH

Acetic Acid

SULFONATION

• **PROBLEM** 11-15

Give structures and names of the principal organic products expected from the monosulfonation of:

(a) cyclohexylbenzene   (d) m-nitrophenol
(b) benzenesulfonic acid   (e) o-fluoroanisole
(c) salicylaldehyde   (f) o-nitroacetanilide
    ($o-HOC_6H_4CHO$)   ($o-O_2NC_6H_4NHCOCH_3$)
              (g) o-xylene

Solution: When there are two substituents on an aromatic ring, one activating and one deactivating, the activating substituent will generally direct the addition of any in-coming electrophiles. If there are two activating substituents on the aromatic ring, the electrophilic substitution will be directed by the more strongly activating substituent. The more strongly activating substituent is the one that can best stabilize the positive charge of the intermediate carbonium ion.

Sulfonation involves the addition of a sulfonyl group (SO_3H) to the aromatic ring. The general reaction for sulfonation may be written as:

$$\text{ArH} + \text{HOSO}_3\text{H} \xrightarrow{\text{SO}_3} \text{ArSO}_3\text{H} \qquad + \text{H}_2\text{O}$$

(A sulfonic acid)

All products of sulfonation may be named as sulfonic acids, with -SO₃H on carbon number one.

(a)

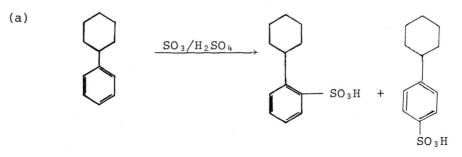

cyclohexylbenzene ⟶ o and p-cyclohexylbenzene
sulfonic acid

The cyclohexyl substituent is an activating one, so that it directs ortho and para.

(b)

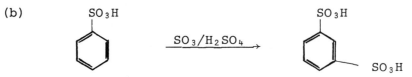

benzenesulfonic acid ⟶ m-benzenedisulfonic acid

The sulfonyl group is deactivating and directs meta.

(c)

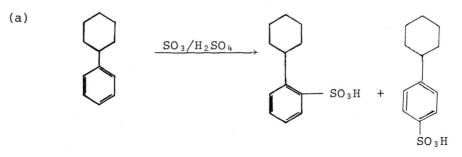

salicylaldehyde

A   3-formyl-2-hydroxybenzenesulfonic acid

B   3-formyl-4-hydroxybenzenesulfonic acid

Even though the -CHO is meta directing, the -OH is strongly activating so that it prevails and directs o and p.

352

(d)

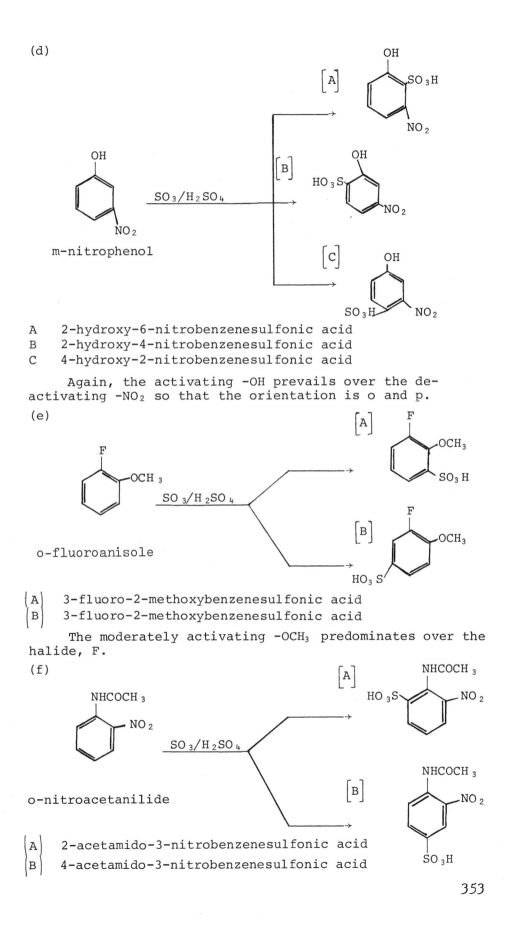

A   2-hydroxy-6-nitrobenzenesulfonic acid
B   2-hydroxy-4-nitrobenzenesulfonic acid
C   4-hydroxy-2-nitrobenzenesulfonic acid

Again, the activating -OH prevails over the deactivating -NO₂ so that the orientation is o and p.

(e)

[A]   3-fluoro-2-methoxybenzenesulfonic acid
[B]   3-fluoro-2-methoxybenzenesulfonic acid

The moderately activating -OCH₃ predominates over the
halide, F.

(f)

[A]   2-acetamido-3-nitrobenzenesulfonic acid
[B]   4-acetamido-3-nitrobenzenesulfonic acid

Both -NHCOCH$_3$ and -NO$_2$ activate the same positions on the ring.

(g)

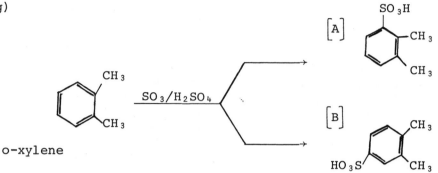

o-xylene

A   2,3-dimethylbenzenesulfonic acid

B   3,4-dimethylbenzenesulfonic acid

The methyl group is activating and directs the sulfonyl group to ortho and para.

EFFECT OF SUBSTITUENTS ON REACTIVITY

• **PROBLEM** 11-16

Explain the following observations: (1) The ortho-para ratio of the products obtained by sulfonation of toluene is lower than that of nitration; (2) The ortho-para ratio of the products obtained by nitration of isopropylbenzene is lower than that of nitration of toluene.

Solution: (1) The sulfonation of aromatic compounds such as toluene occurs by treatment with concentrated sulfuric acid. One has the formation of the electrophilic reagent, SO$_3$:

$$2H_2SO_4 \rightleftarrows H_3O^+ + HSO_4^- + SO_3$$

SO$_3$ is a strong electrophile because of the partial positive charge on the sulfur atom:

In nitration of aromatic compounds, one starts treatment by mixing concentrated nitric and sulfuric acids to form the electrophilic reagent $^+NO_2$, the nitronium ion which attacks the ring

$$2H_2SO_4 + HONO_2 \rightleftarrows {}^+NO_2 + 2HSO_4^- + H_3O^+$$

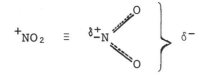

It can be seen from the representation of SO_3 and $^+NO_2$ that the former is more bulky. Thus, the more bulky SO_3 will be more hindered in its attack at the ortho position by CH_3 that is, the lower ratio in the case of sulfonation can be accounted for by steric hinderance by the methyl group of toluene at the ortho position. The larger or more bulky the group that attempts to bind at this position, the more difficult it becomes.

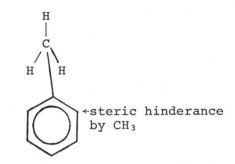

toluene ← steric hinderance by CH_3 If it

is easier to bind somewhere else, the electrophilic reagent will. Methyl directs or activates ortho and para, so that the SO_3 group will prefer to bind to para, which causes the reduced ratio as compared to nitration.

(2) Here, one again deals with steric hinderance. However, this time the variable is not the electrophilic reagent binding, but the substituents on the benzene ring.

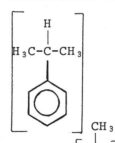

Isopropylbenzene   has a more

bulky substituent than toluene   . Hence for

the same reasons as noted in (1), the isopropylbenzene will hinder binding of the nitronium species at the ortho ring more effectively than toluene due to the bulkiness of the isopropyl.

● **PROBLEM** 11-17

Even in dilute acidic solution, aniline, which exists mainly as the anilinium ion ($C_6H_5NH_3^+$), undergoes o,p-substitution. Account for this.

Solution: In acidic solution, aniline

exists in equilibrium with the anilinium ion $(C_6H_5NH_3^+)$.
Assume that hydrochloric acid was used to acidify an
aqueous solution of aniline. The solution will constantly
be undergoing an acid-base equilibrium as follows:

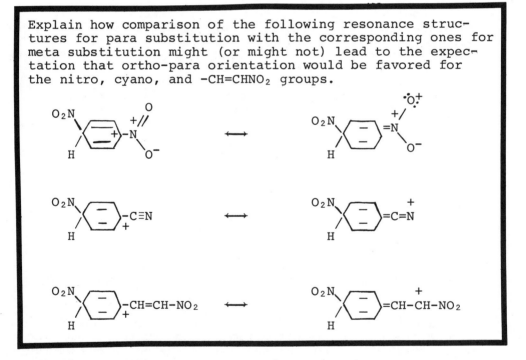

In acidic solution, aniline undergoes o,p-substitution

because it is the ⬡-$\ddot{N}H_2$ in low concentration that reacts

with the electrophile. The amino group (NH_2) is an ortho,
para director because it can stabilize a positive charge.
As more and more aniline is reacted, the acid-base equilibrium is shifted to the right. This produces more aniline
which will react to give o,p-substitution.

● **PROBLEM** 11-18

Explain how comparison of the following resonance structures for para substitution with the corresponding ones for
meta substitution might (or might not) lead to the expec-
tation that ortho-para orientation would be favored for
the nitro, cyano, and $-CH=CHNO_2$ groups.

Solution: The ortho, para orientation for NO_2, CN, and
$\overline{CH=CHNO_2}$ groups leads to an activated complex with an unfavorable distribution of charge. Ortho, para substitution
in aromatic nitro compounds will place two positive charges
in close proximity to one another. This situation is less
stable than the activated complex for meta substitution
where this proximity is relieved.

Ortho, para substitution in aromatic cyano compounds places a partial positive charge on the aromatic carbon bearing the cyano group. The cyano group is an electron withdrawing group because it contains an sp hybridized carbon and a nitrogen, both of which are more electronegative than the sp^2 hybridized carbon to which they are bonded. The electron withdrawing ability of the cyano group causes destabilization by intensifying this positive charge. The meta orientation places no charge on the carbon bonded to the cyano group. This situation is more stable than in ortho, para orientation.

Ortho, para orientation in aromatic compounds bearing the $-CH=CH-NO_2$ group places a positive charge on the carbon adjacent to the electron withdrawing nitro group. This destabilizes the molecule and makes the $-CH=CH-NO_2$ group a ring deactivator. This would normally make the $-CH=CH-NO_2$ group a meta directing group. In actuality, however, the $-CH-CH-NO_2$ group is an ortho, para director with deactivation. The reason for this is that the $-CH=CH-NO_2$ group has a destabilizing effect as well as a stabilizing effect. The destabilizing effect is a result of the electron withdrawing nitrogroup residing next to a positively charged carbon in the activated complex for ortho, para substitution. The nitro group makes the cationic carbon more positive, an inductive effect. $-CH=CH-NO_2$ also has a stabilizing effect. In ortho, para orientation the carbon-carbon double bond is involved in the resonance for the molecule. This resonance effect tends to release electrons and stabilize the molecule. This is more important than the inductive effect for orientation of substituents. Hence, the $-CH=CH-NO_2$ group is an ortho, para directing group with deactivation. This situation is similar to the case of the halogens.

● PROBLEM 11-19

Explain why the $-CF_3$, $-NO_2$, and $-CHO$ groups should be meta-orienting with deactivation.

Solution: All three groups have a full or partial positive charge on the atom directly bonded to the aromatic ring. The three fluorine atoms, being highly electronegative, tend to severely decrease the electron density about the carbon atom. This gives the carbon a partial positive charge. The nitro group is represented by two principal resonance structures, both of which place a full positive charge on the nitrogen. The highly electronegative oxygen atom of the formyl group decreases the electron density about the carbon, which gives the carbon a partial positive charge. SO, $-CF_3$, $-NO_2$, and $-CHO$ will possess a partial or full positive charge on the atom bonded to the aromatic carbon of the ring.

In such a situation, aromatic electrophilic substitution will follow a meta pathway. This is explained by the fact that when an electrophile (an electron-deficient species) attacks the aromatic ring, a carbonium ion results, that is,

positive charge is introduced. If the electrophile added
ortho or para to the substituent, some of this positive
charge would be centered at the aromatic carbon bonded to
the atom of the substituent that already possesses positive
charge. This would be an unfavorable situation because of
the proximity of two like charges. The situation is illustrated using the substituent $-CF_3$ and the nitronium ion
($^+NO_2$) as the electrophile below:

unfavorable

    The nitronium ion added para to $-CF_3$ so that a partial
positive charge now exists under the CF_3, which already has
positive charge character.

    Now, if the electrophile adds meta, this close prox-
imity of like charges is avoided. The positive charge of
the electrophile is not centered directly under the substituent as shown below:

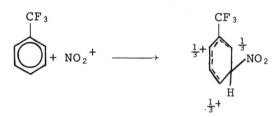

    Since the close proximity of like charges is re-
lieved, this intermediate is more stable. This, then
accounts for the meta-directing orientation of $-CF_3$,
$-NO_2$, and $-CHO$.

    These three groups all withdraw electrons, so that they
intensify the positive charge in the intermediate carbonium
ion. This results in deactivation of the aromatic ring.

● **PROBLEM** 11-20

Starting with the definition of partial rate factor, derive
an expression relating p_f^G to the rate of substitution para
to G in C_6H_5G.

Solution: The partial rate factor compares the rate of
substitution at a single position on C_6H_5G to the rate of
a single substitution on benzene. The partial rate factor

for the para position $\left(p_f^G\right)$ is defined to be

$$p_f^G = \frac{K_p G}{K_H} \qquad \text{where}$$

$K_p G$ = rate of reaction for para attack upon C_6H_5G and

K_H = rate of substitution at one position on benzene.

The rate of substitution para to G in C_6H_5G can be expressed as a function of the overall rate of substitution in C_6H_5G and the fraction of para isomer formed.

$$\text{fraction of para product} = \frac{\% \text{ para product}}{100}$$

$$\frac{\% \text{ para product}}{100} = \frac{K_p G}{K_{C_6H_5G}}$$

where $K_{C_6H_5G}$ = overall rate of reaction of C_6H_5G.

From this equation, we find that:

$$K_p G = \frac{\% \text{ para product}}{100} \times K_{C_6H_5G}$$

Substituting this equality for $K_p G$ into the partial rate factor equation will give us:

$$p_f^G = \frac{\% \text{ para product}}{100} \times \frac{K_{C_6H_5G}}{K_H}$$

Since the overall rate of substitution on benzene must be six times the rate of substitution at any one position on benzene, we can form the following equality:

$$K_H = \frac{1}{6} K_{C_6H_6}, \qquad \text{where}$$

K_H = rate of substitution at one position on benzene

and $K_{C_6H_6}$ = overall rate of substitution on benzene.

Substituting the equality for K_H into the partial rate factor equation will give us an expression relating p_f^G to the rate of substitution para to G in C_6H_5G.

$$p_f^G = \frac{\% \text{ para product}}{100} \times \frac{6 \ K_{C_6H_5G}}{K_{C_6H_6}}$$

Ethylation of chlorobenzene is slower than is ethylation of benzene $(k_{C_6H_5Cl}/k_{C_6H_6} = 0.20)$. Using this, and the product distribution shown below, calculate o_f^{Cl}, m_f^{Cl}, and p_f^{Cl} for this alkylation.

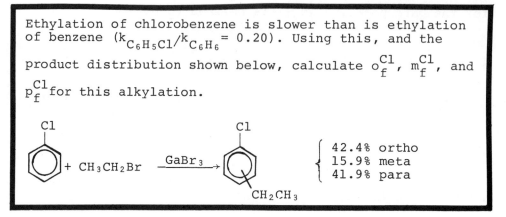

$$+ \; CH_3CH_2Br \xrightarrow{GaBr_3}$$

$$\begin{cases} 42.4\% \text{ ortho} \\ 15.9\% \text{ meta} \\ 41.9\% \text{ para} \end{cases}$$

Solution: The partial rate factors for the ortho, meta and para positions are o_f^G, m_f^G, and p_f^G, respectively. They are defined to be:

$$o_f^G = \frac{K_o G}{K_H}; \quad m_f^G = \frac{K_m G}{K_H}; \quad \text{and} \quad p_f^G = \frac{K_p G}{K_H}, \quad \text{where}$$

$K_o G$ = rate of ortho attack on C_6H_5G

$K_m G$ = rate of meta attack on C_6H_5G

$K_p G$ = rate of para attack on C_6H_5G

K_H = rate of substitution at one position on benzene.

Using these equations, one can derive an expression relating the partial rate factors to the rate of ortho, para, and meta substitution in C_6H_5G.

$$\frac{\% \text{ ortho product}}{100} = \frac{2 K_o G}{K_{C_6H_5G}}$$

$$\frac{\% \text{ meta product}}{100} = \frac{2 K_m G}{K_{C_6H_5G}}$$

$$\frac{\% \text{ para product}}{100} = \frac{K_p G}{K_{C_6H_5G}}$$

where $K_{C_6H_5G}$ = overall rate of substitution on C_6H_5G and the coefficients 2,2 and 1 represent the possible number of sites of attack.

$$K_H = \frac{1}{6} \left(K_{C_6H_6} \right);$$

where $K_{C_6H_6}$ = overall rate of substitution on benzene.

The above equations together with the partial rate factor equations can be used to get the following expressions:

$$o_f^G = \frac{\% \text{ ortho isomer}}{100} \times \frac{3 \ K_{C_6H_5G}}{K_{C_6H_6}}$$

$$p_f^G = \frac{\% \text{ para product}}{100} \times \frac{6 \ K_{C_6H_5G}}{K_{C_6H_6}}$$

$$m_f^G = \frac{\% \text{ meta product}}{100} \times \frac{3 \ K_{C_6H_5G}}{K_{C_6H_6}}$$

Since we are given the ratio

$$\frac{K_{C_6H_5Cl}}{K_{C_6H_6}} = 0.20 \qquad \text{and the product distribution,}$$

we can calculate o_f^G, m_f^G, and p_f^G, where G is chlorine.

$$o_f^{Cl} = \frac{42.4}{100} \times 3(0.20) = 0.25$$

$$m_f^{Cl} = \frac{15.9}{100} \times 3(0.20) = 0.09$$

$$p_f^{Cl} = \frac{41.9}{100} \times 6(0.20) = 0.50.$$

● **PROBLEM** 11-22

Even though 1,3,5-trinitrobenzene (TNB) has more shattering power (more brisance) and is no more dangerous to handle, 2,4,6-trinitrotoluene (TNT) has always been the high explosive in more general use. Can you suggest a reason (connected with manufacture) for the popularity of TNT? (Benzene and toluene are both readily available materials; for many years benzene was cheaper.)

Solution: The difference between toluene and benzene is that toluene has a methyl group substituent on the aromatic ring. The methyl group is an activating group; it releases electrons so that it stabilizes the intermediate carbonium ion in electrophilic aromatic substitution.

The activated complex for nitration of toluene is slightly stabilized by the activating methyl group. Since benzene has no such groups on the aromatic ring, its activated complex for nitration is not as stable as toluene's. Since benzene will have a less stable activated complex than toluene, the rate of reaction is slower for benzene than for toluene. Toluene is more easily nitrated, and therefore more easily polynitrated than benzene.

Arrange the following in order of reactivity toward ring nitration, listing by structure the most reactive at the top, the least reactive at the bottom.

(a) benzene, mesitylene $(1,3,5-C_6H_3(CH_3)_3)$, toluene, m-xylene, p-xylene

(b) acetanilide $(C_6H_5NHCOCH_3)$, acetophenone $(C_6H_5COCH_3)$, aniline, benzene

(c) 2,4-dinitrochlorobenzene, 2,4-dinitrophenol.

Solution: Reactivity towards ring nitration depends upon the energy level of the activated complex. The higher the energy level of the activated complex, the less stable is the activated complex and the slower is the rate of reaction. Conversely, the more stable is the activated complex, the greater are the rate of reaction and reactivity.

(a)   When nitronium ion $(^+NO_2)$ is added to benzene, the positive charge is distributed amongst three secondary carbons. In the case of ortho, para substitution in mesitylene, the positive charge in the activated complex is distributed amongst three tertiary carbons as shown:

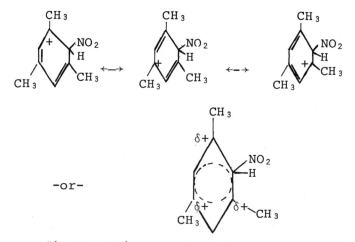

Since tertiary carbocations are more stable than secondary carbocations, the activated complex for mesitylene is more stable than for benzene. Therefore, mesitylene is more reactive toward ring nitration than is benzene. Looking at the other compounds' activated complexes for ortho, para substitution, we find: Toluene has two secondary carbocations and one tertiary carbocation; m-xylene has one secondary carbocation and two tertiary carbocations; p-xylene has two secondary carbocations and one tertiary carbocation. We see that toluene and p-xylene have the same number of secondary and tertiary carbocations in the activated complex. The activated complex for p-xylene is, however, more stable than for toluene because of the presence of an extra methyl group. The methyl group has an activating effect on the entire molecule. From the relative stabilities of the activated complexes, we can show the relative reactivities toward ring nitration to be:

mesitylene > m-xylene > p-xylene > toluene > benzene.

(b) In its activated complex, acetanilide has its positive charge distributed amongst three carbons, one of which is bonded to an acetamido group. The acetamido group activates the ring by stabilizing the positive charge. Acetophenone is an aromatic ring with an acetyl group. The acetyl group destabilizes the ring and will likewise destabilize the activated complex. Aniline is an aromatic ring with an activating amino group. The amino group will stabilize the positive charge in aniline's activated complex more than the acetamido group will stabilize the positive charge in acetanilide's activated complex. This is because the acetyl portion of the acetamido group is electron withdrawing and weakens the full stabilizing effect of the activating substituent. Benzene is an aromatic ring with no substituents. Acetophenone is the least reactive; it is the only compound with a deactivating group. Both aniline and acetanilide are more reactive towards nitration than benzene, because they both have an activating group, whereas benzene has none. The relative reactivity towards ring nitration is:

aniline > acetanilide > benzene > acetophenone.

(c) The activated complex for the nitration of 2,4-dinitrochlorobenzene has some positive charge nearby the deactivating chloro group. The electron withdrawing chloro group destabilizes the positive charge. In the case of 2,4-dinitrophenol, there is some positive charge nearby the activating hydroxyl group. The hydroxyl group stabilizes positive charge in the activated complex. Since both compounds have two nitro groups in the same relative positions, the reactivity towards ring nitration is:

2,4-dinitrophenol > 2,4-dinitrochlorobenzene.

SYNTHESIS

• PROBLEM 11-24

Outline all steps in the laboratory synthesis of the following compounds from benzene and/or toluene, using any needed aliphatic or inorganic reagents. Assume that a pure para isomer can be separated from an ortho, para mixture.

(a) p-nitrotoluene   (d) p-bromobenzoic acid
(b) p-bromonitrobenzene   (e) o-iodobenzoic acid
(c) m-bromobenzenesulfonic acid (f) 1,3,5-trinitrobenzene
                  (g) 3,5-dinitrobenzoic acid

Solution: (a) Nitration of an aromatic compound is the addition of a nitro group (NO_2) to that compound. A nitro group can be added onto an aromatic ring by reacting it with a mixture of concentrated nitric acid (HNO_3) and concentrated sulfuric acid (H_2SO_4). The electrophile in this case is the nitronium ion, $\overset{+}{N}O_2$. The electrophile is supplied by the nitric acid. The purpose of the sulfuric acid is to increase the concentration of nitronium ion by protonating the nitric acid.

$$HONO_2 + 2\ H_2SO_4 \;\rightleftarrows\; \underset{+\ +}{HO-\overset{\overset{\displaystyle H}{|}}{\underset{}{N}}-O^-} + HSO_4{}^- + H_2SO_4$$

$$O=\overset{+2}{N}-O^- + H_3O^+ + 2\ HSO_4{}^-$$
nitronium ion

Nitration of toluene results in the addition of nitronium ion mainly at the ortho and para positions of toluene. This occurs because the methyl group in toluene is an activating group; it will tend to stabilize a nearby positive charge. When the nitronium ion adds to toluene, it introduces a resonance stabilized positive charge onto the aromatic ring. When the nitronium ion adds to the ortho or para positions of toluene, the resonance stabilizing structures place some positive charge on the aromatic carbon bonded to the methyl group. The positive charge is stabilized by the electron release of the methyl group. When the nitronium ion adds to the meta position of toluene, the positive charge is not positioned directly under the methyl group so that the stabilization by electron release is not as extensive. Since chemical reactions tend to occur through the activated complex with the lowest energy (or the greatest amount of stabilization), nitration of toluene will occur mainly at the ortho and para positions.

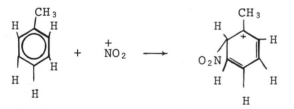

Addition of nitronium ion to ortho position.

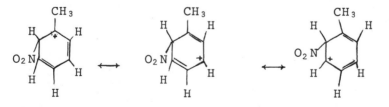

Resonance stabilization of resulting cation. Note that one of the resonance structures has the positive charge on carbon number one, which is especially stable due to the electron release.

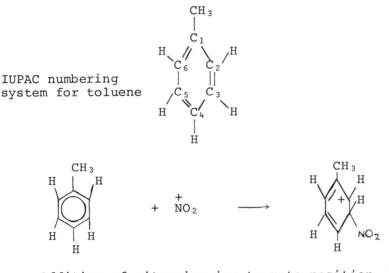

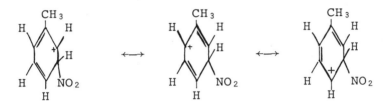

$$+ \quad \overset{+}{N}O_2 \quad \longrightarrow$$

Addition of nitronium ion to meta position.

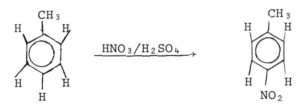

Resonance stabilization of meta substituted toluene.
Note that positive charge does not reside directly under
the methyl group. This is, therefore, not as low in energy
as the ortho and para substituted toluenes. As a result,
the main products of nitration of toluene are o-nitrotoluene and p-nitrotoluene. These can be separated to give
p-nitrotoluene. The synthesis of p-nitrotoluene from
toluene can be summarized as:

$$\xrightarrow{\text{HNO}_3 / \text{H}_2\text{SO}_4}$$

(b)   The problem faced here is which substituent should be
added first: the bromo group or the nitro group? Since we
want p-bromonitrobenzene, the first substituent to be added
should be one which directs the addition of the second substituent in a para position. The nitro group is a meta
director. That is, a nitro group on an aromatic ring destabilizes positive charge and as a result will direct the
addition of a second substituent mainly in a meta position.
The bromo group, however, is an ortho, para director. The
bromo group (a halogen) is a deactivating group; it destabilizes positive charge by its inductive effect, that is,
by its ability to withdraw electrons. Through its resonance
effect, the bromine releases electrons to stabilize the

intermediate carbonium ion. This electron release is effective only for attack at the ortho and para positions. The
resonance effect of the bromo group is possible because of
the free electron pairs on bromine. Knowing that the bromo
group is an ortho, para director, we would want to first
brominate the aromatic ring. Subsequent nitration will result
in mainly ortho and para bromonitrobenzene. These can be
separated to give p-bromonitrobenzene. Bromination of aromatic
compounds is accomplished by reacting with bromine gas and a
metal catalyst, such as iron. Synthesis of p-bromonitrobenzene from benzene is:

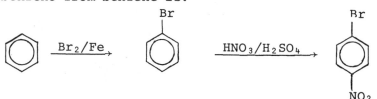

(c)   The sulfonyl (SO₃H) group is a meta director whereas
the bromo group is an ortho, para director. Since we want
to synthesize m-bromobenzenesulfonic acid, we should first
add the sulfonyl group to the aromatic ring so that subsequent bromination will give the desired product. Sulfonation of aromatic compounds is the addition of a sulfonyl
group to the compound. This is accomplished by using fuming
sulfuric acid; that is, sulfur trioxide dissolved in concentrated sulfuric acid. The actual electrophile is sulfur
trioxide, and the reaction as follows:

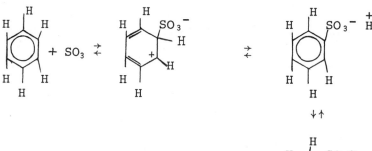

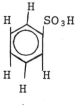

benzenesulfonic acid

Bromination of benzenesulfonic acid will result mainly
in the formation of m-bromobenzenesulfonic acid, because of
the meta directing -SO₃H group. The synthesis of m-bromobenzenesulfonic acid from benzene can be summarized as
follows:

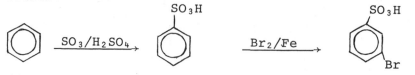

(d)   A carboxylic acid group (-COOH) is a meta director
because it is an electron withdrawing group and will destabilize positive charge. A methyl group, on the other
hand, is an ortho, para director. Since we want to synthesize p-bromobenzoic acid, we should first add a bromo
group to toluene. This will give both o- and p-bromotoluene as the major products. This can be separated to
give p-bromotoluene. Now we can convert the methyl group
on the aromatic ring to a carboxylic acid group. This is
accomplished by using potassium permanganate, a powerful
oxidizing agent. The synthesis of p-bromobenzoic acid from
toluene is:

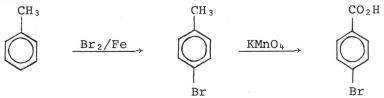

(e)   Vigorous oxidation of any alkylated aromatic compound
will oxidize the alkyl group to a carboxylic acid group. It
can be accomplished by using potassium permanganate. Using
this method we can convert toluene to benzoic acid. Since
the carboxylic acid group is a meta director, direct
iodination will not give the desired product. One way to
get the iodo group substituted at the ortho position is by
thallation. Thallation is the treatment of aromatic compounds
with thallium trifluoroacetate. The products of this reaction
are trifluoroacetic acid and an arylthallium ditrifluoro-
acetate. The reaction involves electrophilic attack by the
(Lewis) acidic thallium upon the aromatic ring. When thallium
trifluoroacetate reacts with benzoic acid, it adds in an
ortho fashion despite the fact that the carboxylic acid
group is a meta director. This is because the electrophile
first complexes with the carboxylic acid group. It is easier
for thallium to move from the substituent to the ortho position than to the meta position.

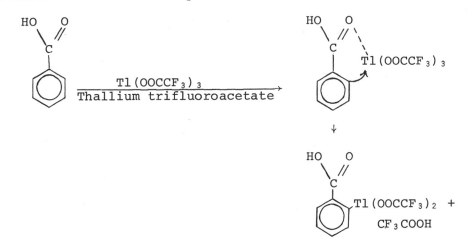

Thallation is almost exclusively para to other substituents because of the bulk of the electrophile. The

process of thallation followed by reaction with iodide ion forms aryl iodide compounds in high yield. The synthesis of o-iodobenzoic acid from toluene is:

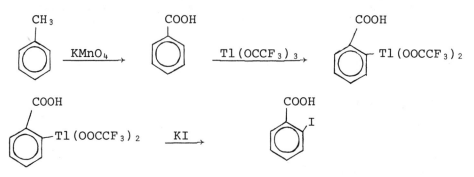

(f) Nitration of benzene is accomplished by using a mixture of concentrated nitric acid and concentrated sulfuric acid. The nitronium ion adds to the benzene ring to give nitrobenzene. The nitro group of nitrobenzene has a destabilizing effect upon the entire aromatic ring. This makes the molecule less reactive to further nitration. Nitration of nitrobenzene can be accomplished by increasing the concentration of the electrophile. The electrophile is the nitronium ion and its concentration can be increased by using fuming nitric acid with concentrated sulfuric acid. Fuming nitric acid is nitrous oxide dissolved in nitric acid. The nitronium ion adds to nitrobenzene in a meta fashion because that is the position where the least destabilization occurs. Further nitration is extremely difficult because of the combined destabilization effect of the two nitro groups. Nitration of m-dinitrobenzene is accomplished by reacting with fuming nitric acid and fuming sulfuric acid. Fuming sulfuric acid increases the acidity of the mixture and increases the concentration of nitronium ion. Nitration occurs in a meta fashion because that is where the least destabilization occurs. The synthesis of 1,3,5-trinitrobenzene from benzene is:

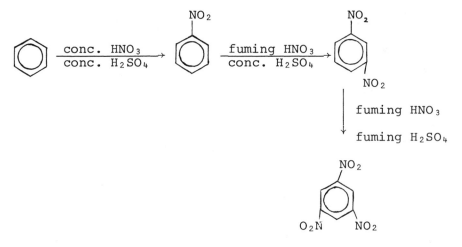

(g) Oxidation of toluene using potassium permanganate will yield benzoic acid. Nitration of benzoic acid occurs

368

slowly at room temperature because of the destabilizing effect of the carboxylic acid group upon the aromatic
ring. The rate of reaction will increase if heat is applied.
Nitration of benzoic acid will produce mainly the meta
substituted compound due to the electron withdrawing
carboxylic acid group. Further nitration will occur very
slowly because of the destabilization effect of both the
carboxylic acid group and the nitro group. The reaction will
progress at an acceptable rate if heated very strongly.
Nitration will occur in a meta fashion because that is where
there is least destabilization. Synthesis of 3,5-dinitro-
benzoic acid from toluene is:

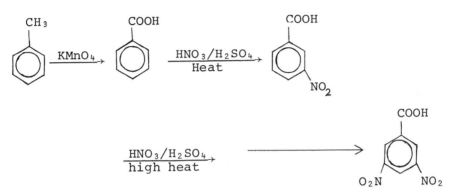

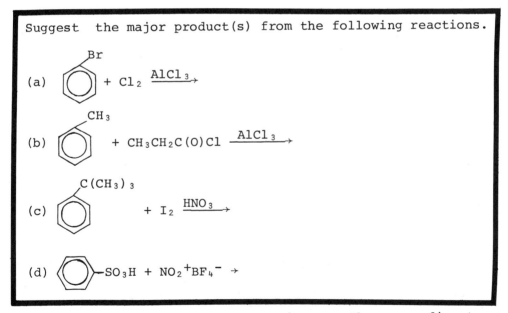

● **PROBLEM** 11-25

Suggest   the major product(s) from the following reactions.

(a) 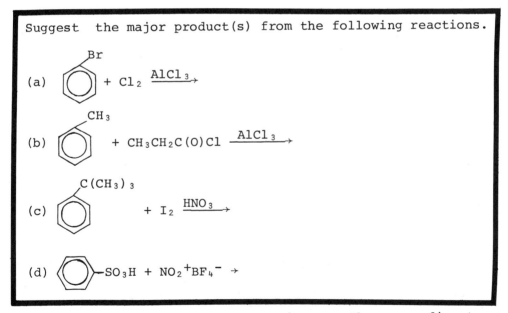 + Cl_2 $\xrightarrow{AlCl_3}$

(b) + $CH_3CH_2C(O)Cl$ $\xrightarrow{AlCl_3}$

(c) + I_2 $\xrightarrow{HNO_3}$

(d) $\langle \bigcirc \rangle$—SO_3H + $NO_2^+BF_4^-$ →

Solution: (a) The bromo group is an ortho, para director.
Although it is a deactivating group by its inductive effect
(due to its great electronegativity), it can stabilize a
positive charge by its resonance effect (due to its free
electron pairs). While reactivity is controlled by the inductive effect, the orientation (ortho, para directing) is
controlled by the resonance effect. When an aromatic com-

pound reacts with chlorine gas and aluminum chloride, chlorination of the aromatic ring will occur.

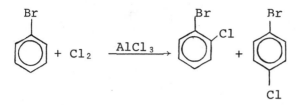

(b)   A methyl group on an aromatic ring releases electrons to stabilize the intermediate carbonium ion. This group directs ortho and para. When an aromatic compound reacts with an acyl chloride in the presence of aluminum chloride, Friedel-Crafts acylation occurs. An acyl chloride has the general formula RCOCl. Acylation of aromatic compounds in-volves the addition of an acyl group (RCO-) to the aromatic ring. The acyl chloride first complexes with aluminum chloride. This complex breaks down to form the acylium ion, R - C = O.   Once formed, the acylium ion undergoes an electrophilic aromatic substitution reaction with the aromatic compound. The product of this acylation reaction is an aromatic ketone. Toluene is acylated by propanoyl chloride to give both ortho and para substituted products.

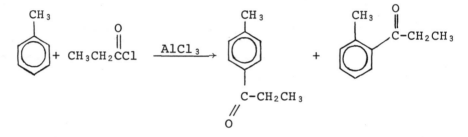

(c)   Bromination and chlorination of aromatic compounds can be accomplished by using the halogen gas with aluminum chloride. Iodination will not occur using these conditions because iodine is too unreactive. Iodination can be ac-complished by using iodine in the presence of an oxidant such as nitric acid.

      t-Butylbenzene can be iodinated only at its para position, even though the t-butyl group is an ortho, para director. This is because of steric hindrance; both the t-butyl group and the iodo group are relatively large. It is too difficult for the iodo group to substitute for the aromatic hydrogen at the ortho position because of "inter-ference" by the large t-butyl group. It is much easier for the iodo group to add para to the t-butyl group. As a result, none or very little ortho substituted product is formed.

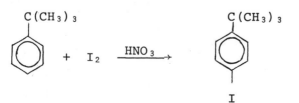

(d)   Nitration of aromatic compounds can be performed
using nitronium tetrafluoroborate, a direct source of
nitronium ion. Benzenesulfonic acid has a meta directing
$-SO_3H$ group. The $-SO_3H$ group is electron withdrawing and
will destabilize the aromatic ring. As a result, benzenesulfonic acid will be nitrated at the meta position.

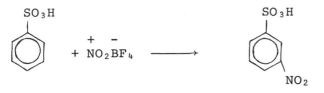

● **PROBLEM** 11-26

2,2'-Dinitrobiphenyl is to be synthesized. Outline the
method of preparation from iodobenzene. No other organic
reagent may be used. Any inorganic reagent may be employed.

Solution: 2,2'-Dinitrobiphenyl can be produced directly
from 2 moles of o-iodonitrobenzene by use of the Ullmann
reaction, which is used for the synthesis of biphenyl
derivatives. The reaction is outlined below:

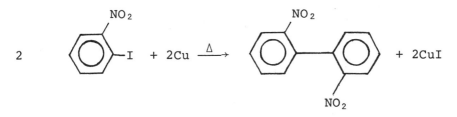

O-iodonitrobenzene   2,2'-Dinitrobiphenyl

      Hence, this synthesis can be performed when iodonitro-
benzene is obtained from iodobenzene. This can be accomplished
by a nitration reaction, where concentrated nitric and sulfuric acids are mixed to produce the nitronium ion ($^+NO_2$)
which is the electrophilic reagent that attacks the ring.
One must consider the direction of the attack. If benzene
possesses an iodine substituent, the iodine will direct
para and ortho, so that one obtains the following upon
nitration:

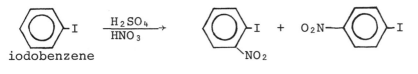

iodobenzene

                         o-iodonitro-   p-iodonitro-
                           benzene   benzene

      These two can be separated. The Ullmann reaction
is performed with the ortho compound and 2,2'-dinitrobi-
phenyl is obtained.

SPECTROSCOPY

Hydrocarbon B, C_6H_6, gave an nmr spectrum with two signals: δ 6.55 and δ 3.84, peak area ratio 2:1. When warmed in pyridine for three hours, B was quantitatively converted into benzene.

  Mild hydrogenation of B yielded C, whose spectra showed the following: mass spectrum, mol. wt. 82; infrared spectrum, no double bonds; nmr spectrum, one broad peak at δ 2.34.

  (a) How many rings are there in C? (b) How many rings are there (probably) in B? How many double bonds in B? (c) Can you suggest a structure for B? for C?

  (d) In the nmr spectrum of B the downfield signal was a triplet. How must you account for these splittings?

Solution: (a) Mild hydrogenation of B yielded C, whose mass spectrum reveals that its molecular weight is 82. The molecular weight of B(C_6H_6) is 78. From this data, we can conclude that B received four hydrogen atoms upon mild hydrogenation. This would give C the molecular formula C_6H_{10}. This formula is of the general form C_nH_{2n-2}, which denotes unsaturation. Since the infrared spectrum of structure C showed that there were no double bonds, the molecular formula suggests that C may be cyclic.

  Ring formation in hydrocarbons can account for unsaturation. As the carbon-carbon single bond is formed, two hydrogens are lost. In other words, when an alkane gives rise to a cycloalkane, two hydrogens are lost from the original molecular formula (C_nH_{2n+2}). To determine how many rings compound C possesses, we shall look at the molecular formula of C (C_6H_{10}). We find that C has four less hydrogens than the corresponding non-cyclic alkane (C_6H_{14}). This means that to go from C_6H_{14} to C_6H_{10}, two rings must have been established. Only with the formation of two rings can four hydrogens be lost to give the molecular formula of C_6H_{10}. Structure C has, therefore, two rings.

(b) To figure out the number of rings in structure B, we can use the same method as in part (a). Structure B accepted four hydrogens under mild hydrogenation in conversion to C. This means that B has either one carbon-carbon triple bond or two carbon-carbon double bonds, since both will accept four hydrogens upon hydrogenation.

  The spectral data seems to support the suggestion that B has two carbon-carbon double bonds. The carbon-carbon triple bond would resonate at about 2.5 to 3.0 parts per million. The lowest absorbance in the nuclear magnetic resonance (nmr) spectrum of structure B is 3.84 parts per million. The carbon-carbon double bond would resonate at about 5.5 to 6.5 parts per million. There is an absorbance at 6.55 in the nmr spectrum of B. This corresponds to the two carbon-carbon double bonds' absorbance. Hence, structure B has two carbon-carbon double bonds. The reason why a carbon-carbon double bond resonates downfield from a carbon-carbon triple bond has to do with shielding effects. The triple bond has a higher electron density about the hydrogens than does a double bond; this means the hydrogens of the carbon-carbon triple bond will be shielded more than the hydrogens of the carbon-carbon double bond. As a result, the carbon-carbon double bond resonates downfield from the carbon-carbon triple bond. We now know that structure B has the molecular formula C_6H_6 and contains two double bonds. The general molecular formula for a non-cyclic diene is C_nH_{2n-2}. The molecular formula for B can be written as C_nH_{2n-6}. As in part (a), for every cyclization two hydrogens are lost. Since we see that B has four less hydrogens than a non-cyclic diene, we can conclude that B has two rings. Structure B contains two rings and two double bonds.

(c)   The structures for B and C that are consistent with the data are as follows:

Structure B: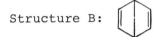

bicyclo [2.2.0] hexa-2,5-diene

This can also be called "Dewar benzene".

Structure C:

bicyclo [2.2.0] hexane

(d)   The tertiary carbons in B are bonded to two equivalent vinylic carbons and to each other.

Since the two tertiary hydrogens are equivalent, they will not split each other. Each tertiary hydrogen will be split into a triplet by the two equivalent vinylic hydrogens. This happens because n equivalent protons lying adjacent to the reference proton will split the reference proton into an n+ 1 multiplet. The two tertiary hydrogens are equivalent and therefore absorb at the same frequency. They appear as one triplet in the nmr spectrum.

● **PROBLEM** 11-28

Mesitylene reacts (- 80°) with ethyl fluoride and boron trifluororide to form a salt. Upon warming to - 15°, this salt is converted to a hydrocarbon whose nmr spectrum exhibits three different types of methyl resonances of relative intensities 2:1:1. Account for this, suggesting a structure for the salt. What would its nmr spectrum be like?

Solution: The reaction of ethyl fluoride (CH_3CH_2F) and boron trifluoride (BF_3) with mesitylene

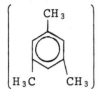 indicates a Friedel-Crafts alkylation is

taking place. One possible mechanism for the reaction is:

(1)   RF   + BF_3 → R^+ + BF_4^-
       (Alkyl halide)   (Lewis Acid)   (Carbonium ion)

(2) R^+ + C_6H_6 ⟶ $C_6H_5 \overset{+}{\underset{H}{\diagdown}} {\diagup}^R$

(3) $C_6H_5 \overset{+}{\underset{H}{\diagdown}} {\diagup}^R$ + BF_4^- ⟶ C_6H_5R + BF_3 + HF

The electrophile that attacks the aromatic compound is a carbonium ion. The Lewis acid functions by abstracting the halide ion from the alkyl halide to create the carbonium ion.

In this problem, boron trifluoride abstracts fluoride ion from ethyl fluoride to produce ethyl cation:

CH_3CH_2F $\underset{\leftarrow}{\overset{BF_3}{\rightarrow}}$ BF_4^- + $CH_3CH_2^+$

The ethyl cation attacks the aromatic ring of mesitylene seeking the rich source of electrons in the 𝜋 cloud. This results in the formation of an intermediate

carbonium ion (the $C_6H_5 \overset{+}{\underset{H}{\diagdown}} {\diagup}^R$ in the mechanism outlined

above). The salt isolated at − 80° in this problem is this intermediate carbonium ion in conjunction with BF_4^-. That is, we have tetrafluoroborate salt of ethyl mesitylene. Subsequent proton loss occurs by heating to give the hydrocarbon. Now, it is important to note that the mesitylene will only be monoalkylated. When an ethyl cation attacks the ring, positive charge is introduced. An additional attack by another ethyl cation would create an unstable situation with the addition of another positive (like) charge. The formation of the hydrocarbon from mesitylene may be illustrated as follows:

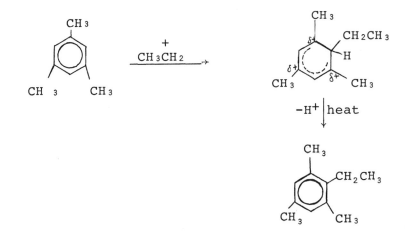

There are three different types of environments in which the methyl groups reside. This means that there are three methyl groups that are non-equivalent. As a result, there will be three different types of methyl chemical shifts in nmr. Since the hydrocarbon contains four methyl groups, two of the four groups must be equivalent to each other. The two equivalent methyl groups are the ones that are bonded to carbon numbers 2 and 6 of the aromatic ring. The numbering system for the aromatic ring of this hydrocarbon is:

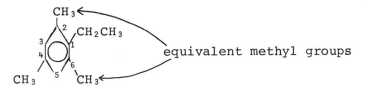

As in the hydrocarbon, the nmr spectrum of the salt would contain three different types of methyl chemical shifts (of relative intensities 2:1:1.). The structure of the salt is:

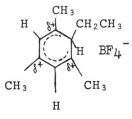

The frequency at which a substituent's proton will absorb depends upon the electronic environment about that substituent. The greater the electron density, the greater shielding there is and the further upfield will be the absorption. The principal resonance structures for the salt are:

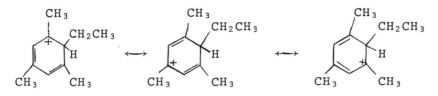

We see from the resonance structures that the positive charge is distributed amongst carbon #2, 4 and 6. The carbons furthest from the positive charge have the greatest electron density, and will absorb at the lowest frequency; that is, their signal will be the most upfield. The nmr spectrum of the salt is as follows:

The methyl portion of the ethyl group at carbon #1 is the carbon that is furthest from the positive charge; it has the greatest electron density and will be the most upfield signal in the spectrum. This methyl group absorbs near 1.0 δ. This methyl absorption also occurs as a triplet; this is the result of the spin-spin splitting by the two protons on the adjacent methylene (-CH_2-) group. The methylene protons will absorb near 1.5 δ and will occur as a quartet. It absorbs downfield from the adjacent methyl group because it is deshielded relative to the methyl group; the methylene is lower in electron density because it is closer to the positive charge. The methylene group occurs as a quartet because of spin-spin splitting by the three protons of the adjacent methyl group. The proton at carbon #1 occurs as a triplet. This happens because there is an adjacent methylene group for spin-spin splitting to occur. The proton absorbs near 1.8 δ, which is characteristic of an R_3CH proton. The methyl groups at carbons #2 and 6 absorb as singlets near 7.0 δ. Absorption occurs at a high δ value because of the low electron density of carbons #2 and 6, due to their partial positive charge. The methyl group at carbon #4 occurs as a singlet near 7.0 δ; it is slightly downfield from the methyl groups at carbons #2 and 6. The methyl groups at carbons #2 and 6 have slightly greater electron density because of the adjacent ethyl group. The two protons at carbons #3 and 5 are equivalent and will absorb at the same frequency. They occur as a singlet and absorb near 7.2 δ. Their signal is the most downfield one in the nmr spectrum of the salt. This is because the electron density is lowest at carbons #3 and 5, and therefore the greatest amount of deshielding occurs at these carbons. As a result, the protons absorb downfield from all the other signals in the nmr spectrum. The nmr spectrum of the salt can be summarized as follows:

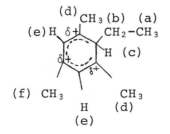

(a) 3H, triplet near 1.0 δ

(b) 2H, quartet near 1.5 δ

(c) 1H, triplet near 1.8 δ

(d) 6H, singlet near 7.0 δ

(e) 2H, singlet near 7.2 δ

(f) 3H, singlet near 7.0 δ (downfield from d)

Note that nH (n is an integer) indicates the relative number of protons in each substituent absorbed.

● **PROBLEM** 11-29

A compound, $C_{10}H_{14}$, has the following nmr and ir spectra. Determine the structure of the compound.

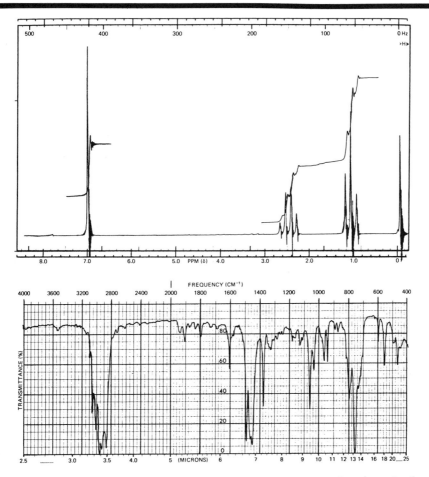

Solution: The nmr spectrum shows a quartet signal down-field from a triplet signal, and a singlet as the most downfield signal. The value of 7.0 δ for the singlet strongly suggests the presence of a benzene ring. The multiplet signals must have occurred as a result of spin-spin splitting. The quartet and triplet indicate that there is a carbon with two protons adjacent to a carbon with three protons. Such is the case with an ethyl group. We are now aware of the presence of an ethyl group and a benzene ring. Since the molecular formula is $C_{10}H_{14}$ and eight carbons (six from benzene and two from ethyl) have been accounted for, we have two carbons still to be solved for. These two carbons make up another ethyl group, because of the fact only the absorption peaks for an ethyl group are seen in the aliphatic region of the nmr. Hence, the nmr suggests the existence of a diethylbenzene.

The infrared spectrum shows a band at 3000 cm^{-1}. This is the characteristic absorption of an aryl C-H bond stretching. The methyl C-H bonds and the methylene C-H bonds absorb in the range of 1430 cm^{-1} to 1470 cm^{-1} for carbon-hydrogen bending. This band is seen in the infrared spectrum, and supports our conclusion that the compound is a diethylbenzene. The only thing left to be determined is the orientation of the ethyl groups on the benzene ring. The infrared spectrum shows a band between 750 - 810 cm^{-1}. This is indicative of a meta orientation on a benzene ring. Hence, the compound with the molecular formula $C_{10}H_{14}$ which is consistent with the spectral data given is m-diethylbenzene.

CHAPTER 12

ARENES

NOMENCLATURE AND STRUCTURE

Draw the structure of:

(a) m-xylene   (g) isopropylbenzene (cumene)
(b) mesitylene   (h) trans-stilbene
(c) o-ethyltoluene   (i) 1,4-diphenyl-1,3-butadiene
(d) p-di-tert-butylbenzene   (j) p-dibenzylbenzene
(e) cyclohexylbenzene   (k) m-bromostyrene
(f) 3-phenylpentane   (l) diphenylacetylene

Solution: To draw these structures, it will be necessary to consider the nomenclature of arenes (compounds that contain both aromatic and aliphatic units).

The simplest of the alkylbenzenes (compounds made up of aromatic and alkane units), methylbenzene, is given the name of toluene. Compounds with longer side chains are named by prefixing the name of the alkyl group to the word

-benzene. For example, n-propylbenzene: $\bigcirc$—CH$_2$CH$_2$CH$_3$.

The name xylene is the special name given to the simplest of the dialkylbenzenes, the dimethylbenzenes. There is o-xylene, m-xylene, and p-xylene. Dialkylbenzenes containing one methyl group are named as derivatives of toluene, while others are named by prefixing the names of both alkyl groups to the word -benzene. A compound containing a very complicated side chain might be named as a phenylalkane (C$_6$H$_5$=phenyl). Examples.

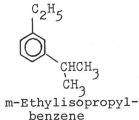

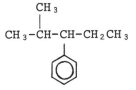

p-Ethyltoluene   m-Ethylisopropyl-   2-Methyl-3-phenyl-
                       benzene   pentane

379

Compounds containing more than one benzene ring are nearly always named as derivatives of alkanes as can be seen in the following example:

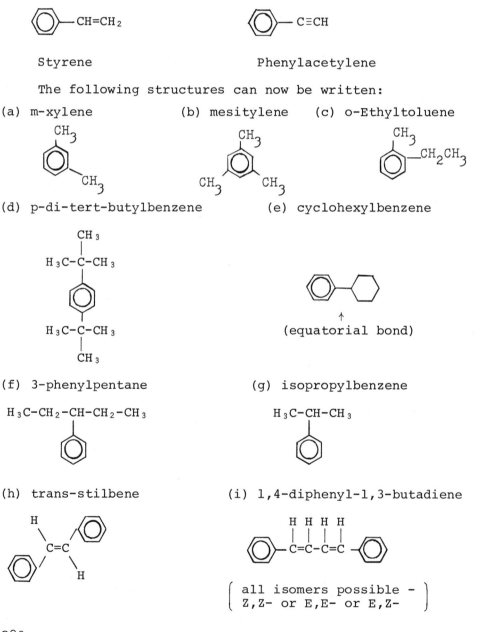

Styrene is the special name given to the simplest alkenylbenzene. Others are generally named as substituted alkenes (sometimes as substituted benzenes). Alkynyl-benzenes are named as substituted alkynes. Examples:

Styrene   Phenylacetylene

The following structures can now be written:

(a) m-xylene   (b) mesitylene   (c) o-Ethyltoluene

(d) p-di-tert-butylbenzene   (e) cyclohexylbenzene

(equatorial bond)

(f) 3-phenylpentane   (g) isopropylbenzene

$H_3C-CH_2-CH-CH_2-CH_3$ $H_3C-CH-CH_3$

(h) trans-stilbene   (i) 1,4-diphenyl-1,3-butadiene

(all isomers possible -
  Z,Z- or E,E- or E,Z-)

(j) p-dibenzylbenzene

(k) m-bromostyrene

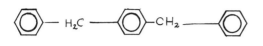

(l) diphenylacetylene

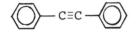

● PROBLEM 12-2

Name each of the following compounds by an accepted system.

(a) $(C_6H_5)_2CHCl$

(b) $C_6H_5CHCl_2$

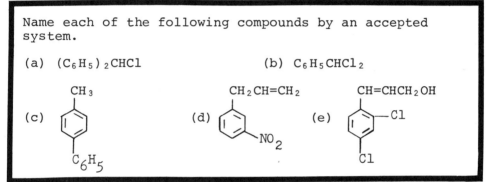

Solution: This problem requires a knowledge of arene nomenclature. Benzene (C_6H_6) is the simplest aromatic hydrocarbon. Benzene compounds can be named as a derivative of benzene or as a phenyl-substituted compound.

(a) In IUPAC (International Union of Pure and Applied Chemistry) nomenclature, a compound having two benzene rings separated by a carbon is named as a methane derivative. Since the compound $(C_6H_5)_2CHCl$ has a chloro group on the middle carbon, it is named as a chloro-substituted compound. There are two phenyl groups (the benzene rings) attached to the methane carbon. Two phenyl substituents can be written as a diphenyl-substituted compound. In IUPAC nomenclature, the names of substituents appear in alphabetical order. Hence, the IUPAC name for the compound $(C_6H_5)_2CHCl$ is chlorodiphenylmethane.   There is no numbering system used for naming methane derivatives because the parent chain is only one carbon long. The compound can alternatively be named as a benzhydrol derivative. Benzhydrol has the formula $(C_6H_5)_2CHOH$. The $(C_6H_5)_2CH-$ portion is called the benzhydryl group. A chloro group in place of the hydroxyl group (-OH) in benzhydrol can be named as a chloride compound. The compound $(C_6H_5)_2CHCl$ can be called benzhydryl chloride.

(b) Benzaldehyde has the formula C_6H_5CHO. The $C_6H_5-\overset{|}{C}H-$ group is called the benzal group. The compound $C_6H_5CHCl_2$ is named as a chloride. The presence of the benzal group gives it the name benzalchloride. In IUPAC nomenclature, the compound $C_6H_5CHCl_2$ would be named as a benzene deriva- tive and not as a methane derivative. The $-CHCl_2$ group is a chloro substituted methyl group. The presence of two chloro groups gives it the name 'dichloromethyl'. Hence the IUPAC name for the compound $C_6H_5CHCl_2$ is dichloro- methylbenzene.

(c)   The compound $C_6H_5-C_6H_5$ is called biphenyl. The compound

whose name we desire (CH_3 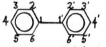 C_6H_5) can be named as a

derivative of biphenyl. The compound is a methyl substituted biphenyl compound. The numbering system of biphenyl is:

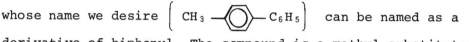

The n,n' nomenclature of biphenyl compounds is used only when there is a substituent on each ring. If only one ring bears substituents, the n nomenclature is used and not the n'. In this problem, the methyl group is the only

substituent in the biphenyl compound CH_3 ◯ C_6H_5.

Hence the methyl is considered to be in the 4 position and not the 4' position. Therefore, the compound is named as 4-methylbiphenyl.

(d)   The compound ◯(NO₂)$-CH_2-CH=CH_2$ is named as a

benzene derivative. There are two substituents on the ring: allyl ($-CH_2-CH=CH_2$) and nitro (NO_2). These groups are located meta with respect to each other

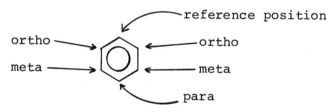

Above: Orientations on a disubstituted benzene ring.

The names of the two groups on the compound appear in alphabetical order. Their relative orientation on the ring is meta (abbreviated as m-) and precedes the name of

the compound. Hence the compound ◯(NO₂)$-CH_2$ $\underset{CH=CH_2}{|}$ is

named m-allylnitrobenzene.

382

(e)   The compound Cl—[ring with Cl]—CH=CH-CH$_2$OH can be named as
a derivative of allyl alcohol (CH$_2$=CH-CH$_2$OH). The numbering

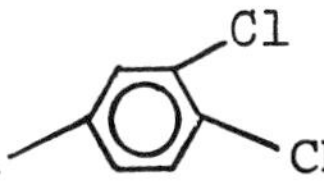

system of allyl alcohol is: $\overset{3}{C}H_2=\overset{2}{C}H-\overset{1}{C}H_2OH$. In the compound
we want to name, there is a substituted phenyl substituent
at carbon # 3 of allyl alcohol. The benzene carbon bonded
to carbon # 3 of allyl alcohol will be carbon # 1 of the

aromatic ring. Hence the substituent   Cl—[ring with Cl]—   is called

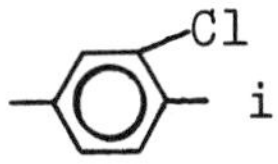

2,4-dichlorophenyl. The compound   Cl—[ring with Cl]—CH=CH-CH$_2$OH is

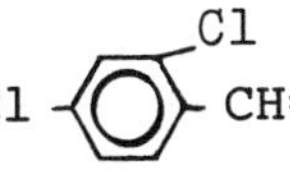

therefore named as 3 -(2,4-dichlorophenyl)-allyl alcohol.

REACTIONS

● **PROBLEM** 12-3

Give structures and names of the principal organic
products expected from the reaction of n-propylbenzene
with each of the following:

(1)   K$_2$Cr$_2$O$_7$, H$_2$SO$_4$, heat   (3) Cl$_2$, Fe
(2)   HNO$_3$, H$_2$SO$_4$ (4) Br$_2$, heat, light
             (5) cyclohexene, HF

<u>Solution:</u>   N-propylbenzene is a compound made up of
aromatic and alkane units. Hence, it belongs in the category
of alkylbenzenes, which, in turn, are part of the group of
compounds known as arenes (compounds that contain both
aliphatic and aromatic units). Such compounds show two sets
of chemical properties. The ring undergoes the electrophilic substitution characteristic of benzene, whereas the
side chain undergoes the free-radical substitution characteristic of alkanes. Each should modify the other. Except
for oxidation and hydrogenation these are the reactions to
be expected for arenes.

(1) 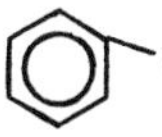   [benzene ring]—CH$_2$CH$_2$CH$_3$ + K$_2$Cr$_2$O$_7$, H$_2$SO$_4$, heat $\xrightarrow{\quad ? \quad}$

          n-propylbenzene

     While benzene and alkanes are very unreactive to
oxidizing agents (KMnO$_4$, K$_2$Cr$_2$O$_7$, etc.) the benzene ring
makes an aliphatic side chain susceptible to oxidation.
Only a carboxyl group (-COOH) remains to indicate the
position of the original side chain after oxidation.
Potassium permanganate (KMnO$_4$), potassium dichromate
(K$_2$Cr$_2$O$_7$) or dilute nitric acid (HNO$_3$) can be used to
oxidize the alkylbenzenes. Consequently, when K$_2$Cr$_2$O$_7$,

H₂SO₄ (heat) is added to n-propylbenzene the n-propyl side chain should be oxidized to the carboxyl group as shown:

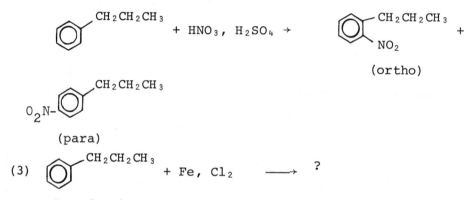

$CH_2CH_2CH_3$ + $K_2Cr_2O_7$, H_2SO_4, heat → $COOH$

(2) $CH_2CH_2CH_3$ + HNO_3, H_2SO_4 ⟶

    The alkyl groups of alkylbenzenes release electrons in electrophilic aromatic substitution so that they activate the ring and direct ortho and para. Hence, when nitric acid and sulfuric acid are mixed to generate a nitronium ion (+NO₂) for a nitration reaction, the ortho and para products are to be expected as shown:

$CH_2CH_2CH_3$ + HNO_3, H_2SO_4 → $CH_2CH_2CH_3$ / NO_2 +

(ortho)

$CH_2CH_2CH_3$ / O_2N-

(para)

(3) $CH_2CH_2CH_3$ + Fe, Cl_2 ⟶ ?

    When ferric halogen and a halogen are added together, aromatic halogenation occurs. In this instance, it would

be chlorination. The attacking species, $Cl_3\overset{-}{Fe}-\overset{+}{Cl}-Cl$, does not react with the side chain of the compound; only the aromatic ring is involved. As mentioned above, the alkyl side chain directs ortho and para, so that the following results:

$CH_2CH_2CH_3$ + Fe, Cl_2 → $CH_2CH_2CH_3$ / Cl +

(ortho)

$CH_2CH_2CH_3$ / $Cl-$

(para)

(4) 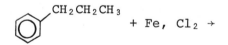 $CH_2CH_2CH_3$ + Br_2, heat, light ⟶ ?

It is known that halogenation of alkanes requires conditions that favor the creation of halogen radicals. High temperature or light is necessary. The halogenation of benzene involves transfer of a positive halogen (X^+) (which is protonated by acid catalysts). This means that the position of attack (whether on the benzene or on the side chain) will depend on the nature of the attacking species (an ion or a radical). Since the conditions in this problem are those that favor the production of bromine radicals, halogenation occurs exclusively to the n-propyl side chain. Hence,

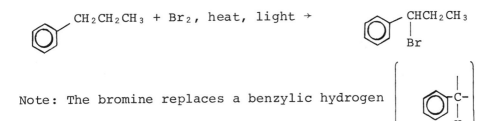

$CH_2CH_2CH_3$ + Br_2, heat, light → ... $CHCH_2CH_3$ | Br

Note: The bromine replaces a benzylic hydrogen

i.e., the hydrogen atom attached to the carbon joined directly to the aromatic ring. These hydrogens are easy to abstract due to resonance stabilization:

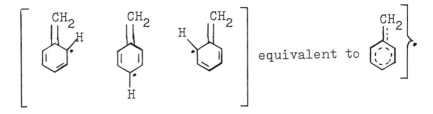

equivalent to

The odd electron is not located on the side chain in the benzyl radical but is delocalized, being distributed about the ring.

(5)  $CH_2CH_2CH_3$ + cyclohexene, HF ———→ ?

This reaction is an example of Friedel-Crafts alkylation, which permits direct attachment of an alkyl group to the aromatic ring. The general reaction may be written as:

R

+ RX $\xrightarrow{\text{Lewis acid}}$ ... + HX

Lewis acid: $AlCl_3$, BF_3, HF, etc. RX may be an alkyl halide, substituted alkyl halide, alkene or alcohol. The Lewis acid functions to generate the electrophile that attacks the ring. Since the n-propyl group is activating, the reaction should occur with orientation ortho and para.

385

Hence,

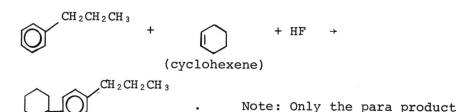

(cyclohexene)

. Note: Only the para product

results. The reason the ortho product fails to be produced derives from the bulkiness of the substituents. There exists

a steric problem when ⬡— and $-CH_2CH_2CH_3$ are ortho

to each other.

• **PROBLEM** 12-4

When 2,4,6-trinitroanisole is treated with methoxide in methanol, a red anion having the composition $(C_8H_8O_8N_3)^-$ is produced. Such anions are called Meisenheimer complexes after the chemist who first suggested the correct structure. What structure do you think he suggested? One of Meisenheimer's experiments compared the product of reaction of 2,4,6-trinitroanisole with ethoxide ion with the product of 2,4,6-trinitrophenyl ethyl ether with methoxide ion. What do you think he found?

Solution: Benzene compounds that possess a potential leaving group and also contain substituents that can stabilize a negative charge by resonance will undergo a nucleophilic aromatic substitution reaction upon treatment with a nucleophilic reagent. The reaction proceeds through an isolable intermediate benzeneanion called a Meisenheimer complex. The nucleophile attacks the carbon in the aromatic ring that bears the leaving group and destroys the aromaticity of the compound. The negative charge is resonance stabilized by the groups on the ring. The greatest stabilization occurs when the stabilizing groups are ortho and para to the leaving group. When 2,4,6-trinitroanisole is treated with methoxide in methanol, the nucleophilic methoxide anion attacks the carbon bearing the methoxy group. The resulting negative charge will be resonance stabilized by the three nitro groups:

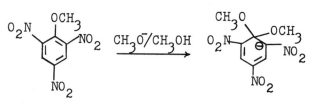

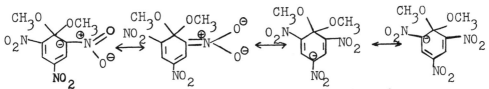

Above: Resonance stabilization of intermediate benzeneanion; shown only for one nitro group. The overall structure for the resonance stabilized species is:

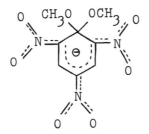

Above: Meisenheimer complex.

When 2,4,6-trinitroanisole is treated with ethoxide
ion, it will produce the same Meisenheimer complex that
2,4,6-trinitrophenyl ethyl ether produces when reacted with
methoxide ion. This Meisenheimer complex can be represented
as follows:

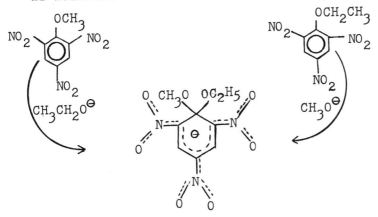

• PROBLEM 12-5

Provide the missing reactant or reaction condition for
the following:

(a) n-heptane + ____?____   →   toluene

(b) Iodobenzene + ____?____   →   biphenyl

(c) $C_6H_5COCH_3$ + ____?____   →   ethyl benzene

Solution: Reaction (a) belongs to the general class of reactions known as dehydrocyclization reactions. An example of such a reaction is

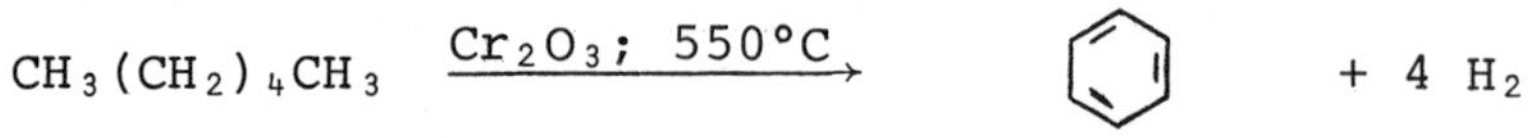

$$CH_3(CH_2)_4CH_3 \xrightarrow{\quad Cr_2O_3;\ 550°C \quad} \text{⬡} + 4\ H_2$$

The reagent involved in the reaction is Cr_2O_3 and the reactants are heated to a temperature of 550°C.

In the given reaction n-heptane changes into cyclic toluene through the same process. Thus,

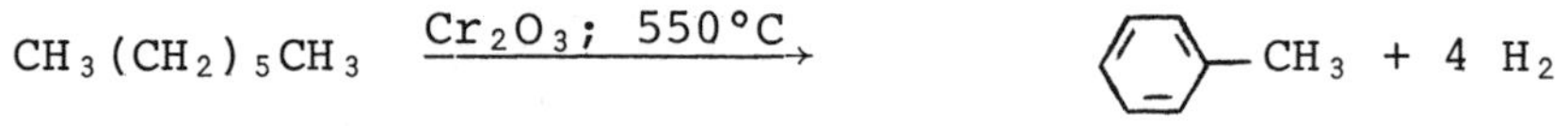

$$CH_3(CH_2)_5CH_3 \xrightarrow{\quad Cr_2O_3;\ 550°C \quad} \text{⬡}-CH_3 + 4\ H_2$$

Reaction (b) is known as an Ullmann reaction. The general reaction is

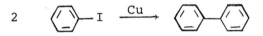

$$2\ R\!-\!\text{⬡}\!-\!I \xrightarrow{\quad Cu \quad} R\!-\!\text{⬡}\!-\!\text{⬡}\!-\!R$$

For reaction (b) the R group is a hydrogen atom and the missing reactant is Cu.

$$2\ \text{⬡}\!-\!I \xrightarrow{\quad Cu \quad} \text{⬡}\!-\!\text{⬡}$$

Reaction (c) is known as a Clemmensen Reduction. The general reaction is

$$\underset{\underset{O}{\|}}{ArCR} \xrightarrow{\quad Zn - Hg,\ HCl \quad} ArCH_2R$$

For the given reaction,

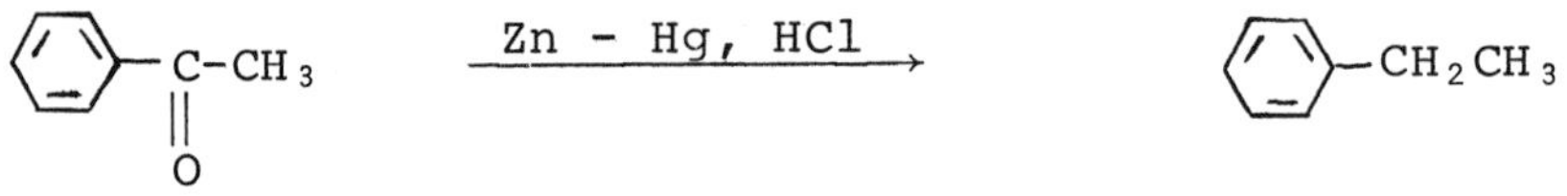

$$\text{⬡}\!-\!\underset{\underset{O}{\|}}{C}\!-\!CH_3 \xrightarrow{\quad Zn - Hg,\ HCl \quad} \text{⬡}\!-\!CH_2CH_3$$

Thus, the reagent used is Zn - Hg in HCl; this produces ethyl benzene from $C_6H_5COCH_3$.

● **PROBLEM** 12-6

Show how to make the following conversions using any necessary reagents:

(a)   Benzene to ethylbenzene
(b)   Toluene to benzyl alcohol
(c)   Iodobenzene to benzene

Solution: Synthesis of complicated organic molecules should be done in such a manner so that each individual step of the synthesis is one that has high yields of reasonably pure product. It is not necessary to complete and balance each equation, however, it is important that each step be given the proper reagents and experimental conditions needed for the reaction to take place.

(a) For the synthesis of ethylbenzene from benzene, first draw these structures and using the knowledge of the reactions of benzene with various reagents set up a series of reactions until the final product has been produced. Thus,

$$C_6H_6 \xrightarrow[\text{FeBr}_3]{\text{Br}_2} C_6H_5Br$$

$$C_6H_5Br \xrightarrow[\text{ether}]{\text{Mg}} C_6H_5MgBr$$

$$C_6H_5MgBr \xrightarrow{\text{Et}_2SO_4} C_6H_5Et$$

These steps can be combined to give:

$$C_6H_6 \xrightarrow[\text{FeBr}_3]{\text{Br}_2} C_6H_5Br \xrightarrow[\text{ether}]{\text{Mg}} C_6H_5MgBr \xrightarrow{\text{Et}_2SO_4} C_6H_5Et$$

(b) The synthesis of benzyl alcohol from toluene can be set up in a similar manner. Using the knowledge previously gained of the reactions of the benzene ring and other organic molecules, the synthesis can be shown as follows:

$$C_6H_5CH_3 \xrightarrow{\text{Cl}_2, \text{ uv light}} C_6H_5CH_2Cl$$

$$C_6H_5CH_2Cl \xrightarrow{\text{OH}^-} C_6H_5CH_2OH$$

Combining these steps:

$$C_6H_5CH_3 \xrightarrow{\text{Cl}_2, \text{ uv light}} C_6H_5CH_2Cl \xrightarrow{\text{OH}^-} C_6H_5CH_2OH$$

(c) For the reaction of iodobenzene to benzene, we can make the Grignard reagent and treat it with an acid (any proton source).

$$C_6H_5I \xrightarrow[\text{ether}]{\text{Mg}} C_6H_5MgI \xrightarrow[\text{H}^+]{\text{H}_2O} C_6H_6$$

389

Provide the missing reactant or reaction condition for the following:

(a) Mesitylene + ___?___ →

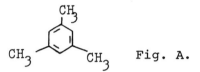

(b) CH₃⟨⟩—MgBr + ___?___ →

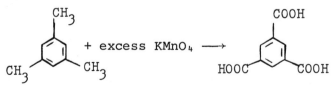

Solution: From a previous problem, the structure of mesitylene (1,3,5-trimethylbenzene) is shown in Figure A.

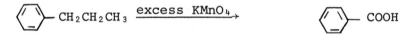

Fig. A.

In reaction (a) the positions of the side chains remain the same. This reaction is a typical example of an oxidation reaction.

Some examples of oxidation reactions are

⟨⟩—CH₂CH₂CH₃ $\xrightarrow{\text{excess KMnO}_4}$ ⟨⟩—COOH

Benzoic Acid

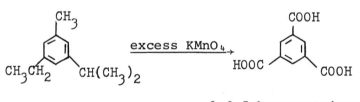

1,3,5-benzenetricarboxylic acid

Note that primary and secondary side chains are oxidized to carboxyl groups but tertiary groups are unaffected. The complete reaction of part (a) is

$$\text{(mesitylene)} + \text{excess KMnO}_4 \longrightarrow \text{(1,3,5-benzenetricarboxylic acid)}$$

Reaction (b) is an alkylation reaction by means of the Grignard reagents. CH₃—⟨⟩—MgBr is the Grignard reagent where -MgBr is replaced by an alkyl group. The only possible alkyl group that would produce the desired result is a

390

benzyl group : 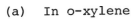 — CH₂-. In this reaction any benzyl halide would work.

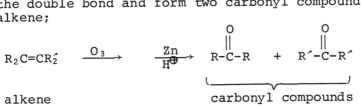

What products would you expect to be formed in the ozonization (with reductive workup) of the following substances (consider carefully which bonds are likely to be most reactive)?

(a) o-xylene
(b) naphthalene

Solution: Ozonization of compounds with carbon-carbon double bonds, followed by reductive workup, will break the double bond and form two carbonyl compounds: In an alkene;

$$R_2C=CR_2' \xrightarrow{O_3} \xrightarrow[H^{\oplus}]{Zn} \underbrace{R-\overset{O}{\overset{||}{C}}-R \quad + \quad R'-\overset{O}{\overset{||}{C}}-R'}_{\text{carbonyl compounds}}$$

alkene

     The ozonization of aromatic compounds is more inter-esting and complex in that each bond in the aromatic system has a certain degree of double bond character and this is reflected in the amounts of ozonization products since this reaction is specific for double bonds. Benzene, for ex-ample, has six bonds of equal double bond character. This can be represented by its two Kekulé resonance structures which we must realize do not denote independent, existing forms but they do approximate the relative amount of double bond character for each bond.

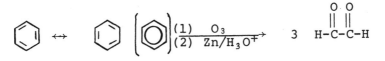

Benzene's
resonance structures

(a)   In o-xylene , we can also represent the structure as two resonance forms but the second of the two seems to be more important in that it contains a double bond substituted by two methyl groups. A methyl group like any alkyl substituent stabilizes a double bond by its electron-releasing inductive effect. Therefore a methyl substituted double bond will be more stable than an un-

methylated one and a dimethyl substituted double bond
would be even more stable

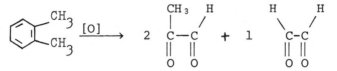

Since the bond between the two methyl groups has the most
double-bond character, it will be most reactive to the
double bond specific ozonization. The ozonization products
for the structure containing this bond:

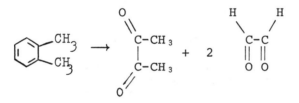

The stabilization of the methyl groups is not that
great and the double bonds not shown in the previous
structure do have significant occurrence and therefore
the compound

$$\begin{array}{cc} CH_3 & CH_3 \\ | & / \\ C - C \\ || & || \\ O & O \end{array}$$

is an additional ozonization

product.

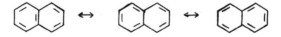

(b)   Naphthalene, a bicyclic, aromatic compound can be
presented as several resonance forms and we can determine
the fraction of double bond character by examining these
structures.

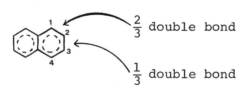

From this we can conclude:

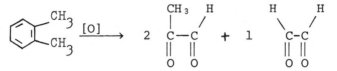

We should therefore expect that the bond with $\frac{2}{3}$
double bond character should react more than the bond with
$\frac{1}{3}$ double bond character. This, coupled with the fact that
the subsequent product is conjugated and retains aromaticity ensures the major reaction to involve cleavage of

392

the C_1-C_2 and C_3-C_4 bonds. Thus, the ozonization of naphthalene is as follows:

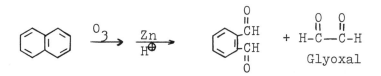

● **PROBLEM** 12-9

The compound indene, C_9H_8, found in coal tar, rapidly decolorizes Br_2/CCl_4 and dilute $KMnO_4$. Only one mole of hydrogen is absorbed readily to form indane, C_9H_{10}. More vigorous hydrogenation yields a compound of formula C_9H_{16}. Vigorous oxidation of indene yields phthalic acid. What is the structure of indene? Of indane?

Solution: An alkene (a compound with a double bond) is best characterized by its property of decolorizing both a solution of bromine in carbon tetrachloride (Br_2/CCl_4) and a cold, dilute, neutral permanganate solution ($KMnO_4$). The fact that indene undergoes these reactions indicates the presence of a reactive double bond. The fact that only one mole of hydrogen is absorbed readily suggests that only one of these reactive double bonds is present, since hydrogen adds across a double bond in a one to one mole ratio. Three more double bonds are present, however; vigorous hydrogenation results in the addition of three more hydrogen molecules (H_2) as can be seen by the fact that the molecular formula changes from C_9H_{10} to C_9H_{16}, a difference of 6 hydrogens. The fact that this hydrogenation is vigorous means the double bonds are especially stable; such a situation may be explained by the resonance stabilization that occurs in aromatic compounds such as benzene.

The evidence so far points to an aromatic group (benzene) and a reactive double bond, which must be part of some substituent attached to the benzene ring. In other words, the presence of an arene is suggested. An arene is a hydrocarbon that contains both aliphatic and aromatic units. The presence of the benzene ring is confirmed by the fact, that vigorous oxidation of indene yields phthalic acid, . This reaction is typical of arenes.

Hot oxidizing agents such as $KMnO_4$ and $K_2Cr_2O_7$ oxidize the side chain (the aliphatic portion) to the carboxyl group (COOH) and leave the benzene ring untouched. The presence of the COOH on the ring indicates where the original side chain was located. Hence, indene must contain the benzene ring, which would account for six carbons of the nine carbons in C_9H_8.

Consider now the compound obtained after all the hydrogenation is completed, C_9H_{16}. It no longer possesses any unsaturated bonds (double bonds), since the hydrogens would have added across them. And yet, it "looks" unsaturated, since the saturated hydrocarbon would possess the formula C_9H_{20} in accordance with the C_nH_{2n+2} rule for saturated alkanes. The absence of the 4 hydrogens (20-16=4) can only be accounted for by ring formation. For each ring formed, two hydrogens are "lost" from the saturated alkane. Here, then, there must be two rings present since 4 hydrogens disappear. The only structure for C_9H_{16} that can possess two rings (with one containing six carbons - recall, one ring must be from the vigorously hydrogenated benzene) is

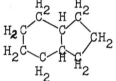

To find the structures of indane and indene just retrace your steps. This compound resulted from vigorous hydrogenation of indane. (Three hydrogen molecules were added across the resonance stabilized double bonds of indane.) Therefore, the structure indane must be:

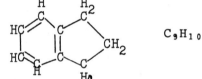 C_9H_{10}

Recall that indane resulted from indene by the addition of one molecule of hydrogen across a reactive double bond. Hence, indene must be:

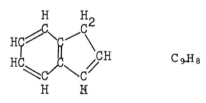 C_9H_8

Notice how the oxidation of this produces phthalic acid with the carboxyls in the correct positions on the benzene ring.

SPECTROSCOPY

● PROBLEM 12-10

There are many isomers of $C_9H_{11}Cl$, even when we specify the presence of a benzene ring. One such compound is 2-chloro-1,3,5-trimethylbenzene.

(a) Sketch its expected nmr spectrum.
    Other isomers are:

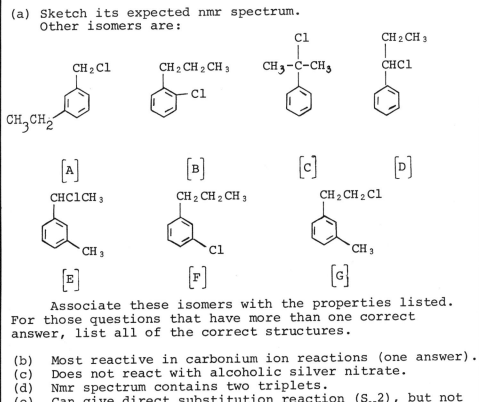

[A]   CH₂Cl (CH₃CH₂ substituent)

[B]   CH₂CH₂CH₃, Cl

[C]   CH₃-C-CH₃ with Cl

[D]   CH₂CH₃, CHCl

[E]   CHClCH₃, CH₃

[F]   CH₂CH₂CH₃, Cl

[G]   CH₂CH₂Cl, CH₃

    Associate these isomers with the properties listed.
For those questions that have more than one correct
answer, list all of the correct structures.

(b)   Most reactive in carbonium ion reactions (one answer).
(c)   Does not react with alcoholic silver nitrate.
(d)   Nmr spectrum contains two triplets.
(e)   Can give direct substitution reaction (S_N2), but not

      elimination (E2).
(f)   Can give both S_N2 and E2 reactions.

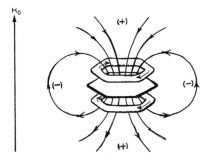

The two magnetic fields
generated by an aromatic ring.

Solution: (a) 2-Chloro-1,3,5-trimethylbenzene has the

following structure:

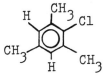

    Its nmr spectrum will show three singlets. The two
aromatic protons are in identical electronic environments
and will therefore absorb at the same frequency. Their
singlet appears near 7.5 δ, the characteristic absorption
of an aromatic proton. The two methyl groups ortho to the

395

chloro group are in identical environments, and will
absorb at the same chemical shift. The methyl group para
to the chloro group is in a different environment than the
other methyl groups. The para methyl group will absorb near
2.0 δ whereas the ortho methyl groups will absorb near
3.0 δ. The ortho methyl groups absorb downfield relative
to the para methyl group because the ortho methyls are deshielded relative to the para methyl. This is due to the
fact that the ortho methyls have a lower electron density
because of the inductive effect of the nearby chloro group.
All signals in the nmr spectrum will occur as singlets
because there are no two non-equivalent protons that lie
on adjacent carbons for spin-spin splitting to occur.

(b)   To determine which isomer is the most reactive in
carbonium ion reactions, we will have to look at the
carbocations formed upon the leaving of Cl⁻. The most stable
carbocation will be the one that reacts fastest, hence the
most reactive. This is because carbocation formation is
the rate determining step in carbonium ion reactions. The
more thermodynamically stable the carbocation, the lower
the activation energy and the faster is the reaction. The
carbocations of these isomers are as follows:

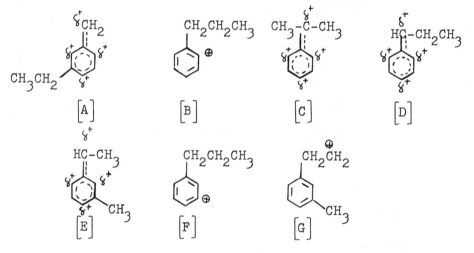

Since cations B, F and G do not undergo electron
delocalization, they are less stable than the other cations.
Cations A, C, D and E have the positive charge distributed
amongst four carbons, three of which are the same (ring
carbons) Since carbocation stability follows the order
3° > 2° > 1°, cation C is the most stable one. Cation C
is a tertiary benzylic cation, cations A, D, and E are
either secondary or primary benzylic cations. Hence,

$$\text{compound C} \quad \left(\begin{array}{c} \text{Cl} \\ | \\ \text{CH}_3\text{-C-CH}_3 \\ \bigcirc \end{array} \right) \quad \text{must be the most reactive in}$$

carbonium ion reactions.

396

(c) Alkyl halides undergo a nucleophilic substitution reaction (either S_N1 or S_N2) when reacted with silver

nitrate $(\overset{+}{Ag}\overset{-}{NO_3})$. The silver cation helps to pull off the halide ion and the resulting silver halide precipitates from the solution. Since aryl halides do not undergo S_N1 or

S_N2 reactions, the halide ion will not leave and no precipitate will form. Hence, by inspection we can predict

that only compounds B 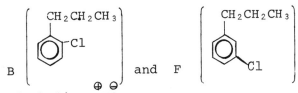 and F

will not react with alcoholic $AgNO_3$.

(d) Triplets in an nmr spectrum occur as a result of spin-spin splitting by two protons. The only compounds that will have two distinct triplets in its nmr spectrum are those that have: (1) a methylene group bonded to two carbons bearing hydrogens; these two carbons must be non-equivalent so that they absorb at different chemical shifts. For example; $Cl-CH_m-CH_2-CH_n-H$ -OR-

(2) two non-equivalent adjacent methylene groups, both of which are bonded to atoms that lack hydrogens. For example;

$$Cl-CH_2-CH_2-\overset{\overset{O}{\|}}{C}-R \quad .$$

According to these conditions, compounds B, D, F and G all have two triplets in their nmr spectrum.

(e) For an arene to be able to undergo an S_N2 reaction but not an E2 reaction (elimination), there must not be any hydrogens adjacent to the carbon undergoing the substitution reaction. Of the compounds A through G, all except B, C and F can undergo S_N2 reactions. Compounds B and F cannot do so because the leaving group (chlorine) is attached to an sp^2 hybridized carbon; S_N2 reactions occur only on sp^3 hybridized carbons. Compound C undergoes S_N1 reactions and not S_N2 reactions because of the stability of a tertiary carbocation(formed only in S_N1). Of the remaining compounds only A will not undergo an E2 reaction (elimination) This is because compound A is the only one that lacks β-hydrogens (hyrdogens adjacent to the carbon bearing the leaving group). Elimination reactions require the presence of β-hydrogens. Hence, compound A

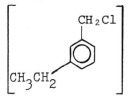   is the only one that will undergo S_N2

but not E2 reactions.

(f) In part (e) we reasoned that only compounds A, D, E, and G were able to undergo S_N2 reactions. We also reasoned that of those compounds only A was not able to undergo an E2 reaction. Since compounds D, E and G have β-hydrogens they can undergo E2 reactions. Hence, compounds D

$$\left[\text{⬡—CHCl-CH}_2\text{CH}_3 \right], \text{ E}$$

$$\left[\begin{array}{c} \text{CH}_3 \\ \text{⬡—CHClCH}_3 \end{array} \right] \text{ and G}$$

$$\left[\begin{array}{c} \text{CH}_3 \\ \text{⬡—CH}_2\text{CH}_2\text{Cl} \end{array} \right] \quad \text{are the only ones that can undergo}$$

both S_N2 and E2 reactions.

What would you predict for the general character of the chemical shifts of the protons of (a) the separate CH_2 groups of 1,4-hexamethylenebenzene as compared with 1,2-hexamethylenebenzene;

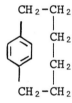

$$\begin{array}{c} \text{CH}_2\text{-CH}_2\text{-CH}_2 \\ \text{⬡} \\ \text{CH}_2\text{-CH}_2\text{-CH}_2 \end{array}$$

1,4-hexamethylenebenzene   1,2-hexamethylenebenzene

(b) cyclooctatetraene

Solution: (a) When an aromatic compound's π system is treated by a magnetic field, a flow of π electrons is induced around the ring (ring current) which generates a secondary magnetic field which opposes the applied magnetic field at the center of the ring but augments it around the vicinity of the benzene protons. The alpha (the benzylic carbon may be considered the α-carbon) methylene protons of 1,2-hexamethylenebenzene as well as its beta protons may be considered to have similar chemical shifts compared to their corresponding sets of protons in 1,4-hexamethylenebenzene because they have the same proximal relationship to the aromatic ring. The auxiliary magnetic field of the ring causes these protons to be shifted downfield (to a higher chemical shift) since they are approximately in the same plane of the aromatic ring. On the other hand, the ring's magnetic field causes the gamma protons of 1,4-hexamethylenebenzene to be shifted upfield, probably because the geometry of the molecule is such that these gamma protons are approximately perpen-

dicular to the aromatic ring. The gamma protons of 1,2-
hexamethylenebenzene do not achieve this degree of
perpendicularity and thus they are not shifted as much
upfield as the gamma protons of 1,4-hexamethylenebenzene.
Therefore, the difference in molecular geometry can lead
to spectroscopic separation of these two compounds.

(b) Cycloöctatetraene, has four double bonds

and a total of 8 π electrons. We note that Hückel's Rule
for aromaticity states that any species containing 4n+2 π
electrons in a cyclic π system will be aromatic. This is
not true of cycloöctatetraene and therefore the compound
is antiaromatic. The compound's protons should have
chemical shifts typical of a vinyl proton of an alkene.

● PROBLEM 12-12

Predict the effect on the ultraviolet spectrum of a solution
of aniline in water when hydrochloric acid is added. Explain
why a solution of sodium phenoxide absorbs at longer wavelengths than a solution of phenol (see Table below).

Table: Effect of Auxochromic Substituents on the
            Ultraviolet Spectrum of the Benzene
                    Chromophore

	Benzene	Phenol	Phenoxide ion	Iodobenzene	Aniline
$\lambda_{max, A}$	1,980	2,100	2,350	2,260	2,300
ε_{max}	8,000	6,200	9,400	13,000	8,600

Solution: In general, the λ max of a UV spectrum will shift
to a longer wavelength for a more conjugated system and a
shorter wavelength for a less conjugated system.   This rule-
of-thumb is derived from the fact that the energy difference
between the π and π* state of a compound decreases as the
system becomes more conjugated.   Since E=hC/λ, the wavelength
will increase as the energy difference decreases.   With this
in mind, let us compare the degree of conjugation between
aniline and aniline hydrochloride:

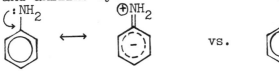

Since the lone-pair   electrons of aniline hydrochloride are not able to conjugate with the ring, it is
less conjugated than aniline.   Therefore it should absorb
at a shorter wavelength as compared to aniline.

When the lone-pair electrons of oxygen in phenol conjugate with the ring, there is charge separation :

But when the lone-pair electrons in the phenoxide ion conjugate with the ring, there is no charge separation:

Since the resonance in the phenoxide ion is more important than that in phenol, the former is much more extensively conjugated than the latter, resulting in phenoxide's absorption at longer wavelengths in the UV spectrum.

SYNTHESIS

● **PROBLEM** 12-13

Outline all steps in the conversion of: (a) ethylbenzene into phenylacetylene; (b) trans-1-phenylpropene into cis-1-phenylpropene.

Solution: (a) The preparation of phenylacetylene, an alkynylbenzene, follows from the chemistry of benzene and the alkynes.
     Recall that the dehydrohalogenation of vicinal dihalides yields alkynes. It may be summarized as:

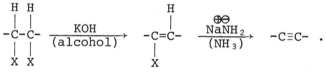

(vinyl halide)
Consequently, if one can obtain

one can readily produce phenylacetylene, the desired product.

C-C-H may be synthesized from the starting

material (ethylbenzene) in the following manner:

     Ethylbenzene may be halogenated in the presence of

light to obtain 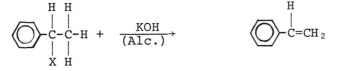 . Next, employ KOH to de-

hydrohalogenate to styrene as shown:

Bromine in carbon tetrachloride may be added to styrene to obtain the vicinal dihalide:

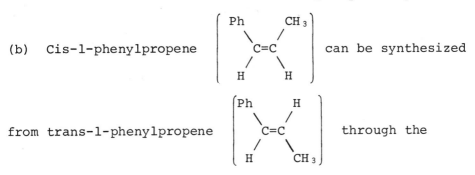

one proceeds to the desired product as previously mentioned. The overall sequence may be written as:

$$PhCH_2CH_3 \xrightarrow[\text{light}]{X_2} PhCHXCH_3 \xrightarrow[\text{(Alc.)}]{KOH} PhCH=CH_2 \xrightarrow[\text{CCl}_4]{Br_2}$$

$$PhCHBrCHBr \xrightarrow[\text{(Alc.)}]{KOH} \xrightarrow[\text{(NH}_3)]{\overset{\oplus\ominus}{NaNH_2}} PhC\equiv CH$$

(phenyl acetylene)

(b) Cis-1-phenylpropene
$$\begin{pmatrix} Ph & CH_3 \\ & C=C \\ H & H \end{pmatrix}$$
can be synthesized

from trans-1-phenylpropene
$$\begin{pmatrix} Ph & H \\ & C=C \\ H & CH_3 \end{pmatrix}$$
through the

alkyne intermediate. Recall that the addition of hydrogen to produce the corresponding alkene can occur in the cis fashion with Pd or Ni-B (P-2) or trans fashion with Na or Li in ammonia. To prepare the alkyne, one wants to produce the vicinal dihalide and dehydrohalogenate as mentioned in (a). Therefore, the following sequence can be employed to make the conversion.

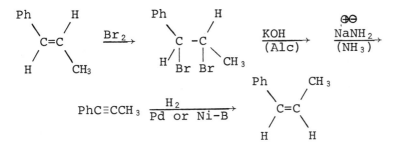

401

What arene derivatives are expected from the oxidation of the following with hot, alkaline potassium permanganate followed by acidification?

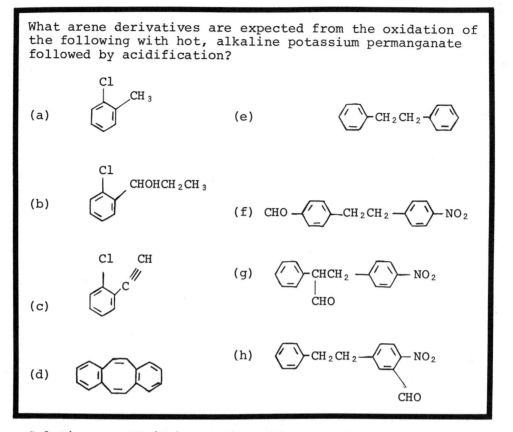

(a)

Cl
CH₃

(b)

Cl
CHOHCH₂CH₃

(c)

Cl   CH
‖
C

(d)

(e)   ⟨⟩—CH₂CH₂—⟨⟩

(f) CHO—⟨⟩—CH₂CH₂—⟨⟩—NO₂

(g) ⟨⟩—CHCH₂—⟨⟩—NO₂
              |
              CHO

(h) ⟨⟩—CH₂CH₂—⟨⟩—NO₂
                        CHO

Solution: It is known that alkanes and benzene are quite inert to oxidation with potassium permanganate in aqueous alkali. However, alkyl and aryl groups attached to benzene rings can be oxidized to carboxyl (-COOH) groups with hot, alkaline permanganate. For example,

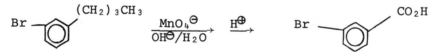

Br—⟨⟩—(CH₂)₃CH₃ $\xrightarrow[\text{OH}^\ominus/\text{H}_2\text{O}]{\text{MnO}_4^\ominus}$ H⊕ →   Br—⟨⟩—CO₂H

With this in mind, we can predict the products of the following reactions:

(a)

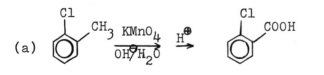

Cl
CH₃ $\xrightarrow[\text{OH}^\ominus/\text{H}_2\text{O}]{\text{KMnO}_4}$ H⊕ →   Cl
COOH

(b)

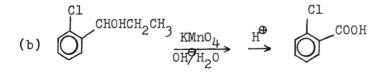

Cl
CHOHCH₂CH₃ $\xrightarrow[\text{OH}^\ominus/\text{H}_2\text{O}]{\text{KMnO}_4}$ H⊕ →   Cl
COOH

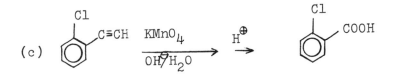

(c)

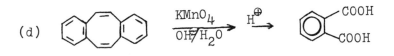

(d)

(e)

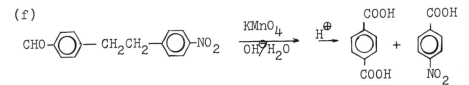

(f)

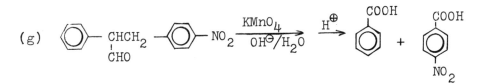

(g)

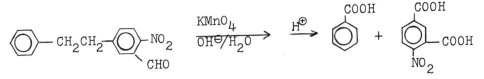

(h)

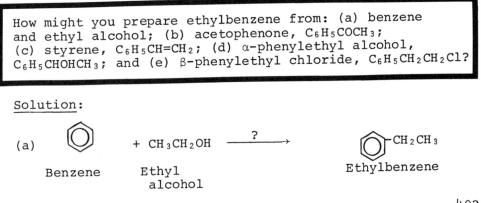

ELECTROPHILIC AROMATIC SUBSTITUTION

• **PROBLEM** 12-15

How might you prepare ethylbenzene from: (a) benzene and ethyl alcohol; (b) acetophenone, $C_6H_5COCH_3$; (c) styrene, $C_6H_5CH=CH_2$; (d) α-phenylethyl alcohol, $C_6H_5CHOHCH_3$; and (e) β-phenylethyl chloride, $C_6H_5CH_2CH_2Cl$?

Solution:

(a) ⬡   + CH_3CH_2OH $\xrightarrow{\quad ? \quad}$ ⬡—CH_2CH_3

    Benzene   Ethyl   Ethylbenzene
                 alcohol

In this problem we want to add an alkyl group to an aromatic ring to obtain an alkylbenzene. Attachment of an alkyl group may be accomplished by Friedel-Crafts alkylation. The general reaction may be written as:

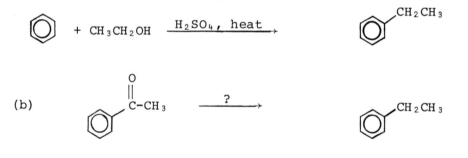

$$\bigcirc + RX \xrightarrow{\text{Lewis acid}} \bigcirc^R + HX.$$

The Lewis acid may be $AlCl_3$, BF_3, HF, etc. RX represents an alkyl halide, alcohol, or alkene, but not an aryl halide. The Lewis acid functions by generating a carbonium ion (R+) from RX, which subsequently attacks the electron rich aromatic (benzene) ring to give the

alkylbenzene, $\bigcirc^R$. Hence, to synthesize ethyl-

benzene from ethyl alcohol and benzene add an acid to the solution (for example, H_2SO_4 and heat). This results in formation of the ethyl cation (CH_3CH_2+) which now attacks the benzene ring to give the desired product. Hence,

$$\bigcirc + CH_3CH_2OH \xrightarrow{H_2SO_4,\ heat} \bigcirc^{CH_2CH_3}$$

(b)

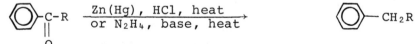

Acetophenone

The task in this case is to reduce the carbonyl group

$\left[\begin{array}{c}\diagdown \\ \diagup\end{array} C{=}O\right]$ to the methylene ($-CH_2-$) group. Such a side chain

conversion may be accomplished by Clemmensen or Wolff-Kishner reduction. In the former, we have amalgamated zinc and concentrated hydrochloric acid, whereas the latter consists of hydrazine (NH_2NH_2) and a strong base like KOH or potassium tert-butoxide. The reaction may be generalized as:

$$\bigcirc\!\!-\!\!\underset{O}{\overset{}{C}}\!-\!R \xrightarrow[\text{or } N_2H_4,\ base,\ heat]{Zn(Hg),\ HCl,\ heat} \bigcirc\!\!-\!\!CH_2R$$

Therefore, we could synthesize ethylbenzene from acetophenone as follows:

(c)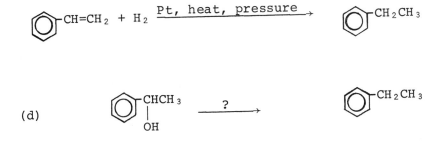

Styrene

   This conversion can readily be made by the addition of hydrogen (H_2) across the carbon-carbon double bond of styrene. This is done by catalytic hydrogenation as shown:

⬡—CH=CH$_2$ + H$_2$ $\xrightarrow{\text{Pt, heat, pressure}}$ ⬡—CH$_2$CH$_3$

(d) ⬡—CHCH$_3$ (OH)   —?→   ⬡—CH$_2$CH$_3$

α-phenylethyl alcohol

   If the alcohol is dehydrated with the use of acid such as H_2SO_4, styrene would be produced. From styrene, we go to ethylbenzene by catalytic hydrogenation as mentioned above. Overall:

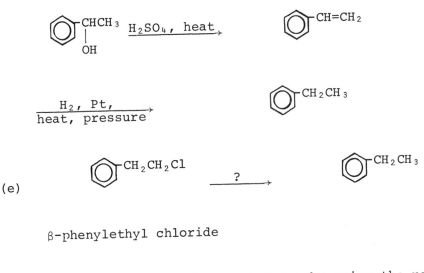

(e) ⬡—CH$_2$CH$_2$Cl   —?→   ⬡—CH$_2$CH$_3$

β-phenylethyl chloride

   This conversion can be carried out by using the reagent KOH (alc) so that a dehydrohalogenation reaction occurs to yield styrene

⬡—CH$_2$CH$_2$Cl $\xrightarrow{\text{KOH (alc)}}$ ⬡—CH=CH$_2$

Styrene can now undergo catalytic hydrogenation to produce ethylbenzene

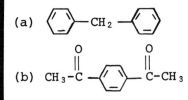

Suggest possible routes for the synthesis of the following compounds:

(a) ⟨ ⟩—CH₂—⟨ ⟩

(b) CH₃-C(=O)—⟨ ⟩—C(=O)-CH₃

(c) CH₃—⟨ ⟩—CH₂CH₃

Solution: (a) Diphenyl methane ($C_6H_5CH_2C_6H_5$) can be prepared by using benzene as our starting material. We would want to add a benzyl group ($C_6H_5CH_2-$) to the benzene ring to get our desired product. A direct method used to accomplish this is the Friedel-Crafts alkylation procedure. In the presence of an alkyl halide (RX) and a Lewis acid (ex: $AlCl_3$) as a catalyst, the benzene ring would become alkylated.   Hence the desired product could be synthesized by reacting benzene with benzyl chloride in the presence of $AlCl_3$:

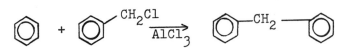

There is a problem associated with the above synthesis. When the benzene ring becomes alkylated, the alkyl group activates the ring. This makes the ring more susceptible to further alkylation; that is, the presence of an activating group on the ring will enhance its susceptibility to alkylation. Therefore, the reaction produces more poly-alkylated than monoalkylated product. One method of synthesis that will not encounter this problem is the Friedel-Crafts acylation. When a benzene ring is treated with an

acyl halide $\left(R\text{-}\overset{\displaystyle O}{\overset{\|}{C}}\text{-}X\right)$ in the presence of a Lewis acid (ex:

$AlCl_3$) catalyst, an acyl group $\left(R\text{-}\overset{|}{C}\text{=}O\right)$ will be added onto

406

the ring. Since an acyl group deactivates an aromatic ring (due to the electron withdrawing carbonyl), diacylation is more difficult than monoacylation. Hence the monoacylated product is the major product in the reaction. When benzene is reacted with benzoyl chloride in the presence of $AlCl_3$, benzophenone is the major product:

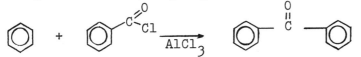

benzoyl chloride   benzophenone

To convert benzophenone to our desired product we must reduce the carbonyl $\left(\begin{smallmatrix} O \\ || \\ -C- \end{smallmatrix}\right)$ to a methylene ($-CH_2-$). This can can be done by using the Clemmensen reduction. If there is a carbonyl group attached to a benzene ring, it will be converted into a methylene group when treated with zinc amalgam and hydrochloric acid. When benzophenone undergoes a Clemmensen reduction, diphenylmethane is produced:

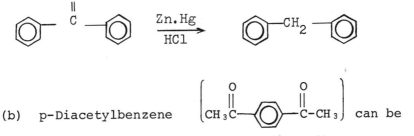

(b)   p-Diacetylbenzene $\left(\begin{smallmatrix} O & & O \\ || & & || \\ CH_3C- & \bigcirc & -C-CH_3 \end{smallmatrix}\right)$ can be

be synthesized by starting with p-diethylbenzene $\left(CH_3CH_2 - \bigcirc - CH_2CH_3\right)$. Free radical chlorination will chlorinate only the methylene groups. This occurs because the reaction proceeds through the most stable benzylic radical:

$$Cl_2 \xrightarrow{hr} Cl\cdot \quad + \quad Cl\cdot$$

$$Cl\cdot + CH_3CH_2 -\bigcirc- CH_2CH_3 \rightarrow HCl + CH_3\overset{\cdot}{C}H -\bigcirc- CH_2CH_3$$

$$Cl_2 + CH_3\overset{\cdot}{C}H-\bigcirc- CH_2CH_3 \rightarrow Cl\cdot + CH_3\underset{\underset{Cl}{|}}{CH} -\bigcirc- CH_2CH_3$$

Above: Mechanism of free radical chlorination.

The overall reaction is:

$$CH_3CH_2 - \bigcirc - CH_2CH_3 \xrightarrow[h\gamma]{Cl_2} CH_3\overset{\overset{\displaystyle Cl}{|}}{\underset{\underset{\displaystyle Cl}{|}}{C}} - \bigcirc - \overset{\overset{\displaystyle Cl}{|}}{\underset{\underset{\displaystyle Cl}{|}}{C}} - CH_3$$

If the chlorinated product is treated with water, a substitution reaction will occur to produce a gem diol $\left(HO-\overset{|}{\underset{|}{C}}-OH \right)$. This gem diol will undergo water loss to form the carbonyl:

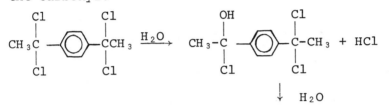

$$\downarrow H_2O$$

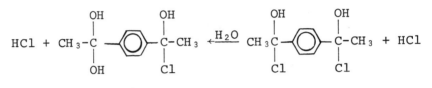

$$\downarrow H_2O$$

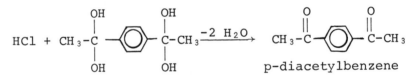

The overall reaction is:

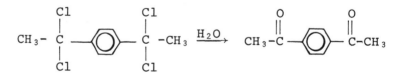

(c) p-Ethyltoluene $\left(CH_3 - \bigcirc - CH_2CH_3 \right)$ can be synthesized

from toluene. An ethyl group can be added onto the ring by using a Friedel-Crafts alkylation. There is the problem of polyalkylation in this case. Hence we can use the method described in part (a): Friedel-Crafts acylation followed by a Clemmensen reduction. If toluene is reacted with acetyl chloride (CH_3COCl) in the presence of $AlCl_3$, the acetyl group will add onto the ring. Toluene will be acetylated at its ortho or para position due to the ortho, para directing methyl group. The reaction is:

408

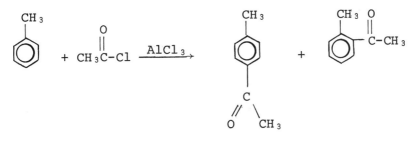

The product mixture can be separated and the para isomer can undergo Clemmensen reduction to give the desired product:

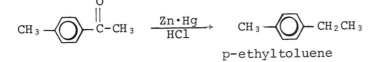

p-ethyltoluene

• PROBLEM 12-17

tert-Pentylbenzene is the major product of the reaction of benzene in the presence of BF_3 with each of the following alcohols: (a) 2-methyl-1-butanol, (b) 3-methyl-2-butanol, (c) 3-methyl-1-butanol, and (d) neopentyl alcohol. Account for its formation in each case.

Solution: The complicated alkylbenzenes such as tert-pentylbenzene are synthesized by Friedel-Crafts alkylation (attachment of an alkyl group) or by Clemmensen or Wolff-Kishner reduction (conversion of side chain). The fact that the Lewis acid, BF_3, is used in association with benzene and the alcohols in (a)-(d) means the Friedel-Crafts alkylation is taking place.

The reaction may be summarized as:

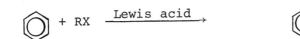

The Lewis acid may be $AlCl_3$, BF_3, HF, etc. RX does not have to be an alkyl halide; it can be an alcohol or alkene, but not aryl halide.

In the mechanism of Friedel-Crafts alkylation, the Lewis acid functions to generate an alkyl carbonium ion. For example:

$$ROH + H^{\oplus} \rightleftharpoons ROH_2^{\oplus} \rightleftharpoons R^{\oplus} + H_2O.$$

This alkyl carbonium ion, an electrophile, attacks the electron rich aromatic ring to give the alkylbenzene. The fact that carbonium ions are involved means it is to be expected they would undergo rearrangement to the most stable carbonium ion. It is this rearrangement of carbonium ions that accounts for the production of tert-pentylbenzene as the major product in (a)-(d). In each case, the tert-pentyl

$$\text{cation} \quad \left[\begin{array}{c} CH_3 \\ | \\ CH_3CH_2-\overset{+}{C}- \\ | \\ CH_3 \end{array} \right] \quad \text{attacks the benzene ring. The}$$

formation of this cation occurs by 1,2 hydride and 1,2 methyl shifts as indicated by the arrows below:

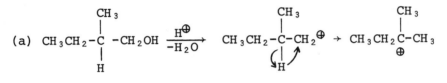

(a)   2-methyl-1-butanol   1° cation

(b)   3-methyl-2-butanol   2° cation

(c)   3-methyl-1-butanol   1° cation   2° cation

$$\rightarrow \quad \begin{array}{c} CH_3 \\ | \\ CH_3CH_2-\overset{\oplus}{C}-CH_3 \end{array}$$

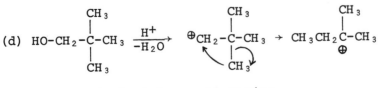

(d)   Neopentyl alcohol   1° cation

From available materials outline a synthesis of

$$\text{⬡}-CH_2-\overset{\overset{\displaystyle CH_3}{|}}{\underset{\underset{\displaystyle CH_3}{|}}{C}}-CH_3$$

Solution: Neopentylbenzene

$$\left[\text{⬡}-CH_2-C(CH_3)_3\right]$$

can be synthesized by starting with benzene. We must add
a neopentyl group $(-CH_2-C(CH_3)_3)$ to the benzene ring to
get our desired product. By using a Friedel-Crafts alkylation we can alkylate the benzene ring. This method involves
the reaction of an aromatic ring with an alkyl halide in
the presence of a Lewis acid catalyst $(AlCl_3)$. When using
this method one encounters the problem of polyalkylation.
When an alkyl group adds onto the ring, it activates the
ring and makes it more susceptible to further alkylation.
Hence the major product will be the polyalkylated product.
To produce the monoalkylated product in an acceptable yield,
we can use a two step method. First we can acylate the
benzene ring by using a Friedel-Crafts acylation (differs
from Friedel-Crafts alkylation in that an acyl halide is

used.) An acyl group $\left(\text{R-}\overset{\overset{\displaystyle O}{||}}{C}\text{-}\right)$ will be added onto the benzene
ring. If benzene is reacted with trimethylacetyl chloride
in the presence of $AlCl_3$, an aromatic ketone will be formed.
Polyacylation is not a problem in this reaction. This is
because when an acyl group adds onto a benzene ring it will
deactivate the ring due to the electron withdrawing carbonyl
group. Deactivation makes the ring less susceptible to
further acylation. Hence the monoacylated product is the
major one. The reaction that forms phenyl-t-butyl ketone is:

To get our desired product we must convert the carbonyl
to a methylene group. This is accomplished by employing a
Wolff-Kishner reduction. This accomplishes the same thing
as the Clemmensen reduction; the difference is that the
Wolff-Kishner reduction is carried out in basic solution
whereas the Clemmensen reduction is carried out in acidic
solution. The aromatic ketone we produced must be reduced
by the Wolff-Kishner method and not the Clemmensen method.
This is because the ketone is unstable in acidic media
(it will undergo a rearrangement). The reagents used in
the Wolff-Kishner reduction are hydrazine (NH_2NH_2) and
potassium hydroxide (KOH). Nitrogen gas is released as a
by-product of the reaction:

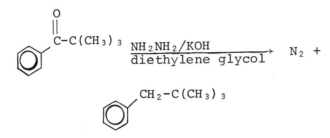

neopentyl benzene

• **PROBLEM** 12-19

Treatment with methyl chloride and $AlCl_3$ at 0° converts toluene chiefly into o- and p-xylenes; at 80°, however, the chief product is m-xylene. Furthermore, either o- or p-xylene is readily converted into m-xylene by treatment with $AlCl_3$ and HCl at 80°.

How do you account for this effect of temperature on orientation? Suggest a role for the HCl.

Solution: This problem is similar in nature to that of addition of HBr to 1,3-butadiene ($CH_2=CH-CH=CH_2$) in which both the 1,2 and 1,4 products are obtained, but the proportions in which they are obtained depend on the temperature at which the reaction is carried out. The proportions of products obtained from low-temperature addition are determined by the rates of addition, whereas for the high-temperature they are determined by the equilibrium control.

Here, the situation can be summarized as follows:

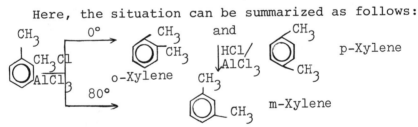

    At the low-temperature (0°) addition, rate-control is being observed. The o- and p-xylenes are formed faster. At the high-temperature (80°) addition, equilibrium-control is shown: m-xylene is the most stable product. The methyl group of toluene activates the ring for electrophilic aromatic substitution and directs substituents to the ortho and para positions. Just as the methyl group favors alkylation at the ortho and para positions, it also favors dealkylation - via electrophilic attack by a proton - at these same positions. This means that while the ortho and para isomers are formed more rapidly, they are also dealkylated more rapidly as shown:

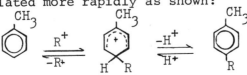

Although the meta isomer forms slowly, it tends to persist (be more stable) once produced.

The function of the HCl is to provide the proton required for the reversal of alkylation:

$$HCl + AlCl_3 \rightleftharpoons H^+ \quad AlCl_4^-$$

It is believed that when the proton attacks the aromatic ring to create an intermediate carbonium ion, the methyl group undergoes a 1,2 shift to give the new orientation. In other words, it is believed the conversion of p-xylene to m-xylene occurs by intermolecular rearrangement (between molecules). A carbon bearing a methyl group in p-xylene is protonated and a methyl cation leaves the ring. This methyl cation attacks another molecule of toluene. This is shown as:

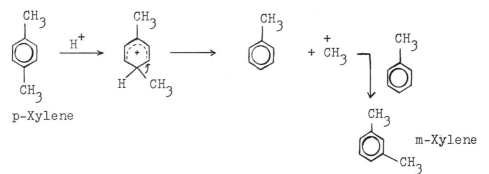

p-Xylene

m-Xylene

The same process occurs for o-xylene.

CHARACTERIZATION TESTS

● **PROBLEM** 12-20

Describe simple chemical tests that would distinguish between: (a) benzene and toluene; (b) bromobenzene and bromocyclohexane; (c) bromobenzene and 3-bromo-1-hexene; (d) ethylbenzene and benzyl alcohol ($C_6H_5CH_2OH$).

<u>Solution</u>:   By writing out the structures of the compounds in each case, the functional groups can be identified. In this way, chemical tests can be selected that differentiate between these functional groups.

(a)

 and

Benzene   Toluene

Toluene is classified as an arene; it contains both aliphatic and aromatic units. While compounds such as benzene and alkanes are rather unreactive toward oxidizing

agents, arenes are quite susceptible to these agents
($KMnO_4$, $K_2Cr_2O_7$, etc.). It is on this basis that benzene
and toluene are distinguished. When the oxidizing agent is
added to the arene, the side chain is oxidized down to the
ring with only a carboxyl (-COOH) group remaining to indicate the position of the original side chain. Therefore,
if hot $KMnO_4$ is added to toluene, benzoic acid results
(accompanied by decolorization of $KMnO_4$):

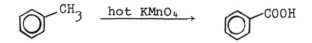

Benzoic Acid

Benzene fails to give this reaction.

(b)

Bromobenzene   Bromocyclohexane

These two compounds are differentiated by the aryl
halide's ability to be sulfonated by - and thus dissolve
in - cold fuming sulfuric acid. Bromocyclohexane fails to
give the sulfonation reaction outlined below for bromohexane:

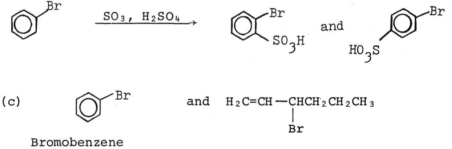

(c)

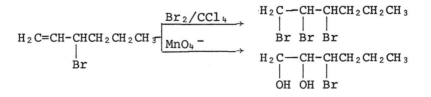 and $H_2C=CH-CHCH_2CH_2CH_3$

Bromobenzene

3-bromo-1-hexene

The aryl halide may be distinguished from the alkene
by the failure of the former to decolorize bromine in
carbon tetrachloride and by the failure to decolorize
cold, dilute, neutral permanganate solutions. 3-bromo-1-
hexene undergoes a reaction with these reagents as shown
below:

$$H_2C=CH-CHCH_2CH_2CH_3 \quad \begin{array}{c} \xrightarrow{Br_2/CCl_4} \\ \xrightarrow{MnO_4^-} \end{array}$$

(d)

        Ethylbenzene   Benzyl alcohol

     Alkylbenzenes can be distinguished from primary and secondary alcohols by their failure to give a positive chromic anhydride test. Recall, primary and secondary alcohols are oxidized by chromic anhydride, CrO_3, in aqueous sulfuric acid. Within two seconds, the clear orange solution turns blue-green and becomes opaque as shown:

   ROH   + $HCrO_4^-$ $\longrightarrow$ Opaque, blue-green

 1° or 2°   Clear, orange

     Benzyl alcohol, a primary alcohol, will give the color change, whereas the ethylbenzene will not.

                                  ● **PROBLEM** 12-21

Describe simple chemical tests (if any) that would distinguish between: (a) styrene and ethylbenzene; (b) styrene and phenylacetylene; (c) allylbenzene and 1-nonene; (d) allylbenzene and allyl alcohol ($CH_2=CH-CH_2OH$). Tell exactly what you would do and see.

<u>Solution:</u>   This problem can be solved by writing down the chemical structure to note the particular functional group the compound possesses and then devising characterization tests to distinguish between the functional groups and, as such, the compounds.

(a)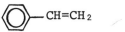

     Styrene   Ethylbenzene

     Both of these arenes (compounds containing both an aromatic and aliphatic unit) possess double bonds. However, only styrene has the double bond (for unsaturation) in its side group where it is extremely reactive to reagents that normally add across double bonds as in alkenes. (The double bonds of the aromatic ring are resonance stabilized so that they are not reactive to these reagents). Hence, these two compounds can be distinguished by the ability to decolorize both a solution of bromine in carbon tetrachloride and a cold, dilute, neutral permanganate solution. Styrene will decolorize since the aliphatic portion ($-CH=CH_2$) behaves as an alkene, whereas ethylbenzene will not (the side chain, $-CH_2CH_3$, behaves as an alkane so that it is inert to these reagents). The following will be seen:

styrene   red   colorless

Ethylbenzene + Br_2/CCl_4 $\longrightarrow$ no reaction

red   red

Purple   Brown ppt.   colorless

Ethylbenzene + MnO_4^- $\longrightarrow$ no reaction

(purple)   (purple)

(b)   Styrene   Phenylacetylene

⬡—CH=CH₂   ⬡—C≡CH

Phenylacetylene can be distinguished from styrene by the former's ability to form a heavy metal acetylides. The acidic acetylenes such as phenylacetylene react with certain heavy metal ions, chiefly Ag^+ and Cu^+, to form insoluble acetylides. The reaction is indicated by the formation of a precipitate. Styrene will not form this precipitate if placed in a solution such as $Ag(NH_3)_2OH$ or $Cu(NH_3)_2OH$. Hence, detection of a precipitate in either of these solutions is the simple chemical test desired.

(c)   ⬡—$CH_2CH=CH_2$ $H_2C=CH(CH_2)_6CH_3$

Allylbenzene   1-nonene

These two compounds can be distinguished by physical properties after oxidation. Upon oxidation with hot $KMnO_4$

or $K_2Cr_2O_7$, allylbenzene and 1-nonene yield   ⬡—COOH

and $C_7H_{15}COOH$, respectively. The melting point of ⬡—COOH

is 122°, whereas the melting point of $C_7H_{15}COOH$ is 16°. This allows one to differentiate between allylbenzene and 1-nonene.

(d)   ⬡— $CH_2CH=CH_2$ $CH_2=CH—CH_2OH$

     Allylbenzene   Allyl alcohol

    Since allyl alcohol is a primary alcohol, it will give a positive chromic anhydride test, whereas allylbenzene will not. Primary and secondary alcohols are oxidized by chromic anhydride, CrO_3, in aqueous sulfuric acid. The clear orange solution turns blue-green and becomes opaque within two seconds in the presence of these alcohols. Hence, allyl alcohol and allylbenzene may be distinguished by the former's ability to give the color change in chromic anhydride.

CHAPTER 13

NUCLEOPHILIC DISPLACEMENT

● PROBLEM 13-1

Explain why $(CH_3)_4\overset{+}{N}$ is neither a nucleophile nor an electrophile.

Solution: An ion or molecule is defined as nucleophilic (nucleus-seeking) if it possesses at least one pair of electrons that it will share with another atom to form a covalent bond. Nucleophiles are therefore Lewis bases. The ion or molecule that accepts electrons is said to be electrophilic (electron-seeking).

In order to fully understand why $(CH_3)_4\overset{+}{N}$ is neither a nucleophile nor an electrophile, all the electrons must be accounted for. The electron dot formula (figure A) shows that $(CH_3)_4\overset{+}{N}$ does not have a lone pair of electrons nor can it accept any electrons. The structure accounts for

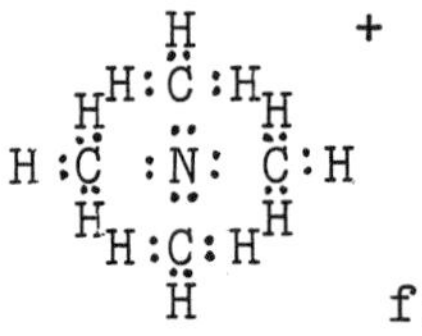

figure A

all of the electrons and for the charge on the ion.

● PROBLEM 13-2

(a) Draw the structures of ethyl, n-propyl, isobutyl, and neopentyl bromides. These structures can be considered methyl bromide with one of its hydrogens replaced by various alkyl groups (GCH_2Br). What is the group G in each case?

(b) The relative rates of reaction (with ethoxide ion) are roughly: methyl bromide, 100; ethyl bromide, 6; n-propyl bromide, 2; isobutyl bromide, 0.2; neopentyl bromide, 0.00002. What is the effect of the size of the group G attached to carbon bearing the halogen?

Solution:(a) Recalling the nomenclature of the fundamental
groups

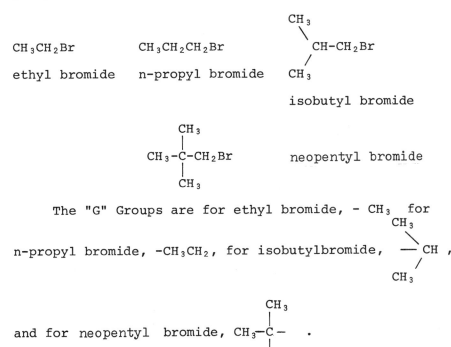

CH_3CH_2Br $CH_3CH_2CH_2Br$

ethyl bromide   n-propyl bromide

isobutyl bromide

neopentyl bromide

The "G" Groups are for ethyl bromide, $-CH_3$ for

n-propyl bromide, $-CH_3CH_2$, for isobutylbromide,

and for neopentyl bromide,

    (b) As the G group grows in size, so does the steric
hindrance which is the actual physical interference caused
by the substituents of a chain. As the interference increases,
the likelihood of a reaction decreases hence lowering the
rate of reaction.

S_N2 REACTIONS

● PROBLEM 13-3

Ethyl chloride (0.1 M) reacts with potassium iodide
(0.1 M) in acetone solution at 60° to give ethyl iodide
and potassium chloride at a rate of 5.44×10^{-7}
mole/liter/sec.

(a) If the reaction proceeded by an S_N2 mechanism, what
would the rate of the reaction be at 0.01 M concentrations of both reactants? Show your method of
calculation.

(b) Suppose the rate were proportional to the square of
the potassium iodide concentration and the first
power of the ethyl chloride (S_N3). What would the
rate be with 0.01 M reactants?

(c) If one starts with solutions initially 0.1 M in
both reactants, the rate of formation of ethyl iodide
is initially 5.44×10^{-7} mole/liter/sec but falls as
the reaction proceeds and the reactants are used up.
Make plots of the rate of formation of ethyl iodide
against the concentration of ethyl chloride as the
reaction proceeds (remembering that one molecule of
ethyl chloride consumes one molecule of potassium
iodide) on the assumption that the rate of reaction
is proportional to the first power of the ethyl
chloride concentration; and to (1) the zeroth power,
(2) the first power, and (3) the second power of the
potassium iodide concentration.

(d) What kind of experimental data would one need to tell
whether the rate of the reaction of ethyl chloride with
potassium iodide is first order in each reactant or
first order in ethyl chloride and zero order in
potassium iodide?

Solution: The rate of any chemical reaction is always
the product of three factors: (1) the collision frequency,
(2) the energy factor and (3) probability factor.

In this problem, the effect of the concentration on a
given reaction will be examined.

In general, if all other conditions remained uniform,
how would changes in concentration affect the rate of a
reaction? A change in concentration would have no effect
on the energy of the reaction, nor would it influence the
percentage of collisions with proper orientation, but a
change in concentration would definitely affect the total
number of collisions. One can liken the situation to that
of a student wishing to breed fruitflies. The greater the
number of fruitflies he has in a given space the greater
the number of new flies because of the increased number of
flies that cross paths. The increase in fruitflies has no
effect on the biochemical factors of mating, nor does it
increase the fraction of fruitfly collisions which are
male-female.

The field of chemistry which deals with rates of
reactions, and in particular the effects of concentration
on the rate of reaction is called kinetics.

(a) The reaction of potassium iodide with ethyl
chloride yielding ethyl iodide is an $S_N 2$ reaction.

As can be seen, the reaction proceeds via the interaction of the iodide anion with ethyl chloride; one would
reasonably conclude that the rate would be dependent on

both the concentration of the nucleophilic anion and ethyl chloride. A doubling of either the iodide anion or ethyl chloride would result in doubling the reaction rate by doubling the number of successful collisions. This proportionality can be expressed in terms of a formula:

$$rate = k \ [I^{\ominus}] \ [CH_3CH_2Cl]$$

Here, k stands for the rate constant, which is characteristic for a reaction under particular conditions (solvent, temperature, etc.). This rate constant would take into account the effects on the rate of reaction other than the concentration of the reactants.

Given that .1 M ethyl chloride reacts with .1 M potassium chloride in acetone at 60° at a rate of 5.44×10^{-7} mole/liters/sec., the rate constant can be calculated.

$$Rate = k[CH_3CH_2Cl] \ [I^{\ominus}]$$

Substituting;

$$5.44 \times 10^{-7} = k \ [.1][.1]$$

$$k = 5.44 \times 10^{-5}$$

5.44×10^{-5} is therefore the rate constant of the potassium iodide - ethyl chloride reaction at 60°.

If one were to now change the concentrations of either of the reactants, the rate of reaction could be calculated.

At (.01) M for both reactants the rate would be equal to:

$$rate = k[CH_3CH_2Cl] \ [I^{\ominus}]$$

$$= 5.44 \times 10^{-5} \ [10^{-2}][10^{-2}]$$

$$rate = 5.44 \times 10^{-9}$$

(b) The equation

$$rate = k[I^{\ominus}] \ [CH_3CH_2Cl]$$

is a second order equation which means that the sum of the exponents of its variables are equal to two. Indeed this is the basis of the name S_N2 (in contrast in S_N1) - a nucleophilic reaction of second order.

If the reaction of the iodide anion with ethyl chloride were such that the rate of the reaction were proportional to the square of the potassium iodide concentration it would be termed an S_N3 reaction.

$$\text{rate} = k[I^\ominus][CH_3CH_2Cl][I^\ominus]$$

or

$$\text{rate} = k[I^\ominus]^2[CH_3CH_2Cl]$$

This is termed a third order reaction because basically three molecules are involved in the reaction's transition state and hence the sum of the exponents is equal to three.

In order to calculate the rate constant of this reaction, the initial information provided is employed.

$$\text{rate} = k[I^\ominus]^2[CH_3CH_2Cl]$$

$$5.44 \times 10^{-7} = k[10^{-1}]^2[10^{-1}]$$

$$k = 5.44 \times 10^{-4}$$

When the concentrations of both reactants are both .01 M, the rate would be:

$$\text{rate} = 5.44 \times 10^{-4}[10^{-2}]^2[10^{-2}]$$

$$\text{rate} = 5.44 \times 10^{-10}$$

(c) If the reaction of ethyl chloride and potassium iodide proceeded in accordance with the mechanism below, it would be termied an S_N1 reaction.

$$CH_3CH_2Cl \ + \ I^\ominus \ \rightleftarrows \ CH_3CH_2^\oplus \ + \ Cl^\ominus \ + \ I^\ominus$$
$$\downarrow\uparrow$$
$$CH_3CH_2I \ + \ Cl^\ominus$$

This reaction would be independent of the concentration of the iodide ion. No matter how much iodide ion is added it will have no effect on the dissociation of the ethyl chloride. The ethyl chloride would dissociate slowly and would recombine in a second fast step. It is the first step (ionization of ethyl chloride) which is the rate determining step. Therefore the kinetic equation of the reaction is as follows;

$$\text{rate} = k[I^\ominus]^0[CH_3CH_2I]$$

Since the reaction is a unimolecular, nucleophilic substitution reaction it is termed S_N1.

Plotting the concentration versus the rate for the S_N1, S_N2 and S_N3 reactions;

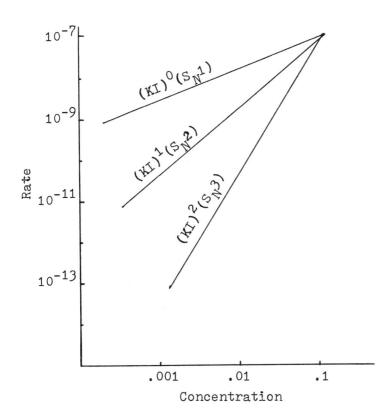

(d) At this point, the reader must be experiencing some confusion as to whether ethyl chloride and potassium iodide would undergo an S_N1, or an S_N2 reaction. This could be determined by a simple experiment whereby the concentration of only the potassium iodide were changed. If a change in the ration rate were observed then one could assume the reaction S_N2 and if there is no change in the reaction rate, then the reaction is S_N1.

As it so happens, the reaction of potassium iodide with ethyl chloride proceeds with an S_N2 mechanism. In fact, all nucleophilic attacks on a primary carbon will always proceed through an S_N2 path. S_N1-type reactions are limited to attack upon compounds that will generate particularly stable carbocations (e.g. tertiary, allylic cations).

● **PROBLEM** 13-4

Suppose a water solution was made up initially to be 0.01 M in methyl bromide and 1.0 M in sodium acetate at 50°. In water, the S_N2 rate constant for reaction of hydroxide ion with methyl bromide at 50° is 30×10^{-4} liters/mole/sec, whereas that of acetate ion at 50° is 1.0×10^{-4} liters/mole/sec. The ionization constant of acetic acid at 50° is 1.8×10^{-5}. In the

423

following, assume perfect solutions and neglect the rates
of reaction of methyl bromide with water or acetic acid
by themselves and any further reactions of methyl acetate:

(a) Calculate the hydroxide-ion concentration in the
initial solution.

(b) Calculate the initial rates of formation of methyl
acetate and methanol.

(c) What kind of information would be needed to predict
what products would be expected from a solution of
methyl bromide and sodium hydroxide in methanol?
Explain.

Solution: (a) In order to determine the hydroxide ion
concentrations, the hydrolysis constant must first be obtained. Hydrolysis refers to the action of the salts of
weak acids and bases with water to form acidic or basic
solutions. Such is the case with sodium acetate.

$$HOAc \rightleftharpoons H^+ + OAc^-$$

$$k = \frac{[H^+][OAc^-]}{[HOAc]} = 1.8 \times 10^{-5}$$

$$H^+ + {}^-OH \rightleftharpoons H_2O$$

$$k_w^{-1} = \frac{[H_2O]}{[H^+][{}^-OH]} = 10^{14}$$

The net equation of the hydrolysis reaction is:

$$HOAc \rightleftharpoons H^+ + {}^-OAc$$

$$H^+ + {}^-OH \rightleftharpoons H_2O$$
_____
$$HOAc + H^+ + {}^-OH \rightleftharpoons H^+ + {}^-OAc + H_2O$$

The equation of the hydrolysis constant is kk_w .

$$k = \frac{[H^+][{}^-OAc]}{[HOAc]} = 1.8 \times 10^{-5}$$

$$k_w^{-1} = \frac{[H_2O]}{[H^+][[{}^-OH]} = 10^{14}$$

$$k_{hyd} = kk_w^{-1} = \frac{[H^+][{}^-OAc][H_2O]}{[HOAc][H^+][{}^-OH]}$$

$$= \frac{[{}^-OAc][H_2O]}{[HOAc][{}^-OH]} = 1.8 \times 10^{9}$$

$$HOAc + {}^-OH \rightleftharpoons {}^-OAc + H_2O$$

In the hydrolysis equation, it will be noted that the

concentrations of acetic acid and hydroxide will be identical. Hence if X = the concentration of the hydroxide ion, then $[HOAc][^-OH] = X^2$.

The initial concentration of sodium acetate is 1 M, hence the concentration of sodium acetate of equilibrium is 1 - X; or the initial concentration minus the amount reacted to yield the X moles of hydroxide ion per liter.

Hence, the hydrolysis equation is:

$$\frac{[^-OAc][H_2O]}{[^-OH][HOAc]} = \frac{1 - X}{X^2} = 1.8 \times 10^9$$

Solving for X;

$$X = 2.2 \times 10^{-5} \text{ moles/liter.}$$

(b)

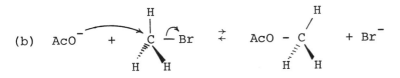

All S_N2 displacements, as in the above reaction, are second order kinetic reactions. That is, the rate of reaction is dependent on the concentrations of both the reactants. The rate of any second order reaction A + B → C + D can be written as

$$\text{rate} = k[A][B],$$

where k is the reaction constant. In the case of the methyl bromide - acetate ion reaction,

$$\text{rate} = k[CH_3Br][^-OAc]$$

Substituting the given values,

$$\text{rate} = 1.0 \times 10^{-4} \times 10^{-2} \times 1.0$$

$$= 1 \times 10^{-6}$$

The rate of the methyl bromide - hydroxide reaction is computed similarly.

$$\text{rate} = k[CH_3Br][OH]^-$$

$$= 3.0 \times 10^{-3} \times 10^{-2} \times 2.2 \times 10^{-5}$$

$$= 6.6 \times 10^{-10} \text{ m/liter/sec.}$$

(c)   Three factors are needed in determining the nature of the products expected.

The first would be the position of the equilibrium of the reaction

$$CH_3OH + NaOH \underset{\leftarrow}{\rightarrow} CH_3O^-Na^+ + H_2O.$$

425

Secondly, the initial concentration of sodium hydroxide would be needed and thirdly, the rate constants of the reactions:

$$CH_3Br \ + \ CH_3OH \ \rightleftharpoons \ CH_3OCH_3 \ + \ HBr$$

$$CH_3Br \ + \ Na(OH) \ \rightleftharpoons \ CH_3OH \ + \ NaBr$$

$$CH_3Br \ + \ CH_3ONa \ \rightarrow \ CH_3OCH_3 \ + \ NaBr$$

● **PROBLEM** 13-5

Predict the product(s) of the S_N2 reaction of each of the following nuclephiles with (±)-2-iodooctane.

(a) Br^-

(b) $CH_3C(O)CH_2^-$

(c) $(R)-CH_3CHCH_2CH_3$
       $\overset{|}{O^-}$

(d) $(R,S)-CH_3CHCH_2CH_3$
       $\overset{|}{O^-}$

Solution: (a)This is an S_N2 displacement reaction with bromide anion acting as a nucleophile and the iodide anion being the leaving group:

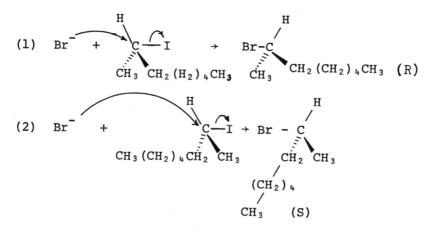

Since equal amounts of the dextrorotatory and the levo-rotatory 2-iodooctane are present, a racemic product will be obtained. Note that a S_N2 displacement proceeds with inversion of configuration at the chiral carbon.

(b)   Here again, the product is a racemic modification.

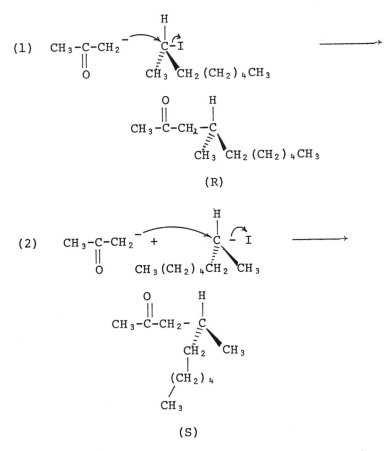

(1) $CH_3-C-CH_2^-$ ... C-I
$\quad\quad\quad\quad || \quad\quad\quad\quad$
$\quad\quad\quad\quad O$

$CH_3 \quad CH_2(CH_2)_4CH_3$

$\quad\quad\quad O \quad\quad H$
$\quad\quad\quad ||\quad\quad\quad |$
$\quad\quad CH_3-C-CH_2-C$
$\quad\quad\quad\quad\quad CH_3 \quad CH_2(CH_2)_4CH_3$

(R)

(2) $CH_3-C-CH_2^- \quad +$ ... C-I
$\quad\quad\quad\quad || \quad\quad\quad\quad\quad$
$\quad\quad\quad\quad O \quad CH_3(CH_2)_4CH_2 \quad CH_3$

$\quad\quad\quad O \quad\quad H$
$\quad\quad\quad ||\quad\quad\quad |$
$\quad CH_3-C-CH_2- \quad C$
$\quad\quad\quad\quad\quad CH_2 \quad CH_3$
$\quad\quad\quad\quad\quad |$
$\quad\quad\quad\quad (CH_2)_4$
$\quad\quad\quad\quad /$
$\quad\quad\quad\quad CH_3$

(S)

(c) In this problem, the nucleophile contains its own chiral center whose configuration is maintained in the product. Therefore, diastereomers are generated.

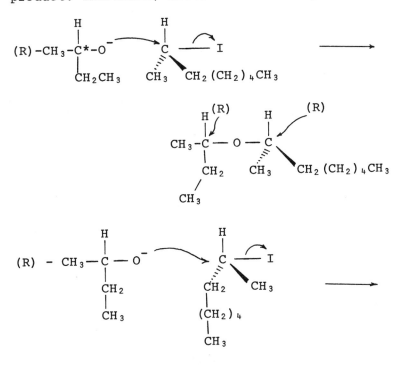

$\quad\quad H \quad\quad\quad\quad H$
$\quad\quad | \quad\quad\quad\quad\quad |$
$(R)-CH_3-C^*-O^- \quad\quad C \quad\quad I$
$\quad\quad | \quad\quad\quad\quad CH_3 \quad CH_2(CH_2)_4CH_3$
$\quad\quad CH_2CH_3$

$\quad\quad\quad\quad\quad\quad H \quad (R) \quad\quad H \quad\quad (R)$
$\quad\quad\quad\quad\quad\quad |\quad\quad\quad\quad\quad\quad |$
$\quad\quad\quad CH_3-C-O-C$
$\quad\quad\quad\quad\quad\quad CH_2 \quad CH_3 \quad CH_2(CH_2)_4CH_3$
$\quad\quad\quad\quad\quad\quad /$
$\quad\quad\quad\quad\quad CH_3$

$\quad\quad\quad\quad H \quad\quad\quad\quad\quad H$
$\quad\quad\quad\quad | \quad\quad\quad\quad\quad\quad |$
$(R) - CH_3-C-O^- \quad\quad C \quad\quad I$
$\quad\quad\quad\quad | \quad\quad\quad\quad CH_2 \quad CH_3$
$\quad\quad\quad\quad CH_2 \quad\quad\quad |$
$\quad\quad\quad\quad | \quad\quad\quad\quad (CH_2)_4$
$\quad\quad\quad\quad CH_3 \quad\quad\quad |$
$\quad\quad\quad\quad\quad\quad\quad\quad\quad CH_3$

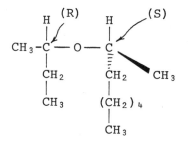

(d) In this displacement, four different stereochemical products would be expected, because the attacking nucleophile is a racemic modification. The stereochemistries of the products are (R, R), (R, S), (S, R) and (S, S). The reaction of the (R) isomer was seen in the last part of this problem.

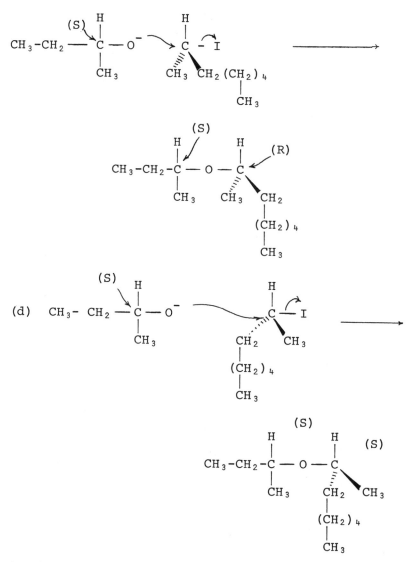

428

S_N1 REACTIONS

Benzyl bromide reacts with H_2O in formic acid solution to yield benzyl alcohol; the rate is independent of $[H_2O]$. Under the same conditions p-methylbenzyl bromide reacts 58 times as fast.

Benzyl bromide reacts with ethoxide ion in dry alcohol to yield benzyl ethyl ether $(C_6H_5CH_2OC_2H_5)$; the rate depends upon both $[RBr]$ and $[OC_2H_5^-]$. Under the same conditions p-methylbenzyl bromide reacts 1.5 times as fast.

Interpret these results. What do they illustrate concerning the effect of: (a) polarity of solvent, (b) nucleophilic power of the reagent, and (c) electron release by substituents?

Solution: The polarity of a solvent can often determine the mechanism by which a given reaction will occur. Ionization of an alkyl halide occurs only because most of the energy needed to reach the transition state is provided for by the formation of dipole-dipole bonds. The more polar the solvent, the stronger the solution forces and the faster the ionization.

(a) In part a, formic acid is more polar than dry alcohol, and hence favors the S_N1 reaction. The less polar solvent, alcohol, favors the S_N2 reaction.

(b) Water would not be a strong enough nucleophile to undergo and S_N2 reaction and displace bromine. The ethoxide ion, however, is a far stronger nucleophile and is more capable of undertaking an S_N2 displacement.

(c) The electron releasing properties at the methyl group will speed up the S_N1 reaction (by stabilizing the transition state). It will have little effect, however, on the S_N2 reaction.

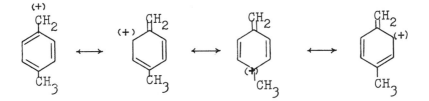

Resonance stabilization of methyl benzyl cation.

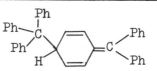

The above dimer decolorizes iodine in the presence of benzene at a rate that is independent of the concentration of iodine, but dependent on the concentration of the dimer. Likewise, if a benzene solution of the dimer is exposed to an NO gas atmosphere, the pressure of the gas drops at a rate independent of the gas but dependent upon the dimer. The rate constants for the above two processes are identical. Account for this.

Solution: Both reactions proceed in an S_N1 manner, where the dissociation of the dimer is the rate determining step.

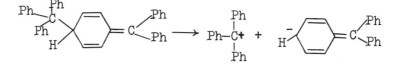

Subsequent steps are fast and have no effect on the rate of reaction.

The rate of this equation, as well as that of the reaction where nitric oxide is the nucleophile is:

$$r = k[dimer]$$

The hydroxyl catalyzed dehydrohalogenation of isopropyl bromide can follow both the El or E2 mechanism. Explain with the use of illustrations both types of mechanisms.

Solution: Elimination reactions may be classified as α eliminations (eliminations of two groups from the same atom) or β eliminations (eliminations of two groups from adjacent atoms yielding unsaturated bonds). Both of these eliminations are catalyzed by bases.

Bimolecular elimination, known as E2, involves the abstraction of a β proton by base attack with the simultaneous departing of the group X. It can be illusrated as follows:

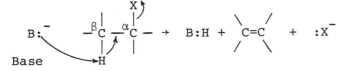

The reaction follows second-order kinetics; the rate of alkene formation depends on the concentrations of both reactants. No rearrangements of the alkyl group are involved in the E2 mechanism.

Unimolecular elimination, known as El, differs from E2 in that the group X leaves the molecule before the attack of base. As a result, one has an intermediate formation of a carbonium ion. The two step reaction of El can be written as:

Step 1: Carbonium ion formation

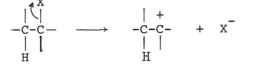

Step 2: Abstraction of proton by base attack:

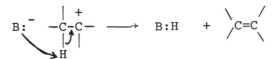

Step 1 is the slower and hence, the rate-controlling step, dependent only on the concentration of the alkyl halide.

STEREOCHEMISTRY OF S_N REACTIONS

● **PROBLEM** 13-9

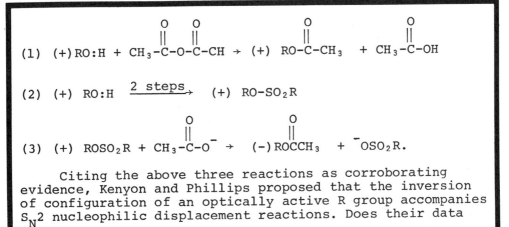

Citing the above three reactions as corroborating evidence, Kenyon and Phillips proposed that the inversion of configuration of an optically active R group accompanies $S_N 2$ nucleophilic displacement reactions. Does their data justify their conclusion?

Solution: Kenyon and Phillips' hypothesis is supported by their data; reaction (3) undergoes an inversion of configuration. However, reaction (3) in itself could not be construed as evidence of configurational inversion. While a change in the sign of rotation occurs, there is no evidence that a change in the optical configuration of the R group occurs. The sign of rotation refers to the rotation of light while passing through an optically active medium; it does not reveal the absolute optical configuration of a molecule.

Reactions (1) and (2), however, do sustain the contention that reaction (3) does undergo inversion of configuration. It is evident that reactions (1) and (3) do not involve a change of configuration of the optically active R group in that in each instance the reaction occurs at the alcohol's oxygen and not at its optically active R group. Hence, the two esters

$$(+) \ RO\text{-}\overset{\overset{\displaystyle O}{\|}}{C}\text{-}CH_3 \qquad and \quad (+) \ RO\text{-}SO_2R \quad must \ have \ the$$

same optical configurations. Moreover, since

$$.(+) \ RO\overset{\overset{\displaystyle O}{\|}}{C}\text{-}CH_3 \qquad and \quad (-) \ ROCCH_3$$

have opposite configurations, then

$$(+) \ R\text{:}OSO_2R \qquad and \quad (-) \ RO\text{-}\overset{\overset{\displaystyle O}{\|}}{C}\text{-}CH_3$$

must also have opposite configurations. Therefore, reaction (3) proceeds with inversion about the R group.

● PROBLEM 13-10

Under S_N1 conditions, 2-bromo octane, of specific rotation - 20.8°, was found to yield 2-octanol of specific rotation + 3.96°. If optically pure 2-bromooctane has a specific rotation of - 34.6° and optically pure 2-octanol has a specific rotation of - 9.9° calculate: (a) the optical purity of reactant and product; (b) the percentage of racemization and of inversion accompanying the reaction; (c) the percentage of front side and of back side attack on the carbonium ion.

Solution: (a) The optical purity of a compound can be expressed as the fraction $\dfrac{r_i}{r_p}$; where r_i is the rotation of the impure compound and r_p is the rotation of the pure compound.

432

In the case of 2-bromooctane, the optical purity is,

$$\frac{20.8}{34.6} \times 100 = 60\%.$$

In the case of 2-octanol;

$$\frac{3.96}{9.90} \times 100 = 40\%.$$

(b) The percentage of racemization and inversion can be obtained by first determining the ratio of the optical purity of the products to that of the reactants. In the case of 2-bromooctane and 2-octanol, this ratio is $\frac{40}{60}$ or $\frac{2}{3}$. If the reaction had proceeded with complete inversion, an optical purity ratio of 1 would have been expected (for every molecule of 2-bromooctane, one molecule of 2-octanol would have formed).

Therefore, if the optical purity ratio is $\frac{2}{3}$, the reaction proceeds with $\frac{2}{3}$ inversion and $\frac{1}{3}$ racemization.

(c) Every molecule that undergoes front-side attack(re-tention) cancels the optical activity of a molecule that is undergoing back-side attack(inversion). In this reaction, $\frac{1}{6}$ front-side attack occurs, cancelling $\frac{1}{6}$ of the back-side attack, giving $\frac{1}{6} + \frac{1}{6}$ or $\frac{1}{3}$ racemization. Therefore, $\frac{1}{6}$ + $\frac{2}{3}$(inversion) or $\frac{5}{6}$ of the molecules undergo back-side attack.

● **PROBLEM** 13-11

(a) What product would be formed if the reaction of cis-4-bromocyclohexanol with OH⁻ proceeded with inversion? (b) Without inversion? (c) Is it always necessary to use optically active compounds to study the stereochemistry of substitution reactions?

Solution: (a) If the S_N2 reaction of cis-4-bromo-cyclohexanol proceeded with inversion, trans(1,4) cyclo-hexadiol will be produced.

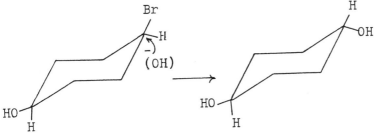

(b) Without inversion (retention):

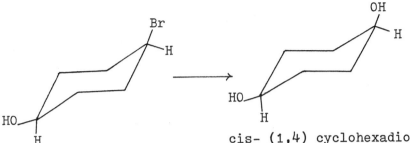

cis- (1,4) cyclohexadiol

(c) It is not necessary to use optically active reactants to study the stereochemistry of substitution reactions. We may use starting materials such as those in this problem which have two chiral centers. Using the proper nucleophile, we can induce the reactants to form diastereomeric products which can be separated by differences in physical properties.

• PROBLEM 13-12

Optically active 2-iodooctane, upon standing in an acetone solution containing NaI^{131}, loses its chirality and exchanges its I^{127} for I^{131}. In addition, while the rate of reaction is dependent on both [RI] and [I$^-$] racemization proceeds twice as fast as isotopic exchange. Explain.

Solution: The reaction goes as illustrated below; an S_N2 displacement

$$^{131}I^- \quad C - I^{127} \rightleftharpoons \quad ^{131}I - C \quad + \quad {}^-I^{127}$$

$$CH_3 \quad CH_2(CH_2)_4CH_3 \qquad CH_3 \quad CH_2-(CH_2)_3-CH_3$$

Racemization proceeds at twice the rate of isotopic exchange because for every molecule that is formed, with inverted configuration, one unreacted molecule of opposite configuration is "cancelled"; and therefore the rate of racemization should be twice the rate of reaction. For example, if we started with four molecules of bromo-deuteriophenylmethane and introduce iodide anions, the optical purity will decrease by 50% (not 25%) after the initial attack. An additional nucleophilic attack will racemize the mixture completely.

STRUCTURAL AND SOLVENT AFFECTS

• PROBLEM 13-13

Draw a reaction coordinate diagram for the solvolysis of 2,2,2-triphenylethyl chloride in acetic acid. Pay special attention to the phenonium-ion intermediate. What would be the difference in this diagram if the phenonium ion were a transition state instead of an intermediate?

Solution: Solvolysis refers to the form of nucleophilic substitution where the solvent is the nucleophile. For example, a dilute solution of methyl iodide will always contain methanol

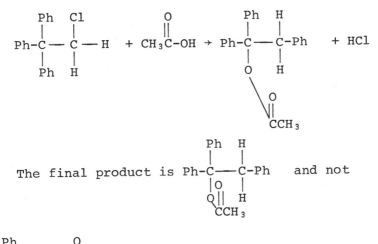

solvent

In this particular case, acetic acid

$\left(CH_3\text{-}\overset{\overset{\displaystyle O}{||}}{C}\text{-}OH \right)$ is the nucleophile displacing a chloride anion

from 2,2,2 triphenylethyl chloride. The net reaction is

The final product is Ph-C——C-Ph and not

because the latter product would

require nucleophilic attack upon a primary carbon. The carbon is too hindered to undergo a S_N2 reaction and the implausibility of a primary cation eliminates the possibility of an S_N1 reaction that does not involve rearrangement. Due to the immense instability of the primary carbocation, 2,2,2-triphenylethyl chloride will under an S_N1 solvolysis with migration of a phenyl group to the carbon which is simultaneously losing a chloride ion. This migration, which stabilizes the transition state, is known as anchimeric assistance. The intermediate phenonium ion is very stable due to participation of the aromatic ring in delocalization of the positive charge. The phenonium ion is analogous to the intermediate in electrophilic aromatic substitution. The reaction coordinate for this reaction, assuming the phenonium ion to be an actual intermediate, appears as follows:

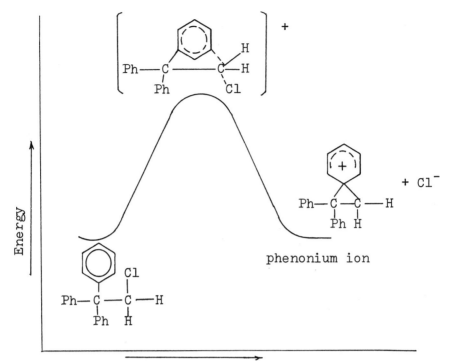

Reaction Coordinate

The phenonium ion will be attacked by acetic acid to give the final products in the second part of this reaction.

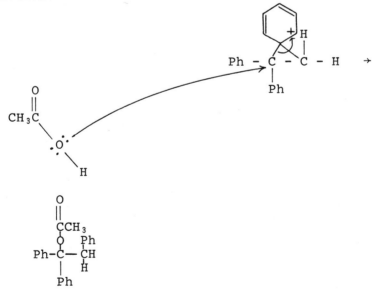

If the phenonium ion were a transition state instead of an intermediate, the reaction coordinate would be:

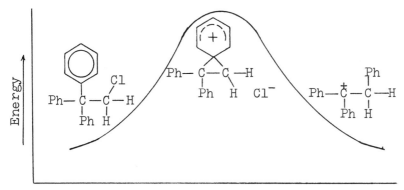

Reaction coordinate

The dibenzylic cation intermediate undergoes nucleo-philic attack by acetic acid to complete the S_N1 reaction.

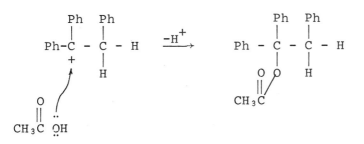

• **PROBLEM** 13-14

Predict either an increase or decrease in the rate of each of the following reactions with an increase in solvent-ionizing power. Specify whether the change would be relatively large or small. Give your reasoning.

(a) $(CH_3)_3COH_2^+ \xrightarrow{S_N1} (CH_3)_3C^+ + H_2O$

(b) $CH_3OSO_2C_6H_5 + OH^- \xrightarrow{S_N2} CH_3OH + OSO_2C_6H_5^-$

(c) $CH_3S(CH_3)_2^+ + OC_2H_5^- \xrightarrow{S_N2} CH_3OCH_2H_5 + S(CH_3)_2$

(d) $CH_3CH_2I + (CH_3CH_2)_3N \xrightarrow{S_N2} (CH_3CH_2)_4N^+ + I^-$

Solution: The polarity of a solvent will often determine by which mechanism a given reaction proceeds. The more polar the solvent, the greater the solvent-ionizing power of the solvent, which in turn increases the S_N1 character of a given reaction. (S_N1 reactions involve the ionization of an alkyl halide.) Hence, an increase in solvent ionizing power will usually serve to increase the S_N1 character of the reaction.

437

Reaction (a) is an exception to this rule. A decrease in S_N1 character would be expected as the charge is spread out slightly more in the transition state than in the reactant.

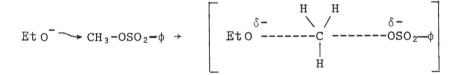

In (b) the S_N2 reaction will also undergo a slight decrease as the transition state has a charge separation only slightly greater than that of the reactant.

$$
Et\,O^- \rightsquigarrow CH_3-OSO_2-\phi \rightarrow \left[\begin{array}{c} H \quad H \\ \delta- \quad \backslash \; / \qquad\qquad \delta- \\ Et\,O \text{------}C\text{------}OSO_2\text{---}\phi \\ | \\ H \end{array} \right]
$$

(c) In this instance, a large decrease in the S_N2 reaction rate would be expected, as transition state undergoes a decrease in charge separation.

$$
\underset{+}{CH_3S(CH_3)_2} + {}^-OEt \rightarrow \begin{array}{c} CH_3 \\ \delta+/ \\ CH_3\text{---}S \\ \backslash \\ CH_3 \\ | \; \delta- \\ OEt \end{array}
$$

(d) A large increase in the rate would be expected as a large charge separation develops in the transition state. The solvent would help to stabilize the transition state, which would increase the overall rate of the reaction.

$$
CH_3CH_2I + (CH_3CH_2)_3N \longrightarrow
$$

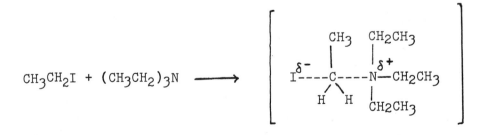

$$
\xrightarrow{\text{solvent}} \underset{+}{(CH_3CH_2)_4N} + I^-
$$

Each of the following cations is capable of rearranging to a more stable cation. Limiting yourself to a single 1,2-shift, suggest a structure for the rearranged cation.

(a) $CH_3CHCH_3CHCH_3$ $\overset{+}{}$

(b) $(CH_3)_3CCHCH_3$ $\overset{+}{}$

(c) $CH_3CH_2CH_2CHCH(CH_3)C(CH_3)_3$ $\overset{+}{}$

(d) $CH_2=CHCH_2CHCH_2CH_3$ $\overset{+}{}$

(e) $CH_3OCH_2CHC(CH_3)_3$ $\overset{+}{}$

Solution: In solving this problem, one must keep in mind that the order of stability of carbocations is allyl > 3° > 2° > 1°; that is, an allyl carbocation will be more stable than a tertiary cation, which in turn is more stable than the secondary form, which is more stable than the primary. The allyl cation is the most stable carbocation owing to its resonance stabilization.

A molecule that can be represented by two or more viable structural forms which vary only in the arrangement electrons about the same atomic nuclei is said to be in resonance.

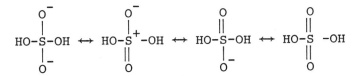

Figure: Resonance forms of Sulfuric Acid (H_2SO_4)

A molecule in resonance cannot be adequately represented by any one of its resonance structures and is viewed as a hybrid of all its resonance structures. The resonance hybrid is more stable than any of its resonance structures. The additional stability of the molecule is its Resonance Energy.

One must keep in mind, however, that only when the contributing structures are of approximately the same energy is resonance important. For example, methane has several resonance forms (A, B, C). However,

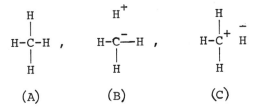

Structure A is of a far more stable energy so as to make the existence of B + C negligible.

In the case of sulfuric acid, where the resonance

forms are of nearly the same energy, the electrons are
spread over several bonds; this is referred to as
delocalization of electrons. Delocalization results in
stronger bonds and a more stable molecule.

The relative stabilities of 3° > 2° > 1° can be
explained by two factors: Hyperconjugation or the delocalization of electrons in alkyl radicals (see below), and
the inductive effect

```
      H                      H+
   +  |                      ||
  -C-C-      ←→        -C=C-
   |  |                 |  |
```

Figure: Hyperconjugation

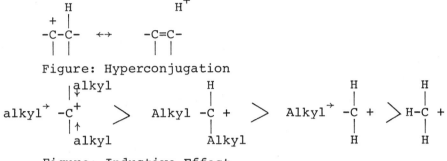

Figure: Inductive Effect

The relative stabilities of 3° > 2° > 1° are explained through hyperconjugation and by the number of
resonance contributing structures. t-butyl cation has nine
contributing structures; 2-butyl cation has five contributing structures; n-butyl cation has two contributing
structures.

The inductive effect relies on the ability of the
alkyl group to release electrons along the σ-bond to
electron deficient atoms. Halogens, because of their high
electronegativities, would destabilize the cation. Within
the alkyl group sp^3 hybridized alkyls would exert a greater
inductive effect than an sp^2 hybridized alkyl which would
have a greater inductive effect than sp hybridized alkyls.
(NOTE: in decreasing order of electronagetivity:
$sp > sp^2 > sp^3$).

(a) The 3-isobutyl cation is a secondary carbocation;
and has four hyperconjugated resonance forms.

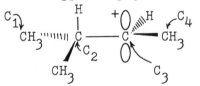

In a situation such as the one above, the 3-isobutyl
cation will undergo a 1-2 (Whitmore) shift whereby the
hydrogen bonded to C_2 and its electrons will migrate to the
positively charged π orbital of C_2. This is otherwise known
as the hydride shift, to distinguish it from other 1-2
shifts; because both hydrogen and its electron pair migrate,
having the net effect of the shift of a hydride ion. This
hydride shift places a positive charge on the second
carbon, thereby converting the secondary cation into the
more stable tertiary form.

(A)

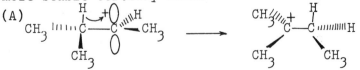

Figures: 1-2(hydride) shift of the 3-isobutyl cation.

440

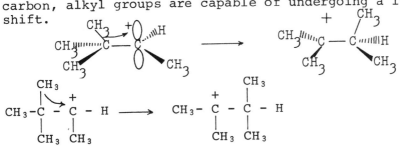

(B)

Part (b). In the absence of a hydride ion on the tertiary carbon, alkyl groups are capable of undergoing a 1-2 shift.

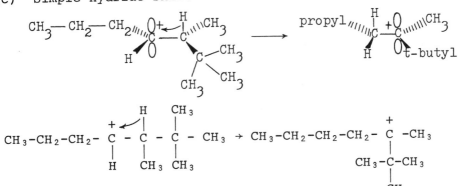

Figure: Migration of methyl group

(c) Simple Hydride Shift

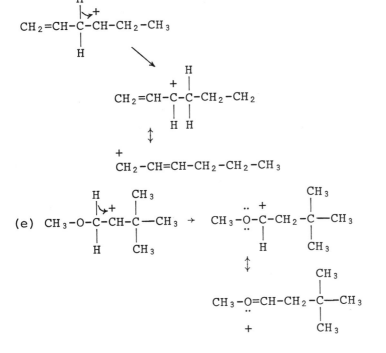

$$CH_3-CH_2-CH_2-\overset{H}{\underset{H}{C}}-\overset{CH_3}{\underset{CH_3}{C}}-\overset{}{\underset{CH_3}{C}}-CH_3 \rightarrow CH_3-CH_2-CH_2-CH_2-\overset{+}{C}-CH_3$$

(d) As the allyl is the most stable of all carbocations, it will form the most readily.

$$CH_2=CH-\overset{H}{\underset{H}{C}}\overset{+}{-}CH-CH_2-CH_3$$

$$CH_2=CH-\overset{+}{\underset{H}{C}}-\overset{H}{\underset{H}{C}}-CH_2-CH_2$$

$$CH_2-CH=CH-CH_2-CH_2-CH_3$$

(e) $CH_3-O-\overset{H}{\underset{H}{C}}-CH-\overset{CH_3}{\underset{CH_3}{C}}-CH_3 \rightarrow CH_3-\overset{..}{O}-\overset{+}{C}-CH_2-\overset{CH_3}{\underset{CH_3}{C}}-CH_3$

$$CH_3-\overset{..}{O}=CH-CH_2-\overset{CH_3}{\underset{CH_3}{C}}-CH_3$$

441

NOTE: A methyl shift is not undergone, as the product
is not resonance stabilized as is the product of the hydride
shift.

Two scientists, working in separate labs, were looking
into the properties of limestone. Two months later, both
published their results in a highly renowned journal
causing a great controversy amoung the cognoscenti of
Organic Chemistry. Said one: "Limestone is quite stable,
it is able to withstand centuries of atmospheric exposure."
The other said, "Limestone is extremely reactive, dissolving very rapidly in HCl to produce CO_2 and $CaCl_2$. The two
statements seem mutually exclusive. Assuming that each
scientist is correct, explain.

Solution: These statements are not paradoxical if one
considers the conditions each scientist worked under. Under
the rather inert conditions used by the first scientist,
the energy applied upon the limestone was not enough to
cause a reaction, because the energy of activation was too
great. In the second scientist's case, the conditions he
worked under were quite drastic and the energy of activation
was easily overcome.

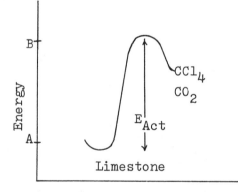

E_{Act} =Activation
energy

As can be seen from the above diagram, the set of
conditions in the first experiment (A) were not sufficient
to overcome the energy of activation, whereas the energy
in the second experiment (B) were more than enough to
affect a reaction.

SPECTROSCOPY

Deduce the structures of the two compounds whose n.m.r.
and infrared spectra are shown below. Assign as many of
the bands as possible and analyze the n.m.r. spectra in
terms of chemical shifts and spin-spin splittings.

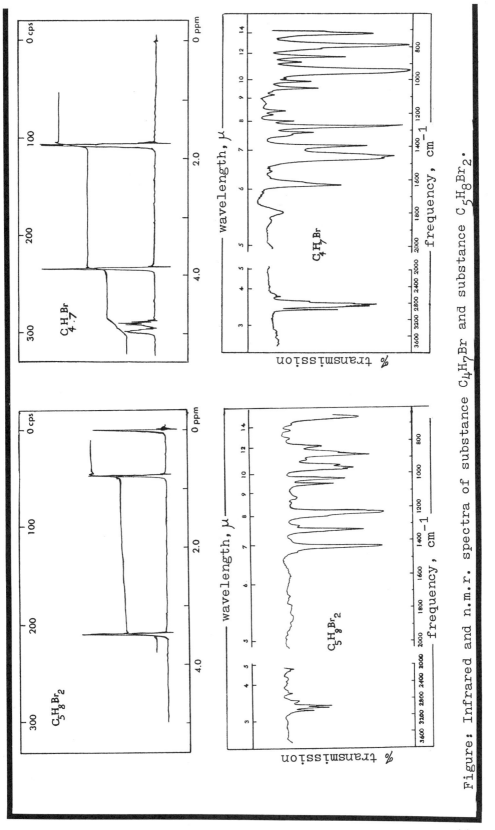

Figure: Infrared and n.m.r. spectra of substance C_4H_7Br and substance $C_5H_8Br_2$.

Solution: (A) Given the empirical formula, C_4H_7Br, and two spectroscopy charts, there is little that can be ascertained immediately. One must piece together all information that can be derived from what is at hand. From the i.r. readout, the characteristic C-H alkane absorption is present at 2800 cm^{-1}. The sharp, symmetric absorption at 1380 cm^{-1} indicates the presence of either a methyl or ethyl but not an isopropyl or t-butyl group. But, the most important piece of information gleaned from an initial observation is the presence of a sharp absorption at 1650 cm^{-1}, which is indicative of a double bond. By consulting Table A, the substitution about the double bond can be established. It will be noted that the i.r. absorptions correspond closely to the

$$\begin{array}{c} R \\ \diagdown \\ C= CH_2 \\ \diagup \\ R \end{array}$$ absorptions. This, by itself, is not enough to

establish any definite representation. However, by coupling the knowledge already known with the n.m.r. chart, one can be established. The hydrogen absorption ratios are 3 : 2 : 2. The multiplet at 1.85 could be that of $-C=C-CH_3$; the singlet at 3.9 could be that of $C=C-CH_2Br$, and the multiplet at 5.0 is that of the non-equivalent $CH_2=$protons. Putting everything together,

$$\begin{array}{c} CH_2Br \\ \diagup \\ H_2C=C \\ \diagdown \\ CH_3 \end{array}$$

can be proposed as a logical structure.

(B) From an initial glance at the i.r. spectra several characteristics of the C_5H_8Br molecule become evident. The first is the lack of any significant ab-sorptions between 1500 and 2700 cm^{-1}, which indicates that a double bond is probably not present. The sharp absorption at 1460 is indicative of some form of cyclic component from the n.m.r. . It can be seen that there are only two types of hydrogens present, and both present in the ratio of 1 : 1. One group of hydrogens is shifted far downfield, while the other lies at approximately 0.85 ppm which is

characteristic of the cyclopropane group. From this information,

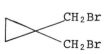

can be proposed as a logical structure that would be consistent with the facts given.

	=C-H Stretch	Overtone	C=C Stretch	C-H out of plane Bending
RCH=CH$_2$	3080-3140 (m)	1800-1860 (m)	1645 (m)	990 (s) 910 (s)
R$_2$C=CH$_2$	3080-3140 (m)	1750-1800 (m)	1650 (m)	890 (s)
(cis) RCH=CHR	3020 (w)	-	1660 (w)	675-725 (m)
(trans) RCH=CHR	3020 (w)	-	1675 (vw)	970 (s)
R$_2$C=CHR	3020 (w)	-	1670 (w)	790-840 (s)
R$_2$C=CR$_2$	-	-	1670 (vw)	-

s = strong absorption
m = medium absorption
w = weak absorption

All absorptions in cm^{-1}.

Table A: Characteristic absorptions of alkenes.

● **PROBLEM** 13-18

(a)   In the liquid form, tert-butyl fluoride and isopropyl fluoride gave the following nmr spectra:

tert-butyl fluoride: doublet, δ 1.30, J = 20 Hz
isopropyl fluoride: two doublets, δ 1,23, 6H,
                                   J = 23 Hz and 4 Hz
                   two multiplets, δ 4.64, 1H
                                   J = 48 Hz and 4 Hz

How do you account for each of these spectra?

(b)   When the alkyl fluorides were dissolved in liquid SBF$_5$, the following nmr spectra were obtained:

tert-butyl fluoride: singlet, δ 4.35
isopropyl fluoride: doublet, δ 5.06, 6H, J = 4 Hz
                   multiplet, δ 13.5, 1H, J = 4 Hz

To what molecule is each of these spectra due? (Hint: What does the disappearance of just half the peaks observed in part (a) suggest?) Is the very large downfield shift what you might have expected for molecules like these?

Solution: The fluorine (^{19}F) nucleus, like that of the hydrogen nucleus, possesses magnetic properties. Hence, it too gives rise to nmr spectra, albeit of a different frequency-field strength than that of the proton. However, fluorine nuclei can be coupled with protons (as well as themselves). Splitting by the fluorine proton of the proton signals can be detected, while absorption by fluorine does not appear on a proton nmr spectrum.

$$
\begin{array}{c}
CH_3 \\
| \\
CH_3-C-F \\
| \\
CH_3
\end{array}
$$

(a)

t-butyl fluoride

In t-butyl fluoride, there exists only one species of hydrogen which is the hydrogen of the methyl groups. This hydrogen is split by the fluorine which results in the doublet. The relative downfield position of the doublet (δ 1.30) is due to the electronegative effects of fluorine.

$$
\begin{array}{c}
F \\
| \\
CH_3-CH-CH_3
\end{array}
$$

isopropyl fluoride

In this molecule, the splitting of the methyl group's hydrogen by the secondary hydrogen and the fluorine results in the presence of the two doublets at δ 1.23; the hydrogen's splitting of the methyl hydrogen (J = 4) followed by the resplitting by the fluoride ion.

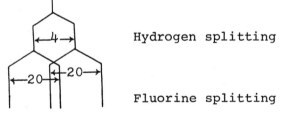

Hydrogen splitting

Fluorine splitting

The multiplet at 4.64 is a result of the tri-splitting of the secondary hydrogen by the methyl hydrogens followed by a single splitting by the fluorine. The secondary hydrogen is split seven times by the methyl hydrogens and then split again by the fluorine resulting in a multiplet of fourteen signals.

(b) The disappearance of half of the peaks observed in (a) should suggest that the fluorine is no longer present, and indeed, it no longer is.

$$
\begin{array}{c}
CH_3 \\
| \\
CH_3-C-F \\
| \\
CH_3
\end{array}
+ SbF_5 \longrightarrow t\text{-but}^+ \; SbF_6^-
$$

446

This would account for both the presence of only a singlet (from the tert-butyl group) and also the down-field shift (accounted for by the cation and its inductive properties).

This can likewise be seen in the isopropyl cation.

$$CH_3-\overset{\overset{\displaystyle H}{|}}{\underset{\underset{\displaystyle F}{|}}{C}}-CH_3 \ + \ SbF_5 \ \longrightarrow \ i\text{-}Pr^+ \ SbF_6^-$$

SYNTHESIS

● PROBLEM 13-19

Each of the following might have been synthesized by an S_N2 reaction. Suggest a combination of substrate and nucleophile which could have led to their production.

(a) CH_3OCH_3

(b) $C_6H_5\overset{\overset{\displaystyle O}{\|}}{C}-O-CH_2C_6H_5$

(c) (R) $CH_3CH(OCH_3)CH_2CH_3$

(d) $(CH_3)_4N^+Cl^-$

(e) $O\overset{\diagup CH_2-CH_2}{\underset{\diagdown CH_2-CH_2}{\big|}}$

(f) $O\overset{\diagup CH_2-CH_2 \diagdown}{\underset{\diagdown CH_2-CH_2 \diagup}{}}O$

Solution: (a) The first thing one must do is to look for a suitable nucleophile. In the case of CH_3OCH_3 (Dimethylether), the only possibility is CH_3O^-.

$$\overset{+}{Na} \ \overset{-}{O}CH_3 \ + \ CH_3I \ \longrightarrow \ \overset{+}{Na} \ I^- \ + \ CH_3OCH_3$$

(b) In this problem, two alternatives for the nucleophile

$$\left(C_6H_5-\overset{\overset{\displaystyle O}{\|}}{C}-O^- \quad \text{and} \quad C_6H_5CH_2O^- \right) \quad \text{are possible.}$$

$C_6H_5CH_2O^-$, however, is a relatively unstable anion, so that $C_6H_5-\overset{\overset{\displaystyle O}{\|}}{C}-O^-$ is the nucleophile in this synthesis.

$$C_6H_5CH_2-Br \ + \ ^-O-\overset{\overset{\displaystyle O}{\|}}{C}-C_6H_5 \ \longrightarrow \ C_6H_5-CH_2-O-\overset{\overset{\displaystyle O}{\|}}{C}-C_6H_5$$

(c) The two substituents of this S_N2 reaction are the

447

methodixe ion and $CH_3-CH-CH_2-CH_3$.   (L being any leaving
group.) The question then becomes whether the butyl
compound is in the (R) or (S) form. Since the product is
in the (R) form, and an inversion of configuration always
accompanies S_N2 reactions then it can be assumed that
the initial butyl compound had an (S) configuration.

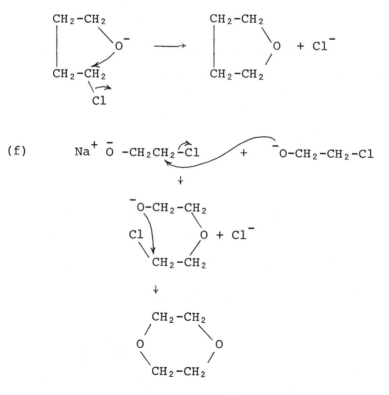

(S) 2-Chlorobutane   (R) 2-methoxy butane

The reader   must remember that the lone pairs of
electrons on nitrogen and oxygen are capable of acting
as nucleophiles.

(e)   The cyclic product can only be formed via an intramolecular S_N2.

(f)

Outline all steps in a possible laboratory synthesis of each of the following, using benzene, toluene, and any needed aliphatic or inorganic reagents.

(a) p-bromobenzyl chloride   (e) m-nitrobenzotrichloride
(b) triphenylchloromethane   (f) 1,2-dichloro-1-phenylethane
(c) allyl iodide   (g) phenylacetylene
(d) benzal bromide   (h) phenylcyclopropane

Solution: (a)This reaction involves bromination of the benzene ring followed by the chlorination of the alkyl side chain.

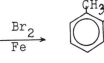

toluene   o-bromotoluene   p-bromotoluene

The bromination of the benzene ring produces both the ortho and para isomers, which are isolable from each other. After isolating the para isomer, the alkyl side chain is chloronated.

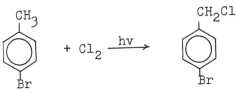

p-bromotoluene   p-bromobenzyl chloride

(b) In this reaction, a variation of the Friedel-Crafts acylation is used with CCl_4 and benzene as the starting products.

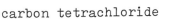

benzene   carbon tetrachloride   phenyl-trichloro
                                                       methane

The phenyl-trichloro methane is isolated and reacted with benzene in the presence of $AlCl_3$.

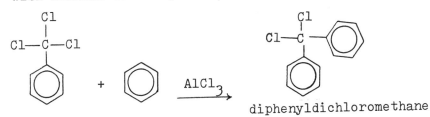

diphenyldichloromethane

The process is repeated once more with diphenyl-dichloromethane.

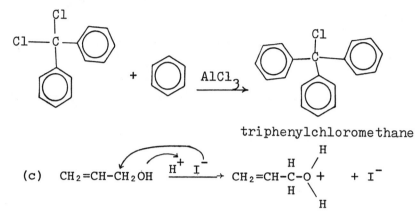

triphenylchloromethane

(c)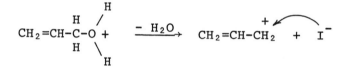

The synthesis begins with the protonation of the hydroxide group. The hydroxide then leaves the molecule as water.

$$CH_2=CH-C-O+ \quad \xrightarrow{- H_2O} \quad CH_2=CH-CH_2^+ \quad + \quad I^-$$

The free iodide anion then attacks the positively charged carbon giving the desired product.

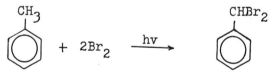

$$CH_2=CH-CH_2^+ \quad + \quad I^- \quad \longrightarrow \quad CH_2=CH-CH_2I$$

Allyl cation   Allyl iodide

(d) The best approach to this synthesis would be through the bromination of the methyl side chain group of toluene, under controlled conditions.

$$CH_3-C_6H_5 \quad + \quad 2Br_2 \quad \xrightarrow{hv} \quad CHBr_2-C_6H_5$$

toluene   benzal bromide

(e) The best mode of attack would be to start with toluene, chloronate the methyl side chain and then nitrate.

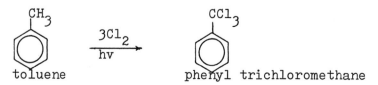

toluene   phenyl trichloromethane

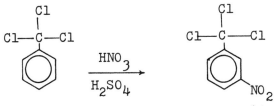

phenyl trichloromethane   m-nitrobenzotrichloride

(f)   The synthesis of 1,2-dichloro-1-phenylethane can best be affected by starting with benzene and performing a Friedel-Crafts reaction using CH_3CH_2Cl.

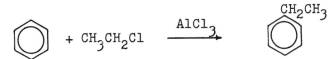

A variety of other substrates, such as ethylene in the presence of hydrogen fluoride, could be utilized.

From this point, a variety of routes may be undertaken, but the best is simply the industrial conversion of the alkane to the alkene.

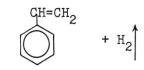

1-phenylethane   1-phenylethylene

From here, the simple chloronation of the double bond will yield the desired product.

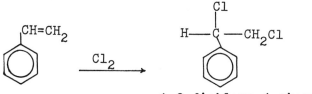

1,2-dichloro-1-phenylethane

(g)   Starting with the product formed in (f), an E2 reaction to convert it to an alkene would be the first step.

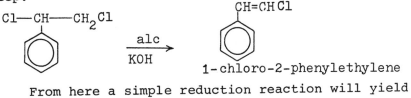

1-chloro-2-phenylethylene

From here a simple reduction reaction will yield the desired alkyne.

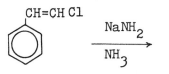

phenylacetylene

(h)   The formation of cyclopropane rings is a relatively simple synthetic process.

(1)   CH₂I₂ + Zn(Cu) ⟶ I CH₂ZnI

The first step consists of the reaction of methylene iodide with a copper zinc couple. The product then reacts with the appropriate alkene in the presence of other to yield the desired product.

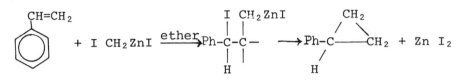

This is a relatively good process which can be carrier out in yields ranging from 30 to 70 percent in the laboratory, however, like most organic syntheses, it is far easier to perform on paper.

REACTIONS

● PROBLEM 13-21

What can be concluded about the mechanism of the acetalysis of n-butyl derivatives from the following reaction?

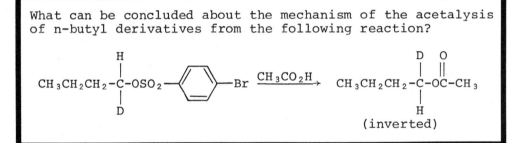

Solution: The reaction depicted is an S$_N$2 displacement. The S$_N$2 reaction always results in inversion of configuration and this pattern is maintained here. Note that the attacked ethylene carbon is a primary carbon and not a secondary one.

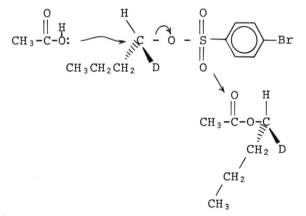

HCN has pK_a = 9.21; acetic acid has pK_a = 4.76.

(a) What is the difference in the standard free energies ($\Delta\Delta G°$) for these two acid-base equilibria?

(b) What is the equilibrium constant and $\Delta G°$ for the reaction

$$HCN + CH_3CO_2^- \longrightarrow CN^- + CH_3CO_2H$$

Solution: (a) The general equation for the standard free energy is $\Delta G° = -2.3$ RT log K_a.

Therefore $\Delta G° = 2.3$ RT pK_a

To find $\Delta\Delta G°$,

$$\Delta\Delta G° = \Delta G_1° - \Delta G_2° = 2.3 \text{ RT } pK_{a_1} - 2.3 \text{ RT } pK_{a_2}$$

$$= 2.3 \text{ RT } (pK_{a_1} - pK_{a_2})$$

Substituting;

$$\Delta\Delta G° = 2.3 \text{ RT } (9.21 - 4.76)$$

$$= (1.36)(4.45) = 6.05 \text{ Kcal/mole}$$

(b)
$$HCN + CH_3\overset{O}{\overset{||}{C}}-O^- \longrightarrow (CN)^- + CH_3-\overset{O}{\overset{||}{C}}-OH$$

In order to determine the equilibrium constant and the $\Delta G°$ of the reaction, the reaction is broken into its component parts.

$$HCN \longrightarrow CN^- \qquad pK_a = 9.21$$

$$CH_3-\overset{O}{\overset{||}{C}}-O^- \longrightarrow CH_3-\overset{O}{\overset{||}{C}}-OH \qquad pK_a = -4.76$$

Since the total equation is the sum of these two half-reactions the pK_a must also be the sum of the two component pK_a's.

Hence 9.21 - 4.76 = 4.45

The K_{eq} is, therefore, the - antilog of 4.45, which is 3.5×10^{-5} The $\Delta G°$ is the same as in part a.

$$\Delta G° = 23 \text{ RT } pK_a$$

$$\Delta G° = (1.36)(4.45)$$

$$\Delta G° = 6.05 \text{ Kcal/mole.}$$

Give the structures and names of the chief organic
products expected from the reaction (if any) of n-butyl
bromide with:

(a) NaOH(aq)   (g) product (f) + D_2O
(b) KOH(alc)   (h) dilute neutral $KMnO_4$
(c) cold conc. H_2SO_4 (i) NaI in acetone
(d) Zn, H^+ (j) $HC \equiv C^- Na^+$
(e) Li, then CuI, ethyl bromide (k) H_2O
(f) Mg, ether   (l) NH_3(aq)

<u>Solution:</u>   (a) Simple S_N2 displacement

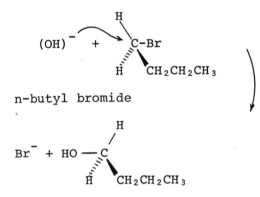

n-butyl bromide

Br^- + HO —— C

1-butanol

(b)   In this reaction alcoholic KOH is utilized in order
to synthesize oxide ion of an alcohol, usually, methanol
or ethanol.

$$CH_3-CH_2OH \quad \overset{-}{\longleftarrow} (OH)K^+ \quad \underset{\leftarrow}{\rightarrow} \quad CH_3-CH_2-O^- + H_2O$$

    The molecule will now undergo an E2 elimination
reaction with EtO^- acting as a base

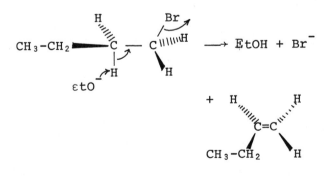

1 -Butene

Note:While in the above reaction the final product has no
isomers, this is not always the case. In order that the

right isomer be derived, make sure that the bonds being broken in the E2 complex are represented as being anti to each other.

(c) No reaction will be undergone, since n-butyl bromide is not unsaturated.

(d) In the presence of a metal, usually zinc, and acid alkyl halides will be reduced to the corresponding alkane.

$$CH_3CH_2CH_2CH_2Br \xrightarrow[H^+]{Zn} CH_3CH_2CH_2CH_3 \quad n\text{-Butane}$$

(e) This problem is an example of the coupling of alkyl halides with organometallic compounds. This reaction occurs in several steps:

$$CH_3CH_2CH_2CH_2Br + Li \rightarrow CH_3CH_2CH_2CH_2Li + Br^-$$

$$CH_3CH_2CH_2CH_2Li + CuI \rightarrow (CH_3CH_2CH_2CH_2)_2CuLi + I^-$$

$$(CH_3CH_2CH_2CH_2)_2CuLi + CH_3CH_2Br \rightarrow n\text{-hexane}$$

(f) Formation of the Grignard Reagent

$$CH_3CH_2CH_2CH_2Br + Mg \xrightarrow{ether} CH_3CH_2CH_2CH_2MgBr$$

Ether is used as the solvent but it cannot donate a proton. If ever performing a Grignard reaction in the lab make sure that it is carried out in a totally water-free environment if not, reaction (g) will occur.

(g) Destruction of the Grignard Reagent

$$CH_3CH_2CH_2CH_2MgBr + D(OD) \rightarrow CH_3CH_2CH_2CH_2D + Mg\overset{\displaystyle Br}{\underset{\displaystyle OD}{\big|}}$$

This reaction will occur similarly with H_2O.

(h) No reaction; the identifying chemical characteristics of alkyl halides are their insolubilities in cold concentrated sulfuric acid (see (c)), their inertness to

(i) S_N2 Displacement

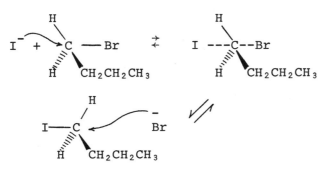

1-iodobutane

(j) S$_N$2 Displacement

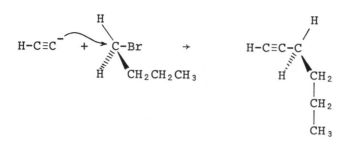

1-Hexyne

(k)   In the absence of a stronger nucleophile, the line pair of electrons on oxygen can act as a nucleophile.

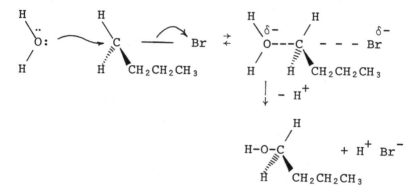

1-butanol

One should note, however, that this reaction is of little practical value as the time of reaction is too slow.

(l) Like the lone pair on oxygen, the electrons on nitrogen can cause it to act as a nucleophile. This is exceedingly important in the synthesis of a class of compounds known as Amines.

Figure: Bonding structure of ammonia

n-butylamine

CHARACTERIZATION TESTS

A certain graduate student at a great metropolitan university took it to heart to surprise the six students in his lab section by handing them unknowns and requiring them to identify the mysterious compound. As it was still too early in the term for unknowns to be distributed, a great hue and cry was raised. The graduate student relented and agreed to give each student a choice of two possibilities:

(a) Student A was given either $CH_3CH_2CH_2CH_3$ or $CH_3CH_2CH_2CH_2Cl$.

(b) Student B was given either $BrCH=CHCH_2Cl$ or $ClCH=CHCH_2Br$.

(c) Student C had to choose between $(CH_3)_3CCl$ and $(CH_3)_2CHCH_2Cl$.

(d) Student D: $CH_3CH=CHCl$ or $CH_2=CHCH_2Cl$

$\qquad\qquad\qquad$ (trans) $\qquad\qquad$ (cis)
(e) Student E: $CH_3CH_2CH=CHCl$ or $CH_3CH_2CH=CHCl$

(f) Student F: $CH_3CH_2CH=CHCl$ or $CH_2=CHCH_2CH_2Cl$.

How would one go about distinguishing chemically between these various compounds?

Solution:$\qquad$(a) n-Butane will not react with alcoholic $\overline{AgNO_3}$. 1-chlorobutane will, upon warming, yielding AgCl as a precipitate.

$$CH_3CH_2CH_2CH_3 + AgNO_3 \xrightarrow[\text{alc.}]{} \quad \text{No reaction}$$

$\qquad$ n-Butane

$$CH_3CH_2CH_2CH_2Br \underset{\longleftarrow}{\overset{Ag^+}{\longrightarrow}} \quad CH_3CH_2CH_2CH_2{}^+ + Ag^+ Br^-$$

This is the reaction used to catalyze S_N1 reactions. Indeed, primary alkyl halides, which will normally undergo S_N2 reactions, will undergo S_N1 reactions in the presence of Ag^+.

(b) Both compounds have halogens in the allylic position, and hence both compounds will react immediately. However, the products will be different.

(1) $BrCH=CHCH_2Cl + AgNO_3 \rightarrow Ag^+Cl^- \downarrow + BrCH=CHCH_2^+$

(2) $ClCH=CHCH_2Br + AgNO_3 \rightarrow Ag^+Br^- \downarrow \quad ClCH=CHCH_2^+$

All one has to do is isolate the precipitate and test for K_{sp}.

(c)   Again, in this reaction, alcoholic $AgNO_3$ is utilized. When Ag^+ cation is reacted with a tertiary chloride, it will react very fast, due to the inductive effect stabilizing the subsequent ion; so that $(CH_3)_3CCl$ will react immediately while $(CH_3)_2CHCH_2Cl$ will react only after heating.

(d) $CH_3CH=CHCl$ will not undergo a reaction with alcoholic $AgNO_3$ because the chlorine is not on the allylic carbon. $CH_2=CHCH_2Cl$, conversely, will undergo an immediate reaction resulting in the precipitation of $AgCl$.

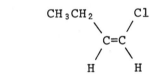

$CH_2=CH-CH_2Cl + AgNO_3 \rightarrow AgCl + CH_2\overset{\frown}{=}CH-CH_2^+$

$^+CH_2-CH\overset{\frown}{=}CH_2$

(e)   These two isomers can be distinguished by the addition of alcoholic $K(OH)$. The cis isomer will undergo an E2 elimination, while the trans isomer will not.

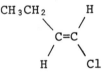

     trans-1-chloro-1-   cis-1-chloro-1-butene
        butene

As is evident from the illustrations, the hydrogen and the chlorine in the cis isomer are in an anti position to each other, ready to undergo an E2 reaction.

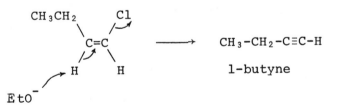

$CH_3-CH_2-C\equiv C-H$

1-butyne

(f)   No reaction will occur upon addition of alcoholic $AgNO_3$ to 1 chloro 1-butene (see (d)). Alcoholic $AgNO_3$ will, however, react with 4 chloro-1 butene upon heating.

$Cl-CH=CH-CH_2CH_3$ $CH_2=CH-CH_2CH_2Cl$

1-chloro-1-butene   4-chloro-1-butene

While the chlorine is not in an allylic position, it is in

458

a primary position, which will allow for a reaction upon heating.

$$CH_2=CH-CH_2-CH_2Cl \xrightarrow[\Delta]{AgNO_3} CH_2=CH-CH_2-\overset{+}{C}H_2 + Ag^+ Cl^-$$

● **PROBLEM 13-25**

A liquid of boiling point 37-44° was insoluble in water, dilute acids or bases, or concentrated H_2SO_4. It did not react with Br_2/CCl_4 or dilute $KMnO_4$. It was subjected to sodium fusion, and the resulting solution was filtered, acidified with nitric acid, and boiled. Addition of $AgNO_3$ gave a precipitate.

(a) On the basis of the table below what compound or compounds might this have been? (b) Several milliliters of CCl_4 were added to a portion of the acidified solution from the fusion, and the mixture was shaken with chlorine water. A violet color appeared in the CCl_4 layer. Which compound or compounds of (a) are still possible? (c) How would each of the other possibilities have responded in (b)?

ALKYL HALIDES

Name	Chloride B.p., °C	Chloride Density at 20°C	Bromide B.p., °C	Bromide Density at 20°C	Iodide B.p., °C	Iodide Density at 20°C
Methyl	−24		5		43	2.279
Ethyl	12.5		38	1.440	72	1.933
n-Propyl	47	.890	71	1.335	102	1.747
n-Butyl	78.5	.884	102	1.276	130	1.617
n-Pentyl	108	.883	130	1.223	157	1.517
n-Hexyl	134	.882	156	1.173	180	1.441
n-Heptyl	160	.880	180		204	1.401
n-Octyl	185	.879	202		225.5	
Isopropyl	36.5	.859	60	1.310	89.5	1.705
Isobutyl	69	.875	91	1.261	120	1.605
sec-Butyl	68	.871	91	1.258	119	1.595
tert-Butyl	51	.840	73	1.222	100d	
Cyclohexyl	142.5	1.000	165			
Vinyl (Haloethene)	−14		16		56	
Allyl (3-Halopropene)	45	.938	71	1.398	103	
Crotyl (1-Halo-2-butene)	84				132	
Methylvinylcarbinyl (3-Halo-1-butene)	64					
Propargyl (3-Halopropyne)	65		90	1.520	115	
Benzyl	179	1.102	201		93¹⁰	
α-Phenylethyl	92¹⁵		85¹⁰			
β-Phenylethyl	92²⁰		92¹¹		127¹⁹	
Diphenylmethyl	173¹⁹		184²⁰			
Triphenylmethyl	310		230¹⁵			
Dihalomethane	40	1.336	99	2.49	180d	3.325
Trihalomethane	61	1.489	151	2.89	subl.	4.008
Tetrahalomethane	77	1.595	189.5	3.42	subl.	4.32
1,1-Dihaloethane	57	1.174	110	2.056	179	2.84
1,2-Dihaloethane	84	1.257	132	2.180	d	2.13
Trihaloethylene	87		164	2.708		
Tetrahaloethylene	121				subl.	
Benzal halide	205		140²⁰			
Benzotrihalide	221	1.38				

459

Solution: (a) An inspection of the chemical properties
of the liquid unknown reveals it to have the properties of
an alkyl halide ,namely   failure to react with Br_2/CCl_4,
dilute $KMnO_4$, or concentrated H_2SO_4. This is confirmed by
breaking the unknown into its component elements, via the
sodium fusion reaction, and obtaining a precipitate upon
reaction with silver nitrate.

An inspection of the table reveals CH_3I (43°),
CH_3CH_2Br (38°), and CH_2Cl_2 (40°) as possible compounds.

(b)   The addition of CCl_4 to the acidified solution would
result in the formation of Br_2 and I_2. The Cl^- ion would be
unaffected. The violet color seen in the CCl_4 layer would
be clearly indicative of I_2. Therefore, the only compound
that the alkyl halide unknown could be is CH_3I.

(c)   If the unknown had been CH_3CH_2Br, then a red-brown
color indicative of Br_2 would have been observed in the
CCl_4 layer. Had the unknown been CH_2Cl_2, no color would
have been observed as Cl^- would not have reacted.

● **PROBLEM** 13-26

An unknown compound is believed to be one of the
following. Describe how you would go about finding out
which of the possibilities the unknown actually is. Where
possible, use simple chemical tests; where necessary,
use more elaborate chemical methods like quantitative
hydrogenation, cleavage, etc. Where necessary, make use
of the table below.

(a)	b.p., °C		b.p., °C
n-decane	174	p-cymene (p-isopropyltoluene)	177
4-methylcyclohexanol	174	limonene (see Problem 17, page 317)	178
1,3-dichloro-2-propanol	176	n-heptyl bromide	180
(b)			
1-phenyl-1-propene	177	n-hexyl iodide	180
benzyl chloride	179	cyclohexylcarbinol	182
2-octanol	179		
(c)			
m-diethylbenzene	182	n-octyl chloride	185
n-butylbenzene	183	trans-decalin (see Problem 8, p. 315)	186
2-ethyl-1-hexanol	184		

CARBOXYLIC ACIDS

Name	Formula	M.p., °C	B.p., °C	Solub., g/100 g H_2O
Formic	HCOOH	8	100.5	∞
Acetic	CH_3COOH	16.6	118	∞
Propionic	CH_3CH_2COOH	−22	141	∞
Butyric	$CH_3(CH_2)_2COOH$	− 6	164	∞
Valeric	$CH_3(CH_2)_3COOH$	−34	187	3.7
Caproic	$CH_3(CH_2)_4COOH$	− 3	205	1.0
Caprylic	$CH_3(CH_2)_6COOH$	16	239	0.7
Capric	$CH_3(CH_2)_8COOH$	31	269	0.2
Lauric	$CH_3(CH_2)_{10}COOH$	44	225^{100}	i.
Myristic	$CH_3(CH_2)_{12}COOH$	54	251^{100}	i.
Palmitic	$CH_3(CH_2)_{14}COOH$	63	269^{100}	i.

Stearic	$CH_3(CH_2)_{16}COOH$	70	287[100]	i.
Oleic	cis-9-Octadecenoic	16	223[10]	i.
Linoleic	cis,cis-9,12-Octadecadienoic	− 5	230[16]	i.
Linolenic	cis,cis,cis-9,12,15-Octadecatrienoic	−11	232[17]	i.
Cyclohexanecarboxylic	cyclo-$C_6H_{11}COOH$	31	233	0.20
Phenylacetic	$C_6H_5CH_2COOH$	77	266	1.66
Benzoic	C_6H_5COOH	122	250	0.34
o-Toluic	o-$CH_3C_6H_4COOH$	106	259	0.12
m-Toluic	m-$CH_3C_6H_4COOH$	112	263	0.10
p-Toluic	p-$CH_3C_6H_4COOH$	180	275	0.03
o-Chlorobenzoic	o-ClC_6H_4COOH	141		0.22
m-Chlorobenzoic	m-ClC_6H_4COOH	154		0.04
p-Chlorobenzoic	p-ClC_6H_4COOH	242		0.009
o-Bromobenzoic	o-BrC_6H_4COOH	148		0.18
m-Bromobenzoic	m-BrC_6H_4COOH	156		0.04
p-Bromobenzoic	p-BrC_6H_4COOH	254		0.006
o-Nitrobenzoic	o-$O_2NC_6H_4COOH$	147		0.75
m-Nitrobenzoic	m-$O_2NC_6H_4COOH$	141		0.34
p-Nitrobenzoic	p-$O_2NC_6H_4COOH$	242		0.03
Phthalic	o-$C_6H_4(COOH)_2$	231		0.70
Isophthalic	m-$C_6H_4(COOH)_2$	348		0.01
Terephthalic	p-$C_6H_4(COOH)_2$	300 subl.		0.002
Salicylic	o-HOC_6H_4COOH	159		0.22
p-Hydroxybenzoic	p-HOC_6H_4COOH	213		0.65
Anthranilic	o-$H_2NC_6H_4COOH$	146		0.52
m-Aminobenzoic	m-$H_2NC_6H_4COOH$	179		0.77
p-Aminobenzoic	p-$H_2NC_6H_4COOH$	187		0.3
o-Methoxybenzoic	o-$CH_3OC_6H_4COOH$	101		0.5
m-Methoxybenzoic	m-$CH_3OC_6H_4COOH$	110		
p-Methoxybenzoic (Anisic)	p-$CH_3OC_6H_4COOH$	184		0.04

Solution: The best way to go about any determination of
a compound is by an elimination system of trial and error.
We are aided here with a chart of the physical properties
of possible unknowns.

The best mode of attack would be to break all
the possibilities into subcategories and differentiate between the subcategories.

(a) In any laboratory determination, the key aspect
to a successful solution is to use a small amount of the
unknown at a time, giving us the ability to perform
many tests. Of the six choices in part (a) only n-heptyl
bromide and 1,3-dichloro-2-propanol are alkyl halides.
It is best to begin with them.

The first step would be to perform a sodium fusion
which would break the alkyl halides into their components
which include halide anions. After acidification and
addition of CCl_4, we shake with Cl_2/H_2O and observe the
results. If the unknown is n-heptyl bromide, the bromide
anions will be oxidized to Br_2, which will be soluble in
CCl_4 layer giving it a distinctive red-brown color. If no
color is observed, 1,3 dichloro-2-propanol could still be
present, as Cl^- is not converted to Cl_2 under the previous
conditions. To test for the dichloro compound, we simply
add $AgNO_3$ with a white precipitate, AgCl indicating the
presence of chlorine.

If the alkyl halides are eliminated as possibilities,
we check for solubility in cold condentrated sulfuric acid

461

since n-decane and p-cymene are insoluble in H_2SO_4. If the unknown is insoluble in cold concentrated sulfuric acid, we test for its solubility in fuming sulfuric acid. n-Decane will not be soluble in fuming sulfuric acid while p-cymene will.

If none of the previous tests have been successful, then either limonene or 4-methyl-cyclohexanol is present. A simple Br_2/CCl_4 test for unsaturation will determine that the unknown is limonene because it will decolorize bromine due to its unsaturation, while the alcohol will not.

It should be noted at this point, that if carrying out this experiment in the lab, one should not be satisfied with one positive test. For best results, a derivative should be synthesized and its melting point should be taken as a confirmatory test.

(b) One would attack the second set of possible compounds in the same manner that the previous six were distinguished. The alkyl halides would be the first to be distinguished.

A sodium fusion test would first be performed on the unknown, breaking it down into its components, and then the unknown would be acidified, mixed with carbon tetra-chloride, and shaken with Cl_2. A purple color would be indicative of I_2, which would indicate n-hexyl iodide as the unknown. If no purple color is observed, we would add $AgNO_3$. The formation of a white precipitate (AgCl) would point to benzyl chloride as the unknown.

If the sodium fusion test fails, the Br_2/CCl_4 test for unsaturation would be next. If there is decolorization of the bromine solution, then the unknown would most likely be 1-phenyl 1-propene, which is the only unsaturated compound.

If none of these tests give positive results, then 2-octanol is most likely present. A confirmatory test would be the iodoform reaction ($I_2/(OH)^-$), converting 2-octanol to heptanoic acid.

Once again, once the compound has been identified, a derivative should be synthesized and tested for melting point.

(c) n-octyl chloride can be identified by sodium fusion followed by the addition of $AgNO_3$. The formation of a white precipitate (AgCl) would indicate n-octyl chloride.

The next step would be to test the solubility of the unknown in fuming sulfuric acid, realizing that it it is insoluble then the unknown is trans-decalin.

The rest of the compounds, being alcohols, could be oxidized to their corresponding acids, and their melting points taken.

CHAPTER 14

ELIMINATION REACTIONS

E2 REACTIONS

Predict the structure of the major alkene formed in the E2 reactions of the following halides.

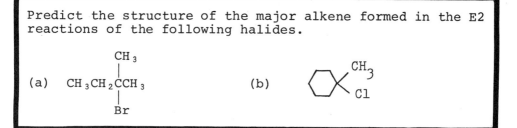

(a) $CH_3CH_2CCH_3$ with CH_3 above and Br below the central carbon

(b)   cyclohexane ring with CH_3 and Cl substituents

Solution: This problem represents an exercise in applying the Saytzeff and Hofmann rules to the mechanism of an E2 reaction. To understand these rules we will go through the E2 mechanism.

An E2 will be favored over an S_N2 reaction in conditions such as low polar media (an alcoholic solvent is generally used), high temperature, and when a strong base is present. Mechanism (general case): Note: ⟶ represents flow of electrons.

$$B:^{\ominus} \longrightarrow H-C_\beta - C_\alpha - X \longrightarrow BH + C_\beta = C_\alpha + X^{\ominus}$$

(anionic base)
nucleophile

This reaction, which like an S_N2 is concerted (occurs in one step), has the same activated complex as an S_N2.

activated
complex in E2 } $$B ----H---- C \stackrel{\delta-}{=\!=\!=} C ---- X$$ with $\delta-$ over B region and $\delta-$ over X

The activated complex shows the concerted process of bond making and bond breaking. In the E2 reaction, a nucleophile ($B:^-$) attacks a hydrogen β to the leaving group (^-X). While this is going on the electron pair of the $H-C_\beta$ bond "swings around" and attacks the carbon (C_α) adjacent to it. C_α, unable to hold ten electrons will simultaneously begin to eject the leaving group along with its two electrons of the $C_\alpha-X$ bond. As the leaving group is ejected, a π bond forms between C_α and C_β, creating a double bond. Note that this process occurs in one continuous step (concerted). A problem arises when there is more than one type of β carbon that bears a hydrogen. For example, in part (a) we are given the compound $CH_3CH_2-\overset{\overset{\displaystyle CH_3}{|}}{\underset{\underset{\displaystyle Br}{|}}{C}}-CH_3$,

and we are asked to predict the major structure of the alkene formed by an E2 reaction.

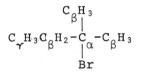

One can readily see that the two β-methyl groups have no difference stereochemically, therefore the question is which alkene will form: $CH_3CH=C\overset{\displaystyle /CH_3}{\underset{\displaystyle \backslash CH_3}{}}$ or $CH_3CH_2-C\overset{\displaystyle //CH_2}{\underset{\displaystyle \backslash CH_3}{}}$

To answer this we follow Saytzeff's rule for most products. It states that the major alkene produced is the most highly substituted one (i.e., the one with the largest number of <u>alkyl</u> groups bonded to the sp^2-hybridized carbons). In part (a) we readily see that $\underset{(1)}{CH_3CH}=C\overset{\displaystyle /(2)\,CH_3}{\underset{\displaystyle \underset{(3)}{\backslash CH_3}}{}}$ has three sub-

stituents bonded to the Csp^2 atoms while with $\underset{(2)}{CH_3CH_2}-C\overset{\displaystyle //CH_2}{\underset{\displaystyle \underset{(1)}{\backslash CH_3}}{}}$

we observe only two substituents. According to Saytzeff, $CH_3CH=C\overset{\displaystyle /CH_3}{\underset{\displaystyle \backslash CH_3}{}}$ is the major alkene compound formed, and it is

thus known as the Saytzeff product while $CH_3CH_2-C\overset{\displaystyle //CH_2}{\underset{\displaystyle \backslash CH_3}{}}$ is

the minor alkene formed and is called the Hofmann product.

464

Hofmann's rule states that the major alkene produced is the least highly substituted one (i.e., the one with the smallest number of alkyl groups bonded to the sp²-hybridized carbons). Hofmann's rule will usually apply when the leaving group is a positively charged species (e.g. $-\overset{+}{N}(CH_3)_3$).

In part (b) we consider which alkene will be produced upon an E2 reaction involving 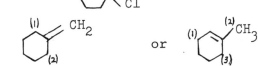 . The major com-

pound will either be   or

Here, Saytzeff's rule applies since the leaving group is Cl⁻, a negatively charged species. Thus the major alkene formed

is   .

● PROBLEM 14-2

Like Markovnikov, Saytzeff states his rule in terms, not of product stability, but of numbers of hydrogens on carbon atoms. (a) Suggest a wording for this original Saytzeff rule. (b) Predict the major product of dehydrohalogenation of 2-bromo-1-phenylbutane on the basis of the original rule. (c) On the basis of the modern rule.

Solution: (a) To state Saytzeff's rule in numbers of hydrogens on carbon atoms, we consider changes in the number of H-C bonds in a Saytzeff elimination. For example in the elimination reaction

$$CH_3CH_2\overset{\overset{\displaystyle Cl}{\displaystyle |}}{C}HCH_3 \xrightarrow[\text{EtOH}]{\text{KOH}} CH_3CH=CHCH_3 \quad (\text{ Saytzeff product })$$

the double bond forms between C_2 and C_3 in the Saytzeff product, and not between C_1 and C_2. C_3 has two hydrogens while C_1 has three hydrogens; thus it is safe to assume that "removal of hydrogen occurs from the carbon carrying the fewer hydrogens."

(b) Let us first look at the structure of 2-bromo-1-phenylbutane, $PhCH_2-CHBr-CH_2CH_3$.

We find that both C_1 and C_3 have two hydrogens, but because of our original rule we cannot have any preference in alkene formation since C_1 and C_3 both have two hydrogens.

(c) By using the modern rule which states that the

more stable alkene will form in elimination, we clearly see that the emphasis is on stability. In the case of $PhCH_2CHBrCH_2CH_3$, we have a choice of product, upon elimination, between $PhCH=CHCH_2CH_3$ and $PhCH_2CH=CHCH_3$. The key word is stability. $PhCH=CHCH_2CH_3$ is the more stable alkene, because the double bond between C_1 and C_2 is conjugated with the highly stable aromatic, phenyl group. $PhCH_2CH = CHCH_3$ has its double bond between C_2 and C_3 which is too far away for the stabilizing effect that is present in conjugation.

It should be mentioned that among the reasons why conjugation stabilizes a system is the fact that with conjugation usually many important contributing structures can be drawn , indicating great delocalization of charge and thus an increase in stability.

● PROBLEM 14-3

Write the products of the following reactions:

(a) $CH_3CH_2CH_2-OH$ $\xrightarrow[\text{heat}]{H_2SO_4}$

(b) $CH_3CH_2CH_2OH + CH_3CH_2OH$ $\xrightarrow[\text{heat}]{H_2SO_4}$

(c) $CH_3O^{\ominus}Na^{\oplus} + (CH_3)_3C - Br \rightarrow$

<u>Solution:</u>   (a) The compound $CH_3CH_2CH_2-OH$ is an alcohol. Alcohols when heated with acid catalysts readily lose a molecule of water to give the corresponding alkene.

The reaction proceeds as follows:

(1) $CH_3CH_2CH_2-OH$ $\xrightarrow[\text{heat}]{H_2SO_4}$ $CH_3CH=CH_2 + H_2O$

   n-propyl alcohol   propene

It is also possible by carefully controlling the temperature to convert alcohols to ethers. The general formula of the reaction is as follows:

$$2\ R - OH \xrightarrow{H_2SO_4} R - O - R + H_2O$$

Since a molecule of water is lost for every pair of alcohol molecules, the reaction is a kind of dehydration. Dehydration is generally limited to the preparation of symmetrical ethers, because a combination of two alcohols usually yields a mixture of three ethers. The reaction proceeds as follows:

(2) 2 $CH_3CH_2CH_2-OH$ $\xrightarrow[-H_2O]{H_2SO_4}$ $CH_3CH_2CH_2-O-CH_2-CH_2-CH_3$

     n-propyl alcohol   n-propyl   ether

Summarizing two steps of the reaction we may write the general equation of the reaction outlined in the problem as follows:

3     $CH_3CH_2CH_2-OH$ $\xrightarrow[\text{heat}]{H_2SO_4}$ $CH_3CH_2CH_2-O-CH_2-CH_2-CH_3$ +

     n-propyl alcohol   n-propyl ether

                 + $CH_3CH=CH_2$ + $2\ H_2O$

                      propene

The reaction mixture contains 3 major compounds: n-propyl alcohol, propene and n-propyl ether.

(b)   The mechanism of the reaction between n-propyl alcohol $CH_3CH_2CH_2-OH$, ethyl alcohol CH_3CH_2OH and hot sulfuric acid is similar to the mechanism outlined above; when alcohols are heated with sulfuric acid they are converted to alkenes. At the same time it is possible by careful control of the temperature to convert alcohols to ethers. The combination of two alcohols usually yields a mixture of three ethers, two symmetrical and one non-symmetrical, and two corresponding alkenes. The reaction outlined in the problem proceeds as follows:

$CH_3CH_2CH_2OH$ + CH_3CH_2OH $\xrightarrow[\text{heat}]{H_2SO_4}$ $CH_3CH_2CH_2OCH_2CH_2CH_3$ +

n-propyl   ethyl   n-propyl ether
alcohol   alcohol

 + $CH_3CH_2OCH_2CH_3$ + $CH_3CH_2CH_2OCH_2CH_3$ + $CH_2=CH_2$ + $CH_3CH=CH_2$

   ethyl ether   ethyl n-propyl   ethylene   propene
                           ether

(c)   This reaction is the reaction of an alkoxide ion (OR^-) with a tertiary alkyl halide. Two possibilities arise. The reaction can proceed by an Sn_1 reaction or it can proceed by an E_2 reaction. The key is that the alkoxide ion $^-OCH_3$ is a much better base than a nucleophile, thus it favors its ability to abstract protons. Its attack on a proton triggers an E_2 elimination. The reaction and products are as follows:

$$CH_3O^{\ominus}Na^{\oplus} + (CH_3)_3C-Br \rightarrow \left[CH_3O----H--CH_2\overset{\overset{\displaystyle CH_3}{|}}{\underset{\underset{\displaystyle CH_3}{|}}{C}}----Br \right]$$

$$CH_2=\overset{\overset{\displaystyle CH_3}{|}}{C}-CH_3 \leftarrow \begin{array}{l} -CH_3OH \\[4pt] -Br^{\ominus} \end{array}$$

There will also be some substitution so $(CH_3)_3COCH_3$ will be a minor product as well.

467

Predict the major products, if any, for the reaction of isobutyl n-propyl ether with:

(a) $H_2Cr_2O_7$, room temperature
(b) Dilute, aqueous H_2SO_4
(c) Hot, concentrated HBr.

Solution: Just as alcohols can be protonated by strong acids, ethers too can donate a pair of electrons to a hydrogen ion to form protonated ethers, or oxonium ions. These ions are formed only in concentrated acid. The general equation of the reaction is as follows:

$$R - \overset{..}{\underset{..}{O}} - R' + H^{\oplus} \rightleftharpoons R - \overset{\oplus}{\underset{\underset{H}{|}}{O}} - R'$$

oxonium salt

The equation for the reaction outlined in the problem is as follows:

$$\underset{\text{isobutyl n-propyl ether}}{CH_3-\overset{\overset{CH_3}{|}}{CH}-CH_2-O-CH_2-CH_2-CH_3} + \underset{\text{chromic acid}}{H_2Cr_2O_7} \xrightarrow[\text{temperature}]{\text{room}}$$

$$\longrightarrow CH_3-\overset{\overset{CH_3}{|}}{CH}-CH_2-\overset{\overset{\oplus}{|}}{\underset{\underset{H}{|}}{O}}-CH_2-CH_2-CH_3$$

oxonium salt

(b) Ethers can be protonated only by concentrated acids, that is why there will be no reaction between the compounds given in the problem, isobutyl n-propyl ether and dilute, aqueous H_2SO_4.

(c) Ethers react with strong acids to form oxonium ions, as we have seen above. If the acidic solution is heated the reaction proceeds as follows:

(1) The oxonium ion forms:

$$R - O - R' + H^{\oplus} \rightleftharpoons R - \overset{\oplus}{\underset{\underset{H}{|}}{O}} - R'$$

(2) The ether is cleaved upon heating:

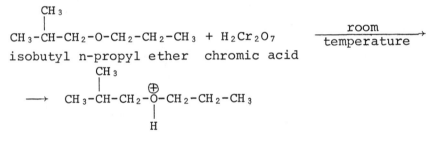

where X is a halide (Cl, Br, I or F). If the acid used is excess HCl, HBr or HI, the alcohols formed will also be converted to alkyl halides by the reaction ROH + HX → R-X + H_2O. The equation for the reaction outlined in the problem is as follows:

$$CH_3-\overset{\overset{\displaystyle CH_3}{|}}{CH}-CH_2-O-CH_2-CH_2-CH_3 + 2\ HBr \xrightarrow{\text{heat}} CH_3-\overset{\overset{\displaystyle CH_3}{|}}{CH}-CH_2-Br$$

isobutyl n-propyl ether   isobutyl bromide

$$+\ CH_3-CH_2-CH_2-Br + H_2O$$

n-propyl bromide

● **PROBLEM 14-5**

An alternative mechanism for E2 elimination is the following:

$$CH_3CH_2Cl + OH^{\ominus} \underset{\longleftarrow}{\xrightarrow{\text{fast}}} \overset{\ominus}{\underset{\cdot\cdot}{CH_2}}CH_2Cl + H_2O \xrightarrow{\text{slow}} CH_2=CH_2 + Cl^{\ominus}$$

(a) Would this mechanism lead to a first-order kinetics with respect to the concentrations of OH⁻ and ethyl chloride? Explain.
(b) This mechanism has been excluded for several halides by carrying out the reaction in deuterated solvents such as D_2O and C_2H_5OD. Explain how such experiments could be relevant to the reaction mechanism.

Solution: To solve part (a) of this problem we must try to determine a rate equation in terms of the concentrations of OH⁻ and ethyl chloride.

Let us first determine which species are the key ones in a rate equation. For all rate equations we are interested in the species involved in the rate determining step. The rate determining step of a reaction is usually the slow part of the reaction, or if a reaction has several slow steps, the rate determining step is the slowest step.

We now look at the alternative E2 mechanism for this reaction:

$$CH_3CH_2Cl + OH^{\ominus} \underset{\longleftarrow}{\xrightarrow{\text{fast}}} \overset{\ominus}{\underset{\cdot\cdot}{CH_2}}CH_2Cl + H_2O \xrightarrow{\text{slow}} CH_2=CH_2 + Cl^{\ominus}$$

Clearly the species involved in the rate determining step are $\underset{\cdot\cdot}{CH_2}CH_2Cl$ (carbanion) and H_2O. We know that the rate equation is dependent upon the concentrations of these two species, so the rate equation can be expressed as follows:

Rate = $k[\overset{\ominus}{\underset{\cdot\cdot}{CH_2}}CH_2Cl][H_2O]$, where k is a constant of

469

proportionality. At this point we now try to get this rate
equation in terms of $OH^{\ominus}$ and CH_3CH_2Cl. This can be done by
creating a new constant, called K, where

$K = [CH_2CH_2Cl][H_2O]/[CH_3CH_2Cl][OH^{\ominus}]$. We substitute this

into our original equation in the following manner:

$$Rate = k[CH_2CH_2Cl][H_2O]$$

$$K = [CH_2CH_2Cl][H_2O]/[CH_3CH_2Cl][OH^{\ominus}]$$

$$[CH_2CH_2Cl][H_2O] = [CH_3CH_2Cl][OH^{\ominus}] K$$

$$Rate = kK [CH_3CH_2Cl][OH^{\ominus}]$$

From observing this final equation, we can see that
this mechanism does lead to first order kinetics with respect to the concentrations of $OH^{\ominus}$ and CH_3CH_2Cl.

(b)   To solve this part we must try to involve the deuterated
solvents, such as D_2O and C_2H_5OD, in the reaction mechanism.
Using the reaction from part (a), as our example, we substitute D_2O for H_2O and $OD^{\ominus}$ for OH^-. Let us now consider
the fast part of this reaction:

$$:CH_2CH_2Cl^{\ominus} + D_2O \xrightarrow{\text{fast}} DCH_2CH_2Cl + OD^{\ominus}$$

In this reaction (which is reversible), we would expect

the carbanion ($\overset{..}{CH_2}CH_2Cl^-$) to exhibit a deuterated exchange
with D_2O when it reverts back to the starting material. If
we find some deuterated starting material present after a
short time we can conclude that this exchange has taken
place, and our mechanism may be correct.

● **PROBLEM 14-6**

Predict the dehydration product(s) of each of the following
alcohols:

(a) $CH_3CH_2CH_2CH_2OH$

n-Butyl alcohol

(b)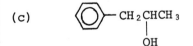

1-Phenyl ethanol

(c)

1-Phenyl-2-propanol

Solution: A very important reaction of alcohols is that of dehydration, which simply is the transformation of an alcohol into an alkene, e.g.

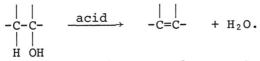

$$\underset{\substack{|\ \ | \\ H\ OH}}{-\overset{|}{C}-\overset{|}{C}-}\ \xrightarrow{\text{acid}}\ \underset{\ }{-\overset{|}{C}=\overset{|}{C}-}\ +\ H_2O.$$

According to the commonly accepted mechanism, dehydration involves (1) formation of the protonated alcohol, $ROH_2^{\oplus}$, (2) its slow dissociation into a carbonium ion, and (3) subsequent expulsion of a hydrogen ion from the carbonium ion to form an alkene. Acid is required to convert the alcohol into the protonated alcohol, which dissociates- by loss of the weakly basic water molecule - much more easily than the alcohol itself. To illustrate these steps:

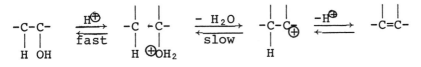

Alcohol   Protonated   Carbonium   Alkene
                   Alcohol   Ion

The acid ordinarily used is sulfuric acid (H_2SO_4), but when writing the synthesis the word "acid" is more often used, as H_2SO_4 is understood to be the acid.

Referring to the above general principles and the general reaction, the products of each alcohol can be predicted.

(a) $CH_3CH_2CH_2CH_2OH$ $\xrightarrow{H_2SO_4 \text{ heat}}$ $CH_3CH=CHCH_3$

       n-butyl alcohol   2-butene

(b)   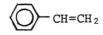 $\xrightarrow{H_2SO_4}$

       1-phenylethanol   Carbonium ion
                                          intermediate

       $\xrightarrow{-\ H^{\oplus}}$

       Styrene

(c)    $\xrightarrow{\text{acid}}$

       1-Phenyl-2-Propanol   1-Phenylpropene

471

E1 REACTIONS

Predict the products of the following reactions:

(a) $CH_3CH_2CBr(CH_3)CH_2CH_3 \xrightarrow[S_N1, E1]{H_2O}$

(b) $(CH_3)_3CCH(CH_3)Cl \xrightarrow[S_N1, E1]{H_2O}$

(c) 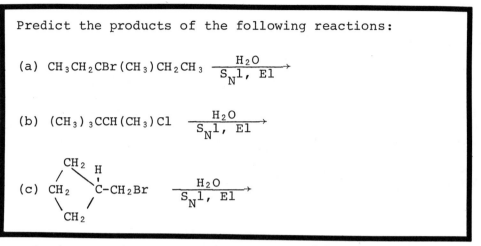 $\xrightarrow[S_N1, E1]{H_2O}$

Solution: The systematic way of solving this problem is to follow each reaction through its designated mechanism, while at each step considering rearrangements for increased stability.

For example, in part (a) we are given the following

problem: $CH_3CH_2-\overset{\overset{\displaystyle CH_3}{|}}{\underset{\underset{\displaystyle Br}{|}}{C}}-CH_2CH_3 \xrightarrow[S_N1, E1]{H_2O}$ E1 products +

S_N1 products. The mechanism for the E1 and S_N1 reactions are presented below:

$\underline{S_N1 \text{ mechanism:}}$

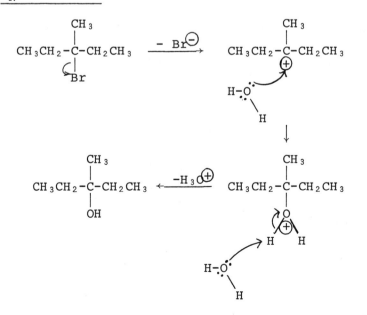

El mechanism:

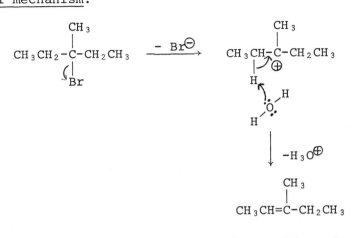

(Saytzeff product)

Looking again at the carbocation we find the mechanism for the Hofmann product to be:

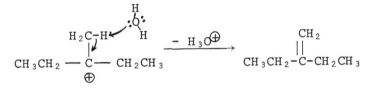

(Hofmann product)

In this case, as in most cases, the Saytzeff product is the major alkene formed.

We follow the same procedure for part (b):

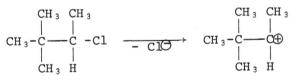

2° carbocation

When this 2° carbocation is formed, something very important happens. Recall that a 3° carbocation is more stable than a 2° carbocation, so it would be nice to be able to form one without the molecule expending too much energy. This formation can be energetically feasible by what is called a methyl shift. A methyl shift occurs when a methyl group attached to a carbon α to the positively charged carbon migrates to the empty orbital in this positively charged carbon thereby making C_α the new positively charged carbon. For example, in part (b) the carbocation rearranges in the following manner:

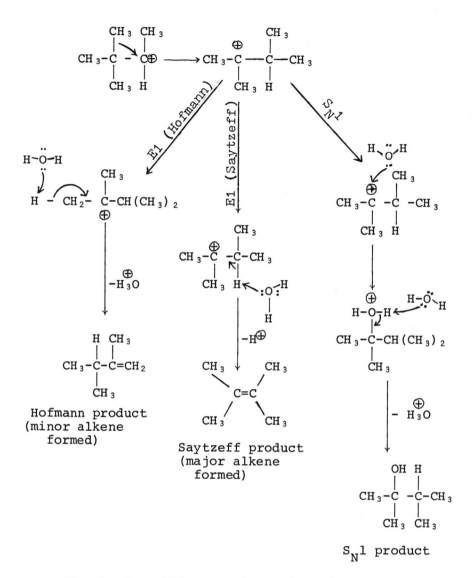

Hofmann product
(minor alkene formed)

Saytzeff product
(major alkene formed)

S_N1 product

S_N1 product

Clearly from this example, and as in our rule, once the methyl shift has taken place the mechanism continues as before.

Again we work systematically in part (c):

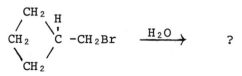

This reaction will begin in an S_N1 fashion because we are working with an alkyl halide with the potential to form a 3° carbocation. Let us see how this works:

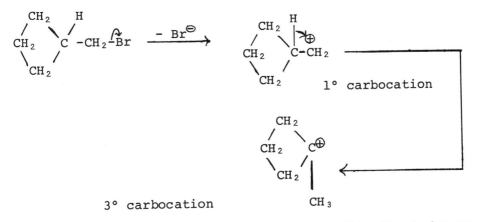

1° carbocation

3° carbocation   CH₃

As the methyl group migrated in part (b), the hydrogen migrates here, forming the more stable 3° carbocation. This migration is called a 1,2-hydride shift. We now continue as in part (b) and obtain the expected products:

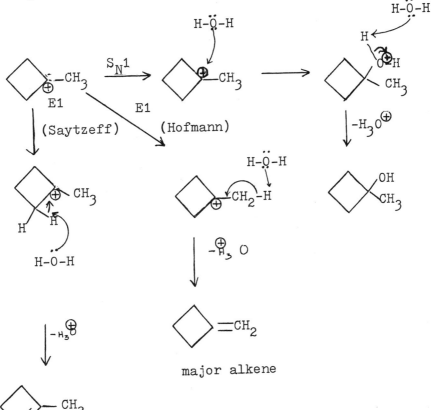

major alkene

minor alkene (because of ring strain)

These compounds would be all the compounds possibly formed by the indicated E1 and S$_N$1 reactions if only there was not yet another possible shift; but there is. Let's look at the starting material:

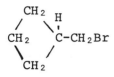

We now, from our study of cycloalkanes, recall that a five membered ring is more stable than a four membered ring. It would be energetically stabilizing if such a five membered ring could be formed. In this case there is a way for this to happen:

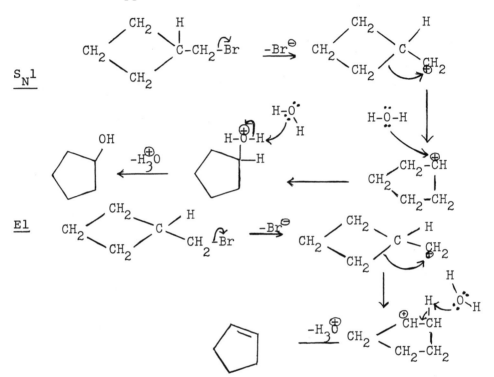

Although this ring shift may seem unlikely, it readily occurs because it increases the molecules' thermodynamic stability. When solving substitution and elimination problems one must always think in terms of stability; the most stable intermediates will form the most often.

● **PROBLEM 14-8**

Explain how $(CH_3)_2CDCHBrCH_3$ might be used to determine whether trimethylethylene is formed directly from the bromide in an El reaction, or by rearrangement and elimination.

Solution: To solve this problem we simply take $(CH_3)_2CDCHBrCH_3$ and run it through, first a direct El reaction, and second a rearrangement and then an El reaction. We then compare the results and look for possible differences that can be isolated from the two methods.

476

Let us now consider the direct El reaction of
$(CH_3)_2CDCHBrCH_3$:

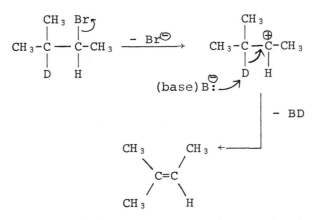

The important thing to note is that no deuterium is
found. We now look at the rearrangement and then El reaction:

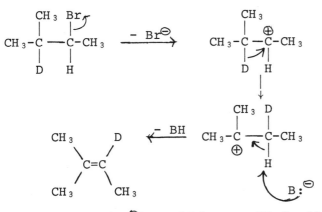

Note: The base $(B:^{\ominus})$ could have pulled off a $D^{\oplus}$ instead
of an $H^{\oplus}$.

Looking at this result the answer comes out. We find,
in this last reaction, two products are formed in equal
yields; one is deuterated while the other one is not. We
can conclude from this that if the reaction is a direct El,
then no deuterium should be detected, and if the reaction
proceeds via rearrangement and then El then about 50% of
the product should be deuterated.
It should be mentioned that in the rearrangement and

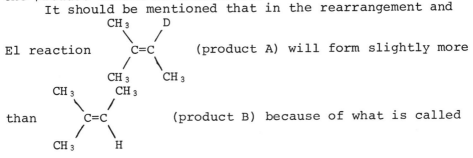

El reaction (product A) will form slightly more

than (product B) because of what is called

the kinetic isotope effect. This is the fact that a C-H bond is easier to break than a C-D bond because D has a greater mass than H. In the above example product A has a C-H bond broken in elimination while product B has a C-D bond broken during elimination. For the purposes of this problem this effect should be ignored.

We can summarize the reaction involving rearrangement and then elimination as:

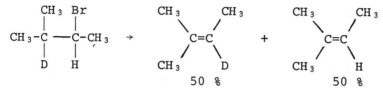

50 %   50 %

STEREOCHEMISTRY

● **PROBLEM** 14-9

Write all the possible staggered conformations for each of the isomers of 2,3-dibromobutane shown in (1) and (2).

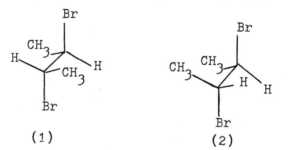

(1)   (2)

Show the structures of the alkenes that could be formed from each by a trans E2 elimination of 1 mole of hydrogen bromide with hydroxide ion. Which alkene should more readily eliminate further to form dimethylacetylene? Explain.

Solution: A staggered conformation is defined as a con-formation with a torsional angle of 60° as seen in a Newman projection. Below are the Newman projections for (1) and (2).

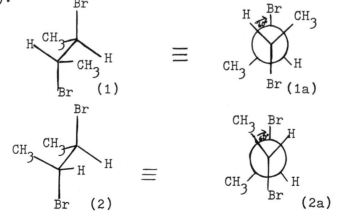

For (1) and (2) the only other Newman projections with torsional angles of 60° and thus the only other staggered conformations, are shown below:

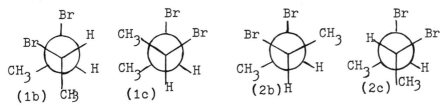

(1b)   (1c)   (2b)   (2c)

We are now asked to show the structures of the alkenes that could be formed from each by a trans E2 elimination of one mole of hydrogen bromide with hydroxide ion. This requires that in each conformation we look for a hydrogen trans to a bromine and then when making the E2 product, converting the projection to an almost planar figure to judge whether or not the alkene is cis or trans. For example let us consider structure 1b:

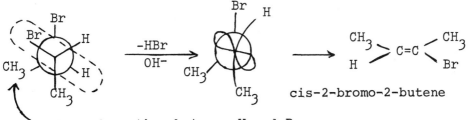

anti-conformation between H and Br

(1c) is done in the same manner:

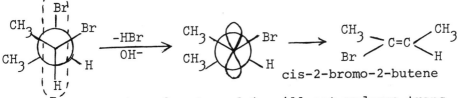

Conformations 2a, 2c and 1a will not undergo trans E2 elimination because there are no hydrogens anti to a bromine. Conformation 2b has two possible trans elimination routes:

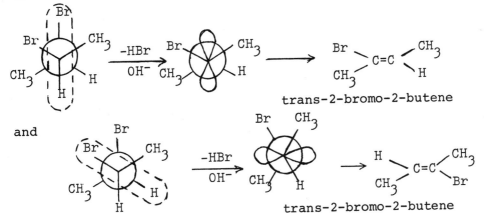

and

479

There is no significance to this since both form the same isomeric alkene, thus the two alkenes that form are trans- and cis-2-bromo-2-butene.

To see which isomer will eliminate more readily we look at the Newman projections for each isomer. Only in the trans isomer is there still another anti H to Br conformation. In the cis isomer H and Br are eclipsed and less stable than the anti conformation. Elimination via an eclipsed conformation is called syn elimination, and it is generally less stable and slower than anti elimination. We conclude the trans isomer (H and Br are anti to each other) will more readily eliminate further to form dimethylacetylene.

● PROBLEM 14-10

Using models, suggest explanations for the following:

(a) On E2 elimination with t-Bu$\overset{-+}{OK}$/t-BuOH, both cis- and trans-2-phenylcyclopentyl tosylates give 1-phenylcyclopentene as the only alkene; the cis isomer reacts 14 times as fast as the trans.

(b) On E2 elimination with n-$C_5H_{11}\overset{-+}{ONa}$/n-$C_5H_{11}OH$ to give 2-chloronorbornene, II reacts about 100 times as fast as its diastereomer, I .

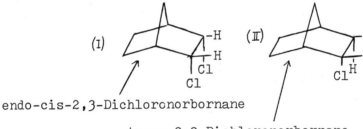

(I)   (II)

endo-cis-2,3-Dichloronorbornane

trans-2,3-Dichloronorbornane

Solution: (a) Let us look at the structure of both cis- and trans-2-phenylcyclopentyl tosylates:

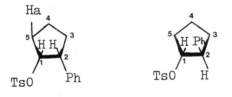

cis-   trans-

For the E2 elimination, the TsO acts as the leaving group in both the cis- and trans-isomers. The question that must be answered is by what mechanisms are the isomers eliminating to form 1-phenylcyclopentene? These mechanisms have one thing in common: they each involve the removal of a leaving group and a hydrogen β to it and the creation of a double bond between C_α and C_β. Sterically it works out

480

that elimination will proceed either with the leaving group
anti to the β hydrogen (anti elimination) or with the leaving group eclipsed to the β hydrogen (syn elimination). The
anti elimination mechanism is the more energetically stable
method because the anti conformation is far more feasible
than the eclipsed conformation.

Visually we can determine that the cis isomer will
undergo an anti elimination because the leaving group, TsO,
has two hydrogens anti to it. Since we are told that only

1-phenylcyclopentene [structure] forms with elimina-

tion from both isomers, we can assume that the trans isomer
must proceed by syn elimination for that is the only available route (the Ph group is in the anti position to the
TsO group). The question is why will the double bond form
only on the C_1-C_2 bond? Let us first go through both
eliminations.

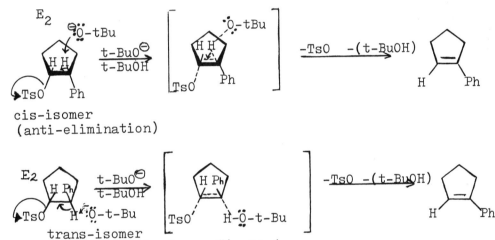

cis-isomer
(anti-elimination)

trans-isomer
(syn elimination)   Figure 1

The answer to our question rests with the phenyl group.
It greatly controls the orientation of elimination because
of the conjugation of the double bond formed by the aromatic,
high stable, phenyl group. This drive for the double bond
to be conjugated is so energetically favorable that it only
forms a double bond between C_1 and C_2.

In Figure 1 we see that the cis isomer undergoes the
highly favorable trans elimination, thus its elimination
reaction goes much faster than that of the trans isomer.

(b) In this part we are dealing with rigid, bicyclic
compounds. By rigid we mean that the compound does not
readily change conformations. This factor is a key point
in dealing with this problem.

Compound I must react via an anti elimination,
which can be formed via a change in conformation of the
compound. Compound II is already in an eclipsed conforma-

481

tion and will thus react via syn elimination. Normally we
would expect the compound using an anti elimination to
react faster than a compound using syn elimination but from
the data given the reverse is true. The main thing to
remember is that the most stable elimination will react the
fastest. In this case, for example, the fact that bicycle
compounds are rigid makes the anti elimination of   I   more
unstable, thus slower than   II .   I   must change its conformation in order to undergo anti elimination, and the
energy needed to change the conformation is relatively
large. The result is that   II   reacts much faster than   I .

The reaction of (±)-2,3-dibromobutane with ethoxide ion
produces trans-2-bromo-2-butene while, under the same
conditions, meso-2,3-dibromobutane produces the corresponding cis isomer. With the aid of three-dimensional
representations, determine whether this is an anti (trans)
elimination. Explain how it is possible for a "trans"
elimination to produce both cis and trans product.

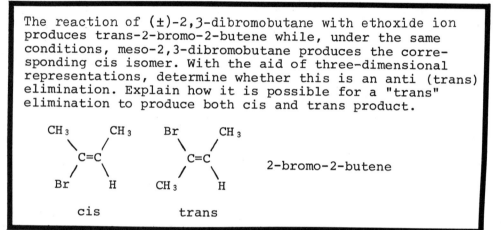

2-bromo-2-butene

cis   trans

Solution: To solve this problem we should look at the
structures of (±)-2,3-dibromobutane and meso-2,3-dibromo-
butane in three dimensional representations:

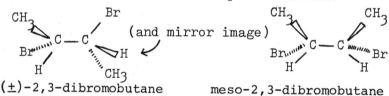

(±)-2,3-dibromobutane   meso-2,3-dibromobutane

     To make things as clear as possible we will present
the meso-2,3-dibromobutane as a Neuman projection:

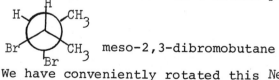

meso-2,3-dibromobutane

     We have conveniently rotated this Newman projection
so that it is ready to undergo a trans-elimination (the
H and Br are anti to each other). The point of this is that
if we get a cis product we know that it does undergo a
trans-elimination, but if we get a trans product then this
meso compound does not undergo a trans-elimination. We now

go through this elimination (E2):

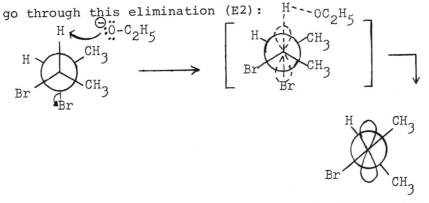

cis-2-bromo-2-butene

We can conclude from this representation that the elimination reaction of meso-2,3-dibromobutane to form cis-2-bromo-2-butene proceeds via a trans-elimination.

To explain how it is possible for a trans elimination to produce both cis and trans product, let us examine the compound $CH_3CH_2CHBrCH_3$ by using the Newman projection:

Fig. 1

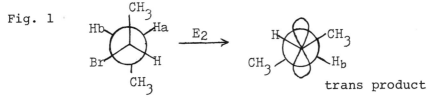

trans product

We labeled the two hydrogens of the methylene group to show two possible routes of anti elimination, figure 1 shows H_a being eliminated and a trans product being formed.

Figure 2 is below:

CH₃   CH₃   Hb   CH₃   H
  E2
Br   H   CH₃   Ha
  Ha   cis product

In this case by labeling the hydrogens to be eliminated we see that there can be both cis and trans products.

ELIMINATION VS. SUBSTITUTION

● **PROBLEM** 14-12

Consider the reaction of isopropyl iodide with various nucleophiles. For each pair, predict which will give the larger substitution/elimination ratio.

(a) I^- or Cl^- (b) $N(CH_3)_3$ or $P(CH_3)_3$ (c) CH_3S^- or CH_3O^-

483

Solution: To solve this problem we consider what properties of a nucleophile will increase the substitution
to elimination ratio.

A very important difference between elimination and
substitution is their emphasis on nucleophilicity and
basicity. Nucleophilicity is the affinity of a base for a
carbon atom in a displacement reaction transition state.
It is measured by the rate of reaction of the nucleophile
with a suitable halide. Judging by the first step of an S_n
reaction, where a base attacks the back lobate orbital of
a suitable carbon, we can state that nucleophilicity is
extremely important in S_n reactions.

Basicity is the affinity of a base for a proton and
is measured by the equilibrium pKa of the conjugate acid
in water. Judging by the first step of an elimination reaction, where a base abstracts a proton from a carbon β
to a halogen causing a series of electron shifts, basicity
is clearly very important in elimination reactions. To
summarize then: In S_n reaction nucleophilicity is the key
while in elimination reactions basicity is the key.

We want to increase the substitution to elimination
ratio; to do this we try to find the nucleophile with the
greater nucleophilicity. The question now arises: what
factors affect nucleophilicity? What it all boils down to
is that the nucleophile with the greater polarizability
will also have the greater nucleophilicity. Larger elements
have relatively diffuse lone pairs of electrons because the
orbitals are larger than in let us say first row elements.
These diffuse lone pairs of electrons tend to bond more
strongly to the more diffuse state of the p orbital in an
S_n2 transition state than to the small, tight 1s orbital of
a hydrogen (if it were acting as a base). From this we can
conclude that larger (second and third row) elements are
more nucleophilic than smaller (first row) elements.

In part (a) we consider I^- and Cl^-. I^- is the larger
element and is thus more polarizable and more nucleophilic,
thereby increasing the substitution to elimination ratio.
In the same way in part (b), $P(CH_3)_3$ is the correct choice
and in part (c), CH_3S^- is the correct choice.

● **PROBLEM** 14-13

Predict the order of reactivity of the following halides
with (a) sodium iodide in acetone; (b) aqueous alcoholic
silver nitrate.

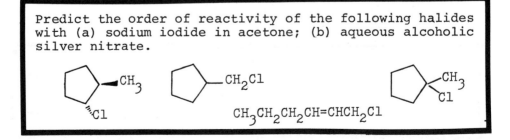

$$CH_3CH_2CH_2CH=CHCH_2Cl$$

<u>Solution:</u>   To solve this problem, we consider various techniques used in figuring the relative reactivities of several compounds in S_N reactions.

The first step to solve this problem systematically, is to consider the reaction conditions. In part (a) the reaction conditions are sodium iodide in acetone. This media favors S_N2 over S_N1 reactions. In part (b) the reaction conditions are aqueous alcoholic silver nitrate. This indicates an S_N1 type media.

We now consider what factors affect reactivity in S_N reactions. The most important factor is the degree of alkylation of the carbon α to the halogen (the carbon bonded to the halide), that is whether this alkyl halide is 1°, 2°, or 3°. For review a 1° (primary) alkyl halide follows the

form H-C-H, a 2° (secondary) alkyl halide follows the form

R-C-R, and a 3° (tertiary) alkyl halide follows the form

R-C-R, where X represents a halogen and R represents an

alkyl or aromatic group. is thus a 2° alkyl

halide, is a 1° alkyl halide and

is a 3° alkyl halide. $CH_3CH_2CH_2CH=CHCH_2Cl$ is a 1° alkyl halide but it is a special case in both S_N1 and S_N2 reactions. In part (a) $CH_3CH_2CH_2CH=CHCH_2Cl$ undergoes an S_N2 reaction as follows: $CH_3CH_2CH_2CH=CHCH_2Cl + I^{\ominus} \xrightarrow{acetone}$
$CH_3CH_2CH_2CH=CHCH_2I + Cl^{-}$. Being an S_N2 reaction the following activated complex is formed:

$$CH_3CH_2CH_2CH=CHCH_2Cl + I^{\ominus} \xrightarrow{\quad acetone \quad}$$

π overlap stabilizing the S_N2 activated complex:

$\longrightarrow C_3H_8CH=CHCH_2I +$
$+ Cl^{\ominus}$

This activated complex has π bonding overlap which tends to stabilize and thus decrease the energy content of the activated complex. The net result of all this is that $C_3H_8CH=CHCH_2Cl$ (1°) will have a greater reactivity than

CH_2Cl because of this effect.

Getting back now to the degree of the alkyl halide, in an S_N2 reaction the order of reactivity is $CH_3X > 1° > 2° > 3°$, while in a S_N1 reaction the order of reactivity is $3° > 2° > 1° > CH_3X$. Thus in part (a) (S_N2 media) the order of reactivity is

$C_3H_8CH=CHCH_2Cl >$ (cyclopentyl)$-CH_2Cl >$ (cyclopentyl)$-CH_3 >$ (methylcyclopentyl with Cl)

In part (b) (S_N1 media) $C_3H_8CH=CHCH_2Cl$ exhibits an-other very interesting effect. You will note that this com-pound has an allylic type group: $C_3H_8 \backslash CH=CH-CH_2Cl$. The com-pound reacts via an S_N1 path in the following way:

$$C_3H_8CH=CHCH_2Cl \xrightarrow{-Cl^\ominus} \overset{\oplus}{C_3H_8CH=CHCH_2} \xrightarrow{I^\ominus} C_3H_8CH=CHCH_2I$$

allylic carbocation intermediate

The allylic carbocation intermediate displays what is called a resonance effect. That is the allylic carboca-tion can be drawn as two identical arrangements of atoms differing only in their electronic distribution. Each ar-rangement is called a resonance or contributing structure. These structures have no physical existence and they are not in equilibrium; rather the real allyl cation is a hybrid of the two main contributing structures (hybrid also in electronic distribution):

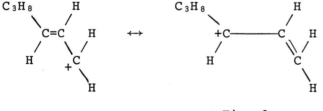

Fig. 1

Notice from Fig. 1 that the positive charge is de-localized amongst the contributing structures. This de-localization of charge greatly stabilizes the carbocation, thus creating an effect whereby $C_3H_8CH=CHCH_2Cl$ is more re-

active via S_N1 than even t-butyl bromide, a tertiary compound.

Taking this resonance effect into account, the order
of reactivity in part (b) is:

$C_3H_8CH=CHCH_2Cl$ > CH$_3$ (3°) > CH$_3$ (2°) > CH$_2$Cl (1°)

Predict the order of reactivity of the following halides
with (a) sodium iodide in acetone; (b) aqueous alcoholic
silver nitrate:

—CH$_2$Br   CH$_3$——Br   CH$_3$Br   [—CHBr]$_2$

Solution: This problem requires an understanding of the
techniques used in predicting the order of reactivity of
various alkyl halides under S_N1 and S_N2 conditions. Taking
a systematic approach in solving this problem we first consider the media in which the reaction takes place. In part
(a), we are told that the reaction takes place in a sodium
iodide/acetone media. These reaction conditions favor an
S_N2 reaction. This means that the compound most favoring an
S_N2 reaction will have the greatest reactivity. We know in
general the order of reactivity in S_N2 reactions is
$CH_3X > 1° > 2° > 3°$. CH_3Br fits the CH_3X brand and is therefore the most reactive species.   —CH$_2$Br is a 1°
(primary) alkyl halide and is thus the next most reactive
species.   —CHBr is a 2° alkyl halide and is the
third most reactive species. CH_3——Br deserves special
mention; because the halide (bromine) is attached to the
phenyl group the compound is classified as an aromatic
halide and because it is so stable it is very unreactive
species and it will not easily undergo any type of S_N reaction. Therefore CH_3——Br is by far the least reactive
species in both part (a) and part (b).

By the same method we consider part (b). The reaction
media is aqueous alcoholic silver nitrate. This is indicative

of S_N1 reaction conditions (aqueous media favors S_N1, while acetone favors S_N2). The order of reactivity by S_N1 for alkyl halides in general, is $3° > 2° > 1° > CH_3X$. Taking this into account we find that the order turns out to be

$$\left[\bigcirc\!\!\!\!\bigcirc \!-CHBr \right]_2 \ (2°) \ > \ \bigcirc\!\!\!\!\bigcirc\!-CH_2Br \ (1°) \ > \ CH_3Br \ (CH_3X)$$

$$> \ CH_3-\bigcirc\!\!\!\!\bigcirc\!-Br.$$

● **PROBLEM** 14-15

The reaction of t-butyl chloride with water is strongly accelerated by sodium hydroxide. How would the ratio of elimination to substitution products be effected thereby?

Solution: To understand the effect of the addition of NaOH to the reaction of t-butyl chloride with water, we should first consider its important chemical properties.

NaOH when placed in water ionizes to a great extent, which causes the pH of the solvent to increase. This increase in pH indicates increased basicity of the water. NaOH ionizes to Na^+ and OH^- ions, with virtually 100 % dissociation in water. Because of this complete dissociation NaOH is a very strong base.

The question is now: what effects does a strong base have on an elimination or substitution reaction? To answer this we consider what a base does. By far the most important use of a strong base is to abstract protons. Thinking now of the mechanisms of elimination and substitution, we see in an E2 reaction the abstraction of a proton β to the halide. Thus we can conclude that the addition of NaOH (a strong base) to the reaction of t-butyl chloride with water would increase the ratio of elimination to substitution.

It should be mentioned that the reason NaOH strongly accelerates the reaction is that it increases the concentration of base present. The reactions of NaOH with t-butyl chloride and water are:

$$NaOH + CH_3-\underset{\underset{CH_3}{|}}{\overset{\overset{CH_3}{|}}{C}}-Cl \xrightarrow[H_2O]{E2} \underset{\underset{CH_3}{\diagdown}}{\overset{\overset{CH_3}{\diagup}}{CH_2=C}} \ + \ NaCl$$

$$NaOH + CH_3-\underset{\underset{CH_3}{|}}{\overset{\overset{CH_3}{|}}{C}}-Cl \xrightarrow[H_2O]{S_N1} CH_3-\underset{\underset{CH_3}{|}}{\overset{\overset{CH_3}{|}}{C}}-OH \ + \ NaCl$$

Which compound of each of the following sets would you
expect to give the higher yield of substitution product
under conditions for bimolecular reaction?

(a) ethyl bromide or β-phenylethyl bromide;
(b) α-phenylethyl bromide or β-phenylethyl bromide;
(c) isobutyl bromide or n-butyl bromide;
(d) isobutyl bromide or tert-butyl bromide.

Solution: To solve this problem we must consider what
physical properties will determine the amount of substitution
produced from each compound in a nucleophilic bimolecular
substitution reaction (S_N2). The properties to be considered
are the degree of substitution on the ∝-carbon (1°, 2°, 3°,
or CH_3X), the leaving group, the nucleophile the reaction
conditions (the polarity of the solvent used and the temperature of the reaction), the degree of substitution at the
β-carbon, and the substituents themselves at the carbon α
and the carbon β. For this problem we do not consider the
reaction conditions since we are told they favor S_N2 nor

do we consider the nucleophile (which is not given), and
the leaving group in each compound is bromine. What we do
consider are the degree of substitution of C-α and at C-β,
and the substituents themselves at C-α and at C-β. The most
favorable conditions for S_N2 arise when C-α is primary

$$\begin{pmatrix} R \\ | \\ H-C-H \\ | \\ X \end{pmatrix}$$ due to the fact that there is less steric hindrance

in the transition state. So therefore the order of reactivity
for S_N2 is $CH_3X > 1° > 2° > 3°$. If both compounds are 1°
(primary) we now consider the substituents at C-β. Again,
due to the lack of steric hindrance, a primary C-β is the
most favorable condition for S_N2. As far as the substituents

themselves are concerned, the larger the substituent the
less S_N2 is favored. In part (a) we consider CH_3CH_2Br and

$PhCH_2CH_2Br$. Usually we can determine that the Ph group at
the C-β position causes $PhCH_2CH_2Br$ to be sterically less
favorable than CH_3CH_2Br therefore ethyl bromide would give
a higher yield than β-phenylethyl bromide under bimolecular
reaction conditions. An important note to this problem is
that the presence of the highly conjugated Ph group causes
E2 (elimination) to easily occur in $PhCH_2CH_2Br$ to produce
a conjugated alkene:

(Styrene)

In part (b) we consider $CH_3CH(Ph)Br$ and $PhCH_2CH_2Br$.
Here there is the very significant fact that $CH_3CH(Ph)Br$

is secondary at C-α while $PhCH_2CH_2Br$ is primary at C-α. This fact outweighs the point that $PhCH_2CH_2Br$ undergoes a significant E2 reaction because steric considerations are extremely important in terms of reaction rate and

$$Br-CH_2-\overset{\overset{\displaystyle CH_3}{|}}{\underset{\underset{\displaystyle CH_3}{|}}{CH}}$$

yield. In part (c) we consider $Br-CH_2-CH$ and

$CH_3(CH_2)_3Br$. Both are primary at C-α site, however, at the C-β site $CH_3CH(CH_3)CH_2Br$ is tertiary while $CH_3(CH_2)_3Br$ is only secondary. This branching in isobutyl bromide creates steric hindrance for an S_N2 but helps stabilize (thermodynamically) the alkene formed by an E2. In part (d) we consider $CH_3CH(CH_3)CH_2Br$ and $CH_3C(CH_3)_2Br$. Using our systematic approach, we immediately see that the C-α of the +-butyl bromide is 3° (tertiary) while the C-α of iso-butyl bromide ($BrCH_2CH(CH_3)CH_3$) is 1° (primary). The extreme steric effect exhibited by t-butyl bromide severely inhibits an S_N2 reaction while the primary isobutyl bromide exhibits virtually no steric effects and easily undergoes an S_N2 reaction. Summarizing our answers:

(a) CH_3CH_2Br - (ethyl bromide)

(b) $PhCH_2CH_2Br$ - (β-phenylethyl bromide)

(c) $CH_3CH_2CH_2CH_2Br$ - (n-butyl bromide)

(d) $CH_3\underset{\underset{\displaystyle CH_3}{|}}{CH}CH_2Br$ - (isobutyl bromide)

● PROBLEM 14-17

Outline a possible laboratory synthesis of each of the following compounds from alcohols and phenols:

(a)   methyl tert-butyl ether
(b)   n-propyl phenyl ether
(c)   cyclohexyl methyl ether

Solution: (a) The compound methyl tert-butyl ether is an asymmetrical ether with the general formula: R-O-R´.

Sodium alkoxides $R-\overset{\ominus}{O}-\overset{\oplus}{Na}$ are used to obtain ethers. Sodium t-butoxide $(CH_3)_3C-\overset{\ominus\oplus}{ONa}$ could be reacted with methyl bromide. This reaction gives the desired product methyl tert-butyl ether $(CH_3)_3C-O-CH_3$.

Sodium alkoxides $R-\overset{\ominus}{O}Na^{\oplus}$ are prepared by reacting an alcohol with sodium.

$$R - OH + Na \rightarrow R - \overset{\ominus}{O}\overset{\oplus}{Na} + H_2 \uparrow$$

sodium
alkoxide

$$R - \overset{\ominus}{O}\overset{\oplus}{Na} + R' - X \rightarrow R - O - R' + \overset{\oplus\ominus}{NaX}$$

sodium	alkyl	Asymmetrical
alkoxide	halide	ether

$$2 \quad CH_3-\underset{\underset{CH_3}{|}}{\overset{\overset{CH_3}{|}}{C}}-O^{\ominus}Na^{\oplus} + CH_3Br \quad CH_3-\underset{\underset{CH_3}{|}}{\overset{\overset{CH_3}{|}}{C}}-O-CH_3 + \overset{\oplus\ominus}{NaBr}$$

Sodium t-butoxide   methyl tert-butyl ether

(b)   The compound n-propyl phenyl ether is a mixed aliphatic-aromatic ether with the general formula Ar-O-R. It can be prepared from the corresponding alcohol and phenol.

Alcohols can be converted into other kinds of compounds having the same carbon skeleton. Alkyl halides are prepared from alcohols by use of hydrogen halides or phosphorus halides. Phosphorus halides are often preferred because they tend less to bring about rearrangement. The general equation for this reaction is as follows:

$$R - OH + PX_3 \rightarrow RX + H_3PO_3$$

where R represents an alkyl group and X a halide (Cl, Br, I or F). The equation for the reaction outlined in the problem is:

$$3 \ CH_3CH_2CH_2OH \quad + \quad PBr_3 \quad \rightarrow \quad 3 \ CH_3CH_2CH_2Br \quad + \quad H_3PO_3$$

n-propyl   n-propyl bromide

Phenols are converted into their salts by aqueous hydroxides. The equation for this reaction is as follows:

$$\text{⬡}-OH + NaOH \rightarrow \quad \text{⬡}-O^{\ominus}Na^{\oplus} + H_2O$$

Phenol   Sodium phenoxide

Sodium phenoxide reacts with n-propyl bromide giving

the desired product n-propyl phenyl ether $CH_3CH_2CH_2O-\text{⬡}$

$$CH_3CH_2CH_2Br + Na^{\oplus\ominus}O-\text{⬡} \longrightarrow CH_3CH_2CH_2O-\text{⬡} + \overset{\oplus\ominus}{NaBr}$$

n-propyl bromide   Sodium phenoxide   n-propyl phenyl ether

(c)   The compound cyclohexyl methyl ether is an asymmetrical ether with the general formula R-O-R´. Ethers can
be prepared by the method of synthesis that uses sodium
alkoxides and alkyl halides. The general equation for this
reaction is as follows:

$$R - \overset{\ominus}{O}\overset{\oplus}{Na} \ + \ R´ - X \rightarrow R - O - R´ \ + \ \overset{\oplus}{Na}\overset{\ominus}{X}$$

a sodium alkoxide   alkyl   asymmetrical
                    halide   ether

where R represents an alkyl group and X a halide (Cl, Br,
I or F). Sodium alkoxides are made by direct action of
sodium metal on dry alcohols:

$$ROH \ + \ Na \ \rightarrow \ R\overset{\ominus}{O}\overset{\oplus}{Na} \ + \ H_2 \uparrow$$

                     a sodium
                     alkoxide

     Alkyl halides are commonly prepared from the alcohols
by use of phosphorus halides:

$$R - OH \ + \ PX_3 \ \rightarrow \ RX \ + \ H_3PO_3$$

                     alkyl
                     halide

     The equations for the reaction outlined in the problem
are:

(1) $\langle hexagon \rangle$—OH + Na → $\langle hexagon \rangle$—$\overset{\ominus}{O}\overset{\oplus}{Na}$ + $H_2 \uparrow$

     cyclohexanol   sodium cyclohexoxide

(2)   3 CH_3OH + PBr_3 → 3 CH_3Br + H_3PO_3

     methyl alcohol   methyl bromide

(3) $\langle hexagon \rangle$—$\overset{\ominus}{O}\overset{\oplus}{Na}$ + CH_3Br → $\langle hexagon \rangle$—$O-CH_3$+ $\overset{\oplus}{Na}\overset{\ominus}{Br}$

     sodium   methyl   cyclohexyl
     cyclohexoxide   bromide   methyl ether

CHAPTER 15

ORGANOMETALLIC COMPOUNDS

PREPARATION

● PROBLEM 15-1

Write balanced equations for the preparation of each of the following organometallic compounds by two different reactions starting from suitable alkyl halides and in-organic reagents. Specify reaction conditions and solvents. In each case, indicate which method of preparation you would prefer from standpoints of yield, convenience, etc.

(a) $(CH_3)_2 Zn$ (c) $(CH_3 CH_2)_4 Pb$
(b) $CH_3 MgCl$ (d) $(CH_3)_2 CHLi$

<u>Solution:</u>   Organometallic compounds can be prepared by a direct or an indirect method. The direct method of prepar-ing alkyl organometallic compound is to react an alkyl halide (RX) with the free metal:

$$R-X + 2 Li \rightarrow Li^+ X^- + R-Li$$

The indirect method of preparing organometallic alkanes involves first the formation of an organometallic alkane that differs from the desired product only by the metal. Next, the free metal of the desired product is reacted with the aforementioned alkyl organometallic compound to give the desired product. For example, methyl sodium can be prepared by first forming methylmagnesium chloride. Sub-sequent reaction with sodium forms methyl sodium, sodium chloride and magnesium:

$$CH_3 Cl \quad \xrightarrow[\text{ether}]{Mg} \quad CH_3 MgCl$$

$$CH_3 MgCl \xrightarrow[\text{n-hexane}]{Na} CH_3 Na + Mg + Na^+ Cl^-$$

Generally, the direct method of preparing organo-metallic alkanes is preferred over the indirect method. This is because the direct method involves only one step and will hence give better yields than the indirect method.

(a)   A direct method of preparing the organozinc compound $(CH_3)_2Zn$ can be shown as:

$$2 CH_3I + 2 Zn \rightarrow (CH_3)_2Zn + ZnI_2$$

An indirect method is as follows:

$$2 CH_3I + Hg(Na)_2 \rightarrow (CH_3)_2Hg + 2 NaI$$

$$(CH_3)_2Hg + Zn \rightarrow (CH_3)_2Zn + Hg$$

The direct method (the first one) is preferred because it gives a better yield and it does not proceed through any highly poisonous intermediates ($(CH_3)_2Hg$ is a very poisonous compound). A good solvent for the preparation and reaction of organozinc compounds is diethyl-ether.

(b)   The direct method of preparing methylmagnesium chloride is:

$$CH_3Cl + Mg \xrightarrow{\text{ether}} CH_3MgCl$$

Methylmagnesium chloride is an example of a Grignard reagent (organomagnesium compounds); ether is a good solvent for reactions of Grignard reagents. An indirect method of preparing CH_3MgCl is:

$$CH_3Cl + 2 Li \rightarrow Li^+Cl^- + CH_3Li$$

$$CH_3Li + MgCl_2 \rightarrow CH_3MgCl + Li^+Cl^-$$

The direct method is preferred; it involves only one step and can be carried out at low temperatures due to methylchloride's low boiling point.

(c)   Tetraethyl lead ($Pb(C_2H_5)_4$) is added to automobile fuel to prevent "knocking" in the engine. A direct method of preparing it is:

$$4 CH_3CH_2Cl + 4Pb(Na) \rightarrow (CH_3CH_2)_4Pb + 4 Na^+Cl^- + 3 Pb$$

An indirect method of preparation is:

$$2 CH_3CH_2Cl + Hg(Na)_2 \rightarrow (CH_3CH_2)_2Hg + 2 Na^+Cl^-$$

$$2 (CH_3CH_2)_2Hg + Pb \rightarrow 2 Hg + (CH_3CH_2)_4Pb$$

The direct method is preferred because it gives a better yield and it does not proceed through any highly poisonous intermediates.

(d)   A direct method for preparing isopropyl lithium is:

$$(CH_3)_2CHBr + 2 Li \rightarrow (CH_3)_2CHLi + Li^+Br^-$$

An indirect method is:

$$(CH_3)_2CHBr + Mg \xrightarrow{\text{ether}} (CH_3)_2CHMgBr$$

$$(CH_3)_2CHMgBr + 2 \text{ Li} \rightarrow (CH_3)_2CHLi + Mg + \overset{+}{Li}\overset{-}{Br}$$

The direct method is preferred and ether can be used as a solvent.

When 10.0 g of n-propylchloride is allowed to react with excess sodium in the Wurtz reaction, how many grams of hexane would be produced assuming a 70 % yield?

Solution: The Wurtz reaction is a method used to couple two short chain alkyl groups to form longer chains. The general equation for this reaction is

$$2 \text{ RX} + 2 \text{ Na} \rightarrow R - R + 2 \text{ NaX}$$

where R represents an alkyl group and X a halide (Cl, Br or I).

The equation for the reaction outlined in the problem is:

$$2 \text{ } CH_3CH_2CH_2Cl + 2 \text{ Na} \rightarrow CH_3(CH_2)_4CH_3 + 2 \text{ NaCl}$$

From this equation, it is seen that for every two moles of n-propylchloride that react, one mole of hexane is formed. We must first determine the number of moles of n-propyl-chloride contained in 10.0 g of the compound. One half of this amount will be the theoretical yield of hexane. The problem states that only 70 % of the theoretical yield is obtained. (MW of $CH_3CH_2CH_2Cl$ = 78.5.)

$$\text{no. of moles of } CH_3CH_2CH_2Cl = \frac{10.0 \text{ g}}{78.5 \text{ g/mole}}$$

$$= .127 \text{ moles}$$

$$\text{theoretical yield of hexane formed } = (0.5)(0.127 \text{ moles})$$

$$= 6.35 \times 10^{-2} \text{ moles}$$

$$\text{experimental yield} = (0.7)(6.35 \times 10^{-2} \text{ moles})$$

$$= 4.45 \times 10^{-2} \text{ moles}$$

The weight of the hexane formed can now be calculated. (MW of C_6H_{14} = 86.)

$$\text{mass of } C_6H_{14} \text{ formed} = (86 \text{ g/mole})(4.45 \times 10^{-2} \text{ moles})$$

$$= 3.82 \text{ g.}$$

What products would you expect to be formed in an attempt to synthesize hexamethylethane from t-butyl chloride and sodium? Write equations for the reactions involved.

Solution: Organosodium compounds are unique in that they are one of the most highly reactive organometallic compounds. Organosodium compounds react rapidly with ethers and alkyl halides. They react with alkyl halides to produce hydrocarbons by either S_N2 and/or E2 reactions. For example, ethylsodium ($CH_3CH_2^-$: Na^+) undergoes S_N2 and E2 reactions with ethyl bromide as shown:

E2 reaction:

$$CH_3CH_2^-:\ Na^+ + H-CH_2-CH_2-Br \rightarrow CH_3CH_3 + Na^+Br^- + CH_2 = CH_2$$

S_N2 reaction (Wurtz coupling reaction):

$$CH_3CH_2^-:\ Na^+ + CH_3CH_2-Br \rightarrow CH_3CH_2CH_2CH_3 + Na^+Br^-$$

When t-butyl chloride is treated with metallic sodium, the organosodium compound (t-butyl sodium) is first formed; sodium chloride is a by-product of this reaction:

$$(CH_3)_3C-Cl + 2\ Na \rightarrow (CH_3)_3C^-:\ Na^+ + Na^+Cl^-$$

As t-butylsodium is formed it reacts with the un-consumed t-butyl chloride to form hydrocarbons. The reaction is strictly E2; there is no Wurtz coupling occurring due to the steric hindrance of the t-butyl groups. Hence the hydrocarbons formed are 2-methylpropane and isobutylene; no hexamethylethane is produced. The reaction can be shown as:

$$(CH_3)_3C^-:\ Na^+ + H-CH_2-\overset{\overset{\displaystyle CH_3}{|}}{\underset{\underset{\displaystyle CH_3}{|}}{C}}-Cl \longrightarrow$$

$$Na^+Cl^- + (CH_3)_3CH + CH_2 = C(CH_3)_2$$

$$\quad\quad\quad\quad\text{2-methyl-}\quad\quad\text{isobutylene}$$
$$\quad\quad\quad\quad\text{propane}$$

The following projected synthesis for n-butane is not very efficient. Why?

$$CH_3CH_2CH_2Br + CH_3Br + 2\ Na \rightarrow CH_3(CH_2)_2CH_3 + 2\ NaBr$$

Solution: This reaction is an example of the Wurtz coupling reaction. The general equation is

$$2 R - X + 2 Na \rightarrow R - R + 2 NaX$$

where R represents an alkyl group and X a halide (Cl, Br or I).

In the above reaction there is both n-propylbromide and methylbromide in the mixture. According to the equation for the Wurtz reaction, these two compounds can couple to form n-butane. But, at the same time free methyl groups can combine with each other as can free propyl groups, forming ethane and hexane. This leads to a decrease in the production of n-butane. A more efficient reaction mixture would be just ethylbromide and Na. Here, the only coupled product would be n-butane

$$CH_3-CH_2-Br + 2 Na \rightarrow CH_3(CH_2)_2CH_3 + 2 NaBr.$$

GRIGNARD REAGENTS

An equilibrium has been suggested to exist between an alkyl-magnesium halide (Grignard reagent) and the corresponding dialkylmagnesium in ether solution according to the following equation:

$$2 RMgX \rightleftharpoons R_2Mg + MgX_2$$

When ether solutions of diethylmagnesium and radio-active magnesium bromide, $\overset{*}{M}gBr_2$, are mixed and allowed to stand for several hours, the magnesium bromide that is subsequently precipitated (by the addition of dioxane,

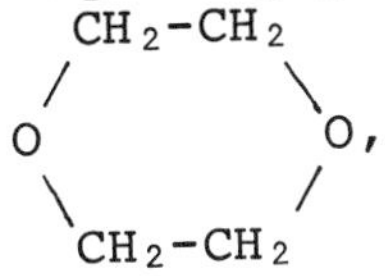

$$O \overset{\displaystyle CH_2-CH_2}{\underset{\displaystyle CH_2-CH_2}{\diagup \diagdown}} O$$, to the solution) has been reported (with

Grignard reagents prepared from at least some specimens of magnesium) to contain almost all the initial radioactivity. What can be deduced from such a result?

Solution: If the proposed equilibrium does exist, then the use of radioactive magnesium bromide should incorporate some radioactive magnesium in all the organomagnesium compounds involved in the equilibrium. This equilibrium between diethylmagnesium, radioactive magnesium bromide ($\overset{*}{M}gBr_2$) and ethylmagnesium bromide is shown as:

$$(CH_3CH_2)_2Mg + \overset{*}{M}gBr_2 \underset{\leftarrow}{\overset{\rightarrow}{}} CH_3CH_2MgBr + CH_3CH_2\overset{*}{M}gBr$$

$$CH_3CH_2MgBr + CH_3CH_2\overset{*}{M}gBr \underset{\leftarrow}{\overset{\rightarrow}{}} \tfrac{1}{2}MgBr_2 +$$

$$\tfrac{1}{2}\overset{*}{M}gBr_2 + \tfrac{1}{2}(CH_3CH_2)_2Mg + \tfrac{1}{2}(CH_3CH_2)_2\overset{*}{M}g$$

The fact that most of the initial radioactivity is contained in the magnesium bromide suggests that the proposed equilibrium does not occur.

Excess methylmagnesium iodide and 0.1776 g of compound A of formula $C_4H_{10}O_3$ react to give 84.1 cc of methane collected over mercury at 740 mm and 25°C. How many active hydrogens does compound A possess? Suggest a possible structure for the compound given that the infrared spectrum shows no carbonyl absorption and the n.m.r. spectrum shows only three types of hydrogen with areas in the ratio of 1:2:2.

Solution: To determine the number of active hydrogens (hydrogens that will react with methyl magnesium halide to form methane) in compound A ($C_4H_{10}O_3$), we must employ some organic stoichiometry. The number of active hydrogens will be the same as the number of moles of methane produced per mole of compound A. In the reaction, 0.1776 g of compound A is reacted. The molecular weight of compound A ($C_4H_{10}O_3$) is $4(12) + 10(1) + 3(16) = 106$. The number of moles of compound A reacted is calculated as:

$$\# \text{ moles} = \frac{\text{g of compound}}{\text{g/mole or MW of compound}}$$

$$\# \text{ moles} = \frac{0.1776}{106} = 0.00168$$

Hence, the number of moles of compound A reacted is 0.00168. All of the compound reacts because it is treated with an excess of methyl magnesium iodide, CH_3MgI. Now we must determine the number of moles of methane produced. The reaction yielded 84.1 cc of methane collected over mercury at 740 mm and 25°Celsius (298° Kelvin). The first thing we must do is to convert the volume of methane collected to its equivalent volume at STP (standard temperature and pressure, 273° Kelvin and 760 mm). Since a cubic centimeter (cc) is equal in volume to one milliliter (ml), 84.1 ml of methane was collected. To convert the number of milliliters of CH_4 to its STP equivalent, the following calculations are performed:

ml CH_4 at STP = ml CH_4 collected ×

$$\frac{\# \text{ of mm over mercury}}{760 \text{ mm}} \times \frac{273° \text{ Kelvin}}{\# \text{ of degrees Kelvin}}$$

ml CH_4 at STP = $84.1 \times \frac{740}{760} \times \frac{273}{298}$

ml CH_4 at STP = 75.0

We can now determine the number of moles of CH_4 collected. Since there are 1000 ml in one liter, and one mole occupies 22.4 liters of space at STP:

$$\# \text{ moles } CH_4 = \frac{\# \text{ ml } CH_4 \text{ collected at STP}}{1000 \text{ ml/liter} \times 22.4 \text{ liters/mole}}$$

$$\text{\# moles CH}_4 = \frac{75.0}{1000 \times 22.4}$$

moles CH$_4$ = 0.00335

We see that there are two moles of methane produced for every mole of compound A reacted:

$$\frac{\text{\# moles CH}_4}{\text{\# moles compound A}} = \frac{0.00335}{0.00168} = 2$$

Hence there are two active hydrogens in compound A.

The problem gives us some infrared (ir) and nuclear magnetic resonance (nmr) spectral data to deduce a possible structure for compound A. The infrared spectrum shows no carbonyl absorption. Since compound A contains oxygens it must be an ether and/or an alcohol. The nmr spectrum shows only three types of hydrogens with relative intensities 1:2:2. Since there are ten hydrogens in compound A, the relative intensities (using the actual number of hydrogens) are 2:4:4. The two active hydrogens in A must be responsible for the relative intensity of "2", since they are different from all the other hydrogens. The only possible structure for compound A that is consistent with all the data is:

$$\text{HOCH}_2\text{CH}_2\text{OCH}_2\text{CH}_2\text{OH}$$

The two active hydrogens are the alcoholic ones. Compound A reacts with methylmagnesium iodide as follows:

$$\text{HOCH}_2\text{CH}_2\text{OCH}_2\text{CH}_2\text{OH} + 2\ \text{CH}_3\text{MgI}\ \text{(excess)} \longrightarrow$$

$$2\ \text{CH}_4 + \text{IMgOCH}_2\text{CH}_2\text{OCH}_2\text{CH}_2\text{OMgI}$$

● **PROBLEM** 15-7

Unknown Q was analyzed and found to contain one atom of bromine per molecule. When the Grignard reagent prepared from Q was treated with water, ethylbenzene was produced. Draw all the possible structures of Q.

Solution: A Grignard reagent can be prepared from an alkyl or aryl halide by reacting it with solid magnesium in dry ethyl ether.

$$\text{R - X} + \text{Mg} \xrightarrow[\text{ether}]{\text{dry}} \text{RMgX}$$

alkyl halide   Grignard reagent

A Grignard reagent is a strong nucleophile. It attacks any slightly positively charged species. Thus, when treated with water, very negligibly acidic, it deprotonates the water molecule.

$$\text{RMgX} + \text{H}_2\text{O} \rightarrow \text{RH} + \text{MgXOH}$$

The unknown Q was made into a Grignard reagent. It deprotonates water to form ethylbenzene. Since Grignard reagent formation and protonation do not change the skeletal structure of a compound, unknown Q must be an aryl halide. The possible structures of unknown Q are shown below as reactants in the process of ethylbenzene synthesis.

UNKNOWN Q   ETHYLBENZENE

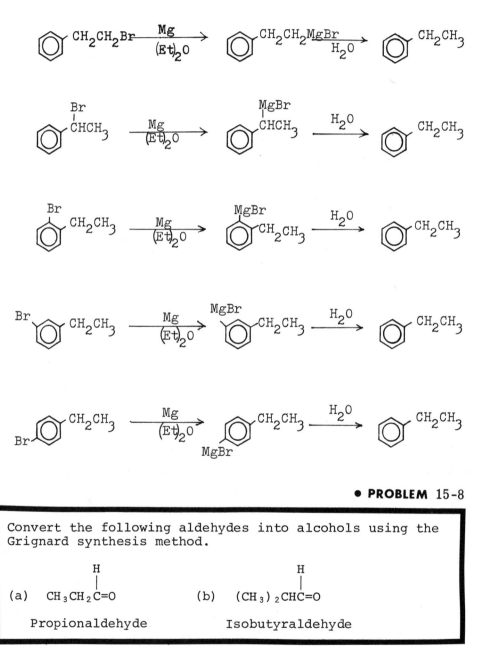

• PROBLEM 15-8

Convert the following aldehydes into alcohols using the Grignard synthesis method.

(a) $CH_3CH_2\overset{\displaystyle H}{\underset{\displaystyle |}{C}}=O$

(b) $(CH_3)_2CH\overset{\displaystyle H}{\underset{\displaystyle |}{C}}=O$

Propionaldehyde   Isobutyraldehyde

Solution: The Grignard synthesis of alcohols is done with one of the most powerful tools used by the organic

chemist, which is the Grignard reagent. The Grignard reagent, as has been shown in previous chapters, has the
formula RMgX, and is prepared by the reaction of metallic
magnesium with the appropriate organic halide. This halide
can be alkyl, allylic, benzylic, or aryl.   The halogen may
be -Cl, -Br, or I. An example of an aldehyde-Grignard
reaction is:

$$
\begin{array}{cccc}
\underset{\displaystyle |}{\overset{\displaystyle H}{}} & & \underset{\displaystyle |}{\overset{\displaystyle H}{}} & \underset{\displaystyle |}{\overset{\displaystyle H}{}} \\
H-C=O + RMgX & \longrightarrow & H-\underset{\displaystyle |}{C}-\overset{- \;+}{O}MgX & \xrightarrow{\ H_2O\ } & H-\underset{\displaystyle |}{C}-OH, \\
& & R & R
\end{array}
$$

showing formaldehyde reacting with the Grignard reagent.
This yields an intermediate that is an organic salt and the
addition of water converts the salt into an alcohol.

   With the principles above, and using the example as a
reference, the aldehydes (a) and (b) can be converted to an
alcohol by reacting with the Grignard reagent.

(a) $CH_3CH_2\overset{\displaystyle H}{\underset{\displaystyle |}{C}}=O + CH_3MgBr \rightarrow CH_3CH_2\overset{\displaystyle H}{\underset{\displaystyle |}{\underset{\displaystyle CH_3}{C}}}\overset{-\;+}{O}MgBr \xrightarrow{\ H_2O\ } CH_3CH_2\underset{\displaystyle CH_3}{\underset{\displaystyle |}{CH}}-OH$

   Propionaldehyde   2-butanol

(b) $(CH_3)_2CH\overset{\displaystyle H}{\underset{\displaystyle |}{C}}=O + CH_3CH_2MgBr \rightarrow (CH_3)_2CH\overset{\displaystyle H}{\underset{\displaystyle |}{\underset{\displaystyle CH_2}{\underset{\displaystyle |}{\underset{\displaystyle CH_3}{C}}}}}\overset{-\;+}{O}MgBr$

   Isobutyraldehyde

$\xrightarrow{\ H_2O\ }$

$$
\begin{array}{c}
CH_3 \\
\diagdown \\
\quad CHCHOH \\
\diagup \quad | \\
CH_3 \quad CH_2 \\
| \\
CH_3
\end{array}
$$

2-methyl-3-pentanol

● **PROBLEM** 15-9

An aromatic dibromide $C_7H_6Br_2$ reacted with aqueous sodium
hydroxide. The product of this reaction had lost only one
bromo group to give the product C_7H_7BrO. When the dibromide
was converted to a Grignard reagent and then hydrolyzed,
the product was toluene. Determine the structure of the
dibromide.

Solution: It is known that alkyl halides can be converted
to alcohols by hydrolysis using a nucleophilic displacement
reaction.(Note: this reaction is NOT the same as dehydrohalogenation where the sodium hydroxide is in alcohol. In
hydrolysis, the sodium hydroxide is in water.) The overall
reaction may be represented by:

$$R\text{---}X + OH^- \xrightarrow{\text{H}_2\text{O}} R\text{---}OH + X^-$$

(Alkyl halide)   (Alcohol)

The fact that the aromatic dibromide reacted indicates
that an alkyl halide group must be attached to the aromatic
(or benzene) ring. Since only 1 bromine was lost, the other
bromine must be directly bound to the aromatic ring, where
NaOH is ineffective in hydrolysis.

The alkyl halide that must be attached to the ring can
be deduced from the chemical formula, $C_7H_6Br_2$. The ring is
composed of 6 carbons, which leaves only 1 carbon to make
up the alkyl halide. Hence, the alkyl halide attached must
be CH_2Br. Recalling that the other bromine must be directly
attached to the ring, the dibromide can now be written:

(Note: the dibromide can be ortho, meta or

para.) By examining this structure, one can now understand
the Grignard reaction which will ultimately lead to toluene.

Alkyl halides and aryl halides can react with magnesium
in anhydrous ether to give alkylmagnesium halides, RMgX,
which are known as Grignard reagents. The Grignard reagents
can then be hydrolyzed by water or acid to the corresponding
hydrocarbon as shown:

$$R\text{---}MgX + HOH \rightleftharpoons R\text{---}H + MgXOH$$

(Hydrogen-
carbon)

The sequence that generated toluene can now be written:

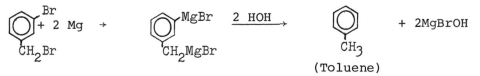

+ 2MgBrOH

(Toluene)

● **PROBLEM** 15-10

Show the product of the following ketones after addition
of the Grignard reagent.

$$\text{(a)} \quad CH_3\overset{\displaystyle O}{\overset{\|}{C}}CH_3 \qquad\qquad \text{(b)} \quad CH_3CH_2CH_2CH_2\overset{\displaystyle O}{\overset{\|}{C}}CH_3$$

Acetone   2-Hexanone

<u>Solution:</u>   The Grignard reagent has been shown in many
other chapters as an organic magnesium halide, with the
structure generally as RMgX. Of course as shown before, the
organic group does not necessarily have to be alkyl; it may
be allyl, aryl, or arenyl. The halogen (X) may be -Cl, -Br,
or -I, and the entire organic magnesium halide reacts with
ketones to yield an alcohol.

The general equation for the reaction is

$$
\underset{O}{\overset{|}{\underset{\|}{-C-}}} + RMgX \longrightarrow \underset{\overset{|}{^-}OMgX}{\overset{|}{-C-R}} \xrightarrow{H_2O} \underset{OH}{\overset{|}{-C-R}}
$$

When the Grignard reagent is added to the carbonyl
group, the double bond is broken and the intermediate is
the magnesium salt of the weakly acidic alcohol and is
easily converted into the alcohol itself by the addition
of the stronger acid, water. Sometimes a diluted solution
of H_2SO_4 or HCl is used instead of water.

With these concepts and by use of the general
equation, problems (a) and (b) can be solved.

(a) CH_3CCH_3 + $CH_3MgBr \longrightarrow CH_3\overset{\overset{-}{O}\overset{+}{M}gBr}{\underset{CH_3}{\overset{|}{C}-CH_3}}$ $\xrightarrow{H_2O}$ $CH_3\overset{OH}{\underset{CH_3}{\overset{|}{CH}-CH_3}}$

$\quad$ acetone

2-methyl-2-propanol

(b) $CH_3CH_2CH_2CH_2\overset{O}{\overset{\|}{C}}CH_3$ +$CH_3MgBr \rightarrow CH_3CH_2CH_2CH_2\overset{\overset{-}{O}\overset{+}{M}gBr}{\underset{CH_3}{\overset{|}{C}-CH_3}}$

$\quad$ 2-hexanone

$CH_3CH_2CH_2CH_2\overset{OH}{\underset{CH_3}{\overset{|}{C}CH_3}}$ $\xleftarrow{H_2O}$

2-methyl-2-hexanol

● **PROBLEM** 15-11

Synthesize a ketone from each of the following precursors
using the reaction of acid chlorides with organocadmium
compounds.

(a) $CH_3CH_2CH_2CH_2MgBr$

$\quad$ Butyl Magnesium Bromide

(b)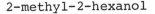

$\quad$ m-Bromotoluene

Solution: Grignard reagents react with dry cadmium
chloride to yield the corresponding organocadmium compounds,
which react with acid chlorides to yield ketones. To make
this concept clearer, the general equation for the synthesis
is:

$$2R'MgX + CdCl_2 \rightarrow R'_2Cd + 2 MgXCl \qquad\qquad \text{Balanced}$$

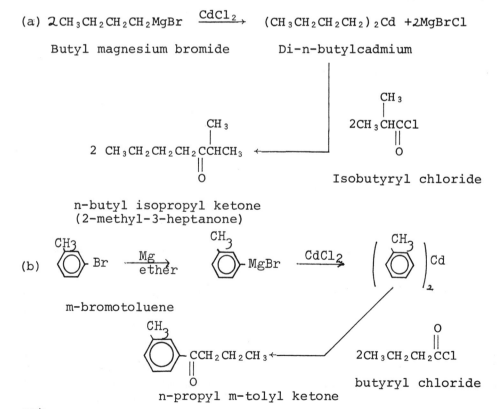

Grignard
reagent

$$2RCCl$$
$$\underset{O}{\|}$$

$$\underset{O}{\overset{O}{\|}}$$
$$\longrightarrow 2R-C-R' + CdCl_2$$
ketone

In this type of synthesis R' must be either aryl or
primary alkyl.

Only organocadmium compounds containing aryl or
primary alkyl groups are stable enough for use. Inspite
of this limitation, the method is one of the most valuable
for the synthesis of ketones.

In this ketone synthesis, (1) the Grignard reagent
reacts with cadmium chloride to yield an organocadmium
compound, plus a magnesium dihalide. (2) The organocadmium
is then reacted with an acid chloride to yield a ketone
plus cadmium chloride.

Solving problems (a) and (b) to yield a ketone:

(a) $2 CH_3CH_2CH_2CH_2MgBr \xrightarrow{CdCl_2} (CH_3CH_2CH_2CH_2)_2Cd + 2MgBrCl$

Butyl magnesium bromide   Di-n-butylcadmium

$$2CH_3\underset{|}{\overset{CH_3}{C}}HCCl$$

Isobutyryl chloride

$$2 \ CH_3CH_2CH_2CH_2\underset{\underset{O}{\|}}{\overset{CH_3}{\underset{|}{C}}}CHCH_3$$

n-butyl isopropyl ketone
(2-methyl-3-heptanone)

(b) m-bromotoluene $\xrightarrow[\text{ether}]{Mg}$ MgBr $\xrightarrow{CdCl_2}$ Cd

m-bromotoluene

$$\underset{\underset{O}{\|}}{C}CH_2CH_2CH_3$$

n-propyl m-tolyl ketone

$$2CH_3CH_2CH_2\overset{O}{\overset{\|}{C}}Cl$$

butyryl chloride

504

Propose a synthesis for n-butane from n-butylbromide using the Grignard Reaction.

<u>Solution:</u>   The Grignard reaction is a common method for synthesizing alkanes from alkyl halides. The general equations for this reaction are as follows:

(i) $R - X \xrightarrow{Mg}$ RMgX

(ii)   RMgX $\xrightarrow{HX/H_2O}$ R - H + MgX$_2$

The Grignard reagent (RMgX) is formed by treating n-butylbromide with clean magnesium in dry ether.

(iii) $CH_3(CH_2)_2CH_2-Br + Mg \xrightarrow[\text{ether}]{\text{dry}} CH_3(CH_2)_2CH_2MgBr$

The desired product, n-butane, can then be synthesized by adding HBr and H$_2$O to the Grignard reagent.

(iv) $CH_3(CH_2)_2CH_2MgBr \xrightarrow[\text{H}_2\text{O}]{\text{HBr}} CH_3(CH_2)_2CH_3 + MgBr_2$

                        n-butane

The intermediate reaction of reaction (iv) is

(v) $CH_3(CH_2)_2CH_2MgBr + HOH \rightarrow CH_3(CH_2)_2CH_3 + MgBrOH$

The bromide ion created by the dissociation of HBr then displaces the OH$^-$ group from MgBrOH to form MgBr$_2$ and water is reformed.

Write structures for the products of the following reactions involving Grignard reagents. Show the structures of both the intermediate substances and the substances obtained after hydrolysis with dilute acid. Unless otherwise specified, assume that sufficient Grignard reagent is used to cause those reactions to go to completion which occur readily at room temperatures.

(a) $C_6H_5MgBr + C_6H_5CHO$

(b) $CH_3MgI + CH_3CH_2CO_2C_2H_5$

(c) $(CH_3)_3CMgCl + CO_2$

(d) $CH_3CH_2MgBr + ClCO_2C_2H_5$

(e) $CH_3MgI + CH_3COCH_2CH_2CO_2C_2H_5$

    (1 mole)   (1 mole)

(f) $C_6H_5MgBr + CH_3O-\overset{\displaystyle O}{\overset{\displaystyle \|}{C}}-OCH_3$

<u>Solution:</u>   Grignard reagents are organomagnesium compounds of the general formula R-Mg-X (X is a halogen). The Grignard

505

reagent has two major resonance structures:

$$R'-\overset{|}{\underset{|}{C}}-MgX \leftrightarrow R'-\overset{|}{\underset{|}{C}}:^{\ominus} \ \overset{\oplus}{MgX}$$

In the presence of carbonyl compounds (compounds that have a $-\overset{O}{\overset{||}{C}}-$ in the molecule), Grignard reagents react to form an alcohol containing a side chain derived from the Grignard. The electron rich Grignard carbon attacks the electron deficient carbonyl carbon (due to oxygen's great electronegativity). The general reaction is written as:

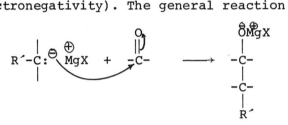

Subsequent acid catalyzed hydrolysis of this intermediate will yield the alcohol:

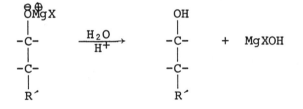

Note: If the carbonyl carbon has a potential leaving group, the group leaves to form another carbonyl compound; this is subject to further attack by the Grignard. The intermediates and hydrolysis products of reactions (a) through (f) are shown below.

(a)   In this reaction there are no potential leaving groups and an alcohol (ROH) will be formed upon hydrolysis of the Grignard salt:

$$C_6H_5MgBr + C_6H_5CHO \rightarrow C_6H_5-\underset{\underset{OMgBr}{\overset{\ominus}{\underset{|}{\oplus}}}}{\overset{|}{CH}}-C_6H_5 \xrightarrow[H^+]{H_2O} (C_6H_5)_2CHOH$$

intermediate (Grignard salt)   final product (alcohol)

(b)   The ethoxy group ($-OCH_2CH_3$) of the ester ($RCOOR'$) is a potential leaving group. When the Grignard reagent reacts with the ester, the ethoxy group leaves once the Grignard salt is formed. This produces a ketone $\left(\overset{O}{\overset{||}{RCR'}}\right)$, which will further react with the Grignard reagent. Hydrolysis will lead to a tertiary alcohol.

506

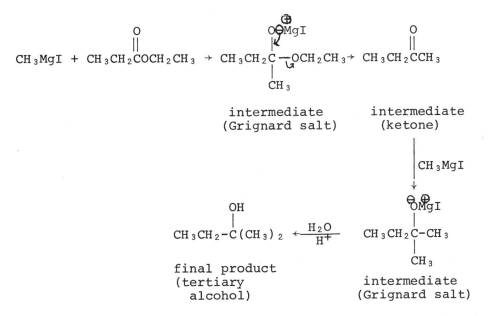

intermediate   intermediate
(Grignard salt) (ketone)

|CH₃MgI

(c) The carbon in CO_2 will be attacked by only one molecule of Grignard reagent; the remaining -C=O bond will not be disrupted by any t-butyl Grignard reagents because the subsequent carboxylate anion is inert to further nucleophilic attack.

The intermediate carboxylate salt will be hydrolyzed to a carboxylic acid (RCO_2H):

$$(CH_3)_3CMgCl + CO_2 \rightarrow (CH_3)_3C\text{-}\overset{O}{\overset{||}{C}}\text{-}\overset{\ominus\oplus}{O}MgCl \xrightarrow[H^+]{H_2O} (CH_3)_3C\text{-}\overset{O}{\overset{||}{C}}\text{-}OH$$

intermediate   final product
        (carboxylic acid)

(d) In this reaction there are two potential leaving groups: the ethoxy group ($-OCH_2CH_3$) and the chloro group ($-Cl$). When the Grignard reagent attacks the carbonyl carbon, the ethoxy group will leave first and not the chloro group; this is because the resulting ethoxide ion is more stable than the chloride ion. Another molecule of Grignard reagent will now

react with the acyl chloride $\left(R\text{-}\overset{O}{\overset{||}{C}}\text{-}Cl \right)$, and the chloride will leave. A third molecule of Grignard reagent will react with the ketone. Hydrolysis will yield a tertiary alcohol:

$$CH_3CH_2MgBr + Cl\text{-}\underset{O}{\overset{||}{C}}\text{-}OCH_2CH_3 \rightarrow CH_3CH_2\text{-}\overset{Cl}{\underset{\underset{\oplus}{O\ominus MgBr}}{C}}\text{-}OCH_2CH_3 \longrightarrow$$

intermediate (Grignard salt)

507

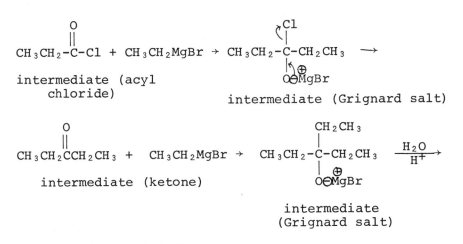

$$CH_3CH_2\text{-}\overset{\overset{\displaystyle O}{\|}}{C}\text{-}Cl \ + \ CH_3CH_2MgBr \ \rightarrow \ CH_3CH_2\text{-}\overset{\overset{\displaystyle Cl}{|}}{\underset{\underset{\displaystyle O\overset{\ominus}{}\overset{\oplus}{M}gBr}{|}}{C}}\text{-}CH_2CH_3 \ \longrightarrow$$

intermediate (acyl chloride)

intermediate (Grignard salt)

$$CH_3CH_2\overset{\overset{\displaystyle O}{\|}}{C}CH_2CH_3 \ + \ CH_3CH_2MgBr \ \rightarrow \ CH_3CH_2\text{-}\overset{\overset{\displaystyle CH_2CH_3}{|}}{\underset{\underset{\displaystyle O\overset{\ominus}{}\overset{\oplus}{M}gBr}{|}}{C}}\text{-}CH_2CH_3 \ \xrightarrow[\;H^+\;]{H_2O}$$

intermediate (ketone)

intermediate (Grignard salt)

$$(CH_3CH_2)_3C\text{-}OH$$

final product (tertiary alcohol)

(e) Since the Grignard reagent is restricted to attacking only one of the two carbonyl groups (since we are reacting one mole of Grignard with one mole of γ-ketoester), the Grignard reagent will selectively attack the keto carbon and not the ester carbon. This is because the keto carbon has a greater partial positive charge than the ester carbon. This is due to the fact that the ester portion undergoes electron delocalization (which spreads about the partial charges of the atoms involved) whereas the keto portion cannot. Hence, the nucleophilic Grignard reagent attacks the more positive keto carbon. Hydrolysis will yield the alcohol.

$$CH_3MgI \ + \ CH_3\overset{\overset{\displaystyle O}{\|}}{C}CH_2CH_2\overset{\overset{\displaystyle O}{\|}}{C}OCH_2CH_3 \ \rightarrow \ CH_3\overset{\overset{\displaystyle CH_3}{|}}{\underset{\underset{\displaystyle \overset{\ominus}{}O\overset{\oplus}{M}gI}{|}}{C}}CH_2CH_2\overset{\overset{\displaystyle O}{\|}}{C}OCH_2CH_3 \ \xrightarrow[\;H^+\;]{H_2O}$$

intermediate (Grignard salt)

$$CH_3\overset{\overset{\displaystyle CH_3}{|}}{\underset{\underset{\displaystyle OH}{|}}{C}}\text{-}CH_2CH_2\overset{\overset{\displaystyle O}{\|}}{C}OCH_2CH_3$$

final product (tertiary alcohol)

(f) Here there are two potential leaving groups of identical structure: $-OCH_3$. When the Grignard reagent attacks the carbonyl carbon, a methoxy group will leave. The carbonyl carbon will again be attacked by another molecule of Grignard reagent and the other methoxy group will leave. This ketone will be attacked by yet another molecule of Grignard reagent. Subsequent hydrolysis will yield a tertiary alcohol.

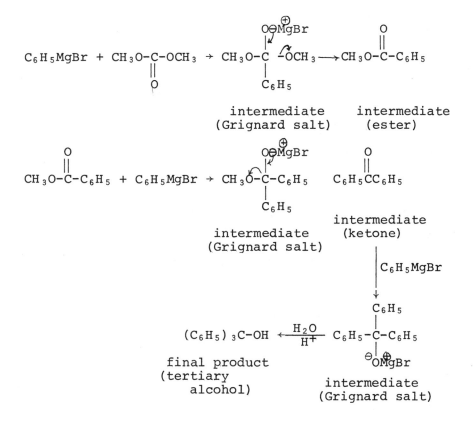

intermediate   intermediate
(Grignard salt)   (ester)

intermediate
(ketone)

C_6H_5MgBr

$(C_6H_5)_3C-OH$ $\xleftarrow[H^+]{H_2O}$ $C_6H_5-\overset{\displaystyle C_6H_5}{\underset{\displaystyle \overset{\ominus}{O}\overset{\oplus}{M}gBr}{C}}-C_6H_5$

final product
(tertiary
alcohol)

intermediate
(Grignard salt)

ORGANOLITHIUM COMPOUNDS

● **PROBLEM** 15-14

The following experimental observations have been reported:

1. t-Butyl chloride was added to lithium metal in dry ether at 35°. A vigorous reaction ensued with evolution of hydrocarbon gases. After all the lithium metal was consumed, the mixture was poured onto Dry Ice. The only acidic product which could be isolated (small yield) was 4,4-dimethylpentanoic acid.

2. t-Butyl chloride was added to lithium metal in dry ether at - 40°. After all the lithium had reacted, the mixture was carbonated and gave a good yield of trimethylacetic acid.

3. t-Butyl chloride was added to lithium metal in dry ether at - 40°. After all the lithium was gone, ethylene was bubbled through the mixture at - 40° until no further reaction occurred. Carbonation of this mixture gave a good yield of 4,4-dimethylpentanoic acid.

    a. Give a reasonably detailed analysis of the results obtained and show as best you can the mechanisms involved in each reaction.

    b. Would similar behavior be expected with methyl

chloride? Explain.

c. Would you expect that any substantial amount of
6,6-dimethylheptanoic acid would be found in (3)
(above)? Explain.

Solution: Of all the organometallic compounds only organosodium and organolithium compounds will react with ether and
have a high reactivity toward alkyl halides. Organolithium
compounds react slowly with ether and the reaction can there-
for be controlled by varying the temperature.

(a) In part (1) there are a number of reactions that occur.
Lithium metal reacts with t-butyl chloride to produce the
organolithium compound, t-butyllithium. At 35° this tertiary
organolithium compound reacts with ether (the solvent for
the reaction) at an appreciable rate by abstracting a methyl
hydrogen from the solvent.   The hydrocarbon, 2-methylpropane,
is emitted as a gas.   t-Butyllithium reacts with ethylene to
produce 3,3-dimethylbutyllithium in low yield.   When this is
reacted with Dry Ice (solid CO_2) and worked up with H_2O,
the product formed is 4,4-dimethylpentanoic acid.   The
reaction sequence and its mechanisms are shown as:

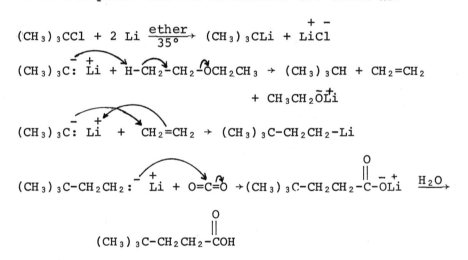

4,4-dimethylpentanoic acid

        In part (2), the reaction was conducted at -40°. At
this low temperature, organolithium compounds will not react with ether at an appreciable rate. Hence the initial
product is t-butyllithium. Carbonation of this will yield
trimethylacetic acid.

$(CH_3)_3CCl + 2\ Li \xrightarrow[-40°]{ether} (CH_3)_3C\overset{+}{-}Li + \overset{-}{Li}\ Cl$

$(CH_3)_3C:\overset{+}{Li} + O=C=O \rightarrow (CH_3)_3C-\overset{O}{\overset{||}{C}}-O\overset{+}{Li} \xrightarrow{H_2O} (CH_3)_3C-\overset{O}{\overset{||}{C}}OH$

trimethylacetic
acid

510

In part (3) t-butyllithium is first produced. It is reacted with ethylene and subsequently carbonated to yield 4,4-dimethylpentanoic acid.

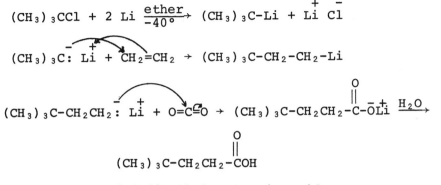

$$(CH_3)_3CCl + 2 Li \xrightarrow[-40°]{ether} (CH_3)_3C\text{-}Li + \overset{+}{Li} \overset{-}{Cl}$$

$(CH_3)_3\overset{-}{C}: \overset{+}{Li} + CH_2=CH_2 \rightarrow (CH_3)_3C\text{-}CH_2\text{-}CH_2\text{-}Li$

$(CH_3)_3C\text{-}CH_2CH_2: \overset{+}{Li} + O=C=O \rightarrow (CH_3)_3C\text{-}CH_2CH_2\overset{O}{\overset{||}{\text{-}C}}\text{-}\overset{-}{O}\overset{+}{Li} \xrightarrow{H_2O}$

$$(CH_3)_3C\text{-}CH_2CH_2\text{-}\overset{O}{\overset{||}{C}}OH$$

4,4-dimethylpentanoic acid

(b) If methyl chloride were used in part (1) instead of t-butylchloride, the organolithium compound (methyl lithium) would be formed. Methyl lithium, however, will not react with ether at 35°. The reason why tertiary organolithium compounds will react with ether whereas primary ones will not is because of the greater basicity of the former. Tertiary organolithium compounds are more basic and will be able to remove an ethereal hydrogen. The greater basicity stems from the fact that tertiary carbanions are less stable, hence more reactive, than primary carbanions. Had methyl chloride been used, the main product of part (1) would have been acetic acid.

In part (2) methyl lithium would be formed. Like t-butyllithium, methyl lithium would become carbonated. The product would be acetic acid.

In part (3) methyl lithium will again be initially formed. Unlike t-butyllithium however, methyl lithium will not react with ethylene. This is because methyl lithium is a primary organolithium compound and is less prone to attack ethylene. The product of part (3) would be acetic acid.

(c) Neohexyllithium is a primary organolithium compound and is thus much less prone to attacking ethylene than t-butyllithium. Hence, no substantial amount of 6,6-dimethyl-heptanoic acid will be formed in part (3).

REFORMATZKY REACTIONS

● **PROBLEM** 15-15

Give structures of compounds A, B and C: ethyl oxalate + ethyl acetate + sodium ethoxide, then $H^+ \rightarrow A(C_8H_{12}O_5)$
A + ethyl bromoacetate + Zn, then $H_2O \rightarrow B(C_{12}H_{20}O_7)$
B + OH^- + heat, then $H^+ \rightarrow C(C_6H_8O_7)$, citric acid.

<u>Solution:</u>   When two different esters (one having an α-

hydrogen and the other lacking α-hydrogen) are reacted in the presence of a base such as an alkoxide salt (M^+OR^-), a crossed Claisen condensation reaction will take

place. An ester has the general formula $R-\overset{\overset{\displaystyle O}{\|}}{C}-OR'$. Both ethyl oxalate and ethyl acetate are esters. In basic solution ethyl acetate will lose its α-hydrogen to form a resonance stabilized enolate anion.

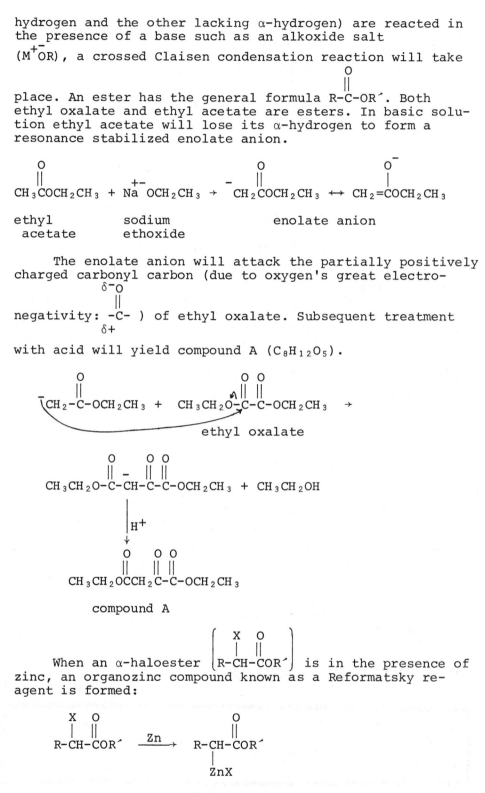

$$CH_3\overset{\overset{\displaystyle O}{\|}}{C}OCH_2CH_3 + Na^+\ ^-OCH_2CH_3 \rightarrow\ ^-CH_2\overset{\overset{\displaystyle O}{\|}}{C}OCH_2CH_3 \leftrightarrow CH_2=\overset{\overset{\displaystyle O^-}{|}}{C}OCH_2CH_3$$

ethyl   sodium   enolate anion
  acetate   ethoxide

    The enolate anion will attack the partially positively charged carbonyl carbon (due to oxygen's great electro-

negativity: $-\overset{\overset{\displaystyle \delta^-O}{\|}}{\underset{\delta^+}{C}}-$) of ethyl oxalate. Subsequent treatment

with acid will yield compound A $(C_8H_{12}O_5)$.

$$^-CH_2-\overset{\overset{\displaystyle O}{\|}}{C}-OCH_2CH_3 + CH_3CH_2O-\overset{\overset{\displaystyle O}{\|}}{C}-\overset{\overset{\displaystyle O}{\|}}{C}-OCH_2CH_3 \rightarrow$$

                           ethyl oxalate

$$CH_3CH_2O-\overset{\overset{\displaystyle O}{\|}}{C}-\overset{-}{C}H-\overset{\overset{\displaystyle O}{\|}}{C}-\overset{\overset{\displaystyle O}{\|}}{C}-OCH_2CH_3 + CH_3CH_2OH$$

$$\Big\downarrow H^+$$

$$CH_3CH_2O\overset{\overset{\displaystyle O}{\|}}{C}CH_2\overset{\overset{\displaystyle O}{\|}}{C}-\overset{\overset{\displaystyle O}{\|}}{C}-OCH_2CH_3$$

      compound A

    When an α-haloester $\left(\overset{\overset{\displaystyle X\ O}{|\ \ \|}}{R-CH-COR'}\right)$ is in the presence of zinc, an organozinc compound known as a Reformatsky reagent is formed:

$$\overset{\overset{\displaystyle X\ \ O}{|\ \ \ \|}}{R-CH-COR'} \xrightarrow{\ Zn\ } \overset{\overset{\displaystyle O}{\|}}{\underset{\underset{\displaystyle ZnX}{|}}{R-CH-COR'}}$$

      Reformatsky reagent

Reformatsky reagents react with aldehydes $\left(\begin{array}{c}O \\ \| \\ R-C-H\end{array}\right)$ and

ketones $\left(\begin{array}{c}O \\ \| \\ R-C-R\acute{}\end{array}\right)$ to form β-hydroxy esters $\left(\begin{array}{c}OH \quad O \\ | \quad | \; \| \\ R"-CH-C-COR\acute{}\end{array}\right)$

after subsequent hydrolysis. Compound A is a polyfunctional compound and can be viewed as a ketone. When ethyl bromoacetate is in the presence of zinc, the Reformatsky reagent will be formed; it will react with compound A to produce a β-hydroxyester derivative.

$$
\underset{\substack{\text{ethyl bromo} \\ \text{acetate}}}{\overset{O}{\underset{}{BrCH_2\overset{\|}{C}OCH_2CH_3}}} \xrightarrow{\;Zn\;} \underset{\substack{\text{Reformatsky} \\ \text{reagent}}}{\overset{O}{\underset{}{BrZnCH_2\overset{\|}{C}OCH_2CH_3}}}
$$

Reformatsky reagents (and organozinc compounds in general) are less reactive than organomagnesium compounds. As a result Reformatsky reagents will not add to esters.

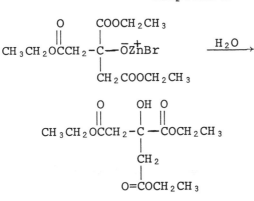

compound A

compound B $(C_{12}H_{20}O_7)$

Compound B has three ester functionalities (-COOR)

and one alcohol functionality $\left(\begin{array}{c}| \\ -C-OH \\ |\end{array}\right)$. Esters will undergo

base catalyzed hydrolysis to yield the corresponding carboxylic acids (R-COOH).

$$\underset{\text{ester}}{\overset{\overset{\textstyle O}{\|}}{R\text{-}C\text{-}OR'}} \quad \xrightarrow[H_2O]{OH^-} \quad \underset{\substack{\text{carboxylic} \\ \text{acid}}}{\overset{\overset{\textstyle O}{\|}}{R\text{-}C\text{-}OH}} \quad + \quad \underset{\text{alcohol}}{R'OH}$$

The carboxylic acid will lose a proton in basic solution:

$$\overset{\overset{\textstyle O}{\|}}{R\text{-}COH} \quad + \quad {}^-OH \quad \rightarrow \quad H_2O \quad + \quad \underset{\text{carboxylate ion}}{\overset{\overset{\textstyle O}{\|}}{R\text{-}C\text{-}O^-}}$$

Alcohols also become deprotonated in basic solution:

$$R'OH \quad + \quad {}^-OH \quad \rightarrow \quad H_2O \quad + \quad \underset{\text{alkoxide ion}}{RO^-}$$

Subsequent acidification will replace all lost protons. Compound B reacts with ^-OH and heat, then with H^+ in the following manner:

$$\underset{\text{compound B}}{\overset{\displaystyle COOCH_2CH_3}{\underset{\displaystyle CH_2COOCH_2CH_3}{HO\text{-}\overset{|}{\underset{|}{C}}\text{-}CH_2COOCH_2CH_3}}} \quad \xrightarrow[H_2O]{^-OH} \quad \xrightarrow{H^+}$$

$$\overset{\displaystyle COOH}{\underset{\displaystyle CH_2COOH}{HO\text{-}\overset{|}{\underset{|}{C}}\text{-}CH_2COOH}} \quad + \quad 3\ CH_3CH_2OH$$

$$\begin{pmatrix} \text{compound C } (C_6H_8O_7) \\ \text{Citric acid} \end{pmatrix}$$

● **PROBLEM** 15-16

Outline the synthesis of the following acids via the Reformatsky reaction:

(a) n-valeric acid; (b) α,γ-dimethylvaleric acid; (c) cinnamic acid.

Solution: (a) n-Valeric acid has the structure: $CH_3CH_2CH_2CH_2COOH$. The Reformatsky reaction is one that occurs between an organozinc compound derived from an α-haloester and an aldehyde or ketone to form a β-hydroxyester. By working backwards, we can devise a method of preparing n-valeric acid by using the Reformatsky reaction. n-Valeric acid can be gotten by the acid catalyzed hydrolysis of ethyl pentanoate, an ester of n-valeric acid. A β-hydroxy-ester of n-valeric acid is β-hydroxyethylvalerate. This can be dehydrated and subsequently hydrogenated to give ethyl-pentanoate. β-hydroxyethylvalerate can be prepared by the Reformatsky reaction between ethyl bromoacetate and propanal. Hence the synthesis of n-valeric acid can be shown as:

$$BrCH_2COOCH_2CH_3 \quad + \quad CH_3CH_2-\overset{\overset{\textstyle O}{\|}}{C}-H \quad \xrightarrow{Zn}$$

ethyl bromoacetate   propanal

$$Br\overset{+}{Z}n\overset{-}{O}-\underset{\underset{\textstyle CH_2COOCH_2CH_3}{|}}{\overset{\overset{\textstyle CH_2CH_3}{|}}{C}}-H \quad \xrightarrow{H_2O} \quad HO-\underset{\underset{\textstyle CH_2COOCH_2CH_3}{|}}{\overset{\overset{\textstyle CH_2CH_3}{|}}{C}}-H$$

β-hydroxyethylvalerate

$$HO-\underset{\underset{\textstyle CH_2COOCH_2CH_3}{|}}{\overset{\overset{\textstyle CH_2CH_3}{|}}{C}}-H \quad \xrightarrow{-H_2O} \quad \xrightarrow{H_2/Ni} \quad CH_3CH_2CH_2CH_2-\overset{\overset{\textstyle CH_3CH_2O}{|}}{C}=O$$

β-hydroxyethylvalerate   ethyl pentanoate

$$\Big\downarrow H_2O/H^+$$

$$CH_3CH_2CH_2CH_2COOH$$

n-valeric acid

(b)   α,γ-dimethylvaleric acid has the structure: $CH_3CHCH_2CHCOOH$. Like n-valeric acid, this compound can

with CH_3 and CH_3 substituents

be synthesized by the sequence: Reformatsky reaction, dehydration, catalytic hydrogenation and hydrolysis. Here the Reformatsky reaction is between 2-methylpropanal and ethyl-α-bromopropionate. The reactions are shown as:

$$CH_3\underset{\underset{\textstyle Br}{|}}{CH}COOCH_2CH_3 \quad + \quad (CH_3)_2CH\overset{\overset{\textstyle O}{\|}}{C}H \quad \xrightarrow{Zn}$$

$$Br\overset{+}{Z}n\overset{-}{O}-\underset{\underset{\underset{\textstyle COOCH_2CH_3}{|}}{\overset{\textstyle CH_3-CH}{|}}}{\overset{\overset{\textstyle H}{|}}{C}}-CH(CH_3)_2 \quad \xrightarrow{H_2O} \quad HO-\underset{\underset{\underset{\textstyle COOCH_2CH_3}{|}}{\overset{\textstyle CH_3-CH}{|}}}{\overset{\overset{\textstyle H}{|}}{C}}-CH(CH_3)_2$$

ethyl-β-hydroxy-α,γ-dimethylvalerate

515

$$\downarrow - H_2O$$

$$\downarrow \quad H_2/Ni$$

$$(CH_3)_2CHCH_2CHCOOCH_2CH_3$$
$$|$$
$$CH_3$$

ethyl-α,γ-dimethylvalerate

$$\downarrow \quad H_2O/H^+$$

$$CH_3CHCH_2CHCOOH$$
$$| \qquad |$$
$$CH_3 \quad CH_3$$

α,γ-dimethylvaleric acid

(c)   Cinnamic acid has the structure: $C_6H_5CH=CHCOOH$. By the same reasoning in part (a), we should look for reactants that, in a Reformatsky reaction, would form a β-hydroxyester of 3-phenylpropanoic acid ($C_6H_5CH_2CH_2COOH$). Ethyl-β-hydroxy-β-phenylpropionate is produced by the Reformatsky reaction between ethylbromoacetate and benzaldehyde. As in part (a), and (b), the β-hydroxyester will lose water to form the alkene. Unlike part (a) and (b), however, we will not perform a catalytic hydrogenation because we want to retain the carbon-carbon double bond. Subsequent acid catalyzed hydrolysis of the ester will lead to the desired product. The reactions are shown as:

$$\overset{\displaystyle O}{\overset{\displaystyle \|}{C_6H_5C-H}} \quad + \quad BrCH_2COOCH_2CH_3 \quad \xrightarrow{\quad Zn \quad}$$

$$\overset{\displaystyle H}{\overset{\displaystyle |}{Br\overset{+}{Z}n\overset{-}{O}-C-C_6H_5}} \quad \xrightarrow{\quad H_2O \quad}$$
$$|$$
$$CH_2COOCH_2CH_3$$

$$\overset{\displaystyle H}{\overset{\displaystyle |}{HO-C-C_6H_5}}$$
$$|$$
$$CH_2COOCH_2CH_3$$

ethyl-β-hydroxy-β-phenyl-propionate

$$\downarrow - H_2O$$

$$C_6H_5-CH=CHCOOCH_2CH_3 \quad \xrightarrow{\quad H_2O/H^+ \quad}$$

$$C_6H_5-CH=CH-COOH$$

cinnamic acid

CHAPTER 16

ALCOHOLS

NOMENCLATURE AND STRUCTURE

What are alcohols and how are they classified?

Solution: Alcohols are hydrocarbon derivatives in which one or more hydrogen atoms have been replaced by the OH (hydroxyl) group. There are many different alcohols, which are either natural or synthetic derivatives of other hydrocarbons. To be more specific, there are:

   I. Monohydroxy Alcohols
      A. Primary
      B. Secondary
      C. Tertiary

  II. Dihydroxy Alcohols

 III. Trihydroxy Alcohols

  IV. Polyhydroxy Alcohols

The monohydroxy alcohols are represented by the general formula R-OH or C_nH_{2n+1} OH.

Specific examples of each are:

Primary $CH_3CH_2CH_2CH_2OH$ 1-Butanol (butyl alcohol)

Secondary $CH_3CH_2CH-CH_3$ 2-Butanol (sec-butyl alcohol)
                           |
                          OH

                   CH_3
                    |
Tertiary CH_3-C-CH_3 2-metyhyl-2-propanol
                    | (tert-butyl alcohol)
                   OH

Dihydroxy and trihydroxy alcohols have two and three hydroxyl groups respectively, on their hydrocarbon molecule. For example:

(a) CH_2-CH_2 1,2-ethanediol (ethylene glycol)
      | | "Dihydroxy Alcohol"
     OH   OH

(b) CH_2-OH 1,2,3-Propanetriol (glycerol)
      | "Trihydroxy Alcohol"
     CH-OH
      |
     CH_2-OH

These alcohols that contain more than one hydroxyl group may be represented by the general formula C_nH_{2n+2-y} (OH)$_y$, where y is two or more. The common poly-hydroxy alcohols usually have one "OH" group on every carbon atom in the molecule.

● PROBLEM 16-2

Name the following alcohols using the IUPAC system of nomenclature:

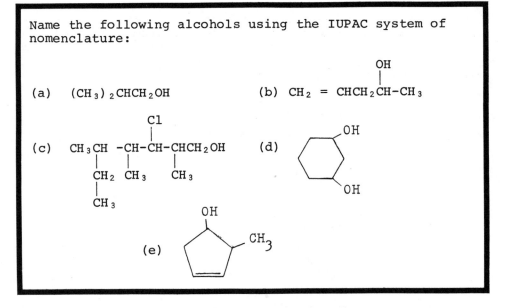

(a) $(CH_3)_2CHCH_2OH$ (b) $CH_2 = CHCH_2\overset{\overset{\displaystyle OH}{|}}{CH}-CH_3$

(c) $CH_3CH-CH-CHCH_2OH$ (d)

(e)

Solution: An alcohol is named as a derivative of the longest continuous carbon chain containing the ⁻OH group. The chain is numbered so as to give the hydroxyl group the lowest number, and the positions of substituents are in-dicated by number. The -ol ending is added to designate an ⁻OH group. For cyclic compounds, the same rules hold true; thus the first carbon number in the ring is the one which possesses the hydroxyl functional group. With these rules in mind, the alcohol compounds can be named.

(a) $(CH_3)_2CHCH_2OH$ 2-methyl-1-propanol

(b) $CH_2 = CHCH_2\overset{\overset{\displaystyle OH}{|}}{CH}-CH_3$ 4-penten-2-ol

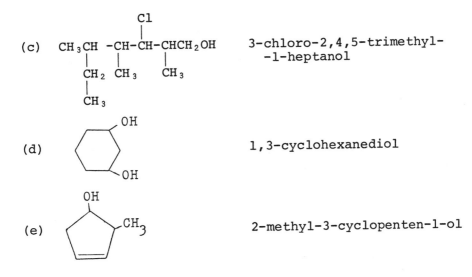

(c) $CH_3CH-CH-CH-CHCH_2OH$ 3-chloro-2,4,5-trimethyl-
                                                  -1-heptanol

(d)   1,3-cyclohexanediol

(e)   2-methyl-3-cyclopenten-1-ol

● **PROBLEM** 16-3

Give each of the following structures IUPAC names:

(a) $(CH_3)_2CHOH$; (b) $(CH_3)_3C-CHOH-CH_3$;

(c) $CH_3-CH_2-CHOH-CH_3$; (d) $CH_3-CH_2COH(CH_3)_2$;

(e) $\text{⟨⟩}-CH_2-CH_2-OH$; (f) $Cl-CH_2-CH_2-CH_2-OH$.

Solution: The hydroxyl group ⁻OH is a frequently
occurring functional group, both in naturally occurring
and in synthetic compounds. When an organic molecule consists of an alkyl group bonded to a hydroxyl group, the
compound is called an alcohol.

      Complicated alcohols are usually named systematically
by the IUPAC system. In the IUPAC system the parent compound
name is found by dropping the alkane ending "e" and adding
the suffix "ol". In long chain alcohols the position of the
hydroxyl group is specified by the appropriate number, just
as is done with alkenes.

      As an example of the IUPAC system of naming alcohols,
the following alcohol (figure A) will be named systematically:

       1   2 3   4 5   6 7   8

                CH_3 Br

$CH_3CHCH_2CCH_2CHCH_2CH_3$

         CH_3 OH

       Figure A.

      1. The longest chain containing the hydroxyl group has
eight carbons; the compound is an octanol.

519

2. The chain is numbered from either side so that the
hydroxyl group is on the lowest possible number; the hydroxyl
group is on the 4 position and the parent name is 4-octanol.

3. Substituents are given the number of the carbon to
which they are attached; the substituents are 2,4-dimethyl
and 6-bromo.

4. Listing the substituents alphabetically, the correct
name of the compound is 6-bromo-2,4-dimethyl-4-octanol.

To name the given compounds, first draw the structure
of each and then name the compound using the IUPAC system.

(a)   (CH₃)₂CHOH is shown in figure B.

$$\begin{array}{ccc} 1 & 2 & 3 \\ C\text{-}C & \text{-}C \end{array}$$
|
OH

figure B.

This structure has been drawn without the accompanying
hydrogen atoms, however, the name of the compound will not
be in any way affected by their deletion. This compound has
a three carbon parent chain and the -OH group on the second
carbon; thus, the name of this compound is 2-propanol.

(b)   (CH₃)₃C-CHOH-CH₃ is shown in figure C.

figure C.

This compound has a four-carbon parent chain with
2 methyl groups on carbon three and the ⁻OH group on
carbon 2; thus, the name of this compound is 3,3-dimethyl-
2-butanol.

(c)   CH₃-CH₂-CHOH-CH₃ is shown in figure D.

C-C-C -C
|
OH

figure D.

This compound has a four-carbon parent chain with
the ⁻OH group on carbon 2; thus, the name of this compound is 2-butanol.

(d)   CH₃-CH₂COH(CH₃)₂ is shown in figure E.

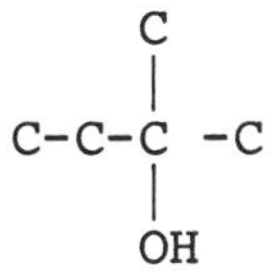

```
          C
          |
    C-C-C -C
          |
          OH
```

figure E.

This compound has a 4-carbon parent chain with the methyl and the ⁻OH groups on carbon 2; thus, the name of the compound is 2-methyl-2-butanol.

(e) -CH₂-CH₂-OH   is shown in figure F.

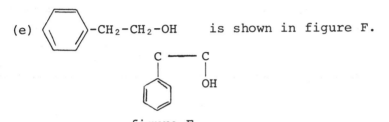

figure F.
This compound has a 2-carbon parent chain with the ⁻OH group on carbon 1 and the benzene ring on carbon 2; thus the name of this compound is 2-phenyl-1-ethanol.

(f) Cl-CH₂-CH₂-CH₂-OH   is shown in figure G.

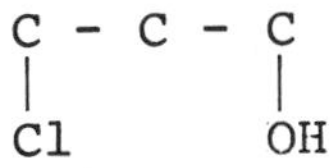

```
     C - C - C
     |       |
     Cl      OH
```
Figure G.

This compound has a 3-carbon parent chain with the ⁻OH group on carbon 1 and a chlorine atom on carbon 3; thus the name of this compound is 3-chloro-1-propanol.

● **PROBLEM** 16-4

Explain how the following alcohols are named using the IUPAC system of nomenclature:

(a)   CH₃CH₂OH   (b) CH₃CH-CH₃   (c) CH₃CH₂CH CH-CH₃
                              | | |
                              OH   OH OH

Solution: Alcohols like all other hydrocarbons have a common name, and an IUPAC name which is derived from its parent hydrocarbon chain, its functional groups and their positions. The IUPAC nomenclature for the alcohols re-places the final "-e" of the hydrocarbon name by "-ol" and prefixes a numeral to indicate the position of the hydroxyl group. When there are two or three hydroxyl (OH) groups on the chain, the suffixes di and tri respectively are added before the -ol moiety.

(a)   CH₃CH₂OH   ethanol (ethyl alcohol)

(b) 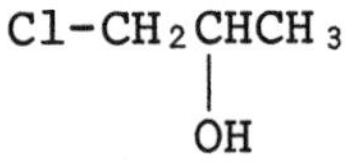   Cl-CH$_2$CHCH$_3$ 1-chloro-2-propanol
        |
        OH

(c) 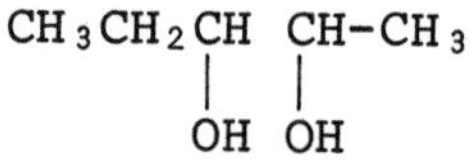   CH$_3$CH$_2$CH CH-CH$_3$ 2,3-pentanediol
        | |
        OH OH

PHYSICAL PROPERTIES

How do you account for the fact that, although ethyl ether
has a much lower boiling point than n-butyl alcohol, it
has the same solubility (8 g per 100 g) in water?

Solution: Examination of the structures of ethyl ether
and n-butyl alcohol shows that they are isomers; they are
different compounds with the same molecular formula (C$_4$H$_{10}$O)

CH$_3$CH$_2$CH$_2$CH$_2$OH   CH$_3$CH$_2$OCH$_2$CH$_3$
n-butyl alcohol   ethyl ether

A consideration of what factors influence boiling
points and solubility will aid in the solution to this
problem.
Associated liquids are ones whose molecules are held
together by hydrogen bonds. It takes considerable energy
to break these hydrogen bonds. Hence, the boiling point is
raised by hydrogen bonding between like molecules of a compound. It can be seen from the structure of n-butyl alcohol, that the alcohol molecules can form hydrogen bonds
to each other and to water molecules. The ether can form
hydrogen bonds to only the water, however. The situation
is depicted below:

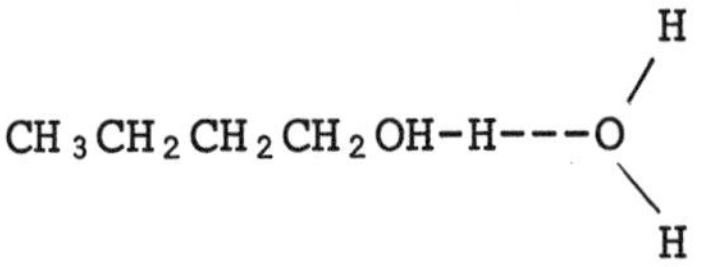

                                    H
                                   /
CH$_3$CH$_2$CH$_2$CH$_2$OH-H---O   ⇐ H-bonding with water 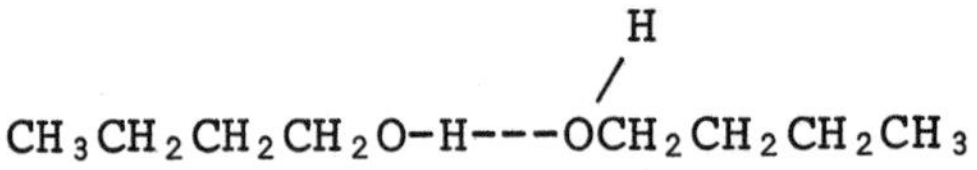
                                   \
                                    H

                             H
                            /
CH$_3$CH$_2$CH$_2$CH$_2$O-H---OCH$_2$CH$_2$CH$_2$CH$_3$ ⇐ H bonding to each
                                                    other

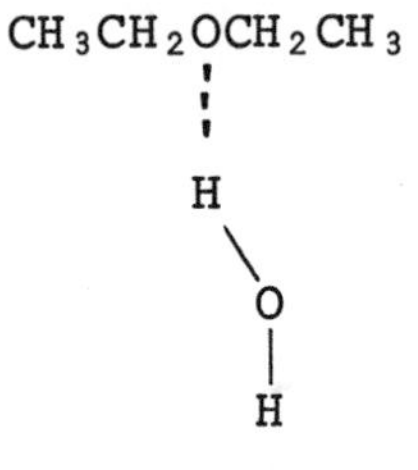

CH$_3$CH$_2$OCH$_2$CH$_3$ ⇐ H-bonding with water only.
        ┆
        ┆
    H
     \
      O
      |
      H

This means the ether must have the lower boiling point. The boiling point is determined, in part, by the hydrogen bonding between (like) molecules, which the ether lacks. This also explains why the alcohol and ether have the same solubility. Solubility reflects and is increased by hydrogen bonding between solute molecules and solvent molecules. In this case, the solute is either the alcohol or ether and the solvent is water. As shown above, both the alcohol and ether may participate in hydrogen bonding with water equally well. Hence, they should possess the same solubility.

● **PROBLEM** 16-6

It has been suggested that there is a weak hydrogen bonding: (a) between chloroform molecules; (b) between HCN molecules. How would you account for this?

<u>Solution</u>:   Hydrogen bonding generally occurs between an electronegative atom and a hydrogen bonded to another electronegative atom (usually N or O). Hydrogen bonding is actually the electrostatic attraction between the partially positively charged hydrogen and the partially negatively charged electronegative atom. For example, water undergoes hydrogen bonding as shown:

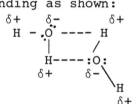

Note: Dotted lines indicate H-bonding.

(a)   The inductive effect of the chlorine atoms in chloroform ($HCCl_3$) makes the molecule highly polar. The three electron withdrawing chlorine atoms makes the carbon and hydrogen atoms electron deficient. As a result, the chlorines have a partial negative charge and the carbon and hydrogen have a partial positive charge:

$$
\begin{array}{c}
\delta- \\
Cl \\
\uparrow \\
Cl \leftarrow C \rightarrow H \\
\downarrow \\
Cl \\
\delta-
\end{array}
$$

Because the molecule is highly polar, the hydrogen has enough of a positive charge to have a weak electrostatic attraction for the partially negatively charged chlorine of another chloroform molecule. Hence there is weak hydrogen bonding in chloroform. This can be shown as:

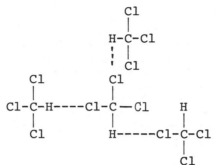

(b)   The carbon atom of hydrogen cyanide (HCN) is sp-hybridized and this will make the hydrogen more electro-positive than an sp^2 or sp^3 hybridized carbon. (Recall that sp-hybridized carbons are more electronegative than sp^2-hybridized carbons, which are more electronegative than sp^3-hybridized carbons.) This plus the fact that nitrogen is an electronegative atom will give hydrogen in

HCN a partial positive charge $\left(\begin{array}{c} \delta- \quad\leftarrow\!\!+\quad \delta+ \\ N \equiv C - H \end{array} \right)$. A combination of these two effects will be strong enough for the forma-tion of hydrogen bonding between nitrogen and hydrogen.

The hydrogen bonds will be weak ones because the hydrogen in HCN is not as positively charged as it would have been, had it been bonded to an electronegative atom such as oxygen or nitrogen. The H-bonding in HCN can be shown as:

$$:N\equiv C-H --- :N\equiv C-H$$
$$:N\equiv C-H --- :N\equiv C-H$$

PREPARATION

● **PROBLEM** 16-7

What are the various methods of preparing alcohols?

<u>Solution:</u>   There are many ways of preparing alcohols through organic reactions, although when one thinks of alcohol preparation, they immediately assume anaerobic sugar fermentation. As yet, it is not possible to introduce hydroxyl groups directly into alkanes, and all synthetic reactions of alcohols start from compounds containing re-active functional groups. The most common methods of pre-paring alcohols are as follows:

(1) Hydration of olefins in the presence of acid.

(2) Hydrolysis of alkyl halides by water or alkali.

(3) Hydrolysis of ethers in strongly acidic conditions.

(4) Hydrolysis of esters

(a) acid catalyzed hydrolysis

(b) alkaline hydrolysis (saponification)

(5) Reduction or catalytic hydrogenation of aldehydes, ketones, carboxylic acids, and esters.

Each of these methods will be explained in detail with many examples as the chapter progresses.

● **PROBLEM** 16-8

Predict the products of each precursor by the hydration of olefins method.

(a) $CH_3CH = CH_2$ (b) $CH_2 = CH_2$

Propylene   Ethene

Solution: Olefins (alkenes) are readily converted into alcohols either by direct addition of water, or by addition of sulfuric acid followed by hydrolysis. The general reaction for this method of preparation is:

$$RCH = CHR + H_2SO_4 \rightarrow RCH-CH_2R + H_2O \rightarrow RCH-CH_2R.$$
$$\qquad\qquad\qquad\qquad OSO_3H \qquad\qquad\qquad OH$$

The addition of H_2SO_4 changes the alkene precursor into alkyl hydrogen sulfate, which is an intermediate in this reaction. This intermediate is hydrated with water which yields an alcohol. From this, the products of precursors (a) and (b) can be obtained by hydration in an acid medium.

(a) $CH_3-CH=CH_2 + H_2SO_4 \rightarrow CH_3CHCH_3 \xrightarrow{H_2O} CH_3CHCH_3$
$$\qquad\qquad\qquad\qquad\qquad\qquad OSO_3H \qquad\qquad OH$$

   Propylene   Isopropanol

(b) $CH_2=CH_2 + H_2SO_4 \rightarrow CH_3-CH_2OSO_3H \xrightarrow{H_2O} CH_3CH_2OH$

   Ethylene   Ethanol
                                                (ethyl alcohol)

● **PROBLEM** 16-9

Show the product of each compound by hydrolysis of alkyl halides:

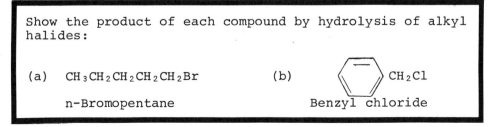

(a) $CH_3CH_2CH_2CH_2CH_2Br$ (b) CH_2Cl

   n-Bromopentane   Benzyl chloride

Solution: This method of preparing an alcohol can be done by adding a concentrated aqueous alkali to the reactant and reflux the mixture. The alkali usually used is sodium hydroxide (NaOH) or potassium hydroxide (KOH) in which the -OH group replaces the halogen on the molecule. The general reaction for this is:

$$RX \quad + \quad KOH \text{ (aqueous)} \rightarrow R - OH \quad + \quad K^+ X^-.$$

Alkyl Halide   Alkyl Alcohol

The R shows the alkyl functional group, and the X signifies the halogen (Br or Cl). With the above facts in mind, the products of the two precursors can be derived by hydrolysis.

(a) $CH_3CH_2CH_2CH_2CH_2Br \xrightarrow{\text{NaOH (aqueous)}} CH_3CH_2CH_2CH_2CH_2OH +$

n-Bromopentane   n-Pentanol

$$+ \overset{+}{Na} \overset{-}{Br}$$

(b) 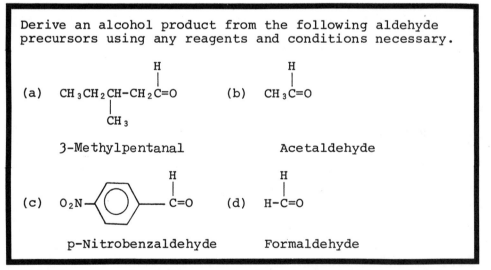 CH_2Cl + KOH (aqueous) →

Benzyl chloride

CH_2OH +

Benzyl alcohol

$$+ K^+ Cl^- .$$

● **PROBLEM** 16-10

Derive an alcohol product from the following aldehyde precursors using any reagents and conditions necessary.

(a) $CH_3CH_2CH-CH_2\overset{\overset{\textstyle H}{|}}{C}=O$
          |
          CH_3

(b) $CH_3\overset{\overset{\textstyle H}{|}}{C}=O$

3-Methylpentanal

Acetaldehyde

(c) $O_2N-\underset{}{\bigcirc}-\overset{\overset{\textstyle H}{|}}{C}=O$

(d) $H-\overset{\overset{\textstyle H}{|}}{C}=O$

p-Nitrobenzaldehyde

Formaldehyde

Solution: Obtaining an alcohol from aldehydes involves aldehyde reduction or catalytic hydrogenation. Reduction involves the use of a strong reducing agent such as lithium aluminum hydride ($LiAlH_4$); alcohols are formed easily and in high yield. Another extremely useful reducing agent is sodium borohydride, $NaBH_4$, but this reagent is limited to the extent that it does not reduce compounds containing carbon-carbon double bonds. Both of these reagents must react in the presence of an acid, either HCl (hydrochloric acid), or acetic acid.

Another method for reducing aldehydes to alcohols is catalytic hydrogenation, which employs the use of hydrogen, and finely divided nickel, palladium, or platinum catalyst.

The general reactions for both of these processes are:

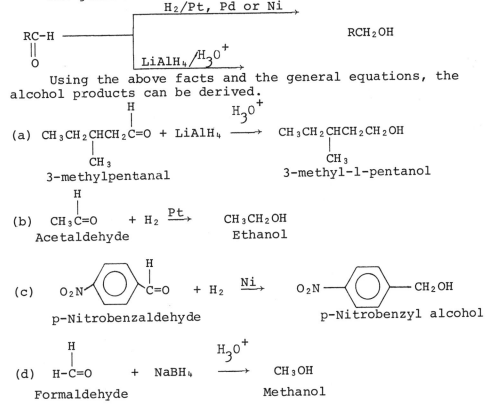

$$RC-H \xrightarrow{\quad H_2/Pt, \ Pd \ or \ Ni \quad} RCH_2OH$$

Using the above facts and the general equations, the alcohol products can be derived.

(a) $CH_3CH_2CHCH_2C=O$ + $LiAlH_4$ $\xrightarrow{H_3O^+}$ $CH_3CH_2CHCH_2CH_2OH$

3-methylpentanal   3-methyl-1-pentanol

(b) $CH_3C=O$ + H_2 $\xrightarrow{Pt}$ CH_3CH_2OH
Acetaldehyde   Ethanol

(c) O_2N⟨⟩$C=O$ + H_2 $\xrightarrow{Ni}$ O_2N—⟨⟩—CH_2OH
p-Nitrobenzaldehyde   p-Nitrobenzyl alcohol

(d) $H-C=O$ + $NaBH_4$ $\xrightarrow{H_3O^+}$ CH_3OH
Formaldehyde   Methanol

● PROBLEM 16-11

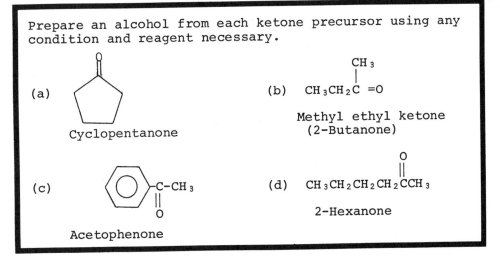

Prepare an alcohol from each ketone precursor using any condition and reagent necessary.

(a) Cyclopentanone

(b) $CH_3CH_2C=O$ with CH_3 group
Methyl ethyl ketone
(2-Butanone)

(c) ⟨⟩$-C-CH_3$
Acetophenone

(d) $CH_3CH_2CH_2CH_2CCH_3$
2-Hexanone

527

Solution: When preparing an alcohol from a ketone,
essentially, the same reaction occurs as with aldehydes.
The difference with ketones is that its carbonyl (C=O)
moiety or functional group is usually between two groups
(alkyl and/or aryl). The reagents used to convert a ketone
to an alcohol is LiAlH₄ (lithium aluminum hydride), or
NaBH₄ (sodium borohydride); and both must be used in
acidic conditions. The acids used are hydrochloric acid or
acetic acid.

    Another way to produce an alcohol from a ketone is
to reduce the ketone by catalytic hydrogenation. This
method involves the use of hydrogen gas with a nickel (Ni),
platinum (Pt), or palladium (Pd), catalyst.

    The general equations for both methods are:

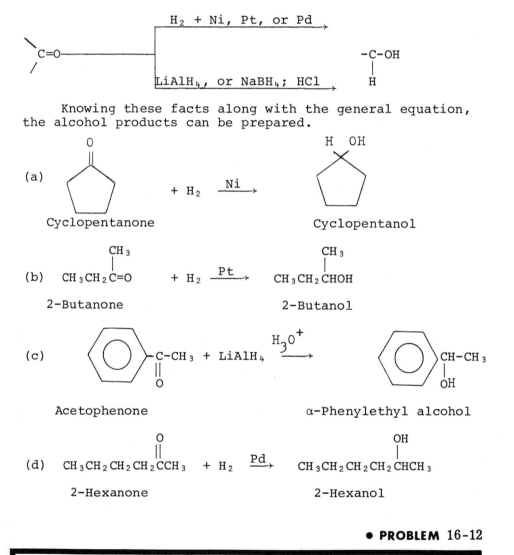

    Knowing these facts along with the general equation,
the alcohol products can be prepared.

(a) Cyclopentanone   + H₂ —Ni→   Cyclopentanol

(b) CH₃CH₂C=O (with CH₃) 2-Butanone   + H₂ —Pt→   CH₃CH₂CHOH (with CH₃) 2-Butanol

(c) Acetophenone C-CH₃ + LiAlH₄ —H₃O⁺→   α-Phenylethyl alcohol CH-CH₃ / OH

(d) CH₃CH₂CH₂CH₂CCH₃ 2-Hexanone + H₂ —Pd→   CH₃CH₂CH₂CH₂CHCH₃ (OH) 2-Hexanol

● PROBLEM 16-12

Prepare an alcohol from each carboxylic acid precursor
given, using any condition and/or reagent necessary.

528

(a) $(CH_3)_3CCOOH$

Trimethylacetic
acid

(b)

$$\text{COOH}$$

m-Toluic acid

Solution: Lithium aluminum hydride, $LiAlH_4$, is one of the few reagents that can reduce a carboxylic acid to an alcohol; the initial product is an alkoxide from which the alcohol is liberated by hydrolysis. The general reaction for this process:

$$4\,RCOOH + 3LiAlH_4 \rightarrow 4H_2 + 2LiAlO_2 + (RCH_2O)_4\,AlLi \xrightarrow{H_2O}$$

$$4\,RCH_2OH$$

In this type of reaction, the intermediate, an alkyl oxide (alkoxide) is the major product, but as seen above lithium aluminum hydride is oxidized to $LiAlO_2$. The intermediate is then protonated through hydrolysis to yield an alcohol.

From these facts and the general equation the alcohol products of the given carboxylic acid can be prepared.

Trimethylacetic acid

(a) $4\,(CH_3)_3CCOOH + 3LiAlH_4 \rightarrow [(CH_3)_3CCH_2O]_4AlLi +$

$$2\ LiAlO_2 + 4H_2 \xrightarrow{H^+} (CH_3)_3CCH_2OH$$

Neopentyl alcohol
(2,2-dimethyl-1-propanol)

(b)

$$\text{COOH}$$

m-Toluic acid

$$\xrightarrow{LiAlH_4} \xrightarrow{H^+}$$

$$\text{CH}_2\text{OH}$$

m-Methylbenzyl alcohol

● **PROBLEM** 16-13

Suggest a Grignard reaction which will produce the following:

(a) $CH_3-\underset{\underset{\textstyle CH_3}{|}}{\overset{\overset{\textstyle OH}{|}}{C}}-CH_2CH_3$

(b) $\begin{array}{l}CH_2-CH_2 \\ |\qquad\ | \\ CH_2-CH-CH_2OH\end{array}$

(d)

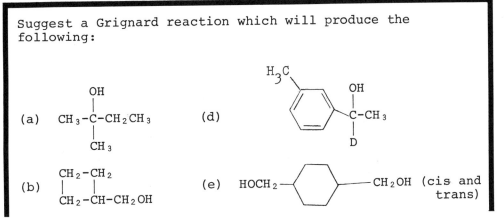

(e) $HOCH_2-\underset{\text{trans)}}{\underset{\text{(cis and}}{\bigcirc}}-CH_2OH$

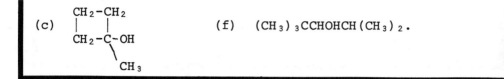

(c)

CH₂-CH₂
| |
CH₂-C-OH
    \
     CH₃

(f) $(CH_3)_3CCHOHCH(CH_3)_2$.

Solution: Grignard reagents (organomagnesium compounds of the general form R-Mg-X, X being a halogen) can react with ketones $\left(R-\overset{\overset{\displaystyle O}{\displaystyle \|}}{C}-R'\right)$ and aldehydes $\left(R-\overset{\overset{\displaystyle O}{\displaystyle \|}}{C}-H\right)$ to form a magnesium halide salt of an alcohol. Subsequent acid catalyzed hydrolysis produces an alcohol. The general reaction is:

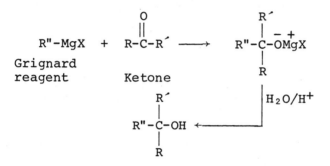

$$R"-MgX \quad + \quad R-\overset{\overset{\displaystyle O}{\displaystyle \|}}{C}-R' \longrightarrow R"-\overset{\overset{\displaystyle R'}{\displaystyle |}}{\underset{\displaystyle R}{C}}-\overset{- \; +}{OMgX}$$

Grignard
reagent   Ketone

$$R"-\overset{\overset{\displaystyle R'}{\displaystyle |}}{\underset{\displaystyle R}{C}}-OH \longleftarrow \quad \Big| H_2O/H^+$$

The Grignard reagent has two major resonance forms:

$$R-\overset{|}{\underset{|}{C}}:\overset{- \; +}{MgX} \longleftrightarrow R-\overset{|}{\underset{|}{C}}-MgX$$

The nucleophilic Grignard carbon attacks the carbonyl carbon to form the magnesium halide salt of the alcohol. The Grignard reactions that will form the compounds (a) through (f) are:

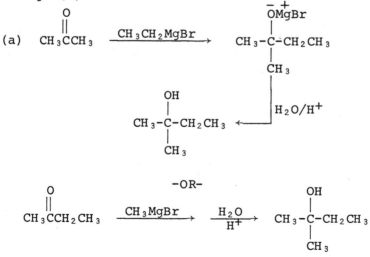

(a) $CH_3\overset{\overset{\displaystyle O}{\displaystyle \|}}{C}CH_3 \quad \xrightarrow{\; CH_3CH_2MgBr \;} \quad CH_3-\overset{\overset{\displaystyle \overset{- \; +}{OMgBr}}{|}}{\underset{\displaystyle CH_3}{C}}-CH_2CH_3$

$$CH_3-\overset{\overset{\displaystyle OH}{\displaystyle |}}{\underset{\displaystyle CH_3}{C}}-CH_2CH_3 \longleftarrow \quad \Big| H_2O/H^+$$

-OR-

$CH_3\overset{\overset{\displaystyle O}{\displaystyle \|}}{C}CH_2CH_3 \quad \xrightarrow{\; CH_3MgBr \;} \quad \xrightarrow[\; H^+ \;]{\; H_2O \;} \quad CH_3-\overset{\overset{\displaystyle OH}{\displaystyle |}}{\underset{\displaystyle CH_3}{C}}-CH_2CH_3$

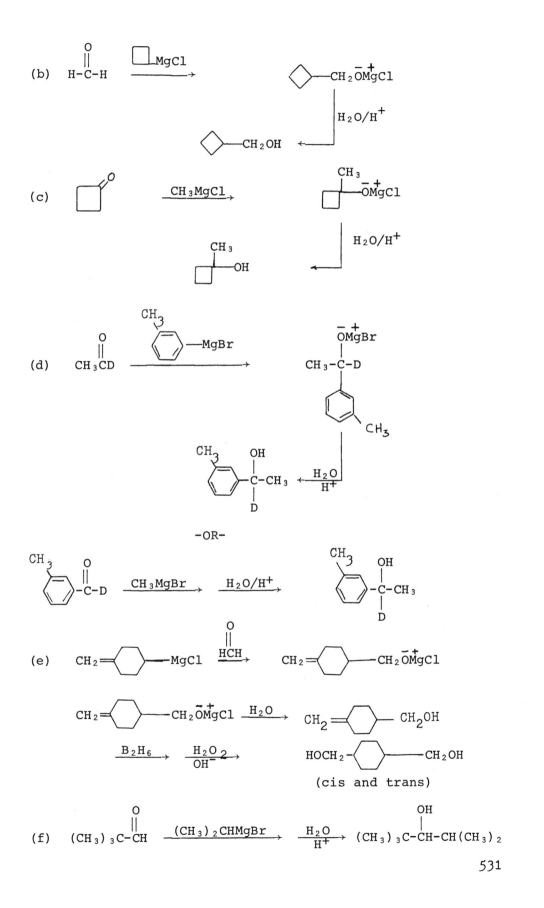

(b) $H-\overset{\overset{\text{O}}{\|}}{C}-H$ $\square\text{-MgCl}$ $\longrightarrow$ $\square\text{-CH}_2\overset{-}{\text{O}}\overset{+}{\text{M}}\text{gCl}$

$\square\text{-CH}_2\text{OH}$ $\longleftarrow$ H_2O/H^+

(c) $\square\!=\!\text{O}$ $\xrightarrow{\text{CH}_3\text{MgCl}}$ $\square\overset{\text{CH}_3}{\underset{}{\text{-}}}\overset{-}{\text{O}}\overset{+}{\text{M}}\text{gCl}$

$\square\overset{\text{CH}_3}{\underset{}{\text{-}}}\text{OH}$ $\longleftarrow$ H_2O/H^+

(d) $\text{CH}_3\text{CD}\overset{\overset{\text{O}}{\|}}{}$ CH$_3$-phenyl-MgBr $\longrightarrow$ $\text{CH}_3-\overset{\overset{-}{\text{O}}\overset{+}{\text{M}}\text{gBr}}{\underset{}{\text{C}}}-\text{D}$ (phenyl-CH$_3$)

$\text{CH}_3\text{-phenyl}\overset{\text{OH}}{\underset{\text{D}}{\text{C}}}\text{-CH}_3$ $\longleftarrow$ $\dfrac{H_2O}{H^+}$

−OR−

$\text{CH}_3\text{-phenyl}\overset{\overset{\text{O}}{\|}}{C}\text{-D}$ $\xrightarrow{\text{CH}_3\text{MgBr}}$ $\xrightarrow{H_2O/H^+}$ $\text{CH}_3\text{-phenyl}\overset{\text{OH}}{\underset{\text{D}}{\text{C}}}\text{-CH}_3$

(e) $\text{CH}_2\!=\!\bigcirc\!-\text{MgCl}$ $\xrightarrow{\text{HCH}\overset{\text{O}}{\|}}$ $\text{CH}_2\!=\!\bigcirc\!-\text{CH}_2\overset{-}{\text{O}}\overset{+}{\text{M}}\text{gCl}$

$\text{CH}_2\!=\!\bigcirc\!-\text{CH}_2\overset{-}{\text{O}}\overset{+}{\text{M}}\text{gCl}$ $\xrightarrow{H_2O}$ $\text{CH}_2\!=\!\bigcirc\!-\text{CH}_2\text{OH}$

$\xrightarrow{B_2H_6}$ $\xrightarrow[\text{OH}^-]{H_2O_2}$ $\text{HOCH}_2-\bigcirc\!-\text{CH}_2\text{OH}$

(cis and trans)

(f) $(\text{CH}_3)_3\text{C-CH}\overset{\overset{\text{O}}{\|}}{}$ $\xrightarrow{(\text{CH}_3)_2\text{CHMgBr}}$ $\xrightarrow{\dfrac{H_2O}{H^+}}$ $(\text{CH}_3)_3\text{C-}\overset{\text{OH}}{\underset{}{\text{CH}}}\text{-CH}(\text{CH}_3)_2$

-OR-

$$(CH_3)_2CH\overset{\overset{\textstyle O}{\|}}{-}C-H \xrightarrow{(CH_3)_3CMgBr} \xrightarrow[H^+]{H_2O} (CH_3)_3C\overset{\overset{\textstyle OH}{|}}{-}CH-CH(CH_3)_2$$

● **PROBLEM** 16-14

Outline the synthesis of n-butyldimethylcarbinol (2-methyl-2-hexanol) from acetone and n-butylbromide.

Solution: Alcohols are compounds of the general formula ROH, where R is any alkyl or substituted alkyl group.

A general synthesis reaction of alcohols from ketones and aldehydes is the Grignard synthesis. The reaction is:

$$RMgX + R'\overset{\overset{\textstyle R''}{|}}{-}C=O \rightarrow R'\overset{\overset{\textstyle R''}{|}}{\underset{\underset{\textstyle R}{|}}{C}}-\overset{-}{O}\overset{+}{M}gX \xrightarrow{H_2O} R'\overset{\overset{\textstyle R''}{|}}{\underset{\underset{\textstyle R}{|}}{C}}-OH$$

where R can be any alkyl group.

To synthesize n-butyldimethylcarbinol we make use of this important reaction. The structure of n-butyldimethylcarbinol is shown in figure A.

$$nC_4H_9-\overset{\overset{\textstyle CH_3}{|}}{\underset{\underset{\textstyle CH_3}{|}}{C}}-OH$$

fig. A.

Thus from the general reaction the three R groups are nC_4H_9-, CH_3-, and CH_3- and the reaction is:

$$n-C_4H_9MgBr + CH_3-C=O \rightarrow n-C_4H_9-\overset{\overset{\textstyle CH_3}{|}}{\underset{\underset{\textstyle CH_3}{|}}{C}}-\overset{-}{O}\overset{+}{M}gBr \xrightarrow{H_2O} n-C_4H_9-\overset{\overset{\textstyle CH_3}{|}}{\underset{\underset{\textstyle CH_3}{|}}{C}}-OH$$

However $n-C_4H_9MgBr$ must be prepared first. This is done by using n-butyl bromide

$$n-C_4H_9Br + Mg \xrightarrow{ether} n-C_4H_9MgBr$$

Thus the total sequence of reactions requires only two steps; the production of the Grignard reagent and the addition of acetone to this reagent.

532

Suggest a mechanism for the conversion of $C_6H_5CHClCH=CH_2$ to $C_6H_5CH=CHCH_2OH$ in water.

Solution: In order for the double bond to be shifted, the reaction must proceed through a free carbocation stage. This is facilitated by the leaving of the chlorine atom. The carbocation formed is resonance stabilized, and will be hydrolyzed to form an alcohol. The mechanism is shown as:

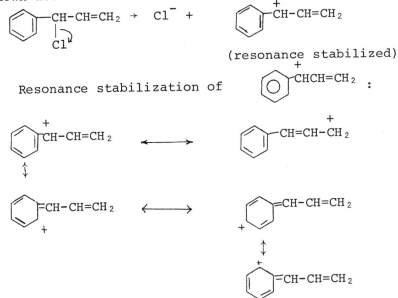

Resonance stabilization of

The resonance stabilized carbocation can be represented as:

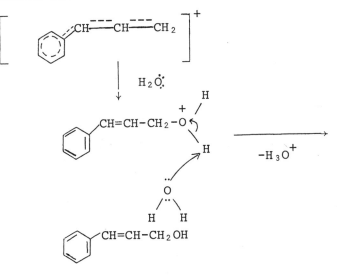

3-phenyl-2-propenol

The ⁻OH adds onto the primary carbon because the positive charge is greatest there. This is because the double bond is conjugated with the aromatic ring:

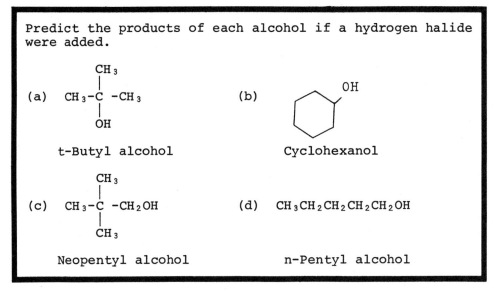

C-OH BOND CLEAVAGE

● PROBLEM 16-16

Predict the products of each alcohol if a hydrogen halide were added.

(a) $CH_3-\underset{\underset{OH}{|}}{\overset{\overset{CH_3}{|}}{C}}-CH_3$

t-Butyl alcohol

(b)

Cyclohexanol

(c) $CH_3-\underset{\underset{CH_3}{|}}{\overset{\overset{CH_3}{|}}{C}}-CH_2OH$

Neopentyl alcohol

(d) $CH_3CH_2CH_2CH_2CH_2OH$

n-Pentyl alcohol

<u>Solution:</u>   The chemical properties of an alcohol, ROH, are determined by its functional group, -OH, the hydroxyl group.

Reactions of an alcohol can involve the breaking of either of two bonds: the C-OH bond, with removal of the -OH group; or the O-H bond, with removal of -H. Either kind of reaction can involve substitution, in which a group replaces the -OH or -H, or elimination, in which a double bond is formed.

Alcohols react readily with hydrogen halides to yield alkyl halides and water. The reaction is carried out either by passing the dry hydrogen halide gas into the alcohol, or by heating the alcohol with the concentrated aqueous acid. Sometimes hydrogen bromide is generated in the presence of the alcohol by reaction between sulfuric acid (H_2SO_4) and sodium bromide.

The general formula for this type of reaction is:

$$R - OH + HX \rightarrow RX + H_2O$$

and by using this formula with the above principles, the
products of the given reactions may be predicted.

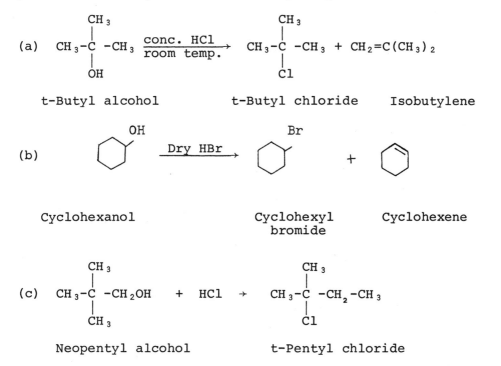

(a)   t-Butyl alcohol   t-Butyl chloride   Isobutylene

(b)   Cyclohexanol   Cyclohexyl   Cyclohexene
                         bromide

(c)   Neopentyl alcohol   t-Pentyl chloride

From solution (c) it is seen that the halogen does
not always become attached to the carbon that originally
held the hydroxyl group. Even the carbon skeleton may be
different from that of the starting material. The reason
is because compounds during reaction seek their most
stable form, and they will rearrange to that form if it is
energetically feasible.

     Neopentyl alcohol arranged as shown:

(d) $CH_3CH_2CH_2CH_2CH_2OH + HCl \xrightarrow[\text{heat}]{ZnCl_2} CH_3CH_2CH_2CH_2CH_2Cl + H_2O$

       n-Pentyl alcohol   n-Pentyl chloride

Would you expect optically active 1-deuterioethanol to
react with HBr and yield 1-deuterioethyl bromide with
inversion of configuration, or with racemization? Explain.

Solution: When an alcohol (ROH) is treated with an acid
of the type HX (X being a halogen), a nucleophilic substitution reaction (S_N) will take place. The acid (HX) will
ionize to produce the nucleophilic halide ion (X^-) which will
replace the hydroxyl (OH) functionality in the alcohol.
Before it leaves the molecule, the hydroxyl group is protonated by the proton from the ionization of HX. This occurs
because the leaving group is now water (H_2O) and not ^-OH;
H_2O is a larger species than ^-OH and is hence a better
leaving group. In the problem optically active 1-deuterio-
ethanol reacts with HBr to yield 1-deuterioethyl bromide.
The reaction is:

$$\underset{\substack{| \\ \text{OH}}}{\overset{\substack{\text{D} \\ |}}{\text{CH}_3\text{CH}}} \ + \ \text{HBr} \ \rightarrow \ \underset{\substack{| \\ \text{Br}}}{\overset{\substack{\text{D} \\ |}}{\text{CH}_3\text{CH}}} \ + \ \text{H}_2\text{O}$$

1-deuterio-   1-deuterioethyl
  ethanol   bromide

     The problem asks whether the reaction occurs with
inversion of configuration or racemization. Inversion of
configuration is characteristic of S_N2 (bimolecular nucleophilic substitution) reactions. This is because the reaction proceeds via a concerted mechanism and the nucleophile attacks the chiral carbon on the side opposite the
leaving group:

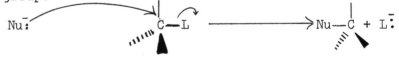

Nu⁻:   = nucleophile
L   = leaving group
C   = chiral carbon

     The S_N reaction that occurs with racemization is
characteristic of an S_N1 reaction (unimolecular nucleophilic substitution). This occurs because the reaction
proceeds through a free carbocation stage; the nucleophile
attacks either face of the carbocation with equal probability:

free carbocation stage
(sp^2 hybridized)

50%   50%

Primary and secondary carbons bearing a potential leaving group will undergo S_N reactions mainly by the bimolecular pathway whereas tertiary carbons will mainly follow the unimolecular pathway. This is due to the relative carbocation stabilities ($3° > 2° > 1° > {}^+CH_3$). Since 1-deuterioethanol is a primary alcohol it will react with HBr mainly via an S_N2 pathway. Since inversion of configuration is characteristic of S_N2 reactions, it will be observed here. The mechanism for the reaction is:

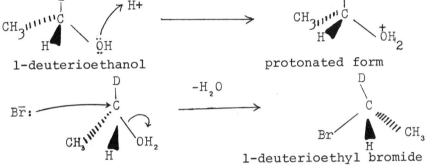

We can see by this mechanism that 1-deuterioethanol reacts with HBr mainly via an S_N2 pathway and hence proceeds with inversion of configuration.

● PROBLEM 16-18

React the following alcohols with a phosphorus trihalide and show the products.

(a)

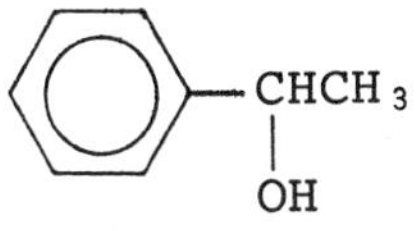

⬡—CHCH₃
       |
       OH

1-Phenylethanol

(b) $CH_3CH_2CH_2CHCH_2CH_2OH$
                    |
                    CH_3

3-Methyl-1-hexanol

(c) CH_3CH_2C —CH_2OH
with CH_3 above and CH_3 below the central C

2,2-Dimethyl-1-butanol

(d) CH_3CH_2OH

Ethyl alcohol

Solution: Alcohols react with phosphorus trihalides to produce alkyl halides with the same carbon skeleton as that of the alcohol. As seen in previous problems, alkyl halides can also be prepared from alcohols with a hydrogen halide, but phosphorus halides are often preferred because they tend less to bring about rearrangement of the carbon skeleton.

The general reaction for this synthesis is:

$$3 \text{ R-OH} + PX_3 \longrightarrow 3 \text{ RX} + H_3PO_3$$

$$(PX_3 = PBr_3, PI_3, PCl_3)$$

This reaction is simple substitution where the halogen, either bromine or iodine will replace the ^-OH group, and the phosphorus forms the by-product phosphorus acid (H_3PO_3). With the above facts and the general synthesis at hand, the products of each reaction can be obtained after reacting the alcohol with a phosphorus trihalide.

(a)   ⬡— CHCH$_3$ + PBr$_3$ →   ⬡— CHCH$_3$ + H$_3$PO$_3$
                | |
                OH   Br

   1-Phenylethanol   1-Bromo-1-
                                          phenylethane

(b) $CH_3CH_2CH_2CHCH_2CH_2OH$ $\xrightarrow{PBr_3}$ $CH_3CH_2CH_2CHCH_2CH_2Br$ + H_3PO_3
                        | |
                        CH_3 CH_3

   3-Methyl-1-hexanol   3-Methyl-1-bromohexane

                CH_3 CH_3
                  | |
(c) $CH_3CH_2C\ CH_2OH$ $\xrightarrow{PI_3}$ $CH_3CH_2C\ CH_2I$ + H_3PO_3
                  | |
                CH_3 CH_3

   2,2-Dimethyl-1-butanol   2,2-Dimethyl-1-iodobutane

(d) CH_3CH_2OH + PCl_3 → CH_3CH_2Cl + H_3PO_3

   Ethyl alcohol   Ethyl chloride

● PROBLEM 16-19

Describe the mechanism for the dehydration of alcohols.

Solution: The dehydration of alcohols begins with the formation of the protonated alcohol. After the dissociation of the acid (H_2SO_4) an H^+ attaches itself to the electronegative oxygen atom. This step is an equilibrium reaction and can go either way depending upon the reaction conditions.

538

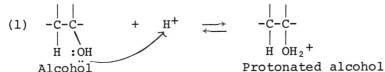

(1)   Alcohol   Protonated alcohol

Next, the protonated alcohol loses a molecule of water to form the most stable carbonium ion that is structurally possible.

(2)

In this step equilibrium lies very far to the left and thus there is a very low concentration of carbonium ions present at any time.

The final step of the reaction is the loss of a proton (or hydrogen ion) from the carbonium ion, restoring the electric neutrality of the molecule and forming a double bond.

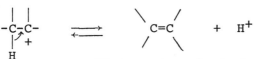

In the overall reaction the hydrogen ions are not consumed and are therefore true catalysts.

The dehydration of some alcohols can result in the formation of more than one alkene. 2-butanol, for example, may eliminate in either of two directions to give 1-butene or 2-butene. This can be seen in figure 1.

$$CH_3 - \underset{\underset{H}{|}}{\overset{\overset{H}{|}}{C}} - \underset{\underset{\lfloor OH \rfloor}{\overset{\overset{H}{|}}{C}}}{} - \underset{\overset{\overset{H}{|}}{C}}{} - H \xrightarrow{H^+} CH_3CH_2CH{=}CH_2 + H_2O$$

$$CH_3 - \underset{\underset{\lfloor H}{\overset{\overset{H}{|}}{C}}}{} - \underset{\overset{\overset{H}{|}}{C}}{} - \underset{\overset{\overset{H}{|}}{C}}{} - H \xrightarrow{H^+} CH_3CH{=}CHCH_3 + H_2O$$

figure 1

In general when two alkenes can be formed from a single alcohol, the alkene that predominates is the one with more alkyl substituents on the double bond. This generalization, known as the Saytzeff rule, is illustrated by the reactions which follow. In the first reaction 2-butanol gives both 2-butene and 1-butene. 2-Butene is the major product because it has two alkyl substituents (two methyl groups) on the double bond.

$$CH_3CHCH_2CH_3 \xrightarrow[\text{heat}]{H_2SO_4} CH_3CH{=}CHCH_3 + CH_2{=}CHCH_2CH_3$$
$$\underset{OH}{|}$$
                                         major product   minor product

2-butanol

539

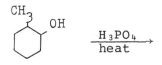

2-methylcyclo-
hexanol

$\xrightarrow[\text{heat}]{H_3PO_4}$

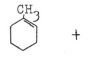

1-methylcyclo-
hexene
major product

+

3-methylcyclo-
hexene
minor product

1-Butene has only one alkyl substituent (one ethyl group) on the double bond and is therefore the minor product. Similarly, the dehydration of 2-methylcyclo-hexanol gives as the major product 1-methylcycohexene (three substituents including the ring carbons) and as the minor product 3-methylcyclohexene (two substituents including the ring carbons).

● **PROBLEM** 16-20

When allowed to react with aqueous HBr, 3-buten-2-ol ($CH_3CHOHCH=CH_2$) yields not only 3-bromo-1-butene ($CH_3CHBrCH=CH_2$) but also 1-bromo-2-butene ($CH_3CH=CHCH_2Br$). (a) How do you account for these results? (b) Predict the product of the reaction between HBr and 2-buten-1-ol ($CH_3CH=CHCH_2OH$).

Solution: (a) These results can be accounted for by the consideration of the allyl cation ($CH_2=CH-CH_2^+$). From in-spection of bond dissociation energies, allyl radicals are unusually stable. From this, it is possible to deduce that the allyl cation, too, is unusually stable. This stability is accounted for by delocalization of the electrons in this carbonium ion. It seems that the allyl cation is a resonance hybrid of two exactly equivalent structures:

$[CH_2=CH-CH_2^+ \leftrightarrow {}^+CH_2-CH=CH_2]$ equivalent to $CH_2\text{---}CH\text{---}CH_2$

$\underbrace{\qquad\qquad}_{+}$

At this point recall the fact that the dehydration of alcohols with acid (such as HBr) occurs through an intermediate carbonium ion with Markovnikov orientation. Hence, when HBr is added 3-buten-2-ol, a carbonium ion is formed as shown:

$$CH_3-\underset{\underset{OH}{|}}{\overset{\overset{H}{|}}{C}}-CH=CH_2 + HBr \rightarrow CH_3-\underset{\underset{{}^+OH_2}{|}}{\overset{\overset{H}{|}}{C}}-CH=CH_2 \xrightarrow{-H_2O} CH_3-\underset{\underset{+}{|}}{\overset{\overset{H}{|}}{C}}-CH=CH_2$$

carbonium ion

The important thing to see is that this is not just a carbonium ion but an allylic cation. Consequently, the true picture of this structure is:

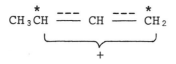

This hybrid allylic cation formed makes available to the bromide ion (Br⁻) two points of attack, which are starred. The result should be two products as indicated:

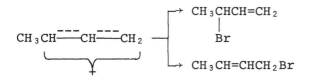

(b) When HBr is added to 2-buten-1-ol, the same hybrid allylic cation results as shown:

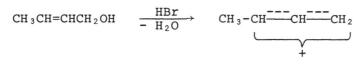

This means that the same two products obtained in (a) will be produced in this reaction.

● PROBLEM 16-21

(a) From the reaction of either (2R,3S) or (2S,3R)-3-bromo-2-butanol with HBr, the product is meso-2,3-dibromobutane. Show how this product is formed. Is the intermediate bromonium ion chiral?

(b) Contrast the reaction of (2R,3S)-3-bromo-2-butanol with HBr and the reaction of the same substrate with sodium ethoxide.

Solution: (a) (2S,3R)-3-bromo-2-butanol has the structure shown below (in Fischer projection form):

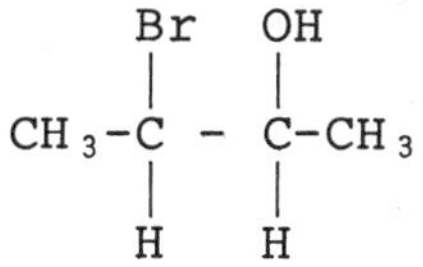

$$\begin{array}{cc} Br & OH \\ | & | \\ CH_3-C & - & C-CH_3 \\ | & | \\ H & H \end{array}$$

When this is treated with HBr, the hydroxyl group (OH) of the alcohol is protonated by a proton from the ionization of HBr. The presence of a nucleophilic group (bromine) on the carbon adjacent to the carbon bearing the protonated hydroxyl makes it possible for an intramolecular S_N2 reaction to occur. A free electron pair on bromine will attack the carbon bearing the protonated hydroxyl group; water will leave the molecule and a cyclic bromonium ion will be formed. Since this is an S_N2 reaction (because the carbon bearing the leaving group, H_2O, is secondary), the nucleophile (Br) will attack the carbon bearing the protonated hydroxyl group on the side opposite the leaving group:

In order for the bromine to react via an S_N2 pathway, it must be anti to the leaving group (H_2O). The conformation of the protonated alcohol that satisfies this requirement is:

Hence,

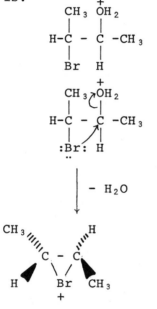

cyclic bromonium ion

The cyclic bromonium ion reacts with the bromide ion, Br^-:, (from the ionization of HBr) via an S_N2 pathway. The nucleophile bromide ion attacks one of the ring carbons on the side opposite the bromine cation. This results in the formation of meso-2,3-dibromobutane:

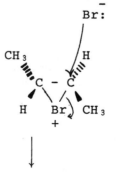

542

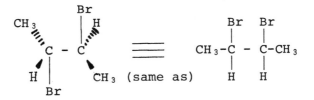

meso-2,3-dibromobutane   (Fischer projection)

The cyclic bromonium ion is a chiral molecule. This is because there is no plane of symmetry for the molecule.

(b)   (2R,3S)-3-Bromo-2-butanol has the structure:

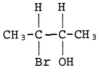

$$CH_3-\overset{\overset{\displaystyle H}{|}}{C}-\overset{\overset{\displaystyle H}{|}}{\underset{\underset{\displaystyle OH}{|}}{C}}-CH_3$$

(with Br below the first carbon, OH below the second)

Reaction of this compound with HBr proceeds through a cyclic bromonium ionic intermediate; the final product is meso-2,3-dibromobutane. When the above compound (the alcohol) is reacted with sodium ethoxide (Na$^+$ $^-$OC$_2$H$_5$), the mechanism is very similar to that shown in part (a). The ethoxide ion removes a proton from the hydroxyl group. The resulting anionic oxygen attacks the carbon bearing the bromine in an intramolecular S$_N$2 reaction; this forms a chiral cyclic intermediate (an epoxide). This intermediate reacts with ethoxide ion in an S$_N$2 reaction to open the ring. The product formed is optically active and is named (2R,3S)-3-ethoxy-2-butanol. The mechanism for these reactions are shown as:

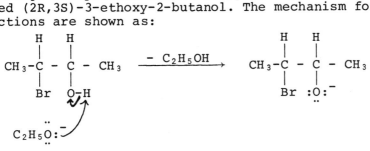

The intermediate must be oriented correctly for an intramolecular S$_N$2 reaction to occur; the oxygen anion must be anti to the bromine. The conformation that satisfies this requirement is:

$$CH_3-\overset{\overset{\displaystyle H}{|}}{C}-\overset{\overset{\displaystyle :O:^-}{|}}{C}-H$$

(with Br below the first carbon, CH$_3$ below the second)

Hence,

$$CH_3-\overset{\overset{\displaystyle H}{|}}{C}-\overset{\overset{\displaystyle O:^-}{|}}{C}-H$$

(with Br below the first carbon, CH$_3$ below the second)

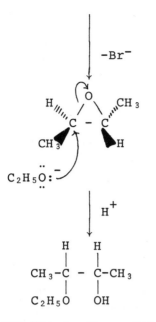

$-Br^-$

chiral, cyclic
intermediate
[(2R,3R)-2,3-epoxybutane]

H^+

$$\begin{array}{ccc} & H & H \\ & | & | \\ CH_3-C & - & C-CH_3 \\ & | & | \\ & C_2H_5O & OH \end{array}$$

(2R,3S)-3-ethoxy-2-butanol

CO-H BOND CLEAVAGE

● **PROBLEM** 16-22

Sodium metal was added to tert-butyl alcohol and allowed
to react. When the metal was consumed, ethyl bromide
was added to the resulting mixture. Work-up of the reaction mixture yielded a compound of formula $C_6H_{14}O$.

In a similar experiment, sodium metal was allowed
to react with ethanol. When tert-butyl bromide was added,
a gas was evolved, and work-up of the remaining mixture
gave ethanol as the only organic material.

(a) Write equations for all reactions. (b) What
familiar reaction type is involved in each case? (c) Why
did the reactions take different courses?

Solution: (a), (b) It is known that alcohols may act
as acids. Alcohols may react with active metals to form
the alkoxide ion, RO^-, and hydrogen gas. The reaction may
be written as:

$$RO - H + M \rightarrow RO^- M^+ + \tfrac{1}{2}H_2,$$

where M=Na, K, Mg, Al, etc. and the reactivity of ROH is
$CH_3OH > 1° > 2° > 3°$. Hence, when sodium metal is added
to tert-butyl alcohol and allowed to react, sodium tert-
butoxide is formed as shown:

$$\underset{\substack{\text{OH} \\ |}}{\overset{\substack{\text{CH}_3 \\ |}}{CH_3\text{-}C\text{-}CH_3}} + Na \longrightarrow \underset{\substack{\overset{\ominus}{O}Na^{\oplus} \\ |}}{\overset{\substack{\text{CH}_3 \\ |}}{CH_3\text{-}C\text{-}CH_3}} + \tfrac{1}{2}H_2$$

t-butyl alcohol   sodium t-butoxide

Alkoxides are useful reagents; they are used as powerful bases (stronger than hydroxide). Sodium t-butoxide and ethyl bromide (CH_3CH_2Br) are mixed together to give $C_6H_{14}O$. This reaction illustrates nucleophilic substitution. Ethyl bromide is an alkyl halide, and nucleophilic substitution is typical of such organic compounds. Nucleophilic substitution may be generalized as

$$R : Z \ + \ : Z \ \rightarrow \ R : Z \ + \ : \overset{\ominus}{X}$$

A nucleo-   Leaving
philic reagent   group

As mentioned, sodium tert-butoxide is a strong base. It is an electron-rich species, so that it may be described as a nucleophile. Consequently, the equation for the reaction with ethyl bromide becomes:

$$\underset{\substack{\text{CH}_3 \\ |}}{\overset{\substack{\text{CH}_3 \\ |}}{CH_3\text{-}C\text{-}\overset{\ominus}{O}Na^{\oplus}}} + CH_3CH_2Br \rightarrow \underset{\substack{\text{CH}_3 \\ |}}{\overset{\substack{\text{CH}_3 \\ |}}{CH_3\text{-}C\text{-}OCH_2CH_3}} \quad (C_6H_{14}O)$$

t-butyl ethyl ether

In a similar experiment, another alkoxide, sodium ethoxide, is obtained when sodium is allowed to react with ethanol. The reaction may be written as follows:

$$CH_3CH_2OH \ + \ Na \rightarrow \ CH_3CH_2\overset{\ominus}{O}Na^{\oplus} \ + \ \tfrac{1}{2}H_2$$

Ethanol   Sodium ethoxide

Due to the fact that the only organic compound present after tert-butyl bromide is added to sodium ethoxide is ethanol, this reaction cannot be the same as the one discussed above (when ethanol was added to sodium t-butoxide). In fact, this reaction is one of elimination. Recall that in the dehydrohalogenation to produce alkenes, the base ($O\overset{\ominus}{H}$) pulled a hydrogen ion away from carbon, and simultaneously a halide ion separated. This is exactly what happens when sodium ethoxide and t-butyl bromide are mixed together, except that in this case the sodium ethoxide replaces OH^- as the base. The reaction may be written as:

$$CH_3CH_2\overset{\ominus}{O}Na^{\oplus} + \underset{\substack{\text{Br} \\ |}}{\overset{\substack{\text{CH}_3 \\ |}}{CH_3\text{-}C\text{-}CH_3}} \rightarrow \underset{\text{(isobutylene)}}{\overset{\substack{\text{CH}_3 \\ |}}{CH_3\text{-}C\text{=}CH_2}} + \underset{\text{Ethanol}}{CH_3CH_2OH} + NaBr.$$

Isobutylene, the alkene produced, is a gas and diffuses away. This leaves only NaBr (inorganic) and ethanol.

(c)   How can the different courses of the two reactions be explained? Examine the nature of the alkyl halide involved in each case. In the first case, ethyl bromide, a primary alkyl halide, was used. In the second case, tert-butyl bromide, a tertiary alkyl halide, was used. Both nucleophilic substitution and elimination are typical reactions of alkyl halides - they can compete with each other. But note the reactivities for each:

E_2 or E_1 elimination: 3° > 2° > 1°

S_N2 (Substitution nucleophilic bimolecular):

   CH_3X > 1° > 2° > 3°.

   Hence, when the primary alkyl halide is used, S_N2 is favored over elimination. Therefore, nucleophilic (S_N2) substitution occurs when ethyl bromide is added to sodium t-butoxide. However, when the tertiary alkyl halide is employed, the elimination reaction predominates, as seen when t-butyl bromide is added to sodium ethoxide.

● **PROBLEM 16-23**

Predict the major products of the following reactions:

(a) $(CH_3)_3CBr$ + $CH_3O^{\ominus}$ →

(b) 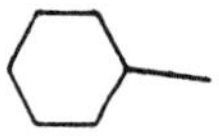   ⬡— Cl + $(CH_3)_3CO^{\ominus}$ →

(c) 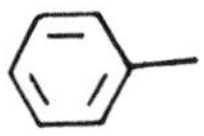   ⬡— CH_2Br + $(CH_3)_2CHCH_2O^{\ominus}$ →

(d) $(CH_3)_2CHCH_2Br$ + $C_6H_5CH_2O^{\ominus}$ →

Solution: When an alkyl halide (RX) is treated with an alkoxide ($RO^{\ominus}$) the major product will be an alcohol (ROH)

and an alkene $\left(\begin{matrix} \diagdown \\ / \end{matrix} C{=}C \begin{matrix} / \\ \diagdown \end{matrix} \right)$ or an ether (ROR´). The alcohol

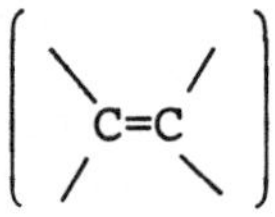

and alkene are products of an elimination (E) reaction. The ether is the product of a nucleophilic substitution (S_N) reaction. When there are no hydrogens α to the carbon bearing the leaving group, elimination cannot occur and the reaction will yield only S_N products. When the reaction is done in the presence of a strong base, and α hydrogens (relative to C-X) are present, elimination will be favored over substitution. The basicity of alkoxides follows the order: 3° > 2° > 1° > $CH_3O^{\ominus}$. This is because the acidity of their conjugate acids (the alcohols) follow the order: CH_3OH > 1° > 2° > 3°.

546

Elimination will also be favored over substitution when the alkyl portion of the alkyl halide can have a fairly stable carbocation (i.e.: tertiary alkyl halides), and if the alkyl portion is a larger group (because of steric considerations, elimination will predominate over substitution). With this in mind, we may predict the major products of reactions (a) through (d).

(a)   This is mainly an elimination reaction due to the tertiary alkyl halide; the t-butyl group is a large moiety and it has a fairly stable carbocation.

$$(CH_3)_3C-Br + CH_3O^\ominus \rightarrow (CH_3)_2C=CH_2 + CH_3OH + Br^\ominus$$

isobutylene   methanol

(b)   As in part (a) the major reaction will be an elimination; this is because of the relatively strong base, t-butoxide.

cyclo-   t-butanol
hexene

(c)   Since the alkyl halide has no hydrogens α to the carbon bearing the bromine, elimination cannot occur and the reaction is strictly S_N.

benzyl-isobutyl ether

(d)   Elimination will be favored over substitution in this reaction because of the fairly large isobutyl group of the alkyl halide and the good basicity of the benzoxide anion. There will, however, be some substitution because of the nucleophilic nature of the alkoxide and because the alkyl halide is primary.

$$(CH_3)_2CHCH_2Br + C_6H_5CH_2O^\ominus \rightarrow (CH_3)_2C=CH_2 + C_6H_5CH_2OH + Br^\ominus$$

isobutylene   benzyl
alcohol

There will also be some:

$$(CH_3)_2CHCH_2OCH_2C_6H_5$$

benzyl-isobutyl ether

In the esterification of an acid with an alcohol, how could you distinguish between C-O and O-H cleavage of the alcohol using heavy oxygen (^{18}O) as a tracer?

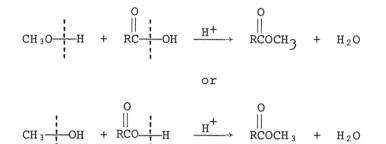

or

What type of alcohols might conceivably react by C-O cleavage, and what side reactions would you anticipate for such alcohols?

Solution: We can distinguish between C-O and O-H bond cleavage in the alcohol in Fischer esterification reactions by using ^{18}O-labeled alcohol. In the problem, methanol (CH_3OH) is the alcohol used. If ^{18}O-labeled methanol was reacted with a carboxylic acid $\left(R-\overset{\overset{O}{\|}}{C}-OH\right)$, the methyl ester $\left(R-\overset{\overset{O}{\|}}{C}-OCH_3\right)$ would contain heavy oxygen, if the O-H bond was broken and the water would be free of ^{18}O. If the C-O bond was broken, the methyl ester would be unlabeled and the water would contain heavy oxygen. These reactions are shown as:

O-H cleavage

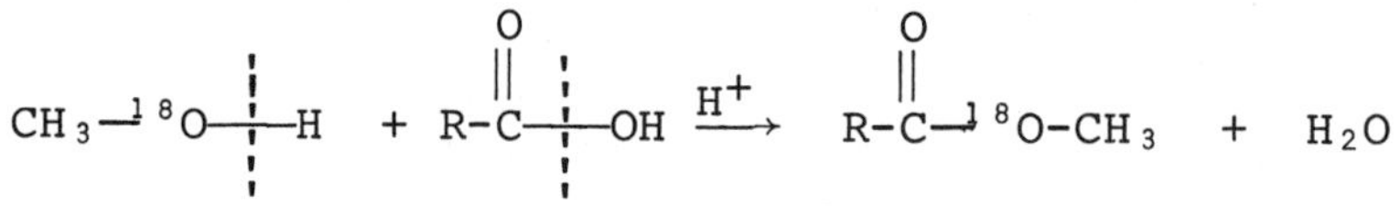

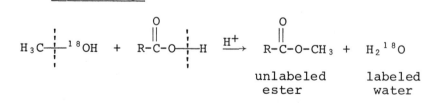

labeled ester unlabeled water

C-O cleavage

unlabeled ester labeled water

Alcohols that might conceivably react by C-O cleavage are those that can form fairly stable carbocations, such as tertiary or allylic alcohols:

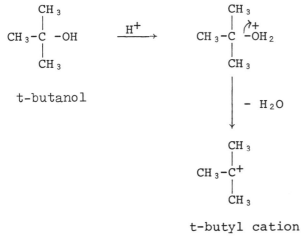

t-butanol

t-butyl cation

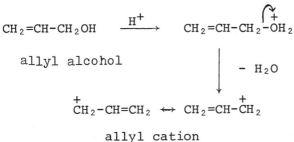

allyl alcohol

$$\overset{+}{C}H_2-CH=CH_2 \longleftrightarrow CH_2=CH-\overset{+}{C}H_2$$

allyl cation

The side reactions expected to occur for such alcohols would be ether and alkene formation as shown:

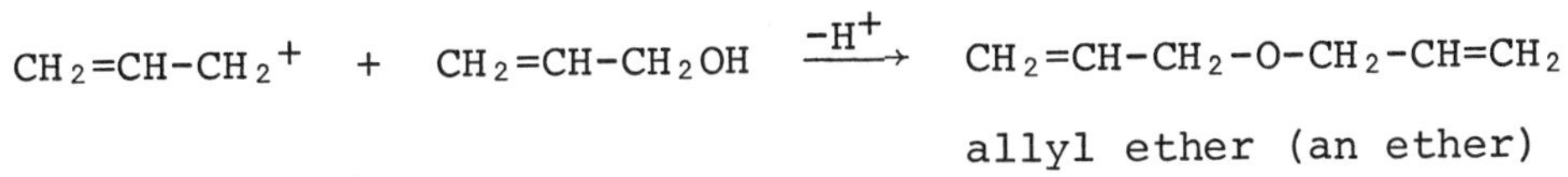

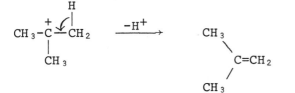

allyl ether (an ether)

2-methylpropene
(an alkene)

• **PROBLEM** 16-25

You prepare sec-butyl tosylate from alcohol of $[\alpha]$ + 6.9°. On hydrolysis with aqueous base, this ester gives sec-butyl alcohol of $[\alpha]$ - 6.9°. Without knowing the configuration or optical purity of the starting alcohol, what (if anything) can you say about the stereochemistry of the hydrolysis step?

<u>Solution:</u>   Base catalyzed hydrolysis of a sulfonyl
ester (R'-SO_3R) will yield an alcohol (ROH) and a sulfonic
acid salt ($R'SO_3^-$). Sec-butyl tosylate is a sulfonyl ester
and will be hydrolyzed to sec-butanol and the anion of p-
methylbenzenesulfonic acid. The reaction is shown as:

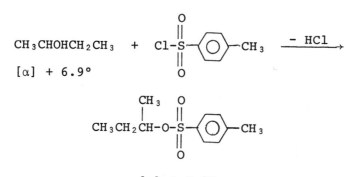

sec-butyltosylate

anion of
p-methylbenzenesulfonic
acid
(tosylate ion)

$CH_3CHOHCH_2CH_3$

sec-butanol

   This reaction proceeds via an S_N2 pathway where the
hydroxide ion (OH^-) acts as a nucleophile and the tosylate
ion acts as the leaving group. As in all S_N2 reactions,
this one will proceed with inversion of configuration; that
is, if the starting material is optically active, the
product will have the same optical rotation as the reactant, only it will have the opposite sign (i.e.: if reactant has optical rotation of + 20°, product will have
optical rotation of - 20°). The problem states that the
sec-butyl alcohol produced from sec-butyltosylate has a
[α] (optical rotation) of - 6.9°. Since the reaction that
produces the sec-butyl alcohol is an S_N2 reaction, we may
conclude that the sec-butyltosylate has a [α] of + 6.9°.
Since the sec-butyltosylate was prepared from an alcohol
of [α] + 6.9°, we can see that the reaction that produced
sec-butyltosylate proceeded with retention of configuration.
This is explained by the fact that the O-H bond and not the
C-OH bond is broken in the alcohol to form the tosylate.
The reaction can be written as:

$CH_3CHOHCH_2CH_3$ +   (structure) $\xrightarrow{\text{- HCl}}$

[α] + 6.9°

(structure)

[α] + 6.9°.

OXIDATION

Give the product of each alcohol below after oxidation
with any reagent necessary.

(a) $CH_3CH_2CH-CH_2OH$ (b)

            |
          CH_3

   2-Methyl-1-butanol

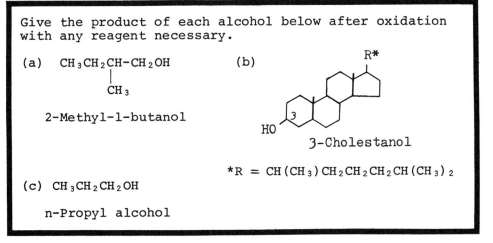

3-Cholestanol

$*R = CH(CH_3)CH_2CH_2CH_2CH(CH_3)_2$

(c) $CH_3CH_2CH_2OH$

   n-Propyl alcohol

Solution: The product that is formed by oxidation of
an alcohol depends upon the number of hydrogens attached
to the carbon bearing the hydroxyl, -OH group, i.e. upon
whether the alcohol is primary, secondary, or tertiary.
The products formed are aldehydes, ketones and carboxylic
acids, and their preparation by the oxidation of alcohols
is of great value in organic synthesis.

     Some oxidizing reagents (such as $K_2Cr_2O_7$) are highly
selective reagents which operate on only one functional
group in a complex molecule, and leave the other functional
groups unchanged. Of the many reagents that can be used to
oxidize alcohols, only the most common ones will be considered here, those containing manganese (Mn), and chromium
(Cr).

     The general reactions for these oxidations are:

(1) Primary Alcohols

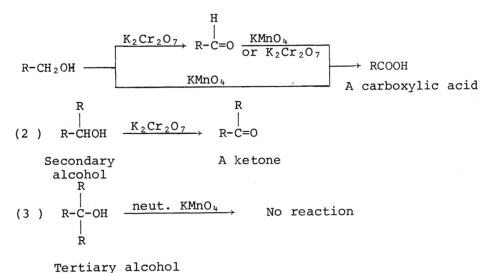

Tertiary alcohol

From the general reactions, it can be seen that primary alcohols are oxidized to carboxylic acids either directly or via an aldehyde, depending upon the oxidizing reagent. For example, take problem (a).

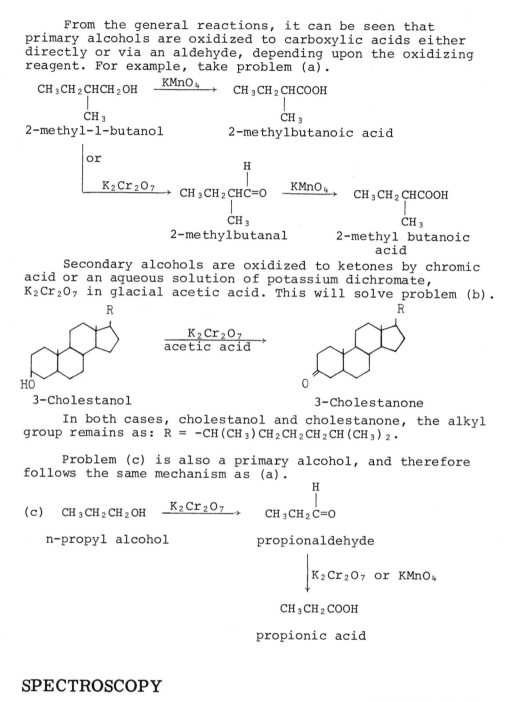

$$CH_3CH_2CHCH_2OH \xrightarrow{KMnO_4} CH_3CH_2CHCOOH$$

$$| \qquad\qquad\qquad\qquad\qquad |$$

$$CH_3 \qquad\qquad\qquad\qquad\qquad CH_3$$

2-methyl-1-butanol   2-methylbutanoic acid

or

$$\xrightarrow{K_2Cr_2O_7} CH_3CH_2CHC\overset{\overset{\textstyle H}{|}}{=}O \xrightarrow{KMnO_4} CH_3CH_2CHCOOH$$

$$\qquad\qquad\qquad | \qquad\qquad\qquad\qquad\qquad\quad |$$

$$\qquad\qquad\qquad CH_3 \qquad\qquad\qquad\qquad\qquad CH_3$$

2-methylbutanal   2-methyl butanoic acid

Secondary alcohols are oxidized to ketones by chromic acid or an aqueous solution of potassium dichromate, $K_2Cr_2O_7$ in glacial acetic acid. This will solve problem (b).

$$\xrightarrow[\text{acetic acid}]{K_2Cr_2O_7}$$

HO   O

3-Cholestanol   3-Cholestanone

In both cases, cholestanol and cholestanone, the alkyl group remains as: R = $-CH(CH_3)CH_2CH_2CH_2CH(CH_3)_2$.

Problem (c) is also a primary alcohol, and therefore follows the same mechanism as (a).

(c) $CH_3CH_2CH_2OH \xrightarrow{K_2Cr_2O_7} CH_3CH_2C\overset{\overset{\textstyle H}{|}}{=}O$

n-propyl alcohol   propionaldehyde

$$\downarrow K_2Cr_2O_7 \text{ or } KMnO_4$$

$$CH_3CH_2COOH$$

propionic acid

SPECTROSCOPY

• **PROBLEM** 16-27

(a) Very dry, pure samples of alcohols show spin-spin splitting of the O-H signals. What splitting would you expect for a primary alcohol? a secondary alcohol? a tertiary alcohol? (b) This splitting disappears on the addition of a trace of acid or base. Write equations to show just how proton exchange would be speeded up by an

Solution: (a) Proton exchange at the hydroxyl group occurs very slowly in dry, pure samples of alcohol. As a result, a given hydroxyl proton remains bonded to the oxygen long enough for spin-spin splitting to occur (due to the protons of the carbon adjacent to the oxygen). Hence the two protons on the neighboring carbon in primary alcohols ($-CH_2-OH$) will split the hydroxyl signal into a triplet. The single proton on the carbon in secondary

alcohols $\left(-\overset{\displaystyle |}{C}H-OH\right)$ will split the hydroxyl signal into a doublet. The hydroxyl proton will not undergo spin-spin

splitting in tertiary alcohols $\left(-\overset{\displaystyle |}{\underset{\displaystyle |}{C}}-OH\right)$ because there are

no hydrogens on the carbon adjacent to the oxygen. Hence the hydroxyl signal will occur as a singlet.

(b) When an alcohol is in the presence of a trace of acid, or base, proton exchange is speed up as follows:

By Acid:

$$R*OH* \quad + \quad H:B \quad \rightleftharpoons \quad \left[\begin{array}{c} R*OH* \\ | \\ H \end{array}\right]^{+} \quad + \quad B:^{-}$$

$$\text{alcohol} \qquad \text{acid}$$

$$\left[\begin{array}{c} R*OH* \\ | \\ H \end{array}\right]^{+} + \quad ROH \quad \rightleftharpoons \quad R*OH \quad + \quad \left[\begin{array}{c} ROH \\ | \\ H* \end{array}\right]^{+}$$

$$\left[\begin{array}{c} ROH \\ | \\ H* \end{array}\right]^{+} + \quad B:^{-} \quad \rightleftharpoons \quad ROH* \quad + \quad H:B$$

By Base:

$$R*OH* \quad + \quad B: \quad \rightleftharpoons \quad R* O^{-} \quad + \quad [B:H*]^{+}$$

$$\text{alcohol} \qquad \text{base}$$

$$R* O^{-} \quad + \quad ROH \quad \rightleftharpoons \quad R*OH \quad + \quad RO^{-}$$

$$RO^{-} \quad + \quad [B:H*]^{+} \quad \rightleftharpoons \quad ROH* \quad + \quad B:$$

As a result of this increase in proton exchange, the hydroxyl proton does not remain bonded to the oxygen long enough for spin-spin splitting to occur.

The infrared spectrum of cis-1,2-cyclopentanediol has an O-H stretching band at a lower frequency than for a free -OH group, and this band does not disappear even at high dilution. trans-1,2-Cyclopentanediol shows no such band. Can you suggest a possible explanation?

Solution: A consideration of the structure of cis-1,2-cyclopentanediol and the factors that might shift the characteristic absorption band of a group in the infrared spectrum will aid in solving this problem.

It is known that the absorption band of a group may be shifted by various structural features: conjugation, electron withdrawal by a neighboring substituent, angle strain or van der Waals strain, and hydrogen bonding. The structure of cis-1,2-cyclopentanediol (below) reveals an interesting fact.

The hydroxyl groups located on the same face can undergo intramolecular hydrogen bonding, as indicated by the dashed line. This phenomenon is referred to as chelation, the holding of a hydrogen or metal atom between two atoms of a single molecule. Intramolecular hydrogen bonding appears to occur whenever the structure of a compound permits. This phenomenon explains the fact that even at high dilution the shifted absorption band does not disappear. Under high dilution conditions, the chance of intermolecular hydrogen bonding (that is, hydrogen bonding between molecules) is remote, but intramolecular hydrogen bonding still occurs.

At this point, examine the structure of trans-1,2-cyclopentanediol as shown:

Here, the structure of the compound does not permit intramolecular hydrogen bonding. Consequently, there should be no band at high dilution.

The cis-isomer has an O-H stretch band at a lower frequency because the O-H stretch is greater in the cis-isomer than in a free -OH group. This is because the relatively weak intramolecular hydrogen bond pulls the O-H bond further apart; that is the bond is stretched more.

SYNTHESIS

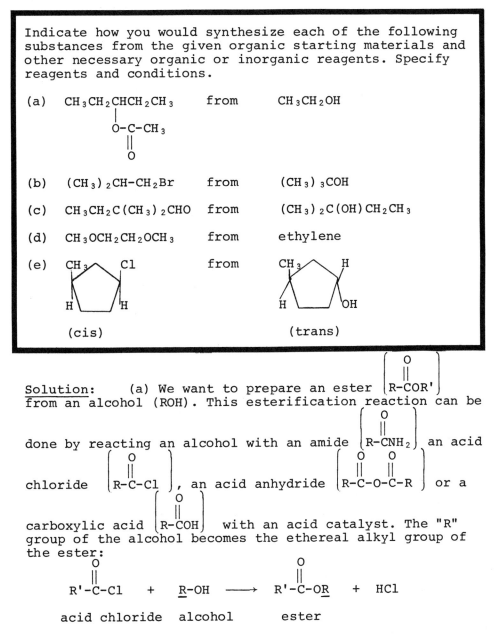

Indicate how you would synthesize each of the following substances from the given organic starting materials and other necessary organic or inorganic reagents. Specify reagents and conditions.

(a) $CH_3CH_2CHCH_2CH_3$ from CH_3CH_2OH

           $O-C-CH_3$
               $\parallel$
               O

(b) $(CH_3)_2CH-CH_2Br$ from $(CH_3)_3COH$

(c) $CH_3CH_2C(CH_3)_2CHO$ from $(CH_3)_2C(OH)CH_2CH_3$

(d) $CH_3OCH_2CH_2OCH_3$ from   ethylene

(e)   (cis)   from   (trans)

Solution: (a) We want to prepare an ester $\left(\begin{array}{c} O \\ \parallel \\ R-COR' \end{array} \right)$ from an alcohol (ROH). This esterification reaction can be done by reacting an alcohol with an amide $\left(\begin{array}{c} O \\ \parallel \\ R-CNH_2 \end{array} \right)$ an acid chloride $\left(\begin{array}{c} O \\ \parallel \\ R-C-Cl \end{array} \right)$, an acid anhydride $\left(\begin{array}{c} O \;\; O \\ \parallel \;\; \parallel \\ R-C-O-C-R \end{array} \right)$ or a carboxylic acid $\left(\begin{array}{c} O \\ \parallel \\ R-COH \end{array} \right)$ with an acid catalyst. The "R" group of the alcohol becomes the ethereal alkyl group of the ester:

$$\begin{array}{ccccccc} O & & & & O & & \\ \parallel & & & & \parallel & & \\ R'-C-Cl & + & \underline{R-OH} & \longrightarrow & R'-C-\underline{OR} & + & HCl \end{array}$$

     acid chloride   alcohol   ester

     To prepare our desired product (an ester), we must first synthesize the alcoholic portion of the ester (3-pentanol) from the starting material (ethanol). This can be done by a Grignard reaction. Grignard reagents (organo-magnesium compounds of the type R-Mg-X) will react with carbonyl compounds to produce alcohols upon hydrolysis. The alkyl group of the Grignard reagent adds onto the carbonyl carbon. If the carbonyl carbon bears a potential leaving group, that group will leave to form another carbonyl compound, which will react with another molecule

555

of Grignard reagent. Once 3-pentanol is formed, we can react it with acetyl chloride to produce our desired product.
The synthesis is as follows:

First step - an S_N reaction

$$CH_3CH_2OH \ + \ HBr \longrightarrow \ CH_3CH_2Br$$

ethanol   ethyl bromide

Second step - preparation of Grignard reagent

$$CH_3CH_2Br \ + \ Mg \xrightarrow{\ ether\ } CH_3CH_2MgBr$$

ethyl magnesium bromide

Third step - reaction with carbonyl compound

$$2 \ CH_3CH_2MgBr \ + \ \underset{\displaystyle \overset{\displaystyle O}{\|}}{H-C-OCH_3} \rightarrow \underset{\displaystyle \underset{\displaystyle CH_2CH_3}{|}}{CH_3CH_2-\overset{\displaystyle \overset{-\ \ +}{OMgBr}}{\underset{|}{C}}-H} \xrightarrow{H_2O} \underset{\displaystyle 3\text{-pentanol}}{\overset{\displaystyle \overset{OH}{|}}{CH_3CH_2CHCH_2CH_3}}$$

Fourth step - reaction with an acid chloride

$$\underset{\displaystyle \underset{OH}{|}}{CH_3CH_2CHCH_2CH_3} \ + \ \overset{\displaystyle \overset{O}{\|}}{CH_3C-Cl} \rightarrow \ \underset{\displaystyle \underset{\displaystyle \underset{O}{\|}}{O-C-CH_3}}{CH_3CH_2CHCH_2CH_3} \ + \ HCl$$

3-pentylacetate

(b) We want to synthesize an alkyl bromide (isobutyl
bromide) from an alcohol (t-butanol). Since the two com-

$$\begin{pmatrix} C \\ | \\ C-C-C \end{pmatrix}$$

pounds have the same carbon skeleton , and the
bromine of the alkyl bromide is on a carbon adjacent to
the one that holds the hydroxyl group in the alcohol,
an elimination reaction must first be performed. Once
the alkene is formed we must add a bromine atom in the
orientation that will yield the desired product. Elimination reactions occur fastest with a strong base. Tertiary
alkoxides are of sufficient basicity so as to yield mainly
elimination products. To add a bromine to the alkene (isobutylene) in the orientation that will yield the desired
product, we must use a free radical hydrobromination reaction. This reaction proceeds with an anti-Markovnikov
addition to the alkene because (1) a bromine radical and
not a hydrogen radical reacts first with the π system of
the alkene, and (2) the most stable radical is formed
most rapidly. Hence the synthesis of isobutyl bromide from
t-butanol is:

$(CH_3)_3C-OH$ $\xrightarrow[-\ H_2O]{K^+\ ^-OC(CH_3)_3}$ $(CH_3)_2C=CH_2$

t-butanol   isobutylene

$(CH_3)_2C=CH_2$ $+$ HBr $\xrightarrow{\begin{array}{c}\overset{O}{\overset{\|}{C_6H_5C}}-O-O-\overset{O}{\overset{\|}{C}}-C_6H_5 \\ \text{(dibenzoyl peroxide} \\ -\ \text{a radical initiator)}\end{array}}$

$$\overset{\displaystyle CH_3}{\underset{\displaystyle |}{CH_3-CH}}CH_2Br$$

isobutyl bromide

(c)   We want to synthesize an aldehyde (R-CHO) from an alcohol. Since the carbon skeleton of the aldehyde

$$\left(\begin{array}{c} C \\ | \\ C-C-C-C \\ | \\ C \end{array} \right)$$ has one more carbon that that of the alcohol

$$\left(\begin{array}{c} C \\ | \\ C-C-C \\ | \\ C \end{array} \right)$$, and that carbon is bonded to the carbon that

bears the hydroxyl group in the alcohol, we can use a

Grignard reaction with formaldehyde $\left(H-\overset{O}{\overset{\|}{C}}-H \right)$ to bring us closer to our desired product. Subsequent hydrolysis will yield 2,2-dimethylbutanol; our desired product is 2,2-dimethylbutanal. Oxidation of the primary alcohol to the aldehyde can be accomplished with Sarett's reagent, a combination of chromium trioxide (CrO_3) with pyridine. The Grignard reagent can be prepared by first converting the alcohol to the alkyl bromide (S_N1) and then reacting with magnesium in dry ether. The synthesis of 2,2-dimethyl-butanal from 1,1-dimethylpropanol is:

$$\underset{\displaystyle |}{\overset{\displaystyle CH_3}{\overset{\displaystyle |}{CH_3CH_2-C-OH}}} \quad \xrightarrow{\text{HBr}} \quad \underset{\displaystyle CH_3}{\overset{\displaystyle CH_3}{\overset{\displaystyle |}{CH_3CH_2-C-Br}}}$$

$$\Big\downarrow \ \text{Mg/ether}$$

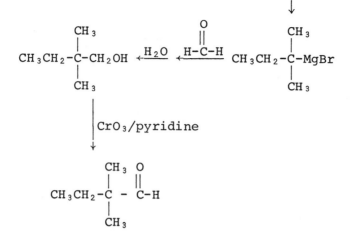

2,2-dimethylbutanal

(d) We want to synthesize 1,2-dimethoxyethane from
ethylene; this can be done by proceeding through an epoxide

$\begin{pmatrix} & O & \\ & / \backslash & \\ -C & - & C- \\ | & & | \end{pmatrix}$. The desired product is very similar to methyl

cellosolve ($CH_3OCH_2CH_2OH$) and is synthesized from ethylene
in a similar fashion. Ethylene is converted to ethylene
oxide (an epoxide) by reacting with peroxybenzoic acid

$\begin{pmatrix} & O & \\ & || & \\ C_6H_5C-O-OH \end{pmatrix}$. Ethylene oxide will react with two moles of
methanol, with an acid catalyst, to produce the desired
product. The electron rich oxygen of methanol attacks a
carbon of ethylene oxide to form methyl cellosolve. The
hydroxyl group becomes protonated and reacts with a second
molecule of methanol. The synthesis is:

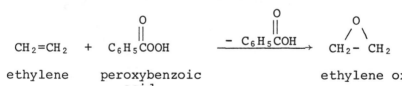

| ethylene | peroxybenzoic acid | | ethylene oxide |

$\underset{\text{methanol}}{\overset{O}{\underset{}{\overset{/\backslash}{CH_2- CH_2}}}}$ + 2 CH_3OH $\xrightarrow[- H_2O]{H^+}$ $\underset{\text{1,2-dimethoxyethane}}{CH_3OCH_2CH_2OCH_3}$

(e) We want to synthesize cis-3-methylcyclopentyl
chloride from trans-3-methylcyclopentanol. The inversion
of configuration can be accomplished by an S_N2 reaction.
Since the hydroxyl group is a poor leaving group, it will
leave only in protonated form; that is, it will leave only
as water. If the starting material reacted with HCl, the
reaction would be more S_N1 than S_N2; therefore racemization

558

and not inversion of configuration would occur. If the
hydroxyl group was replaced by a better leaving group (e.g.
chloride ion), the reaction would proceed mainly via an
S_N2 pathway. This is accomplished by reacting the starting

material with tosyl chloride $\left(CH_3-\bigcirc-\overset{\overset{O}{\|}}{\underset{\underset{O}{\|}}{S}}-Cl \right)$; the O-H

bond of the alcohol is broken and the product has a

tosylate group $\left(CH_3-\bigcirc-\overset{\overset{O}{\|}}{\underset{\underset{O}{\|}}{S}}-O- \right)$ in place of the hydroxyl

group. The tosylate group has excellent leaving group
abilities and will proceed mainly via an S_N2 pathway when
the compound is reacted with chloride ion. The synthesis
is as follows:

trans-3-methyl-
cyclopentanol

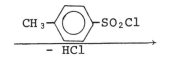
$CH_3-\bigcirc-SO_2Cl$
$\xrightarrow{\text{- HCl}}$

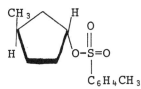

trans-3-methyl
cyclopentyl tosylate

$\Big\downarrow$ $Na^+ Cl^-$

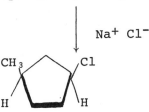

cis-3-methyl-cyclopentyl
chloride

● **PROBLEM** 16-30

Outline all steps in a possible laboratory synthesis of
each of the following compounds from cyclohexanol and any
necessary aliphatic, aromatic, or inorganic reagents.

(a) cyclohexanone ($C_6H_{10}O$) (e) trans-2-methylcyclohexanol
(b) bromocyclohexane   (f) cyclohexylmethylcarbinol
(c) 1-methylcyclohexanol   (g) trans-1,2-dibromocyclohexane
(d) 1-methylcyclohexene   (h) cyclohexanecarboxylic acid
              (i) adipic acid HOOC(CH$_2$)$_4$COOH

559

(a) Like most secondary alcohols $\left(R\text{-}\overset{\overset{\displaystyle R'}{|}}{\underset{}{C}}HOH\right)$,

cyclohexanol will be oxidized to a ketone $\left(R\text{-}\overset{\overset{\displaystyle O}{||}}{C}\text{-}R'\right)$ by oxidizing solutions such as potassium dichromate $(K_2Cr_2O_7)$ in aqueous sulfuric acid or chromium trioxide (CrO_3) in aqueous acetic acid. The synthesis of cyclohexanone from cyclohexanol is:

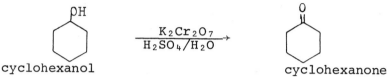

cyclohexanol   cyclohexanone

(b)   Alcohols will react with phosphorous tribromide to form an alkyl bromide. The hydroxyl group is replaced by a bromine atom and this occurs by an S_N displacement reaction. Bromocyclohexane is prepared from cyclohexanol as shown:

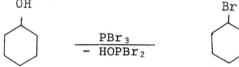

(c)   1-Methylcyclohexanol differs from cyclohexanol in that there is a methyl group bonded to the carbon bearing the hydroxyl group. This extra carbon can be added to cyclohexanol by a Grignard reaction. A Grignard reagent with a one carbon alkyl group (a methylmagnesium halide compound) will react with cyclohexanone to form the Grignard salt of the desired product. Subsequent hydrolysis will lead to 1-methylcyclohexanol. The synthesis is:

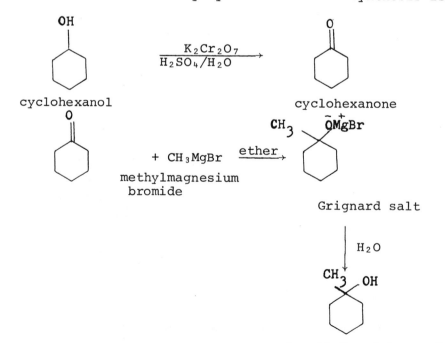

(d)   1-Methylcyclohexene can be prepared from 1-methyl-
cyclohexanol by a dehydration reaction; in acidic solution
an alcohol will have its hydroxyl group protonated and will

undergo an elimination reaction to form an alkene .

If there is more than one alkene that could possibly be
formed (as in our case), the most highly substituted alkene
will be the major product because it is the most stable
one; this product is called the Saytzeff product. The less
substituted alkene (the minor product) is known as the
Hofmann product. Hence 1-methylcyclohexene is synthesized
from cyclohexanol as follows:

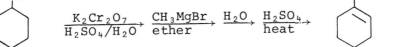

cyclohexanol   1-methylcyclohexanol

$\dfrac{H_2SO_4}{heat}$ →   + H_2O

1-methylcyclohexene

(e)   Trans-2-methyl-cyclohexanol can be prepared from 1-
methylcyclohexene by the hydroboration-oxidation method of
synthesizing alcohols from alkenes. This method involves
the reaction of an alkene with diborane (B_2H_6); the diborane adds cis to the alkene (the hydrogen and boron
atoms add onto the double bond from the same side) and in
an anti-Markovnikov fashion. Oxidation of the alkylborane
(R_3B) by a basic solution of hydrogen peroxide (H_2O_2) will
yield the alcohol. The synthesis of our desired product
from cyclohexanol is:

 $\dfrac{K_2Cr_2O_7}{H_2SO_4/H_2O}$ → $\dfrac{CH_3MgBr}{ether}$ → H_2O, $\dfrac{H_2SO_4}{heat}$ →

cyclohexanol   1-methylcyclo-
                                                hexene

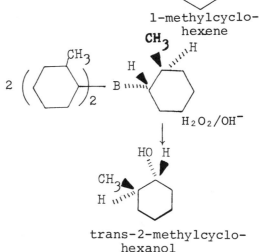

trans-2-methylcyclo-
hexanol

561

Note that the hydroxide ion replaces the boron with retention of configuration. Hence the trans configuration in the alkyl borane is retained in the final product.

(f) The desired product can be synthesized from cyclohexanol by a Grignard reaction. Cyclohexanol must first be converted to the alkyl halide. We can convert it to an alkyl bromide (cyclohexyl bromide) by reacting it with PBr_3. The Grignard reagent can then be made by reacting cyclohexyl bromide with magnesium in dry ether. Reaction of the Grignard reagent with a carbonyl compound consisting of two carbons (acetaldehyde) will lead to the desired product after hydrolysis. The synthesis of cyclohexylmethyl-carbinol from cyclohexanol is:

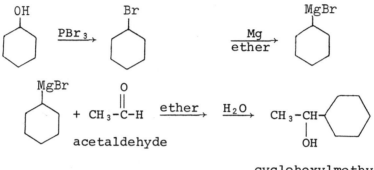

cyclohexylmethyl-
carbinol

(g) Trans-1,2-dibromocyclohexane can be synthesized from cyclohexene by reaction with bromine in carbon tetrachloride. The reaction proceeds through an intermediate cyclic bromonium ion. A bromide ion reacts with the intermediate in a trans fashion to give a trans-product from the alkene. Cyclohexene can be produced from cyclohexanol by a dehydration (elimination) reaction. This is done by heating cyclohexanol with a strong acid.

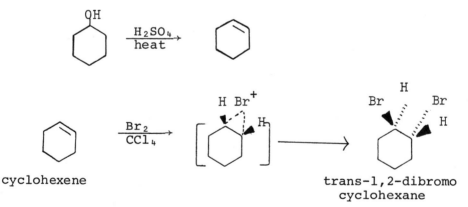

cyclohexene   trans-1,2-dibromo
                                                   cyclohexane

(h) Cyclohexanecarboxylic acid can be prepared by the oxidation of cyclohexylcarbinol by potassium permanganate. Cyclohexylcarbinol in turn can be prepared by the Grignard reaction of cyclohexylmagnesium bromide with formaldehyde. Hence we can synthesize cyclohexanecarboxylic acid as follows:

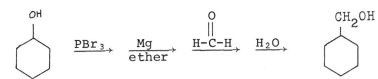

cyclohexanol   cyclohexanolcarbinol

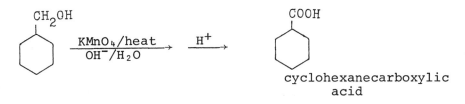

cyclohexanecarboxylic
acid

An alternate route of synthesis uses the reaction of cyclohexylmagnesium bromide with carbon dioxide. Subsequent acidification will yield the desired product:

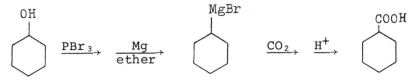

(i) Adipic acid can be synthesized from cyclohexene by an ozonolysis reaction with an oxidative workup. Alkenes react with ozone (O_3) to cleave the σ and π bonds. Upon reaction,

a molozonide $\begin{array}{c} | \quad | \\ -C - C- \\ | \quad | \\ O \quad O \\ \diagdown \diagup \\ O \end{array}$ is formed, which spontaneously

changes to an ozonide $\begin{array}{c} O \\ \diagdown \diagup \diagdown \diagup \\ C \quad C \\ \diagup \diagdown \diagup \diagdown \\ O-O \end{array}$ Oxidative workup of

the ozonide with an acidic solution of hydrogen peroxide (H_2O_2) will yield ketones and/or carboxylic acids and/or carbon dioxide and water. The oxidation products depend upon the degree of substitution of the alkene. Some examples are:

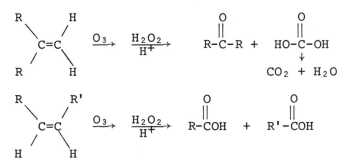

Cyclohexene will undergo an ozonolysis reaction to yield adipic acid upon oxidative workup. Cyclohexene is produced from cyclohexanol by a dehydration (elimination) reaction. The synthesis of adipic acid from cyclohexanol is:

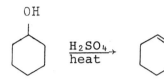

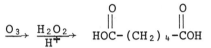

cyclohexanol   cyclohexene   adipic acid

● **PROBLEM** 16-31

A naive graduate student attempted the preparation of $CH_3CH_2CDBrCH_3$ from $CH_3CH_2CDOHCH_3$ by heating the deuterio-alcohol with HBr and H_2SO_4. He obtained a product having the correct boiling point, but a careful examination of the spectral properties by his research director showed that the product was a mixture of $CH_3CHDCHBrCH_3$ and $CH_3CH_2CDBrCH_3$. What happened?

Solution: In acidic media alcohols will become protonated at their hydroxyl oxygen. Subsequent loss of water will produce a carbocation which will react with bromide ion to produce an alkyl bromide. 2-Deuterio-2-butanol reacts with HBr to form a secondary carbocation; a 1,2-hydride shift might occur to give another secondary carbocation; this type of rearrangement readily occurs because there is no change in stability. Hence 2-deuterio-2-butanol reacts with HBr in the following manner:

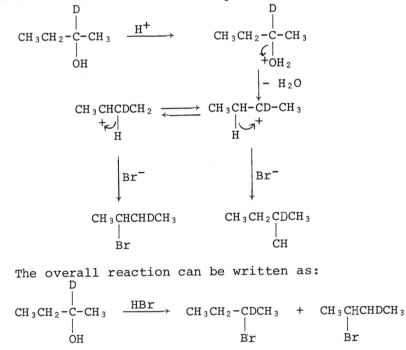

The overall reaction can be written as:

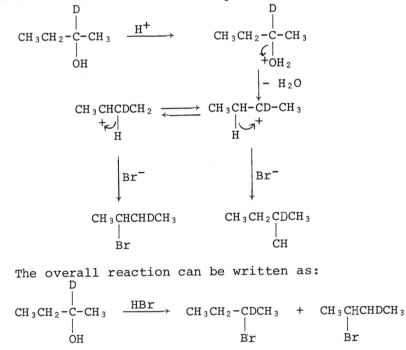

Either t-butyl alcohol or isobutylene treated with strong
sulfuric acid and hydrogen peroxide gives a mixture of
two liquid compounds (A and B), the ratio of which depends
on whether the hydrogen peroxide or organic starting material is in excess. Both substances are reasonably stable and
A is $C_4H_{10}O_2$, whereas B is $C_8H_{18}O_2$.

Treatment of A and B with hydrogen over a nickel
catalyst results in quantitative conversion of each compound to t-butyl alcohol. A reacts with acyl halides and
acid anhydrides, whereas B is unaffected by these reagents.
Treatment of 1 mole of A with excess methylmagnesium iodide
in diethyl ether solution produces 1 mole of methane and
1 mole each of t-butyl alcohol and methanol. One mole of
B with excess methylmagnesium iodide gives 1 mole of methyl
t-butyl ether and 1 mole of t-butyl alcohol.

When B is heated with vinyl chloride it causes polymerization to occur.

Work out structures for A and B from the above data.
Write equations for all the reactions involved, showing the
mechanisms and intermediates that are important for each.

Solution:　　The molecular formula (M.F.) of compounds A
and B are of the type $C_nH_{2n+2}O_2$. This indicates that the
compounds are saturated (there are no C=O or C=C bonds or
rings) and belong to any one of the following classes of
compounds:

(1) dialcohol (a diol)

(2) monohydroxy ether

(3) diether (compound with two ether linkages)

(4) peroxide.

Catalytic hydrogenation of compounds A and B gave
the same product: t-butanol.　The fact that compounds A
and B underwent catalytic hydrogenation indicates that they
are peroxide compounds and cannot be any of the other types
of compounds listed above. This is because catalytic hydrogenation acts upon π bonds (generally C=O and C=C). Since
diols, monohydroxy ethers and diethers do not posses π bonds
they will not undergo catalytic hydrogenation. Peroxides
also lack π bonds but they will undergo catalytic hydrogenation to yield alcohols:

$$R-O-O-R' \xrightarrow{H_2/Ni} R-OH \quad + \quad R'-OH$$

peroxide   alcohol   alcohol

This is because the σ bond between the two oxygens is
a relatively weak bond. The strength of this σ bond is
closer to a C=C π bond than to a C=C σ bond. Hence the

oxygen-oxygen σ bond of peroxides will be broken upon catalytic hydrogenation. t-Butanol ((CH$_3$)$_3$C-OH) was the sole product of the catalytic hydrogenation of A and B. This means that both A and B have their carbons arranged in the same way that t-butanol is structured; that is, the

carbon skeleton of A and B is
$$\begin{array}{c} C \\ | \\ C-C \\ | \\ C \end{array}$$
. Since the M.F. of

compound A is C$_4$H$_{10}$O$_2$, this restricts A to four carbons and hence on t-butyl group. The M.F. of compound B (C$_8$H$_{18}$O$_2$) restricts B to eight carbons and hence two t-butyl groups. Since A and B are peroxides and their catalytic hydrogenation product is t-butanol (which has the -OH on the tertiary carbon), the peroxide linkage (the -O-O- portion) must be located on the tertiary carbon of the t-butyl group(s). Thus a possible structure for compound A is:

$$\begin{array}{c} CH_3 \\ | \\ CH_3-C-O-O-H \\ | \\ CH_3 \end{array}$$

And for Compound B:

$$\begin{array}{c} CH_3 \qquad\ CH_3 \\ | \qquad\qquad | \\ CH_3-C-O-O-C-CH_3 \\ | \qquad\qquad | \\ CH_3 \qquad\ CH_3 \end{array}$$

The reaction for catalytic hydrogenation of these compounds is:

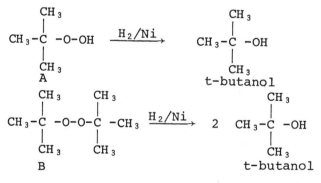

We will try to explain the other experimental results by referring to our suggested structures for A

and B. Compound A reacts with acyl halides $\left(\begin{array}{c} O \\ || \\ R-C-X \end{array} \right)$ and

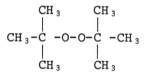

acid anhydrides $\left(\begin{array}{c} O\ \ O \\ ||\ \ || \\ R-COCR \end{array} \right)$ while compound B will not. This can be explained by the fact that A has an -OH functionality

566

whereas B does not. Compounds that have an -OH portion will react with acyl halides and acid anhydrides; the electronegative oxygen will attack the electropositive carbonyl

carbon $\left(\begin{matrix} O^{\delta-} \\ || \\ -C- \\ \delta+ \end{matrix}\right)$ to displace a halide ion or a carboxylate

anion. Subsequent proton loss from the -OH portion results

in ester $\left(\begin{matrix} O \\ || \\ R-C-OR' \end{matrix}\right)$ formation. In our case a peroxy ester

$\left(\begin{matrix} O \\ || \\ R-C-O-O-R' \end{matrix}\right)$ will be formed. The reaction of A with an acyl halide and an acid anhydride is shown below:

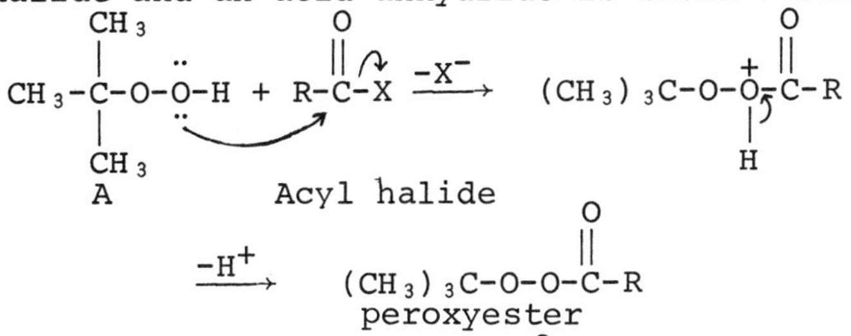

$$\underset{\underset{\underset{A}{CH_3}}{|}}{\overset{\overset{CH_3}{|}}{CH_3-C-O-O-H}} + \underset{Acyl\ halide}{\overset{\overset{O}{||}}{R-C-X}} \xrightarrow{-X^-} (CH_3)_3C-O-\overset{+}{\underset{H}{O}}-C-R$$

$$\xrightarrow{-H^+} \underset{peroxyester}{(CH_3)_3C-O-O-\overset{\overset{O}{||}}{C}-R}$$

$$\underset{A}{(CH_3)_3COOH} + \underset{acid\ anhydride}{R-\overset{\overset{O}{||}}{C}-O-\overset{\overset{O}{||}}{C}-R} \xrightarrow{-\ RCOH} \underset{peroxy\ ester}{(CH_3)_3C-O-O-\overset{\overset{O}{||}}{C}-R}$$

Grignard reagents (R'-Mg-X) will react with peroxides of the type R-O-O-H to remove the active hydrogen (ROOH) and form a hydrocarbon (R'H) and a Grignard salt (ROO-MgX). If there is excess Grignard reagent, it will react with ROOMgX to form two Grignard salts which will be converted to alcohols upon hydrolysis:

$$ROOH\ +\ R'MgX\ \longrightarrow\ \underset{hydrocarbon}{R'H}\ +\ ROOMgX$$

$$ROMgX\ +\ R'OMgX\ \xleftarrow{R'MgX}$$
$$\Big\downarrow H_2O$$
$$\underset{alcohols}{ROH\ +\ R'OH}$$

Peroxides of the type ROOR will react with excess Grignard reagent to form an ether and an alcohol (after hydrolysis of the Grignard salt):

$$ROOR\ +\ R'MgX\ \longrightarrow\ ROMgX\ +\ \underset{ether}{ROR'}$$

$$\Big\downarrow H_2O$$

$$\underset{alcohol}{ROH}$$

Compounds A and B react with excess methylmagnesium iodide as follows:

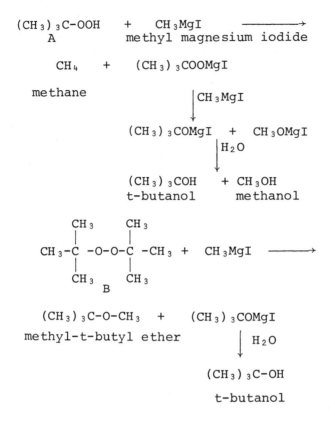

$(CH_3)_3C-OOH$ + CH_3MgI $\longrightarrow$
A   methyl magnesium iodide

CH_4 + $(CH_3)_3COOMgI$

methane

$\downarrow CH_3MgI$

$(CH_3)_3COMgI$ + CH_3OMgI

$\downarrow H_2O$

$(CH_3)_3COH$ + CH_3OH
t-butanol   methanol

$CH_3-\underset{\underset{CH_3}{|}}{\overset{\overset{CH_3}{|}}{C}}-O-O-\underset{\underset{CH_3}{|}}{\overset{\overset{CH_3}{|}}{C}}-CH_3$ + CH_3MgI $\longrightarrow$
B

$(CH_3)_3C-O-CH_3$ + $(CH_3)_3COMgI$

methyl-t-butyl ether

$\downarrow H_2O$

$(CH_3)_3C-OH$

t-butanol

Peroxides of the type ROOR are often used as radical initiators in free radical polymerization reactions. According to our suggested structures, compound B is a peroxide of the type ROOR. Vinyl chloride will undergo a free radical polymerization to form polyvinylchloride (PVC). Polymerization occurs in a head to tail fashion; the growing end of the polymer chain is the most stable radical possible. Hence the growing end of the PVC chain will be

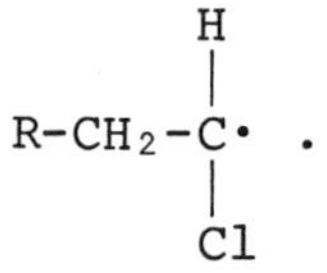

$$R-CH_2-\underset{\underset{Cl}{|}}{\overset{\overset{H}{|}}{C}}\cdot \quad .$$

When peroxides are heated, the weak oxygen-oxygen σ bond is broken and an alkoxy radical ($R-\overset{..}{O}\cdot$) is formed. This is the initiation step in free radical polymerization.

Compound B reacts with vinyl chloride to form PVC when heated as follows:

initiation { $(CH_3)_3C-\overset{..}{\underset{..}{O}}-\overset{..}{\underset{..}{O}}-C(CH_3)_3$ $\xrightarrow{\text{heat}}$ $2 (CH_3)_3C-\overset{..}{O}\cdot$

$$\text{propagation}\begin{cases}
(CH_3)_3C\text{-}\ddot{O}\cdot \; + \; CH_2{=}CHCl \quad \longrightarrow \\[2em]
(CH_3)_3C\text{-}O\text{-}CH_2\text{-}\underset{\underset{Cl}{|}}{\overset{\overset{H}{|}}{C}}\cdot \; + \; n(CH_2{=}CHCl) \quad \longrightarrow \\[2em]
(CH_3)_3C\text{-}O{\left(CH_2\text{-}CHCl\right)}_{\!n}CH_2\text{-}\underset{\underset{Cl}{|}}{\overset{\overset{H}{|}}{C}}\cdot
\end{cases}$$

$$\text{termination}\begin{cases}
2 \; (CH_3)_3CO{\left(CH_2CHCl\right)}_{\!n}CH_2\underset{\underset{Cl}{|}}{\overset{\overset{H}{|}}{C}}\cdot \quad \longrightarrow \\[2em]
(CH_3)_3CO{\left(CH_2CHCl\right)}_{\!2n+2}OC(CH_3)_3 \\[1em]
\qquad\quad - \text{ and/or } - \\[1em]
2 \; (CH_3)_3CO{\left(CH_2CHCl\right)}_{\!n}CH_2\text{-}\underset{\underset{Cl}{|}}{\overset{\overset{H}{|}}{C}}\cdot \quad \text{—} \\[2em]
(CH_3)_3CO{\left(CH_2CHCl\right)}_{\!n}CH_2CH_2Cl \; + \\[1em]
(CH_3)_3CO{\left(CH_2CHCl\right)}_{\!n}CH{=}CHCl \\[1em]
\qquad\quad - \text{ and/or } - \\[1em]
(CH_3)_3CO{\left(CH_2CHCl\right)}_{\!n}CH_2\underset{\underset{Cl}{|}}{\overset{\overset{H}{|}}{C}}\cdot \; + \; (CH_3)_3C\ddot{O}\cdot \\[2em]
\qquad\qquad\qquad \downarrow \\[1em]
(CH_3)_3CO{\left(CH_2CHCl\right)}_{\!n+1}OC(CH_3)_3
\end{cases}$$

Since all the reactions of compounds A and B have been accounted for by our suggested structures, compounds A and B must be the ones we suggested.

HYDROBORATION

Identify the alcohol that will be produced by the hydroboration-oxidation of the following:

(a) $D_2C=CHCH_3$
(b) $CH_3CH=CHCH_3$ (Z isomer)   (d)
(c) $CH_3CH=CHCH_3$ (E isomer)

Solution: Alcohols can be synthesized from alkenes by
a hydroboration-oxidation procedure. This method involves
the reaction of diborane (B_2H_6) with the alkene; subsequent
oxidation by a basic solution of hydrogen peroxide (H_2O_2)
will yield the alcohol. Diborane adds cis to the alkene
and in an anti-Markovnikov fashion. The general reaction
is shown as:

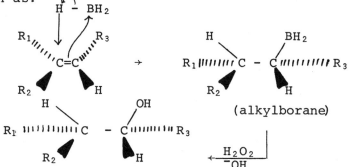

        With this information we can predict the hydrobora-
tion-oxidation products of alkenes (a) through (d).

(a)   Diborane adds to the alkene in an anti-Markovnikov
fashion; that is, the carbon bearing the least number of
hydrogens (or deuterons) will be protonated. Hence,

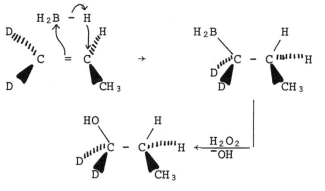

The product is $HO-CD_2CH_2CH_3$, 1,1-dideuteriopropanol.

(b)   The Z isomer of 2-butene is called cis-2-butene; it
has the structure:

The hydroboration-oxidation of cis-2-butene is shown as:

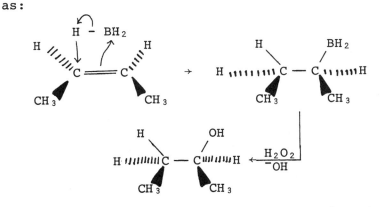

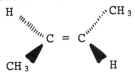

Either carbon of the alkene can receive the hydrogen since they are equivalent. BH$_3$ can attack either face of the double bond equally well and hence the product will be a racemic mixture of dextrorotatory and levorotatory 2-butanol. The product is therefore (d,ℓ)-2-butanol.

(c)   The E isomer of 2-butene is called trans-2-butene and has the structure:

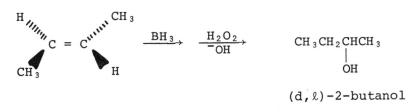

Either one of the sp^2-hybridized carbons can receive the hydrogen from BH$_3$ because they are equivalent. Since BH$_3$ can attack either face of the double bond equally well the product will be a racemic mixture of 2-butanol. This is the same product formed in part (b).

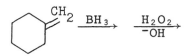

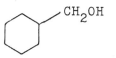

(d,ℓ)-2-butanol

(d)   Hydroboration-oxidation of methylene cyclohexane would place the hydroxyl group on the =CH$_2$. Hence the product is cyclohexylcarbinol.

methylene
cyclohexane

cyclohexylcarbinol

Predict the products of hydroboration-oxidation of:
(a) cis-2-phenyl-2-butene; (b) trans-2-phenyl-2-butene;
(c) 1-methylcyclohexene.

Solution: When diborane, $(BH_3)_2$, is added to alkenes,
they undergo hydroboration to yield alkylboranes, R_3B.
These compounds give rise to alcohols on oxidation. This
hydroboration oxidation may be illustrated as:

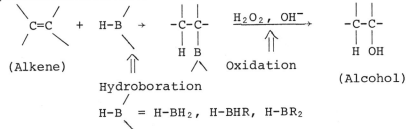

It is important to recognize that this reaction
gives products corresponding to anti-Markovnikov addition
of water to the carbon-carbon double bond. This behavior
evidently results because carbonium ions are not intermediates - rearrangement does not occur in hydroboration.
The stereochemistry of this reaction involves syn addition,
that is, addition to the double bond is on the same face
of the alkene.
    With this in mind, the following products can be
predicted after hydroboration-oxidation:

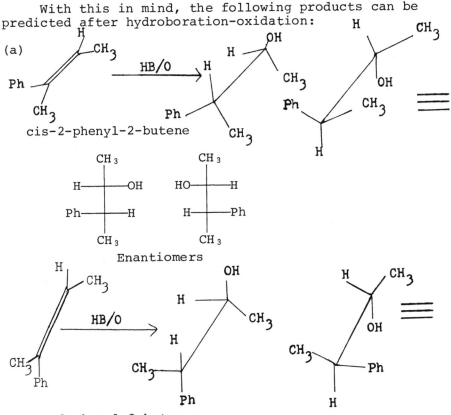

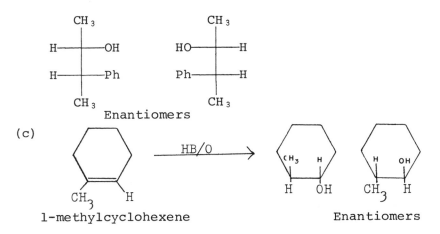

Enantiomers

(c)

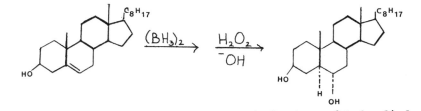

1-methylcyclohexene   Enantiomers

In each case, the reaction proceeds with syn-addition (hydration) and anti-Markovnikov orientation.

● **PROBLEM** 16-35

(a) As shown in the diagram below, cholesterol is converted into cholestane-3β,6α-diol through syn-hydration by hydroboration-oxidation. What stereoisomeric product could also have been formed by syn-hydration? Actually, the reaction gives a 78% yield of cholestane-3β,6α-diol, and only a small amount of its stereoisomer. What factor do you think is responsible for this particular stereospecificity?

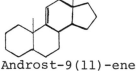

cholesterol   cholestane-3β,6α-diol

$$CH_3$$
$$C_8H_{17} = -CH-CH_2CH_2CH_2CH(CH_3)_2$$

(b) Hydroboration of androst-9(11)-ene gives 90% of a single stereoisomer. Which would you expect this to be?

Androst-9(11)-ene

Solution: (a) Hydroboration-oxidation occurs with cis addition to the alkene in an anti-Markovnikov fashion. Diborane can add onto either face of the alkene. Since the overall hydration process occurs in a cis fashion, hyd-

roboration-oxidation gives syn hydration. Hydration of
cholesterol occurs from "beneath" to yield cholestane-
3β,6α-diol (β positions are cis to the ring substituents,
α positions are trans) and from "above" to yield the
stereoisomeric coprostane-3β,6β-diol:

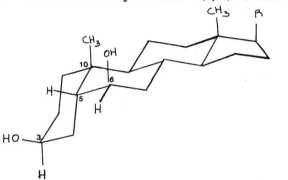

Note:

$R=C_8H_{17}$

Coprostane-3β,6β-diol

   Attack from "above" has greater steric hindrance
than from "below" because of the substituents projecting
"upward", particularly the methyl group at carbon number
ten. Hence, the 3β,6α-diol is formed in greater yield
than the 3β,6β-diol.

(b) Syn-hydration would occur mainly from the side that
is less sterically hindered; that is, from "beneath". The
main product has an α-OH at carbon number eleven and an
α-H at carbon number nine.

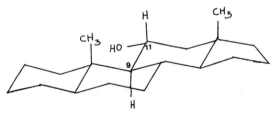

CHAPTER 17

ETHERS

NOMENCLATURE AND STRUCTURE

● PROBLEM 17-1

Name each of the following compounds:

(a) $CH_3-O-CH_2-CH(CH_3)_2$

(b) $(CH_3CH_2CH_2)_2-O$

(c) $(CH_3)_2CH-O-CH_2CH_2CH_2CH_3$

(d) $CH_3-O-CH_2CH_2-O-CH_3$

(e) $CH_3CH_2-O-CH_2CH_2CH_2CH_2CH_2-OH$

(f)
$$\begin{array}{c} Cl \\ | \\ CH_3CHCH_2CH-CH_2 \\ \diagdown \quad \diagup \\ O \end{array}$$

<u>Solution:</u>   Ethers have the general formula of R-O-R, where R may represent an alkyl or aryl group. To name many ethers, one usually names the two groups that are attached to oxygen, and follow these names by the word "ether".

(a)   The compound $CH_3-O-CH_2CH\begin{smallmatrix} CH_3 \\ \diagup \\ \diagdown \\ CH_3 \end{smallmatrix}$ has the oxygen of the ether linkage bonded to methyl and an isobutyl groups. It is called isobutyl methyl ether.

(b) $CH_3CH_2CH_2-O-CH_2CH_2CH_3$ is a symmetrical molecule because the two groups bound to the oxygen are identical. In this compound, the two groups are n-propyls. Thus, it is named dipropyl ether, or n-propyl ether. It is understood that if the name only contains one substituent group, the compound is symmetrical.

(c)   The compound $\begin{smallmatrix} CH_3 \\ \diagdown \\ CH-O-CH_2CH_2CH_2CH_3 \\ \diagup \\ CH_3 \end{smallmatrix}$ contains an isopropyl group and an n-butyl group. It is called n-butyl isopropyl ether.

(d) When an ether contains groups which do not have simple names, the compound may be named as an alkoxy derivative. The alkoxy functional group can be written as RO, where R may be an alkyl group. Since $CH_3-O-CH_2CH_2-O-CH_3$ contains two ether functional groups, which make naming very complicated, one may name the compound as a derivative of ethane. The two substituent groups are both methoxy (CH_3O-) at carbons 1 and 2, respectively. Thus, the compound can be named as 1,2-dimethoxy-ethane.

(e) $CH_3CH_2-O-CH_2CH_2CH_2CH_2CH_2OH$ has two functional groups, alkoxy (or ether) and hydroxy (or alcohol). In the IUPAC system, the alcohol functional group takes precedence over the ether in naming. (Exception can be made if the naming is overly complicated when named as an alcohol.)

The compound in question can be named as an alcohol with an alkoxy substitution. The hydrocarbon containing the hydroxyl has five carbons. Thus, the compound is a derivative of n-pentanol. The alkoxy substitution is an ethoxy (CH_3CH_2O-) group at the number five carbon (the hydroxyl group is attached to the first carbon). The complete name for the compound is 5-ethoxy-1-pentanol.

(f) The compound $CH_3CCHCH_2CH-CH_2$ contains a three member

$$\underset{Cl}{\overset{\displaystyle |}{}}\quad\overset{O}{\underset{\diagdown\diagup}{}}$$

ring which includes an oxygen atom. Such compounds are called epoxides. The epoxides are named by numbering the alkyl chain and indicating the two carbons to which the oxygen is attached. The prefix "epoxy" denotes this functional group. Here, the alkyl group contains five carbons; it is a pentane. The epoxide oxygen is attached to carbons 1 and 2, so that the name becomes 1,2-epoxy-pentane. The compound also has a chlorine substitution at carbon number four. The full name for

$$\underset{Cl}{\overset{\displaystyle |}{}}$$
$CH_3CHCH_2-CH-CH_2$ is 4-chloro-1,2-epoxypentane.
$$\overset{O}{\underset{\diagdown\diagup}{}}$$

• PROBLEM 17-2

Write structural formulas for:

(a) methyl ether
(b) isopropyl methyl ether
(c) 3-methoxyhexane
(d) 1,2-epoxypentane

Solution: The characteristic functional group in ethers
is the oxygen atom single bonded to two carbon atoms. The
general formulas for these compounds are R'OR, ROAr and
Ar'OAr, where R and R' are either different or identical
alkyl groups and Ar and Ar' represent different or identical
aryl groups.

When naming simple ethers, both of the attached groups
are named in alphabetical order followed by the word 'ether'.
For example,

$$CH_3-O-CH_2CH_3$$

is called ethyl methyl ether.

(a)   If both of the attached groups are the same, the compound is a symmetrical ether, and only one group need be
named. For example, the compound $CH_3CH_2-O-CH_2CH_3$ is usually
called ethyl ether. Often to avoid confusion this compound
is referred to as diethyl ether. The structure for methyl
ether is analogous to this. There is one methyl group on
each side of the oxygen. The structure can be written as
follows:

$$CH_3-O-CH_3.$$

This compound is also called dimethyl ether.

(b)   isopropyl methyl ether. This is a simple asymmetrical
ether. From its name, one knows that there is a methyl
group on one side of the oxygen and an isopropyl group on
the other. The structure for this compound is written:

$$CH_3-O-CH-CH_3$$
$$|$$
$$CH_3$$

(c)   In more complicated ethers, the ether grouping, R-O-
(an alkoxy group), may be named as a substituent on a
longer chain. A methoxy group is written $-O-CH_3$. In 3-
methoxyhexane, the methoxy group is attached to the carbon
at the 3 position of the hexane chain.

$$CH_3-CH_2-CH-CH_2-CH_2-CH_3$$
$$|$$
$$O-CH_3$$

3-methoxyhexane

(d) Epoxides are a class of cyclic ethers in which the
ether oxygen is included in a three-membered ring,

$- \overset{|}{C} - \overset{|}{C} -$. Ethylene oxide is drawn as shown: $CH_2 - CH_2$
with O below.

The epoxides are named by numbering the alkyl chain and
indicating the two carbons to which the oxygen is attached.
The prefix 'epoxy' denotes this functional group. Ethylene

oxide can also be called epoxyethane. In 1,2-epoxypentane, the oxygen is bound to the first two carbons of the pentane chain.

$$CH_2 - CH-CH_2-CH_2-CH_3$$
$$\diagdown O \diagup$$

1,2-epoxypentane

A compound of MW 74 did not react with acetyl chloride, $KMnO_4$, phenylhydrazine, or Schiff's reagent. It dissolved in concentrated H_2SO_4. Suggest three possible structures.

Solution: The molecular weight indicates that it is a small molecule, having at most five carbons. Since it is inert with respect to acetyl chloride, one can make several assumptions.

(1) It contains no amino (NH_2) group, or it would have formed an amide linkage $\left(\begin{array}{c} O \\ \| \\ C \\ \diagup \diagdown \diagup \\ NH \end{array} \right)$.

(2) It is not an alcohol because alcohol and acetyl chloride can undergo an esterification reaction to give

$$\begin{array}{c} O \\ \| \\ C \\ \diagup \diagdown \\ O-R \end{array}$$

(3) It is not aromatic because it does not undergo Friedel-Crafts acylation to give a methyl aryl ketone $\left(\begin{array}{c} O \\ \| \\ Ar-C-CH_3 \end{array} \right)$.

Since $KMnO_4$ is an oxidizing reagent for olefins, and the compound is unreactive to $KMnO_4$, it is not an olefin. It does not react with phenylhydrazine or Schiff's reagent; therefore, it is not a carbonyl compound. (Phenylhydrazine can react with the carbonyl group of aldehydes and ketones to form phenylhydrazone; Schiff's reagent is used to identify aldehydes.) Since the compound dissolves in concentrated sulfuric acid, the presence of an oxygen atom is indicated.

Putting all the information together, one obtains a compound with general formula of C_nH_mO. Since oxygen has MW 16, C_nH_m must have MW 58. Keeping in mind the rule C_NH_{2N+2} and the weight limitation of 58, the combination of carbon and hydrogen that fits is C_4H_{10}. (The molecular weights of carbon and hydrogen are, respectively, 12 and 1. Hence, $12(N) + 1(2N + 2) = 58$; $n = 4$.) The molecular formula becomes, therefore, $C_4H_{10}O$. Such a compound may be either an alcohol or ether. Alcohols have already been eliminated by the compounds failure to react with acetyl chloride. Hence, $C_4H_{10}O$ must be an ether. The three possible structures with this molecular formula are as follows:

(1) $CH_3OCH_2CH_2CH_3$ (methyl propyl ether)

(2) $CH_3CH_2OCH_2CH_3$ (diethyl ether)

(3) $CH_3OCH-CH_3$ (isopropyl methyl ether)
   $\quad\quad\quad |$
   $\quad\quad\quad CH_3$

PREPARATION

● PROBLEM 17-4

Outline a method of synthesizing α-phenylethyl tert-butyl ether from styrene and tert-butyl alcohol. Any inorganic reagents may be employed.

Solution: α-phenylethyl tert-butyl ether

$$\begin{pmatrix} C_6H_5CHCH_3 \\ | \\ OC(CH_3)_3 \end{pmatrix}$$ may be produced from styrene ($C_6H_5CH=CH_2$)

and tert-butyl alcohol (($CH_3)_3COH$) by using the alkoxy-mercuration-demercuration reaction. In this reaction, alkenes react with mercuric trifluoroacetate

$$\begin{pmatrix} +2 & - \\ Hg & (OOCCF_3)_2 \end{pmatrix}$$ in the presence of an alcohol to give

alkoxymercurial compounds which on reduction yield ethers. Overall, the general reaction may be written as:

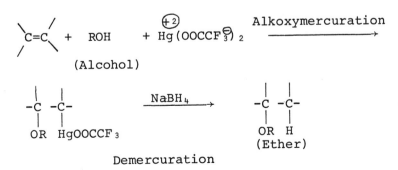

This reaction has great utility in that it is fast, convenient, gives good yields, has little or no rearrangement, and has no competing elimination reaction. Therefore, the following equation can be written for the synthesis of α-phenylethyl tert-butyl ether:

$$C_6H_5CH=CH_2 + (CH_3)_3COH \xrightarrow{\overset{\oplus}{Hg}(OOCCF_3)_2 \overset{\ominus}{}} \xrightarrow{NaBH_4} C_6H_5CHCH_3$$
$$\underset{OC(CH_3)_3}{|}$$

● **PROBLEM** 17-5

Starting with any alcohols, outline all steps in the synthesis of n-hexyl isopropyl ether, using the Williamson method.

Solution: The Williamson synthesis of ethers is important because of its versatility in the laboratory. This method of synthesis can be used to make asymmetrical ethers as well as symmetrical ethers. In the Williamson synthesis, an alkyl halide is allowed to react with a sodium alkoxide (or sodium phenoxide).

$$R - X \quad + R' - O^- Na^+ \rightarrow \quad R-O-R' + Na^+X^-,$$
Alkyl halide Sodium alkoxide   Ether

where R represents an alkyl group and X a halide (Cl, Br, I or F). [The yield from RX is: $CH_3 > 1° > 2° (>3°)$.] The sodium alkoxide is made by direct action of sodium metal on dry alcohols:

$$R - OH + Na \rightarrow \quad R - O^- Na^+ \quad + \tfrac{1}{2} H_2 \uparrow$$
Sodium alkoxide

As an example,

$$CH_3- CH_2OH \quad + \quad Na \quad \rightarrow \quad CH_3-CH_2-O^- Na^+$$

Ethanol   Sodium ethoxide

Alkyl halides can be prepared from alcohols by use of phosphorus trihalides:

$$R - OH + PX_3 \quad \rightarrow \quad RX \quad + \quad H_3PO_3$$

Alkyl halide

As an example,

$$\underset{\text{Isobutyl alcohol}}{\overset{\overset{\displaystyle CH_3}{|}}{CH_3-CH -CH_2OH} + PCl_3} \qquad \underset{\text{Isobutyl chloride}}{\overset{\overset{\displaystyle CH_3}{|}}{CH_3-CH-CH_2Cl}} \qquad + \quad H_3PO_3$$

The Williamson synthesis involves nucleophilic substitution of the alkoxide ion for the halide ion.

The compound n-hexyl isopropyl ether is an a-symmetrical ether with the formula

$$CH_3(CH_2)_4CH_2-O-\overset{\overset{\displaystyle CH_3}{|}}{CH}-CH_3 \quad \text{and can be prepared from the}$$

corresponding alcohols, n-hexyl alcohol and isopropyl alcohol. The complete reactions are:

$$\overset{\overset{\displaystyle CH_3}{|}}{CH_3-CH-OH} \quad + \text{ Na} \longrightarrow \quad \overset{\overset{\displaystyle CH_3}{|}}{CH_3-CH-O^-Na^+}$$

Isopropyl   Sodium isopropoxide
alcohol

$$CH_3(CH_2)_4CH_2OH \quad + \quad PBr_3 \longrightarrow \quad CH_3(CH_2)_4CH_2Br + H_3PO_3$$

n-Hexyl alcohol   n-Hexyl bromide

$$CH_3(CH_2)_4CH_2Br \quad + CH_3-\overset{\overset{\displaystyle CH_3}{|}}{CH}-O^-Na^+ \rightarrow CH_3(CH_2)_4CH_2-O-\underset{\underset{\displaystyle CH_3}{|}}{CH}-CH_3 + NaBr$$

n-Hexyl bromide +   isopropoxide   n-Hexyl isopropyl
                                            ether

● **PROBLEM** 17-6

In ether formation by dehydration, as in most other cases of nucleophilic substitution, there is a competing elimination reaction. What is this reaction and what products does it yield? For what alcohols would elimination be most important?

Solution: Ethers have the general formula R-O-R, where R can be aryl and/or alkyl. Ethers can be formed by two alcohols molcules in the presence of strong acid to release a water molecule. This is called acid-catalyzed dehydration of alcohols to form ethers.

The mechanism of this reaction resembles that of substitution. It involves the protonation of one alcohol and release of a water molecule to form a carbonium ion. A carbonium ion is a strong electrophile. It attacks the electron-rich oxygen of another alcohol, which releases a proton to form an ether.

$$R-O-H \quad \xrightarrow[\text{heat}]{H_2SO_4} \quad R^\oplus \; + \; H_2O$$

$$R^\oplus + \quad \overset{\displaystyle ..}{:O}-R \longrightarrow \quad R-O-R \; + \; H^\oplus$$
$$\quad\quad\quad \underset{\displaystyle H}{|}$$

581

Under closer scrutiny, one can see that in the
process of strong acid protonation of alcohol, another
reaction can occur instead of the substitution attack on
another alcohol. A carbonium ion is a highly reactive
species. It can participate in a substitution reaction,
as in ether formation, or undergo an elimination reaction
to form an alkene. The latter reaction is most prominent
in tertiary alcohols.

A tertiary alcohol has the general formula of

R
|
R-C-OH . It is a bulky molecule. This bulkiness makes the
|
R

positively-charged carbon of the carbonium ion formed less
accessible. Therefore, the tertiary carbonium ion can release a proton (H$^\oplus$) to obtain the alkene, which will be
stabilized by the alkyl substituents.

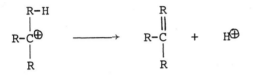

The dehydration of alcohols to ethers rather than
alkenes also reflects the choice of reaction conditions.

● **PROBLEM** 17-7

An alkyl bromide, $C_5H_{11}Br$ reacted rapidly with water to
give an alcohol $C_5H_{12}O$, but when the alkyl bromide was
treated with sodium methoxide in an attempt to convert
it to an ether, the only product was an alkene, C_5H_{10}.
Ozonolysis of this alkene gave two carbonyl compounds as
products, a ketone C_3H_6O and an aldehyde C_2H_4O. What was
the structure of the alkyl bromide?

Solution: One method of synthesizing an ether is by
reacting sodium alkoxide (Na$^+$$^-$O-R´) with an alkyl halide.
Such a preparation is referred to as Williamson synthesis.
Since the alkoxide is nucleophilic and a halide is a good
leaving group, a substitution reaction may occur. The rate
of a substitution reaction depends on the degree of alkylation of the carbon bearing the halide. A primary alkyl
halide can undergo a substitution reaction faster than a
secondary alkyl halide, which is faster than a tertiary
alkyl halide. For a tertiary alkyl halide, the substitution
reaction is so slow that the competing elimination reaction
begins to predominate. Elimination should be particularly
serious when tertiary alkyl halides are present due to the
strong basicity of the alkoxide reagent. (Keep in mind that
the tendency for alkyl halides to under dehydrohalogenation,
an elimination reaction, is 3°>2°>1°.)

The fact that the alkyl bromide, $C_5H_{11}Br$, gave an elimination product, an alkene, and not the ether when treated with sodium methoxide strongly suggests it is

$$\text{tertiary, that is, } R-\overset{\displaystyle R}{\underset{\displaystyle Br}{C}}-R, \text{ where R represents alkyl groups.}$$

Each alkyl group must possess at least one carbon atom, so that the tertiary alkyl halide may be rewritten as: $C-\overset{\displaystyle C}{\underset{\displaystyle Br}{C}}-C.$

The molecular formula, $C_5H_{11}Br$, indicates the existence of a total of five carbon atoms, and the above structure accounts for four. The fifth carbon can only be bonded to one of the three available carbon atoms, which are all equivalent. Hence, the carbon skeleton (plus bromine) must

be $C-\overset{\displaystyle C}{\underset{\displaystyle Br}{C}}-C-C.$ Filling the hydrogens, the structure becomes

$H_3C-\overset{\displaystyle CH_3}{\underset{\displaystyle Br}{C}}-CH_2CH_3$. This fits the molecular formula for the

alkyl halide and represents the structure in question.

This determination could have been made in another fashion - by analysis of the products of ozonolysis. It will be remembered that ozone (O_3) with Zn and H_2O cleaves carbon-carbon double bonds to give aldehydes

$\left(\overset{\displaystyle O}{\underset{\displaystyle R-C-H}{\|}} \right)$ and ketones $\left(\overset{\displaystyle O}{\underset{\displaystyle R-C-R}{\|}} \right)$. A doubly bonded oxygen

is found attached to each of the originally doubly-bonded carbons. The aldehyde obtained here was C_2H_4O, which can only have the structure: $H_3C-\overset{\displaystyle C}{\underset{\displaystyle H}{C}}=O.$ Likewise, the ketone,

C_3H_6O, can only be written as: $H_3C-\overset{\displaystyle C}{\underset{\displaystyle CH_3}{C}}=O.$ Working backwards,

this means that the alkene originally oxidized was:

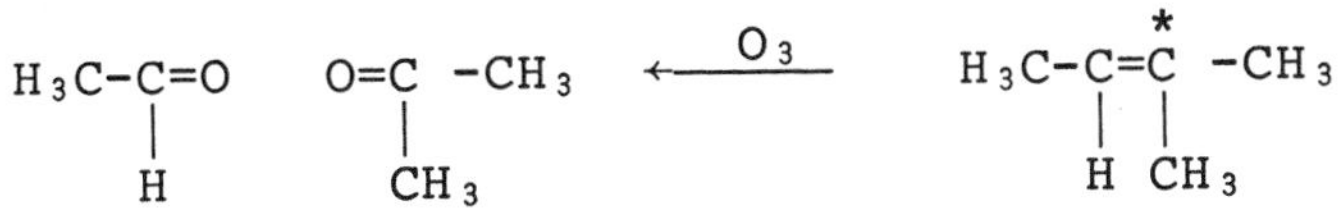

$$H_3C-\overset{\displaystyle C}{\underset{\displaystyle H}{C}}=O \quad O=\overset{\displaystyle C}{\underset{\displaystyle CH_3}{C}}-CH_3 \quad \xleftarrow{\quad O_3 \quad} \quad H_3C-\overset{\displaystyle \quad *}{\underset{\displaystyle H\ CH_3}{C}=C}-CH_3$$

Now, recall that the alkyl bromide from which this alkene was obtained must be tertiary. The only way this could happen is if the bromine is positioned on the starred (*) carbon, that is, the structure must be:

$$
\begin{array}{c}
\text{Br} \\
| \\
\text{H}_3\text{C-CH}_2\text{-C -CH}_3 \\
| \\
\text{CH}_3
\end{array}
$$

● **PROBLEM** 17-8

The following compounds are commercially available for use as water-soluble solvents. How could each be made?

(a) $CH_3CH_2-O-CH_2CH_2-O-CH_2CH_2-OH$ Carbitol

(b) $C_6H_5-O-CH_2CH_2-O-CH_2CH_2-OH$ Phenyl carbitol

(c) $HO-CH_2CH_2-O-CH_2CH_2-OH$ Diethylene glycol

(d) $HO-CH_2CH_2-O-CH_2CH_2-O-CH_2CH_2-OH$ Triethylene glycol

Solution: (a) Carbitol ($CH_3CH_2-O-CH_2CH_2-O-CH_2CH_2-OH$) may be synthesized by making use of the chemistry of epoxides. When acid is added to epoxides, they become protonated epoxides which can then undergo attack by any number of nucleophilic reagents. The overall result is acid-catalyzed cleavage of epoxides as written below:

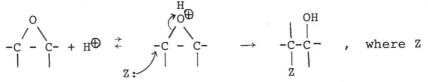

is the nucleophile. Now, the reaction of epoxide with alcohol and acid generates a compound that is both an ether and an alcohol as shown:

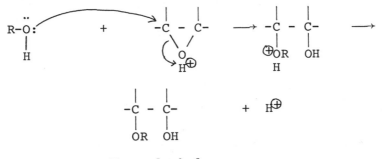

An alkoxyalcohol
(A hydroxyether)

Examination of the structure of carbitol reveals the fact that this compound is both an alcohol and an ether,

584

but with two ether linkages. Hence, its synthesis must be of the same nature as that pictured above.

In the first step of the synthesis, ethanol (CH_3CH_2OH) is taken as the starting material. Ethylene oxide

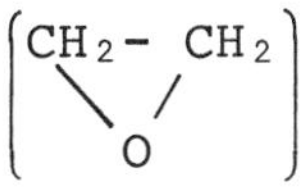

$\left(\begin{array}{c} CH_2- CH_2 \\ \diagdown \diagup \\ O \end{array} \right)$ is then added in the presence of acid. The

product then becomes 2-ethoxyethanol ($CH_3CH_2OCH_2CH_2OH$). The reaction may be written as:

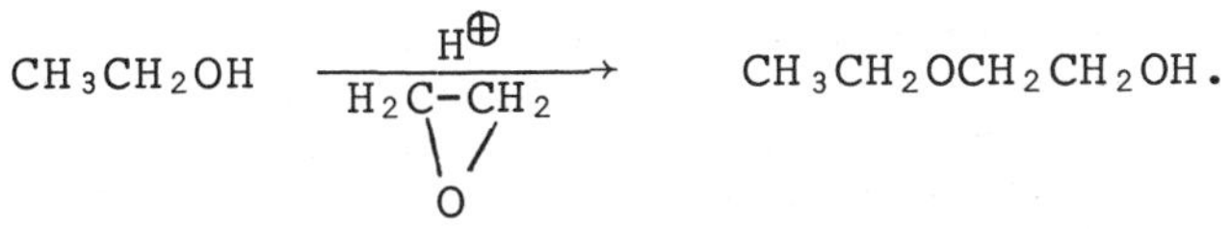

$$CH_3CH_2OH \xrightarrow[\substack{H_2C-CH_2 \\ \diagdown \diagup \\ O}]{H^{\oplus}} CH_3CH_2OCH_2CH_2OH. \qquad \text{At this}$$

point, another ethylene oxide must be added (with acid) to synthesize carbitol. ($CH_3CH_2OCH_2CH_2OH$ possesses a hydroxyl (OH) group so that it may act as the nucleophile when the ethylene oxide is protonated by acid.) Consequently,

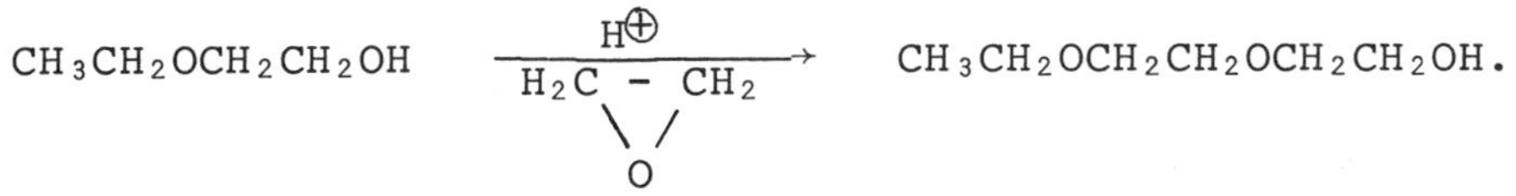

$$CH_3CH_2OCH_2CH_2OH \xrightarrow[\substack{H_2C - CH_2 \\ \diagdown \diagup \\ O}]{H^{\oplus}} CH_3CH_2OCH_2CH_2OCH_2CH_2OH.$$

(b) Phenyl carbitol can be synthesized in the same fashion as carbitol, except that the starting material is

phenol $\left[\bighexagon - OH \right]$, not ethanol.

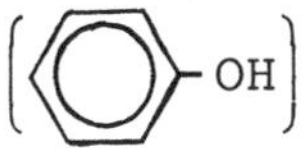

(c) Diethylene glycol is also synthesized in a manner similar to that of carbitol. Here, though, ethanol is replaced by water (HOH).

(d) Triethylene glycol may be readily manufactured if the product from part (c), diethylene glycol, is used as the starting material. Ethylene oxide and acid (H^+) could be added to diethylene glycol to obtain triethylene glycol as illustrated:

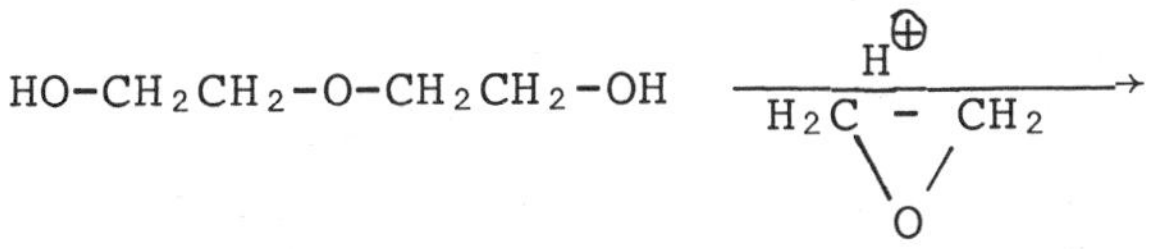

$$HO-CH_2CH_2-O-CH_2CH_2-OH \xrightarrow[\substack{H_2C - CH_2 \\ \diagdown \diagup \\ O}]{H^{\oplus}}$$

$$HO-CH_2CH_2-O-CH_2CH_2-O-CH_2CH_2-OH \text{ (triethylene glycol)}$$

● **PROBLEM** 17-9

Synthesize trans-1-methoxy-2-methylcyclopentane from 1-methylcyclopentene using any needed reagents.

<u>Solution:</u>   The problem asks for the following conversion:

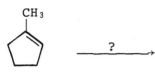

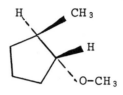

1-methylcyclopentene

trans-1-methoxy-2-methyl-
cyclopentane

Since the groups participating in the ether linkage
are not identical, the ether to be synthesized is a-
symmetrical. One method of producing asymmetrical ethers
is through the Williamson synthesis. In this reaction,
an alkyl halide (or substituted alkyl halide) is allowed
to react with a sodium alkoxide or a sodium phenoxide as
shown:

$$R - X \quad\quad + \quad Na^{\oplus} \; {}^{-}O\text{-}R \quad\quad \rightarrow \quad R\text{-}O\text{-}R' \quad + \quad Na^{\oplus} \; X^{\ominus}$$

(Alkyl halide)   (Sodium alkoxide)   (Ether)

$$R - X + Na^{\oplus} \; {}^{-}O\text{-}Ar \quad\quad \rightarrow \quad R\text{-}O\text{-}Ar \quad + Na^{\oplus} \; X^{\ominus}$$

(Sodium phenoxide)

The yield from RX is: $CH_3 > 1° > 2° (>3°)$. Hence, to
produce ether efficiently, a methyl halide or primary
halide should be selected. The sodium alkoxides are made
by the addition of sodium metal to alcohols: ROH + Na
$RO^{-} Na^{+} + \frac{1}{2}H_2$. Due to the appreciable acidity of phenols,
sodium phenoxides are made by the action of aqueous
sodium hydroxide to phenols:

ArOH + NaOH $\rightarrow$ ArO$^{\ominus}$Na$^{\oplus}$ + H_2O.

In this problem, 1-methylcyclopentene, an alkene, is
the starting product. This must be converted into the
alcohol so that it may be then transformed into the sodium
alkoxide for use in the Williamson synthesis. (One does
not want to convert 1-methylcyclo-pentene into an alkyl
halide because a secondary or tertiary structure would
result, and this is not very efficient, as mentioned previously.) Now, there exist a number of ways to synthesize
an alcohol from an alkene. The method of choice, however,
is the one that provides us with the required stereochemistry. Recall that the final product must be a trans
isomer. If hydroboration-oxidation of the alkene is used,
addition occurs in a cis fashion and the trans isomer
will be the net result. That is, the -H and -OH add trans
to the methyl group.

Hydroboration-oxidation gives anti-Markownikoff
addition of water across the carbon-carbon double bond.
The alcohol that results will have the hydroxyl group
trans with respect to the methyl substituent on the ring.

586

Consequently, the following hydroboration-oxidation reaction is performed:

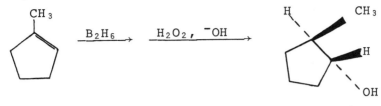

1-methylcyclopentene   trans-2-methyl-1-
                                           cyclopentanol

At this point, sodium metal must be added to convert this alcohol into a sodium alkoxide as illustrated:

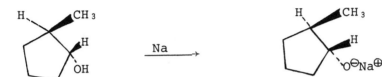

If a methyl halide, say methyl bromide, is added, the desired product results as shown:

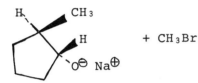 + CH₃Br   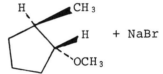 + NaBr

                                    trans-1-methoxy-2-methyl
                                           cyclopentane

REACTIONS

• **PROBLEM** 17-10

(a) Upon treatment with sulfuric acid, a mixture of ethyl and n-propyl alcohols yields a mixture of three ethers. What are they? (b) On the other hand, a mixture of tert-butyl alcohol and ethyl alcohol gives a good yield of a single ether. What ether is it likely to be? How can the good yield be accounted for?

Solution: (a) Ethers can be synthesized by the acid-catalyzed dehydration of alcohols. However, this reaction mechanism is only useful for the synthesis of symmetrical ethers (ROR, where both alkyl or aryl groups are identical). It is inefficient in the synthesis of unsymmetrical ethers (where the alkyl and/or aryl groups are not identical) be-cause it gives a mixture of products. This can be explained by the reaction mechanism.

The reaction in question is an acid-catalyzed de-hydration. The first step of this reaction is the protona-tion of alcohol by the acid, H_2SO_4. Since the reaction

587

mixture contains two different alcohols, each one of them can be protonated. This results in two different kinds of carbonium ions after release of water molecules. Each of these two carbonium ions can attack either alcohol to form an ether. If the ethyl cation $(CH_3CH_2^+)$ reacts with ethyl alcohol, diethyl ether is formed. If the n-propyl cation $(CH_3CH_2CH_2^+)$ reacts with n-propyl alcohol, di-n-propyl ether is formed. And if ethyl cation reacts with n-propyl alcohol, or n-propyl cation reacts with ethyl alcohol, ethyl n-propyl ether is formed. Since ethyl and n-propyl cations are formed at the same rate, the product will contain a mixture of diethyl ether, di-n-propyl ether, and ethyl n-propyl ether.

(b) In a mixture of tert-butyl alcohol and ethyl alcohol, the major product is ethyl t-butyl ether. This product is in good yield due to the kinetic effect.

As mentioned earlier, the first step of an acid-catalyzed dehydration of alcohol is the protonation of the alcohol. The elimination of a water molecule to form the carbonium ion from the protonated alcohol is the slowest step. Therefore, it is the rate-limiting step. The rate at which a carbonium ion forms is dependent on its stability. It can be formed fastest if there are e-lectron-releasing groups to stabilize the positive charge. The rate of carbonium ion formation is: $3°>2°>1°>$ methyl. This is also the order of stability of carbonium ions. Since tert-butyl alcohol can form a $3°$ cation, whereas ethyl alcohol can only form a $1°$ carbonium ion, tert-

$$\text{butyl-cation } \left[\begin{array}{c} CH_3 \\ | \\ CH_3-\overset{+}{C} \\ | \\ CH_3 \end{array} \right] \text{ should form the fastest and pre-}$$

dominate over ethyl cation $(CH_3CH_2^+)$ in the mixture.

Since the tert-butyl group is bulky, the 3° carbonium ion formed tends to attack ethyl alcohol more often than tert-butyl alcohol in the subsequent substitution reaction. The reactions are shown below:

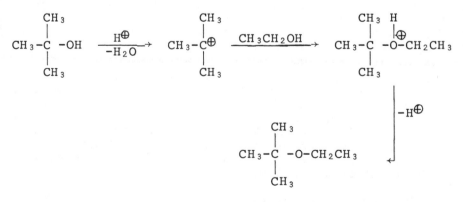

ethyl t-butyl ether

In conclusion, the ethyl t-butyl ether should be

the predominate ether because of the speed in which t-butyl cation forms and the difficulty of this cation attacking the t-butyl alcohol for steric reasons.

Poly(oxypropylene)glycols,

$$\underset{\substack{\displaystyle | \\ \text{HO-CH-CH}_2\text{-O}}}{\overset{\displaystyle \text{CH}_3}{}}\left[\underset{\substack{\displaystyle | \\ \text{CH}_2\text{CH-O}}}{\overset{\displaystyle \text{CH}_3}{}}\right]_n\underset{\substack{\displaystyle | \\ \text{-CH}_2\text{CHOH}}}{\overset{\displaystyle \text{CH}_3}{}}$$

which are used in the manufacture of polyurethane foam rubber, are formed by the action of base (e.g., hydroxide ion) on propylene oxide in the presence of propylene glycol as an initiator. Write all steps in a likely mechanism for their formation.

Solution: To write the mechanism for the formation of poly(oxypropylene)glycols, two facts must be understood. The first fact to be recognized is that alcohols may act as acids; the polarity of the O-H bond should facilitate the separation of the relatively positive hydrogen as the ion. The second fact is that epoxides $\left(\begin{array}{c}\text{O}\\ \diagup\diagdown\\ \text{-C - C-}\\ |\quad\ |\end{array}\right)$ may

undergo base-catalyzed cleavage as illustrated below:

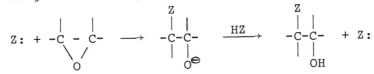

The epoxide undergoes nucleophilic attack by the nucleophile (base), Z:.

With this in mind, the mechanism may be written. When the initiator, propylene glycol, is mixed with base, hydroxide ion, one of the OH groups of the glycol may act as an acid to create an alkoxide-like molecule and water as shown:

$$\text{CH}_3\text{CHOHCH}_2\text{OH} \quad + \text{ OH}^{\ominus} \rightarrow \text{CH}_3\text{CHOHCH}_2\text{O}^{\ominus} \quad + \quad \text{H}_2\text{O}$$

    propylene glycol   alkoxide-like
                                     ion

The ion formed is sufficiently nucleophilic to attack the propylene oxide to cause cleavage as shown:

$$\text{CH}_3\text{CHOHCH}_2\text{O}^{\ominus} \quad + \quad \underset{\underset{\text{O}}{\diagdown\diagup}}{\text{H}_2\text{C - C}}\overset{\text{CH}_3}{\overset{|}{\rule{0pt}{0pt}}} \quad \rightarrow \quad \text{CH}_3\text{CHOHCH}_2\text{O-CH}_2\text{-CH}\overset{\text{CH}_3}{\overset{|}{\rule{0pt}{0pt}}}\text{-O}^{\ominus}$$

                propylene oxide

589

The ion generated in the above reaction can also act as a nucleophile to attack another propylene oxide molecule. This process proceeds on and on until a water molecule is added to form the poly(oxypropylene)glycol. The sequence is written below:

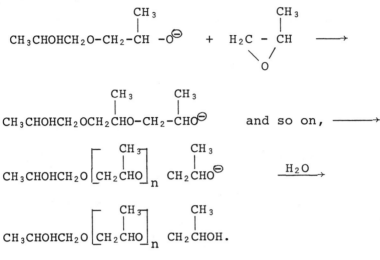

$$CH_3CHOHCH_2O-CH_2-\overset{\overset{\displaystyle CH_3}{|}}{CH}-O^{\ominus} \quad + \quad H_2C-\overset{\overset{\displaystyle CH_3}{|}}{CH} \longrightarrow$$

$$CH_3CHOHCH_2O\overset{\overset{\displaystyle CH_3}{|}}{CH_2CHO}-CH_2-\overset{\overset{\displaystyle CH_3}{|}}{CHO}^{\ominus} \quad \text{and so on,} \longrightarrow$$

$$CH_3CHOHCH_2O\left[\overset{\overset{\displaystyle CH_3}{|}}{CH_2CHO}\right]_n \overset{\overset{\displaystyle CH_3}{|}}{CH_2CHO}^{\ominus} \qquad \xrightarrow{H_2O}$$

$$CH_3CHOHCH_2O\left[\overset{\overset{\displaystyle CH_3}{|}}{CH_2CHO}\right]_n \overset{\overset{\displaystyle CH_3}{|}}{CH_2CHOH}.$$

poly(oxypropylene)glycol

● PROBLEM 17-12

Write an equation for each of the following. (If no reaction occurs, indicate "no reaction.")

(a) potassium tert-butoxide + ethyl iodide
(b) tert-butyl iodide + potassium ethoxide
(c) ethyl alcohol + H_2SO_4 (140°)
(d) n-butyl ether + boiling aqueous NaOH
(e) methyl ethyl ether + excess HI (hot)
(f) $C_6H_5OC_2H_5$ + hot conc. HBr
(g) $C_6H_5OC_2H_5$ + HNO_3, H_2SO_4.

Solution: The parts in this problem test understanding of the preparation and reactions of ethers and epoxides.

$$\text{(a)} \quad H_3C-\overset{\overset{\displaystyle CH_3}{|}}{\underset{\underset{\displaystyle O^{\ominus}K^{\oplus}}{|}}{C}}-CH_3 \quad + \quad CH_3CH_2I \qquad \longrightarrow \qquad ?$$

potassium
tert-butoxide   ethyl iodide

These two reactants illustrate a most versatile method in the preparation of ethers, the Williamson synthesis. In this synthesis, an alkyl halide (or substituted alkyl halide), such as ethyl iodide, is allowed to react with a sodium alkoxide (RO^-Na^+) or a sodium phenoxide (ArO^-Na^+) to produce the ether as shown:

590

$$\text{R-X} \qquad + \text{Na}^{\oplus}\ ^{\ominus}\text{O-R}' \rightarrow \text{R-O-R}' + \text{Na}^{\oplus}\text{X}^{\ominus}$$
$$(\text{K}^+)$$

(alkyl halide)

$$\text{R-X} \quad + \quad \text{Na}^{\oplus}\ ^{\ominus}\text{O-Ar} \quad \rightarrow \quad \text{R-O-Ar} \quad + \quad \text{Na}^{\oplus}\text{X}^{\ominus}$$
$$(\text{K}^+)$$

The yield from RX is: $CH_3 > 1° > 2° (>3°)$. Hence,

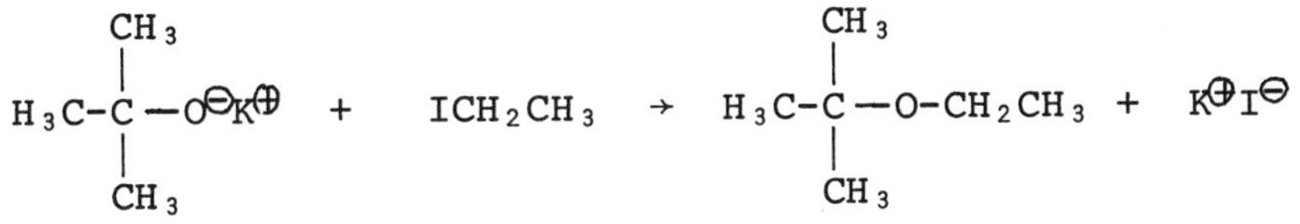

$$\begin{array}{c} \text{CH}_3 \\ | \\ \text{H}_3\text{C-C}\ ^{\ominus}\text{O}^{\ominus}\text{K}^{\oplus} \\ | \\ \text{CH}_3 \end{array} + \quad \text{ICH}_2\text{CH}_3 \quad \rightarrow \quad \begin{array}{c} \text{CH}_3 \\ | \\ \text{H}_3\text{C-C}-\text{O-CH}_2\text{CH}_3 \\ | \\ \text{CH}_3 \end{array} + \quad \text{K}^{\oplus}\text{I}^{\ominus}$$

(t-butyl ethyl ether)

(b) $\qquad \begin{array}{c} \text{CH}_3 \\ | \\ \text{H}_3\text{C-C}-\text{I} \\ | \\ \text{CH}_3 \end{array} + \quad \text{CH}_3\text{CH}_2\text{O}^{\ominus}\text{K}^{\oplus} \quad \longrightarrow \quad ?$

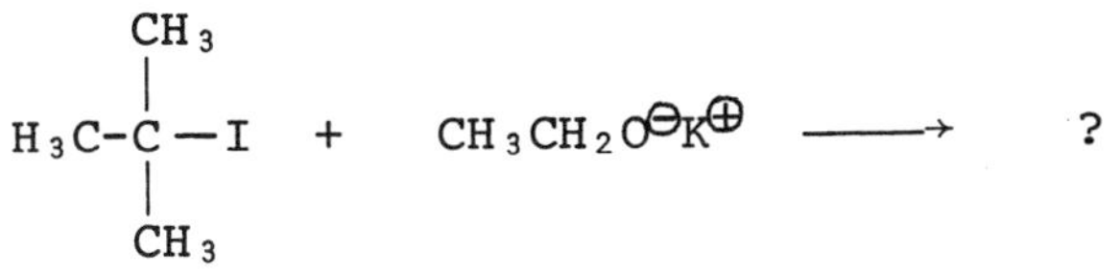

These reactants would seem to follow the pattern for Williamson ether synthesis outlined above. Afterall, an alkyl halide and an alkoxide are again reacting. But note, this time the alkyl halide is tertiary and, as shown above [part (a)], such a halide gives a very low yield. In fact, the use of tertiary halides to produce ethers in this fashion is usually not feasible, for elimination will be favored over substitution (which is what occurs when the ether is generated). Recall that the tendency for alkyl halides to undergo dehydrohalogenation (an elimination reaction) is: $3° > 2° > 1°$. With the strong basicity of the alkoxide reagent, elimination should be particularly serious. Hence, when these two reagents, t-butyl iodide and potassium ethoxide, combine, a dehydrohalogenation reaction occurs as illustrated:

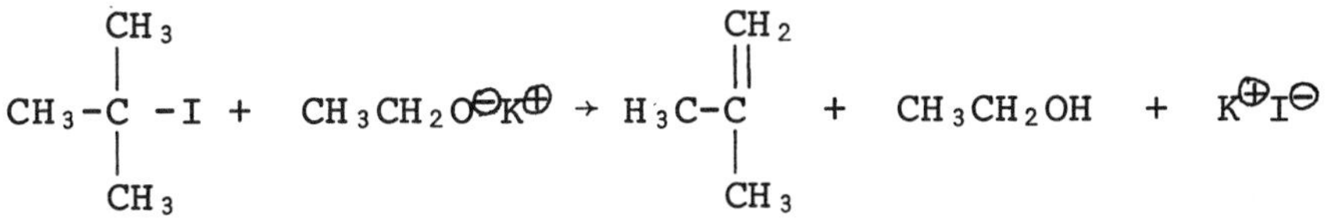

$$\begin{array}{c} \text{CH}_3 \\ | \\ \text{CH}_3\text{-C -I} \\ | \\ \text{CH}_3 \end{array} + \text{CH}_3\text{CH}_2\text{O}^{\ominus}\text{K}^{\oplus} \rightarrow \begin{array}{c} \text{CH}_2 \\ || \\ \text{H}_3\text{C-C} \\ | \\ \text{CH}_3 \end{array} + \quad \text{CH}_3\text{CH}_2\text{OH} \quad + \quad \text{K}^{\oplus}\text{I}^{\ominus}$$

(isobutylene) (ethanol)

(c) $\quad CH_3CH_2OH + H_2SO_4 \ (140°) \longrightarrow \quad ?$

Ethyl alcohol

Some symmetrical ethers containing the lower alkyl groups may be prepared by reactions of the corresponding alcohols with sulfuric acid (H_2SO_4). A water molecule is lost for every pair of alcohol molecules so that the reaction is termed dehydration. (Recall that alcohols can be dehydrated also to alkenes. The conditions determine whether the alkene or ether results.) The dehydration to ethers is written below:

$$2R-O-H \xrightarrow{\text{H}_2\text{SO}_4, \text{ heat}} R-O-R + H_2O.$$

This is exactly the reaction that occurs with ethyl-alcohol in H_2SO_4 at 140°. Hence,

$$2CH_3CH_2OH \xrightarrow{\text{H}_2\text{SO}_4, \text{ 140}°} CH_3CH_2OCH_2CH_3 + H_2O$$

$$\text{ethyl ether}$$

(d) $CH_3CH_2CH_2CH_2OCH_2CH_2CH_2CH_3$ + boiling aqueous NaOH → ?

n-butyl ether

Ethers may be characterized as comparatively unreactive compounds. The ether linkage is quite stable toward oxidizing agents, reducing agents, and bases. Hence, when the boiling aqueous base of NaOH is added to n-butyl ether there is no reaction.

(e) $CH_3OCH_2CH_3$ + excess HI (hot) $\longrightarrow$

methyl ethyl ether

Under vigorous conditions (high concentration and high temperatures), ethers may be cleaved by acids as shown:

$$R-O-R' + HX \rightarrow R-X + R'OH$$

$$\text{(Alkyl halide)} \quad \text{(Alcohol)}$$

$Ar-O-R + HX \rightarrow R-x + Ar-OH.$ The R'OH, in the presence of HX, will proceed to alkyl halide, R-X, also.

The reactivity of HX is: HI > HBr > HCl.

Cleavage by acid involves the nucleophilic attack by halide ion on the protonated ether, with the weakly basic alcohol molecule being displaced as shown:

$$\ddot{R}\ddot{O}R' + HX \rightleftarrows \overset{\overset{H}{\overset{\cdot\cdot}{\oplus}}}{R\ddot{O}R'} + X^- \quad \overset{S_N 1}{\underset{\text{or}}{\underline{}}} \quad RX + R'OH.$$
$$S_N 2$$

When excess HI (hot) is added to methyl ethyl ether, cleavage of the ether can be expected:

$$CH_3OCH_2CH_3 + \text{excess HI (hot)} \rightarrow CH_3I + CH_2CH_3I$$

$$\qquad\qquad\qquad\qquad\qquad\qquad\text{methyl} \quad\text{ethyl}$$
$$\qquad\qquad\qquad\qquad\qquad\qquad\text{iodide} \quad\text{iodide}$$

(f) $-OC_2H_5$ + hot conc. HBr $\longrightarrow$?

ethyl phenyl
  ether

Again, cleavage of the ether can be expected due to the presence of an acid, HBr, with vigorous conditions. The important point to understand is that the cleavage of an aryl alkyl ether yields a phenol and an alkyl halide. This derives from the fact of low reactivity at the bond between oxygen and an aromatic ring, so that it undergoes cleavage at the alkyl-oxygen bond. Therefore,

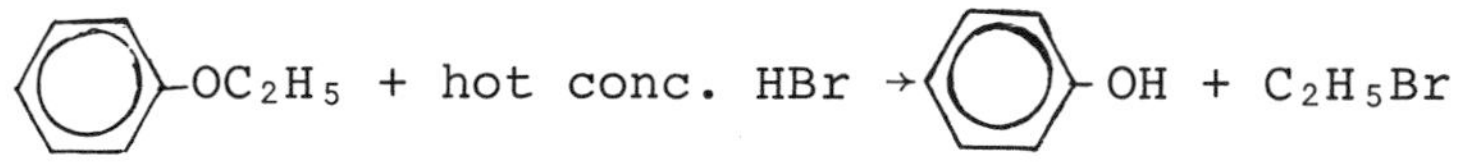

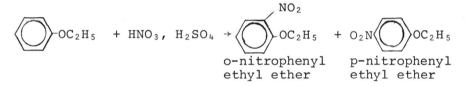

$\langle O \rangle$-OC$_2$H$_5$ + hot conc. HBr → $\langle O \rangle$-OH + C$_2$H$_5$Br

$\qquad\qquad\qquad\qquad\qquad\qquad$ phenol $\qquad$ ethyl bromide

(g) 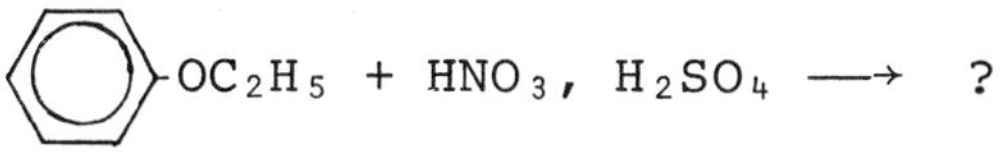 $\langle O \rangle$-OC$_2$H$_5$ + HNO$_3$, H$_2$SO$_4$ ⟶ ?

phenyl ethyl
  ether

This problem involves electrophilic substitution in aromatic ethers. The alkoxy group, -OR, is moderately activating and so directs ortho, para. Consequently, the nitro group can be expected to be positioned ortho, para to the OC$_2$H$_5$ group in phenyl ethyl ether as shown:

$$\langle O \rangle\text{-OC}_2\text{H}_5 + \text{HNO}_3, \text{H}_2\text{SO}_4 \rightarrow \overset{\text{NO}_2}{\langle O \rangle}\text{-OC}_2\text{H}_5 + \text{O}_2\text{N}\langle O \rangle\text{OC}_2\text{H}_5$$

$\qquad\qquad\qquad\qquad\qquad\qquad\qquad$ o-nitrophenyl $\qquad$ p-nitrophenyl
$\qquad\qquad\qquad\qquad\qquad\qquad\qquad$ ethyl ether $\qquad\quad$ ethyl ether

● **PROBLEM** 17-13

What are the structures of A-D in the scheme shown?

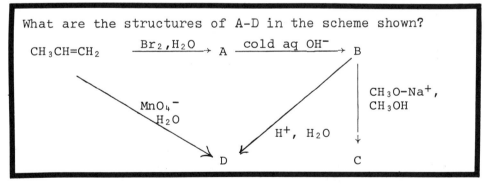

CH$_3$CH=CH$_2$ $\xrightarrow{\text{Br}_2,\text{H}_2\text{O}}$ A $\xrightarrow{\text{cold aq OH}^-}$ B

MnO$_4^-$ / H$_2$O

CH$_3$O-Na$^+$, CH$_3$OH

H$^+$, H$_2$O

D $\qquad$ C

Solution: The sequence commences with propylene, an alkene. When chlorine or bromine is added in the presence of water to alkenes, they yield compounds containing halogen and hydroxyl groups on adjacent carbon atoms. Such compounds are called halohydrins. Hence, compound A must be a halohydrin as shown below:

CH$_3$CH=CH$_2$ $\xrightarrow{\text{Br}_2,\text{H}_2\text{O}}$ CH$_3$-CH-CH$_2$
$\qquad\qquad\qquad\qquad\qquad\qquad\qquad$ | |
$\qquad\qquad\qquad\qquad\qquad\qquad\qquad$ OH Br

(propylene bromohydrin)

Compound B comes about from compound A by the action of a base, hydroxide ion. This suggests the formation of an epoxide. It is known that halohydrins can be converted into epoxides by the action of base as in the general re-

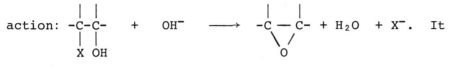

(epoxide)

can then be said that compound B is an epoxide as illustrated:

$$CH_3-CH-CH_2 \xrightarrow{\text{cold aq OH}^-} CH_3-CH-CH_2$$

with OH Br below the left and O below the right (epoxide).

Compound A   Compound B

It is possible to cleave epoxides under alkaline con- ditions. The epoxide undergoes nucleophilic attack by the such nucleophilic reagents as alkoxides, phenoxides, and ammonia. The general reaction of this base-catalyzed cleavage is written below:

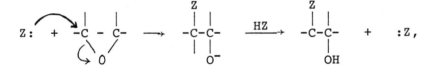

where Z: represents the nucleophile.

The reagent $CH_3O^-Na^+$ is an alkoxide so that it should cause base-catalyzed cleavage of the epoxide (compound B) as shown:

$$CH_3-CH-CH_2 \xrightarrow[CH_3OH]{CH_3O^-Na^+} CH_3CHCH_2OCH_3$$

with O below the left and OH below the right.

Compound B   Compound C

Compound B also generates compound D when H^+, H_2O is added. This reaction denotes acid-catalyzed cleavage of epoxides. An important characteristic of this reaction is the production of compounds with two functional groups. The general reaction is:

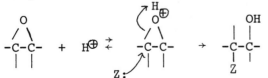

Reaction with water generates a glycol as shown:

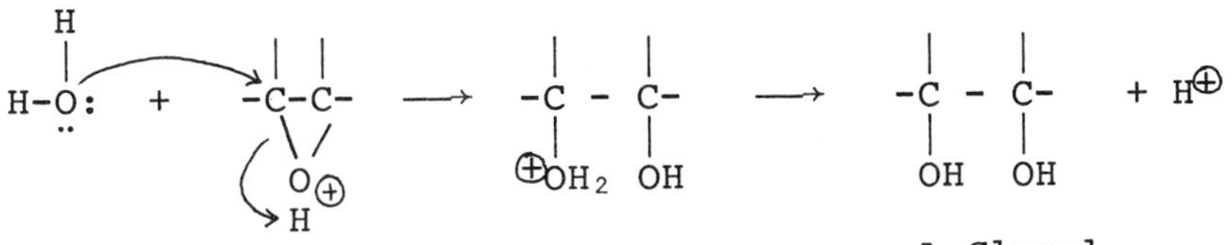

A Glycol

Compound D must be a glycol. Its formation is depicted in the following equation:

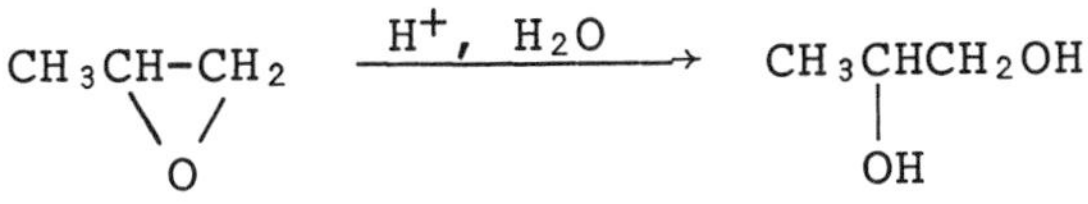

Compound B Compound D

Propylene also gives rise to compound D when H_2O, MnO_4^- is added. This reaction is typical of alkenes. Certain oxidizing agents (such as $KMnO_4$) convert alkenes into glycols. This is a hydroxylation reaction.

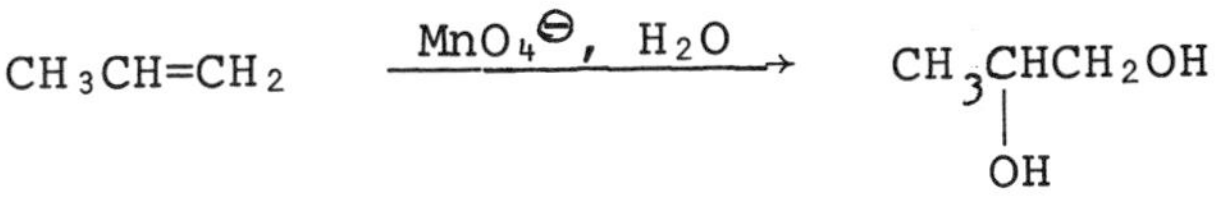

• PROBLEM 17-14

In so far as the ether linkage is concerned, ethers undergo just one type of reaction, cleavage by acids. Discuss this reaction in terms of the mechanism, conditions, and products obtained.

Solution: While the ether linkage (R-O-R) is stable toward bases, reducing agents, and oxidizing agents, they can be cleaved by acids as illustrated:

$$R\text{-}O\text{-}R' + HX \rightarrow R\text{-}X + R'OH \xrightarrow{HX} R'X$$

$$Ar\text{-}O\text{-}R + HX \rightarrow R\text{-}X + Ar\text{-}OH$$

This reaction will occur only under vigorous conditions (that is, concentrated acids at high temperatures). The alkyl ether reacts with the acid to yield an alkyl halide and an alcohol. The alcohol may continue to react with acid to generate a second mole of alkyl halide. An aryl alkyl ether yields a phenol and an alkyl halide because cleavage occurs at the alkyl-oxygen bond, and not the aryl-oxygen due to the latters low reactivity. For example,

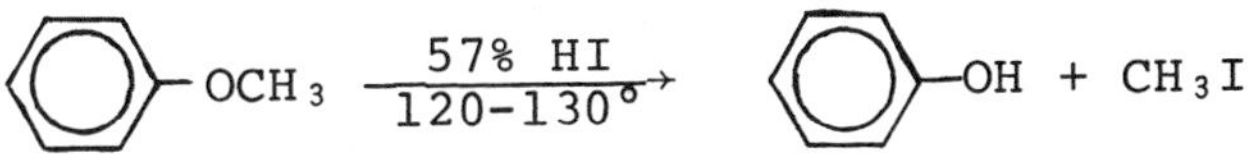

Anisole Phenol Methyl iodide

Selection of the acid can be important because of their different reactivities as indicated:

Reactivity of HX: HI > HBr > HCl.

The cleavage of the ether by acid involves nucleophilic attack by halide ion on the protonated ether. This causes displacement of the weakly basic alcohol molecule as illustrated:

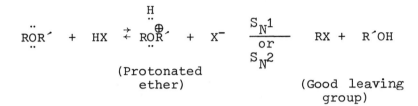

$$\overset{..}{R}\overset{..}{O}R' \; + \; HX \; \rightleftarrows \; R\overset{H}{\underset{..}{O}}\overset{\oplus}{R'} \; + \; X^- \quad \overset{S_N1}{\underset{S_N2}{or}} \quad RX \; + \; R'OH$$

(Protonated ether)

(Good leaving group)

As mentioned, the reaction may proceed by substitution nucleophilic unimolecular (S_N1) or substitution nucleophilic bimolecular(S_N2). The conditions and structure of the ether will determine which way the reaction goes. S_N1 and S_N2 are outlined below.

$$S_N1$$

(1) $\quad R\overset{H}{\underset{}{\overset{|}{\underset{}{O}}}}\overset{\oplus}{R'} \quad \xrightarrow{\text{slow}} \quad R^+ \; + \; HOR'$

(2) $\quad R^{\oplus} \; + \; X^- \quad \xrightarrow{\text{fast}} \quad R\text{-}X$

$$S_N2$$

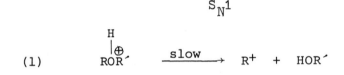

$$R\overset{H}{\underset{}{\overset{|}{\underset{}{O}}}}\overset{\oplus}{R'} \; + \; X^- \; \longrightarrow \; \left[\begin{array}{c} H \\ | \\ \overset{\delta-}{X}\text{---}R\text{---}\overset{}{O}R' \\ \delta+ \end{array} \right] \; \longrightarrow \; RX \; + \; HOR'$$

Since the S_N1 mechanism proceeds through an intermediate carbonium ion, it might be expected that a tertiary alkyl group undergoes S_N1 displacement, whereas a primary aklyl group undergoes S_N2 displacement.

● **PROBLEM** 17-15

A homogeneous solution is known to contain equal parts of diethyl ether and pentane. These liquids have similar boiling points and cannot be separated by fractional distillation. Devise a method for separating them.

Solution: Ethers have the general formula of R-O-R,

where the R's stand for alkyl and/or aryl groups. They are unreactive towards most compounds, and are often used as solvents for a wide variety of organic compounds. The solution in question is homogeneous, meaning that diethyl ether and pentane are completely miscible. Since they cannot be separated by fractional distillation, one must look into their differences in properties.

While ethers resemble hydrocarbons (such as pentane) in chemical behavior because of the low reactivity of the functional group, they can be distinguished by the ether's solubility in cold concentrated sulfuric acid through formation of oxonium salts. When diethyl ether is mixed with cold concentrated sulfuric acid, the following takes place:

$$CH_3CH_2OCH_2CH_3 \xrightarrow[\text{H}_2\text{SO}_4]{\text{cold concentrated}} CH_3CH_2\overset{\overset{\displaystyle H}{|}}{O}CH_2CH_3 \atop \overset{\oplus}{\ominus}HSO_4$$

diethyl ether   oxonium salt

The hydrocarbon, pentane, fails to produce the oxonium salt.

The oxonium salt formed by diethyl ether is soluble in H_2SO_4. Thus, diethyl ether leaves the homogeneous solution and dissolves in the acid. Pentane does not dissolve in the acid so that a second phase is established. With two phases present, the compounds may be separated by extraction.

● **PROBLEM** 17-16

The unsaturated cyclic ether furan can readily be made from substances isolated from oat hulls and corncobs; important uses of furan involve its conversion into (a) tetrahydrofuran and (b) 1,4-dichlorobutane. Show how these conversions can be carried out.

Solution: The structure of furan,

```
   HC-CH
   //  \\
   HC    CH  ,   shows it to be a cyclic ether. The pre-
    \   /
     O
```

paration and properties of most cyclic ethers do not vary from the other ethers; the ether linkage is basically the same whether it forms part of an open chain or part of an aliphatic ring.

To synthesize tetrahydrofuran,

```
   H2C-CH2
   /     \
  H2C     CH2 ,  from furan, hydrogen (H2) must add across
    \    /
     O
```

the two carbon-carbon double bonds of furan. Such a reaction is hydrogenation of alkenes as shown:

$$C_NH_{2N} \xrightarrow{\text{H}_2 + \text{ Pt, Pd, or Ni}} C_NH_{2N+2}$$

Alkene   Alkane

Therefore, it can be written:

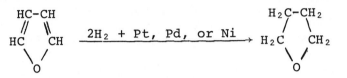

The ether linkage will remain undamaged in this reaction for it is stable toward reducing agents (and oxidizing agents and bases).

To produce 1,4 dichlorobutane, $ClCH_2CH_2CH_2CH_2Cl$, the
starting material should be the tetrahydrofuran synthesized
previously. This conversion will take advantage of the fact
that cyclic ethers can be cleaved by acid. The general
equation for cleavage by acids is shown below:

$$R-O-R' + \text{ HX} \rightarrow R-X + R'OH \xrightarrow{\text{HX}} R'-X \ .$$

Ether   Acid   Alkyl   Alcohol   Alkyl
                 halide   halide

An alkyl ether when mixed with acid (HI>HBr>HCl in reactivity) under vigorous conditions (high concentration
and temperature) yields an alkyl halide and an alcohol;
the alcohol may react further with acid to yield a second
mole of alkyl halide.

Therefore, if HCl is added to tetrahydrofuran in
concentration form at high temperatures, the ether linkage
should be cleaved as shown:

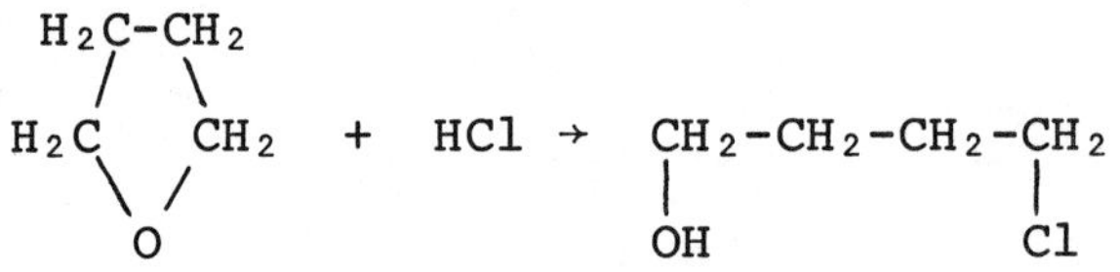

$$
\begin{array}{c}
\text{H}_2\text{C-CH}_2 \\
/ \qquad \backslash \\
\text{H}_2\text{C} \qquad \text{CH}_2 \\
\backslash \quad / \\
\text{O}
\end{array}
\; + \; \text{HCl} \; \rightarrow \;
\begin{array}{l}
\text{CH}_2\text{-CH}_2\text{-CH}_2\text{-CH}_2 \\
\quad | \qquad\qquad\qquad | \\
\quad \text{OH} \qquad\qquad\quad \text{Cl}
\end{array}
$$

(4-chloro-1-butanol)

The hydroxyl group and halide end up on the same
molecule because of the cyclic nature of the ether. When
a cyclic ether is cleaved, it cleaves to one molecule,
not two. 4-chloro-1-butanol can continue to react with HCl
to produce the desired product, 1,4-dichlorobutane, as
indicated:

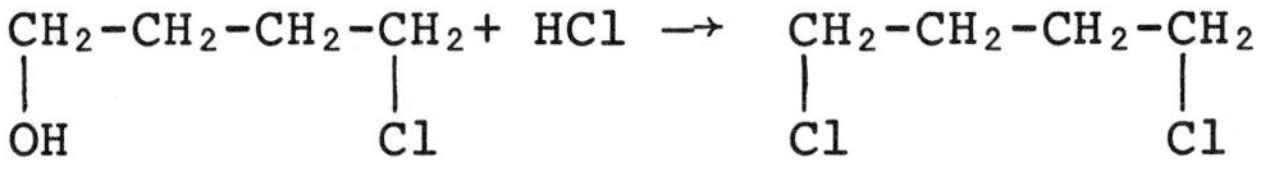

$$
\begin{array}{l}
\text{CH}_2\text{-CH}_2\text{-CH}_2\text{-CH}_2 + \text{ HCl} \; \longrightarrow \; \text{CH}_2\text{-CH}_2\text{-CH}_2\text{-CH}_2 \\
\; | \qquad\qquad\qquad\quad | \qquad\qquad\qquad\quad | \qquad\qquad\qquad\qquad | \\
\; \text{OH} \qquad\qquad\qquad \text{Cl} \qquad\qquad\qquad \text{Cl} \qquad\qquad\qquad\quad \text{Cl}
\end{array}
$$

1,4-Dioxane is prepared industrially (for use as a water-soluble solvent) by dehydration of an alcohol. What alcohol is used?

Solution: 1,4 dioxane is a symmetrical cyclic ether containing two ogygens,

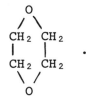

Since it is symmetrical, having identical alkyl groups, preparation by dehydration of an alcohol is efficient. Also, since the compound contains two oxygens, a compound with two hydroxyl groups as the main functional groups, a diol, must have been used. The dihydroxy compound having two carbons is called ethylene glycol, $HO-CH_2CH_2-OH$. The reaction is shown below.

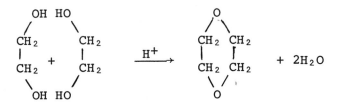

For every two moles of ethylene glycol used, one mole of 1,4-dioxane is formed, and two moles of water are released.

EPOXIDES (OXIRANES)

Draw structures showing stereochemistry where necessary for the products you would expect from the following reactions.

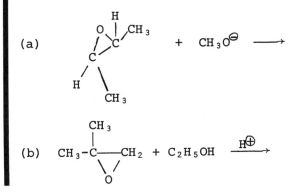

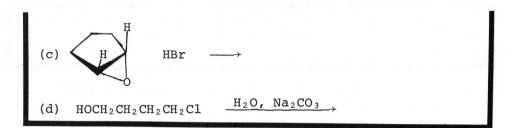

(c)   HBr $\longrightarrow$

(d) $HOCH_2CH_2CH_2CH_2Cl$ $\xrightarrow{H_2O,\ Na_2CO_3}$

Solution: All the products in (a) - (d) come about as a result of the preparation or reactions of epoxides. Consequently, a knowledge of the chemistry of epoxides is necessary to solve this problem.

(a)   Unlike most ethers, epoxides react easily with many strongly nucleophilic reagents. There exists base-catalyzed cleavage of epoxides by such nucleophilic reagents as alkoxides, phenoxides, and ammonia. The reaction may be generalized as:

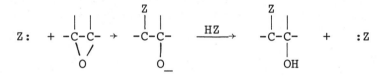

The stereochemistry of the reaction is consistent with an S_N2 mechanism, since inversion of configuration at the site of attack occurs. Here, CH_3O^-, an alkoxide, attacks the epoxide to cause cleavage and gives a trans configuration in the product as shown:

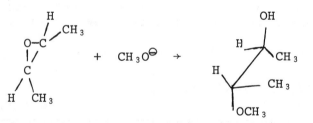

(b)   This reaction involves acid-catalyzed cleavage of epoxides. The acid converts the epoxide into a protonated epoxide, which is then susceptible to any number of nucleophilic reagents. It may be generalized as shown:

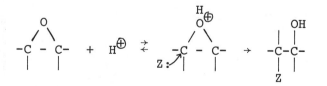

An important feature of this reaction is the fact the compounds formed contain two functional groups. Reaction with water generates a glycol, whereas reaction with an alcohol produces a compound that is both ether and alcohol.

600

Hence,

$$CH_3-\underset{\underset{O}{\diagdown\diagup}}{\overset{\overset{CH_3}{|}}{C}}-CH_2 \quad + \quad C_2H_5OH \quad \xrightarrow{H^+} \quad CH_3-\underset{\underset{OC_2H_5}{|}}{\overset{\overset{CH_3}{|}}{C}}-CH_2OH$$

(c)   This reaction is also acid-catalyzed cleavage. The only thing that distinguishes this reaction from (b) is that the nucleophile in this instance is bromide (Br⁻) ion. It is therefore possible to write the following:

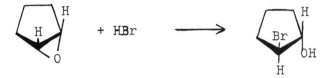

(d)   This reaction illustrates a method of preparation of epoxides. Halohydrins may be converted into epoxides by the action of base. This method may be described as an adaptation of the Williamson synthesis. The generalized reaction is depicted below:

$$-\overset{|}{C}=\overset{|}{C}- \quad \xrightarrow{X_2,\ H_2O} \quad -\underset{\underset{X}{|}}{\overset{|}{C}}-\underset{\underset{OH}{|}}{\overset{|}{C}}- \quad + \quad OH^{\ominus} \quad \longrightarrow$$

(alkene)   (halohydrin) (base)

$$-\underset{\underset{O}{\diagdown\diagup}}{\overset{|}{C}}-\overset{|}{C}- \quad + \quad H_2O \quad + \quad X^{\ominus}$$

(epoxide)

The base need not be hydroxide ion. It could be sodium carbonate (Na_2CO_3). Consequently, when Na_2CO_3 is added to the halohydrin $HOCH_2CH_2CH_2CH_2Cl$, one might expect an epoxide to form. But note, the HO and Cl are at opposite ends, so that a cyclic ether forms as shown below:

$$HOCH_2CH_2CH_2CH_2Cl \quad \xrightarrow{H_2O,\ Na_2CO_3} \quad \underset{\underset{O}{\diagdown\diagup}}{\overset{\overset{CH_2-CH_2}{\diagup\quad\diagdown}}{CH_2 \qquad CH_2}}$$

● **PROBLEM** 17-19

Predict the product(s) of the reaction of ethylene oxide with

(a) $H_3O^{\oplus}$
(b) $OH^{\ominus}/H_2O$, then $H_3O^{\oplus}$
(c) $CH_3S^{\ominus}Na^{\oplus}$
(d) $CH_3CH_2CH_2MgBr$, then $H_3O^{\oplus}$

This problem focuses on the reactions of

epoxides $\left(\begin{array}{c} | \quad | \\ -C - C- \\ \diagdown / \\ O \end{array} \right)$, which include acid-catalyzed cleavage,

base-catalyzed cleavage, and organometallic (e.g. Grignard reagents) cleavage. The general equations for these re-actions may be written as follows:

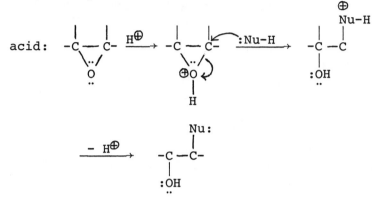

acid:

The epoxide is converted by acid ($H^{\oplus}$) into the

protonated epoxide $\left(\begin{array}{c} | \quad | \\ -C - C \\ \diagdown / \\ O \\ \oplus | \\ H \end{array} \right)$ which can then undergo attack

by any number of nucleophilic reagents (:Nu-H). Absence of acid:

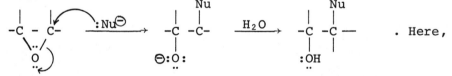

the epoxide, not the protonated epoxide, undergoes nucleo-philic attack.

To solve for the products of (a) - (d), substitute into one of the two general equations. The different products reflect the different nucleophilic reagents.

(a) $H_2C \underset{\diagdown \diagup}{\overset{}{\underset{O}{-}}} CH_2$ + $H_3O^{\oplus}$ $\longrightarrow$ $H_2C \underset{\diagdown \diagup}{\overset{}{\underset{\underset{H}{O_\oplus}}{-}}} CH_2$

Ethylene
oxide

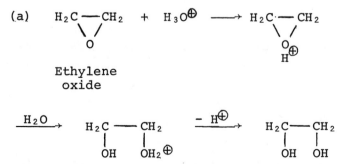

$\xrightarrow{H_2O}$ $H_2C \underset{OH}{\overset{}{|}} \longrightarrow CH_2 \underset{OH_2 \oplus}{\overset{}{|}}$ $\xrightarrow{- H^{\oplus}}$ $H_2C \underset{OH}{\overset{}{|}} \longrightarrow CH_2 \underset{OH}{\overset{}{|}}$

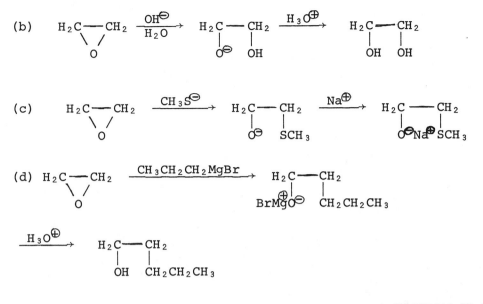

(b) $H_2C \overline{} CH_2$ $\xrightarrow[H_2O]{OH^{\ominus}}$ $H_2C \overline{} CH_2$ $\xrightarrow{H_3O^{\oplus}}$ $H_2C \overline{} CH_2$

(c) $H_2C \overline{} CH_2$ $\xrightarrow{CH_3S^{\ominus}}$ $H_2C \overline{} CH_2$ $\xrightarrow{Na^{\oplus}}$ $H_2C \overline{} CH_2$

(d) $H_2C \overline{} CH_2$ $\xrightarrow{CH_3CH_2CH_2MgBr}$ $H_2C \overline{} CH_2$

$\xrightarrow{H_3O^{\oplus}}$ $H_2C \overline{} CH_2$

• **PROBLEM** 17-20

Write equations for the reaction of ethylene oxide with
(a) methanol in the presence of a little H_2SO_4; (b) methanol
in the presence of a little $CH_3O^{\ominus}Na^{\oplus}$; (c) aniline.

Solution: Ethylene oxide $\left(\begin{array}{c} H_2C - CH_2 \\ \diagdown \diagup \\ O \end{array} \right)$ is an epoxide, a

compound containing the three-membered ring $-\overset{|}{C} - \overset{|}{\underset{\diagdown \diagup}{\underset{O}{C}}}-$.

Epoxides are highly reactive due to the ease of opening of
the highly strained three-membered ring. Epoxides can undergo base and acid-catalyzed cleavage. Reactions in (a) - (c)
are examples of such cleavages.

(a)   The reaction of ethylene oxide with methanol and H_2SO_4
illustrates the acid-catalyzed cleavage of epoxides. An
epoxide when mixed with acid is converted into the protonated
epoxide, which can then undergo attack by any of a number of
nucleophilic reagents. The general mechanism of the reaction
may be written as:

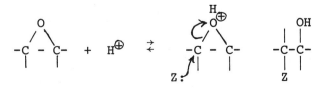

where Z: represents the nucleophilic reagent. In this problem,
methanol is the nucleophilic reagent and attacks the pro-

tonated ethylene oxide to produce an alkoxyalcohol (a hydroxyether) as shown:

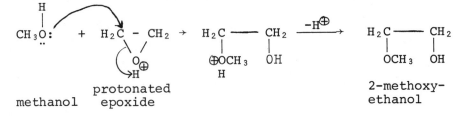

protonated
methanol   epoxide

2-methoxy-
ethanol

Hence, 2-methoxyethanol is the product of the reaction of ethylene oxide with methanol and acid.

(b)   Methanol in the presence of a little $CH_3O^{\ominus}Na^{\oplus}$ will react with ethylene epoxide to give the same product in (a), 2-methoxyethanol. However, the product comes about by a different mechanism, base-catalyzed cleavage of epoxides. Here, the epoxide itself, not the protonated epoxide, undergoes nucleophilic attack as indicated in the general mechanism below:

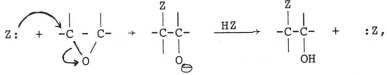

where Z: denotes the nucleophile. Here, CH_3O^- is the nucleophile that attacks ethylene oxide as shown:

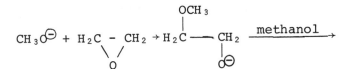

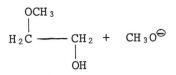

(2-methoxyethanol)

(c) Aniline, is considered to have appreciable

basicity due to the pair of non-bonded electrons on the nitrogen atom. Hence, when aniline is added to ethylene epoxide, base-catalyzed cleavage may be expected as shown:

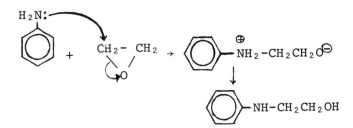

Draw the structure of the epoxide(s) produced by epoxidation of: (a) 1-hexene, (b) 2-hexene.

Solution: One method of synthesis of an epoxide $\begin{pmatrix} | & | \\ -C-C- \\ \backslash / \\ O \end{pmatrix}$

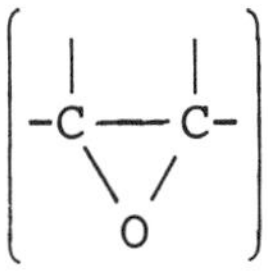

is by oxidation of an alkene $\begin{pmatrix} | & | \\ -C=C- \end{pmatrix}$. Peroxyacids are frequently the oxidants used in this epoxidation reaction. It is believed that both carbon-oxygen bonds of the epoxide are formed simultaneously. This means the stereochemistry of the alkene will be retained in the epoxide. Thus, cis alkenes produce cis epoxides and trans alkenes produce trans epoxides. With this in mind, it is possible to draw the structures required.

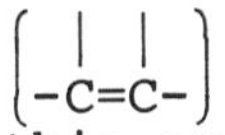

(a) 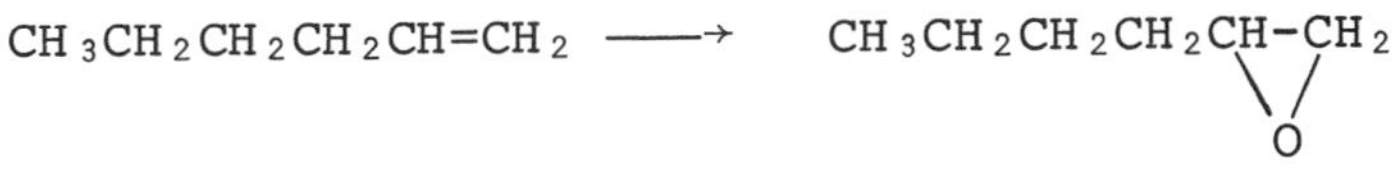 $CH_3CH_2CH_2CH_2CH=CH_2 \longrightarrow CH_3CH_2CH_2CH_2\underset{\backslash / \atop O}{CH-CH_2}$

(1-hexene)

(b)   2-hexene exists in cis and trans forms. Hence,

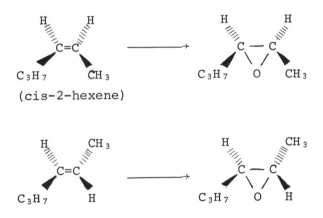

(cis-2-hexene)

(trans-2-hexene)

Note how the cis, trans stereochemistry is retained in each case.

Propylene oxide can be converted into propylene glycol by the action of either dilute acid or dilute base. When optically active propylene oxide is used, the glycol obtained from acidic hydrolysis has a rotation opposite to that obtained from alkaline hydrolysis. What is the most likely interpretation of these facts?

Propylene oxide, 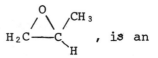 , is an

epoxide because it contains the three-membered ring $-\overset{|}{C}-\overset{|}{C}-$.
$\underset{O}{\diagdown\diagup}$

Due to the ease of opening this strained ring, it is highly reactive. Dilute acid or base can hydrolyze it into propylene glycol; CH_3CHCH_2.
$\qquad\overset{|}{O}H\overset{|}{O}H$

If optically active propylene glycol is used, depending on the method of hydrolysis, two different enantiomers are formed. Enantiomers are mirror image isomers whose chemical and physical properties are the same, except for the ability to rotate plane polarized light in opposite directions.

Acid hydrolysis begins with the protonation of the epoxide (see the diagram below). A water molecule then attacks a carbon adjacent to the oxygen. It attacks the more highly substituted carbon. In this case, the carbon attacked is a chiral carbon, that is, a carbon with four different atoms or groups of atoms. Since the water attacks at the chiral carbon, inversion of configuration results to change the rotation of plane polarized light.

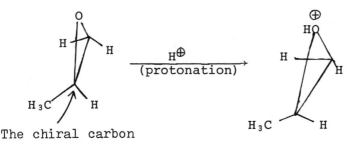

The chiral carbon

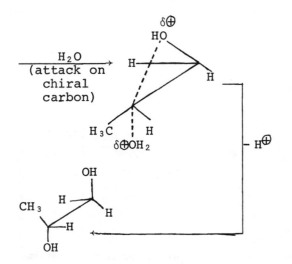

Base hydrolysis takes place with retention of configuration. The attack of hydroxide is at the 1° carbon, where no bond to the chiral carbon is broken. Hence, the rotation of plane polarized should not be altered.

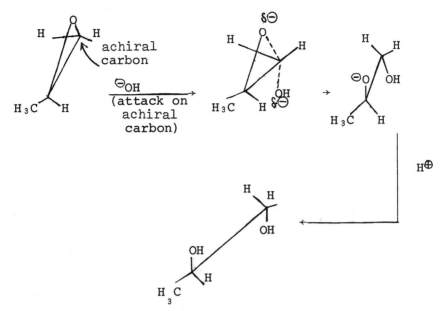

The products by base and acid hydrolysis are mirror images of each other. They rotate plane-polarized light in opposite directions.

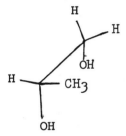

from base hydrolysis

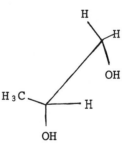

from acid hydrolysis

● **PROBLEM** 17-23

Write a mechanism for the reaction of trans-2-butene with trifluoroperacetic acid which is consistent with the fact that the rate is first order in each participant and gives cis addition.

Solution: One of the most important methods of preparing epoxides or oxiranes involves oxidation or epoxidation of an alkene with a percarboxylic acid, $\overset{\overset{O}{\|}}{R C}OOH$. One such per-

carboxylic acid is trifluoroperacetic acid, CF$_3$COOH. The
$$\overset{\|}{O}$$

net result of reaction is addition of oxygen across the
carbon-carbon double bond. This proceeds only in the cis
configuration. Therefore, when trifluoroperacetic acid is
added to trans-2-butene, trans-2-butene oxide should result.

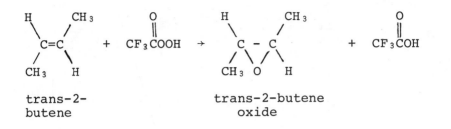

trans-2-
butene

trans-2-butene
oxide

It is believed the peracid furnishes the $^+$OH to the
double bond as shown in the mechanism outlined below:

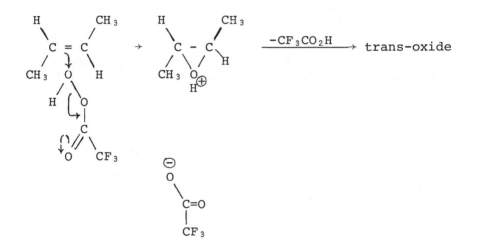

Note: The arrows indicate the shifting of pairs of
electrons.

Kinetically, the rate is first order for each
participant because all that is needed to produce one
molecule of product is one molecule of each reactant.

SPECTROSCOPY

● **PROBLEM** 17-24

The nmr spectra are those of anisole and p-methoxyanisole. Assign the correct structure to each of these
spectra.

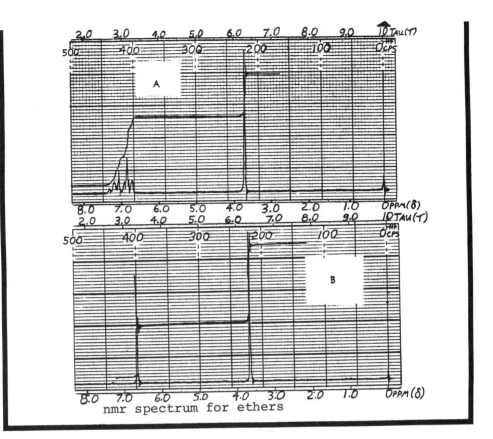

nmr spectrum for ethers

Solution: Spectrum A can be assigned the structure of

anisole, CH$_3$O—⬡ . To see this, consider the hydrogens

of the methyl group. Such hydrogens, HC-OR, normally have
a chemical shift of 3.3-4, where R represents an aryl or
alkyl group in the ether linkage. R is aryl, as will be
shown below, so that it may be expected that such protons
absorb downfield (approximately 3.7 δ) relative to an alkyl
R due to the powerful deshielding from the circulation of
the π electrons in the aryl ring. Therefore, it may be
concluded that the peak at 3.7 δ indicates the existence
of HC-OR. It is known that aromatic hydrogens absorb between
6 and 8.5 δ. The spin-spin splitting that occurs in this
region in spectrum A must signify the hydrogens of the
aromatic group. Note that two different chemical shifts are
present to illustrate the different electronic environments
of the aromatic hydrogens. The hydrogens closest to the
ether linkage absorb upfield from the other aromatic
hydrogens because of the high electron density of oxygen.

At this point, the structure must be H$_3$C-O—⬡ . There

exist no other peaks, so that it cannot possibly be the
other given structure.

Spectrum B can only be p-methoxyanisole,

CH₃O——OCH₃. This structure is determined by referring

back to spectrum A, anisole. A comparison of the two shows that the only difference is the presence of only one peak in the 6 to 8.5 δ region with no spin-spin splitting. Recall that this region indicated aromatic hydrogens. Now, for spectrum B to have only one peak with no spin-spin splitting indicates that all of its aromatic hydrogens are equivalent; they exist in the same electron environment.

If anisole has the structure CH₃O—⬡ with non-equi-

valent aromatic hydrogens, then the only way to have the same spectrum except for equivalent aromatic hydrogens, is to have another CH₃O linkage located para to the first one,

that is, the structure must become CH₃O—⬡—OCH₃, which

is p-methoxyanisole.

● **PROBLEM** 17-25

Give a structure or structures for the compound whose infrared spectrum is shown.

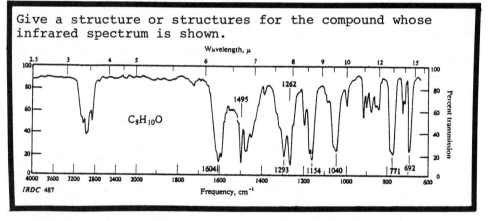

IRDC 487

Solution: Examination of this infrared spectrum

establishes this compound as some kind of aryl ether, ⬡ OR .

The most characteristic feature in the spectroscopic analysis of ethers is the strong band of C-O stretching. It occurs in the 1060-1300 cm⁻¹ range. In this region, many bands are present, but this alone does not establish the presence of an ether. For note, alcohols, carboxylic acids, and esters also show C-O stretching. They can be eliminated as possibilities, however, by the fact alcohols would also show the strong and broad O-H stretch in the 3200-3600 cm⁻¹, carboxylic acids $\left(\begin{matrix} O \\ \| \\ -C-OH \end{matrix}\right)$ would show carbonyl (C=O) absorption

at about 1700 cm^{-1}, and esters $\left(\begin{matrix} O \\ \| \\ -C-O- \end{matrix}\right)$ would do the same.
The fact that none of these bands is present leaves only
the functional group of an ether as one that can exhibit
C-O stretching. This ether could be aryl or alkyl. That it
must be aryl can be determined by looking at the specific
positions of the bands for C-O stretching. Aryl ethers
show C-O stretching between 1200 and 1275 cm^{-1} (and,
weaker at 1020-1075 cm^{-1}). At 1040 cm^{-1} and approximately
1075 cm^{-1} two bands are present. This fits into the pattern
expected for aryl ethers. Note: If it were an alkyl ether,
the C-O stretching would have been between 1060-1150 cm^{-1},
and no such band can be detected.

Hence, it is now established that an aryl ether is
present. This accounts for, then, 6 carbons (of benzene
portion) and one oxygen (the ether linkage). Now subtracting these atoms from the given molecular formula, $C_8H_{10}O$,
leaves C_2H_{10}. The two carbons to be accounted for must be
part of the substituents on the aromatic ring. This means
they will influence the out-of-plane C-H bending for aromatic
rings. While out-of-plane bending gives strong absorption in
the 675-870 cm^{-1} region, the exact location will depend upon
the number and position of the substituents (mono-substituted,
o, m, p-disubstituted). The bonds at 771 cm^{-1} and 692 cm^{-1}
indicate a m-disubstituted benzene exists, for such a compound
shows C-H out-of-plane bending at 690-710 cm$^-$ and 750-810
cm^{-1}. In summary, it is now known that $C_8H_{10}O$ is an aryl
ether with a m-disubstituted benzene. One of the substituents
must be linked to the oxygen to establish an ether. Because
only C_2H_{10} is available after the aryl ether atoms are considered, the second substituent is an alkyl group.

The question at this point is what other group is the
oxygen attached to and what is the specific alkyl group
mentioned above. A little thought indicates that if only
two carbons (and some hydrogens) are available, methyl
(CH$_3$) groups must be the answer. One methyl group would be
attached to the oxygen atom to complete the ether linkage,
while the other would be a substituent of benzene in the

meta position. The picture becomes: [structure: benzene ring with OCH$_3$ and CH$_3$ substituents]   The

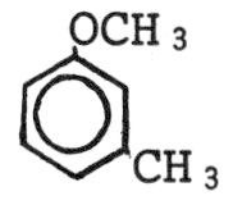

two methyls account for two carbons and six hydrogens. Since
C_2H_{10} was available, only four hydrogens are still to be
determined. They are bonded to the four carbons of the
benzene ring that lack a substituent. The structure shown
above is, therefore, the compound depicted in the infrared
spectrum. It is named m-methylanisole.

CHARACTERIZATION TESTS

Specify a simple chemical test to distinguish the following pairs of compounds. Give the reagent to be used and the observation that you would make.

(a) Diisopropyl ether and diallyl ether
(b) Diethyl ether and methyl iodide
(c) Dibutyl ether and n-butyl alcohol

Solution: A good way to approach this type of problem is to write out the structures of the compounds involved to discern the functional groups present. Then try to select reagents that would distinguish between the compounds on the basis of the functional groups.

(a) $CH_3-\overset{\overset{H}{|}}{C}-O-\overset{\overset{H}{|}}{C}-CH_3$ $CH_2=CH-CH_2-O-CH_2-CH=CH_2$
         $\underset{|}{CH_3}$ $\underset{|}{CH_3}$

   Diisopropyl ether   Diallyl ether

   The use of reagents that would reveal the presence of an ether would be useless in this case. Both compounds would give a positive test. Note, however, that diallyl ether contains carbon-carbon double bonds. It is unsaturated. An excellent method for characterizing carbon-carbon double bonds is by using a solution of bromine in carbon tetrachloride, which has a reddish color. The bromine will add across the double bond, thereby decolorizing the solution. Since the diisopropyl ether lacks a double bond, it will not decolorize the Br_2/CCl_4 solution. Hence, the two ethers may be distinguished on this basis.

(b) $CH_3CH_2OCH_2CH_3$ CH_3I

   Diethyl ether   Methyl iodide

   Methyl iodide is a primary alkyl halide. It is possible to test for such halides by placing them in aqueous alcoholic silver nitrate. If the alkyl halide exists, a silver halide should precipitate out of solution. Hence, methyl iodide can be expected to produce AgI, the silver halide, slowly after being added to aqueous alcoholic silver nitrate. The ether fails to give a precipitate, so that the compounds are distinguished on this basis.

(c) $CH_3CH_2CH_2CH_2-O-CH_2CH_2CH_2CH_3$ $CH_3CH_2CH_2CH_2OH$

   Dibutyl ether   N-butyl alcohol

   The alcohol may be distinguished from the ether by the fact that the former can act as an acid to form the alkoxide ion, RO^-. The acidity of alcohols is shown by their reaction with active metals (such as sodium, Na) to form hydrogen gas as shown:

$$ROH \quad + \quad Na \quad \rightarrow \quad RO^{\ominus}Na^{\oplus} \quad + \quad \tfrac{1}{2} H_2 \, .$$

Consequently, if sodium pieces are allowed to come into contact with n-butyl alcohol hydrogen gas should be seen bubbling off. The dibutyl ether will fail to liberate hydrogen, so that it is this observation that differentiates the two compounds.

● **PROBLEM** 17-27

An unknown compound is believed to be one of the following. Describe how you would go about finding out which of the possibilities the unknown actually is. Where possible, use simple chemical tests; where necessary, use more elaborate chemical methods like quantitative hydrogenation, cleavage, etc. Make use of any needed tables of physical constants.

(a)   n-propyl ether (b.p. 91°) and 2-methylhexane (b.p. 91°)
(b)   benzyl ethyl ether (b.p. 188°) and allyl phenyl ether (b.p. 192°)
(c)   methyl p-tolyl ether (b.p. 176°) and methyl m-tolyl ether (b.p. 177°)

Solution: (a) N-propyl ether $(CH_3CH_2CH_2OCH_2CH_2CH_3)$ and

2-methylhexane $\left(CH_3CHCH_2CH_2CH_2CH_3 \atop \qquad | \atop \qquad CH_3 \right)$ may be distinguished on

the basis of physical properties, specifically solubility. Since the C-O-C bond angle of ethers is not 180°, there exists a net dipole moment. Ethers possess weak polarity, so that they show solubility in water comparable to that of alcohols. Apparently, the hydrogen bonding between water molecules and ether molecules accounts for the solubility as shown:

$$
\begin{array}{ccc}
R-O & \cdots & H-O \\
| & & | \\
R & & H
\end{array}
$$

Hence, N-propyl ether should show some solubility in water. Also, it will be soluble in cold concentrated sulfuric acid through formation of oxonium salts. 2-methylhexane, being an alkane, is non-polar. Consequently, it will be insoluble in these same solutions.

(b)   The structures of benzyl ethyl ether and allyl phenyl ether are, respectively,

   ⬡–$CH_2OCH_2CH_3$ and   ⬡–$OCH_2-CH=CH_2$.

The structure of allyl phenyl ether shows a unit of unsaturation. This means that a method of distinguishing the two ethers is by oxidation with the agent $KMnO_4$. The ether linkage, itself, is relatively unreactive. It is

613

stable toward bases, oxidizing agents, and reducing agents. Carbon-carbon double bonds are, however, very reactive, so that when KMnO₄ is added, only the allylic ether is oxidized due to the region of unsaturation.

(c)   The structures of the two compounds to be differentiated can be written as follows:

     methyl p-tolyl ether   methyl m-tolyl ether

    Again, oxidation will distinguish these compounds. Addition of KMnO₄ will oxidize the methyl group (CH_3) to the carboxyl group ($-COOH$) so that the following compounds result:

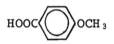

     HOOC⟨ ⟩OCH₃ and m-OCH₃ structures

  p-methoxybenzoic acid   m-methoxybenzoic acid

(Recall, the ether group is unreactive toward oxidizing agents such as KMnO₄.) These two compounds have significant melting point differences. The melting points of the para and meta compounds are, respectively, 184°C and 110°C. This means a melting point determination should identify which of the two compounds is present. In this way, by working backwards, the correct methyl tolyl ether can be discerned.

CHAPTER 18

ALDEHYDES AND KETONES I

NOMENCLATURE AND STRUCTURE

● PROBLEM 18-1

What is a ketone?

Solution: The main functional group of a ketone is the

carbonyl group $\left[\diagdown \atop \diagup C{=}O \right]$. In a ketone there are two alkyl

or aryl groups. attached to the carbonyl carbon. They
can either be the same or different groups. The traditional
representation of a ketone is

$$R' - \underset{\underset{O}{\|}}{C} - R$$

where R' and R represent alkyl or aryl groups. In general
ketones are named by replacing the final "e" of the hydrocarbon name by the suffix "one". For example

$$H_3C - \underset{\underset{O}{\|}}{C} - CH_3 \qquad .$$

is called propanone (its trivial name is acetone) and

$$H_3C{-}\underset{\underset{O}{\|}}{C}{-}CH_2 CH_2 CH_3$$

is called 2-pentanone.

        In case there are two or more functional groups
present, the suffix takes the form of "dione," "trione,"
etc. and the "e" ending remains. For example

$$H_3C -\underset{\underset{O}{\|}}{C}{-}CH_2{-}CH_2{-}\underset{\underset{O}{\|}}{C}{-}CH_3$$

is called 2,5 hexanedione.

Name the following compounds according to an acceptable nomenclature (IUPAC or common):

(a)　　$CH_3-C-CH_2CH_3$
　　　　　　　$\overset{\displaystyle \|}{O}$

(d)　$CH_3-C-CH_2-C-CH_3$
　　　　　$\overset{\displaystyle \|}{O}$　　　$\overset{\displaystyle \|}{O}$

(b)　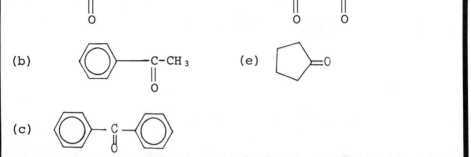

(e)

(c)　

Solution:　　By looking at the above compounds one can

$$\overset{\displaystyle O}{\overset{\displaystyle \|}{}}$$

see that they all follow the general formula $R'-C-R$, which indicates that they are all ketones. The suffix used to describe ketones is "one". Ketones are named by replacing the "e" of the hydrocarbon name with "one". In cases where there are two or three carbonyl groups

$\left(\begin{array}{c}\diagdown \\ {\diagup}\end{array}C{=}O\right)$　the suffixes dione and trione are used respec-

tively, and the "e" ending of the hydrocarbon name remains.

(a)　$CH_3-C-CH_2CH_3$　　The parent compound is the four
　　　　　$\overset{\displaystyle \|}{O}$

carbon alkane, butane. Since two alkyl groups must be attached to the carbonyl group, the carbonyl group must be at C2 or C3. Since these two carbons are equivalent the lower number is used in naming the compound. This compound is named 2-butanone.

(b)　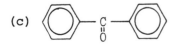　　Another method for naming ketones

is to place the names of the two alkyl groups as prefixes to the word ketone. Here, one alkyl group is a methyl group and the other is a phenyl group. The groups are named in alphabetical order and the compound is methyl phenyl ketone.

(c)　　　The two aryl groups are benzene

rings (phenyl groups). The compound can be named di-
phenyl ketone; its trivial name is benzophenone.

(d) 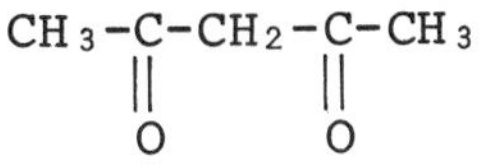 $CH_3-C-CH_2-C-CH_3$ The parent compound is the

five carbon alkane, pentane. Since there are carbonyl
groups at both C2 and C4, the suffix used is "dione"
instead of "one". The name of this compound is 2,4-
pentanedione.

(e) 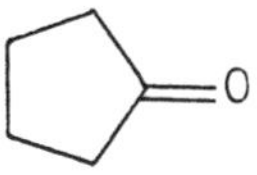   The parent compound is the cyclic five

carbon alkane, cyclopentane. The ketone is named cyclopentanone.

● PROBLEM 18-3

What is an aldehyde?

Solution: The functional group which differentiates an
aldehyde from other organic molecules is a carbonyl atom
(C=O) joined to another carbon atom and to a hydrogen atom.
In general, the formula for an aldehyde is

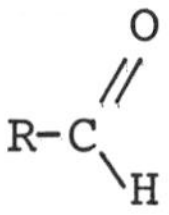

$$R-C\overset{\displaystyle O}{\underset{\displaystyle H}{\big/\big/}}$$

where R symbolizes an alkyl or aryl group. Aldehydes are
named by adding either "al" or "aldehyde" to the end of the
name of the parent compound. Substituent groups attached to
the alkyl group are taken into account by prefixes before
the name of the parent compound.

An example of an aldehyde is acetaldehyde which is
composed of two carbons. It can be drawn as

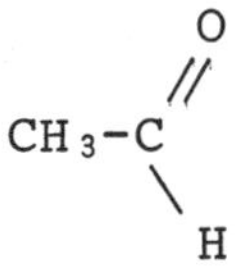

acetaldehyde

● PROBLEM 18-4

Name the following structures:

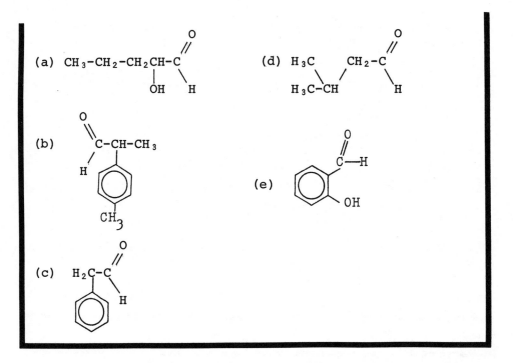

(a) $CH_3-CH_2-CH_2CH-C\overset{O}{\underset{\underset{\displaystyle OH}{|}}{\overset{//}{}}}\underset{H}{\diagdown}$

(d) $H_3C\diagdown\underset{H_3C-CH}{}\diagup CH_2-C\overset{O}{\overset{//}{}}\diagdown H$

(b) $\overset{O}{\overset{\|}{}}C-CH-CH_3$ with H and benzene ring bearing CH_3

(e) benzene ring with $C\overset{O}{\overset{\|}{}}-H$ and OH

(c) $H_2C-C\overset{O}{\overset{//}{}}\diagdown H$ with benzene ring

Solution: First we will determine the parent structure
and then the functional groups. The names and locations of
the functional groups are added as prefixes to the name of
the parent compound. In general the suffix 'al' (IUPAC
nomenclature) or aldehyde (common name) is added to the
parent names of aldehydes (according to the nomenclature
used).

(a) $CH_3-CH_2-CH_2CH-C\overset{O}{\underset{\underset{\displaystyle OH}{|}}{\overset{//}{}}}\underset{H}{\diagdown}$ The parent compound

is the five carbon aldehyde, pentanal or pentaldehyde.
There is an alcohol moiety attached to the carbon adjacent
to the aldehyde functional group. For aldehydes the carbons
beginning with the one attached to the carbonyl carbon are
labelled, alpha, beta, gamma (α, β, γ), etc. for the common
name and 2,3,4, etc. for the IUPAC name. The name of this
compound is therefore 2-hydroxypentanal or α-hydroxypent-
aldehyde.

(b)   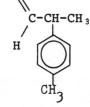   Normally   in naming the
parent compound one deter-
mines the longest carbon

chain to find the root. The parent compound here would be
the three carbon aldehyde propanal or propionaldehyde.

There is a phenyl group with a methyl substituent in the para position attached to the α carbon. The name of this compound is thus 2-p-tolylpropanal or α-p-tolylpropi.-onaldehyde.

(c) 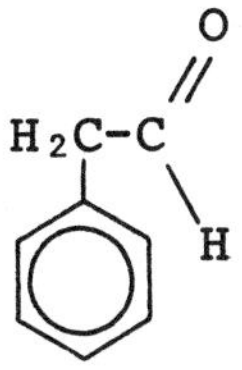   The parent compound is the two carbon aldehyde acetaldehyde

or ethanal. There is a benzene group attached to the α or "2" carbon, which gives the compound the name 2-phenylethanal or α-phenylacetaldehyde.

(d) 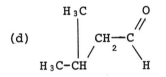 The parent compound is the

four carbon aldehyde, butanal or butyraldehyde. There is a methyl group attached to the "3" or β-carbon. The name of the compound is therefore 3-methylbutanal or β-methylbutyraldehyde.

(e) 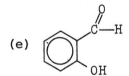 The parent compound is the

aromatic aldehyde, benzaldehyde. There is a hydroxy group ortho to the aldehyde group. The name of this compound is o-hydroxybenzaldehyde. There is also a trivial name for this compound which is salicylaldehyde.

● PROBLEM 18-5

Give the structural formulas of the following:

(a) formaldehyde
(b) glyceraldehyde
(c) 2-hydroxybutanal

(d) benzaldehyde
(e) β-aminopropionaldehyde

Solution: Aldehydes have the general structural formula

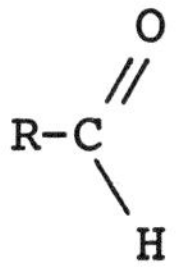

(a) Formaldehyde is the simplest aldehyde. It contains only one carbon and can be written as

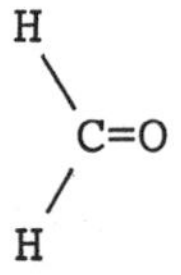

formaldehyde

(b) The structural formula for glycerol is

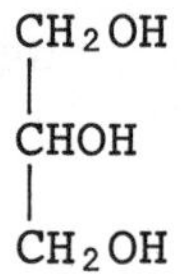

CH_2OH
|
$CHOH$
|
CH_2OH

One of the alcohol functions on the end is oxidized to form the aldehyde, glyceraldehyde.

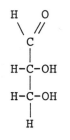

glyceraldehyde

(c) 2-hydroxybutanal. The parent structure is butyraldehyde:

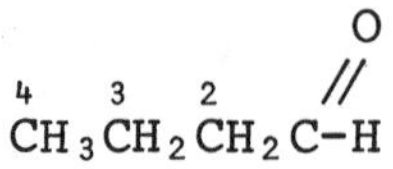

$$\overset{4}{CH_3}\overset{3}{CH_2}\overset{2}{CH_2}\overset{O}{\overset{\|}{C}}-H$$

butyraldehyde

The carbons proceeding from the carbonyl carbon towards the end of the chain are labelled two, three and four.

The hydroxy group is attached to carbon number two.

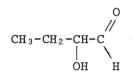

2-hydroxybutanal

(d) Benzaldehyde, as its name implies is a benzene group with an aldehyde function attached.

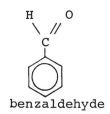

benzaldehyde

(e) β-aminopropionaldehyde The structure of this compound is determined in a manner similar to that used for 2-hydroxybutanal. The parent compound is propionaldehyde.

The carbons are labelled beginning with the first carbon after the carbonyl carbon.

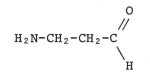

β-aminopropionaldehyde

THE CARBONYL GROUP

● **PROBLEM** 18-6

Arrange the following pairs of compounds in order of expected reactivity toward addition of a common nucleophilic agent such as hydroxide ion to the carbonyl bond. Indicate your reasoning.

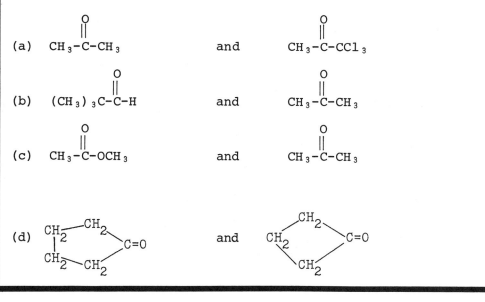

Solution: To solve this problem, we consider what properties of carbonyl compounds favor a reaction with a nucleophilic reagent.

The primary property of carbonyl compounds is the inherent charge separation in the $\diagdown C=O \diagup$ bond. This charge separation is great enough to lead to a significant contribution of the dipolar resonance form with oxygen negative and carbon positive:

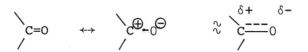

A carbonyl carbon is more susceptible to nucleophilic attack when it is highly electropositive. The nucleophile will more readily contribute its electron pair to a highly electron deficient species in order to relieve the partial positive charge on the carbonyl carbon.

Another important factor in determining reactivity is steric hindrance. The bulkier the substituents on the $\diagdown C=O \diagup$ group , the less room they have to move freely and thus the less reactive they are, as illustrated in the following comparison:

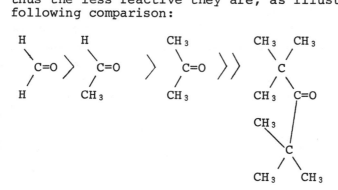

When comparing cyclic ketones and their open chain analogs in terms of reactivity, the cyclic ketones are almost always more reactive:

This is because the freely rotating alkyl groups on the open chained ketone will often "swing around" and block a nucleophilic attack on the carbonyl group. In a cyclic compound the substituents cannot rotate freely

about the $\diagdown$C=O single bonds and the carbonyl carbon is $\diagup$

less sterically hindered.

      In part a we look at $CH_3-\overset{\overset{\textstyle O}{\|}}{C}-CH_3$ and $CH_3-\overset{\overset{\textstyle O}{\|}}{C}-CCl_3$. The electron withdrawing power of the trichloromethyl group creates a greater electropositive charge on the carbonyl carbon in $CH_3-\overset{\overset{\textstyle O}{\|}}{C}-CCl_3$. This electron withdrawing effect of $-CCl_3$ is called an inductive effect. The compound $CH_3-\overset{\overset{\textstyle O}{\|}}{C}-CCl_3$ is thus more reactive to nucleophilic attack by $OH^{\ominus}$ then $CH_3-\overset{\overset{\textstyle O}{\|}}{C}-CH_3$.

      In part b we consider $(CH_3)_3C-\overset{\overset{\textstyle O}{\|}}{C}-H$ and $CH_3-\overset{\overset{\textstyle O}{\|}}{C}-CH_3$. The very bulky t-butyl group creates great steric hindrance around the carbonyl carbon thus making a nucleophilic attack by $OH^{\ominus}$ very difficult. For this reason, $CH_3-\overset{\overset{\textstyle O}{\|}}{C}-CH_3$ is the more reactive compound.

      Part c brings an unexpected answer. By considering the inductive effect of $-OCH_3$ we would expect $CH_3-\overset{\overset{\textstyle O}{\|}}{C}-OCH_3$ to be more reactive. This is not the case. The carbonyl carbon loses some electropositive charge because of the charge stabilization brought about by the following contributing structures:

$$CH_3-\overset{\overset{\textstyle O}{\|}}{C}-OCH_3 \quad \longleftarrow \quad CH_3-\overset{\overset{\textstyle \overset{\ominus}{O}}{|}\,\oplus}{C}=OCH_3$$

      Because of this decrease in electropositive charge and the bulk of the $-OCH_3$ group, the carbonyl carbon of $CH_3-\overset{\overset{\textstyle O}{\|}}{C}-OCH_3$ is less reactive than that of $CH_3-\overset{\overset{\textstyle O}{\|}}{C}-CH_3$ towards nucleophilic attack.

      On this point we should note that the carbonyl carbon is sp^2 hybridized, and that upon nucleophilic attack it becomes sp^3 hybridized. In part d, cyclobutane has an angle strain of 30° (120° sp^2 bond angle -

90° cyclobutane bond angle = 30° angle strain.) Upon
nucleophilic addition the angle strain is reduced to 19.5°
(109.5° sp³ bond angle - 90° = 19.5° angle strain). For
cyclobutanone this is a significant reduction of angle
strain. In the case of cyclopentanone angle strain is
not as important as the eclipsing interactions between
non-bonded atoms on adjacent carbons.

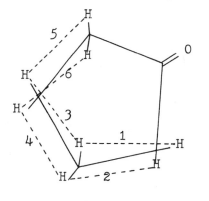

six eclipsing
interactions

H₂O

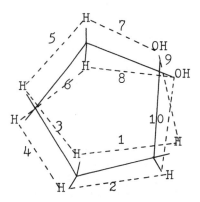

ten eclipsing
interactions

   These eclipsing interactions put more energy in the
compound's bonds, thus destabilizing the compound. Increasing the number of these interactions will destabilize
the compound, thus nucleophilic addition in cyclopentanone
is not favorable and cyclobutanone is the more reactive
species.

● **PROBLEM** 18-7

The attack of the nucleophile always occurs at carbon
rather than oxygen in a carbonyl compound; this is true
when the reaction is kinetically controlled, and it is
also true when the reaction is thermodynamically controlled.
Explain.

<u>Solution:</u>   A carbonyl compound is characterized as having

a $-\underset{/}{C}=O$ group within it. The C=O bond has a very important

contributing structure which shows the inherent separation of charge between the carbon and oxygen:

$$\underset{/}{\overset{\backslash}{C}} = O \quad\longleftrightarrow\quad \underset{/}{\overset{\backslash}{C}} \overset{\oplus}{-} \overset{\ominus}{O}$$

A carbonyl is thus more accurately represented with partial charges:

$$\left[\; \underset{/}{\overset{\backslash}{C}} \overset{\delta+}{\underset{}{\text{---}}} \overset{\delta-}{O} \;\right]$$

Kinetically this means that the carbonyl carbon is somewhat electrophilic (desires electrons because it is electron deficient) and thus the nucleophile will attack here.

Thermodynamically we could have the following intermediates upon nucleophilic attack:

$$B \text{——} \underset{/}{\overset{\backslash}{C}} - \overset{\ominus}{O} \qquad or \qquad \underset{/}{\overset{\backslash}{C}}{}^{\ominus} - O - B,$$

where "B" represents a base.

$B - \underset{/}{\overset{\backslash}{C}} - \overset{\ominus}{O}$ is the more stable intermediate because

it is more favorable to have the negative charge on the more electronegative atom (oxygen has a greater electronegativity than carbon).

● **PROBLEM** 18-8

The equilibrium constant for hydration is especially large for formaldehyde, trichloroacetaldehyde, and cyclopropanone. Explain.

Solution: To solve this problem we must consider what conditions will strongly favor hydration and then see if these conditions are present in the questioned compounds.

Favorable hydrate formation will result when there is a destabilization of charge separation that is inherent

in carbonyl groups $\left(\begin{array}{c} \overset{\delta-}{O} \\ \parallel \\ -C- \\ \delta+ \end{array} \right)$ caused by a group that is close to it. When there is a steric disadvantage in the carbonyl compound it can sometimes be relieved by formation of the hydrate.

In the case of formaldehyde $\left(\begin{array}{c} O \\ \parallel \\ H-C-H \end{array} \right)$, there is no alkyl group present. Alkyl groups stabilize positively charged centers to which they are bonded, therefore formaldehyde is destabilized, relative to most aldehydes by the absence of these alkyl groups. It exists completely in its hydrated form in aqueous solution.

Trichloroacetaldehyde $\left(\begin{array}{c} O \\ \parallel \\ CCl_3-C-H \end{array} \right)$ has a trichloro-methyl group ($-CCl_3$) bonded to the carbonyl carbon. This group induces a significant inductive effect (change in distribution of charge in atoms due to distortions of electron density caused by large electronegativity differences), which destabilizes the charge separation present in the carbonyl group. Chlorine, a very electronegative element, is the cause of this destabilizing inductive effect. The hydrated compound looks like this:

$$\begin{array}{c} OH \\ | \\ CCl_3-C-H \\ | \\ OH \end{array}$$

Cyclopropanone $\left(\text{} \right)$ has a large K (equilibrium constant for hydration) value because of steric effects. The bond angle in cyclopropanone is 60°. The carbonyl carbon, being sp^2 hybridized, prefers a bond angle of 120°. The angle strain is thus 60° (120° - 60°). In hydrate form this carbon becomes sp^3 hybridized. The preferred bond angle changes from 120° to 109.5° and the angle strain decreases from 60° to 49.5° (109.5° - 60° = 49.5°).

SYNTHESIS

● PROBLEM 18-9

Outline all steps in a possible laboratory synthesis of each of the following from alcohols of four carbons or fewer, using any needed inorganic reagents:

(a) $CH_3CH_2CCH_3$
　　　　　$\parallel$
　　　　　O

(b) CH_3-C-CH_3
　　　　$\parallel$
　　　　O

Methyl ethyl ketone

Acetone

Solution: Ketones can be prepared by oxidation of secondary alcohols with a variety of reagents, such as CrO_3 (chromium trioxide) or $K_2Cr_2O_7$ (potassium dichromate) with acid. The compound that is formed by oxidation of an alcohol depends upon the number of hydrogens attached to the carbon bearing the -OH group, that is upon whether the alcohol is primary, secondary or tertiary. For example, in the first problem, to synthesize the product, methyl ethyl ketone, a secondary alcohol is used that has the same number of carbon atoms as the product. In this case sec-butyl alcohol is used as the precursor.

$$\text{(a)} \quad \underset{\text{sec-butyl alcohol}}{CH_3CH_2\overset{\displaystyle OH}{\overset{|}{C}}HCH_3} \xrightarrow{CrO_3} \underset{\text{methyl ethyl ketone}}{CH_3CH_2\overset{\displaystyle O}{\overset{||}{C}}CH_3}$$

To obtain the product only requires one step where sec-butyl alcohol is oxidized directly to methyl ethyl ketone with chromium trioxide.

An example of a longer synthesis in preparation of a ketone is producing acetone from a two-carbon alcohol. The only two carbon alcohol is ethanol, so this will be the precursor.

$$\text{(b)} \quad \underset{\text{Ethanol}}{CH_3CH_2OH} \xrightarrow[H^{\oplus}]{K_2Cr_2O_7} CH_3\overset{\displaystyle O}{\overset{||}{C}}H + CH_3MgBr \xrightarrow{H_2O} CH_3\overset{\displaystyle OH}{\overset{|}{C}}HCH_3$$

$$\underset{\text{Acetone}}{CH_3\underset{\displaystyle O}{\overset{||}{C}}CH_3} \xleftarrow{CrO_3}$$

This synthetic reaction involves oxidation of the alcohol to yield acetaldehyde. To add another carbon atom to this first product, the Grignard reagent methyl magnesium bromide (CH_3MgBr) is added for methylation. Upon hydrolysis this yields a three carbon compound, isopropanol, which is a secondary alcohol. As shown previously, secondary alcohols are oxidized to ketones with chromium trioxide, thus yielding the final product, acetone.

● **PROBLEM** 18-10

Undecanal is a sex attractant for the greater wax moth (Galleria mellonella). Show how to synthesize this compound efficiently from

(a) 1-nonanol   (b) 1-decanol   (c) 1-dodecanol

Solution: In a synthesis problem of this type, where
one specific compound must be synthesized from various
other starting materials, it is a good idea to see what
differences there are between the final product and the
starting material. The idea is then to synthesize this
difference onto the starting material.

For example, in part (a) 1-nonanol $(CH_3(CH_2)_7CH_2OH)$,
the starting material, must gain two carbons to obtain the
carbon skeleton in the final product, undecanal
$(CH_3(CH_2)_9CHO)$.

Some methods of adding two carbons to the alcohol
involves the use of an ethyl Grignard reagent or an
acetylene anion. Of these methods, the use of the acetylene
anion is the most feasible; it will react with an alkyl
halide via an Sn_2 mechanism. The alkyne formed can then be
converted into the desired product. The synthesis which
employs this method is shown below:

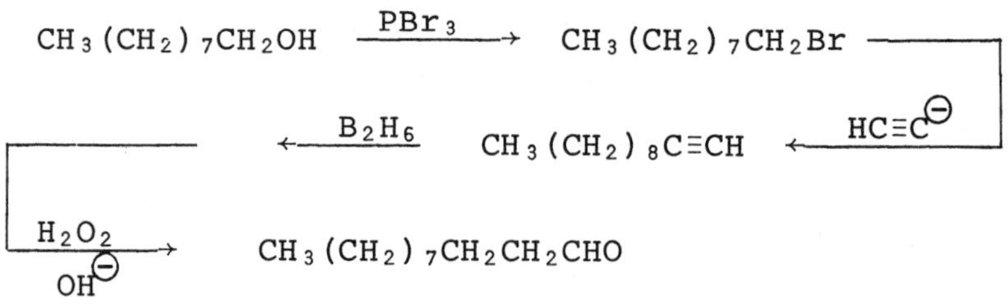

$$CH_3(CH_2)_7CH_2OH \xrightarrow{\text{PBr}_3} CH_3(CH_2)_7CH_2Br$$

$$\xleftarrow{\text{B}_2\text{H}_6} CH_3(CH_2)_8C\equiv CH \xleftarrow{HC\equiv C^\ominus}$$

$$\xrightarrow[\text{OH}^\ominus]{H_2O_2} CH_3(CH_2)_7CH_2CH_2CHO$$

In part b we follow the same rationale used in part
a. In this case we must add one carbon to the starting
material. This can be accomplished by a Grignard reagent
or through cyanohydrin formation. In this case a Grignard
reagent may either react with the ten carbon compound
(1-decanol) or be formed from the ten carbon compound.
Since 1-decanol will react with a Grignard reagent to produce
an alkane and a Grignard salt, we will form the Grignard
from the alcohol:

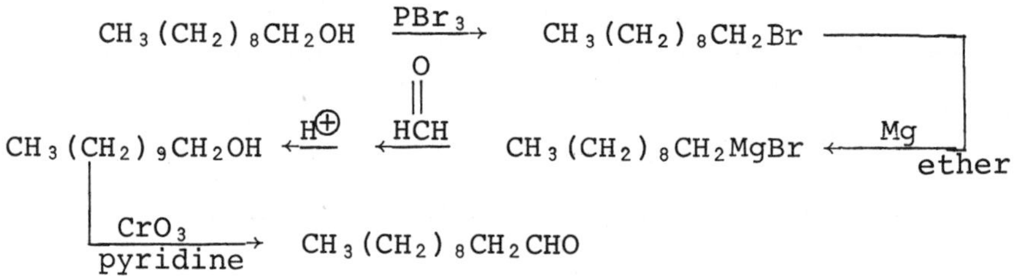

$$CH_3(CH_2)_8CH_2OH \xrightarrow{\text{PBr}_3} CH_3(CH_2)_8CH_2Br$$

$$CH_3(CH_2)_9CH_2OH \xleftarrow{H^\oplus} \xleftarrow{\overset{O}{\overset{||}{HCH}}} CH_3(CH_2)_8CH_2MgBr \xleftarrow[\text{ether}]{Mg}$$

$$\xrightarrow[\text{pyridine}]{CrO_3} CH_3(CH_2)_8CH_2CHO$$

The last reagent used, CrO_3 with pyridine,
is an oxidizing agent that oxidizes a primary alcohol to an
aldehyde.

In part c, the starting material must lose one carbon
to form the desired product. Some methods of losing one
carbon involve the oxidation of a terminal alkene by ozone
(followed by a workup) or by hot, basic $KMnO_4$ solution;
another method involves the Hoffman degradation of an amide
$(RCONH_2)$ to an amine (RNH_2). This last method is impractical

628

since the formation of a terminal alkene is much easier than the formation of an amide (from an alcohol). We will use an ozonolysis reaction (followed by reductive workup) to form the desired aldehyde.

$$CH_3(CH_2)_9CH_2CH_2OH \xrightarrow{PBr_3} CH_3(CH_2)_9CH_2CH_2Br$$

$$CH_3(CH_2)_9CHO \xleftarrow[CH_3COOH]{Zn} \xleftarrow{O_3} CH_3(CH_2)_9CH=CH_2 \xleftarrow[alcohol]{KOH}$$

● **PROBLEM** 18-11

Write equations for all steps in the synthesis of the following from acetophenone, using any other needed reagents:

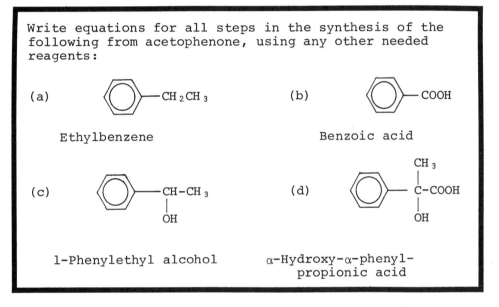

(a) —CH₂CH₃ ... Ethylbenzene

(b) —COOH ... Benzoic acid

(c) —CH–CH₃ / OH ... 1-Phenylethyl alcohol

(d) CH₃ / —C–COOH / OH ... α-Hydroxy-α-phenyl-propionic acid

Solution: Reactions involving acetophenone almost exclusively take place at the carbonyl (C=O) moiety of the molecule. To make this concept clearer the chemical structure of acetophenone is illustrated for comparison with the products wanted:

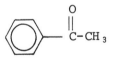

Acetophenone.

In problem (a), ethylbenzene is synthesized from acetophenone by a process called the Clemmensen reduction, which reduces the ketone to its corresponding hydrocarbon. The carbonyl is reduced to a hydrocarbon by the action of amalgamated zinc [Zn(Hg)] and concentrated hydrochloric acid. The general equation for the reaction is:

$$-\underset{\underset{O}{\|}}{C}- \xrightarrow[\text{conc. HCl}]{\text{Zn(Hg)}} -\underset{\underset{H}{|}}{\overset{\overset{|}{}}{C}}-H \text{ , thus solving problem (a).}$$

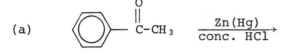

(a) Acetophenone → Zn(Hg), conc. HCl → Ethylbenzene

In problem (b), the product desired is benzoic acid which is synthesized by the oxidation of methyl ketones. This reaction involves sodium hypoiodite (NaOI) and sulfuric acid (H_2SO_4) wherein NaOI has the special property of only attacking the methyl group on methyl ketones. The methyl group is then tri-halogenated with the iodine and the $-CI_3$ group is replaced by an $-O^{\ominus} {}^{\oplus}Na$ portion. This compound formed is known as the intermediate and must be treated with concentrated sulfuric acid to complete the oxidation to a carboxylic acid. Problem (b) can now be solved illustrating the entire synthesis:

(b) Acetophenone → NaOI → (Sodium Benzoate) + CHI$_3$ → H_2SO_4 → Benzoic acid

Acetophenone   + CHI$_3$ Benzoic acid

Sodium Benzoate

+ Iodoform

Problem (c) involves the reduction of ketones to yield an alcohol. As shown many times previously most organic compounds can be reduced with hydrogen gas and a metal catalyst such as nickel, platinum or palladium. Even more common, reductions of ketones are done by the use of lithium aluminum hydride (LiAlH$_4$) or sodium borohydride (NaBH$_4$), then treating the compound with H_2SO_4 or HCl. The alcohol produced from ketones is a secondary alcohol after reduction and may be illustrated as follows:

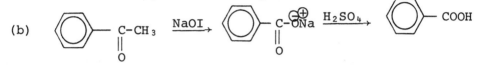

(c) Acetophenone → LiAlH$_4$, HCl → 1-Phenylethyl alcohol

Acetophenone   1-Phenylethyl alcohol

In problem (d), cyanohydrin formation is used. Cyanohydrins are nitriles, and their principal use is based on the fact that, like other nitriles, they undergo hydrolysis; in this case the products are α-hydroxyacids or unsaturated acids. The general equation for this type of reaction is:

$$-\underset{\underset{O}{\|}}{C}- + Na\overset{\oplus}{C}\overset{\ominus}{N} \xrightarrow{H_2SO_4} -\underset{\underset{OH}{|}}{C}-CN \xrightarrow[H_2O]{H_2SO_4} -\underset{\underset{OH}{|}}{C}-COOH$$

Ketone   Cyanohydrin   α-Hydroxyacid

630

The hydrocarbon group adjacent to the carbonyl is either aryl(Ar) or alkyl (R) and does not change at all during the synthesis because the reagents used are specific for the carbonyl moiety.

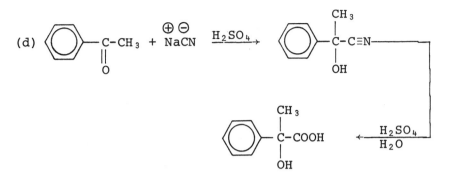

α-Hydroxy-α-phenyl propionic acid

● **PROBLEM** 18-12

Propose a reasonable mechanism for the synthesis of benzaldehyde diethyl acetal from benzene.

Solution: Benzene can be halogenated in the presence of a catalytic amount of iron (Fe). The halobenzene can form a Grignard reagent, which can be carbonated to give a carboxylic acid. Reduction of a carboxylic acid can give an aldehyde; an   acetal is an aldehyde derivative. The complete synthesis is broken down into various steps, and is shown below:

1.)   Chlorobenzene synthesis:

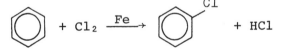

2.)   Grignard formation:

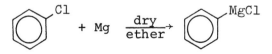

3.)   Carbonation:

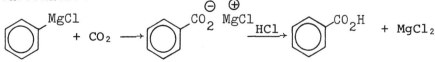

4.)   Rosenmund reduction of carboxylic acid:

631

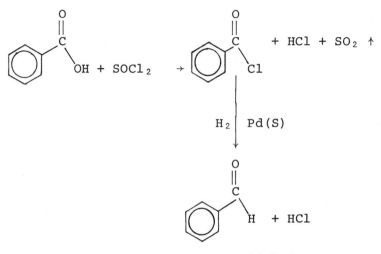

Benzaldehyde

5.) Acetal synthesis:

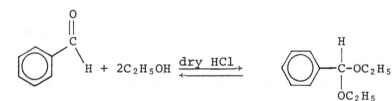

Benzaldehyde diethyl
acetal

● PROBLEM 18-13

One of the compounds that was initially formed in the
primitive atmosphere was formaldehyde ($H_2C=O$). It is one
of the precursor molecules that came to make up living
organisms. It can be formed photolytically as shown in
the following equation:

$$CH_4 + H_2O \xrightarrow{h\nu} H_2C=O + 4H\cdot$$

Propose a mechanism for this reaction.

Solution: When ultraviolet light ($h\nu$) is the energy
source for a reaction, free radicals are usually involved.

When methane (CH_4) is exposed to ultraviolet light
the following fragmentation will occur.

(i) $CH_4 \xrightarrow{h\nu}$ $\cdot CH_3$ + $H\cdot$

methyl radical   hydrogen radical

Since there is water in this system, it will also be exposed to the ultraviolet rays, causing it to break up into radicals.

(ii) $2H_2O$ $\xrightarrow{h\nu}$ $2HO\cdot$ $+ 2H\cdot$

In designing a mechanism, one attempts to build molecules that look increasingly like the desired products. The system now contains the $HO\cdot$, $H\cdot$ and $CH_3\cdot$ radicals. If $HO\cdot$ and $CH_3\cdot$ combine, a product resembling formaldehyde is made.

(iii) $\cdot CH_3 + HO\cdot$ $\longrightarrow$ $HO-CH_3$

methanol

To produce formaldehyde two hydrogen atoms must be removed from this product; one from the oxygen and one from the carbon.

(iv) $HO-CH_3$ $\xrightarrow{h\nu}$ $HO-\overset{\bullet}{C}H_2$ $+ H\cdot$

Remember that ultraviolet light will cause the formation of radicals. In the next reaction the other hydrogen will be removed in a different way. An $\cdot OH$ radical will add to the product formed in reaction (iv) and a transition state will form which will lead to the production of one molecule of formaldehyde, and one molecule of water. The brackets indicate the intermediate transition state.

(v) $HO-\overset{\bullet}{C}H_2 + HO\cdot$ $\longrightarrow$ $\left[\begin{array}{c} OH \\ | \\ HO-CH_2 \end{array} \right]$ $\longrightarrow$ $\begin{array}{c} H \\ \diagdown \\ C=O + H_2O \\ \diagup \\ H \end{array}$

If reactions (i) through (v) are added together one regains the given overall reaction.

REACTIONS

What are the products from the reaction of 1,1-diphenyl-1,2-ethanediol with strong acid? Propose a reasonable mechanism for the reaction.

Solution: Polyhydric alcohols with hydroxyl groups on different carbons are relatively stable, but in strong acid they tend to dehydroxylate to form carbonium ions. If the alcohol is a 1,2-diol, the carbonium ion can rearrange to give a more stable carbonyl compound.

1,1-diphenyl-1,2-ethanediol is a polyhydric alcohol
having the structure

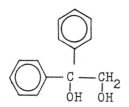

In the presence of strong acid, the carbonium ion can be
formed at either carbon, depending upon the method of
control employed (kinetic or thermodynamic). If the hydroxyl
group at the carbon with the diphenyl is protonated, a
benzylic cation is formed. If the other hydroxyl group is
protonated, a primary carbocation is formed. The rate of
carbocation formation depends upon the stability of the ion
formed. The order of stability of carbocations is:

    benzylic > tertiary > secondary > primary.

Thus, if kinetic (rate) control is used, the hydroxyl
group on the tertiary carbon is protonated to form a
tertiary benzylic cation. The loss of water followed by
a hydride shift gives the final product, diphenylacetaldehyde.

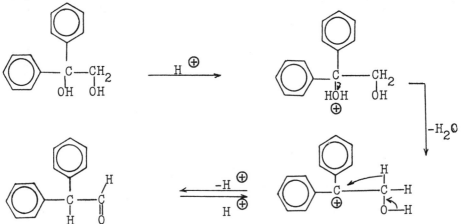

    However, if the reaction is left standing for a
period of time, a different product is formed. This product
is formed slower and is more stable than diphenylacetaldehyde,
thus, the pathway of formation is equilibrium-controlled. It
occurs at a slower rate because it is formed by protonation
of the hydroxyl group on the primary carbon to give a primary
carbocation. This primary carbocation undergoes a phenyl
shift instead of a hydride shift, in the process of carbonyl
formation. This results in a more stable compound because
there is more resonance stabilization arising from the carbonyl group being conjugated to a phenyl than lying adjacent
to a hydrogen. The final product of this slower equilibrium
pathway is benzyl phenyl ketone.

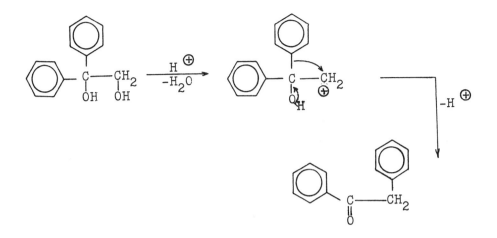

● **PROBLEM** 18-15

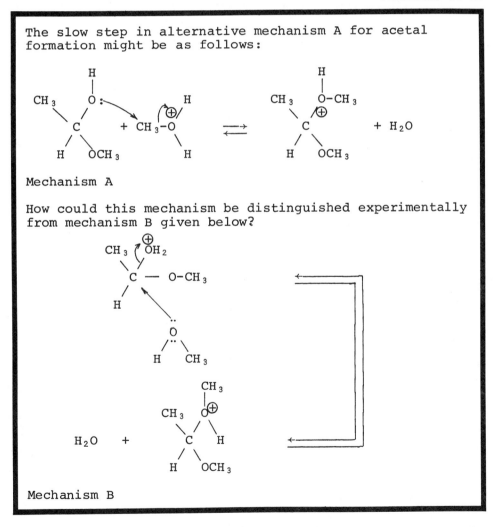

The slow step in alternative mechanism A for acetal formation might be as follows:

Mechanism A

How could this mechanism be distinguished experimentally from mechanism B given below?

Mechanism B

Solution: The major difference between the two mechanisms lies in the initial step of acetal formation: protonation.

In mechanism A the methanol was protonated whereas in mechanism B the hemiacetal $\left(\begin{array}{c} \text{OH} \\ | \\ \text{CH}_3\text{-CH-OCH}_3 \end{array} \right)$ was protonated at the hydroxyl oxygen. Mechanism A shows the cleavage of the C-O bond in methanol; mechanism B shows the cleavage of the C-O bond in the hemiacetal. If we were to use methanol labeled with heavy oxygen (O^{18}), the two mechanisms may be distinguished. If mechanism A was the actual reaction mechanism, heavy oxygen would be found only in the water and methanol, and none of the O^{18} would be incorporated in the acetal. If mechanism B were the actual one, heavy oxygen would be found in the acetal and methanol, and none would be found in the water.

● **PROBLEM** 18-16

Write a plausible reaction mechanism for the trimerization of acetaldehyde to paraldehyde with a trace of acid. How does this mechanism compare to the acid-catalyzed depolymerization of paraldehyde?

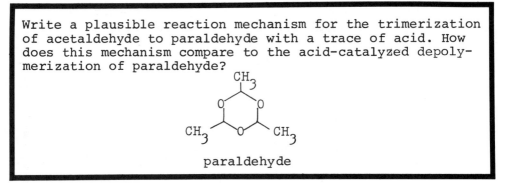

paraldehyde

<u>Solution:</u>   In a slightly acidic solution, only some of the acetaldehyde is protonated. A protonated acetaldehyde contains a carbon bearing a positive charge; this species is fairly reactive and will seek out an electron rich species with which to react. There are four species in this solution: $\text{CH}_3\overset{\text{O}}{\overset{||}{\text{C}}}\text{-H}$, $\overset{\oplus}{\text{H}}$, $\text{CH}_3\underset{\oplus}{\overset{\text{OH}}{\overset{|}{\text{CH}}}}$ and H_2O.

The protonated acetaldehyde may react with H_2O or $\text{CH}_3\text{-}\overset{\text{O}}{\overset{||}{\text{C}}}\text{-H}$.

Reaction with H_2O will yield the initial reactants, $\text{CH}_3\overset{\text{O}}{\overset{||}{\text{C}}}\text{-H}$ and $\overset{\oplus}{\text{H}}$. Reaction with $\text{CH}_3\overset{\text{O}}{\overset{||}{\text{C}}}\text{-H}$ however, at the cationic carbon, will result in the formation of an acetaldehyde dimer bearing a positive charge. This dimer will react with another $\text{CH}_3\overset{\text{O}}{\overset{||}{\text{C}}}\text{-H}$ molecule to form a trimer of acetaldehyde. This trimer has a cationic carbon on one end and an -OH group on the other end; the electronegative -OH oxygen will bond to the cationic carbon. This cyclization is accompanied

636

by proton loss to stabilize the positive charge. Only the acetaldehyde trimer will undergo cyclization (and not the dimer) because of the stability of the six-membered ring formed. A four-membered ring, formed by cyclization of the dimer, is less stable than a six-membered ring due to greater angle strain. The mechanism of paraldehyde formation is shown as:

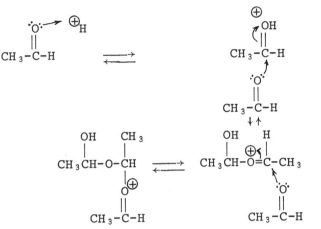

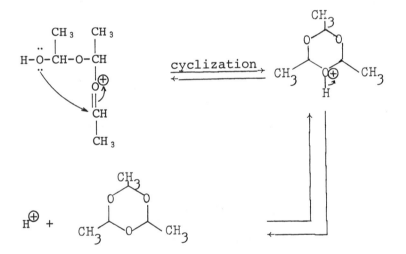

Paraldehyde

Since the polymerization of acetaldehyde to paraldehyde has both forward and reverse directions, the depolymerization of paraldehyde to acetaldehyde follows the reverse mechanism of paraldehyde formation.

● **PROBLEM** 18-17

Aqueous solutions of glutaraldehyde are potent biocides, used in hospitals to destroy bacteria, viruses, and spores on environmental surfaces. An nmr investigation has shown that the major component of a 25% solution of glutaral-dehyde is a cyclic hydrate. Suggest a mechanism for its formation and reversion to glutaraldehyde.

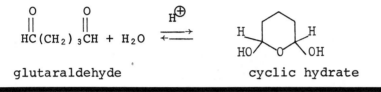

glutaraldehyde   cyclic hydrate

Solution: In acidic solution, glutaraldehyde, like any other aldehyde, will be protonated at one of its carbonyl oxygens. The protonated glutaraldehyde has a positively charged carbonyl carbon which will react with any available nucleophile. A potential nucleophile in this media is water.

The free electron pair on oxygen causes water to act as a nucleophile upon the positively charged carbonyl carbon. Subsequent proton loss rids the molecule of its charge and forms a δ-oxo-gem diol

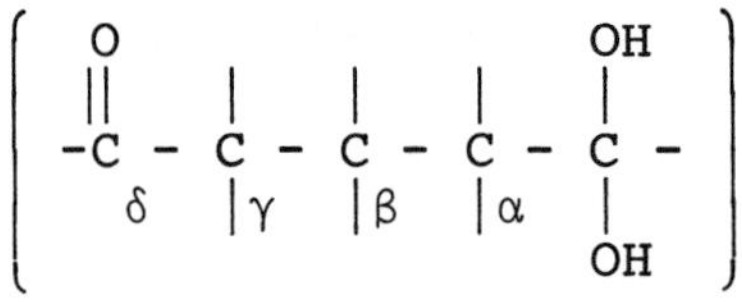

$$
\left(
\begin{array}{ccccc}
O & & & & OH \\
\| & | & | & | & | \\
-C & - C & - C & - C & - C - \\
\delta & |\gamma & |\beta & |\alpha & | \\
& & & & OH
\end{array}
\right)
$$

The molecule is neutral and is protonated at the remaining carbonyl oxygen. The oxygen of a hydroxyl group will form a bond with the positively charged carbonyl carbon that resulted from the second protonation. This cyclization step is thermodynamically favorable due to the formation of a six-membered ring; six-membered rings consisting of sp^3-hybridized carbons (and one oxygen atom in this case) are fairly stable because they have very little angle strain. The cyclic structure formed thus far has a positively charged ring oxygen; subsequent proton loss will neutralize the molecule and give us the cyclic hydrate of glutaral-dehyde.

Reversion of the cyclic hydrate back to glutaraldehyde follows the reverse mechanism of cyclic hydrate formation. This is because all the steps in the mechanism of cyclic hydrate formation are in equilibrium; they have both forward and backward directions. The mechanism of cyclic hydrate formation from glutaraldehyde and its reversion back to glutaraldehyde is shown below:

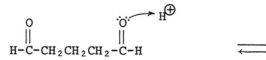

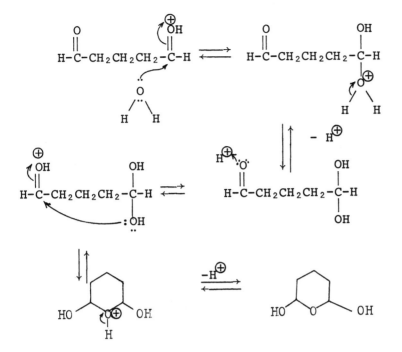

One way we can explore the acidity of hydrogens with an organic molecule is to dissolve the compound in D_2O in the presence of NaOD. If a hydrogen is removed by the base, it will be replaced by deuterium. For example, acetaldehyde, CH_3CHO, in D_2O/NaOD is quickly converted to CD_3CHO. What deuterio compounds would you get from each of the following compounds under those conditions?

(a) acetone
(b) ethyl alcohol

(c) cyclohexanone
(d) benzaldehyde

Solution: The α-hydrogens of aldehydes, ketones, esters and their derivatives are slightly acidic. The α-hydrogens are those hydrogens joined to the carbon atom which is adjacent to the carbon atom bonded to the oxygen. These α-hydrogens are acidic enough so that small but chemically significant amounts of carbanions are produced simply by dissolving carbonyl compounds in basic solutions.

     When an oxygen containing organic compound is dissolved in the basic D_2O/NaOD solution the α-hydrogens are replaced by D. When the compound is placed in the basic solution, these hydrogens dissociate due to their acidities.

(a)   In acetone, H_3CCOCH_3, all six hydrogens are positioned on α-carbons and will therefore be replaced with deuterium atoms.

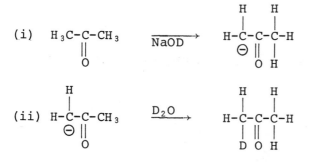

(i) $H_3C-C-CH_3$ $\xrightarrow{\text{NaOD}}$

$H-\overset{H}{\underset{\ominus}{C}}-C-\overset{H}{\underset{}{C}}-H$

(ii) $H-\overset{H}{\underset{\ominus}{C}}-C-CH_3$ $\xrightarrow{D_2O}$ $H-\overset{H}{\underset{D}{C}}-\overset{}{\underset{O}{C}}-\overset{H}{\underset{H}{C}}-H$

The above sequence of reactions will occur until all of the α-hydrogens are replaced.

(b)   In alcohols the most acidic hydrogen is the one bonded to the oxygen atom.

$$C_2H_5-OH \xrightarrow[\text{NaOD}]{D_2O} C_2H_5OD$$

The hydrogen attached to the carbon bonded to the oxygen is not acidic enough and will not be replaced. The α-hydrogens will not be replaced either because the negative charge on the oxygen is dispersed by both the hydrogen and the carbon bound to it causing the α-hydrogens to be much less acidic than they are in the presence of a carbonyl group.

(c)   There are four α-hydrogens in cyclohexanone, two on each α-carbon. All four of these will be replaced by deuterium.

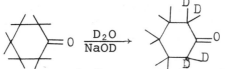

(d)   There are no α-hydrogens in benzaldehyde and no deuterio compounds will be formed.

● PROBLEM 18-19

The ketone tropone, ⟨structure⟩, is exceptionally basic in character, forming much more stable salts with HCl than simple ketones. How can this be explained?

Solution: The ability of a compound to accept or release a proton depends on the stability of the resulting compound. Simple ketones are not basic because the pro-tonated compound is too unstable. For example, a pro-tonated acetone has a positively charged oxygen,

$H_3C-C-CH_3$, and no other possible structure. Since oxygen

is very electronegative, it tends to lose the positive
charge by releasing the proton. Thus, acetone's basicity
is negligible.

The ketone tropone is very different from most other
ketones.   It displays some aromaticity, although it is not
a fully aromatic compound.   However let us look at its
protonated form:

It has six π electrons in a conjugated ring system.
It satisfies Hückel's rule and is thus aromatic.

The protonation of tropone creates a positively
charged oxygen. However, this positive charge can be
shared by all the ring carbons. This is a characteristic
property of the aromatic system. The sharing of the positive charge, that is the resonance structures, give extra
stabilization to the resulting compound. Thus, tropone is
more readily protonated. The resonating protonated tropones
are shown below.

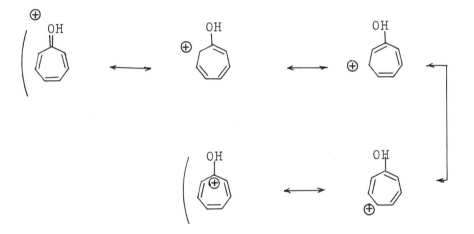

The aromaticity that tropone acquires in its protonated
form thus represents a great increase in stability. For this
reason tropone forms a much more stable salt with HCl than
simple ketones.

● **PROBLEM** 18-20

Chloral (CCl₃CHO) reacts rapidly with methanol to give
the hemiacetal but only very slowly to give the corresponding acetal. Explain.

Solution: Chloral (CCl₃CHO) will react rapidly with
methanol (CH₃OH) because of the inductive effect of the
trichloromethyl group (-CCl₃) in chloral. This effect
creates a highly electropositive carbonyl carbon, making

it very susceptible to nucleophilic attack. In hemiacetal
formation the following reaction will occur:

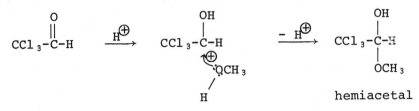

For the acetal to form from the hemiacetal, the
following would have to happen:

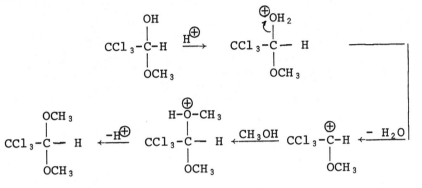

acetal

The key to this acetal formation is the protonation of
the -OH group of the hemiacetal so that dehydration (loss

of H_2O) may occur, and the species CCl_3-$\overset{H}{\underset{\oplus}{C}}$-$OCH_3$ may be

formed.

Chloral strongly hydrates in aqueous media because of
the inductive effect of the -CCl_3 group. In acetal formation we encounter dehydration, which is highly unfavorable.

Also, the cation formed, CCl_3-$\overset{OCH_3}{\underset{\oplus}{C}}$-H , will be unstable be-

cause of the inductive effect of the -CCl_3 group. For
these reasons acetal formation will occur very slowly.

• PROBLEM 18-21

Write balanced equations, naming all organic products, for
the reaction (if any) of phenylacetaldehyde with:

(1)   Tollens' reagent   (5) $NaBH_4$
(2) CrO_3/H_2SO_4 (6) C_6H_5MgBr, then H_2O
(3)   cold dilute $KMnO_4$ (7) $NaHSO_3$
(4) $KMnO_4$, H^+, heat   (8) CN^-, H^+
          (9) 2,4-dinitrophenylhydrazine

Phenylacetaldehyde undergoes

those reactions that are typical of aldehydes.

(1)   Tollens' reagent contains the silver ammonia ion, $Ag(NH_3)_2^{\oplus}$. Its utility stems from the detection of aldehydes, in particular for differentiating them from ketones. This reagent oxidizes the aldehyde to a carboxylic acid; it is accompanied by reduction of silver ion to free silver (in the form of a mirror under the proper conditions). Hence

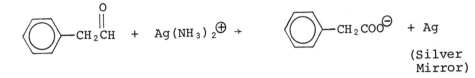

(Silver Mirror)

(2)   Aldehydes can be easily oxidized to carboxylic acids by chromic acid. Therefore

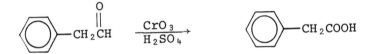

(3)   Under the conditions of cold dilute potassium permanganate ($KMnO_4$), the aldehyde is oxidized to the carboxylic acid with the carbon skeleton number unchanged. Hence,

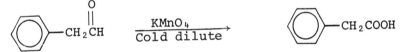

(4)   Prolonged hot treatment of a side chain on an aromatic ring with $KMnO_4$ results in its oxidation down to the ring, only a carbonyl group (-COOH) remaining to indicate the position of the original side chain.

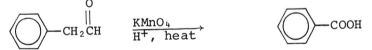

(5)   Sodium borohydride, $NaBH_4$, can be used to reduce carbonyl compounds to alcohols. This reagent has the special advantage of not reducing carbon-carbon double bonds, not even those conjugated with carbonyl groups. Consequently, it is useful for the reduction of such unsaturated carbonyl compounds to unsaturated alcohols. Therefore,

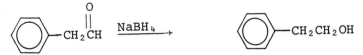

(6)   The addition of Grignard reagents to aldehydes is an important route to secondary alcohols (primary alcohols in

the case of formaldehyde). Thus

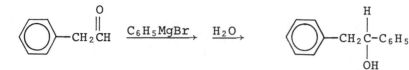

(7)   Sodium bisulfite adds to aldehydes (most of them) to
form bisulfite addition products. This utility is in
separating a carbonyl compound from non-carbonyl compounds.
The reaction is illustrated as follows:

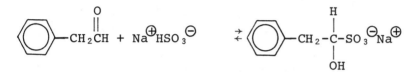

(8)   Hydrogen cyanide (HCN) can be added to the carbonyl
group of aldehydes and ketones to yield compounds known as
cyanohydrins. The reaction is often carried out by adding
mineral acid to a mixture of the carbonyl compound and
aqueous sodium cyanide. Thus,

(9)   Certain compounds that are derivatives of ammonia
such as 2,4 dinitrophenylhydrazine add to the carbonyl
group to form derivatives useful for the characterization
and identification of aldehydes and ketones. The products
possess a carbon-nitrogen double bond that was produced
from elimination of a molecule of water from the initial
addition products. Hence,

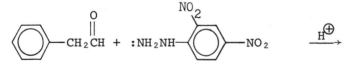

(2,4 dinitrophenylhydrazine)

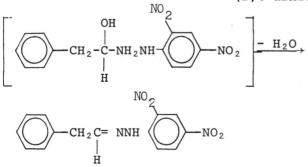

Account for the following reactions:

(a) $C_6H_5CHO + CH_3NO_2 \xrightarrow{KOH} C_6H_5CH=CHNO_2 + H_2O$

(b) $C_6H_5CHO + C_6H_5CH_2CN \xrightarrow{NaOC_2H_5} C_6H_5CH=C-CN \quad + H_2O$
$\qquad\qquad\qquad\qquad\qquad\qquad\qquad\qquad\qquad\quad \underset{\displaystyle C_6H_5}{|}$

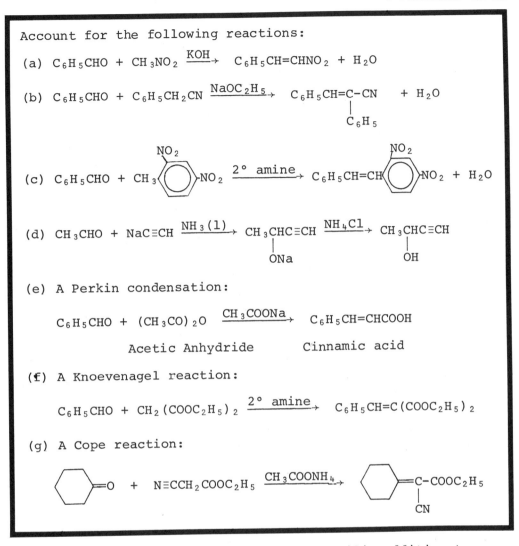

(c) $C_6H_5CHO + CH_3$ ⬡ $NO_2 \xrightarrow{2° \text{ amine}} C_6H_5CH=CH$ ⬡ $NO_2 + H_2O$

(d) $CH_3CHO + NaC\equiv CH \xrightarrow{NH_3(1)} CH_3CHC\equiv CH \xrightarrow{NH_4Cl} CH_3CHC\equiv CH$
$\qquad\qquad\qquad\qquad\qquad\qquad\qquad\quad \underset{\displaystyle ONa}{|} \qquad\qquad\qquad \underset{\displaystyle OH}{|}$

(e) A Perkin condensation:

$\qquad C_6H_5CHO + (CH_3CO)_2O \xrightarrow{CH_3COONa} C_6H_5CH=CHCOOH$

$\qquad\qquad\qquad$ Acetic Anhydride $\qquad\qquad$ Cinnamic acid

(f) A Knoevenagel reaction:

$\qquad C_6H_5CHO + CH_2(COOC_2H_5)_2 \xrightarrow{2° \text{ amine}} C_6H_5CH=C(COOC_2H_5)_2$

(g) A Cope reaction:

⬡$=O \quad + \quad N\equiv CCH_2COOC_2H_5 \xrightarrow{CH_3COONH_4}$ ⬡$=C-COOC_2H_5$
$\qquad\qquad\qquad\qquad\qquad\qquad\qquad\qquad\qquad\qquad\qquad\qquad\qquad \underset{\displaystyle CN}{|}$

<u>Solution:</u>   A consideration of nucleophilic addition to
carbonyl compounds (using an aldol condensation as an
example) will aid in the solution to this problem.

It is known that under the influence of dilute base
two molecules of an aldehyde or a ketone may combine to
form a β-hydroxyaldehyde or a β-hydroxyketone. Such a
reaction is called an aldol condensation. Using acetaldehyde as an example, the mechanism for the base-catalyzed
condensation may be written as follows:

(1) $CH_3CHO \quad + \quad OH^{\ominus} \rightleftarrows H_2O \qquad H_2\overset{\displaystyle \ominus}{C}-\overset{\displaystyle O}{\overset{\displaystyle ||}{C}}-H$

$\qquad$ (Acetaldehyde)   (Base Catalyst) $\qquad\quad$ (I)

The hydroxide ion ($OH^{\ominus}$) abstracts a hydrogen ion
from the α-carbon of the aldehyde to form carbanion I.

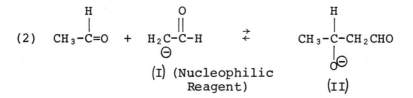

(2) $\quad CH_3-\overset{\overset{\displaystyle H}{|}}{C}=O \;+\; H_2C-\overset{\overset{\displaystyle O}{||}}{C}-H \quad \overset{\rightarrow}{\leftarrow} \quad CH_3-\overset{\overset{\displaystyle H}{|}}{\underset{\underset{\displaystyle O^{\ominus}}{|}}{C}}-CH_2CHO$

$\qquad\qquad\qquad\;\; \underset{\ominus}{}$

$\qquad\qquad$ (I) (Nucleophilic $\qquad\qquad\qquad$ (II)
$\qquad\qquad\qquad$ Reagent)

The carbanion I attacks the carbonyl carbon to form carbanion II, an alkoxide.

(3) $\quad CH_3-\overset{\overset{\displaystyle H}{|}}{\underset{\underset{\displaystyle O\ominus}{|}}{C}}-CH_2CHO \;+\; H_2O \quad \overset{\rightarrow}{\leftarrow} \quad CH_3-\overset{\overset{\displaystyle H}{|}}{\underset{\underset{\displaystyle OH}{|}}{C}}-CH_2CHO \;+\; OH^{\ominus}$

$\qquad\qquad$ (II) $\qquad\qquad\qquad\qquad\qquad\qquad$ (III)

The alkoxide abstracts a proton from water to form the β-hydroxyaldehyde III, regenerating the hydroxide ion. The purpose of the OH$^\ominus$ was to form the carbanion I, which is the actual nucleophilic reagent. The carbonyl group provides the unsaturated linkage at which addition occurs (step 2) and makes the α-hydrogen acidic enough for carbanion formation (step 1) to take place.

With this information, note that in (a) - (g) (except (d)) there exists a base (KOH, NaOC$_2$H$_5$, 2° amine, NH$_3$, CH$_3$COONa, CH$_3$COONH$_4$) that abstracts a proton that is alpha to one or more electronic withdrawing groups (- NO$_2$, -C≡N, -C=O, and 2,4-(NO$_2$)$_2$C$_6$H$_3$-) to give the following anions: (a) [CH$_2$NO$_2$]$^\ominus$, (b) [PhCHCN]$^\ominus$

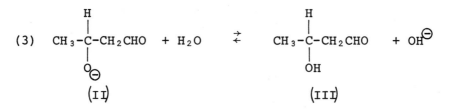

(c) [2,4-(O$_2$N)$_2$C$_6$H$_3$CH$_2$]$^\ominus$ $\qquad$ (d) HC≡C$^\ominus$

(e) $\left[\overset{..}{}CH_3C-O-C\overset{---}{}CH_2 \right]^{\ominus}$ $\qquad$ (f) [CH(COOEt)$_2$]$^\ominus$
$\qquad\;\; \overset{||}{\underset{O}{}} \quad \overset{|\vdots}{\underset{O}{}}$

(g) [CH(CN)(COOEt)]$^\ominus$. Hence the bases in (a) - (g)

serve the same purpose as the hydroxide ion in the aldol condensation - the production of anions.

At this point, the anions produced add to the aldehyde or ketone present (C$_6$H$_5$CHO, CH$_3$CHO,

⬡=O) to give an aldol-like product, the alkoxy

group is protonated, and water is lost. Note that in (e) the hydrolysis of an intermediate anhydride is needed as well.

CARBONYL REACTIONS WITH AMMONIA DERIVATIVES

● PROBLEM 18-23

Find all possible structures of the ketone that reacts

with hydroxylamine to form an oxime which contains 13.9% nitrogen.

Solution: Ketones $\begin{pmatrix} R \\ \diagdown \\ C=O \\ \diagup \\ R \end{pmatrix}$ can undergo a condensation

reaction with derivatives of ammonia such as hydroxylamine (H_2NOH) to form stable crystalline solids such as oximes $\begin{pmatrix} \diagdown \\ C=N-OH \\ \diagup \end{pmatrix}$ with the loss of a water (H_2O) molecule.

The reaction of the ketone to be determined with hydroxylamine can be written as:

$$\begin{array}{c} R \\ \diagdown \\ C=O \\ \diagup \\ R \end{array} \quad + H_2NOH \quad \longrightarrow \quad \begin{array}{c} R-C=N-OH \\ \diagup \\ R \end{array} \quad + H_2O$$

(ketone)   hydroxylamine   (oxime)

The problem indicates that oxime is 13.9% nitrogen (N) and asks that the ketone, specifically the R groups, be found. The percentage of nitrogen in the oxime is a measure of the atomic weight of nitrogen times the number of nitrogen atoms divided by the molecular weight of the oxime times 100:

$$\frac{(\text{AW of N})\ (\text{No. of atoms})}{(\text{MW of oxime})} \times 100 = \%\ \text{of N}$$

One knows the following: No. of N atoms is one, MW of N is 14, MW of carbon is 12, MW of H is 1, and the MW of O is 16. If one represents the total weight of the hydrocarbon R groups by X, then it can be written that:

$$\frac{14}{14 + 16 + 1 + 12 + X}\ (100) = 13.9$$

Solving for X,   X = 57.7.

This means the total weight of the carbon and hydrogen atoms in the R groups is 57.7 Through a little trial and error, one will find this total weight measures a toal of 4 carbon atoms (4 × 12 = 48) and 10 hydrogen atoms (10 × 1 = 10). This means the R groups could each be CH_3CH_2, or one could be $CH_3CH_2CH_2$ and the other CH_3. Consequently, the ketone is either diethyl ketone or methyl N-propyl (or isopropyl) ketone as shown:

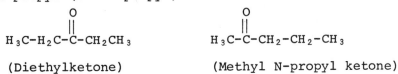

$$\begin{array}{cc} O & O \\ \parallel & \parallel \\ H_3C-H_2C-C-CH_2CH_3 & H_3C-C-CH_2-CH_2-CH_3 \end{array}$$

(Diethylketone)   (Methyl N-propyl ketone)

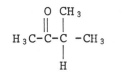

(Methyl isopropyl ketone)

Semicarbazide (1 mole) is added to a mixture of cyclohexanone (1 mole) and benzaldehyde (1 mole). If the
product is isolated immediately, it consists almost entirely of the semicarbazone of cyclohexanone; if the
product is isolated after several hours, it consists
almost entirely of the semicarbazone of benzaldehyde.
How do you account for these observations?

Solution: Semicarbazide ($:NH_2NHCONH_2$), a derivative of
ammonia, can add to the carbonyl group of aldehydes and
ketones to form the derivative semicarbazone. The reactions
with cyclohexanone and benzaldehyde
can be written as follows:

$$\text{cyclohexanone}=O + :NH_2NHCONH_2 \xrightarrow{H^{\oplus}} \text{cyclohexanone}=NNHCONH_2 + H_2O$$

$$C_6H_5-C(H)=O + :NH_2NHCONH_2 \xrightarrow{H^{\oplus}} C_6H_5-C(H)=NNHCONH_2 + H_2O$$

     When the product is isolated immediately, most of it
consists of the semicarbazone of cyclohexanone, whereas
hours later it is mostly the semicarbazone of benzaldehyde.
These observations strongly suggest semicarbazide formation
is reversible. Cyclohexanone reacts more rapidly, but
benzaldehyde gives the more stable product so that it will
predominate in time. Initially, one isolates the product
of rate control (the compound that reacts with greatest
speed). Later, after the equilibrium is established, one
isolates the product of equilibrium control (greatest
stability).

Calculate the pH which would give the most rapid reaction
rate for a carbonyl compound with $K_B = 10^{-14}$ and an RNH_2
derivative with $K_B = 10^{-11}$ assuming 1 M concentrations
for the reactants, and the slow step being as in Eq.(1).
How many times faster is the rate at this pH than at
pH 0? Than at ph 7?

$$
\begin{array}{c}
\underset{CH_3}{\overset{CH_3}{\diagdown}} \hspace{-0.3cm} C \overset{\oplus}{=} \overset{}{O}H \quad + \quad :NH_2-R \quad \rightleftharpoons \quad \underset{CH_3 \quad OH}{\overset{CH_3 \quad \overset{\oplus}{N}H_2R}{\diagdown \diagup C \diagdown}} \hspace{2cm} (1)
\end{array}
$$

Solution: We approach this problem by trying to find a rate equation for the whole reaction and then, by using the given equilibrium constants, substitute the correct concentrations and by using calculus find the pH value of the maximum reaction rate.

Being that this example involves a great deal of mathematics, we try to simplify as much as possible. Let us now introduce symbols to represent concentrations of various species.

Let $A = [(CH_3)_2CO]$

$B = [RNH_2]$

$H = [H^+]$

$AH = [(CH_3)_2CO^{\oplus}H]$

$BH = [RNH_3^{\oplus}]$

$OH = [O\overset{\ominus}{H}]$

The rate of reaction (expressed by the symbol ν) is equal to the concentration of one reactant multiplied by the concentration of the other reactant times k (constant for reaction rate).

Equation (2) $\nu = k \cdot AH \cdot B$

We now try to solve for the concentrations of AH and B. We accomplish this by using the equilibrium equation for each of these species. The equilibrium equation that we are speaking of is the equilibrium that occurs when each of the reactant species is isolated in aqueous media. The equilibrium equation for B is:

$$K_B = \frac{BH \cdot OH}{B}$$

This is derived from the chemical equation

$$RNH_2 \;+\; H_2O \;\rightleftharpoons\; RNH_3^{\oplus} + OH^{\ominus}$$

We know that the reactants of Eq. (1) are present in one molar concentrations, thus we can say that BH + B = 1 or BH = 1 - B. From general chemistry we know that $K_w =$ OH $\cdot$ H, thus OH $= \dfrac{K_w}{H}$. By substitution we can change our equilibrium equation as follows:

$$K_B = \frac{(1 - B) \cdot OH}{B}$$

$$= \frac{(1 - B) \cdot K_w}{B \cdot H}$$

Solving for B we get

$$B = \frac{1}{1 + (K_B/K_w) \ H}$$

We now follow the same procedure for expressing AH in terms of its K_B (call it $K_{B'}$):

$$K_{B'} = \frac{AH \cdot OH}{A}$$

Since AH + A = 1, then   A = 1 - AH

$$K_{B'} = \frac{AH \cdot OH}{1 - AH}$$

$$K_w = H \cdot OH, \qquad OH = \frac{K_w}{H}$$

$$K_{B'} = \frac{AH \cdot K_w}{(1 - AH) \cdot H}$$

$$AH = \frac{H}{H + (K_w/K_{B'})}$$

We can now express our original rate equation by the following:

Eq. (3) $$v = k \cdot \frac{H}{H + (K_w \ / \ K_{B'})} \cdot \frac{1}{1 + (K_B/K_w) \cdot H}$$

Since K_w is always equal to 10^{-14}, and we are given that $K_B = 10^{-11}$ and $K_{B'} = 10^{-14}$, we can now substitute these values into our rate equation:

$$v = k \cdot \frac{H}{H + (10^{-14}/10^{-14})} \cdot \frac{1}{1 + (10^{-11}/10^{-14}) \cdot H}$$

$$v = k \ \frac{H}{H + 1} \cdot \frac{1}{1 + 1000 \cdot H}$$

$$v = k \cdot \frac{H}{1000 \cdot H^2 + 1001 \cdot H + 1}$$

At this point we are interested in finding a value for H that will maximize the reaction rate, v. We find this value by applying a method used in Calculus; the first derivative of the rate equation with respect to H (expressed as $\frac{dv}{dH}$) is calculated. We then solve for H by setting the derivative equal to zero. The value for H is expressed in terms of pH to obtain the final asnwer. The calculations for this are shown below:

$$\frac{dv}{dH} = k \cdot \left[\frac{(10^3H^2+1001\ H+1)\frac{dH}{dH} - H\ \frac{d(10^3H^2+1001\ H + 1)}{dH}}{(10^3H^2 + 1001\ H + 1)^2} \right]$$

$$\frac{dv}{dH} = k \cdot \left[\frac{(10^3H^2+1001\ H + 1)(1) - H(2000\ H^2 + 1001)}{(10^3H^2 + 1001\ H + 1)^2} \right]$$

$$\frac{dv}{dH} = k \cdot \frac{1 - 1000\ H^2}{(10^3H^2 + 1001\ H + 1)^2}$$

Since k, like all rate equation constants is not equal to zero, when the derivative (dv/dH) is set equal to zero, the equation to be solved is:

$$O = 1 - 1000\ H^2$$

$$H^2 = .001, \qquad H = \sqrt{.001} = 3.2 \times 10^{-2}$$

$$pH = -\log H = -\log(3.2 \times 10^{-2}) = 1.5$$

We are now asked to compare the rate at this pH to rates at other pH's. To find the rates at this pH and other pH's we substitute the various H values into equation (3). The v values are then compared to each other. The rate equation constant k, should be ignored for it is the same at any pH. The comparisons are shown below:

At pH = 0,   H = 1

$$v_1 = \frac{1}{(1 + 1)(1 + 10^3)} = \frac{1}{2002} = .0004995$$

At pH = 1.5,   H = $\sqrt{.001}$

$$v_2 = \frac{\sqrt{10^{-3}}}{(1 + \sqrt{10^{-3}})(1 + 10^{3/2})} = .0009396$$

At pH = 7.0,   H = 10^{-7}

$$v_3 = \frac{10^{-7}}{(1 + 10^{-7})(1 + 10^{-4})} = \frac{.0000001}{1.00010010001}$$

$$v_3 \approx 10^{-7}$$

$$\frac{v_2}{v_1} = 1.88 \approx 1.9 \qquad\qquad \frac{v_2}{v_3} \approx 10^4$$

The reaction at pH = 1.5 will take place 1.9 times faster than the reaction at pH = 0 and 10^4 times faster than the reaction at pH = 7.

651

HALOGEN REACTIONS

Predict the product of each of the following ketone precursors after base-promoted or acid-catalyzed halogenation.

(a)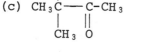

(b) CH_3CCH_3
      $\overset{\|}{O}$

Cyclohexanone

Acetone

(c) $\overset{\displaystyle CH_3}{\underset{\displaystyle CH_3}{CH_3C}}\!\!-\!\!\overset{\|}{\underset{O}{C}}\text{-}CH_3$

3,3-Dimethyl-2-butanone

Solution: There are two ways to halogenate ketones; one is called base-promoted halogenation and the other is acid-catalyzed halogenation. In essence, acids and bases speed up the halogenation of ketones, thus they are considered to be catalysts in these reactions. The general synthesis for both proceeds as:

$$-\overset{|}{\underset{H}{C}}\text{-}\overset{|}{\underset{O}{C}}\text{-} \;+\; X_2 \;\xrightarrow{\;H^+ \text{ or } OH^-\;}\; -\overset{|}{\underset{X}{C}}\text{-}\overset{\|}{\underset{O}{C}}\text{-} \;+\; HX \qquad X_2 = Cl_2,\; Br_2,\; I_2$$

The kinetics of acid-catalyzed halogenation show the rate of halogenation to be independent of halogen concentration, but dependent upon ketone concentration and acid concentration.

In both types of halogenation the products are the same, except in acid-catalyzed halogenation racemization can occur; i.e. isomers of the product are formed.

To solve problems a, b, and c the above concepts and the general equation are followed.

(a)

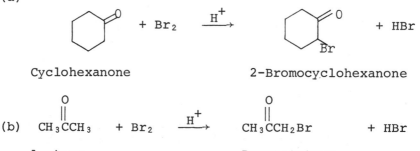

Cyclohexanone   2-Bromocyclohexanone

(b) $CH_3\overset{O}{\overset{\|}{C}}CH_3$ + Br_2 $\xrightarrow{\;H^+\;}$ $CH_3\overset{O}{\overset{\|}{C}}CH_2Br$ + HBr

Acetone   Bromoacetone

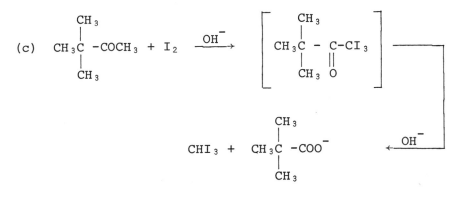

(c) $CH_3\overset{\underset{\displaystyle |}{CH_3}}{\underset{\underset{\displaystyle |}{CH_3}}{C}}-COCH_3 + I_2 \xrightarrow{OH^-}$ $\left[CH_3\overset{\underset{\displaystyle |}{CH_3}}{\underset{\underset{\displaystyle |}{CH_3}}{C}} - \overset{\underset{\displaystyle \|}{}}{\underset{\underset{\displaystyle O}{}}{C}}-CI_3 \right]$

$CHI_3 + CH_3\overset{\underset{\displaystyle |}{CH_3}}{\underset{\underset{\displaystyle |}{CH_3}}{C}}-COO^- \xleftarrow{OH^-}$

Iodoform Trimethylacetate ion

The first product in reaction (c) is an unstable compound so more base is added to take the reaction to equilibrium, thus forming the above product and by-product, trimethylacetate ion and iodoform, respectively.

● **PROBLEM** 18-27

Write a reasonable mechanism for the reaction of hydrogen chloride and methanol with formaldehyde to give methyl chloromethyl ether that is consistent with the fact that the reaction occurs under conditions where neither methylene chloride nor methyl chloride are formed.

$$\overset{\overset{\displaystyle O}{\underset{\displaystyle \|}{}}}{H-C-H} + HCl + CH_3OH \rightleftharpoons CH_3OCH_2Cl + H_2O$$

Solution: Both methanol and formaldehyde will become protonated when they are in separate acidic solutions. When a single solution of methanol and formaldehyde is made acidic, only one of these (the stronger base) is protonated. The fact that no methyl chloride was formed indicates that formaldehyde was protonated and methanol was not, that is, formaldehyde is more basic than methanol. This conclusion is based on the fact that methanol must first be protonated in order to undergo a substitution reaction (to form methyl chloride). The protonated formaldehyde will tend to react with a nucleophilic species. There are two available nucleophilic species: $Cl^{\ominus}$ and CH_3OH. Reaction with $Cl^{\ominus}$ would form $ClCH_2OH$; this would undergo a substitution reaction to form methylene chloride faster than CH_3OH would react to form methyl chloride. This is because $\overset{\oplus}{C}H_2Cl$ (formed by H_2O loss from $ClCH_2\overset{\oplus}{O}H_2$) is more stable than $CH_3^{\oplus}$ (formed by H_2O loss from $CH_3\overset{\oplus}{O}H_2$)   due to resonance. Since no methylene chloride is formed, the protonated formaldehyde must react with CH_3OH rather than $Cl^{\ominus}$. This is shown as:

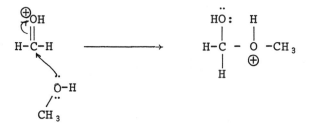

A subsequent proton shift occurs from the CH_3O- to the $-OH$ as follows:

Loss of water will form a reasonance stabilized cation of the type:

$$\overset{\oplus}{C}H_2-\overset{..}{\underset{..}{O}}-CH_3 \longleftrightarrow CH_2=\overset{\oplus}{O}-CH_3$$

Reaction with $Cl^\ominus$ forms the desired product. The mechanism of the reaction can be written as:

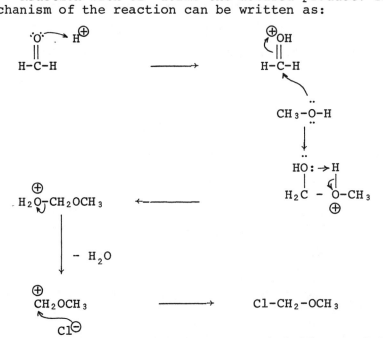

$Cl-CH_2-OCH_3$

methylchloromethyl ether

● PROBLEM 18-28

Work out reasonable mechanisms for the reactions of phosphorus pentachloride and sulfur tetrafluoride with carbonyl groups. A reasonable first step with phosphorus pentachloride is dissociation into $PCl_4^\oplus$ and $Cl^\ominus$.

Solution: The reaction of phosphorus pentachloride (PCl₅) with a ketone results in the conversion of the

carbonyl group $\left(\begin{array}{c} O \\ \| \\ -C- \end{array}\right)$ to a dichloromethylene group

$\left(\begin{array}{c} Cl \\ | \\ -C-Cl \\ | \end{array}\right)$. We are given the first step:

$$PCl_5 \longrightarrow {}^{\oplus}PCl_4 + Cl^{\ominus}$$

The carbonyl oxygen of a ketone is nucleophilic enough to react with the $\overset{\oplus}{P}Cl_4$ species. The resulting

cation will react with $Cl^{\ominus}$ to form $R_2\overset{\overset{Cl}{|}}{C}OPCl_4$. The penta-coordinated phosphorus will lose a $Cl^{\ominus}$ to form a positively charged species. This will react with $Cl^{\ominus}$ in a S_N type re-

action. The mechanism is shown as:

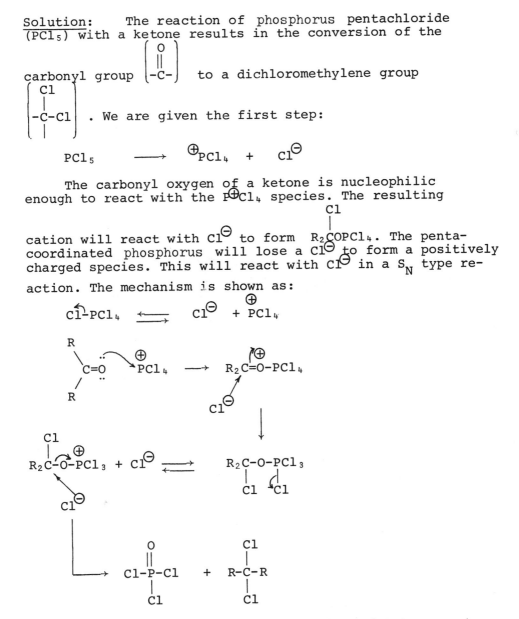

The reaction of sulfur tetrafluoride with ketones is very similar to that of phosphorus pentachloride. Sulfur tetrafluoride will lose a fluoride ion to form the more

stable $\overset{\oplus}{S}F_3$ species (more stable because sulfur now has an octet of electrons). The mechanism of SF_4 with R_2CO is analogous in every aspect to that of PCl_4 and R_2CO. The mechanism is shown below:

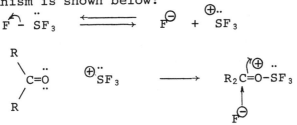

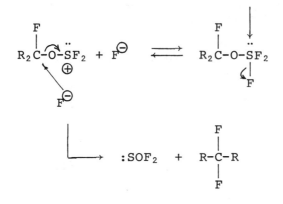

● **PROBLEM** 18-29

Chloroform was at one time synthesized commercially by the action of sodium hypochlorite on ethanol. Formulate the reactions that might reasonably be involved. What other types of alcohols might be expected to give haloforms with halogens and base?

Solution: The net reaction that we are interested in is:

$$CH_3CH_2OH \xrightarrow{\overset{\oplus\ \ominus}{Na\ OCl}} CHCl_3$$

Chloroform ($CHCl_3$) is formed via the base-catalyzed chlorination of a methyl ketone or acetaldehyde by the following reaction sequence:

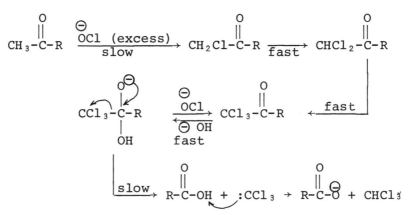

The key then to solving this problem is to create a

$$\overset{\displaystyle O}{\underset{\displaystyle \|}{CH_3-C-}}$$ group from ethanol (CH_3CH_2OH). We also need to

create a basic solution with a significant amount of $OH^{\ominus}$ ions present. $OH^{\ominus}$ ions could form if -OCl could be substituted for -OH. This could occur by the following mechanism:

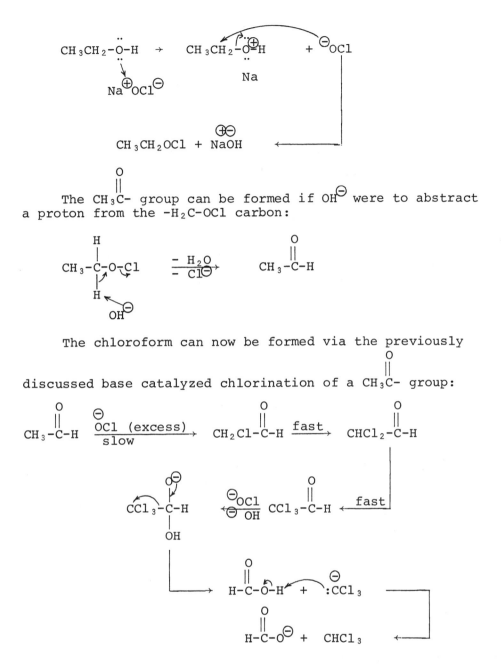

The $CH_3\overset{\overset{O}{\|}}{C}-$ group can be formed if $OH^{\ominus}$ were to abstract a proton from the $-H_2C-OCl$ carbon:

The chloroform can now be formed via the previously discussed base catalyzed chlorination of a $CH_3\overset{\overset{O}{\|}}{C}-$ group:

REDUCTION

● PROBLEM 18-30

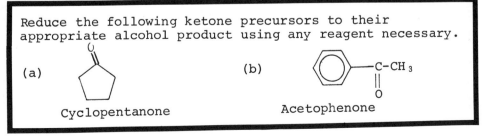

Reduce the following ketone precursors to their appropriate alcohol product using any reagent necessary.

(a)

Cyclopentanone

(b)

Acetophenone

Solution: Ketones can be reduced to secondary alcohols either by catalytic hydrogenation or by use of chemical reducing agents such as lithium aluminum hydride, LiAlH₄. Such reduction is useful for the preparation of certain alcohols because of the higher yields than for other methods. The general equation for the reaction is:

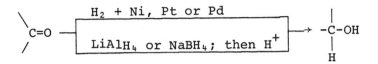

Sodium borohydride, NaBH₄, does not reduce carbon-carbon double bonds, not even those conjugated with carbonyl groups, and is thus useful for the reduction of such unsaturated carbonyl compounds to unsaturated alcohols. For example:

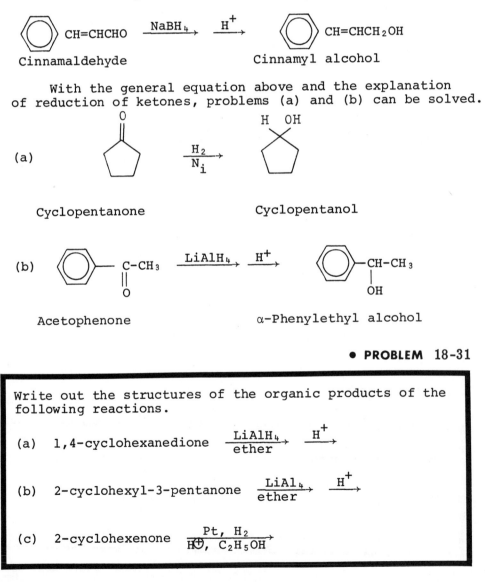

With the general equation above and the explanation of reduction of ketones, problems (a) and (b) can be solved.

(a) Cyclopentanone → Cyclopentanol

(b) Acetophenone → α-Phenylethyl alcohol

● PROBLEM 18-31

Write out the structures of the organic products of the following reactions.

(a) 1,4-cyclohexanedione $\xrightarrow[\text{ether}]{\text{LiAlH}_4}$ $\xrightarrow{\text{H}^+}$

(b) 2-cyclohexyl-3-pentanone $\xrightarrow[\text{ether}]{\text{LiAl}_4}$ $\xrightarrow{\text{H}^+}$

(c) 2-cyclohexenone $\xrightarrow[\text{HO, } C_2H_5OH]{\text{Pt, } H_2}$

Solution: The three reactions shown above are all reductions, either by catalytic hydrogenation with molecular hydrogen and a platinum, nickel, or palladium catalyst, or by reduction with lithium aluminum hydride ($LiAlH_4$) or sodium borohydride ($NaBH_4$) plus acid.

Ketones are reduced to secondary or tertiary alcohols depending upon the structure of the precursor under reduction. This method of producing alcohols is the most favorable in organic synthesis because of the high yield produced in proportion to the amount of ketone with which was started. To begin solving the problems, the precursors' structure should be drawn:

Note that a reduction reagent would react at the carbonyls.

1,4-cyclohexadione

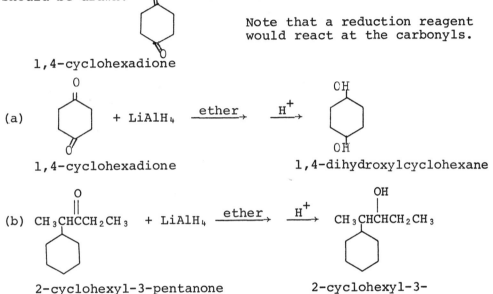

(a)

1,4-cyclohexadione

1,4-dihydroxylcyclohexane

(b) $CH_3CHCCH_2CH_3$ + $LiAlH_4$ $\xrightarrow{ether}$ $\xrightarrow{H^+}$ $CH_3CHCHCH_2CH_3$

2-cyclohexyl-3-pentanone

2-cyclohexyl-3-pentanol

In both problems (a) and (b) ether is the solvent in which the reaction is carried out. This yields an unstable intermediate that is treated with an acid to obtain an alcohol. In problem (c) the reducing process is changed where hydrogen attacks the carbonyl moiety with the facility of a metal catalyst, platinum. The double bond is also reduced by the addition of hydrogen to yield a cycloalkane. The solvent used to carry out the catalytic hydrogenation is ethanol.

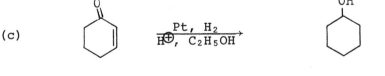

(c)

2-cyclohexenone

cyclohexanol

● **PROBLEM** 18-32

Reduce the following ketones to their appropriate hydrocarbons by the Clemmensen reduction method.

(a) 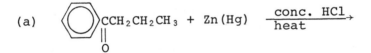 CCH$_2$CH$_2$CH$_3$ (b)   CH$_3$C(CH$_2$)$_5$CH$_3$
         ‖   ‖
         O   O

   n-Butyrophenone   2-Octanone

(Phenyl n-propyl ketone)

Solution: The Clemmensen reduction is the reaction used
to reduce ketones and aldehydes to their respective hydrocarbons by the action of amalgamated zinc and concentrated
hydrochloric acid. This reaction has the general equation
of:

$$-\overset{\|}{\underset{O}{C}}- \quad \xrightarrow{\text{Zn(Hg), conc. HCl}} \quad -\overset{|}{\underset{H}{C}}-H$$

for compounds that are sensitive to base. Amalgamated zinc
is an alloy of mercury (Hg) fused with zinc and is used
as a catalyst in the reaction. The reaction reduces the
carbonyl moiety to a simple one-carbon hydrocarbon, thus
changing the acyl group in problem (a) to the corresponding
aliphatic chain.

    The Clemmensen reduction is heterogenous, involving
an organic layer, an aqueous layer containing concentrated
hydrochloric acid, and solid amalgamated zinc. Since the
reaction is first order in ketone, the rate-determining
step cannot be the production of hydrogen atoms, which
would react very rapidly if formed. Present evidence indicates that reduction occurs at the surface of the zinc, and
that alcohols are not intermediates since they seem to be
unreactive under Clemmensen conditions. With the above information and the general equation for the reaction,
problems (a) and (b) can be solved as follows:

(a) CCH$_2$CH$_2$CH$_3$ + Zn(Hg) $\xrightarrow[\text{heat}]{\text{conc. HCl}}$
        ‖
        O

   n-Butyrophenone

(Phenyl n-propyl ketone)

        CH$_2$CH$_2$CH$_2$CH$_3$ +   ZnCl + H$_2$O + Hg

   n-Butylbenzene

(b) CH$_3$C(CH$_2$)$_5$CH$_3$ + Zn(Hg) $\xrightarrow[\text{heat}]{\text{conc. HCl}}$ CH$_3$(CH$_2$)$_6$CH$_3$+ZnCl+H$_2$O+Hg
        ‖
        O

        2-Octanone   Octane

660

The reduction of 2-butanone with magnesium amalgam produces, after hydrolysis, two isomeric glycols. What are their structures?

Solution: The structure of 2-butanone is as follows:

$$CH_3-\overset{\overset{\displaystyle O}{||}}{C}-CH_2CH_3$$

Its reaction with magnesium amalgam and water proceeds by the following mechanism:

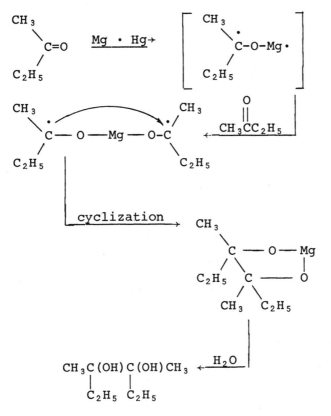

$$CH_3C(OH)C(OH)CH_3$$
$$\underset{C_2H_5 \quad C_2H_5}{|\quad\quad\quad|}$$

The compound shown can be formed in two ways, as a meso compound or as a d,l compound:

$$\underset{\underset{C_2H_5\;C_2H_5}{|\quad\;\;|}}{CH_3-\overset{\overset{OH\;\;OH}{|\quad\;\;|}}{C}-\overset{}{C}-CH_3}$$

$$\underset{\underset{C_2H_5\quad OH}{|\quad\quad\;|}}{CH_3-\overset{\overset{OH\;C_2H_5}{|\quad\;\;|}}{C}-\overset{}{C}-CH_3}$$

meso compound   d, l compound

661

Those compounds, which fit the type R R' COH COH R R' where R' may also be R, are known as pinacols. Pinacols, under acidic conditions, form ketones by what is called a "pinacol-pinacolone" rearrangement. This rearrangement is shown in the following reaction:

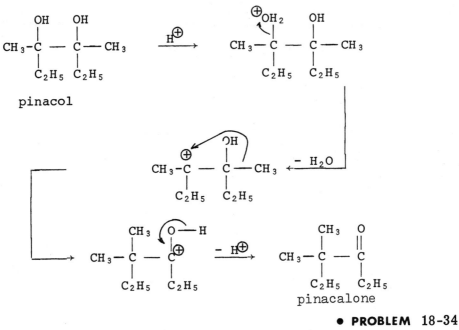

pinacol

pinacalone

● **PROBLEM** 18-34

Suppose n-butyraldehyde-1-^{2}H(CH$_3$CH$_2$CH$_2$CDO) were reduced with aluminum tri-s-butoxide made from optically active s-butyl alcohol. Assuming the cyclic reduction mechanism, would you expect the first 10 per cent of n-butanol-1-^{2}H to be optically active? Explain. What would be the products at equilibrium?

Solution: We approach this problem by trying to draw the two different cyclic intermediates formed in the reduction reaction between CH$_3$(CH$_2$)$_2$CDO and aluminum tri-sec-butoxide. Once having done this we see if the intermediates should react equally fast or if one intermediate will react faster than the other.

The cyclic reduction mechanism that we are referring to is known as the Meerwein-Ponndorf-Oppenauer-Verly method and it is shown in the following generalized form:

RCHO   + Al(OCHR'R")$_3$ $\longrightarrow$

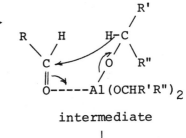

intermediate

$\downarrow$

$$R-CH_2-O-Al(OCHR'R'')_2 + R'-\overset{\overset{\displaystyle O}{\|}}{C}-R''$$

Let us apply this generalized mechanism to our specific case and consider the intermediates:

$$CH_3(CH_2)_2CDO \quad + \quad Al(O\overset{\overset{\displaystyle CH_3}{|}}{C}HCH_2CH_3)_3 \quad \longrightarrow$$

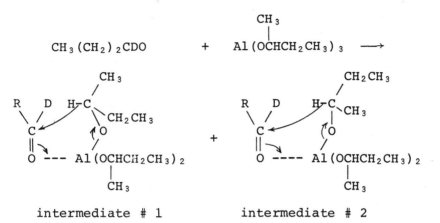

intermediate # 1   intermediate # 2

To show orientation in space and thus bring out the differences between the intermediates, we show them in six membered ring chair-conformations:

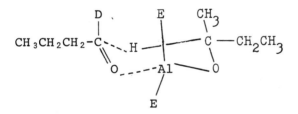

intermediate # 1

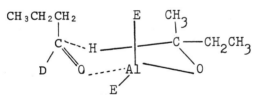

intermediate # 2

In both intermediates shown above, the sec-butoxy group $\left(\begin{array}{c} CH_3 \\ | \\ -OCHCH_2CH_3 \end{array}\right)$ is represented by "E". Intermediate # 2 has the n-propyl group in an axial position; the n-propyl group and the "E" group are above the ring. Intermediate # 1 has the n-propyl group in an equatorial position; the n-propyl group is further away from the "E" group had it been in an axial position. Hence intermediate # 1 has less steric hindrance than # 2 and the alcohol formed from intermediate # 1 will be produced at a faster

663

rate than that produced from intermediate # 2. Therefore
the first 10% of product formed should exhibit some optical
activity.

At equilibrium the amount of d- and ℓ-isomers of
$CH_3CH_2CH_2CHDOH$ are equal, and thus form a racemic mixture
which has no optical activity.

OXIDATION

● PROBLEM 18-35

Write an equation for a reasonable synthesis of 1,5-
pentane dialdehyde from cyclopentanone.

Solution: Cyclopentanone has the structure

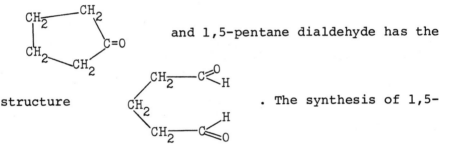

and 1,5-pentane dialdehyde has the

structure   . The synthesis of 1,5-

pentane dialdehyde from cyclopentanone involves the
breaking of a carbon-carbon bond to open the ring. In
general, cyclic hydrocarbons are resistant to ring-opening,
thus the C-C bond to be cleaved must be about the carbonyl
carbon. Since ketone carbon-carbon bonds are relatively
stable, one must modify the keto group first.

The carbonyl can be reduced to a secondary alcohol,
which can be dehydrated to form a cycloalkene. The necessary dialdehyde can be synthesized from the cycloalkene by
ozonolysis.

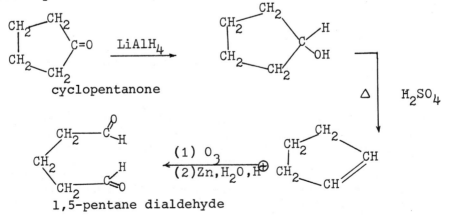

1,5-pentane dialdehyde

Benzaldehyde (C_6H_5CHO) is oxidized to benzoic acid
($C_6H_5CO_2H$) by acid permanganate. The rate of the oxidation
is proportional to the concentrations of $H^\oplus$, benzaldehyde,
and $MnO_4^\ominus$. The reaction is much slower with C_6H_5CDO than
with C_6H_5CHO. When the reaction is carried out in $H_2^{18}O$
with C_6H_5CHO and $MnO_4^\ominus$, the product is $C_6H_5CO_2H$. With
C_6H_5CHO, H_2O, and $Mn^{18}O_4^\ominus$, the $C_6H_5CO_2H$ contains ^{18}O.
Write a mechanism for the reaction which is consistent
with all the above facts. (Note that the C_6H_5 group is not
involved.) Give your reasoning.

<u>Solution</u>:   Since the rate of oxidation is dependent on
the concentrations of $H^\oplus$, benzaldehyde, and $MnO_4^\ominus$, the slow
step in the reaction mechanism must involve these species.
The slow step or rate-determining step of this mechanism
also involves the breaking of a C-H bond of the aldehyde
group as evidenced by the isotope effect, that is, the reaction is much slower with ϕ-C(=O) -D than with ϕ-C(=O) -H. The next
clue gives us the picture for the rate-determining step.
That is, the second oxygen of the carboxyl group comes from
MnO_4 and not H_2O. This conclusion arises from the fact that
when the reaction is carried out in $H_2^{18}O$ with ϕ-C(=O) -H
and $MnO_4^\ominus$, the product is ϕ-C(=O) -OH, while the reaction with
ϕ-C(=O) -H, H_2O, and $Mn^{18}O_4^\ominus$ gives ϕ-C(=O) -OH with ^{18}O. With
this information, we can now write out the rate-determining
step:

     First, we know that $H^\oplus$, ϕ-C(=O) -H, and $MnO_4^\ominus$ is in-
volved. Second, an aldehydic C-H bond breaks:

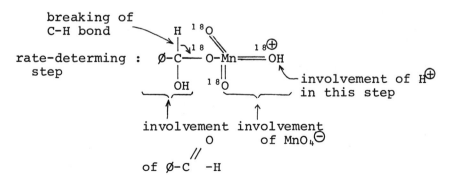

     Let us now examine this system. In order for $H^\oplus$ to

play a part in the rate of this step, an O-Mn bond must
break, otherwise the concentration of H⊕ would be irrelevent
in this rate-determining step; compare the rate of the
following two mechanisms:

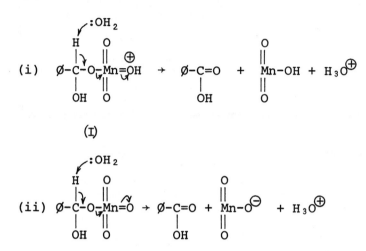

(i)   (I)

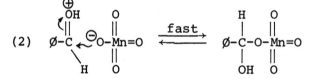

Since mechanism (i) goes from a charged species to
a neutral species, it is the faster reaction.

Since this step gives us the desired products, this
must be the last step in the reaction mechanism. We can
now write out the entire mechanism by writing steps that
are much faster than the rate-determining step, and which
culminates with species I.

$$\text{(1)} \quad \phi\text{-C}-\text{H} \quad \xrightleftharpoons[\text{}]{\text{fast}} \quad \phi\text{-C}-\text{H}$$

Protonation reactions are fast reactions.

$$\text{(2)} \quad \xrightleftharpoons[\text{}]{\text{fast}} \quad \phi\text{-C}-\text{O}-\text{Mn}=\text{O}$$

From previous experience we know that nucleophilic

attack on -C- carbon is a fast reaction.

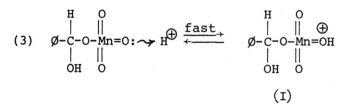

$$\text{(I)}$$

666

(4) $\emptyset$-C-O-Mn=OH $\xrightarrow{\text{slow}}$ $\emptyset$-C$\overset{O}{\diagup}$-OH + MnO$_3$H + H$_3$O$^{\oplus}$

(I)

This mechanism accounts for all experimental data.

Certain aldehydes decompose to hydrocarbons and carbon monoxide when heated in the presence of peroxides.

$$(CH_3)_2CHCH_2CHO \xrightarrow[\Delta]{ROOR} (CH_3)_2CHCH_3 + CO$$

Write a reasonable chain mechanism for such reactions.

Solution: Reactions that proceed through a chain mechanism (initiation, propagation, termination) usually involve free radical intermediates. Peroxides will readily decompose to alkoxy radicals (RO·) upon heating. This must be the initiating step of the chain mechanism for this reaction.

Carbon monoxide (CO) is formed in the reaction and it must have come from the formyl group $\left(\begin{matrix}O\\||\\-CH\end{matrix}\right)$ of the aldehyde. The loss of carbon monoxide from an aldehyde (decarbonylation) has the same mechanism as the loss of carbon dioxide from a carboxylic acid (decarboxylation). The hydrogen of the formyl group is removed by the highly reactive alkoxy radical. This results in the formation of an alcohol and an acylium radical (R-Ċ=O). The loss of carbon monoxide from this radical will produce an alkyl radical, which will abstract a hydrogen from another aldehyde molecule to produce an alkane and another acylium ion. These reactions constitute the propagation step of the chain mechanism. Termination can be accomplished by dimerization, disproportionation and/or hydrogen abstraction. The mechanism can be written as:

initiation   ROOR $\xrightarrow{\Delta}$ 2 RO·

propagation

$$RO· + (CH_3)_2CHCH_2CH\overset{O}{\overset{||}{}} \rightarrow ROH + (CH_3)_2CHCH_2-C·\overset{O}{\overset{||}{}}$$

$$(CH_3)_2CHCH_2-C·\overset{O}{\overset{||}{}} \rightarrow {:}C{\equiv}O^{\oplus}\text{-} + (CH_3)_2CHCH_2·$$

$$(CH_3)_2CHCH_2· + (CH_3)_2CHCH_2CH\overset{O}{\overset{||}{}} \rightarrow (CH_3)_2CHCH_3 + (CH_3)_2CHCH_2-C·\overset{O}{\overset{||}{}}$$

667

termination
{
^{1}dimerization

$$2(CH_3)_2CHCH_2\cdot \rightarrow (CH_3)_2CHCH_2CH_2CH(CH_3)_2$$

^{2}disproportionation

$$2(CH_3)_2CHCH_2\cdot \rightarrow (CH_3)_2CHCH_3 + (CH_3)_2C=CH_2$$

^{3}hydrogen abstraction

$$RO\cdot + (CH_3)_2CHCH_2\cdot \rightarrow ROH + (CH_3)_2C=CH_2$$
}

CANNIZZARO REACTION

● **PROBLEM** 18-38

From examination of the mechanism, can you suggest one
factor that would tend to make a crossed Cannizzaro
reaction involving formaldehyde take place in the particular
way it does?

<u>Solution:</u>   An investigation into nucleophilic attack on
carbonyl compounds and the mechanism of the Cannizzaro reaction will aid in the solution.

    The carbonyl group, C=O, provides a site for nucleo-
philic addition. The funtional group contains mobile π
electrons that pull strongly toward oxygen, this makes the
carbonyl carbon electron-deficient and the carbonyl oxygen
electron-rich. The molecule is flat due to the sp² hybridization of the carbon. Consequently, it is open to relatively unhindered attack from above or below. Since the
carbonyl carbon is electron-deficient, it is susceptible
to attack by electron-rich, nucleophilic reagents such as
bases. This typical reaction of aldehydes and ketones may
be written as:

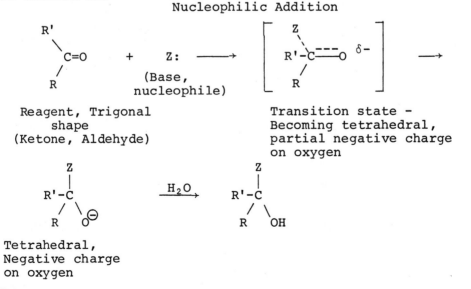

Aldehydes will generally undergo this reaction more readily than ketones. The reason stems from a combination of steric and electronic factors. In the transition state, carbon begins to acquire the tetrahedral configuration; the attached groups are being brought closer together. Hence, one might anticipate moderate steric hindrance. In other words, larger groups will tend to resist crowding more than smaller groups. The hydrogen of aldehydes is the smallest possible group. Therefore, it will not resist the crowding to the same extent as the alkyl or aryl group on the ketone. The electronic factor also comes into play when one considers the fact that an alkyl group releases electrons, and thus destabilizes the transition state by intensifying the negative charge developing on oxygen. This means an aldehyde, which will have less electrons being released, should not destabilize the transition state to the same extent as the ketone.

Consider the Cannizzaro reaction. Here, aldehydes with no α-hydrogens undergo self-oxidation-and-reduction to produce a mixture of an alcohol and a salt of a carboxylic acid. Two aldehydes will generally undergo a Cannizzaro reaction to yield all possible products. However, if one aldehyde is formaldehyde, the reaction almost exclusively yields sodium formate and the alcohol corresponding to the other aldehyde. For example,

$$ArCHO + HCHO \xrightarrow{\text{conc. NaOH}} ArCH_2OH + HCOO^{\ominus}Na^{\oplus}$$

(formal-   (sodium formate)
dehyde)

The mechanism of the Cannizzaro reaction seems to be the addition of hydroxide (nucleophilic attack) in step 1 (see figure below) to give intermediate I. Then, in step 2, one has addition of a hydride ion to a second molecule of aldehyde. Overall, it may be written (with ArCHO as an example) as:

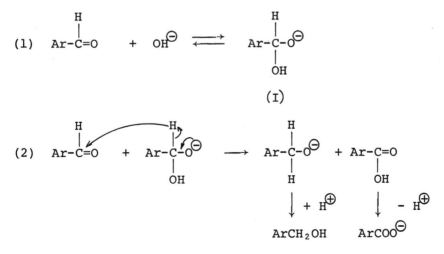

Formaldehyde should be the most favored aldehyde to

undergo the nucleophilic attack by OH⁻ in step one.

Formaldehyde $\left(\begin{array}{c} O \\ \parallel \\ H\text{-}C\text{-}H \end{array} \right)$ contains no alkyl groups, so that
electron release does not occur to intensify and, as
such, destabilize the negative charge developing on oxygen
in the transition state. Also, the two hydrogens are, as
previously mentioned, the smallest possible groups, so
that any other aldehyde will have larger substituents
which means it will resist the crowding that occurs in the
transition state.

This means that if step 1 of the Cannizzaro reaction
is rate-limiting, HCHO is the chief hydride donor (and not
any other aldehyde in solution), since (from the steric
and electronic factors discussed) it will react with OH⊖
faster than any other aldehyde. The equilibrium will be
positioned farther to the right. Note how the carboxylate
salt will derive only from the hydride donor.

Now, if step 2 is rate-limiting, HCHO is still the
chief hydride donor because the equilibrium from step 1
provides more I derived from HCHO than from the other
aldehyde. It turns out that kinetic studies indicate step 2
is indeed rate-limiting.

In essence, formaldehyde behaves the way it does
because of both steric and electronic factors.

● **PROBLEM** 18-39

Phenylglyoxal, C_6H_5COCHO, is converted by aqueous sodium
hydroxide into sodium mandelate, $C_6H_5CHOHCOONa$. Suggest a

likely mechanism for this conversion.

Solution: A characteristic reaction of aldehydes
without α-hydrogens is the oxidation-reduction they undergo
in the presence of a strong base. This is the Cannizzaro
reaction. It involves the attack of a hydroxyl ion upon
the aldehyde's carbonyl carbon, followed by a hydride shift
to give a carboxyl group. A possible mechanism is illustrated
below.

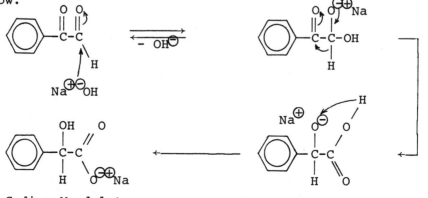

Sodium Mandelate

Assume that an equimolar mixture of formaldehyde and trimethylacetaldehyde (each undergoes the Cannizzaro reaction
by itself) is heated with sodium hydroxide solution. Write
equations for the various possible combinations of Cannizzaro
reactions which might occur. Would you expect formaldehyde
used in excess to primarily reduce or oxidize trimethylacetaldehyde? Why?

Solution:　　The Cannizzaro reaction involves treatment of
an aldehyde lacking an α hydrogen with concentrated base to
produce a primary alcohol and the salt of the corresponding
carboxylic acid. This disproportionation (simultaneous reduction and oxidation of the aldehyde) reaction is specific
to aldehydes without an α hydrogen because abstraction of
such a proton will lead to an aldol condensation instead of
a Cannizzaro reaction.

　　　The mechanism for this reaction involves a hydride
shift which is a rare occurrence. For example, in the case
of the general aldehyde RCH:

$$\overset{O}{\overset{\|}{RCH}}$$

net process:

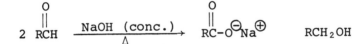

mechanism:

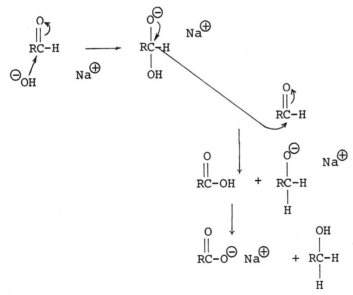

　　　The proton shift that results in the final product
occurs because a carboxylic acid is a stronger acid than
the alcohol. When two different aldehydes (both lacking
α hydrogens) are treated in concentrated base, the reaction

is known as a crossed Cannizzaro reaction. In the case at hand, we have four theoretical reactions, of which one does not readily occur.

$$\underset{\substack{\text{formal-}\\\text{dehyde}}}{\overset{\overset{\displaystyle O}{\|}}{HCH}} \quad + \quad \underset{\substack{\text{trimethylacetal-}\\\text{dehyde}}}{\overset{\overset{\displaystyle O}{\|}}{(CH_3)_3CCH}} \quad \overset{OH^\ominus}{\longrightarrow} \quad \overset{\overset{\displaystyle O}{\|}}{HCO^\ominus} \quad + \quad \underset{\overset{\displaystyle |}{H}}{\overset{\overset{\displaystyle OH}{|}}{(CH_3)_3CCH}}$$

main reaction

$$\overset{\overset{\displaystyle O}{\|}}{2HCH} \quad \overset{OH^\ominus}{\longrightarrow} \quad \overset{\overset{\displaystyle O}{\|}}{HCO^\ominus} + CH_3OH$$

side reaction

$$\overset{\overset{\displaystyle O}{\|}}{2(CH_3)_3C-CH} \quad \overset{OH^\ominus}{\longrightarrow} \quad \overset{\overset{\displaystyle O}{\|}}{(CH_3)_3CC-O^\ominus} + (CH_3)_3CH_2OH \quad \text{side reaction}$$

$$\overset{\overset{\displaystyle O}{\|}}{HCH} + \overset{\overset{\displaystyle O}{\|}}{(CH_3)_3CCH} \quad \overset{OH^\ominus}{\longrightarrow} \quad CH_3OH + \overset{\overset{\displaystyle O}{\|}}{(CH_3)_3CCO^\ominus} \quad \text{does not occur}$$

As seen from these equations, formaldehyde will reduce and not oxidize trimethylacetaldehyde. The reason for this can be traced to the fact that the first step of the Cannizzaro reaction involves attack of a carbonyl by the hydroxide ion. The aldehyde which is attacked in this way will eventually be oxidized to the carboxylic salt. Formaldehyde's carbonyl group is more easily attacked than that of trimethylacetaldehyde for both steric and electrostatic reasons. Formaldehyde's carbonyl group does not have trimethylacetaldehyde's bulky t-butyl group and is easily attacked by a nucleophile. Also, formaldehyde has a more intense positive charge on the carbonyl carbon since it lacks the inductively stabilizing t-butyl group.

$$\overset{\overset{\displaystyle O}{\|}}{H-C-C(CH_3)_3} \quad \longleftrightarrow \quad \underset{\oplus}{\overset{\overset{\displaystyle O^\ominus}{|}}{H-C}} \overset{\leftarrow\!\!+}{-\!\!-\!\!-} C(CH_3)_3$$

For these reasons, formaldehyde will always be converted to its carboxylate ion when it is used in a crossed Cannizzaro reaction.

● **PROBLEM** 18-41

The compound pentaerythritol, $C(CH_2OH)_4$, used in making explosives, is obtained from the reaction of acetaldehyde and formaldehyde in the presence of calcium hydroxide. Outline the probable steps in this synthesis.

Solution: In the presence of calcium hydroxide, a strong base, two carbonyl compounds with at least one containing α-hydrogens, can undergo an aldol condensation to form a hydroxy-carbonyl compound. This condensation reaction can repeat itself until all three of the α-hydrogens are replaced.

When the reactants are acetaldehyde and formaldehyde, the aldol condensation product is tri-methylol acetaldehyde. This compound can undergo a Cannizzaro reaction to give pentaerythritol. The reaction mechanisms are shown in equation form below.

(1) Ionization:

$$CH_2\text{-}\overset{\overset{\displaystyle O}{\|}}{C}\text{-}H \quad \xrightarrow{\ominus OH} \quad \ominus:CH_2\text{-}\overset{\overset{\displaystyle O}{\|}}{C}\text{-}H \quad + H_2O$$

with an H below the first carbon.

(2) Nucleophilic addition:

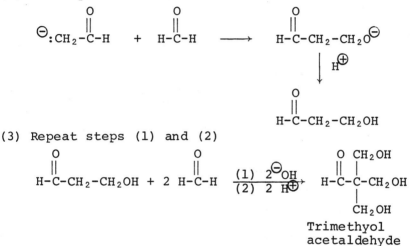

(3) Repeat steps (1) and (2)

$$H\text{-}\overset{\overset{\displaystyle O}{\|}}{C}\text{-}CH_2\text{-}CH_2OH + 2\ H\text{-}\overset{\overset{\displaystyle O}{\|}}{C}\text{-}H \quad \xrightarrow[\text{(2)}\ 2\ H\oplus]{\text{(1)}\ 2\ \ominus OH} \quad H\text{-}\overset{\overset{\displaystyle O}{\|}}{C}\text{-}\overset{\overset{\displaystyle CH_2OH}{|}}{\underset{\underset{\displaystyle CH_2OH}{|}}{C}}\text{-}CH_2OH$$

Trimethyol
acetaldehyde

(4) Cannizzaro reaction:

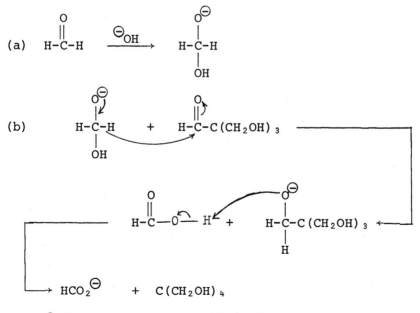

formate   pentaerythritol

CHARACTERIZATION TESTS

A certain test for aldehydes and most ketones depends upon a color-change when the compound is added to a solution of hydroxylamine hydrochloride and an acid-base indicator. Explain the basis of this test.

Solution: A characteristic of both ketones and aldehydes is the carbonyl functional group they possess. Thus, to characterize and identify ketones and aldehydes, reactions with the carbonyls are often done. Since oxygen is more electronegative, (electron-attracting) than carbon, the carbonyl carbon becomes susceptible to nucleophilic attack. Hydroxylamine, derived from its hydrochloride salt, can act as a nucleophilic reagent.

Hydroxylamine hydrochloride ($HO-NH_3^{\oplus}\overset{\ominus}{C}l$) is a derivative of ammonia. It can react with the carbonyl carbon to form a carbon-nitrogen double bond. The reaction rate is enhanced by acid. This can be readily seen in the reaction mechanism. The proton attaches itself to the carbonyl oxygen rendering a more positive dipole to the carbon, which is now more susceptible to nucleophilic attack by nitrogen. The mechanism is shown below, R' can be hydrogen or alkyl group.

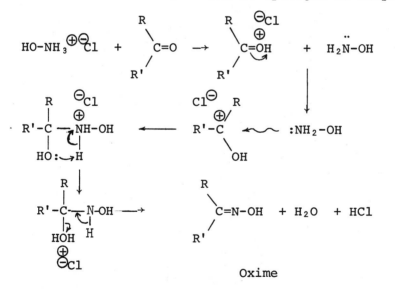

Oxime

The basis of this test is the pH change of the reaction solution which is manifested by the color change in the acid-base indicator. The pH change is due to the oxime formation which consumes the base hydroxylamine. The initial solution is slightly acidic because some acids are needed to protonate the carbonyl oxygen, facilitating the nucleophilic attack on the carbon. However, the concentration of unprotonated nucleophiles must not be too low, thus, the solution cannot be too acidic. As the reaction proceeds, the bases are being consumed. This lowers the pH of the solution which causes the color change, due to the increase in acidity.

Describe a simple chemical test that would serve to distinguish between:

(a) n-valeraldehyde   and   ethyl ketone
(b) propionaldehyde   and   ethyl ether

Solution: To decide on which chemical test to use to distinguish between compounds, one must first look at the structures of the compounds involved, their characteristic functional groups, and their similarities and differences.

(a) n-Valeraldehyde is a five-carbon straight chain aldehyde. Ethyl ketone is a five-carbon symmetric ketone. They are both carbonyl compounds, thus, tests involving the carbonyl oxygen, for example, oxime formation, are useless.

Looking at their structures, one can see that the ketone's carbonyl group is situated between two carbons, while the aldehyde's carbonyl group is between a carbon and a hydrogen. This suggests that aldehydes can be further oxidized than ketones and the two compounds can be distinguished by an oxidation test.

Tollen's test is a characteristic criteria for detecting aldehydes by oxidation. The final products include a silver mirror which can be observed as a sign of the aldehyde's presence. If the compound is not an aldehyde, there is no reaction. The reaction mechanism is shown below.

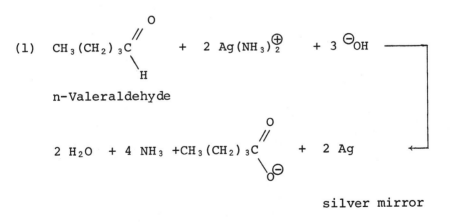

(1) $CH_3(CH_2)_3C\overset{O}{\overset{//}{}}{\diagdown}_H$ +   2 Ag$(NH_3)_2^{\oplus}$ + 3 $^{\ominus}OH$

n-Valeraldehyde

2 H_2O + 4 NH_3 + $CH_3(CH_2)_3C\overset{O}{\overset{//}{}}{\diagdown}_{O^{\ominus}}$ +   2 Ag

silver mirror

(2) $CH_3CH_2\overset{O}{\overset{||}{C}}CH_2CH_3$ +   2 Ag$(NH_3)_2$ $\rightarrow$ no reaction

Ethyl ketone

(b) Propionaldehyde is a three-carbon aldehyde and ethyl ether is a four-carbon symmetric ether. Their structures are CH_3CH_2CHO and $CH_3CH_2OCH_2CH_3$, respectively. Since they have different functional groups, they can readily be distinguished by simple chemical tests.

Tollen's test, described previously, can be used to distinguish between the aldehyde and the ether. Also, oxime formation with hydroxylamine, and Schiff test with the fuchsin-aldehyde reagent to form a characteristic magenta color can be used.

$$CH_3CH_2\overset{\overset{\displaystyle O}{||}}{C}H \quad + \quad NH_2OH \quad \xrightarrow[H\oplus]{- H_2O} \quad CH_3CH_2CH=NOH$$

propionaldehyde   hydroxylamine   oxime

$$CH_3CH_2OCH_2CH_3 \quad + \quad NH_2OH \quad \xrightarrow{H\oplus} \quad \text{no reaction}$$

ethyl ether

• **PROBLEM** 18-44

Describe a simple chemical test which can distinguish between:

(a) phenylacetaldehyde   and   benzyl alcohol
(b) diethyl acetal   and   n-propyl ether

Solution: (a) Phenylacetaldehyde ($C_6H_5CH_2CHO$) and benzyl alcohol ($C_6H_5CH_2OH$) have different functional groups, carbonyl and hydroxyl, respectively. They can be distinguished readily by Tollen's test. The appearance of a silver mirror is a positive test for aldehydes.

$$C_6H_5CH_2CHO \quad + \quad 2 \ Ag(NH_3)_2^\oplus \quad + 3 \ ^\ominus OH$$

Phenylacetaldehyde

$$C_6H_5CH_2CO_2^\ominus \quad + \ 2 \ H_2O \ + \ 4 \ NH_3 + 2 \ Ag$$

silver mirror

(b) Both n-propyl ether and diethyl acetal are ethers. To distinguish them, modification of either compound into a compound with a different functional group may be used.

Diethyl acetal $\left(\begin{array}{c} H \\ | \\ CH_3-C-OC_2H_5 \\ | \\ OC_2H_5 \end{array} \right)$ is a derivative of

of acetaldehyde. It is formed by acid-induced alcoholysis in the following manner.

$$CH_3\overset{\overset{\displaystyle O}{//}}{C}\underset{\diagdown H}{} \quad + \ 2 \ C_2H_5OH \quad \underset{\longleftarrow}{\overset{H\oplus}{\longrightarrow}} \quad \begin{array}{c} H \\ | \\ CH_3-C-OC_2H_5 \\ | \\ OC_2H_5 \end{array} \ + \ H_2O$$

Acetaldehyde   Diethyl acetal

Since the acetals are unstable in presence of acid, addition of acid can reverse the reaction to give acetaldehyde.

Therefore, to distinguish between n-propyl ether and diethyl acetal, one can add acid to both compounds and then perform either Tollen's test or Schiff test; both tests are described in previous problems. The appearance of a silver mirror can identify it as acetaldehyde, that is, the compound is diethyl acetal.

● **PROBLEM** 18-45

Describe a simple chemical test that would serve to distinguish between trioxane and 1,4-dioxane.

<u>Solution:</u>   Trioxane ( ) and 1,4-dioxane ( )

have similar chemical names, but they are functionally very different. Trioxane belongs to the family of cyclic aldehydes and dioxane belongs to the family of cyclic ethers. Dioxane is formed by acid-catalyzed dehydration and cyclization of two ethylene glycol molecules. Trioxane is formed by polymerization of three formaldehyde molecules and cyclization.

To distinguish between dioxane and trioxane, one can decyclize trioxane back into formaldehydes by adding acid and heating and then perform the Tollen's test or Schiff test.

CHAPTER 19

ALDEHYDES AND KETONES II

PROPERTIES AND REACTIONS OF ENOLATE ANIONS

● **PROBLEM** 19-1

What is a carbanion? How is it formed. Briefly discuss its properties and reactions.

Solution: Carbanion is a compound which contains a carbon with a negative charge due to a nonbonded pair of electrons $\left(R-\overset{\displaystyle |}{\underset{\displaystyle |}{C}}\!:^{\ominus}\right)$. The anion is commonly formed by the ionization of an α-hydrogen of a carbonyl compound. The α-hydrogen is more susceptible to ionization than any other hydrogen in the molecule, with the exception of the carboxylic acid proton. The acidity of the α-hydrogen is enhanced by the resonance stability of the carbanion formed. Formation of carbanion and its resonanization is illustrated below.

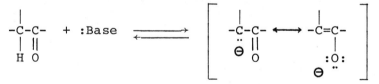

The resonance structure is usually written as:

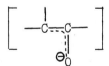

Since oxygen is more electronegative than carbon, most of the negative charge is carried by the oxygen. Thus,

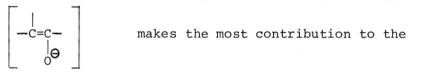
makes the most contribution to the

stability of the carbanion.

Carbon has a normal valence of four. Therefore, having an unbonded electron-pair, the carbanion is exceed-

ingly reactive. It is very basic and behaves like a nucleophile. The carbanion can attack a carbon to form a carbon-
carbon bond. Carbanions also participate in halogenation
of ketones, aldol condensations, Claisen condensation,
and nucleophilic aliphatic substitutions, and various
other reactions.

● PROBLEM 19-2

Suggest a reason for the observed stabilities of the two
enolates of 2-methylcyclohexanone

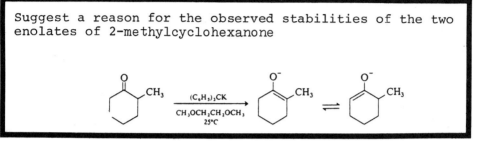

Solution: When in acid media, a carbonyl compound that
has no equivalent α-hydrogens can undergo enolization to
produce more than one enol. In aprotic basic media non-
equivalent α-hydrogens may be extracted to produce more than
one enolate anion. 2-Methylcyclohexanone has two types of
α-hydrogens in the ratio of 2 : 1. Hence in a solution of
potassium triphenylmethide ($(C_6H_5)_3C^\ominus K^\oplus$) two enolates will
be formed; the secondary α-hydrogen may be removed to form
one enolate and the tertiary α-hydrogen may be removed to
form another enolate.

     At equilibrium there will be a greater amount of
the more stable enolate. In our problem this means that,
at equilibrium, the enolate with the more highly substituted
double bond will exist in greater amounts than the enolate
with the lesser substituted double bond. This is because
thermodynamic stability is directly proportional to the
degree of substitution on a carbon-carbon double bond; the
greater the substitution, the more stable the compound.

It is for this reason that [structure] is more stable
than [structure] .

● PROBLEM 19-3

Write the mechanism for the aldol condensation of propionaldehyde, for which the net reaction is shown below.

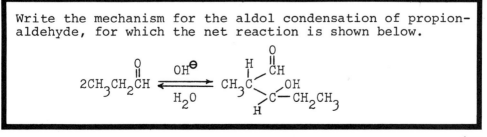

<u>Solution:</u>   The aldol condensation is concerned with the conversion of an aldehyde (not so much a ketone) to a β-hydroxyaldehyde in the presence of acid or base.

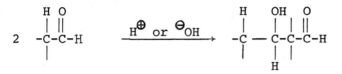

The mechanism for a base catalyzed aldol condensation is shown below. We will use acetaldehyde as our starting material.

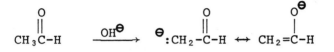

Enolate anion

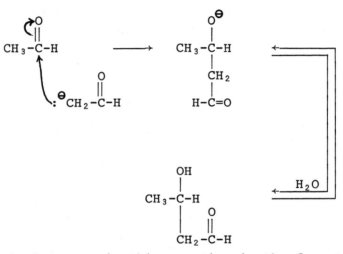

The key step in this reaction is the formation of the carbanion.

All that remains is to apply this mechanism to the given starting material, propionaldehyde.

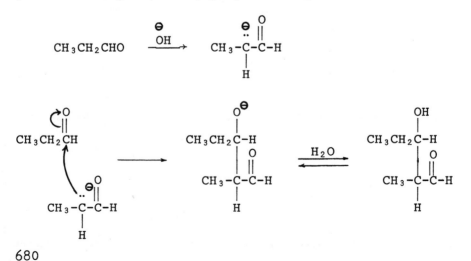

680

Predict the principal products to be expected in each of the following reactions; give your reasoning:

(a) $CH_3CHO + (CH_3)_2CO$ $\xrightarrow{NaOH}$

(b) $(CH_3)_2C(OH)CH_2COCH_3$ $\xrightarrow{NaOH}$

(c) $CH_2O + (CH_3)_3CCHO$ $\xrightarrow{NaOH}$

(d) $CH_2O + (CH_3)_2CHCHO$ $\xrightarrow{Ca(OH)_2}$

Solution: (a) Aldol condensation reactions involve the acidity of the α-hydrogens of carbonyl compounds. The degree of acidity depends upon the stability of the subsequently formed carbanion. In a basic solution of acetaldehyde and acetone (two carbonyl compounds possessing α-hydrogens) a hydroxide ion ($OH^\ominus$) will remove an α-hydrogen from both compounds. These are acid-base equilibrium reactions where the resulting carbanion is stabilized by resonance:

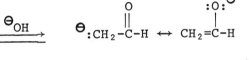

acetaldehyde

resonance stabilization
of resulting carbanion

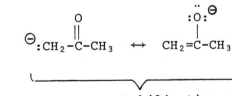

acetone

resonance stabilization of
resulting carbanion

The acetaldehyde and acetone carbanions will seek an electron deficient species with which to react. The formation of the carbanions is an equilibrium situation which involves the reactant (acetone and acetaldehyde) and the product (the respective carbanions).

The carbonyl carbons of these reactants are partially positively charged (electron deficient) and may react with any available carbanion. The carbonyl carbon of acetaldehyde has a greater partial positive charge than that of acetone. This is because acetaldehyde has only one electron releasing alkyl group (methyl) whereas acetone has two such groups. Hence the carbanions will react faster

681

with acetaldehyde than with acetone. This occurs also due
to the steric reasons in that acetone's carbonyl carbon
has greater steric hindrance towards carbanion attack than
acetaldehyde's carbonyl carbon (two methyl groups in
acetone vs. one methyl group in acetaldehyde). The major
product will be the one formed by the attack of the acetone
carbanion upon acetaldehyde. This is because as acetaldehyde
is used up, the equilibrium shifts to the left, hence de-
pleting the acetaldehyde carbanion concentration. The major
product is formed by the following mechanism:

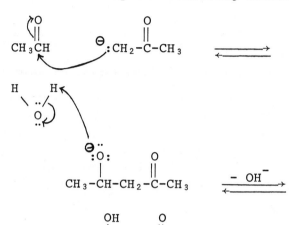

Other products formed by the same general mechanism,
but in smaller amounts, are:

$$\underset{CH_3CHCH_2C-H,}{\overset{OH\quad\;O}{\overset{|\qquad||}{}}} \qquad \underset{(CH_3)_2C-CH_2C-CH_3,}{\overset{OH\quad\;O}{\overset{|\qquad||}{}}} \qquad \underset{(CH_3)_2C-CH_2C-H.}{\overset{OH\quad\;O}{\overset{|\qquad||}{}}}$$

(b) The reactant, diacetone alcohol, is the product of the
base catalyzed aldol condensation of acetone. In basic
solution diacetone alcohol will follow the reverse mechanism
of its formation to produce acetone. This mechanism is
shown as:

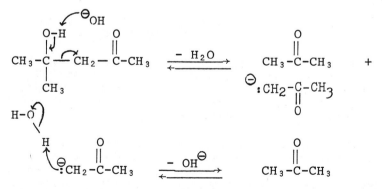

Diacetone alcohol is thermodynamically less stable
than acetone and hence the equilibrium for this reaction
lies far to the side of the acetone. Another reason why

682

diacetone alcohol formation is difficult is that it involves attack of a ketone upon a ketone

$$\left(\overset{\ominus}{:}CH_2\text{-}\overset{\overset{O}{\|}}{C}\text{-}CH_3 \quad \text{attacks} \quad CH_3\text{-}\overset{\overset{O}{\|}}{C}\text{-}CH_3 \right) . \quad \text{The}$$

steric hindrance from the alkyl groups raises the activation energy. Hence the major product of diacetone alcohol in NaOH is acetone, $CH_3\text{-}\overset{\overset{O}{\|}}{C}\text{-}CH_3$.

(c)   Aldehydes that lack α-hydrogens will undergo a Cannizarro reaction in basic solution. This is an oxidation-reduction reaction whereby some of the aldehyde is oxidized to a carboxylic salt and an equal amount is reduced to an alcohol. When two aldehydes that lack α-hydrogens are reacted in basic solution, a crossed Cannizarro reaction will occur. The more easily oxidized aldehyde will be converted into the carboxylic salt and the other aldehyde will be reduced to the alcohol. Formaldehyde and trimethylacetaldehyde are aldehydes that lack α-hydrogens. In basic solution, formaldehyde is oxidized to the formate salt and trimethylacetaldehyde is reduced to the alcohol. This happens because formaldehyde is more prone to attack by OH$^{\ominus}$ (to form the carboxylic salt) than trimethylacetaldehyde due to steric and electrostatic reasons. The reaction mechanism is shown as:

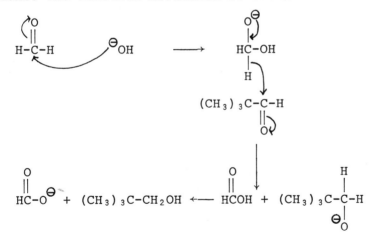

(d)   In a basic solution of formaldehyde and dimethyl-acetaldehyde, the latter will lose its α-hydrogen and undergo an aldol condensation with formaldehyde. The reaction mechanism is shown as:

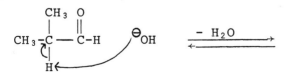

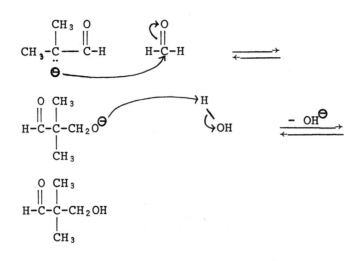

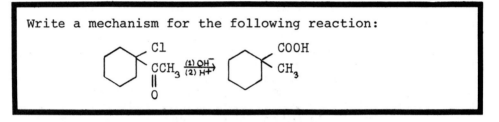

Write a mechanism for the following reaction:

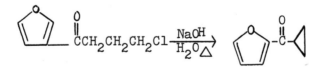

Solution: Ketones that are capable of enolization
may be converted to their corresponding enolates by treatment with base in an aprotic media. The enolates may act
as nucleophiles in S_N2 reactions in which alkyl chains
are added to the reactant. Intramolecular alkylations
are possible; being most feasible when ring closure is
favorable. For example

An interesting example of such an intramolecular
alkylation is the Favorskii rearrangement which involves
treating an α-halo ketone with hydroxide and producing a
carboxylate salt via a rearrangement of the carbon skeleton. The first step involves the formation of the
resonance stabilized enolate ion whose anionic carbon can
displace the halide also present in the compound. The
intermediate cyclopropanone cannot be isolated because
the hydroxide ion will attack the carbonyl group, opening
the ring. A proton shift where the newly formed carboxylic
acid group transfers a proton to the highly basic carbanion
is the final step in this process. The entire process may
be depicted as:

First step:

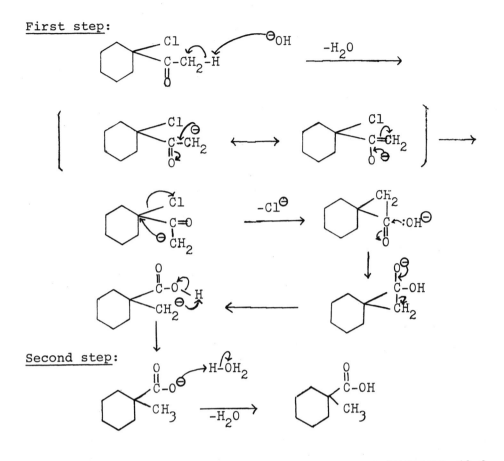

Second step:

• **PROBLEM** 19-6

Pentaerythritol, $C(CH_2OH)_4$, can be obtained by condensing acetaldehyde and formaldehyde together in the presence of sodium hydroxide. Write a mechanism for this reaction.

Solution: Pentaerythritol is a quadri-substituted methyl. Therefore, it is reasonable to take acetaldehyde as the main compound and formaldehyde as the substituents.

Since hydrogens alpha to a carbonyl are acidic, in presence of sodium hydroxide, acetaldehyde is ionized to form a carbanion. Carbanions are strong nucleophiles. It attacks the carbonyl carbon of formaldehyde in an aldol condensation reaction to form a hydroxy-carbonyl compound. This series of reactions can repeat until all three α-hydrogens are replaced by CH_2OH.

In presence of a strong base, formaldehyde can undergo a nucleophilic addition to form $H_2C-O^{\ominus}$.   This

$$\begin{array}{c} \\ | \\ OH \end{array}$$

compound can react with the tri-substituted acetaldehyde in a cross-Cannizzaro reaction to produce pentaerythritol. The reaction mechanisms are shown below:

685

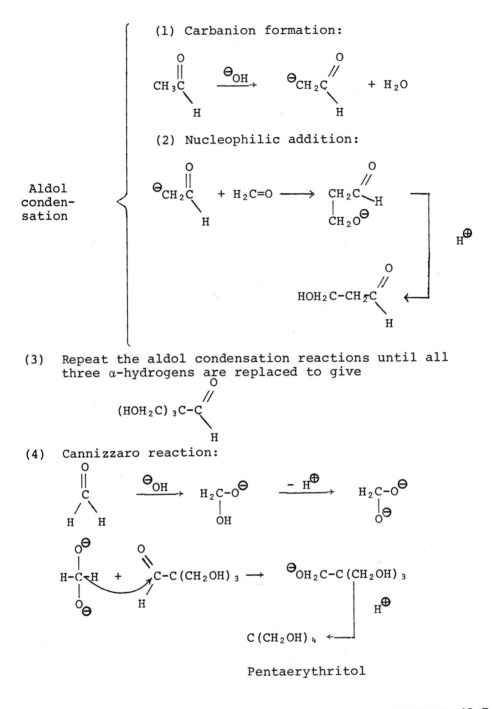

(1) Carbanion formation:

(2) Nucleophilic addition:

Aldol condensation

(3) Repeat the aldol condensation reactions until all three α-hydrogens are replaced to give

$$(HOH_2C)_3C-C{\overset{O}{\underset{H}{<}}}$$

(4) Cannizzaro reaction:

C(CH₂OH)₄

Pentaerythritol

● **PROBLEM** 19-7

An aldol condensation was carried out on equal amounts of propionaldehyde and butyraldehyde. The reaction gave rise to four distinct products. What were their structures, and how did each arise?

<u>Solution</u>: The aldol condensation is an addition reaction

between two carbonyl compounds, at least one of which
contains an α-hydrogen. It utilizes the fact that an α-
hydrogen to a carbonyl is acidic. It can be ionized by a
strong base to form a carbanion, which is an extremely
strong nucleophile. This nucleophile can attack the
positively dipoled carbonyl carbon to form an α,β-hydroxy-
carbonyl compound.

The determining, or rate-limiting step of an aldol
condensation is the ionization of an α-hydrogen from one
of the reactants. If both reacting carbonyl compounds are
identical   or if only one of them contains an α-hydrogen,
the resulting product is pure. But if the reactants are
nonidentical and both contain α-hydrogens, the result will
be a mixture of products. The reaction in question is of
the latter case.

Propionaldehyde, CH_3CH_2CHO, and butyraldehyde,
$CH_3CH_2CH_2CHO$, are both carbonyl compounds having α-
hydrogens. In the presence of strong bases, both α-
hydrogens can be ionized to form carbanions. These carbanions can react with the unionized aldehydes to form aldol
compounds. Depending on the reacting carbanion and aldehyde different aldol products are formed. The products
and reaction processes are shown below.

(1) Carbanion of propionaldehyde and propionaldehyde;

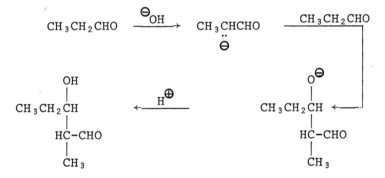

2-Methyl-3-hydroxypentanal

(2) Carbanion of propionaldehyde and butyraldehyde:

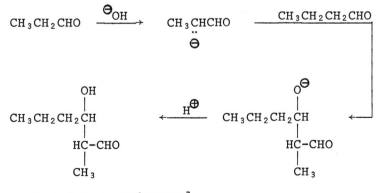

2-Methyl-3-hydroxyhexanal

(3) Carbanion of butyraldehyde and propionaldehyde:

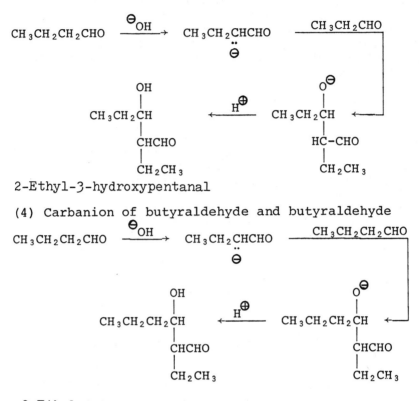

$$CH_3CH_2CH_2CHO \xrightarrow{\overset{\ominus}{O}H} CH_3CH_2\underset{\overset{\ominus}{\cdot\cdot}}{CH}CHO \xleftarrow{CH_3CH_2CHO}$$

$$\underset{\substack{\overset{|}{CH}CHO \\ | \\ CH_2CH_3}}{CH_3CH_2\overset{OH}{\overset{|}{CH}}} \xleftarrow{\overset{\oplus}{H}} \underset{\substack{\overset{|}{HC}-CHO \\ | \\ CH_2CH_3}}{CH_3CH_2\overset{\overset{\ominus}{O}}{\overset{|}{CH}}}$$

2-Ethyl-3-hydroxypentanal

(4) Carbanion of butyraldehyde and butyraldehyde

$$CH_3CH_2CH_2CHO \xrightarrow{\overset{\ominus}{O}H} CH_3CH_2\underset{\overset{\ominus}{\cdot\cdot}}{CH}CHO \xleftarrow{CH_3CH_2CH_2CHO}$$

$$\underset{\substack{\overset{|}{CH}CHO \\ | \\ CH_2CH_3}}{CH_3CH_2CH_2\overset{OH}{\overset{|}{CH}}} \xleftarrow{\overset{\oplus}{H}} \underset{\substack{\overset{|}{CH}CHO \\ | \\ CH_2CH_3}}{CH_3CH_2CH_2\overset{\overset{\ominus}{O}}{\overset{|}{CH}}}$$

2-Ethyl-3-hydroxyhexanal

● **PROBLEM** 19-8

Propose a likely reaction mechanism and name the end-product(s) for the reaction of a solution containing phenylacetaldehyde and dilute sodium hydroxide.

Solution: Phenylacetaldehyde has two potentially reactive functional groups, the carbonyl and the α-hydrogens. However, in a dilute sodium hydroxide solution, only the α-hydrogens are readily attacked by the hydroxide ions. The ionization results in a carbanion which is a potent nucleophile. It attacks the positively dipoled carbonyl carbon to form a carbon-carbon bond. The resulting oxide ion is protonated by the water molecules present. The final product is 2,4-diphenyl-3-hydroxy-butyraldehyde. The complete reaction mechanism is called the aldol condensation.

(a) Ionization of α-hydrogen (carbanion formation):

(b) Condensation:

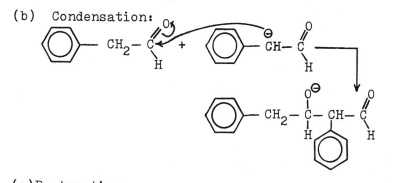

(c) Protonation:

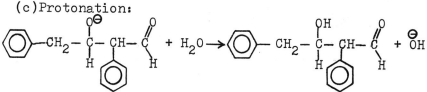

2,4-Diphenyl-3-hydroxy-
butyraldehyde

● **PROBLEM** 19-9

In the manufacturing of methyl isobutyl ketone (MIBK), large quantities of acetone are used. Propose a reasonable mechanism of synthesis for MIBK.

Solution: First, consider the structures of the reactant and product. Acetone is a three-carbon compound, and the product, methyl isobutyl ketone (MIBK) is a six-carbon compound. The three extra carbons in MIBK appear as an isopropyl substituent at the methyl carbon.

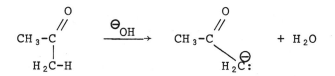

Acetone   MIBK

From the similarity in structure of the isopropyl substituent to a reduced acetone, one may suggest that the reaction is a condensation between two acetones. The mechanism of an aldol condensation of two acetones is shown below:

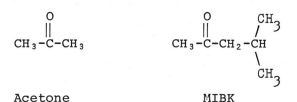

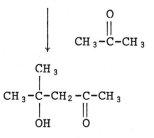

CH₃

$$CH_3-\overset{CH_3}{\underset{\underset{OH}{|}}{C}}-CH_2-\overset{O}{\underset{\|}{C}}-CH_3$$

Diacetone alcohol

The aldol condensation of two ketones results in the formation of diacetone alcohol. This compound can be dehydrated, and then hydrogenated to give MIBK.

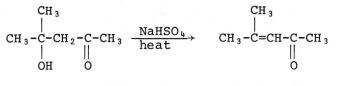

Diacetone alcohol

Diacetone alcohol   Mesityl oxide
(4-Methyl-3-penten-2-one)

H₂, Ni

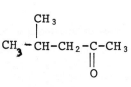

MIBK

(Methyl Isobutyl Ketone)

● **PROBLEM** 19-10

Determine whether acetylacetone (2,4-pentanedione) or acetone is more acidic. Which are the most acidic hydrogens?

Solution: Acetylacetone and acetone are both carbonyl compounds, the former contains two carbonyl groups while the latter only has one. All hydrogens in both compounds are α-hydrogens, however, their acidities are different. This is so because the carbanions formed have different stabilities.

For acetone, all hydrogens are equivalent, that is, they all have a similar environment, therefore, they are all of the same acidity. Ionization of an α-hydrogen will give

690

The negative charge is stabilized by the oxygen.

Acetylacetone is considerably different. It has two different groups of equivalent α-hydrogens; one group contains hydrogens attached to carbons 1 and 5, the other contains the two hydrogens at carbon 3.

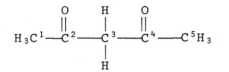

Ionization of different α-hydrogens will result in different carbanions with varying stabilities. If a hydrogen from either carbon 1 or 5 is ionized, a primary carbanion is formed.

If the hydrogen is from carbon 3, a secondary carbanion is formed.

$$H_3C-\overset{\overset{\displaystyle O}{\|}}{C}-CH_2-\overset{\overset{\displaystyle O}{\|}}{C}-CH_3 \quad \xrightarrow{-\ H^{\oplus}} \quad H_3C-\overset{O}{C}\overset{\ominus}{\underset{\underset{\displaystyle H}{|}}{C}}\overset{O}{C}-CH_3$$

In this carbanion, the negative charge is shared by two oxygens. This extra stabilization lowers the energy level of the anion, making the hydrogen more readily released. Thus, for acetylacetone, the hydrogens attached to carbon 3 are more acidic. The carbanion

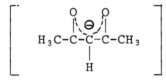

is predominant in an ionized solution.

To compare acid strength between acetone and acetyl-acetone, one considers the stabilities of the carbanions formed. The carbanion of acetone is similar to the carbanion formed by ionization of a hydrogen from carbon 1 or 5 of acetylacetone. Since the predominant carbanion for acetyl-acetone is formed by carbon 3 ionization, it is more stable than the acetone carbanion, therefore, more readily formed. This implies that acetylacetone is more acidic than acetone.

● **PROBLEM** 19-11

In alkaline solution, 4-methyl-4-hydroxy-2-pentanone is partly converted into acetone. Show all steps of a likely mechanism. What does this reaction amount to?

Solution: In alkaline solution, 4-methyl-4-hydroxy-2-pentanone is ionized. The process is shown in equation form below.

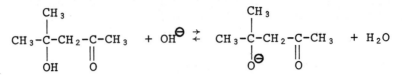

The oxyanion formed can undergo an electronic rearrangement. This involves the breaking of a carbon-carbon bond and formation of a carbonyl double bond.

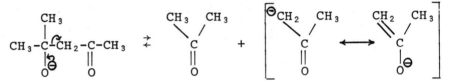

These ions can ionize the water molecules present to form neutral acetone molecules.

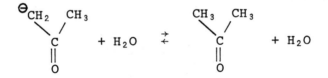

Taking all the steps together, one can see that it is a reverse of the aldol condensation of acetone.

CONTINUED IN VOL. II